RESEARCH DESIGN IN COUNSELING

THIRD EDITION

P. Paul Heppner
University of Missouri, Columbia

Bruce E. Wampold
University of Wisconsin, Madison

Dennis M. Kivlighan, Jr.
University of Maryland, College Park

THOMSON

BROOKS/COLE

Australia • Brazil • Canada • Mexico • Singapore • Spain
United Kingdom • United States

Research Design in Counseling, **Third Edition**
P. Paul Heppner
Bruce E. Wampold
Dennis M. Kivlighan, Jr.

Senior Acquisitions Editor: Marquita Flemming
Assistant Editor: Samantha Shook
Editorial Assistant: Meaghan Banks
Technology Project Manager: Julie Aguilar
Marketing Manager: Meghan McCullough
Marketing Communications Manager: Shemika Britt
Content Project Manager, Editorial Production:
  Rita Jaramillo
Creative Director: Rob Hugel

Art Director: Vernon Boes
Print Buyer: Rebecca Cross
Permissions Editor: Roberta Broyer
Production Service: Aaron Downey, Matrix Productions Inc.
Copy Editor: Toni Ackley
Cover Designer: Bill Stanton
Cover Image: Picture Quest/Creatas Images
Cover and Text Printer: West Group
Compositor: International Typesetting and Composition

Printed in the United States of America
  2 3 4 5 6 7 11 10 09 08 07

Library of Congress Control Number: 2006931761
ISBN-13: 978-0-534-52348-0
ISBN-10: 0-534-52348-X

Thomson Higher Education
10 Davis Drive
Belmont, CA 94002-3098
USA

For more information about our products, contact us at:
Thomson Learning Academic Resource Center
1-800-423-0563
For permission to use material from this text or product,
submit a request online at
http://www.thomsonrights.com.
Any additional questions about permissions can be submitted
by e-mail to
thomsonrights@thomson.com.

To my bright, energetic, inquisitive, passionate, and dedicated students; and to Mary, my true, affirming, and loving partner in all aspects of my life—your kindness, friendship, support, wisdom, and love have all added greatly to my life.
P.P.H.

To my students, whose passion for investigation provides renewal and inspiration; and to Anna and all of our children, whose love and support provide the foundation on which all else is built.
B.E.W.

To Mary Suzanne, Mary Clayton, and Martin, my real research support group.
D.M.K.

CONTENTS

v

CHAPTER 11   **Qualitative Research** 256

Yu-Wei Wang

PART 3 | METHODOLOGICAL ISSUES 297

CHAPTER 12   **Designing and Evaluating the Independent Variable** 298

CHAPTER 20   **Scale Construction   494**
Dong-gwi Lee and Hyun-Woo Lim

PREFACE

The seeds of great discoveries are constantly floating around, but they only take root in minds well prepared to receive them.
—Joseph Henry

So much of the field of counseling is discovery; discovering new techniques for helping people lead better, healthier, more enhanced lives. As Galileo said, "All truths are easy to understand once they are discovered; the point is discovering them." The counseling field is in many ways a new profession, and there are many truths left to be discovered. We are writing this book for the next generation of discoverers—those students and young researchers who will take the field to the next level of understanding. This discovery process is so important to the growth, health, and productivity of the specialty, as well as the next generation of practitioners and scholars who are the stewards of the profession. In this book we hope to provide a foundation to make those discoveries.

The third edition of *Research Design in Counseling* represents a substantial revision from the second edition. Because the first and second editions were well received by students and faculty, we retained the original organization and basic content coverage. However, even though we have maintained the original format, each chapter has been revised and updated to reflect new information developed since the second edition was published in 1999. Another change is the addition of stimulus questions or exercises at the end of each chapter to further students' thinking about the material presented in the chapter. We encourage the reader to use these questions to deepen awareness and understanding of the important content that each chapter represents. By working with the ideas of the chapters and talking to others about them, these skills of designing rigorous research can become integrated more thoroughly into the way students think about important issues in the field. In addition, we have added three new chapters, one focusing exclusively on multicultural issues, another on scale construction, and a third on research training. We have greatly revised the other chapters as well to have a stronger emphasis on diversity issues to portray the increasing breadth of knowledge bases across populations, as well as the increasing complexities in the counseling profession.

There are several challenges in teaching the next generation of counselors and counseling psychologists to be inquisitive and competent researchers. Perhaps first and foremost, many students learn about research methods in general research methods courses in education or psychology, which utilize what seem like very distant and even sometimes irrelevant examples from other disciplines. Subsequently, students in the counseling profession often do not see the utility or full applicability of research methods taught abstractly or apart from the typical domains of counseling research. In addition, when counseling students learn research methods when applied to, let's say clinical psychology or higher education, our students do not learn about the recent counseling literature and the creative approaches being utilized by contemporary scholars in our profession. Such a lack of knowledge and role models makes it difficult for students to acquire strong research interests in topics related to the counseling profession. Although the book is not comprehensive of all research in counseling, it provides beginning graduate students an overview of some of the studies of many of the foremost researchers in the profession.

As with the first and second editions, our goal for this new edition was to facilitate a conceptual understanding of research design, with an emphasis on acknowledging the strengths and weaknesses of all the designs including quantitative and qualitative. Moreover, in this edition, we devote a chapter to some of the unique conceptual and methodological issues related to research addressing multicultural topics. The book does not favor one design over another per se, but rather often emphasizes the need to consider the types of questions being addressed, as well as the inherent strengths and weaknesses in the previous research literature.

The third edition is divided once again into four parts. Part 1 focuses on Philosophical, Ethical, and Training Issues. Basic philosophical and paradigmatic issues are introduced, as are the ethical responsibilities of the researcher. Each of the chapters has been updated with current conceptual perspectives and methodological issues. A major change from the second edition is in Chapter 1, where we provide a more extensive and broadened discussion of the philosophical foundations of counseling research and qualitative approaches. Moreover, we broadened the focus on subsequent chapters to more explicitly include qualitative approaches, such as in discussions relating to research questions and hypotheses. A second major change in Part 1 is a chapter totally devoted to graduate research training (Chapter 2). We not only highlight the current research on this topic, but also discuss implications for students' development in acquiring research competencies. In addition, we are very pleased that this edition includes quotes from seasoned researchers from around the country who share critical aspects of their research journey. With openness and candor they share some of their own fears as well as joys along their path of becoming experts in their own research areas. Chapters 3–5 have been updated to highlight the critical issues involved in identifying research topics, choosing research designs, and the ever-present validity issues. These issues are critical because they build the foundation on which solid, rigorous investigations can be built. Chapter 6, "Ethics" has been updated to include a number of changes in the ethical code of the American Psychological Association (APA) as well as the fifth edition of the *APA Publication Manual* (2001). It is obviously important to maintain the highest ethical standards within our research endeavors; it is only through gaining a thorough understanding about the ethical guidelines that we can be sure we are working within their spirit and intent. Science and ethics really do need to go hand in hand, and this chapter offers many examples and support in making sure they do. In the appendices of this text we also provide copies of the most recent APA and American Counseling Association (ACA) Guidelines.

Part 2 of the book examines the major research designs that counselors use in their work. We have substantially updated these chapters and have provided new examples from the counseling literature about how these designs are being used to discover new truths about our field. In Chapter 10, we particularly focused on the revision to the quantitative descriptive designs because these are being used increasingly in our professional literature. For example, we have included some of the latest thinking and writing about the importance of examining mediating and moderating variables in our research, and address the latest issues in all of these "regression family" kind of designs.

In addition, Chapter 11, "Qualitative Research," has been significantly revised by Dr. Yu-Wei Wang. The chapter defines qualitative research and places it within constructivism and critical theory paradigms. The chapter describes three strategies of qualitative inquiry that have a great deal of applicability for counseling research: grounded theory, phenomenology, and consensual qualitative research. In addition, the chapter discusses common strategies to gather and analyze data, and also provides a wide range of references for further study on qualitative methods.

Part 3 of the book focuses on a broad array of methodological issues. In this section of the book we provide updated chapters on designing and evaluating the independent and dependent variables (Chapters 12 and 13), and update our discussion of population issues (Chapter 14), various forms of bias (Chapter 16), analogue research (Chapter 17), outcome research (Chapter 18), and process research (Chapter 19). The chapter on outcome research is particularly important in our view because counselors need to ensure that the interventions they use are effective. Although the designs used in outcome research are variations of designs discussed in several earlier chapters, particular issues arise when testing whether interventions are effective or are more effective than other interventions; these issues are discussed and various procedures to establish validity within outcome research are presented.

We particularly want to highlight three chapters in this section. First, we point the reader to Chapter 15 on conceptual and methodological issues related to multicultural research, which was written by Dr. Kevin Cokley and Dr. Germine H. Awad. Their careful thought and keen conceptual work raises many critical questions for researchers to consider in the field of multicultural research. Although we have attempted to infuse issues of diversity throughout the text, this new chapter brings together the latest thinking on these issues, and we hope it will be of great support to all researchers. Another new chapter (Chapter 20), which discusses scale construction issues, was written by Dr. Dong-gwi Lee and Dr. Hyun-Woo Lim. Our research can only be as strong as the measurement of our constructs, so this is a critical chapter for researchers who are conducting scale construction projects, as well as those who want to understand more about the psychometric properties of existing inventories. Drs. Lee and Lim not only take the reader through the steps of scale construction, but also offer a cross-national perspective on creating and validating scales with cross-national populations. This addition is empirically important to our field as the counseling profession becomes increasingly global in scope. The third chapter we particularly want to highlight is Chapter 21 on program evaluation, which has been updated by Dr. Matrese Benkofske and Clyde C. Heppner. The field of counseling has increasingly become one that emphasizes intervention and social change at the program and systems level. Many counselors have jobs where conducting program evaluation and assessing the efficacy of interventions is a critical part of their position. This chapter offers many insights about the field of program evaluation and provides a great deal of information and support for researchers involved in assessing the effectiveness of programs and services.

Part 4 of the book, "Professional Issues," includes a chapter on professional writing. This chapter has been substantially revised to include as many helpful tools for scholars as possible. A great deal of research is being conducted by counselors, but good research questions and even well-designed studies often do not get published in our journals. Certainly good research questions and well-designed studies are necessary components, but strong writing skills are needed to accurately depict the study and explain the results. This chapter is aimed at helping students and young researchers with the unique skills of scientific writing.

We have so many individuals to thank for their contributions to this book. We especially want to thank the staff of Brooks/Cole for all of the technical support, patience, and help through this revision process; we very much appreciate the guidance of Caroline Concilla and Marquita Flemming, as well as Samantha Shook for her technical assistance. In addition, we are very appreciative of Aaron Downey at Matrix Productions and our copyeditor, Toni Ackley, for her very careful and thorough polishing of the text. Although a number of staff have changed over the years, the early vision of Claire

Verduin lives on in this third edition, and she deserves special attention for her good judgment and patience in developing the first edition of this book. We also want to thank Young-Ju Cho and M. Meghan Davidson, both graduate students, as well as Amy Simpson, an undergraduate student, all at the University of Missouri-Columbia, and Zachary Imel at the University of Wisconsin, who helped to locate relevant articles, compile references, and assisted in writing and editing; their contributions were deeply appreciated.

In addition, we thank the authors of the chapters, who added greatly to the depth and breadth of critical topics within research design. And a special thanks to the researchers who have been willing to share some of their journey of becoming researchers; their voices added greatly to the discussion of the developmental process of becoming a researcher. In addition, we want to thank so many of you for sending in your comments about the book—how it was helpful to you and also where you would like more examples or suggestions.

We are also deeply appreciative of the scholars who provided detailed reviews of the second and early drafts of the third edition of this book; your feedback was very helpful in guiding the third edition: Richard Balkin, Texas A&M University at Commerce; Janet Carlson, Texas A&M University at Galveston; Y. Barry Cheung, Georgia State University; Stephen Cook, Texas Tech University; David Dixon, Ball State University; Marie S. Hammond, Tennessee State University; Steven Hoover, St. Cloud State University; Marlene Hyde, San Diego State University; Michael LeBlanc, SUNY Oswego; Ed Mauzey, Southeastern Oklahoma State University; Karen Multon, University of Missouri at Columbia; Joseph Ponterotto, Fordham University at Lincoln Center; and Christopher Stankoich, University of Dayton. In essence, we hope many of you see your voices and suggestions reflected in this new edition.

Thanks also to the following students who so graciously gave of their time to contribute to the final outcome of the book, and in doing so enhanced the quality: Chiao, Hung; Meghan Davidson; Lizette Ojeda; Amy Simpson; and Tsai, Chia-Lin.

Finally, we would like to thank all of the authors of the articles and books that we cite in this book; their dedication to conducting high quality research provides the profession not only with important new knowledge, but also with very helpful models on the "how to's" of conducting meaningful research.

As American folklorist Zora Neale Hurston commented "Research is formalized curiosity. It is poking and prying with a purpose." We hope this text gives you many tools to "poke and pry with a purpose" and discover important truths for the betterment of humankind.

Philosophical, Ethical, and Training Issues

I CHAPTER | SCIENCE AND COUNSELING

Counselors help people with a wide variety of personal, educational, and career-related problems. For many years, people have gone to counselors because they have problems they are unable to solve (Dixon & Glover, 1984; Fretz, 1982; Heppner, 1978a; Heppner, Cooper, Mulholland, & Wei, 2001; Horan, 1979). We as professionals assume responsibility for not only promoting the welfare of the people who seek our services, but also protecting clients from harm. Thus, as professionals we need to continually update and extend our knowledge about human nature and the field of counseling as well as evaluate our services, especially because the applied nature of our work affects the daily existence of thousands of people.

Consider the real-life example of a husband and wife who sought career planning assistance. After a thorough intake, they were assigned to a computerized career planning program. Both of them completed the program and were amazed to learn that they received exactly the same results.

Careful checking of the program revealed that the program was reporting scores accurately for the first individual who used the program each day. The second and all subsequent users that day, however, were getting an identical printout of the first user's results. The first user's results continued to appear until the machine was turned off. In essence, every user, except the initial user each day, was receiving invalid results. For us, this resulted in many hours of calling clients to inform them that they had received invalid results. After expressing our shock to the manufacturer, we were told simply: "Oh, yes, we found that out a month ago and it has been fixed on new disks. We'll send you a new set." One wonders how many other career centers never found this error and continued to use a program that gave users blatantly invalid results. (Johnston, Buescher, & Heppner, 1988, p. 40)

This example involves a computer programming error that was not caught through careful evaluation. Many other examples could be listed in which clients receive less than desirable treatments because of outdated information, ineffective or inappropriate counselor interventions, or erroneous knowledge about human behavior and the change process.

Medical professionals also aid people, although they obviously focus primarily on medical problems. The medical profession has advanced over the centuries and has become increasingly more sophisticated. Important lessons can be learned from the trials and tribulations of the medical profession. Consider the historical lesson from the so-called thalidomide babies. In the early 1960s a drug called thalidomide was prescribed in England, Canada, the United States, and several other countries for pregnant women experiencing morning sickness. The drug was administered before adequate empirical tests had been completed. Some medical scientists in England argued that the effects of the drug should have been tested scientifically, especially in comparison with groups of women who did not receive the drug. Others, however, argued more convincingly that it was unethical to withhold (from the comparison group) a drug that was "known" to greatly ease women's problems with pregnancy. For some time after the drug was introduced, a number of medical professionals observed an increase in the number of deformed babies whose arms and legs resembled buds that precede limb development in the human embryo. Years later, after appropriate empirical tests had been completed, researchers discovered that thalidomide administered to women during the critical embryonic period caused these major deformities in the babies. Although the drug was quickly taken off the market, for thousands of infants the damage had already been done. How do we know whether we are promoting the welfare of or actually harming those who seek our services in the counseling profession? None of us in the profession would intentionally want to harm clients. Counseling, however, can have detrimental effects on people (e.g., Lambert, Bergin, & Collins, 1977).

How do we know our interventions are effective? This question has led to identifying what were referred to initially as empirically validated treatments (Wampold, Mondin, Moody, Stich, Benson, & Ahn, 1997) and more recently as evidence-based practice (Chwalisz, 2003). In addition, this has led to the "great psychotherapy debate," regarding which therapy models and methods are most effective. (For more details, see Wampold, 2001, who not only traces this debate over time, but also concludes that successful outcomes are more dependent upon general therapeutic effects than any one theory or method.) What is sufficient proof that we as a profession can afford to accept? If someone proclaims that a certain intervention is effective, should we believe it? If your supervisor maintains that a certain technique is effective, is that sufficient evidence? What kind of *knowledge* must a profession be based on to succeed?

The answers to these questions rest on the manner in which the profession has developed its knowledge base.

Consider this true story of a group of faculty who were ardent believers in Freud's conception of psychoanalysis. These faculty members were relatively isolated from other professionals and had a habit of hiring only their own graduates. (They noted that because they rarely had a faculty opening and the job market was so restricted, they would feel like traitors if they hired someone else's student instead of one of their own.) These people believed that clients' paranoid fantasies were major obstacles to uncovering unconscious psychological conflicts.

Consequently, they would not allow any live recording (audio or visual) or direct observation of their therapy sessions. Nor would they allow any kind of written self-report data to be collected from clients. Their primary method of knowing seemed to be the method of authority (Freud), and it included little opportunity to objectively confirm or disconfirm Freud's ideas. Moreover, they so firmly believed in their truths that they scoffed at the utility of other therapeutic techniques such as systematic desensitization, the Gestalt empty chair, and reflection. Consequently, this group of psychologists, in the absence of any objective data, discovered very little beyond Freud's early formulations of the therapeutic process. The bottom line is that this group did not advance the knowledge of their field; by today's standards (as well as their students' evaluations), their therapy practices were archaic, and their training philosophies and methods totally inadequate.

The purpose of this chapter is to examine how the counseling profession has developed its knowledge base. This chapter focuses on the role of science in the counseling profession, including ways of knowing, philosophical foundations of science, and our views of four key issues for a philosophy of science in counseling.

THE ROLE OF SCIENCE IN COUNSELING

Science plays an essential role in developing the knowledge upon which the counseling profession is based. In this section we take a close look at science as it relates to counseling. We first discuss different ways of knowing, and particularly the scientific way of knowing. Then we discuss philosophical foundations of human behavior and introduce you to some of the issues under debate in the philosophy of science. Finally, we discuss some issues pertaining to a philosophy of science for the counseling profession. These philosophical issues are complex and intricate; our purpose is to introduce you to the basic issues, and thus we provide only a brief overview. Nonetheless, these issues form the foundation for future research and training in the profession.

SCIENCE AS A WAY OF KNOWING

Charles Peirce, a nineteenth-century American mathematician, philosopher, and logician, stated that there are at least four ways of knowing, or of "fixing belief" (Buchler, 1955). The first method is the method of tenacity—that whatever belief one firmly adheres to is truth. These "truths" are known to be true because we have always known them to be true; Kerlinger and Lee (2000) noted that frequent repetition of these "truths" seems to enhance their validity. A second method of knowing is the method of authority. If noted authorities such as the president of the United States, a state governor, a well-known psychologist, or a clinical supervisor say it is so, then it is the truth. A third method of knowing is the a priori method, or method of intuition (e.g., Cohen & Nagel, 1934). This method is based on the notion that what agrees with reason, what makes sense, is true. The fourth method of knowing is the scientific method, which involves empirical tests to establish verifiable facts. We would add a fifth way of knowing—what is learned through one's own direct experiences in the world. Through countless experiences, each individual construes a "reality" of the world; some of his or her perceptions may match those of others with similar experiences, whereas other perceptions and conclusions about the world may not match those of others. Dangers exist if this method is used alone because biases can develop or information can be distorted. Moreover, the events we experience can represent a biased sample, which in turn can lead to inaccurate conclusions.

Given the overwhelming complexity of life and the vast amounts of knowledge needed even in daily living, people most likely acquire "truths" through all five of these ways of knowing. Obviously, error can be involved in any of them. Such error, if it affects the knowledge on which counseling is based, can be dangerous for the counseling profession and our clients. To be credible, reliable, and effective, a profession must be built on dependable facts or truths, rather than on tenacity, decrees from authority figures, or subjective opinions.

A profession that aims to facilitate growth and positive change in clients must be based as much as possible on knowledge that exists in a reality outside of professionals' personal beliefs and biases. The scientific method has been developed to create such knowledge.

Basically, the scientific method is a set of assumptions and rules about collecting and evaluating data. The explicitly stated assumptions and rules enable a standard, systematic method of investigation that is designed to reduce bias as much as possible. Central to the scientific method is the collection of data that allows investigators to put their ideas to an empirical test, outside of or apart from their personal biases. In essence, the proof of the science is in the data. "Stripped of all its glamour, scientific inquiry is nothing more than a way of limiting false conclusions about natural events" (Ruch & Zimbardo, 1970, p. 31).

There are obvious costs to acquiring knowledge by using the scientific method. Conducting empirical investigations is costly in terms of time, energy, and resources. Putting complex and internal cognitive and affective processes to empirical test is a difficult and elusive task. Sometimes when we try to identify specific processes or variables we become mechanistic and lose the gestalt, or whole picture. Sometimes the lack of sophistication of our research methods results in conclusions that tell us little about real-life processes.

But the risks of building a profession on nonscientific evidence are far greater. The thalidomide babies are one clear example of the risks associated with not empirically testing one's opinions. Conducting therapy based only on personal hunches and opinions is risky and might well result in harming clients (e.g., Lambert, Bergin, & Collins, 1977). It is important that the knowledge on which the profession is built be based on objective or verifiable information that can be put to empirical or quantifiable tests. In this way, the methods used to establish our "truths" have a built-in self-correction process; each empirical test is independent of previous findings and can either verify or disconfirm the previous knowledge. In contrast, subjective ways of knowing that do not involve empirical tests run the risk of creating myths. These myths can result in ineffective or even harmful counseling, and hinder the progress of a profession.

This does not mean that the professionals' beliefs, hunches, and even biases are not useful in exploring ideas and perhaps extending the field's knowledge. We can undoubtedly learn a great deal about human behavior from the more subjective ways of knowing; it is clear that many ideas and breakthroughs regarding therapeutic orientations and techniques have initially sprung from practitioners' direct experience with people. However, it is important to note that these ideas must be empirically tested. In fact, no major orientation has been maintained in the profession without substantial empirical support. Parenthetically, even though the scientific method tends to provide data that are prone to less bias or distortion, Howard (1982) cogently recommended that we "periodically obtain evidence demonstrating the adequacy" of the various assumptions or procedures involved in the scientific method (p. 324).

In short, the knowledge of a profession must be empirically based and verifiable rather than subjective and untestable. Even though the scientific method has costs and is not problem-free, building a helping profession without it is too risky. Without a strong scientific foundation, the credibility of a profession is significantly challenged.

PHILOSOPHICAL FOUNDATIONS OF HUMAN BEHAVIOR

In the mid-1800s there was much confusion and speculation about the nature of human behavior. John Stuart Mill suggested that "the backward state of the moral (human) sciences can be remedied by applying to them the methods of physical science, duly extended and generalized" (Mill, 1843/1953). Mill's suggestion not only was adopted by the newly emerging social and behavioral sciences, but also has dominated research in these areas for many years (see Polkinghorne, 1983, 1984). The basic philosophy of science that has been generalized from the physical sciences has been referred to as the received view (Putman, 1962) or the standard view of science (Manicas & Secord, 1983), and has drawn heavily on the logical positivism of the 1930s (Hanfling, 1981). The received view, however, has come under attack from philosophers of science (e.g., Bhaskar, 1975; Harre, 1970, 1972; Kuhn, 1970; Lakatos, 1970; Suppe, 1977; Toulmin, 1972). As a result, an alternative paradigm referred to as the realist's view of science has emerged (see Manicas & Secord, 1983, for a brief overview). Basically, this view proposes that: (1) knowledge is a social and historical product and cannot be obtained only by studying the individual in isolation; (2) the experiences of an individual, whether observable or not, are appropriate topics of study; and (3) the focus of research should not be on events and finding relationships among events, but rather on examining the underlying "causal properties of structures that exist and operate in the world" (Manicas & Secord, 1983, p. 402). The received view also has been criticized by counseling psychologists (e.g., Howard, 1984; Patton, 1984; Polkinghorne, 1984). Critics have maintained that observations are not absolute, but instead are filtered through the subjective, phenomenological world of the observer (e.g., Patton, 1984; Polkinghorne, 1984).

Our philosophical foundations not only guide our understanding of the world, but also affect how scientists conduct research to increase our knowledge relevant for the counseling profession. We will briefly discuss four philosophical underpinnings of research: positivism, postpositivism, constructivism, and critical theory. The basic assumptions of any given paradigms involve the following dimensions: ontology (the nature of reality), epistemology (the relationship between the inquirer and the known), and methodologies (the methods of gaining knowledge of the world). Table 1.1 (adopted from Lincoln and Guba, 2000, p. 168) contrasts the philosophical foundations of positivism and postpositivism (on which quantitative research is based) with the philosophical foundations of constructivism-interpretivism and critical theory (which constitute the philosophical underpinnings of qualitative research). In general, all qualitative paradigms assume relativist ontology (there are multiple realities that are socially and individually constructed) and transactional epistemology (the knower and the known are inextricably intertwined), as well as dialogic/interpretive methodology (Guba & Lincoln, 1994).

It is important for a researcher to familiarize him- or herself with various paradigmatic strands and yet understand that the boundaries between the paradigms are also in constant flux. Lincoln and Guba (2000) used a participatory paradigm proposed by Heron and Reason (1997) as an example to illustrate how this form of inquiry is informed by postpositive, postmodern, and critical theory. They argued that it is inevitable that various paradigms have begun to "interbreed" so that "two theorists previously thought to be in irreconcilable conflict may now appear, under a different theoretical rubric, to be informing one another's arguments" (p. 164). Because research methods are interwoven with the philosophical paradigms, it is not surprising to witness the recent rise of mixed methods research design. This type of approach is beyond the scope of the current chapter. For additional information we encourage interested readers to consult references such as Bamberger, 2000; Beck, 2005; Creswell, 2003; Goodyear, Tracey, Claiborn, Lichtenberg, and Wampold, 2005; Green and Garacelli, 1997; Hanson, Creswell, Clark, Petska, and Creswell, 2005; Newman and Benz, 1998; Tashakkori and Teddlie, 2003. With this caveat, a brief discussion of four paradigms (positivism, postpositivism, constructivism, and critical theory) is presented in the following sections, with an emphasis on their differences and contradictions.

POSITIVISM Positivism is the paradigm that is best represented by the scientific method as traditionally taught in the physical sciences. According to this paradigm, the nature of the universe can be known, and the scientist's goal is to

	Aspect	Quantitative	Qualitative
TABLE 1.1 QUANTITATIVE VERSUS QUALITATIVE RESEARCH	Reality	Truth exists; behavior is governed by rules and laws and is discoverable	Reality is a social construction; there are no truths to be discovered.
	Representation of the world	Mathematical or verbal description of quantitative results	Linguistic; symbolic
	Domain knowledge and theory	Used to construct hypotheses; theory-driven; deductive	Data-driven; previous knowledge can bias results; inductive
	Intellectual bases	Mathematics, statistics, logic, physical sciences	Linguistics, philosophy, anthropology, literature
	Level of inquiry	Reductionistic, atomistic	Holistic
	Role of investigator	Objective, dualistic	Subjective, interactive
	Role of subjects/ participants	Subjects: naive to experimental hypotheses and are acted upon; deception is an ethical issue	Participants: involved in research, are fully informed, and can be involved in analysis and results
	Generalizability	A sample is used to generalize to population; deductive	Applicability is more important than generalizability; inductive
	Bias	Problematic; must be reduced	Accepted and acknowledged
	Validity	Involves minimizing alternative explanations	Involves effect on audience and social utility; uses triangulation
	Reliability	Involves measurements without error; seeks quantitative results that reflect true scores	Not relevant

discover the natural laws that govern each and every object in the universe, and their relationship to each other. Physical laws that describe gravitation, magnetism, and electricity are examples of positivistic statements about the universe that are universal in terms of both time and context. A key principle is that "truth" exists, and given enough time, brilliant scientists, and sophisticated methods, discoveries will be made that illuminate the truth. In the positivistic realm, the scientist is "objective"; that is, the scientist neither affects the world that is studied nor is affected by it. Scientists are interchangeable in that a given experiment should lead to the same outcome and conclusion, regardless of who conducts it. Surely, some scientists are more insightful and creative than others, but in the end, experiments yield results that are self-evident to the scientific community.

TABLE I.I
QUANTITATIVE
VERSUS
QUALITATIVE
RESEARCH
(*Continued*)

Aspect	Quantitative	Qualitative
Product	Research report in scientific journal; contains mathematical or statistical results, a verbal description of quantitative results, and domain-specific language (jargon)	Results written in everyday language or presented in other media; accessible to audience regardless of domain-specific knowledge; may or may not be published in scientific outlets; available, understandable, and relevant to participants
Audience	Academic community; policy implications for others are made by academics	Academic and nonacademic audiences; policy implications are integral to the product
Control	Involves controlling extraneous influences, manipulating variables, and detecting causal relationships	Involves understanding complex relationships among various factors
Goals of study	To discover truth; to explain and predict; to confirm conjectures; to extend knowledge	To describe, interpret, critique, revise, and change
Researcher's voice	That of detached, objective scientist	That of involved investigator, participant, and transformative expert
Power structure	The dominant view in the academic community in terms of publication, funding, promotion, and tenure	Is acquiring recognition; recognition from outside the scientific community is important

Confidence in results derives from the scientific method, not from the scientist; the operations of the experiment produce the results while the scientist observes objectively from the sidelines.

The scientific method involves well-defined steps. First, the scientist makes a conjecture about the nature of the universe. After that, the scientist designs an experiment such that its results will either confirm or disconfirm the conjecture. Knowledge, as opposed to mere opinion, is contained only in statements based on or linked to direct observation. The only kinds of statements free from personal bias (and thus distortion) are those grounded in observation. If the data conform to the prediction, the conjecture is verified. On the other hand, if the data do not conform to the prediction, the scientist concludes that the phenomenon being studied does not follow the conjecture, which is then abandoned as an explanation of truth. The hypothetico-deductive (that is, deductions made from testing hypotheses) nature of this process is characteristic of positivism. Several classic experiments provide vivid examples of positivism: Galileo dropping balls from the Tower of Pisa, the bending of light to prove Einstein's theory of relativity, Madame Curie's observations of radioactivity, and changing pressure and volume related to the gas laws.

There are other important characteristics of positivistic research. First, relations typically are expressed in terms of causality—X causes Y. Second, theories are reductionistic in that complex processes are understood by breaking them down into simpler subprocesses, which can be studied more easily. Third, laws are usually expressed mathematically, measurements are quantitative, and conclusions dichotomous (either the data conform to the prediction, or they do not), resulting in the conclusion that the law is true or not. Thus, the accumulation of facts or knowledge will result in general laws of human behavior. Human nature is lawful; the goal of science is to identify the causal relationships among variables.

The overall goal of science is to develop theories of human behavior, which consist of a network of knowledge statements that are grounded in observation and tied together by deductive logic. The idea of a rigorous link among observations, hypotheses, and theory was appealing; after all, "the hard-nosed scientist," like the proverbial Missourian, wants to be "shown" the evidence (Manicas & Secord, 1983). In addition, the notion of discovering laws of human behavior based on the accumulation of objective data promised credibility as well as utility for a young profession.

Clearly, the description of positivistic research calls to mind the type of science conducted in the physical sciences, such as chemistry or physics, or perhaps that in the biological sciences, but certainly not research in the social sciences (except maybe psychophysics or perception). The positivistic tradition has evolved into the postpositivism paradigm, which recognizes the impossibility of making dichotomous conclusions when systems are complex and the behavior of organisms has multiple determinants.

POSTPOSITIVISM   Postpositivism shares with positivism the belief in a "real" reality and in the goal of discovering "truth." However, postpositivists recognize that truth cannot be fully known, and that, consequently, at best we make probabilistic statements rather than absolute statements about truth. The statistical models that underlie research in the social sciences are saturated with this probabilistic interpretation. The values of p associated with statistical tests are probabilities of obtaining the data, given the assumption that the null hypothesis is true. Statistical tests assert that there is truth, but that we can never conclude with certainty that our results can differentiate among competing hypotheses. When we reject the null hypothesis (that is, obtain a statistically significant result), we decide to accept the alternate hypothesis knowing that there is a small probability that we made the wrong conclusion.

Although the probabilistic nature of statistics exemplifies the postpositivistic nature of most research in the social sciences, it is only one aspect of the research process that diverges from a strict positivistic methodology. Because of the ambiguities related to recognizing that the "truth" cannot be known for certain, the logic of the positivistic scientific method is altered. In the postpositivistic paradigm, theories lead to conjectures, and the statements about truth are altered to recognize that the inferences are probabilistic. If the data are consistent with the conjecture, then confidence in the theory as an accurate description of "truth" is increased.

Often the word *corroborated* is used to indicate that a study produced results consistent with prediction and that the conjecture has thus survived another test. On the other hand, if the data are inconsistent with theoretically derived conjectures, and the study is valid, then the theory has failed to be corroborated. In the postpositivist realm, it would be difficult to give up belief in a theory based on one experiment. However, a succession of studies that fail to conform to prediction would constitute evidence that the theory should be revised or abandoned. The goal in postpositivistic research is to produce, through a succession of experiments, descriptions that are closer approximations to the truth. For example, to prove that smoking causes disease, multiple experiments of various types (for example, passive designs, experimental designs using lab animals) were needed to come to the conclusion that smoking in fact leads to various detrimental health outcomes.

An examination of research methods demonstrates the degree to which postpositivism permeates what we do. Classical test theory rests on the proposition of "true scores," which is the true amount of a characteristic that a person possesses; however, any measurement is actually an obtained score that contains error (that is, obtained score = true score + error). The mere mention of reliability and validity implies that constructs exist, but that random error renders our assessments of these constructs imperfect. In statistics, population parameters are "truths" about which we collect data for the purpose of estimation or hypothesis testing.

Postpositivism also recognizes that there is bias in the scientific process, and that the conclusions researchers make are influenced by the person of the researcher. Truths are not self-evident but must be arbitrated by the scientific community. The process of peer review is an admission that the validity of a conclusion is open to interpretation, and that it is scientists' opinions about the veracity of a claim that dictate whether or not a result adds to the cumulative knowledge of a field. Clearly, there are canons that must be followed (that is, the study must be valid, as described in Chapter 5) if a study is to be conclusive, but it is scientists, rather than some algorithm, who determine whether the conclusions add to knowledge.

Whereas positivism and postpositivism share the view that certain truths exist and that research can shed light on these truths, constructivism and critical theory, two worldviews on the opposite ends of the worldview continuum, have a very different conceptualization of reality. We discuss these two views next.

CONSTRUCTIVISM   In the constructivism paradigm, notions of "truth" and "reality" are abandoned in favor of the notion that ideas about the world, especially the social world, are constructed in the minds of individuals. These constructions, based on the experiences of individuals as they interact with the physical and social environment, are shaped by culture and may be idiosyncratic. Constructions exist and can be described, but they are not representations of truth. Constructions can be simple or complex, naive or sophisticated, uninformed or informed, but they cannot be proven true or false. An individual's constructions may change over time—as a result of education, increased experience with the environment, or maturation.

Constructivists believe that reality is created by the participants of any system. It is true that some event occurs, but it is the meaning attributed to that event that is important socially. Suppose that one is a childhood abuse survivor. Constructivists recognize the reality of the event (childhood abuse), but then argue that it is the meaning that is attributed to that event that is important in determining social relations and behavior. One survivor might believe that the abuse occurred because her parents failed their responsibilities as primary caregivers, thus estranging herself from her parents and later in life having difficulties in trusting other people. Another survivor might feel that her parents hurt her because they were struggling with their own survival and transferring their anger toward her. Growing up in such a familial environment, she learned to be a caretaker for her parents and others at a young age. This example demonstrates that multiple constructions of an event are possible. The important point is that constructivists believe it is the meaning that is attributed to an event, rather than the event itself, that is the important aspect for understanding behavior and social relations.

Because constructions do not represent universal truths, the investigator and the object under investigation cannot be conceived of separately. Social constructions are developed through interactions with the environment and involve mental representations and interpretations of those interactions. The investigator and the person investigated are linked, and through the investigation process the constructions of the participants become accessible to the investigator. Because the construction of a participant is internal, it is only through the interaction between the investigator and the participant, or the interaction between the investigator and the world of the participant, that the constructions of an individual can be understood.

Moreover, the constructions of the investigator cannot be separated from her or his understanding of the participant's constructions. The general methods of understanding in a constructivist world involve both hermeneutics and dialectics. *Hermeneutics* refers to the activity of interpretation, whether the data to be interpreted are language, behavior, text, artifacts, or other aspects of human behavior or thought. The constructivist must use these data to develop an interpretation that, in a sense, is a description of the constructions of the participants. *Dialectics* refers to the interaction between the participant and the investigator. At the most benign level, the interaction is a conversation in which words are exchanged and interpretations of the language lead to an understanding of constructions. At the next level, the exchange involves discussing these constructions, as when an investigator shares her or his interpretations with the participant. At the most extreme level, dialectics involve changing constructions in the process of interpretation. This last level of dialectics (and some would say the essence of dialectics) is more characteristic of critical theory (see the next section) than of constructivism.

In the constructivist paradigm, there are no truths to be discovered; therefore, there can be no conjectures (that is, predictions based on hypothesized truths) or tests of conjectures. Thus, data are not collected with the aim of determining whether or not observations are consistent with conjecture. Rather, data lead to interpretations that then lead the investigator in directions that may not have been anticipated, causing the investigator to reinterpret already collected data or to collect additional data, often in ways unimaginable when the investigation began. Positivistic and postpositivistic methods are linear, whereas constructivist (and critical theory) methods are recursive (that is, the results and method influence each other).

CRITICAL THEORY   Critical theory posits that people's social constructions are shaped by the social, political, cultural, historical, and economic forces in the environment, particularly forces created by powerful individuals. Over time, the constructions take on the appearance of reality; that is, the social reality, which has in fact grown out of the social context, is assumed to be truth. Because the constructions are so deeply embedded in society (including in the researchers themselves), it is extremely difficult to comprehend that these constructions were spawned in the societal context and are not truths. For example (and any examples chosen are necessarily controversial), the belief that the monogamous union of one male and one female for the purpose of reproduction (that is, heterosexual marriage) is natural is a socially derived position.

Critical theorists would concede that it could be argued that marriage is necessary and important for the social order (as we know it), but they would contend that marriage, as an institution, was generated by the social system; that there are alternatives (same-sex unions, polygamous marriages); and that the "truth" of any "natural" propensity to marry is specious.

Ponterotto (2005b) reminded us that "there is no single critical theory" but "there are commonalities among the variants of critical theory" (p. 130). In critical theory, the investigator and the participant form a relationship, and the values of the investigator are vital to the activity. Inquiry, in critical theory, involves the level of dialectism that changes constructions. That is, the investigation involves a dialogue between investigator and other in such a way that the other comes to realize that her or his understanding of the world is derived from the precepts of the social order, and that these precepts can (and should) be altered. In other words, the goal of critical theory is to have the participants view structures for what they are—socially constructed beliefs—rather than as unchangeable truths. Moreover, the dialectic should lead to the participants' understanding that social action is needed to change the social order, thereby being emancipated from oppression (e.g., oppression resulting from racism, classism, able-bodism, heterosexism, or sexism).

For example, feminist theory falls into the critical theoretical realm in that it contends that traditional roles for women have been socially determined, that the power in society has been allocated to males, and that these social realities can be altered. Feminism seeks to "raise the consciousness" of women so that they do not consider their place in society to be fixed as truth, but instead understand both the historical context that led to the current social situation and that the first step in change is to reject the traditional roles. Many critical theorists would contend that this worldview involves more than social action, which tends to change society at the margins, and instead necessitates radical change that dramatically replaces current social structures with others (e.g., Marxism).

SUMMARY OF THE PHILOSOPHICAL FOUNDATIONS   We have contrasted four paradigms that bear on the research process, albeit overly simplistically. Philosophers, since the beginning of humankind, have wrestled with ideas about knowledge and knowing. It is impossible (or irrelevant) to "prove" that one of these paradigms is correct, more appropriate, better, or more useful than another. They are different systems for understanding the world, but no method, either logical or empirical, can establish the superiority of any given view. Nevertheless, it is vital to understand the philosophical foundations of various paradigms so that our methods match our belief systems, and so that the research approach is appropriate for answering research questions within the context of existing knowledge. Morrow, Rakhasha, and Castañeda (2001) made several recommendations on how to select paradigms in accordance with an individual's personal and mental models, research question, and discipline. A researcher should reflect on the compatibility of a particular paradigm with her or his own personal values, beliefs, personality, previous research experience, and research interests.

The debate over the philosophy of science is exceedingly complex and intertwined with our view of human nature, the adequacy of our research methods, the content of our research investigations, and the perceived utility of our research findings. The interested reader might explore these issues further by examining some of the following: Bhaskar (1975), Caple (1985), Dar (1987), Harre (1974, 1980), Lakatos (1970), Lincoln and Guba (2000), Manicas and Secord (1983), Meehl (1978, 1987), Morrow, Rakhasha, and Castañeda (2001), Morrow and Smith (2000), Polkinghorne (1983), Schutz (1964), Serlin (1987), Serlin and Lapsley (1985), Toulmin (1972), as well as two special issues in the *Journal of Counseling Psychology* (Polkinghorne, 1984; Haverkamp, Morrow, & Ponterotto, 2005).

FOUR ISSUES FOR A PHILOSOPHY OF SCIENCE FOR THE COUNSELING PROFESSION

With regard to a philosophy of science for the counseling profession, we will discuss our views on four issues: (1) the goals of science in counseling, (2) the importance of methodological diversity, (3) the need to examine and expand our assumptions regarding human nature, and (4) our responsibility for applying research tools. The upshot of these issues is that counseling psychology has become more sophisticated in its philosophy of science, and subsequently more sophisticated in the methodologies that are found in today's journals.

GOALS OF SCIENCE IN COUNSELING   Science is a mode of controlled inquiry for reducing bias and developing credible "ways of knowing." Historically, the basic functions of the scientific approach were typically considered as twofold (e.g., Kerlinger, 1986; Kerlinger & Lee, 2000). The first function was to advance knowledge, to make discoveries, and to learn facts in order to improve some aspect of the world. The second function was to establish relations among events and develop theories, thereby helping professionals to make predictions of future events. We will now discuss philosophical issues related to each of these functions, specifically within the field of counseling.

In our view, the goal of the scientific method in counseling is multifaceted, and indeed is to advance knowledge, make discoveries, increase our understanding of human behavior, and acquire facts about counseling. However, in the realm of counseling, phenomena of interest include both observable events and subjective, self-reported experiences. Researchers for some time have examined a wide range of phenomenological or self-report variables in counseling (e.g., client satisfaction with counseling, perceived counselor expertise, client's problem-solving self-efficacy, supervisee self-efficacy, and client reactions to counselor statements). The expansion of our knowledge is often guided, in part, by pressing societal needs as well as questions or problems that professionals have in the field. For example, one pressing question has been whether client expectations about the counselor or the counseling process affect later outcomes in counseling, such as problem resolution or premature termination (e.g., Hardin, Subich, & Holvey, 1988; Tinsley, Bowman, & Ray, 1988). Or the pressing question may result from a practitioner's dissatisfaction with her or his inability to help certain clients make effective decisions about their career plans. (See Rubinton, 1980, for a study that explored the utility of different career interventions for clients with different decision-making styles.) Our research is also guided by current societal needs that merit immediate attention, such as social advocacy and social justice for previously marginalized groups. (For more details, see Speight & Vera, 2003; Toporek, Gerstein, Fouad, Roysircar, & Israel, 2005.) Another social need pertains to a number of students' needs in school environments; it has been suggested that counseling psychologists are well positioned to collaborate with school counselors to address a host of issues facing school age students (Hoffman & Carter, 2004; Romano & Kachgal, 2004). Another pressing societal need is the rapid globalization and increasingly interdependent nature of the world economically, socially, and culturally (see Heppner, 2006). In essence, "the world is internationalizing at a much faster pace than the field of psychology" (Leong & Ponterotto, 2003, p. 383), and thus there are growing demands for cross-cultural competencies in the next generation of a wide range of professionals, including counselors (Heppner, 2006). Thus, scientific research is designed, in part, to provide answers to pressing questions or societal problems. In this way, research in counseling can be very practical; in fact, one view is that the adequacy of our research can be evaluated by how relevant the findings are for practitioners (Krumboltz & Mitchell, 1979). Scientific research in counseling can thus advance our knowledge base or understanding of human behavior by providing data that describe and help us understand a wide range of human behaviors, and how such behaviors can be altered through counseling interventions.

It is also important to develop knowledge bases and research perspectives that emphasize the social and historical context of the individual. A common defining element of the counseling profession is that we typically conceptualize a person's behavior as a function of the environment that they experience (Fretz, 1982). People do not think, feel, or behave in isolation, but rather in the context of a rich personal and social history. Research that increases understanding of how individuals interact within a broader social and personal environmental context is crucial to the development of knowledge about counseling. Thus, the goal of science is to expand our knowledge not only about individuals, but also about the interactions between individuals and a larger personal, social, cultural, and historical context. In fact, it has been maintained that to ignore the larger social, cultural, and historical context ignores critical elements in understanding current behavior, and in this sense can lead to ineffective and even inappropriate interventions and unethical behavior (American Psychological Association [APA], 2003; Toporek & Williams, 2005).

Research, however, is guided by more than practical problems and societal needs. To achieve scientific understanding, the researcher often needs to organize observations and facts into a logical framework that explains some aspect of behavior. Thus, research is often guided by theoretical issues within a line of work and seeks to establish general relations and conditional statements among events that help professionals to understand phenomena. The accumulation of facts or knowledge will not likely result in general laws or broad scale theories of human behavior as it was earlier conceived. Human behavior is multi-determined; that is, a single action can be determined by any one of several preceding events. Moreover, human actions consist of complex chains in which preceding events increase or decrease the probability that some subsequent action will occur, but behavior is not a uniform process across individuals or even within individuals over time. Meehl (1978) likewise concluded that for a variety of reasons (such as individual differences, polygenic heredity, random events, nuisance variables, and cultural factors), human psychology is difficult to scientize and that "it may be that the nature of the subject matter in most of personology and social psychology is inherently incapable of permitting theories with sufficient conceptual power" (p. 829). Thus, the range of human variability and complexity does not much lend itself to description by general principles or broad theories, and even less to prediction.

In short, we are suggesting that it is exceedingly difficult to develop broad scale theories aimed at predicting human behavior in general. However, skilled therapists are able to make better predictions about individual people when they combine research knowledge about specific relations among variables with a host of qualifying information, namely the biographical, social, and cultural history of the individual. In this way, therapists use "the discoveries of science, but in order to bring about changes in the everyday world, also employ a great deal of knowledge that extends beyond science" (Manicas & Secord, 1983, p. 412). Thus, it is useful for counseling professionals to continue to organize facts and knowledge into theoretical frameworks that can be used as ingredients within more complex and conditional models of behavior. Theoretical frameworks that consist of sets of conditional statements that can be qualified by specific information about an individual may allow both the needed specificity and complexity in explaining and predicting individuals' behavior. In sum, we believe that the second function of science is to promote understanding, as well as help explain and predict human action, but in a much more complex and idiographic manner than acknowledged in the traditional received view.

THE IMPORTANCE OF METHODOLOGICAL DIVERSITY   Inherent in the traditional view of science was the assumption that the "best" knowledge (and thus best research methodology) could be obtained from tightly controlled, experimental research that used randomization and control groups. There was an implicit hierarchy, with experimental studies at the top and correlational and descriptive studies at the bottom, seemingly based on an assumption that experimental investigations resulted in superior information. We disagree with such assumptions and maintain instead that the selection of the research method must fit both the phenomenon under investigation and the type of information sought (e.g., Ford, 1984; Howard, 1982, 1984; Patton, 1984; Polkinghorne, 1984). For example, we believe that far too often we attempt to do experimental, between-groups studies before we have an adequate description of some phenomenon; thus, in some cases, descriptive studies might very well yield more useful and important information than a controlled experimental investigation. A central thesis of this book is that it is essential to match the research design to the existing knowledge on a particular topic and the next best research questions of interest.

Since the 1980s, there has been a growing consensus for methodological diversity within counseling (e.g., Borgen, 1984a, 1984b, 1992; Gelso, 1979, 1982; Goldman, 1982; Harmon, 1982; Hoshmand, 1989; Howard, 1982, 1983, 1984; Polkinghorne, 1984, and Ponterotto, 2005b). We strongly agree that greater creativity and flexibility in using existing research methods is needed to examine important questions within counseling. Howard (1982) provided a parable that underscores the notion that different methods present advantages and limitations:

> In practice, one never demonstrates that one methodological approach is always superior to another. An elaboration and extension of a parable by the astronomer Eddington might draw this point into sharp relief. Eddington tells of a scientist who wished to catalogue the fish in the sea (the research question). He took a net of two-inch mesh (a research method) and cast it into the sea repeatedly. After carefully cataloguing his findings he concluded that there were no fish in the sea smaller than two inches. In this apocryphal example, the scientist's trust in the adequacy of his method was somewhat misplaced and led the researcher to draw an inaccurate conclusion. However, if someone had doubted the adequacy of the netting procedure and performed an investigation specifically to test its adequacy relative to

some specific alternative procedure, the misinterpretation might have been recognized. For example, our researcher might have considered an alternative research method: namely damming a small inlet of the sea, draining the water, and examining the bodies of the fish left behind. In finding fish smaller than two inches, the limitations of the netting procedure would become apparent. One would not be surprised, however, to find that the largest fish obtained via the damming approach was substantially smaller than was obtained with the netting approach: another potential problem. Therefore, research testing the adequacy of research methods does not prove which technique is better but provides evidence for the potential strengths and limitations of each. From this information, researchers can determine when one of two approaches, or both, should be the method of choice. (p. 319)

Methodological diversity spanning a range of quantitative and qualitative designs is essential for important advances in the counseling profession.

THE NEED TO EXAMINE AND EXPAND OUR VIEW OF HUMAN NATURE   The assumptions one makes regarding the basic qualities of human nature (that is, cognitive, affective, behavioral, and physiological processes) affect how one conceptualizes human behavior. Moreover, our view of human nature affects the research problems we examine in counseling. Our views of human nature have changed dramatically in the past century and are still evolving. Consistent with the beliefs of some of the previously mentioned writers (e.g., Borgen, 1984a; Howard, 1984; Patton, 1984; Polkinghorne, 1984), we believe there is a need to expand our view of how human beings operate, particularly within counseling. One increasingly accepted major change of view concerning human nature pertains to human rationality. For example, Gelatt (1989) noted that his view of human decision making, especially within a counseling context, changed dramatically in the previous 25 years. In 1962 he stressed rational processes in decision making, whereas in 1989 he stressed intuitive processes and positive uncertainty (that is, accepting uncertainty and inconsistencies). Gelatt's 1989 perspective was consistent with those of a host of other writers who at that time emphasized non-rational and unsystematic processes (chance events or luck) within human decision making (e.g., Heppner, 1989; Meehl, 1978; Strohmer & Blustein, 1990; Tversky & Kahneman, 1981). Meehl has cogently argued that our view of human nature should also include chance events: "luck is one of the most important contributors to individual differences in human suffering, satisfaction, illness, achievement, and so forth, an embarrassingly 'obvious' point that social scientists readily forget" (Meehl, 1978, p. 811).

Over the last 20 years, a number of suggestions have been made for how we might expand our view of human beings, such as human agency (e.g., Howard, 1984), phenomenological perspectives within language (e.g., Patton, 1984; Pepinsky, 1984), cognitive mediational processes (e.g., Martin, 1984), and information processing (e.g., Heppner & Krauskopf, 1987), particularly in nonlinear causal chains (e.g., Ford, 1984; Maruyama, 1963). It is striking that all these suggestions are process-oriented, thus suggesting that it may be fruitful to examine more dynamic and microscopic processes at this point within counseling research. Our view of human nature also pertains to our worldview, and assumptions that we make about race/ethnicity, age, gender, socialization, social class, sexual orientation, and those who are physically challenged (see APA, 2003). Our worldview also tends to be culture bound, or related to our cultural background, which often makes it difficult to understand the human nature in cultures quite different than our own culture. The major point here is that our view of human nature affects the research problems we examine in counseling. Thus, counseling researchers must examine their assumptions about human nature and investigate human behavior from a wide range of perspectives. Sometimes other areas of psychology (such as social psychology, developmental psychology, community psychology, and cross-cultural psychology) provide rich sources of information for investigation in a counseling context.

OUR RESPONSIBILITY FOR APPLYING A WIDE VARIETY OF RESEARCH TOOLS   Much of the responsibility for adequately applying the scientific method to counseling phenomena rests with researchers. Over 20 years ago, Strong (1984) aptly delineated this issue as follows:

> Scientific development in counseling psychology has not been as helpful to the pragmatic enterprise of counseling and therapy as we would like. It would be wrong to conclude that it has not been helpful, as many practices of counseling today have grown out of scientific efforts, such as behavior therapy, relationship skills, and psychological tests. There is a frustration that scientific efforts have had less pragmatic import than desired. I believe that this state of affairs is not the result of inherent limitations of the scientific enterprise, but of inadequacies in our conceptions of the objects of inquiry—human beings and the phenomenon of behavior change through interpersonal interaction. (pp. 472–473)

Although our science has clearly affected counseling practice today, the essential point is that the methods of science are only the tools we use to obtain knowledge about phenomena. A flashlight is a good analogy. A flashlight is a useful tool, but it will shine light only where we point it. If we cannot find the object we are looking for with a flashlight, it does not necessarily follow that we should throw the flashlight away, but rather that we should change the direction of the light. Similarly, our research methods will give us information only about the content we examine. If we are dissatisfied with the results, it does not necessarily follow that we should eliminate the research methods, but rather that we should try new angles with our research methods. It is possible, however, that we may need a bigger flashlight, or perhaps a flashlight that can bend around a corner. Thus, sometimes new research methodologies may be needed to help us acquire new or different types of knowledge. Developing new methodologies or alternative ways of collecting data obviously challenges the problem-solving and creative abilities of researchers. Presently, there are many ideas that we cannot examine adequately because we do not have the appropriate methodologies or measurement instruments. Researchers must be creative and versatile not only in the methodologies they use, but also in the types of data they collect in examining the phenomena that are central to counseling and human development.

SUMMARY AND CONCLUSIONS

The counseling profession helps people with a wide variety of personal, educational, and career-related problems. Most of all, we must be very cognizant that we are working with real people, many of whom need critically important information, and/or are experiencing psychological pain of some sort, and are in need of professional assistance. In this introductory chapter, we have discussed different ways to acquire knowledge in the counseling profession. To be credible, reliable, and effective, the profession must be built on a dependable knowledge base, rather than on tenacity, decrees from authority figures, or subjective opinions.

Science represents a way of knowing, a way of establishing relevant knowledge bases for the profession. We can debate about the best way of establishing suitable knowledge bases for our profession, and indeed, different underlying philosophical paradigms (e.g., positivism, postpositivism, constructivism, and critical theory) have led to very different beliefs as to what our science should look like. Regardless of the perspective, it is critical that it is understood that science plays an essential role in developing the knowledge upon which the counseling profession is based. Without a strong science to promote the continual development of our field, our profession will be significantly weakened. In this regard, it is incumbent upon the counseling profession to protect and promote the development of science to continually refine a wide range of knowledge relevant for the diverse forms of counseling practice.

Although our science promotes the development of relevant knowledge bases, it is also essential that the members of our profession are careful in applying our knowledge bases, and careful not to automatically assume that any particular knowledge base about a topic represents a "truth" that can be applied in many cases, across different personal and historical contexts. In fact, we are often at most risk when we consciously or unconsciously assume universal truths within counseling research and practice. For example, by the 1970s the utility of Rogerian conditions was well-documented and accepted in the United States (see Orlinsky, Grawe, & Parks, 1994). Moreover, in later years research has often documented that the working alliance, which is typically based at least in part on the Rogerian conditions, is one of the best predictors of counseling outcomes (Orlinsky et al., 1994). Not surprisingly, teaching of the Rogerian conditions has been widely adopted in many U.S. counselor training programs, as well as in other countries around the world. During my first visit to Taiwan in 1989, I (Heppner) was quite surprised to hear that counselors in Taiwan were finding that the Rogerian conditions were perceived as helpful but lacking is some significant ways in the process of counseling. My Taiwanese colleagues indicated that in Taiwan's culture, counselors were also viewed as teachers, and that clients typically expected a directive, advice-giving counseling style from an elder counselor/teacher. In essence, although there seemed to be some generalizabilty for the U.S. research about the Rogerian conditions to Taiwan, there also seemed to be significant differences in the application of the U.S. "knowledge." Later counseling research in Taiwan has suggested that the counselors' active problem solving and resolution of the clients' presenting problem are also important factors in the counseling process (Wei & Heppner, 2005). In sum, although our science is critically important in establishing relevant knowledge bases for the counseling profession, it is equally important to be vigilant in applying even well-documented findings, especially across different social and cultural contexts.

Thus, we end this introductory chapter on the role of science in counseling with two main conclusions. First, the role of science is essential for the counseling profession, not only for the well-being and growth of the profession, but also for its very survival. Second, and equally important, the ability of the members of the counseling profession to appropriately apply our scientific knowledge to facilitate the development of a diverse clientele is essential; to this end, the ability of all of our members to question assumptions, biases, and stereotypes, and to think scientifically is of utmost importance, and will be discussed more fully in the next chapter.

STIMULUS QUESTIONS

REFLECTIONS ON SCIENCE IN COUNSELING

The purpose of the following exercise is to promote additional reflection on the role of science and practice in the field of counseling. We suggest you answer each question in writing, and then discuss your responses with a peer in class to further discuss and explore these issues.

1. What do you see as the primary value of science in the counseling profession?
2. Which philosophical paradigm is most appealing to you personally? What do you see as some of the advantages and disadvantages of this paradigm?
3. What is the second philosophical paradigm that is most appealing to you? What do you see as some of the advantages and disadvantages of this paradigm?
4. In what ways do you think methodological diversity is necessary in the counseling profession?
5. What do you see as the most important outcome of research in counseling?
6. What role does your worldview play in how you might engage in research and practice? What do you see as the disadvantages and advantages of your worldview for both research and practice?
7. Given all of the complexities in different philosophical paradigms, which one do you want to learn more about? Why?

2 CHAPTER | RESEARCH TRAINING

It takes many years to become truly skilled at a complex set of tasks, such as becoming a skilled potter. For example, in Japan, it is common for an apprentice potter to make the same vase form for many months just to acquire the specific skills to consistently make 15–20 identical vases in a row. Expertise develops over time within an environment that fosters development. In this chapter we discuss the process of becoming a skilled researcher, and the type of training environments that seem to be most helpful for students to acquire the necessary skills and attitudes. For many students in counseling, graduate school is their first introduction to research design, and it evokes many emotional reactions that come with any novel experience, from joy and excitement to anxiety and disenchantment. We seek to prepare students to approach research with enthusiasm for the creativity involved and with a willingness to learn the intricacies of the craft. In addition, we want to promote an awareness of the anxiety that may be created by learning a technical skill that may not be central to one's interests but is required to accomplish a goal (that is, obtaining a graduate degree and becoming a professional in counseling).

We begin the chapter by providing a brief overview of the scientist-practitioner model, and discuss the value as well as some concerns about this popular training model. Next we identify and discuss some issues related to the developmental process of acquiring research competencies, specifically the joy as well as the challenges and fears. Then we specifically discuss ways in which counselors and counseling psychologists can train others to become competent, eager, and productive researchers. In this part of the chapter, we discuss what is known about research training, and how training environments can be structured to create the opportunity for students both to learn about research and to consume and produce quality research products. Finally, we discuss ways to broaden the concept of scientific training to include scientific thinking skills as well as research application skills. Most important, throughout this chapter we emphasize the developmental process of acquiring skills step by step to become a skilled researcher and scientist.

THE SCIENTIST-PRACTITIONER MODEL

Most graduate training programs in counseling espouse the scientist-practitioner model of training. Basically, this model consists of training in both scientific and practitioner activities; the basic assumption is that students trained in both science and practice will be better prepared for the multitude of employment demands in the counseling profession. The scientific activities include courses that focus on the philosophy of science, qualitative and quantitative designs and methods, statistics, evaluation, counseling research literature, and often involvement in research projects (Larson & Besett-Alesch, 2000). The practice-oriented side includes courses such as counseling methods, counseling theories, personality, assessment, and involvement in a variety of practica experiences. When students enter a graduate training program in counseling, they typically have a wide range of interests along the scientist-practitioner continuum. These interests often change over time, not only during graduate training but also throughout their career; thus, students need to prepare themselves broadly to allow for career changes over time.

The scientist-practitioner model goes back almost 50 years. The first national conferences for the training of clinical and counseling psychologists were held in Boulder, Colorado, and Ann Arbor, Michigan, in 1949 and 1950, respectively. One major purpose of the Boulder conference was to develop a broad model of training. After two weeks of meeting daily, the clinical psychologists developed what they dubbed the scientist-practitioner model of training, which is also referred to as the Boulder model (Raimy, 1950). The creators of that model stressed the philosophy that in addition to learning the skills of the practitioner, students also need to be trained to do research, and that the integration of these two skill sets creates a strong foundation for future research and practice. Counseling psychologists affirmed this model in Ann Arbor. In addition, the field of counseling psychology has repeatedly reiterated its commitment to the scientist-practitioner model, most notably in 1951 at the Northwestern conference (Whiteley, 1984), in 1964 at the Greystone conference (Thompson & Super, 1964), and again in 1987 at the Atlanta conference (Meara et al., 1988). In the 1990s there was "an increasingly active interest in and commitment to making the scientist-practitioner model work" (Watkins, 1994, p. 318). This interest has been maintained into 2007, although there has been varying degrees of emphasis on science and practice across programs (Neimeyer, Saferstein, & Rice, 2005).

Meara et al. (1988) succinctly captured the scientist-practitioner model:

> Those at the Georgia [Atlanta] conference agreed that because psychology is a science, both the generation and application of psychological knowledge are based on scientific views of the world. Psychologists, whatever their work, are professionals and their attitude toward their work is scientific.
>
> The scientist-professional model is an integrated approach to knowledge that recognizes the interdependence of theory, research, and practice. The model emphasizes systematic and thoughtful analyses of human experiences and judicious application of the knowledge and attitudes gained from such analyses. An attitude of scholarly inquiry is critical to all the activities of those educated in the scientist-professional model.
>
> The model encompasses a variety of research methods, assessment techniques, and intervention strategies. The counseling psychologist is engaged in the pursuit and application of psychological knowledge to promote optimal development for individuals, groups, and systems (including families), and to provide remedies for the psychological difficulties that encumber them. To implement these goals, the scientist-professional psychologist adopts a scientific approach based on observation of psychological phenomena. This approach generates theoretical constructs and propositions, which are in turn tested as hypotheses (Claiborn, 1987; Pepinsky & Pepinsky, 1954). (p. 368)

CONCERNS WITH THE MODEL

Especially in the earlier years, writers from both counseling and clinical psychology questioned the utility of the scientist-practitioner model (e.g., Albee, 1970; Gelso, 1979). In addition, writers questioned the value of psychological research for practitioners (e.g., Goldman, 1976; Howard, 1984; Polkinghorne, 1983). They contended that most practitioners do not use research findings in their practice, and that, in fact, research findings are often meaningless. This contention led some writers to the conclusion that research training is not necessary for practitioners (e.g., Frank, 1984; Hughes, 1952; Meehl, 1971). Others suggested that students are not receiving adequate training in how to think scientifically, whether it is about clients or about research (e.g., Anderson & Heppner, 1986; Claiborn, 1984; Goodyear & Benton, 1986).

The debate regarding the utility of the scientist-practitioner model is a complex one involving multiple factors. For instance, the model itself could be unrealistic and impossible to fulfill in reality (e.g., Albee, 1970; Gelso, 1979). Conversely, perhaps the training students receive in scientific activities is inadequate or even inappropriate (e.g., Anderson & Heppner, 1986; Gelso, 1979; Goodyear & Benton, 1986; Heppner, Gelso, & Dolliver, 1987; Royalty, Gelso, Mallinckrodt, & Garrett, 1986; Wampold, 1998).

Moreover, it could also be that graduate training in practitioner activities does not adequately incorporate scientific activities, and vice versa (e.g., Anderson & Heppner, 1986; Goodyear & Benton, 1986). It does seem questionable whether graduate students are taught to think about applied problems and to process information as scientists (e.g., Betz, 1986; Claiborn, 1987).

Perhaps the type of research being conducted is too distant from the reality of the practitioner (e.g., Howard, 1984; Polkinghorne, 1984), or perhaps our research methods reduce counseling phenomena to meaningless numbers (e.g., Goldman, 1976). Or maybe our professional journals are structured in ways that make it cumbersome for practitioners to find and assimilate the information they need (e.g., Gelso et al., 1988; Heppner, Carter, et al., 1992). Yet another factor could be that students admitted to graduate programs have predominantly social or interpersonal interests (e.g., Magoon & Holland, 1984) or have been selected on a very narrow range of criteria (Bernstein & Kerr, 1993).

Another issue is how the scientist-practitioner model has been conceptualized in the past. Sometimes the model has been interpreted as a 50–50 split of performing science and practice activities. The type of model in its ideal form (that is, implicitly 50% practitioner and 50% scientist/researcher) may be just that—an ideal that is rarely found in reality. Gelso (1979) proposed that it may be more realistic to train students in both domains (in varying degrees depending on their interests) with the expectation that students will find a suitable place for themselves in performing relevant activities on the scientist-practitioner continuum. Thus, one student might prefer a 20–80 split while another might choose a 75–25 split. Sometimes there have been implicit values attached to either science or practice; that is, some educators might value science more than practice, and thus feel more satisfaction when a new graduate obtains the "best" job, which to them is an academic position complete with a myriad of scientific pursuits. We strongly believe that science and practice are both highly valued activities in the counseling profession, and that as a profession we are stronger (and only can survive) when we train students to be competent in both science and practice. In short, it is important for the profession to equally value various points along this performance continuum.

We prefer to conceptualize the *core* of the scientist-practitioner in terms of scientific or critical thinking. In short, we are suggesting that the role of scientific or critical thinking is a central outcome of the scientist-practitioner model and forms the core of a wide range of science and practice activities. The choice of whether a graduate engages in science or practice activities is not the most important outcome, but rather whether the graduate can utilize scientific or critical thinking in whatever professional activities he or she chooses. For example, a counseling center staff member might be engaged primarily in direct client service and, say, one program evaluation project (see Chapter 21); this might be a 5%–95% science-practice split of *professional activities*. A faculty member (three-quarters time) with a quarter-time direct service appointment in the counseling center might have a 75%–25% split of professional activities. Regardless of the type of professional activities a person selects along the scientist-practitioner continuum, we maintain that both of these individuals could reflect the goals of the scientist-practitioner model through their scientific thinking within their practice and science activities.

Hans Strupp, a noted clinical psychologist with a great deal of experience in practice, research, training, and professional affairs, concluded in 1981 that inadequate training in scientific thinking has been a major problem in the development of the mental health profession, notably in terms of:

> Failure to inspire students to become critical and independent thinkers; failure to teach students abiding respect for empirical data and rival hypotheses; insufficient attention to clinical realities—patient selection, formulation of treatment goals, bold experimentation with alternative technical approaches, systematic exploration of the limits of existing approaches, and the like. . . . Harry Stack Sullivan once expressed amazement at how difficult it is for most people to think seriously of even one alternative hypothesis to explain clinical observations. In short, clinical training must not only be comprehensive and thorough, but it must educate students to become thinking clinicians who can effectively apply quality control in their daily practice. Unless we succeed in selecting and training clinicians who can exercise this kind of self-surveillance, who practice responsibly and effectively while being mindful of their human and professional limitations, it is predictable that governmental controls and bureaucratic rules will make a charade of professional work in this area. It may already be later than we realize. (pp. 217–218)

In the end, there is no doubt that research has enhanced the practice of counseling. Even though a practitioner may not be able to cite a specific reference, his or her graduate school training was likely based on a tremendous amount of research data, all the way from personality theory to intervention strategies. The accumulation may be slow, but the data eventually advance our working knowledge of the field (Heppner & Anderson, 1985). The scientific method and research have advanced the field, but they could be even more helpful. In addition, training in both science and practice has become more sophisticated with not only more integration, but also more emphasis on scientific thinking, which is the core of all science and practice activities of the counseling profession. For more information on a broad array of recommendations for enhancing training in the scientist-practitioner model, see Heppner, Carter, and colleagues (1992).

JOYS AND CHALLENGES IN ACQUIRING RESEARCH COMPETENCIES

Students will often experience a number of different reactions to research training, and these emotional reactions can change throughout the course of their graduate training, and actually many years beyond. Sometimes students will be elated with the joy of discovering new and useful information from their research. Other times students will become restless and disgruntled with the minutiae associated with research. In addition, some students will experience obstacles such as negative self-talk, procrastination, perfectionist tendencies, and a range of "shoulds" (e.g., I should be better at math; see Heppner & Heppner, 2004).

The developmental process of acquiring research competencies takes considerable time, years in fact, and often differs across students. Below and throughout this chapter are reflections from experienced and skillful researchers who provide some useful glimpses into this developmental process of acquiring an array of research competencies. A great deal of wisdom is communicated by these prolific and creative scholars, and we appreciate their candid perspectives on their own developmental process.

After graduating from college with degrees in Biology and Sociology (and a minor in Women's Studies), I worked in an inner city battered women's shelter. At the shelter, I became interested in what differentiated women who returned to the abuser from women who struggled to create nonviolent lives for themselves and their children. Without any knowledge of psychological research, I developed a survey and collected information from the women in the shelter. Around this time, I missed being in school and decided to enroll in a course of interest to me. The professor (Nancy Murdock) encouraged me to join her research team and pursue a doctoral degree. With her help, I completed a thesis related to shelter workers' perceptions of battered women. I loved how my work in the shelter informed and was informed by my research. I also began to see that while helping people individually was rewarding to me, I could really make a difference through sharing my knowledge and research findings with others. My doctoral program solidified my passion for research as I was given the opportunity to study topics of interest to me that had real-world applications. Helping women to achieve economic self-sufficiency developed as a focus of my work. I sometimes struggled with a component of research (e.g., collecting data from difficult to obtain samples), but as soon as this task became unbearable, the next step in research brought new and exciting challenges (e.g., analyzing those data!). As a new assistant professor at the University of Kansas, my favorite part of my job was pursuing questions of interest with a talented (and fun) research team. Today, mentoring students as they become involved in research that makes a difference is a meaningful aspect of my work as an associate professor at the University of Maryland.

—Karen O'Brien, Ph.D.

I love research! I say this in all honesty. I've always loved research—learning about theories, thinking about relations among and between phenomena, finding ways to better understand processes that I think are personally interesting and socially meaningful, and empirically testing ideas. Although research has provided me with a rich intellectual life and has been a rewarding aspect of my career, the process of conducting research has been one of the most challenging personal and professional journeys. I say process because developing competencies in research is not an event. Instead, it is a slow journey; as some markers are achieved, new competency goals quickly surface. Do I feel like I have arrived? No. However, I continue to derive satisfaction as I grow and develop.

As a racial minority woman researcher, I have found the journey of developing competencies particularly challenging for a variety of reasons. On a personal level, I have often doubted whether my ideas were "good," and make a "significant contribution"; I have questioned whether I could in fact "do it" and produce a meaningful product. I think that when I began my career, research on race, racism, and cultural processes in counseling psychology was not always valued. There were significantly fewer racial and ethnic minority researchers in the field to chart the way. Outsiders who examined some of the research that I conducted on general and cultural factors related to the stress and coping processes of Black Americans informed me of the importance of comparing the experiences of racial minorities to those of Whites and that my focus on Black participants was too narrow. Thus, I had to contend with my own feelings of inadequacies in my research skills and I had to rationalize to others why studying Black Americans in and of themselves is important.

I did not always hear the encouraging words from others about my ability to carry out a project or the importance of the work. I instead focused on the negative messages that I received. So, part of my journey has been to develop efficacy in my abilities, to honestly identify growth areas, and to tune out naysayers; in essence, I have had to learn how to believe in what I do and in my ideas.

I have struggled with issues of "voice" at different times throughout my career. I have had to acknowledge that I have an interpretation of events that is worthy of consideration. One of the most helpful suggestions that I have received came from my partner (Sundiata Cha-Jua). I received a rejection letter for a manuscript on a project on the influence of color-blind racial ideology on attitudes and behaviors, one of my central areas of research. I shared the reviews with my partner and his response was very reassuring. He said "Oh, they just don't like your project." The point here is that not everyone is going to like what I do or how I approach the topic area and that is okay. This does not mean that the research is not valuable and that it does not make a contribution. My co-author and I revised the manuscript based on the reviews and subsequently the article was published in another journal.

One last way in which I have developed as a researcher has been to observe colleagues in different departments. Many of my colleagues know that research is a process that requires feedback and input from a number of sources. To help develop a research project, it is absolutely essential to share your work with others and get feedback at all stages. I have learned that it is okay to have a project be underdeveloped in its initial conceptualization. I now realize that others do not judge me (or the research team) on where I start, but rather on where I end up. That is, how I have incorporated the ideas and suggestions from others and how much the project has developed over time. Knowing this has provided me the space to make mistakes, learn, and grow.

—Helen Neville, Ph.D.

These reflections, as well as others throughout the chapter, depict various aspects of the developmental process of acquiring research competencies. From our collective experiences as authors of this text, we have observed that many students question whether they can adequately learn the skills associated with research and science: How can I, a mere graduate student, come up with a good research idea? What if I get bogged down in my research and never finish my degree? Statistics scare me—what if I make a mistake in analyzing my data? We contend that these and other fears are common and developmentally normal. We believe it is essential to discuss the negative affective and cognitive components associated with research, and thus the first section focuses on such common student reactions, namely: (1) performance anxiety and efficacy; (2) threats, unrewarding training, and disenchantment; (3) the false dichotomous conceptualization as research versus practice; and (4) belief in oneself as a researcher and science in general.

PERFORMANCE ANXIETY AND EFFICACY   From our experience working with students, we have found that performance anxiety is a central and crucial affective issue. Other educators have come to similar conclusions (e.g., Claiborn, 1984; Gelso, 1979). For example, common student disclosures include: "I don't know enough to conduct any meaningful research on my own. How can I do a thesis?" "Any study that I could do would be so basic and bland as to make it worthless." "I feel completely inadequate in even conceiving a study that comes at counseling from a unique perspective." "Although I made it through the statistics and research design courses, once I start to do some research, I'll be 'found out'; I am a fraud, and really don't know how to do research." "What if I make a mistake and report inaccurate findings?" "I've had trouble writing before, and I'm scared to death that I will run into debilitating writing blocks again in my research." "I am afraid that my results will be statistically nonsignificant, and all of my research efforts and time will just be one big waste." "I've seen other students in the throes of a dissertation. The whole process seems overwhelming, tedious, long, anxiety-producing, confusing, and complicated."

It is important to put these and similar feelings into the context of the typical entering graduate student. Most incoming graduate students have had some experience (or even a lot) with helping other people, and consequently the benefits of counseling and other practitioner activities are abundantly clear. Moreover, for most of us, helping people is a personally rewarding experience, and students have an understanding of those rewards. Conversely, it has been our experience that most incoming students have had considerably less experience with science. Typically, students do not imagine themselves making contributions to the profession by publishing in our professional journals. Since students have had little, if any, research experience, they often have legitimate reasons to question and doubt their skills and abilities—these feelings, concerns, and fears are thus developmentally normal. In fact, it is not uncommon for faculty to experience performance anxiety and question their efficacy. This suggests to us that acquiring the necessary research and thinking skills occurs over a long period of time; it does not happen all at once. Just as it is unreasonable to expect to become an Olympic downhill skier in four years, it is also unreasonable to expect to become an expert researcher in four years of graduate education (Nancy Downing, personal communication, June 28, 1990).

My experience in research began as a master's level student at the University of Hawaii with counseling faculty who were working on issues of multiculturalism and diversity. As I understood it at that time, the "multicultural movement" was largely a political movement, fueled by the Civil Rights Movement of 1960 and couched within the field under improving the ethical practice of counselors. The professors at UH, however, understood the importance of research to establish a firm empirical basis for the "movement." I, as a student committed to these issues, volunteered for several research teams with them. However, not having had a solid research training background, my contributions, I would guess, were largely limited to my enthusiasm.

After earning my master's degree in school counseling, I had the good fortune of becoming Donald Atkinson's doctoral advisee in counseling psychology at the University of California, Santa Barbara. Here, I learned first hand via Don's work the power of research—that is, good research work can lead to dramatic changes in our profession and society (e.g., the field's current attention to client's cultural background). It was also during this period that my research training became more solidified through several courses on research methods and a statistics course (by the way, the first edition of this book was the textbook used in my main research methods course and it couldn't have offered me a better start!). Most importantly, however, it was really the day-to-day work on several research studies with Don that taught me the intricacies of research, starting from problem conceptualization and moving into research design, data collection, data analyses, and manuscript submission. So in hindsight, I mostly "LEARNED BY DOING." And, I've come to understand that there is no magic formula to becoming a good researcher but to have a good guide and lots of enthusiasm. Of course, like others have said in this chapter, having a research manuscript accepted for publication, which I see as an opportunity to share my work with a larger audience, also has reinforced my enthusiasm and energy. So, my recommendation is: "GET INVOLVED, JOIN RESEARCH TEAMS, STUDY THE TOPICS OF YOUR PASSION, AND HAVE FUN!"

—Bryan S. K. Kim, Ph.D.

As students acquire and begin to apply their knowledge about research design, we have been struck by *many* students' surprise and actual delight about research as they get past their initial fears. We often have heard comments like, "I'm actually *enjoying* this research course"; "I never thought I would be a researcher; now I'm beginning to reconsider my career goals"; "This research stuff is contagious; I'm starting to think about research studies a lot and I want to collect data now!" In sum, the major point is that beginning graduate students often have considerably less information about research and science than about practitioner activities. Moreover, there is evidence that as students obtain more experience with research activities (especially if it is early in their training), their research interests increase and they place a higher value on the role of research (e.g., Gelso, Raphael, Black, Rardin, & Skalkos, 1983; Royalty et al., 1986).

Thus, our advice to students regarding performance anxiety is first of all to recognize that feelings of anxiety and doubt associated with research are normal, and often reflect where one is in the developmental process of acquiring new competencies, in this case research competencies. Second, we strongly recommend that students get involved with research projects to slowly develop various research competencies. We believe the best way to create a sense of research efficacy is to learn and perform those skills. For example, students might offer to volunteer to help on a research project to learn the basic research skills, and slowly work their way up to learn the more advanced skills. In essence, both our experience and our research have suggested that the more students get involved in research, the more self-efficacy they tend to feel; the more efficacious students feel about conducting research, the more positive they are about the training environment (Gelso, Mallinckrodt, & Judge, 1996; Kahn & Scott, 1997; Phillips & Russell, 1994) and interest in research (Kahn & Scott, 1997).

In many ways, I was a late bloomer academically. I had been kicked out of high school and somehow made my way through college on raw ability, luck, and the kindness of others. I had little crystallized understanding of the world. I could read and write well enough but I didn't have clear, cogent thoughts on many subjects. I also had few academic role models in my life. My parents and two older brothers had never finished college and I felt tremendous pressure to be a success. So when I began graduate school at Virginia Commonwealth University, I had many doubts about my abilities and talents. I had a healthy dose of ambition and motivation but a larger dose of uncertainty and insecurity. If I had to identify a key turning point in graduate school, it had to be when I got my first manuscript, based on my master's thesis, accepted for publication in Journal of Counseling Psychology. *I was overwhelmed with pride and joy. Here was validation for all my effort. I finally started to really believe in myself as a researcher who could make a difference. Today, I often tell my graduate students that the first publication is like the first taste of blood. You either want more of it or you realize it isn't for you. I guess I liked that first taste because it definitely gave me the confidence and motivation to engage in more research.*

—*Richard Lee, Ph.D.*

THREATS, UNREWARDING TRAINING, AND DISENCHANTMENT   For any of a number of reasons, students' research training is often less than rewarding, and actually often rather threatening, all of which can result in student disenchantment. Consider this not-too-hypothetical example, offered by Gelso (1979):

> Harold/Hannah Helpful, our typical student, enters graduate school with much ambivalence and anxiety about the scholarly requirements of that situation, as well as the role of science in his/her career. He/she knows he/she has done quite well in school all along, but the scholarly demands of a doctoral program are a different ball game for him/her. Yet he/she is indeed ambivalent, not negative.
>
> At the same time, he/she probably endows the faculty with some degree of omniscience. What the student runs into during the first year is a bewildering array of requirements, including courses (unfortunately, sometimes even in his/her specialty) that are demanding but unexciting. Usually this includes one or two statistics

courses that teach little if anything about counseling research, but seem wedded to the scientific enterprise. These courses often deepen the student's anxiety and deaden motivation. The task is to get through them.

Toward the end of the first year our hypothetical student must start thinking thesis. More anxiety. Up to that point he/she has done no research, acquired no confidence, and at best has gotten through statistics unscathed.

The student does not know how to generate ideas that later may be translated into scientifically answerable questions. The process goes on, through the preliminary meeting with the advisor, the thesis proposal meeting, and the thesis orals. All steps along the way are all too often filled with more threat and anxiety than pleasure of discovery. The fortunate student gets by without massive revisions of the thesis and can take a deep breath until the next major scientific hurdle, the dissertation. When assessed against the criterion of, "Is it positively reinforcing?" this unfortunately not very exaggerated description of the scientific regimen of graduate school hurdles is a dreadful failure. (p. 28).

Unfortunately, when students have little experience with research and science, one bad experience can create tremendous attitudinal and motivational damage and move a student a long way from future scientific activities. Indeed, there is some evidence that some training programs actually decrease students' interest in research (Royalty et al., 1986).

The profession has come a long way in enhancing research training over the last two decades. Consideration of students' affective reactions, values, and individual differences, and of the training environment will most likely continue to enhance the development of students' research efficacy. In addition, consideration of cultural values and social connections are especially important issues for some racial/ethnic minority and international students whose cultural values make it more difficult to seek and participate in the research groups without others' invitation or help.

THE FALSE DICHOTOMOUS CONCEPTUALIZATION OF SCIENCE VERSUS PRACTICE   Another developmental issue is how students conceptualize science and research, and their relationship to practice. A common statement is, "I just want to practice; I am not interested in science/research." Thus, science and research are conceptualized as totally distinct from practice, and for some students, science is perceived as irrelevant for practice. In the past, counseling has been characterized frequently as *either* an art *or* a science, but, as Goodyear and Benton (1986) note, this is a rather narrow view:

This dichotomy, however, oversimplifies the situation and perhaps exists because of a misunderstanding of the scientist role. Scientists are too often confused with technicians, the people who apply the findings of science but without theoretical understanding . . . . The best scientists overlap with the best artists in their capacity for alternative ways of perceiving, in their creativity, and in their openness to new experiences. (p. 290)

In short, sometimes the scientific enterprise is erroneously conceptualized as totally separate from applied work in counseling. Thus, a false dichotomy is established, science versus practice.

In 1989, Michael Patton became president of the Division of Counseling Psychology (Division 17 of the American Psychological Association); he chose "Practice into Science: Science into Practice" as his presidential theme. In essence, Patton's theme depicted the interplay between practice and science, and how each one informed the other; that is, not only do the results of our science inform practice, but the results of our practice in turn inform our science as well. In this sense, science and practice are not independent entities, but rather are intertwined activities. Our belief is that those students who develop skills in both arenas will be better equipped to do the work of the counseling profession.

Moreover, one of the hallmarks of graduate work in counseling is to acquire critical thinking skills, the ability to identify and process information with fewer biases, stereotypes, and assumptions; formulate hypotheses; gather data; and make informed decisions. These critical thinking skills are essential in both the practice and science arenas. Our advice to students is to avoid a narrow conceptualization of research and science and to not prematurely conclude that research and science have little or nothing to offer the practitioner. Rather, we encourage practice-oriented students to be open to learning more about the research process as well as the research literature, and how these experiences can inform practice and improve their counseling competence. The scientific method is simply a set of tools to establish a controlled mode of inquiry about all of our professional activities, research and practice.

DISBELIEF IN ONESELF AS A RESEARCHER AND SCIENCE IN GENERAL   A critically important belief in the process of becoming a competent researcher is believing in one's ability to conduct meaningful research as well as belief in the utility of research, that research does contribute to the profession's knowledge bases, and that our research can and does make a difference in clients' lives.

It is common for students to not initially feel efficacious as a researcher nor to believe that our research in counseling can make a difference in the profession. Most beginning students do not have much of an understanding of the role of science in our profession, and since they do not have a long history in the profession they are unable to identify how previous research has contributed to the profession. Similarly, students do not have a clear understanding of the utility of the scientific method as a way of thinking about either research or clients. Finally, the student typically has had relatively little experience of expanding his or her understanding about clients and applied problems by engaging in research, reading the professional literature, and contemplating the implication of empirical findings. One unfortunate outcome is that students sometimes fill this void with misinformation, like "science = statistics." Or students believe that "science is too intellectual, too cognitive, and unrelated to the experiences of real people." Or "the scientific method is so mechanical and reductionistic that it cannot be used adequately to study the complexities of real human behavior." Conversely, seasoned researchers understand both the challenges of conducting meaningful research and the gradual but steady accumulation of knowledge from our research. Even though it is rare that any one study has a major impact on the profession, programmatic research often does result in the accrual of knowledge over time, and often achieves significant conclusions. For example, many of the chapters in the *Handbook of Counseling Psychology* (Brown & Lent, 2000) are based on extensive literature reviews, and nicely reflect the utility of our research in creating knowledge as well as enhancing the sophistication of our conceptualization of relevant constructs in counseling.

Clara Hill, a creative and prolific counseling researcher, was invited to write a personal account of her evolution as a researcher. Her account illustrates how she made decisions, how complex the process of research can be, and how she coped with the ups and downs along the way and, most important, her "crisis of faith in research":

> After this series of studies I underwent a crisis in terms of research. I had achieved tenure, had my first baby, and turned 30. I started questioning everything. Because I could see so many imperfections in my research, I was not very proud of my work. It had taken an incredible amount of time for little "hard information." I could not even remember the results of many of my studies. Further, I seemed woefully far from even describing what happens in the counseling process let alone understanding what counselor behaviors were useful in effecting change. I despaired that counseling was far too complex to be studied. I had previously had lots of doubts about my research, but it was mostly related to self-confidence in my research abilities. This crisis seemed to have more to do with whether I felt that research was a viable means to answer questions about the counseling process. (Hill, 1984, p. 105)

Hill's behind-the-scenes disclosures are illuminating as well as often relieving for many students and faculty. We strongly encourage students to read this article, perhaps during their first course on research methods. We have found that Hill's frustrations, jubilations, feelings of inadequacy, and doubts about the role of research resonate strongly with students. The evolution of Hill's confidence in the utility of conducting research in her own way not only sends a useful message, but also illuminates the developmental processes of students and faculty in becoming skilled and competent researchers.

When I started graduate school my dream was to become a director of a counseling center at some small liberal arts college. Research was not a part of my career dreams, and I had no sense that I could ever actually publish an article in a professional journal. Moreover, I had little to no interest in research. In my first semester, a friend and I conducted a small research project on prose learning for a class requirement. The results of our pilot study motivated both of us to conduct a large scale investigation on the same topic the following semester. From this work I gained a modicum of research self-efficacy, but more importantly, became very excited about the process of discovering new information through research.

Two years later another student and I conducted a study on perceived counselor expertise for a statistics class requirement; we submitted the paper for editorial review, and to our great excitement, it was accepted (pending revisions)! Around the same time, Mary (my wife) and I submitted a paper to another journal on counseling rape victims, and after initial rejection, it too was accepted for publication. In retrospect, these initial successes were critical to my development as a researcher, as they not only propelled me into more research projects with faculty (which greatly enhanced my learning), but also allowed me to experience the joys of discovery as well as a sense of accomplishment in contributing to the professional literature. These and subsequent research experiences with my advisor, David Dixon, in graduate school shifted my career aspirations toward academia.

—Puncky Heppner, Ph.D.

From our experience, it is critical not only that researchers feel efficacious in conducting relevant and important research, but also that they begin to perceive that their research is important, that it contributes useful information to our professional knowledge bases, and that it can make a difference in the profession as well as the lives of our clients. Such beliefs often are the result of identifying implications of your research findings to practice, being cited in the professional literature in meaningful ways, or seeing either that others are using your research findings in applied settings or that your research is helping other researchers subsequently ask other important questions.

Belief in the utility of research can also result from reading the professional literature to learn the impact of others' research. Our advice is for students to not only read and reflect on the literature, but also to read literature reviews in particular (see Major Contributions in *The Counseling Psychologist* or review papers in *Psychological Bulletin*). In addition, we advise students to get involved in conducting research on topics that are really important to them, either topics that they are very interested in or ones that reflect their personal values in some way.

Becoming a researcher has truly been a developmental process for me. From coming up with a topic, to developing a research question, to determining how to answer the research question, each aspect of becoming a researcher is honed with practice over time. Early on in graduate school I knew that I was interested in racial identity as a broad topic, but I did not know how to develop a research question based on my interest. So, I began to immerse myself in the racial identity literature. The more I read, the more I began to understand the construct, and most importantly, the more I began to see some gaps and unanswered questions in the literature.

I firmly believe that the best researchers usually have a connection and passion about their research. I developed my research program, in part, to help me understand and make sense of my own experiences as an African American man in a predominantly White college environment struggling to do well academically, while at the same time trying to learn more about my history and culture. This desire to better understand myself and the experiences of other people like me led to a dissertation, my first publication, and several other articles. The lesson to be learned is that the more you can take ownership of the research topic, the greater the chances that you will feel excited about conducting research in that area. Perhaps the most important lesson that I have learned has been to be tenacious and resilient. Everyone has experienced challenges in writing and conducting research at some point, and everybody has experienced rejection when trying to publish something. I have learned that it is not always the "smartest" people who can successfully carry out a research project and publish it, but often it is those individuals who are the most resilient.

—*Kevin Cokley, Ph.D.*

A MODEL FOR RESEARCH TRAINING

The purpose of this section is to discuss a number of factors that are important in enhancing research training. Our goal is not only to enhance students' awareness of what appears to be some of the major constructs in research training, but also to promote additional attention and research on this important developmental process. Several early articles identified a number of variables that might be related to effective research training (e.g., Gelso, 1979; Holland, 1986; Magoon & Holland, 1984; Osipow, 1979). Subsequently, researchers have empirically examined the effects of some of these variables on such research outcomes as research productivity (see, for example, Brown, Lent, Ryan, & McParland, 1996; Gelso, Mallinckrodt, & Judge, 1996; Gelso et al., 1983; Kahn & Gelso, 1997; Kahn & Scott, 1997; Mallinckrodt, Gelso, & Royalty, 1990; Phillips & Russell, 1994; Royalty & Magoon, 1985; Royalty & Reising, 1986; Royalty et al., 1986). This research has culminated in the development and testing of the complex model of research training (Kahn & Scott, 1997) presented in Figure 2.1. We will discuss this model and the empirical evidence that supports parts of it, as well as add a few other important aspects of research training not included in the model. We begin by discussing each of the major constructs in the model: (1) personality type, (2) research training environment, (3) research self-efficacy, (4) research interest, (5) research productivity, and (6) career goals in research.

CONSTRUCTS OF THE MODEL

PERSONALITY TYPE   Most students in counseling and counseling psychology can be categorized into one of Holland's (1992) three personality types: social, artistic, or investigative.

Research has shown that the personality of counseling students is related to interest in research and in research courses (Betz & Taylor, 1982; Mallinckrodt et al., 1990), to choice of graduate research programs with traditions of producing research (Mallinckrodt et al. 1990), and to research productivity (Krebs, Smither, & Hurley, 1991; Tinsley, Tinsley, Boone, & Shim-Li, 1993). Specifically, it appears that students who are investigative types have more interest in research activities and ultimately produce more research. Accordingly, Kahn and Scott (1997) predicted that a student's Holland personality type would be directly related to research interest, which in turn

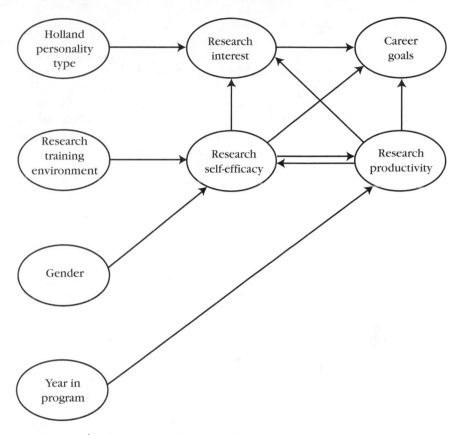

FIGURE 2.1 | HYPOTHESIZED RELATIONSHIPS AMONG THE CONSTRUCTS OF
A STRUCTURAL EQUATION MODEL FOR RESEARCH TRAINING

From Kahn & Scott, *The Consulting Psychologist*, *25*(1), p. 40. Copyright © 1997 by
the Society of Counseling Psychology of the American Psychological Association.
Reprinted by permission of Sage Publications, Inc.

would be related to research productivity and career goals related to research
(see Figure 2.1). In particular, investigative types are hypothesized to be more
interested in research, and social types less interested.

*Research satisfies, for me, two primary characteristics of my personality: (a) the
desire to investigate, and (b) the need to contribute to the well-being of members
of our society, particularly those who are not privileged. After many years of
research on various areas related to counseling psychology, including the process
of counseling and psychotherapy and interpersonal environments in scientific
laboratories, I found myself teaching a course on research on individual psychological interventions. The text for the class was a handbook that reviewed
many areas of counseling and psychotherapy. A class assignment involved taking*

a conclusion made by the author of each chapter, reading the original research that was cited to support the conclusion, and deciding whether or not the research did indeed support the conclusion. We found that authors often claimed that a particular treatment was superior to another when the research cited did not support that conclusion. This practice was offensive to me because it tended to privilege some treatments (mainly, cognitive and behavioral treatments) over others, without scientific basis. To support my and my students' contention that the conclusion that some treatments were superior to others was not justified by research evidence, we conducted a meta-analysis of all studies that compared two treatments intended to be therapeutic and found that these treatments were uniformly efficacious (Wampold, Mondin, Moody, Stich, Benson, & Ahn, 1997). This line of research has continued and the results demonstrate that (a) all treatments intended to be therapeutic produce comparable benefits, regardless of the diagnosis; (b) the therapist accounts for a large proportion of the variability in outcomes; (c) clients of therapists in clinical settings attain outcomes comparable to those attained by therapists in clinical trials with fewer sessions; and (d) the factors common to all treatments are responsible for the benefits of counseling and psychotherapy (see Wampold, 2001). This research has been the basis for arguing that managers of mental health services should not mandate treatments nor restrict access to services. That is, clients should have access to effective therapists who deliver services that are consistent with the attitudes, values, and culture of the client. I feel that my investigative spirit has yielded results that honors clients' access to a variety of effective services; I find this immensely gratifying.

—*Bruce Wampold, Ph.D.*

RESEARCH TRAINING ENVIRONMENT   Gelso (1979, 1993) discussed 10 components of graduate training programs hypothesized to foster positive attitudes toward research. Based on the initial research related to research training, nine of these components have been identified as important features of the research training environment: (1) modeling appropriate scientific behavior and attitudes, (2) reinforcing students' research efforts, (3) involving students in research early and in minimally threatening ways, (4) teaching relevant statistics and the logic of design, (5) teaching that all research is flawed and limited, (6) teaching varied approaches to research, (7) wedding science and practice in training, (8) facilitating students' introspection for research ideas, and (9) conducting science as a partly social experience.

Gelso and colleagues (Gelso et al., 1996; Kahn & Gelso, 1997; Royalty et al., 1986) developed an instrument (the Research Training Environment Scale, RTES, and its revision, RTES-R) that operationalized these nine components of the training environment. Because it was unlikely that these aspects are independent, Kahn and Gelso (1997) factor-analyzed the RTES-R and found that two factors underlie the nine aspects operationalized by the RTES-R. The first factor, labeled *instructional factor,* contains aspects of the environment that are present because of curricular components of graduate training, which included teaching statistics and the logic of design, teaching students to look inward, teaching that experiments are flawed, teaching varied approaches, and wedding science and practice. The second factor, labeled *interactional factor* because the components involved the interaction of trainer and trainee, includes modeling, reinforcing, involving students early, and conducting science as a social experience. In the model, Kahn and Scott (1997) hypothesized that environmental influences affect research self-efficacy, which in turn affects research interest, career goals related to research, and research productivity.

Although the nine components of the research environment can be reduced to two factors statistically, the examination of the individual components that follow reveals how research trainers can construct curricula and experiences to foster the development of skilled and motivated consumers and producers of research. The components have been modified since their original conceptualization; nevertheless, we recommend that professionals involved in research training read Gelso's (1979) seminal article on research in counseling.

Modeling Appropriate Scientific Behavior and Attitudes   Clearly, modeling is a potent way to transfer a variety of skills from master to novice. However, Gelso's conceptualization was that the important aspects of modeling went far beyond the transfer of skills and involved having research mentors exhibit healthy attitudes toward research (Gelso, 1979; Gelso et al., 1996). The primary attitude to be modeled is enthusiasm for the research endeavor. This enthusiasm often comes from two sources. First is the fact that the research endeavor is a creative task and has much intrinsic pleasure because of the act of creation. Second is the inherent pleasure researchers feel when they discover something new. The ability of research mentors to model this enthusiasm and foster it can make a substantial difference in their mentees' feelings about the research process. Gelso (1979) was careful to note that modeling also involves expressing the disappointment involved in research—the rejections, the data that do not inform, the low rate of participation by respondents, and so forth. "The process of scientific discovery, including its trials and tribulations as well as its excitement, must be modeled at least as much as its products" (Gelso, 1979, p. 28).

As I was approaching the end of my doctoral training and about to start my dissertation study, I vividly remember a meeting with Puncky Heppner, one of my mentors in graduate school. This meeting stands out clearly to me because he not only helped me to start thinking about a career as a researcher, but he advised me on what I could do as a graduate student to start laying a foundation and to prepare for this. He suggested that I consider doing my dissertation study in an area that could develop into a programmatic line of research—and that this area be one that will sustain my interest over the years and one that fills a void in the current literature. This incident and many other teaching moments from valued mentors have taught me that the world of research operates on a unique time frame that requires patience, perseverance, and good planning because we often don't see immediate outcomes for the behaviors we are engaged in as researchers.

—Lisa Flores, Ph.D.

Reinforcing Students' Research Efforts   An unspoken code pervades the academy: Calling attention to one's own accomplishment is a sign of insecurity regarding scholarly worth. The corollary of this code is that noticing and commenting on others' accomplishments is also avoided. Gelso (1979) commented on a student "who published a fine research paper in a well-refereed journal and made three national convention presentations in one year—and received no acknowledgment from any faculty member for her excellence" (p. 28). Because academics are trained to act as if scholarship is its own reward, we expect students to act similarly, but students (as well as academics) need recognition for their accomplishments. Honest expressions of reinforcement all along the way in the research process are an important part of building interest in the process.

Involving Students in Research Early and in Minimally Threatening Ways   As early as possible, students should be involved in research in ways that are interesting and involving but consistent with their skill level (Gelso, 1979; Gelso et al., 1996). Asking students to perform tasks for which they are not trained (for example, running a statistical analysis) most likely will create anxiety; asking students to perform menial and uninteresting tasks (for example, repetitively scoring protocols) will create boredom. We have found that students can be stimulating thinkers at any point in their training and should be involved in the conceptualization of research projects. In research groups, students of various levels can participate to the extent that they feel comfortable and have something to contribute. New students often have ideas not shaped by conventional approaches to a problem and make suggestions that are insightful and critical in designing an innovative study.

Teaching Relevant Statistics and the Logic of Design   Many counseling students have little fondness for statistics and are turned off to research because they equate doing research with studying for statistics examinations. Gelso et al. (1996) have suggested that this unfortunate situation be countered by pedagogy in statistics classes that "is sensitive to students' needs" (p. 311) and by emphasizing the logic involved in designing research. The basis of this recommendation is that poorly taught or overly technical statistics classes create unnecessarily negative attitudes toward research.

I entered graduate school in psychology after 10 years of public school teaching, working on a doctorate in English, and abandoning my then-in-progress dissertation on Keats' Odes. My intention at that time was to become a drama therapist and help adolescents build better lives. Learning to write like a psychologist was my first graduate school challenge, and overcoming my abject terror of statistics was my second major hurdle. I almost flunked out of graduate school my first semester (I had the lowest grade in the stat class of about 100 students), and it was only through Nancy Betz' generous intervention that I passed—superb teacher that she is, she essentially taught me that entire course in three afternoons. A short time later I discovered Structural Equation Modeling and I was hooked on being a researcher—I loved making pictures with little circles and squares, and I was thrilled that one could actually study things this way! I also became involved in Division 17 activities, and I connected with many wonderful people who became role models and mentors for my emerging identity as a researcher and academic. I still wanted to help people build better lives, but now I knew that research was an important tool in that effort.

When I re-examine my own JCP articles on methodology (on SEM [1987] and grounded theory [2005]) that anchor the two decades of my career thus far, I am surprised and pleased at how far I've traveled in developing my confidence and voice as a researcher, and how comfortable I've become with a variety of paradigms. I teach my students that research is a political act with social consequences, and I have accepted the responsibility implicit in that reality—that every single moment of my scholarly life counts for something. I am helping people build better lives, just as I wanted to do so many years ago.

—Ruth Fassinger, Ph.D.

Teaching That All Research Is Flawed and Limited   In this book we will consistently suggest that any one study cannot rule out all threats to validity, and that knowledge accumulates through repeated investigations. Students should not feel pressure to design the perfect study; rather, they should feel motivated to create a study that can address the research question, taking the principles of research design as well as practical constraints into account. Requiring students to meet standards and achieve excellence is appropriate; forcing students to clear unrealistic hurdles is not.

Teaching Varied Approaches to Research   The conventional advice to "use the appropriate research method to answer the research question" contains wisdom, but it ignores the person of the researcher. By the nature of their personalities and their interests, students will be attracted to some approaches to knowing more than others. Some students will be attracted to quantitative methods and others to qualitative methods, and these preferences should be respected and honored. Not only do students benefit by using a method that they enjoy, but the field benefits from this methodological pluralism (Gelso et al., 1988).

Wedding Science and Practice in Training   Much has been written about the integration of science and practice. However, as Gelso (1979) noted, research motivation stemming from clinical experience is often discounted. This component recognizes that a true integration of science and practice will make research more attractive, especially to the majority of students whose primary interest is in practice. Courses that carefully draw the intimate connection between science and practice, taught by instructors who feel comfortable with the connection and have skills in each area, are truly motivating to students. Research in applied settings also fosters interest.

Facilitating the Students' Introspection for Research Ideas   For many students, looking inward is to rely on clinical experience, so this component clearly overlaps the wedding of science and practice. When research mentors discount ideas generated from the "person," the person is discounted. It is not productive for students to get the idea that legitimate research ideas should be generated only from an objective reading of the literature. It is our belief that those students who have a deep interest in their topic finish their dissertations faster than those who are motivated to finish their programs but who pick a convenient topic of study.

Conducting Science as a Partly Social Experience   Many aspects of conducting science involve working alone, but because many counseling students are socially oriented, increasing the social aspects of research will increase the attractiveness of the endeavor for them. Gelso (1979) suggested two opportunities for social interactions: advising and research teams. The advisor can provide a variety of roles from helping to generate ideas, to allying fears, to consulting on design issues. When the advisor and advisee have a close relationship in which research is an important component, this can help meet the social needs of the student.

Research teams also provide social interactions. Although they offer opportunities for social interaction, research teams have a task—to conduct meaningful research. Consequently, the team leader must keep the group focused while accommodating the need for social interaction and facilitating skill development in team members. Clearly, the leader must use group facilitation skills as well as research skills.

I think it was the issue of sexual assault that made me really excited to do research on how to better intervene in preventive ways. I can't say that I came into my research career with a lot of confidence or expertise, but I had been involved in rape prevention programming on college campuses and I did want to know more about how we can develop more effective programs to change men's attitudes about sexual violence. That desire led me to a rich and meaningful road conducting large scale prevention studies, eventually obtaining grant funding to support my research and really finding myself enjoying working with my research team on these important issues. I love doing research on teams where we each contribute our own unique skills to the process and learn from one another. My research in the areas of sexual violence prevention is meaningful to me and the process of doing the research with students and colleagues has been a very stimulating and enjoyable part of my career. In a world where sexual violence is becoming more and more prevalent, it feels like an important issue to try to understand and prevent.

—*Mary Heppner, Ph.D.*

RESEARCH SELF-EFFICACY   Social cognitive models of academic and career interest and choice hypothesize that self-efficacy mediates the relationship between direct and vicarious experiences and attainment of goals (Lent, Brown, & Hackett, 1994). In the present context, research self-efficacy is defined as "one's confidence in being able to successfully complete various aspects of the research process" (Kahn & Scott, 1997, p. 41). Kahn and Scott, based on social cognitive models and past research in this area (see, for example, Brown et al., 1996; Phillips & Russell, 1994), predicted that research training and research productivity (that is, experiences with research) would predict research self-efficacy, which in turn would predict research interest and research career goals (see Figure 2.1).

RESEARCH INTEREST   Kahn and Scott (1997) hypothesized that research interest mediates the relationship between personality type and career goals and research productivity. Put another way, the established relationship between personality type and research productivity (and presumably career goals) is due to interest. Investigative types have more interest in research and therefore have goals related to research and produce more research products.

RESEARCH PRODUCTIVITY   One of the outcome constructs in the Kahn and Scott model (1997) is research productivity, which was defined broadly to include journal articles, unpublished empirical manuscripts, manuscript submission and research in process, presentations presented or in process, intensive case studies, program evaluations, informal research, and involvement in the analysis of data. Research productivity has a long history as an outcome variable due to many observations that the research productivity of graduates from counseling programs is low (see, for example, Watkins, Lopez, Campbell, & Himmell, 1986, who found that the modal number of publications of counseling graduates is zero).

It should be noted that research productivity as a goal is somewhat controversial. Increasing research productivity has often been advocated by leaders in the field. For example, Whiteley (1984) stated that "counseling psychologists need to increase their research productivity" (p. 46), and Magoon and Holland (1984) made suggestions that were aimed at "increasing the proportion of graduates who will become producers of research" (p. 63). Others (Fong & Malone, 1994) have commented on the lack of quality in research on counseling. Wampold (1986b) noted that the focus on quantity rather than on quality would have deleterious effects:

> If the quality of research presently conducted by counseling psychologists is poor [which we are not convinced is the case], then increasing the number of individuals who publish is not likely to increase the quality of the research and may only result in a greater volume of research with questionable value. It is vital that counseling psychology programs develop training models that will produce graduates who can conduct quality research. (p. 38)

Moreover, the number of counseling psychologists who publish research is about equal to that of other fields, including the sciences (Price, 1963, cited in Magoon & Holland, 1984). The point is that we feel that the quantity of research published by students, before and after they graduate, should not be the primary indicator of the quality of a training program. We think students should be skilled researchers who can conduct quality research (and who do so in their dissertations), but who also can intelligently consume research, cogently think about scientific issues, balance research and practice from an informed standpoint, appreciate and value the scientific method, and most important apply critical thinking skills to a broad range of research and applied contexts. Hill (1997) noted that even though few of her students had taken academic positions or produced much research, she should not as a result be judged as an inadequate research mentor.

CAREER GOALS IN RESEARCH   In Kahn and Scott's (1997) model, the second outcome construct was goals related to research, which was defined as preferences for postdoctoral positions as researchers rather than as practitioners. Although this is an appropriate construct for their research, we agree with Hill (1997) that training programs should not be judged by the proportion of students going into research-related careers. Instead, programs should graduate students who are trained consistent with the mission of the program, which we believe should include the acquisition of research skills, appropriate attitudes toward research, and most important, critical thinking skills.

TESTING THE MODEL

Kahn and Scott (1997) tested the structural equation in their model and then modified the model. This modified model fit the data well. The structural part of the modified model is presented in Figure 2.2. Several aspects of the modified model are informative. The critical mediating construct was research interests rather than research self-efficacy. This is not surprising if one assumes that most students should feel that they *can* conduct research as a result of their training, although they may choose not to (again, see Hill, 1997). This research highlights the importance of selecting students with research interests and then providing the kind of research environment that helps to foster those interests. See Kahn and Scott for more details.

RESEARCH COMPETENCE—THE MISSING CONSTRUCT

From our perspective, the missing construct in the Kahn and Scott (1997) model is research competence. As counselors and counseling psychologists we appropriately attend to how we structure environments to foster positive attitudes and self-efficacy. However, having competencies to conduct and consume research is also critical to producing quality research. Wampold (1986b) found that training programs did not teach their students various statistical procedures that were used in typical counseling research. In addition, Royalty and Reising (1986) surveyed professionals and found that respondents felt confident of their research skills, with the exception of statistical and computer skills, two skills that were highly correlated with productivity. Although the respondents indicated that graduate programs adequately contributed to their skill level, they became less confident of their skills later in their careers, and they indicated that it is unlikely that they would augment their research skills after graduation. In the empirical model presented in Figure 2.2, the positive path from year in program to research self-efficacy can

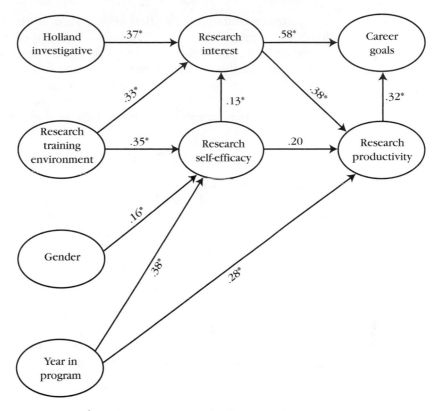

FIGURE 2.2 | PARAMETER ESTIMATES FOR THE MODIFIED STRUCTURAL MODEL OF KAHN AND SCOTT (1997)

Asterisks indicate *p* <.05.

From Kahn & Scott, *The Counseling Psychologist, 25,* p. 55. Copyright © 1997 by the Society of Counseling Psychology of the American Psychological Association. Reprinted by permission of Sage Publications, Inc.

be interpreted from a competence perspective. Self-efficacy is due in part to a research environment that fosters positive attitudes toward research, but it is also built upon competencies. We suspect that year in program is most likely a proxy for increased competence because students acquire research skills as a result of experience in the program.

Based on the empirical evidence for competence in statistics and design, Wampold (1986b, p. 44) listed the following design and statistics competencies: (1) knowledge of designs including, but not limited to, traditional experimental designs, quasi-experimental designs appropriate for field settings, single-subject designs, survey designs, and qualitative designs; (2) an understanding of design issues, such as validity, methods of sampling, and power; (3) knowledge of the statistical analyses commonly used in counseling research;

(4) an understanding of statistical issues, such as the role of assumptions, hypothesis testing strategies, and confirmatory versus exploratory analyses, and (5) the ability to perform analyses with computer assistance, when appropriate. It is hoped that this book, statistics classes, and other experiences will provide readers these competencies. In addition, professional writing skills, which are covered in the last chapter of this book and in a more detailed way in Heppner and Heppner (2004), are critically important skills for students to develop.

THE NEED TO BROADEN SCIENTIFIC TRAINING

Most counselor training programs have a number of training components aimed at promoting the development of an array of research competencies (e.g., research design, statistics). We want to discuss two additional competencies that merit attention: basic scientific or critical thinking skills and basic research application skills.

TRAINING IN BASIC SCIENTIFIC THINKING SKILLS

All counselors, regardless of where their professional activities fall on the scientist-practitioner continuum, need basic scientific or critical thinking skills. Scientific thinking refers to a controlled method of inquiry and reasoning, typically to collect data of some kind for the purpose of testing a hypothesis. A crucial characteristic of a professional counselor is the integration of scientific thinking into the daily activities of professional practice (e.g., Anderson & Heppner, 1986; Berdie, 1972; Claiborn, 1984, 1987; Gambrill, 2005; Goodyear & Benton, 1986; Hoshmand, 1994; Pepinsky & Pepinsky, 1954). Scientific thinking can be instrumental in how counselors process information about a specific client during counseling as well as evaluate the counseling process.

How a person thinks is an exceedingly complex process (e.g., Anderson, 1983; Neisser, 1976). It is becoming increasingly clear over time that human beings often think or process information in both rational and irrational ways, in systematic and unsystematic ways, and in linear and nonlinear ways (e.g., Fiske & Taylor, 1991; Gambrill, 1990, 2005; Heppner, 1989; Kanfer & Busemeyer, 1982; Nisbett & Ross, 1980; Strohmer & Blustein, 1990; Tversky & Kahneman, 1974). Moreover, there is reason to believe that one's cognitive processes (that is, how one thinks) interact with one's affective processes and behaviors, thereby creating a complex triadic process (Heppner & Krauskopf, 1987). Research clearly indicates that people do not think as "objective computers," but rather are selective or biased in the type of information to which they attend (Gambrill, 1990, 2005; Nisbett & Ross; Turk & Salovey, 1988). In particular, people often attend to information that confirms their existing beliefs or discount information that is contrary to their existing beliefs (e.g., Lichtenberg, 1984; Slusher & Anderson, 1989). Such biases can lead to problems for professional counselors as they process information about clients and evaluate the effectiveness of their work. (For more details, see Abramson, 1988; Heppner & Frazier, 1992; Ingram, 1986; Turk & Salovey.)

Carl Rogers was very aware of this danger of counselor bias; in 1955 he observed that he could "deceive himself in regard to my creatively formed subjective hunches" about a client (p. 275). He believed that the scientific method, as a way of thinking, led him to check "the subjective feelings or hunch or hypothesis of a person with the objective fact" (p. 275). Rogers would often check his hunches very directly by asking the client, "Do you mean this?" or "Could it be this?" Rogers would sometimes go a step further and develop a written transcript of an interview to analyze the relationships between counselor and client statements. Years later his face would still light up with excitement about what he would learn about a particular client, or the counseling process, by stepping back from the immediacy of an interview to analyze those transcripts (Rogers, personal communication with P. P. Heppner and L. A. Lee, January 1984).

Pepinsky and Pepinsky (1954) initially articulated a prescriptive model of counselor thinking based on the scientific method. Strohmer and Newman (1983) succinctly summarized their model:

> The counselor observes the client, makes inferences about his or her current status and the causal inferences, and then, based on these inferences, makes a tentative judgment about the client. The counselor then proceeds in an experimental fashion to state the judgment as a hypothesis and to test it against independent observations of the client. Through a series of such tentative judgments and tests based on these judgments, the counselor constructs a hypothetical model of the client. This model then serves as the basis for making predictions (e.g., which treatment approach is most appropriate) about the client. (p. 557)

In essence, Pepinsky and Pepinsky (1954) were suggesting that the counselor incorporate a scientific or critical thinking model by (a) generating hypotheses based on (b) the data that the client presents, followed by (c) empirical testing of the hypotheses, to develop (d) a model that can be used (e) to make predictions about the client. The essence of this approach is that it is *data-based* or *empirical*, which lessens the chance of personal biases or subjectivity. Scientific thinking in this way involves a continual generation and evaluation of hypotheses based on data. Spengler, Strohmer, Dixon, and Shivy (1995) nicely extended the Pepinskys' model by integrating it with the human inference literature, which effectively operationalized scientific thinking and identified a number of inferential errors commonly made in counseling.

Training in scientific thinking may be particularly important in evaluating counseling outcomes. Goodyear and Benton (1986) have referred to a particular counselor bias in assessing counseling outcomes, a bias they call a "walk-through empiricism" mentality:

> That is, as the counselor has successes, he or she will form impressions of what techniques are proving useful. Although this walk-through empiricism can be valuable, it is also subjective and therefore unreliable if it is used as the sole source of data. An analogy might be drawn from medicine where not so long ago a frequent remedy was to treat people by bleeding them of "bad blood." Physicians believed a cause-effect relationship—that the bleeding caused a cure—and continued to offer this as a common treatment for many years. Yet, the treatment was

no doubt responsible for many patient deaths that might have been avoided if the procedure had been tested empirically. (p. 291)

Thus, training in scientific thinking and methodologies can help counselors evaluate the effectiveness of counseling interventions more objectively and with less personal or subjective bias.

More recently, there has been a strong movement for empirically validated treatments or evidence-based practice to enrich the training and practice of counselors (Chwalisz, 2003; Waehler, Kalodner, Wampold, & Lichtenberg, 2000). Scientific thinking is a crucial feature that distinguishes the counselor from a nonprofessional layperson, in large part because of its self-corrective characteristics. That is, whereas laypeople tends to fit what they see or hear into preconceived notions of their world view, well-trained counselors tend to view their assumptions or observations as subject to change as additional information is collected (Pepinsky & Pepinsky, 1954).

Thus, Claiborn (1987) concluded that the difference between the counselor-as-scientist and the scientist is more a matter of goals than of procedure. We believe that it would be worthwhile to pursue more thorough training in basic scientific thinking skills to reflect training outcomes associated with a more integrated scientist-practitioner model. To facilitate the development of scientific thinking, particularly with practice-oriented students, Hoshmand (1994); developed a practice-oriented approach to research supervision; her experiences led her to conclude that a practice-oriented approach engages students' interest and prepares them for contributing scholarly research relevant to practice. At this point, more attention is needed on the efficacy of different approaches of scientific thinking for different types of students. "The process of critical thinking, hypothesis-testing, and other elements of the scientific method should be engendered and integrated into all aspects of training" (Belar & Perry, 1992, p. 72).

TRAINING IN BASIC RESEARCH APPLICATION SKILLS

The counseling research literature contains a great deal of information about client populations, counseling processes and outcomes, assessment, interventions, crisis intervention, professional issues, and a variety of special topics (see reviews by Betz & Fitzgerald, 1993; Borgen, 1984a; Gelso & Fassinger, 1990; Heppner, Casas, Carter, & Stone, 2000; Watkins, 1994). In short, the counseling research literature, as well as the literature from other areas in psychology and education, contains a wealth of information about counseling and human behavior. This information is obviously essential for any person engaging in counseling research and practice. This information also can be an extremely useful database or tool in helping a practitioner solve particular client problems. Anderson and Heppner (1986) observed that counselors' knowledge bases can quickly become out of date. While preparing a book of readings on recent innovations in counseling, Anderson was impressed with the number of articles being published on topics that only 10 years earlier were not taught to counselors in training (such as bulimia, sleep disorders, and spouse abuse). Thus, counselors in the field need to train themselves continually to work effectively with new client problems.

Gelso (1985) has also observed that reading the research literature affects his thinking about the counseling process:

> I would offer that it is important to think about research as that which helps us use our heads more clearly and less prejudicially. It helps us think about what we do and organize our ever-changing personal theory of the processes in which we are involved, be they counseling, psychotherapy, consultation, supervision, and so on. We should not expect empirical research to capture the felt essence of those processes. Only the practice of them will do that.
>
> Most of the research findings that I read are relevant to my clinical practice in the following way: they help me think in a less biased way, they help me further refine my usually private theory of my practice, and they allow me to add small pieces of new information to my conceptual system. (p. 553)

In essence, the professional research literature is a resource that can both provide a wealth of useful information about specific client problems and suggest topics for additional research. Moreover, reading the literature may affect the counselor's thinking and refine his or her conceptualizations of the counseling process. Thus, a basic activity for all graduate students in counseling is to become active consumers of research (e.g., Goodyear & Benton, 1986). The research literature has at times been criticized for having limited value for the practitioner for a wide variety of reasons (e.g., Goldman, 1976, 1982; Howard, 1985). Learning how to use the research literature (e.g., becoming familiar with the types of articles in different journals, learning how to access information most efficiently) and making the literature a part of one's problem-solving repertoire does not simply happen, but rather typically involves specific training.

SUMMARY AND CONCLUSIONS

The trainers of future researchers are the students of today. In this chapter we have discussed some basic issues related to research training, which we hope will help to create positive attitudes toward research as well as increase research competence not only for future researchers, but also for future research trainers.

We strongly believe that there can be a much greater integration between the science and practice domains, not only within counselor training, but also within the professional activities of all counselors. Carl Rogers's hope for the future was that "each researcher would be a practitioner in some field and each practitioner would be doing some research" (Heppner, Rogers, & Lee, 1984, p. 19). This is one type of integration; we have also suggested that scientific research training be broadened to emphasize scientific

thinking and basic research application skills. In our personal experience, our research has clearly been facilitated by observations made during many hours of counseling practice. Moreover, our experience has been that our thinking and counseling skills have been sharpened, extended, and clearly enhanced by subjecting our thinking to empirical tests as well as contemplating and applying new ideas from the research literature. Integration might also happen on another level: between those who are primarily research-oriented and those who are practice-oriented. In some ways, the people who have the most well-developed set of observations of the counseling process are those who are heavily engaged in counseling practice; it behooves the typical researcher to develop collaborative relationships with such practitioners. In short, we suspect that both scientific and practice-oriented professional activities could be enhanced by a more complete integration of the two domains.

We have also maintained that a basic issue in scientific training is scientific thinking. Those at the Atlanta conference in 1987 concluded that "an attitude of scholarly inquiry is critical to all the activities of those educated in the scientist-professional model" (Meara et al., 1988, p. 368). Such an outcome requires not only scientific skills, but also scientific values. The latter are also important goals and need specific attention in training (perhaps by way of discussions about the philosophy of science, research methods, the slow but steady accumulation of knowledge, and students' own research experiences).

An attitude of scholarly inquiry goes beyond scientific thinking and involves curiosity, inquisitiveness, healthy skepticism, exploration, and a desire to learn. In a way, all counseling professionals are pioneers in extending the boundaries of their own knowledge throughout their careers, and possibly extending the knowledge bases of the profession as well. In this way, scholarly inquiry involves discovery, excitement, and even a sense of adventure. Not surprisingly, pioneers in the field of counseling and development report that they were motivated to achieve, in part, by the joys of intellectual discovery,

"the thirst to know something" (Pepinsky, cited in Claiborn, 1985, p. 7).

Maintaining a pioneering attitude in professional scholarly inquiry can also be a way of life. Enos Mills was an early pioneer in the mountainous area of Colorado that is now Rocky Mountain National Park. In the following quote, Mills (1924) aptly describes the qualities of a pioneer's life. Even though he was referring to pioneering in the American West, the qualities of life he describes also apply to the pioneering attitude involved in discovering professional knowledge through scholarly inquiry:

> Those who live pioneer lives are usually the most fortunate of people. They suffer from no dull existence. Each hour is full of progressive thought, and occasions which call for action accompanied by the charm of exploration—action that makes their lives strong, sincere, and sweet. Their days are full of eagerness and repose, they work with happy hands. The lives of pioneers are rich with hope and their future has all the promise of spring. (p. 9)

We hope that your life in the counseling profession will be a good place for you to be a pioneer and that scientific thinking will enrich your life with discoveries that are exciting to you and beneficial to the various clienteles we serve.

STIMULUS QUESTIONS

REFLECTIONS ON RESEARCH TRAINING

1. Why do you think some scholars are advocating a need to broaden scientific training in counseling?
2. In what ways do you think scientific thinking might be useful for both practice and science activities?
3. Identify five activities you can do to incorporate scientific thinking into your counseling practice.
4. If the counseling profession more strongly emphasized the scientist role rather than the practitioner role, what would be the advantages and disadvantages?
5. If the counseling profession more strongly emphasized the practitioner role rather than the scientist role, what would be the advantages and disadvantages?
6. What do you see as the most important advantages of integrating science and practice in the counseling profession?
7. What do you feel very passionate about in your future as a counselor? Can you see any way that research could help you enhance the work you will do within the areas that excite you the most?
8. What concerns, obstacles, and fears do you have about scientific training?
9. Examine the reactions you listed in question 8; why do you think you have these reactions?

IDENTIFYING AND OPERATIONALIZING RESEARCH TOPICS

The purpose of this chapter is to provide an overview of the process of selecting a research topic and developing the research idea into a testable hypothesis. The chapter describes the five main components of this process: identifying research topics, specifying research questions and hypotheses, formulating operational definitions, identifying research variables, and collecting and analyzing data. We present these activities in separate sections in order to adequately discuss each of the five components. However, in reality these activities are often intertwined, and researchers often intersperse thinking and planning across all of these activities as they progress from identifying the topic to developing specific research hypotheses.

IDENTIFYING RESEARCH TOPICS

A wide range of experiences can play a role in helping the researcher develop research ideas. At times, developing a research idea can involve a great deal of creativity as the researcher integrates information from diverse sources and in novel ways. Sometimes successful theses and dissertations extend previous well-established studies one step further by examining one new variable, collecting data from different groups, or using a new methodology (Heppner & Heppner, 2004). It is often exciting to identify topics and innovative ideas that may lead to important contributions of new knowledge, and it is exhilarating to think that no one has thought of this idea before (at least for a short period of time!). Various pioneers in the field of counseling have commented on the joys of discovery and learning they have experienced by engaging in research. Interested students might read some of the interviews with early counseling pioneers that appeared in the "Pioneers in Guidance" and "Lifelines" series in the *Journal of Counseling and Development,* as well as in the "Legacies and Traditions" forum of *The Counseling Psychologist.* For example, Anne Roe, in reflecting on her career, stated simply that "nothing is as much fun as research. . . . I miss that (in retirement)" (Wrenn, 1985, p. 275).

Sometimes developing research ideas may seem difficult for inexperienced researchers; they cringe at the thought of developing an original research idea that *no one* has *ever* had before. Typically, the experienced researcher has little difficulty in developing research ideas. In fact, often the veteran researcher has too many research ideas, and a more difficult problem is deciding which ideas to pursue.

Several ingredients differentiate the experienced researcher from the inexperienced. The experienced researcher usually has a very large knowledge base, not only about a given topic, but also about several other topics. Such a researcher can most likely process information about these topics in sophisticated ways, identifying the most important findings, combining research findings, dovetailing an idea from one topic with another, and elaborating on or extending ideas in novel ways. In addition, the experienced counseling researcher often has a considerable wealth of information from his or her applied counseling experiences that can be the source of many ideas and hypotheses. The veteran researcher also typically knows a great deal about the skills needed to conduct research, such as knowledge of research design, methodology, assessment, statistics, data collection, data analysis, and technical writing. All of these knowledge bases are important tools in facilitating the processing of large amounts of information about specific research projects in sophisticated and often novel ways. Perhaps equally important, the experienced researcher typically has confidence that he or she can effectively conduct research, and thus has the needed level of self-efficacy.

In contrast, the inexperienced researcher has far less knowledge about specific research topics and often has trouble identifying the most important or relevant information. The novice often has less applied experience in counseling, and most likely has less-developed conceptualizations of the counseling process. The inexperienced researcher has perhaps only a vague sense of the various research activities (such as recruitment of participants and data collection) and harbors doubts about his or her ability to do research well. In fact, in many counseling programs, well-articulated guidelines for conducting research are not available to students, leaving the impression that the research process is rather mystical. Drew (1980) noted that a logical place to turn for information is a college or departmental catalog that describes a thesis or dissertation project. Typically such documents say something to the effect that the thesis "must be an original contribution to the field." When viewed literally, the word *original* can engender considerable anxiety as the trainee tries to develop a completely novel research idea. In addition, the idea must represent "a contribution to the field," which makes the task seem even more formidable. It is the rare trainee who believes at the outset that he or she can make a "real contribution" to the field; after all, we are talking about *science*! Sometimes the inexperienced researcher interprets "original contribution" much too broadly and tries to develop a new topic area by creating a new assessment instrument to measure new constructs, a new research methodology to collect data previously not collected, and new statistical procedures to handle old problems. In reality, most experienced researchers would feel quite a sense of accomplishment if they did all of these things during an entire *career*. In short, the inexperienced researcher often takes on too much in trying to develop an original contribution. Not surprisingly, our experience has been that graduate students in beginning research design courses ask questions about how to identify "good" research topics and "good" research ideas. Also not surprisingly, they often ask whether a particular idea is "enough" for a thesis.

We will make some suggestions in this chapter to help beginning researchers to identify a research topic. Essentially, the task is to identify some general topic that may (1) contribute to the profession's knowledge bases in meaningful ways, and (2) simultaneously stimulate and motivate students to explore and learn more about the topic. Most inexperienced researchers in counseling need to learn more about the body of knowledge and the directions of current research efforts. Thus, for such students we do not simply recommend sitting and thinking hard about research topics and hoping that the ideal research question will present itself, but rather taking a more active, information-collecting approach.

A good first step in identifying possible research topics is to start collecting information about previous research, both within and outside of counseling. Thus, read widely in the professional journals and books. Reading widely not only will provide you with information about what is being published, but also may help you to clarify what topics are of most interest to you. Sometimes it is useful to start with a general review of the counseling literature (see Betz & Fitzgerald, 1993; Borgen, 1984a; Gelso & Fassinger, 1990; Heppner, Casas, Carter, & Stone, 2001; Mackay, Barkham, Rees, & Stiles, 2003, or peruse the various handbooks related to the counseling profession). Another strategy is to begin by looking for more focused literature reviews on specific topics. (The *Psychological Bulletin* is a journal devoted to evaluative and integrative reviews; see Dolliver [1969] for an excellent example of an evaluative review of measured versus expressed vocational interest, as well as another excellent example by Oyserman, Coon, and Kemmelmeier [2002] evaluating theoretical assumptions of individualism and collectivism.) Books on specific topics are often useful resources. For example, a student interested in conducting research with racial/ethnic minorities would be wise to examine Ponterotto and Casas (1991). In short, there is no substitute for this time-consuming process of reading the relevant literature; at first you might peruse and read abstracts to develop a broad overview. A good beginning is to spend at least five hours a week reading and exploring the journals for six weeks or more.

In addition to regularly reading the journals, capitalize on the faculty and student resources on your campus. Although this sounds simplistic, it often provides useful information. Talk with these people about their past and present research projects. What are they most excited about now? What was the most stimulating idea at a recent national, regional, or state convention they attended? What do they consider as hot or promising topics? Heppner and Heppner (2004) also encouraged consultation with professionals and experts in the field in a prepared and respectful manner. Follow up your discussions with these people with readings they might suggest to you.

In addition to faculty in general, your advisor or research supervisor is often an invaluable resource. Typically, the advisor's role is to facilitate students' work on their thesis/dissertation. Thus, another strategy is to begin research training by working closely within the advisor's research interests; this approach resembles an apprenticeship model. An advantage of this strategy is that your advisor can more easily facilitate the identification of relevant readings, workable research ideas, methods, obstacles, and procedures (Heppner & Heppner, 2004).

Although we said earlier that we do not recommend simply sitting and thinking hard, we do recommend thinking and reflecting *after* you have collected a wide variety of information. What do you like and dislike about a particular line of research? Pay attention to what bothers you about a study. Was something omitted? How could you improve the study? Also try to bring your own observations and beliefs into your research topics. Many experienced counselors use their own observations about a topic (for example, the counselor supervision process, or counselor self-disclosure) as a source of ideas for research topics. This is riskier for the inexperienced counselor and researcher, however, because a lack of experience may provide less reliable observations. To facilitate reflecting and brainstorming, sometimes it is helpful to record ideas, observations, and questions in a journal or log.

While reading and thinking about previous research in counseling, it is important to keep in mind at least four issues: the utility of research in answering real-life applied questions that address important societal needs, your particular interests, a way to build on previous research, and the role of theory. Perhaps one of the most basic reasons for conducting research is to develop knowledge bases that in one way or another can help people by addressing pressing societal needs. In essence, in order for the counseling profession to be of value to the larger society, our research must address important issues and problems in society. Thus, we encourage students to reflect on some of the most significant current societal issues to identify research topics. For example, a researcher might have questions about effective interventions for treating sexually abused children. Child sexual abuse has been the topic of a great deal of attention (even debate) and has stimulated research on the efficacy of a number of psychosocial interventions (see Enns, McNeilly, Corkery, & Gilbert, 1995). Or a researcher might consider whether improvements could be made to increase the effectiveness of various treatment programs (such as smoking cessation, anger management, substance abuse, or parental training) or outreach programs (for example, rape prevention or alcohol awareness programs). Or are there some important questions that an agency director or some other helping professional needs more information about in order to improve their services? Perhaps a counseling center director would like to know how clients would react to a detailed, computer-assisted intake like CASPER (see Farrell 1999; McCullough & Farrell, 1983; McCullough, Farrell, & Longabaugh, 1986). For example, Farrell found significant differences between the pretreatment and posttreatment CASPER, and also found correlations with client symptoms and therapists' ratings on global assessment. In short, unresolved societal problems or questions about applied aspects of counseling are a rich source of research topics.

It is also essential to continually assess which topics are most important to you. Are there certain topics that you are motivated to pursue, or perhaps feel a special commitment to investigate because of your beliefs or values? What important topics have previous researchers overlooked? In short, pursuing research topics that you are motivated and dedicated to pursue will likely provide both the drive and intellectual stimulation needed to sustain you through the various research tasks.

It is also important to realize that a great deal of research in counseling involves extending the results of previous research. Typically, our research proceeds by adding one or two new pieces of information per study. Thus, a researcher might extend a previous study by adding one or two new constructs or by developing a new assessment instrument to operationalize a construct. Often a researcher uses a data collection method similar to that used in previous research, or instruments used in three or four previous studies. In short, it is essential to focus on investigating a few constructs only, and not to try to do too much in developing an "original contribution." Most often our knowledge bases in counseling increase in small steps by building only slightly on previous research.

A considerable amount of research within counseling applies or tests theories about personality, human behavior, and the change process as they apply to topics in counseling. Testing theory can be an important contribution to the counseling field because it helps refine our theories, especially because many theories have not been tested on diverse populations (Heppner & Heppner, 2004). For example, Stanley Strong (1968) initially conceptualized counseling as a social influence process and used research and theory on persuasion from social psychology to develop a two-phase model of influence within counseling. Subsequently, a great deal of research has examined the persuasion or social influence process within counseling (see reviews by Corrigan, Dell, Lewis, & Schmidt, 1980; Heppner & Claiborn, 1989; Heppner & Dixon, 1981; Heppner & Frazier, 1992; Hoyt, 1996; Strong, Welsh, Corcoran, & Hoyt, 1992). Likewise, another theoretical perspective that is influencing counseling research is that of developmental models in counselor training (see Bernard & Goodyear, 1998; Holloway, 1987, 1992, 1995; Watkins, 1997).

Sometimes a new model or theory is developed by integrating different bodies of research. For example, McCarn and Fassinger (1996) developed a model of lesbian identity formation by integrating literature on lesbian/gay identity, racial/ethnic identity, and gender issues related to identity development; subsequently, a number of research directions were proposed. Or sometimes research will test and extend either competing theories or different conceptualizations of the same phenomena. For example, in 1971 Cross published a model on black racial identity that has been modified by refinements and elaborations (see, for example, Cross, 1978; Cross & Vandiver, 2001; Helms, 1990; Helms & Parham, 1996; Nghe & Mahalik, 2001; Parham, 1989; Parham & Helms, 1981, 1985b). Subsequently, a number of white racial identity models have been proposed, debated, and empirically tested (see, for example, Atkinson, Morten, & Sue, 1989; Behrens, 1997; Behrens, Leach, Franz, & LaFleur, 1999; Gushue & Carter, 2000; Helms, 1990; Helms & Carter, 1990; Rowe & Atkinson, 1995; Rowe, Bennett, & Atkinson, 1994; Sue & Sue, 1990; Thompson, 1994).

Similarly, sometimes theory and research from one topic can be extended to another related topic. For example, women's career development has been the focus of both theoretical models and empirical research for some time (see, for example, Betz & Fitzgerald, 1987; Farmer, 1985; Farmer, Wardrop, Anderson, & Risinger, 1995; Fassinger, 1990; Harmon, 1977; Walsh & Heppner, 2006; Walsh & Osipow, 1994). Models of women's career development were then integrated with empirical research on lesbians' career development to develop a minority group model of career development (Morgan & Brown, 1991). This model of career development was extended to the career development of highly achieving women with physical and sensory disabilities (Noonan et al., 2004). Thus, another strategy in identifying research topics is to examine any theories, whether they are found within the counseling literature or outside the counseling literature, that might be helpful to the work of counselors.

In summary, ideas for research projects can come from a wide range of sources. It is often useful for students to use a combination of strategies as they enter the world of research.

SPECIFYING RESEARCH QUESTIONS AND HYPOTHESES

Typically, the purpose of research is to answer questions, address pressing societal problems, refine theories of interest to counseling, and ultimately add to the existing knowledge in the field. It is one thing to identify a *topic* you want to research. It is another thing to move beyond the research topic to develop a specific research question or hypothesis that can guide your research. In fact, developing testable research questions is often quite troublesome for inexperienced researchers.

After identifying a possible research topic (for example, counselor supervision), it is important that you become knowledgeable about the previous research on that topic, perhaps even by writing a formal review paper. There is no substitute for becoming thoroughly knowledgeable about a topic by identifying current research findings, previous research obstacles, and previous researchers' suggestions for future research. As we indicated earlier, many times developing a specific research idea means extending a line of research one logical step further. Thus, examining key studies or incisive reviews is essential. Pay particular attention to the discussion section in those studies. Often there is explicit discussion of future research needs or of the next logical step. The authors often identify these needs by phrases such as "future research should" or "additional research might examine." These suggestions could be the basis of your research idea.

After reading a number of articles on your general topic, begin to attend more closely to the constructs that have been used in the previous research. What variables or processes are interesting and important to researchers in the field? What questions have researchers been addressing in the research literature? *Research questions* are key elements in developing a topic area, and in essence are questions that explore the relations among or between constructs. For example, "Does the client's level of dysfunction affect the working alliance formed in counseling?" is a research question. In contrast, a *research hypothesis* is more specific in that it states the expected relationship between the constructs, as in "More-dysfunctional clients will form poorer alliances in counseling than will less-dysfunctional clients." Often, distinctions are not made between questions and hypotheses. However, it should be kept in mind that hypotheses specifically state the expected relationship.

From our experience, students have difficulty developing research questions and hypotheses for several reasons. Perhaps most frequently, students may lack a theoretical structure for their investigation and thus cannot conceptualize relevant research hypotheses that will empirically test or extend previous research. Research questions and hypotheses are often deduced from theory (Wampold, Davis, & Good, 1990). At other times, students select constructs they have no way of measuring or testing. For example, one doctoral student was stymied because he could not clearly assess what he meant by counselor personal power and autonomy. Sometimes students have not thought in depth beyond the research topic and have not asked themselves what specific constructs they are most interested in examining. Thus, they may be unable to be more specific than being interested in "something about computerized career information services." Students also may be reluctant to decide on specific constructs, choosing instead to delay or procrastinate for an array of conscious and unconscious reasons. All these difficulties in developing research questions and hypotheses are not atypical for inexperienced researchers. Most important, such difficulties suggest that additional reading and thinking are necessary. Researchers can make serious errors by proceeding to select participants and assessment instruments without ever clarifying their research questions or hypotheses and exactly what they are looking for in their research.

Drew (1980) has identified three useful general categories of research questions (or hypotheses): descriptive, difference, and relationship. *Descriptive questions* essentially ask what some phenomena or events are like. Sometimes we have questions about counseling events or phenomena that are best answered by collecting information on inventories, surveys, or interviews to describe events. Experimental manipulations typically are not used in these studies.

Because there are many types of studies that examine descriptive research questions, we will provide a number of illustrative examples. For example, a researcher might want to use a survey to describe the types of events that trigger counselor anger (Fremont & Anderson, 1986) or the themes in AIDS support groups for gay men (Stewart & Gregory, 1996). Other times qualitative studies might use interviews to understand therapists' experiences addressing racial issues in counseling (see Knox, Burkard, Johnson, Suzuki, & Ponterotto, 2003). Similarly Swagler and Ellis (2003) used interviews to study the cross-cultural adjustment of Taiwanese graduate students in the United States; the results revealed themes of language barriers, confidence about speaking English, social contract, and cultural differences. Later, focus groups were conducted to provide a more complete conceptualization of the relations among the constructs. If a researcher wanted to identify the professional needs and experiences of ethnic and racial minority psychologists, a survey might be a useful strategy to collect information, which was precisely the approach chosen by Constantine, Quintana, Leung, and Phelps (1995). Another survey study was conducted by Johnson and Hayes (2003) to examine the prevalence of religious and spiritual concerns among counseling center clients. At other times we use statistical procedures such as factor analysis (see Tinsley & Tinsley, 1987) or cluster analysis (see Borgen & Barnett, 1987) to describe how people or events might be categorized. For example, one group of researchers used cluster analysis to describe different types of career indecision in students (Larson, Heppner, Ham, & Dugan, 1988). Similarly, Kim, Atkinson, and Yang (1999) developed the Asian Values Scale to measure the adherence to cultural values that play an important role in counseling through factor analysis. Liang, Li, and Kim (2004) also used factor analysis to develop the Asian American Racism-Related Stress Inventory; in this study they also supported their initial factor structure with confirmatory factor analysis. Descriptive research is discussed more fully in Chapters 10 and 11.

Difference questions ask if there are differences between groups of people, or even within individual participants. The key feature in this type of question is a comparison of some sort. Such research questions tend to focus on groups of individuals; the groups may differ on some dimension or may receive different treatments. For example, a study by Mallinckrodt and Helms (1986) examined a difference question in determining whether counselors who are physically challenged have certain therapeutic advantages relative to able-bodied counselors. Likewise, Tracey, Leong, and Glidden (1986) compared help seeking and problem perception in Asian-American and white clients. Similarly, Kelly and Achter (1995) examined differences between high self-concealers (people who keep secrets) and low self-concealers on attitudes toward counseling; they found that high self-concealers had more negative views about counseling when they were told that counseling involves revealing highly personal information. Difference questions are often examined in between-group and within-group designs (see Chapter 7).

Relationship questions explore the degree to which two or more constructs are related or vary together. Such questions tend to use correlational statistics or more complex regression analyses. For example, a study by Marx and Gelso (1987) examined a relationship question by studying the relationship between client satisfaction with termination and five client variables suggesting loss in the termination process. Similarly, Smith and Ingram (2004) studied the relationships among workplace heterosexism, unsupportive social interaction, and adjustment of lesbian/gay/bisexual individuals. Likewise, Good et al. (1995) examined the correlations between gender role conflict and several other inventories (for example, attitudes about masculinity, fear of intimacy, social desirability) to provide estimates of construct validity for the Gender Role Conflict Scale (O'Neil, Helms, Gable, David, & Wrightsman, 1986). Cournoyer and Mahalik (1995) extended this line of research by using canonical analysis, a multivariate approach to examining relations among multiple variables. Relationship research questions are discussed more fully in Chapters 10 and 11.

What constitutes a testable research question? According to Kerlinger and Lee (2000), a research question (a) asks a question about (b) the relationships between two or more constructs that can be (c) measured in some way. First, the question should be worded clearly and unambiguously in question form. Second, the research question should inquire into a relationship between two or more constructs, asking whether construct A is related to construct B. (If a particular relationship is stated, the research question becomes a hypothesis.) This second criterion pertains mostly to difference and relationship questions, whereas descriptive questions often seek to collect or categorize information. Finally, not only is a relationship between constructs examined, but somehow this relationship also must be measurable.

For example, consider a research question like, "Is supervision effective?" One might immediately ask, "Effective at what?" Is the researcher interested in the effectiveness of supervision to lower a trainee's stress level to conceptualize clients, or to intervene with clients? In short, such a question lacks specificity. Now consider the research questions developed by Wiley and Ray (1986), who were interested in the topic of the changing nature of supervision over the course of training. In particular, they were interested in testing Stoltenberg's (1981) counselor complexity model concerning developmental levels of counselor trainees. (Stoltenberg proposed that counselor trainees develop in a predictable way over the course of graduate training, and that counseling supervision environments should be adapted in ways that match the needs of the trainee.) Wiley and Ray developed three specific research questions, each of which inquired about relationships between two or more constructs and was amenable to being measured or tested in some way. For example, one of their questions was: To what extent do supervision dyads with a more congruent person–environment match on developmental level report higher satisfaction and learning than those with a less congruent match? The construct of the congruent person–environment match was concretely operationalized via the use of an assessment instrument called the Supervision Level Scale. Likewise, satisfaction and learning were operationalized in terms of a brief outcome instrument. Parenthetically, although Wiley and Ray obtained results that provided some support for conceptualizing supervisees and supervision environments developmentally, mean satisfaction and learning ratings did not differ by person–environment congruency.

In short, the function of a testable research question or hypothesis is to provide direction for experimental inquiry. The testable research question or hypothesis not only identifies the topic, but also identifies specific constructs of interest within that topic. For more examples about writing research questions, see Heppner and Heppner (2004). After a researcher has developed a specific research question or hypothesis, he or she can then proceed to determine what instruments to use, how data can be collected, what participants to use, and so on. Many of these methodological decisions are directly dependent on the investigator's specific question or hypothesis.

Although the research question provides direction for designing a study, it is important to note that in the formative stages—as an investigator continues to develop the design and methodology of a particular study—it is not uncommon to revise or change the original research question. The investigator may encounter measurement or participant availability problems, which may dictate a slightly different research question. Or the researcher may find new data that suggest additional complexity in the topic and thus require revision of the research question.

In short, any of a number of events may lead the researcher to process more information and subsequently to revise or sharpen the research questions in the formative stages of study design.

Sometimes graduate students get discouraged about their false starts and begin to feel a sense of inadequacy because they "couldn't get it right the first time." There often is an assumption that a "real researcher" proceeds through a logical series of ordered steps, starting first of all with a brilliant, incisive research question. Our experience has been that effective researchers generally examine a wide range of design issues when developing a research question, such as choosing instruments and participants or examining external validity issues. In short, revision of research questions is typical during the formative design stages, and often it is desirable. Of course, once data collection has begun, revision of the research question is no longer functional or appropriate.

FORMULATING OPERATIONAL DEFINITIONS

After the initial development of the research question or hypothesis, it is crucial that all terms or constructs in the question be defined concretely so that the research idea can be empirically tested. More specifically, each construct must be operationally defined, which means specifying the activities or operations necessary to measure it in this particular experiment. Kerlinger (1986) referred to operational definitions as a sort of manual of instructions that spells out what the investigator must do to measure or manipulate the variables during the procedures of the study.

For example, considerable interest has been shown concerning developmental models of supervision, which in essence postulate that trainees' skills and supervisory needs change over time as trainees attain different developmental levels (see Ellis, Ladany, Krengel, & Schult, 1996; Holloway, 1987, 1992, 1995). A critical issue is how one operationally defines developmental level. Some of the initial investigations operationally defined developmental level as the training level of the student, such as beginning practicum student, advanced practicum student, and doctoral-level intern (see, for example, Heppner & Roehlke, 1984; Reising & Daniels, 1983; Worthington, 1984). Thus, developmental level was concretely or operationally defined in terms of training level.

The primary function of an operational definition is to define the constructs involved in a particular study. In a way, the operational definition provides a working definition of the phenomenon (Kazdin, 1980). Thus, the operational definition allows the researcher to move from general ideas and constructs to more specific and measurable events. A problem arises when researchers investigate a given construct but develop different operational definitions for it. Consider again the example of developmental levels of counseling trainees. Whereas developmental level was initially defined as trainee level (see, for example, Reising & Daniels, 1983), Wiley and Ray (1986) defined developmental level in terms of supervisors' ratings on an instrument (the Supervision Level Scale) that assesses the trainee developmental level along five dimensions. Wiley and Ray's definition is more specific and is based on Stoltenberg's (1981) theoretical model. Interestingly, Wiley and Ray found that these two definitions of developmental level result in quite different categorizations of trainees.

This example aptly depicts the problem of different operational definitions for the same construct. As research information accrues over several investigations, it becomes difficult to summarize information on supervisees' developmental level because of the different operational definitions. More important, different operational definitions sometimes lead to very different results. This is a crucial point for the inexperienced researcher to comprehend, because it implies that the results from a particular study must be qualified or restricted according to the operational definitions used in the study. It is also important to note that as research within a topic progresses and becomes more complex, operational definitions often undergo revision as knowledge accumulates and researchers become more sophisticated, as in the supervision literature.

IDENTIFYING RESEARCH VARIABLES

Up to this point we have referred to variables rather generally. Often there is confusion and debate about the terms used to describe or designate the variables in a research study. We hope to alleviate some of this confusion by using specific terms throughout this book to describe the various types or classes of variables found in research designs. Specifically, the terms *independent variable* and *dependent variable* have been used in both experimental and descriptive research to define different types of variables. In true experimental designs (see Chapter 7), the researcher attempts to examine causality by systematically varying or altering one variable or set of variables and examining the resultant changes in or consequences for another variable or set of variables. In such experiments, the variable that is varied or altered is called the independent variable. More specifically, the independent variable is the variable that is manipulated or controlled in a study. Usually an experiment involves two or more levels of the independent variable (for example, treatment and no treatment), sometimes referred to as conditions. For example, in a study that compares cognitive versus interpersonal treatments for depression, the type of treatment (cognitive vs. interpersonal) would be the independent variable.

To examine the effects of the manipulation of the independent variable, concomitant changes in another variable, the dependent variable, are observed. In an experimental study, changes in the dependent variable are supposed to depend on or be influenced by changes or variations in the independent variable. In the previous example, the comparison between cognitive versus interpersonal treatments is made by measuring some dependent variable.

One example of a dependent variable is the depression scores on a standardized test (for example, the MMPI-Depression scale). In a true experimental design we infer that a change (if one exists) in the dependent variable was caused by the manipulation of the independent variable. Thus, the terms *independent variable* and *dependent variable* have causal implications. These terms are sometimes used to describe the variables in nonexperimental studies as well. For instance, the predictor variables in a regression equation are sometimes referred to as independent variables, and the criterion variable is sometimes referred to as a dependent variable. This can be confusing because of the notions of causality implied in the terms. To alleviate this type of confusion, we will primarily utilize the terms *independent variable* and *dependent variable* to describe variables in experimental studies, although some exceptions will have to be made. Independent and dependent variables are discussed further in Chapters 12 and 13.

COLLECTING AND ANALYZING DATA

Once the constructs referenced in the research question or hypothesis have been operationally defined and the design of the study determined, the researcher collects data. The actual process of data collection depends, of course, on the design of the experiment. The design of the study must be determined—and that is the primary focus of the remaining chapters of this book. The final step of collecting and analyzing data, which is most appropriately discussed in various statistical books, will be briefly addressed in several statistical issues presented throughout the book.

Once the data are collected, sense must be made of them. Data usually consist of numbers that index characteristics of the participants. The data are summarized and analyzed with the express purpose of testing the research question or hypothesis. Specifically, the data are examined to determine whether the hypothesized relationship indeed exists. Inevitably, decisions need to be made during the course of a study. At these times, always think about how various alternative methods will affect your ability to shed light on the original question. Will a course of action obscure or clarify the original research question?

SUMMARY AND CONCLUSIONS

The purpose of this chapter is to provide an overview of the process of selecting a research topic and developing the research idea into a testable hypothesis. A number of activities are involved in narrowing a general topic to a series of specific, testable research hypotheses, such as developing research questions or hypotheses, identifying specific variables, and operationalizing variables.

Typically, researchers intersperse thinking and planning into all of these activities as they proceed in reading relevant research literature and developing a particular topic. The outcome should be a specific, well-defined, clearly articulated research hypothesis.

We want to emphasize that it is normal, and even expected, for inexperienced researchers to make false starts and to modify aspects of their research project as they hone the final research question and hypothesis. Sometimes students get the impression that once they have had courses in research methods, statistics, and counseling theory, they ought to be able to produce research questions that have all the bugs worked out. They fear that if they do not perform flawlessly, not only will their competence as a researcher be questioned, but it will be clear that they do not have "the right stuff" to complete the program

or have a research career. Regardless of how many courses a student has taken, there is no reason to expect a graduate student to be an expert researcher. Rather, it may be useful for students to regard their initial research attempts as training opportunities.

It is also important to note, especially for beginning researchers, that all research studies have limitations of one kind or another (such as lack of experimental control or concerns regarding generalizability). Gelso (1979) referred to this phenomenon as the Bubble Hypothesis and suggested that all research studies have some type of flaw or weakness. Sometimes inexperienced researchers create problems for themselves by trying to develop the perfect study or dissertation. In truth, these entities do not exist. Thus, it is essential for the inexperienced researcher to keep in mind the goal of developing a study that provides the profession with another piece of information, not *the* definitive study. Most often our knowledge bases in counseling are increased by adding one or two more pieces of information per study, with each study building on the previous research in some relatively small way. Over time, these small pieces accumulate and our knowledge about a particular topic is substantially increased.

STIMULUS QUESTIONS

INITIAL REFLECTIONS ON POSSIBLE RESEARCH TOPICS

The purpose of this exercise is to promote reflection on possible research topics. You might want to respond to these questions now, or spend several hours examining recent articles in some counseling journals and then consider these questions.

1. Brainstorm a list of topics that excite and motivate you. Are there any themes in this list? Rate the degree to which each topic addresses an important and pressing societal need (1 = low, 10 = high).

2. Can you narrow the list and identify two to three topics on which you might like to conduct a study? Evaluate each of the topics (1 = low, 10 = high) in terms of how passionate you are about this topic as well as how proud you would feel about contributing your scholarly efforts. Indicate why you rated each topic as you did.

3. Now list as many resources as possible in your environment to help you find relevant literature on each of these topics to expand your knowledge.

4. Who in particular could help you to learn more about these topics?

5. Consider your responses to the questions above, and rank order the two to three topics that might be most appropriate to further examine.

6. Finally, spend a few days beginning to explore the top ranked topic, finding a few recent articles on this topic, talking to relevant peers and faculty to collect additional information about the topic, and seeing how you now evaluate this topic. Has your interest increased or decreased? Why?

If this topic continues to interest and intrigue you, continue to learn more about it by searching the literature and talking to knowledgeable faculty. Conversely, if the first topic loses appeal, you might want to explore your second ranked topic to obtain additional information to determine if this topic might better fit your interests.

Choosing Research Designs

The purpose of this chapter is to provide an overview of some of the issues and trade-offs related to what is commonly referred to as research design. We begin by defining research design as a central component of scientific inquiry. Here we briefly introduce a key concept in research: drawing inferences or conclusions from our data. The data may be of both a quantitative and qualitative nature. Next we discuss the "research design myth," which is the conclusion that one design, a priori, is "better" than others. The third and major section of the chapter introduces one way of classifying research designs; the central theme is the balance between experimental control and generalizability of the research findings. The final section revisits the goal of choosing the best research design for a particular study, and we suggest that it is inappropriate to focus only on the merits of any specific design without considering other factors, especially the match between the prior research knowledge, one's resources, and the type of research questions being examined.

SCIENTIFIC INQUIRY AND RESEARCH DESIGN

In Chapter 1 we identified the role of science as extending the profession's knowledge bases and theoretical underpinnings. Moreover, we maintained that the best way to establish credible knowledge bases (ways of knowing) was through a systematic and controlled method of inquiry, known as the scientific method.

In this chapter, as well as the next, we will focus more on what we mean by *systematic* and *controlled*.

The basic task of the experimenter is to design research in such a way as to describe a phenomenon or identify relationships between constructs while ruling out as many plausible rival hypotheses or explanations as possible. The goal, put simply, is to more fully understand a phenomenon or construct, even though many sources of bias and confounding variables might distort that understanding. Perhaps an analogy might help. Ever since human beings began harvesting grains, there has been a need to separate the grain itself (the wheat) from its protective shield (the chaff), a dry, coarse, inedible material. In a way, the chaff gets in the way of digesting the wheat. In a similar way, the researcher wants to isolate the constructs of interest to his or her research question (the wheat) and remove as much as possible of any other constructs (the chaff) that might contaminate, confound, bias, or distort the constructs of interest. Although the analogy of separating the wheat from the chaff is an oversimplification, it does highlight the essential task of the scientific method: isolating the constructs of interest and trying to draw useful conclusions about those constructs. Any particular study can never completely eliminate all the explanations; some types of explanations will be left untested. This is a very crucial point to understand about research design; we will elaborate on this point throughout the chapter.

How does the researcher separate the "wheat" from the "chaff"? The basic tool of the researcher is what we call research design. Research design involves developing a plan or structure for an investigation, a way of conducting or executing the study that reduces bias, distortion, and random error. Different research designs have different strengths and weaknesses, and each will minimize different types of bias. Sometimes bias is also referred to as error, error variance, or noise. One of the most critical decisions in research is selecting a research design whose strengths and weaknesses help the researcher to examine specific research questions in a valid and systematic manner by reducing as many rival hypotheses or explanations as possible while isolating the relevant variables of interest. Research design, then, is a set of plans and procedures that researchers use within scientific inquiry to obtain empirical evidence (data) about isolated variables of interest. From the evidence, or data, the researcher then draws inferences about the constructs in his or her research question. We say "inferences" because the researcher can never rule out all of the rival hypotheses between, say, two constructs, A and B.

WHAT IS THE BEST DESIGN?

In the past, researchers have examined questions like: Does counseling/therapy work? What is the best type of counseling? Which clients benefit the most from therapy? The common thread among these three questions, and many like them, is their assumption of what Kiesler (1966) labels a uniformity myth. Simply stated, we have oversimplified counseling to assume that psychotherapeutic treatments are a standard (uniform) set of techniques, applied in a consistent (uniform) manner, by a standard (uniform) therapist, to a homogeneous (uniform) group of clients. Kiesler believed that these myths have greatly hampered progress in unraveling and understanding psychotherapy research; subsequently, he advocated research that addresses the question of what the best types of treatments are for particular types of clients across different settings.

No doubt, the uniformity myth has hampered and continues to hamper research within counseling. We believe that counseling researchers often operate under an equally pervasive, often subtle, and definitely hindering uniformity myth about research design; we call this the "research design myth." The research design myth is not that all research designs are alike, but rather that one design is a priori "better" than others. Sometimes students will ask, "What is the best research design?" Often students and, unfortunately, experienced researchers believe that there is one right or best type of research design, apart from the type of research question they are examining. Research design is like a tool to help researchers examine specific research questions. But just as a carpenter has many different kinds of tools (for example, hammers, pliers, and screwdrivers), each with different functions, different research designs have different types of functions. For example, if a carpenter wanted a large nail in an oak plank, a hammer would likely be a good tool to choose, but this does not mean that using a hammer every time the carpenter needed a tool would be a wise strategy—it would take a much longer time for the carpenter to remove a screw from the oak plank with a hammer. In short, it is an oversimplification to assume that there is one best type of research design. Rather, it is more appropriate to consider what knowledge is already known in a particular topic, and what type of research question is now being examined. Thus, we maintain that the more helpful question is, "What is the best research design for this particular problem at this time?"

A CLASSIFICATION OF RESEARCH DESIGNS

Historically, several broad categorizations of research designs have been described. Campbell and Stanley (1963) discussed design in terms of pre-experimental designs, experimental designs, and quasi-experimental designs. Kazdin (1980) referred to experimental designs, quasi-experimental designs, and correlational designs. But methodology and research designs are constantly evolving. We will describe and discuss these and other major types of designs later in the book. Here we note that the different types of research designs may present particular strengths or weaknesses with regard to internal and external validity. In short, researchers must consider various trade-offs.

Two major issues affecting the inferences that researchers might make are experimental control and generalizability. It is an oversimplification to conceptualize research design in terms of these two issues alone; in Chapter 5 we will discuss these two issues in considerable depth, and we will also introduce two more issues affecting valid inferences. At this point, however, we want to highlight experimental control and generalizability in terms of the tension or trade-offs between these two issues in selecting a particular research design. Note that our discussion follows a positivistic and postpositivistic mode of thinking; see Chapter 11 for alternative ways of knowing that focus on qualitative designs.

Briefly, on one side of this trade-off the experimenter might use a particular research design to exercise as much experimental control as possible to ensure an accurate investigation of his or her research question. Kerlinger (1986) described this process as the "MAXMINCON" principle. He observed that the researcher first of all tries to *max*imize the variance of the variable or variables pertaining to the research questions. Second, the researcher tries to *min*imize the error variance of random variables, particularly due to errors of measurement or individual differences of participants. Third, the experimenter tries to *con*trol the variance of extraneous or unwanted variables that might affect or bias the variables in question. Although the MAXMINCON principle applies most directly to traditional experimental research (between-group or within-group designs), the essence of Kerlinger's principle applies to all research designs: Control the experiment so as to obtain the most accurate or complete investigation of the research question. Experimental control allows researchers to make more inferences about causal relationships between variables, which is referred to as the internal validity of the study. (Internal validity is discussed in greater depth in Chapter 5.) Studies that are high in control typically use random selection of participants, random assignment of treatments, and manipulation of an independent variable or variables to permit the researcher to make inferences about causality. Studies that are low in control lack either or both random assignment to treatments (quasi-experimental studies) or manipulation of an independent variable (descriptive studies and ex post facto designs). In low-control studies, researchers can make inferences about relationships but not about causality.

At the same time, it is important to emphasize that counseling is first and foremost an applied specialty. It is therefore important to ascertain that the phenomenon one wishes to examine has some relevance to counseling. Whereas experimental control is a central ingredient of research design, a second key issue is generalizability of the results to applied settings, which is referred to as external validity. (For more details regarding external validity, see Chapter 5.) Our research knowledge must be grounded in and responsive to applied counseling interventions. For example, some studies use participants from the population of interest in a naturally occurring form, such as real clients seeing experienced therapists, or students who are truly undecided about a major or career choice. Inferences from these studies tend to be more generalizable to actual counseling applications.

It is important to note that in an applied field such as counseling, experimental control is often difficult and sometimes unethical. For example, it is often difficult to minimize error variance due to individual differences across clients, and there may be ethical dilemmas associated with particular treatment interventions or experimental manipulations. In short, within an applied context that involves the lives of real people who are struggling and need

Internal validity

High · Low

	High	Low
High	Experimental field	Descriptive field
Low	Experimental laboratory	Descriptive laboratory

External validity

FIGURE 4.1 | TYPES OF RESEARCH DESIGNS CLASSIFIED BY LEVELS OF EXTERNAL AND INTERNAL VALIDITY

psychological assistance, experimental control often presents obstacles for the researcher. Moreover, the more steps a researcher takes to maximize control, the more simplified (or even artificial) the research context can become. Thus, a major research design issue for the counseling researcher is the balance and trade-offs between experimental control and generalizability.

Gelso (1979) used the concepts of external and internal validity to create a typology of research designs that we find helpful. Gelso essentially proposed that we can organize counseling research along two dimensions—that research can be either high or low in control (internal validity) and can be conducted in either a field or a laboratory setting (external validity). Gelso acknowledged that although these categories were inevitably simplifications, they were nonetheless useful in understanding the strengths and limitations of types of research designs.

Figure 4.1 is a representation of the different types of research using Gelso's (1979) two (high and low internal validity) by two (high and low external validity) matrix. We have made one change in Gelso's classification system to reflect a broader set of operations. The change involves using the label *descriptive* instead of Gelso's label *correlational* to describe studies low in internal validity. The term *correlational* seemed to unnecessarily limit our thinking about the nature of studies low in internal validity; *descriptive*, in contrast, does not imply the restriction of these designs to one statistical operation (correlation), but also includes a broader range of methods such as qualitative methods.

DESCRIPTIVE LABORATORY STUDIES

Descriptive laboratory studies have low external and low internal validity. These studies are characterized by investigations that do not exercise experimental controls (such as randomization or manipulation of independent variables) and that are conducted in a laboratory setting of some kind. A descriptive laboratory study is low in external validity because it uses a setting that in some ways can only simulate a real-life setting. For instance, a study of some aspect of the counseling process could use undergraduate students as clients and trainees as counselors. Such "counseling" may or may not be like that which takes place between real clients and experienced counselors. In other words, there would certainly be questions about the extent of generalizability of findings from this type of study.

A descriptive laboratory study is low in internal validity because it lacks experimental control in the sense of manipulation of an independent variable or randomization of participants. Rather, the descriptive laboratory study involves describing in detail some aspect of counseling, by identifying, labeling, or categorizing data, as well as obtaining basic descriptive statistics such as means, standard deviations, and correlations among variables. Returning to the counseling example, a researcher may want to determine the likelihood of client self-exploration given certain counselor responses. Rather than manipulating counselor responses, the researcher may want to study their natural occurrence. In this way, the study is descriptive, not experimental.

If internal and external validity are so important, why would a researcher conduct a study that is low along both dimensions? There are two main reasons for conducting these types of studies. First, a laboratory setting allows the researcher some control over extraneous variables, even though the experimenter may choose not to manipulate some of them. Data can be more easily collected, the researcher need not worry as much about experimental variables adversely affecting the therapeutic assistance a client receives, and the researcher can expect and encourage more involvement from the participants. A second reason for conducting descriptive laboratory studies is that it is impossible to study some phenomena in a field or real-life setting. The data collection procedures may be so extensive and/or intensive that the very presence of these procedures alters the process under examination to the extent that it is no longer natural or real.

Elliott's (1985) study of helpful and nonhelpful events in counseling interviews is a good example of a descriptive laboratory study. He had counselor trainees conduct an interview with a recruited client. After the interview, the client reviewed a videotape of the interview and rated each counselor statement on a nine-point helpfulness scale. Most and least helpful counselor statements from each counseling dyad were then given to judges who sorted the statements into categories. Cluster analysis was then used to put the statements into categories. In this manner, Elliott was able to develop a taxonomy of helpful and nonhelpful events in early counseling interviews.

This study is low in internal validity because no manipulation of counselor statements occurred. Rather, statements were classified as helpful or nonhelpful on the basis of an a posteriori (after the fact) rating of helpfulness. The study is low in external validity because counselor trainees and recruited clients served as the participants, and because the video-recall procedure probably altered aspects of the counseling. This study does, however, provide important information about the counseling process that certainly advances our understanding of an important concept—perceived helpfulness to clients of counselor statements. For another example of a descriptive laboratory study, see Mohr, Israel, and Sedlacek (2001).

For the researcher considering a descriptive laboratory study, Chapter 17 contains information about the conduct of analogue research, with special emphasis on the issue of generalizability of laboratory studies. In addition, Chapters 10 (on quantitative descriptive research) and 11 (on qualitative research) contain information on different types of descriptive designs.

DESCRIPTIVE FIELD STUDIES

Descriptive field studies have high external and low internal validity. These studies are characterized by investigations that do not exercise experimental controls (randomization, manipulation of variables) and are conducted in a real-life setting. A descriptive field study is often high in external validity because a sample of participants can be taken directly from a population of interest. In counseling research, for example, this could mean the study of real clients seeing actual therapists. A descriptive field study is low in internal validity because variables are studied as they occur naturally rather than being manipulated.

For a study to be truly high in external validity, the data-gathering procedures must not have sufficient impact on the participants to disrupt their normal set of actions. The two most common examples of this type of study are retrospective studies that use data routinely collected as part of an agency policy, and single-subject studies of individual counseling. A classic study representing descriptive field research is the Menninger project (Wallenstein, 1989), a very large study conducted over a 35-year period that examined the effectiveness of counseling (thus, an outcome study) with patients who received more than 1,000 hours of analysis. Client–therapist pairs were selected for this study only after counseling had formally ended. As Wallenstein stated, clients and therapists were totally unaware during treatment of which cases would be analyzed. In addition, the study used only data that were routinely collected during treatment. Because of the lack of experimental control in this study, a number of problems regarding internal validity are raised, such as threats from history and selection (terms that will be explained more fully in Chapter 5). The real-life nature of this study makes it intriguing because it has high external validity and applicability, even though the findings are only suggestive at best.

A study by Liddle (1996) demonstrates some of the advantages and disadvantages of descriptive field studies. The author was interested in examining whether gay and lesbian clients would benefit from choosing a gay or lesbian therapist, as well as relating specific therapist practices to therapy outcomes. Participants were 392 lesbians and gay men living in 29 states and 3 Canadian provinces. The results revealed that gay, lesbian, and bisexual therapists of both genders, and heterosexual female therapists were all rated as more helpful than heterosexual male therapists. In a second analysis, Liddle examined the relations between 13 therapist practices (9 negative and 4 positive) and (1) client ratings of a therapist as unhelpful, and (2) termination of therapy after one session. (One example of a negative therapist practice was some indication by the therapist of the assumption that the client was heterosexual before the client indicated his or her sexual orientation.) Eight of the nine negative therapist practices were significantly associated with both outcome variables. The three negative therapist practices that had the strongest association with the outcome variables were the therapist blaming the client's problems on the client's sexual orientation, the therapist's refusal to see the client after the client disclosed his or her sexual orientation, and the therapist's indication that he or she believed that a gay or lesbian identity is bad, sick, or inferior. Conversely, all four of the positive therapist practices (for example, the therapist's willingness to deal with the client's sexual orientation when it was relevant) were inversely related to the counseling outcomes.

These findings have some important practical implications:

> The therapists whom these clients find helpful tend to be those who have educated themselves about issues of concern to gay and lesbian clients (including societal prejudice, internalized homophobia, relationship issues, and community resources) and those who help their clients work toward a positive gay or lesbian identity. (Liddle, 1996, p. 399)

This study is high on external validity because of its large number of participants and because the sample was obtained from across the United States and Canada. Conversely, it is not known how many people were asked but declined to participate, or whether the methods of recruiting participants resulted in any systematic biases in the sample. The study is low on internal validity, because no variables were manipulated. Thus, it is not possible to make causal statements concerning the effects of therapist practices on therapeutic outcomes. In addition, any of a number of other counselor behaviors may have affected the counseling process and outcome. The study used an open-ended (free recall) format with an unspecified time (for example, one or five years ago), which might have resulted in some distortion. For other examples of descriptive field studies, see Erdur, Rude, and Baron (2003); Lichtenberg and Tracey (2003); and Woodhouse, Schlosser, Crook, Ligiero, and Gelso (2003).

For researchers interested in conducting descriptive field studies, Chapter 9 (on single-subject designs) and Chapter 19 (on process research) provide guidance, with an emphasis on therapeutic counseling. Chapters 10 and 11 provide an overview of some common quantitative descriptive designs and qualitative designs in particular, whereas Chapter 8 covers quasi-experimental designs.

EXPERIMENTAL LABORATORY STUDIES

Experimental laboratory studies have low external and high internal validity. These studies are characterized by manipulation of independent variables and are conducted in a laboratory setting. An experimental laboratory study is low in external validity because instead of using participants directly sampled from a population of interest, the experimenter sets up a situation to resemble a naturally occurring one. This research is often high in internal validity because the experimenter can randomly assign participants to treatments and manipulate one or more independent variables. Because these studies are high in internal validity, the researcher can and does make inferences about causality. The extent to which these inferences about causality can be generalized to the populations and settings of interest is the critical question about experimental laboratory studies.

A study by Worthington and Atkinson (1996) typifies some of the advantages and limitations of experimental laboratory studies. The researchers were interested in examining the effects of a counselor's attributions or beliefs about the specific causal agents that are antecedents to physical or psychological distress. Forty undergraduate students volunteered to serve as clients for three sessions of counseling role plays with 11 graduate-student counselors. The students were then told of the counselor's attributions of the cause of their problems, which were manipulated to either agree or disagree with the student's own attributions. The results revealed that clients whose attributions agreed with the counselor's rated their counselor as a more credible source of help.

These findings suggest that client–counselor attributional similarity is beneficial to some counseling outcomes. Because of the experimental controls used, the authors could conclude with a high degree of certainty that the similarity or dissimilarity of the client–counselor attributions affects client ratings of counselor credibility. Thus, the study has a high degree of internal validity. However, the study is low in external validity, and it is unclear whether these results would generalize to real counseling interviews involving real clients presenting real problems. For more examples of experimental laboratory studies, see Day and Schneider (2002); Hill, Rochlen, Zach, McCready, and Dematatis (2003); and Kim, Hill, et al. (2003).

For readers interested in using an experimental laboratory design, Chapter 17 details issues in the conduct of analogue research. Chapter 7 describes between-groups and within-subjects designs, which are what many authors refer to as "true" experiments.

EXPERIMENTAL FIELD STUDIES

Experimental field studies have moderate external and internal validity. These studies are characterized by investigations that manipulate independent variables and are conducted in a real-life setting. An experimental field study attempts to examine causality through random assignment of treatments and control of independent variables. Such experimental control moves the study away from the examination of naturally occurring counseling. At best, the researcher has a study moderately high in external validity. Even though an experimental field study attempts to examine causality in a naturally occurring setting, the researcher can never exercise the same control in the field as in the laboratory. Hence, an experimental field study can be at best only moderately high in internal validity. An experimental field study allows for the best combination of inferences about cause and generalizability that is attainable within a single study. Typically, though, an experimental field study can obtain neither the same level of certainty about causality as is possible in an experimental laboratory study nor the same level of certainty about generalizability as in a descriptive field study.

Hogg and Deffenbacher (1988) offer an example of an experimental field study. These authors were interested in comparing an interpersonal and a cognitive approach in the group treatment of depression. They also included a no-treatment control condition in the design. External validity was emphasized by using clients seeking help at a university counseling center and experienced group therapists. However, threats to external validity existed because of the use of pretesting and possible reactions to experimental procedures (tape recordings).

Internal validity was emphasized by random assignment of clients to interpersonal and cognitive groups and by standardized treatment for the two conditions. Internal validity was threatened by the nonrandom assignment of clients to the control condition. (Clients who came to treatment late in the semester were used to form the control group.) This study is a good example of the sacrifices that researchers must often make in external and internal validity considerations in order to conduct an experimental field study. For another example of an experimental field study, see Dennin and Ellis (2003). Researchers wanting to do experimental field studies should read Chapter 7 describing between-groups and within-subjects designs, and Chapter 8 on quasi-experimental designs.

ON CHOOSING A RESEARCH DESIGN

We now return to the question of choosing the best research design. If, as we have argued, there is no a priori best design, then one might conclude that the choice of design does not matter; all designs are equally good and bad. This, of course, would be true only if research were conducted in a vacuum. It might be true that there is no one best design for research within the counseling profession as a whole, *but at any particular time in the history of a topic area there may be more or less useful ways to approach a specific research question.* We propose that the usefulness of a particular research design for examining a specific research question is a function of the following factors: (1) the existing knowledge bases pertaining to the specific research question, (2) the types of research designs used and inferences made to develop the existing knowledge bases, (3) the resources available to the researcher, (4) the specific threats to the validity of the particular design being considered, and (5) the match or fit between previous research knowledge (factors 1 and 2), the design being considered (factor 4), and one's resources (factor 3). Moreover, we believe that it is essential to be aware of Gelso's (1979) Bubble Hypothesis (the idea that all experiments will be flawed somehow), and thus we maintain that both paradigmatic diversity (including mixed methods) and programmatic research are also basic considerations in selecting a design.

Typically, research on a particular question is conducted within an existing body of knowledge. Thus, it is imperative for the researcher to ascertain both what the previous research suggests about a particular topic area and the kinds of questions that remain unanswered. As a researcher forms a particular research question, it is important to ask what kind of knowledge will add to the existing literature. At the same time, the researcher must evaluate what type of research design will provide the kind of knowledge that is needed. Perhaps a qualitative study would add the most useful knowledge or basic normative information about a topic. Or perhaps an experimental study that isolates the interactive effects of two independent variables would help explain previous contradictory findings. Thus, the utility of a research design needs to be evaluated in the context of the existing research knowledge in a given area.

Equally important is the type of research design used and the inferences drawn to develop the existing knowledge bases. The types of research designs used affect the types of inferences made in developing a knowledge base. Thus, if a particular topic has been predominantly researched in laboratory settings, then perhaps research focused on field settings will now add the most useful knowledge that would address questions about external validity in that area. Or if a topic has been investigated through tightly controlled experimental studies, then perhaps descriptive studies might now add some useful information. Any type of design can be overused in a particular area, a condition that can produce an unbalanced and subsequently weak knowledge base. (In Chapter 17 we present a brief overview of the social influence literature in counseling, and we provide details of an example of this problem of overusing any particular design.)

Many times inexperienced researchers do not read the method sections of research reports. One of this book's authors admits (sheepishly) to committing this sin during much of his early graduate studies. Instead, students usually read the introduction and then skip to the discussion. Although this might suffice for obtaining content knowledge in an area, it misses the important aspect of learning about how the studies were conducted. We suggest a simple technique that inexperienced researchers can use in examining a body of literature. Make a copy of Figure 4.1, and as you read the method sections of various studies within a topic area, place the study into the appropriate cell. It should quickly become apparent which designs have been used and perhaps overused in a particular topic area.

It is also important to note that different designs require different resources and have different costs. For instance, a researcher might decide that a descriptive field study was needed to examine the relationship between counselor techniques and a client's perception of the working alliance. But should she do a correlational study or use an intensive single-subject design? The answer to this question should be obtained, in part, by examining the resources available. To do the correlational study, the researcher would probably need to find 30 to 50 client–counselor dyads. It may take a great deal of work to find these dyads, but the data analyses may be fairly easy and pain-less. On the other hand, for an intensive single-subject study the researcher may have an easy time finding one dyad willing to participate. However, a rather involved, intensive process of analyzing the data will likely ensue. Thus, a researcher must not only examine the resources available, but also look at the costs of choosing a particular design.

In choosing a research design, it is also of utmost importance to remember that each experiment has strengths and weaknesses, and moreover that each experiment is typically flawed in some way. Gelso (1979) understood this idea when he offered the Bubble Hypothesis, which suggests that doing research is similar to trying to apply a sticker to a car windshield. When an air bubble forms between the sticker and the windshield, the owner presses the bubble in an attempt to eliminate it. No matter how hard he or she tries, however, the bubble reappears somewhere else. The only way to get rid of the bubble is to throw the sticker away, but then the owner is left without a sticker. In a similar manner, every piece of research and every research design is flawed (has a bubble). The different research designs will have different limitations and strengths (the different designs may change the location of the bubble), but no single design can entirely eliminate the bubble. The researcher can either stop doing research (throw the sticker away) or be cognizant of the size and location of the bubble for any given design.

The Bubble Hypothesis clearly points out that if only one type of research design is advocated by a discipline, then the bubble will always be in a similar place on the sticker—all the research will contain similar flaws or blind spots. On the other hand, if multiple research designs are advocated, each with dif-ferent bubble locations, then the cumulative effect will be a clearer, more accu-rate picture of the topic under examination. Viewed in this manner, the usefulness of a particular design at a particular time is determined by the loca-tions of the bubbles in the studies that have previously addressed this ques-tion. This type of reasoning led Gelso (1979) to suggest that all types of research designs are useful and that knowledge can be advanced only when the same problem is examined using multiple design strategies. He thus ar-gued for paradigmatic diversity. Over the years there has been a growing con-sensus within (and outside) the field of counseling that the discipline is strengthened when alternative designs are used (see, for example, Creswell, 1994; Hanson, et al., 2005; Haverkamp, Morrow, & Ponterotto, 2005; Polkinghorne, 1984; Tashakkori & Teddlie, 2001).

The Bubble Hypothesis and the need for paradigmatic diversity under-score the importance of programmatic research on a particular topic. Put another way, a series of investigations, conducted by the same or different researchers, that successively extends our knowledge bases along a particular line of research on a particular topic is highly desirable for the profession. The reason is that a series of related investigations that build on each other tends to accumulate more useful knowledge bases than does a series of isolated investigations. Consider the following examples and notice how the researchers used different research methods for different purposes.

Hill and her colleagues (Hill, Helms, Spiegel, & Tichenor, 1988) used a descriptive laboratory study as the first step in developing a client reactions system. Recruited clients seen by counselors-in-training used a preliminary version of the reactions system to record their reactions to interviews. Based on client feedback and item analysis, a revised reactions list was formulated and then used in a descriptive field setting. Thus, Hill's group initially used a descriptive laboratory strategy to develop a measure and then followed it up with a descriptive field design that evaluated both the utility of the measure and the implications of the findings. In short, once appropriate measures have been found or developed, it is then important to examine how these variables operate in real-life settings.

A study by Marx and Gelso (1987) also illustrates programmatic research. Because little research had been done on the termination of individual counseling, these authors sought to describe the termination process using a descriptive field study. They did this in two ways: by using content analyzing termination sessions and by examining variables that correlated with client satisfaction concerning termination. One variable that related to satisfaction with termination was the amount of time spent talking about termination. This finding could serve as a springboard for the next step in a program of research, perhaps an experimental field study. One might wonder if there is a causal relationship between the amount of time the counselor spends talking about termination and client satisfaction with termination. Actual clients and counselors could be used to examine this question. For instance, dyads could be randomly assigned to a high or a low termination-discussion condition. Subsequently, more refined questions could be asked, such as how soon (for example, in a middle session or the next-to-last session) the counselor should begin to address termination.

As we and others have advocated for paradigmatic diversity over the years, does this also suggest that a researcher could combine two different methodologies, let's say quantitative and qualitative in the same study? Simply put, yes. Creswell (1994) traces some of the history of the combination of methods and designs; combined methods is defined as using multiple methods of data collection and analysis (Creswell). Advantages of such combined methods are to seek convergence of the results across methods, perhaps providing complementary or different facets of a phenomenon, adding additional breadth to a study, and using one method to inform the second (Greene, Caracelli, & Graham, 1989). The mixed model designs offer some compelling advantages, and have the potential of creating more inclusive knowledge bases in counseling psychology (see also Creswell, 1994; Ponterotto & Grieger, 1999).

SUMMARY AND CONCLUSIONS

In this chapter we have extended our discussion of science and the scientific method to basic research design considerations. We have maintained that the basic task of the experimenter is to design research in such a way as to simultaneously identify relationships between constructs and eliminate as many rival hypotheses as possible. Kerlinger (1986) has labeled this the MAXMINCON principle. Research design involves developing both a plan and a structure for an investigation and a way of executing the study that simultaneously reduces certain kinds of error and helps the researcher obtain empirical evidence (data) about isolated variables of interest.

We have further maintained that two central issues in research design are experimental control and generalizability, and that different types of research designs represent different trade-offs between these two central issues. Although it can be debated which of these issues is of greater importance, or which issue should take priority in beginning a line of research (see Campbell & Stanley, 1963; Gelso, 1979; Stone, 1984), we believe that in an applied specialty such as counseling, both issues are essential. Although internal validity may be the sine qua non (Campbell & Stanley), the applied nature of our work in counseling cannot be ignored and indeed must be emphasized. We have maintained that internal and external validity are not independent, but they also are not incompatible, especially across multiple investigations. Thus, we need programmatic research that is designed to maximize the benefits of both internal and external validity across investigations. Moreover, within such an investigative blend there is a useful place for laboratory research in extending theoretical issues. As Stone (1984) has argued, "a preoccupation with immediate application can lead us to dismiss important research" (p. 108) that extends our theoretical understanding. In essence, we are underscoring the need for balance in our research; we suggest that investigative styles that disregard certain types of research (such as naturalistic research) are dangerous because they reduce the possibility of gaining certain types of knowledge.

We have also suggested that the goodness of a particular design hinges not only on the threats to validity it allows, but also on the context provided by previous research and existing knowledge bases. Thus, in addition to evaluating the threats to validity for a particular study, the researcher needs to consider (1) the existing research content, (2) the type of research designs used in creating the existing knowledge bases on the topic, and (3) the resources currently available for study. The researcher must choose a research design with strengths and weaknesses that match the needs of the research question, a design that will provide the type of knowledge needed at this particular time in history. In this way, a series of research studies, each with different strengths and weaknesses, may add the greatest breadth to our knowledge bases. Thus, we strongly encourage using programmatic research that emphasizes paradigmatic diversity to build broad knowledge bases for the counseling profession.

STIMULUS QUESTIONS

Following are two exercises that are designed to help students to apply some of the material from Chapter 4 to further explore the advantages and disadvantages of different types of research designs.

Examining the Advantages and Disadvantages of Different Types of Research Designs

The purpose of this first exercise is to become more aware of different types of research designs, their advantages and limitations, and which designs might be most useful for you to utilize in a study you are contemplating. First find several published studies that are interesting and appeal to you.

1. What kinds of designs have been used in those studies?
2. What do you see as the strengths and limitations of the designs of those studies in terms of the types of conclusions that can be made?

3. Identify research questions or research hypotheses that occur to you that could now add exciting new knowledge to the topic.
4. Would the design increase experimental control or external validity (relative to the previous research)?
5. What could you do to enhance both the internal and external validity of the research questions/hypotheses you are contemplating?

Utilizing Different Types of Research Designs to Investigate Your Topic of Interest

Sometimes researchers study a topic by utilizing the same type of research designs over and over. (See Chapter 17 for the consequences of overutilizing analogue methodologies.) It is often useful to initially consider a wide range of research designs when developing a study to determine what type of study you want to do. The purpose of this exercise is to practice conceptualizing studies with different types of research designs on a topic of interest to you.

1. In your topical area of interest, conceptualize a study that utilizes a descriptive laboratory design.
   a. What would be the intended purpose of this study?
   b. Describe the methods you would utilize to conduct the study.
   c. Would this study be high or low on experimental control and external validity?
   d. What outcomes would you predict would be found from the study?
   e. What are the advantages or limitations of the design on the conclusions you could draw from the study?

2. In your topical area of interest, conceptualize a study that utilizes a descriptive field design.
   a. What would be the intended purpose of this study?
   b. Describe the methods you would utilize to conduct the study.
   c. Would this study be high or low on experimental control and external validity?
   d. What outcomes would you predict would be found from the study?
   e. What are the advantages or limitations of the design on the conclusions you could draw from the study?
3. In your topical area of interest, conceptualize a study that utilizes an experimental laboratory design.
   a. What would be the intended purpose of this study?
   b. Describe the methods you would utilize to conduct the study.
   c. Would this study be high or low on experimental control and external validity?
   d. What outcomes would you predict would be found from the study?

e. What are the advantages or limitations of the design on the conclusions you could draw from the study?

4. In your topical area of interest, conceptualize a study that utilizes an experimental field design.

   a. What would be the intended purpose of this study?

   b. Describe the methods you would utilize to conduct the study.

c. Would this study be high or low on experimental control and external validity?

d. What outcomes would you predict would be found from the study?

e. What are the advantages or limitations of the design on the conclusions you could draw from the study?

VALIDITY ISSUES IN RESEARCH DESIGN

To draw valid conclusions about research questions, the researcher must design a study that minimizes the potential to generate alternative explanations for the study's results. Whereas we discussed the trade-off between internal and external validity in Chapter 4, this chapter provides a more detailed analysis of four major inferences made by researchers in evaluating the validity of a particular research design. Specifically, the purpose of this chapter is to define and discuss threats to (1) statistical conclusion validity, (2) internal validity, (3) construct validity, and (4) external validity.

FOUR TYPES OF VALIDITY AND THE THREATS TO EACH

Chapter 3 presented an overview of the research process. Based on theory, clinical practice, or observation, the researcher first states one or a set of research hypotheses. Recall that a research hypothesis is a conjecture about the relationship between or among constructs. The next step is to operationalize the constructs so that they can be measured. In a true experimental design, the independent variable is manipulated by the researcher to assess the effect of the manipulation on a dependent variable. Statistical methods are often (although certainly not always) used to help the researcher decide whether the manipulation had the hypothesized effect.

As an illustration, consider the following example. Suppose that a researcher suspects that cognitive treatments of social anxiety have had only limited success because the interventions do not generalize to behavioral situations. The researcher hypothesizes that in vivo behavioral exercises added to cognitive therapy will improve the efficacy of the therapy. In vivo behavioral exercises are operationalized carefully by designing homework that involves a progressive set of situations in which clients first smile at a stranger, later engage strangers in a short conversation, and finally arrange a social encounter. Social anxiety is operationalized by having the participants report on the (fictitious) ABC Anxiety Test the anxiety that they experienced after talking with a stranger that the researcher arranged for them to meet (called a confederate). The independent variable is manipulated by randomly assigning the participants to one of two conditions: cognitive therapy alone or cognitive therapy plus behavioral exercises. Further suppose that 40 participants are randomly chosen from people who (1) answered an advertisement for a program to treat social anxiety and (2) were assessed by the researcher in a clinical interview to be socially anxious. After the 10-week program, anxiety is assessed using the confederate and the ABC Test; a statistical test indicates that there is a reliable difference between the groups in the hypothesized direction. That is, the mean level of anxiety, as indicated on the ABC Test, is lower for the group that received the exercises, and this difference has a low probability of occurring by chance.

Pleased with these results, the researcher concludes that (1) a true relation exists between the independent variable and the dependent variable (that is, participants who receive in vivo exercises in addition to cognitive therapy have reliably lower scores on the ABC Test than participants who receive cognitive therapy only), (2) the manipulation of the independent variable was indeed the cause of the difference in scores (that is, the exercises were the cause of the lower anxiety scores), (3) behavioral exercises increase the effectiveness of the cognitive treatment of social anxiety, and (4) the results are applicable to socially anxious participants generally (and not just to the participants in this particular study). These conclusions, or more specifically the inferences, seem reasonable in this case; however, there are always flaws in any research, and it is appropriate to keep in mind that one or more of these inferences may be incorrect.

The degree to which inferences reflect how things actually are is referred to as validity. If in vivo exercises in fact reduce anxiety, then the inferences made by the researcher in our example are valid. The purpose of this section is to discuss the principles of validity so that researchers and consumers of counseling research can evaluate the probable validity of the inferences made in a particular study. There are several considerations to keep in mind when reviewing threats to validity.

The first issue is that the conceptual specifics of validity and threats to validity are not concretely fixed as innate properties of research. These concepts are deeply embedded in the philosophy of science and evolve over time as philosophers ponder what it means to conduct research and make inferences about their findings. Thus, it is not the categories of validities per say or their descriptions that are important—what is important is that an understanding of threats to validity will lead to research that yields conclusions that have a reasonable probability of being correct and that decisions made using those conclusions will result in clinical activities and policies that ultimately result in benefits to those people with whom counseling psychologists work. Although there are many ways to look at the validity of research, the framework presented by Shadish, Cook, and Campbell (2002) represents the current state of this evolution. Shadish et al. have created a taxonomy that classifies validity into four types: statistical conclusion validity, internal validity, construct validity, and external validity. This typology was derived from Campbell and Stanley's (1963) original conception of internal and external validity, as further refined by Cook and Campbell (1979). Other discussions of validity are presented by Bracht and Glass (1968) and by Wampold, Davis, and Good (1990).

A second issue is that no study will be able to rule out every threat to the validity of the conclusions reached. A study for which the threats to validity are not severe enough to discredit the conclusions completely will remain useful scientifically because the conclusions reached can be tentatively accepted. Additional studies should be designed that will rule out the threats that plagued the original study. Through the accumulation of studies, threats to a conclusion can be ruled out and a strong statement can be made. For example, no single study of smoking and health has unequivocally established a causal relationship between smoking and disease; however, the accumulation of many studies (and there have been thousands) rules out, with near absolute certainty, any threats to this conclusion. (At one time, the Tobacco Institute claimed that no *one* study had ever scientifically established an unequivocal causal relationship between smoking and disease—in isolation, this is a true statement, but it ignores the accumulation of evidence.)

A third issue is that, more or less, most threats discussed here are *possibly* present in any study. However, more important is the determination of the *plausibility* of a threat in a particular study and its *implication* for the conclusion. Thus, the validity of a conclusion is suspect if a threat is plausible and the threat created conditions that could have produced the evidence supporting the conclusion. For example, suppose that it is concluded that a treatment was effective based on superior outcomes obtained when the treatment was administered to volunteers vis-à-vis the outcomes of nonvolunteers who did not receive the treatment. Given evidence that volunteers respond differently than nonvolunteers (e.g., Rosenthal & Rosnow, 1969), it is plausible that the nonrandom assignment affected the outcomes; moreover, it would be expected that volunteers would perform better given their enthusiasm for the treatment, and thus the nonrandom assignment is not only a plausible threat, but also could well have explained the superiority of the treatment found in this study. Thus, the validity of the conclusion is suspect because a threat was plausible and provided an alternative explanation. On the other hand, had the same study produced a result that supported the conclusion that the treatment was no more effective than no treatment (i.e., no significant differences between the two groups), the threat remains plausible but would not likely have accounted for the result because even with volunteers, the treatment did not produce superior outcomes compared to no treatment. In the latter case, the conclusion retains some degree of validity despite the plausibility of the threat.

On the other hand, some threats, although logically possible, are not plausible. Suppose that a treatment is found to be effective in reducing depression related to career-ending knee injuries to athletes, and the conclusion is made that the treatment is useful for the treatment of career-ending orthopedic injuries. Technically, the experiment did not include participants with non-knee orthopedic injuries, but there is little reason to believe that depression or its treatment would differ for patients with knee injuries versus those with shoulder injuries. So although a threat exists, the plausibility that it renders the conclusion invalid is low.

A fourth issue is that there are often tradeoffs to be made in the design and implementation of research. Designs that increase the certainty of both causal inferences (internal validity) and statistical conclusion validity may decrease the certainty of generalizing inferences from samples to populations (external validity) or the meaning of the operations (construct validity). Likewise, designs that increase the certainty of inferences from samples to populations or about constructs may do so at the expense of decreasing the certainty of inferences about the extent of relationships or causality. The point is that there may be trade-offs with different types of research designs, not only with regard to these four types of inferences, but also with respect to other factors. Gelso (1979) used the metaphor of trying to eliminate a bubble underneath a sticker to describe these trade-offs—removing the bubble in one place creates a new bubble somewhere else. Nevertheless, a bubble that casts grave doubts on the conclusions made from a study cannot be discounted simply because the presence of bubbles is inevitable.

A final issue is that considerations of validity are important for those who design and conduct research and those who consume research. A researcher who designs a study should consider each of the possible threats vis-à-vis the possible outcomes of the study to determine whether when the study is finished relatively valid conclusions may result—if not, the study should not be undertaken. The design of a study should be modified to reduce threats to validity, and sometimes various ancillary aspects can be incorporated to address various threats—such aspects will be discussed throughout this book. Of course, there are no guarantees that the study will produce valid conclusions, because despite the researcher's best efforts unexpected events occur. Furthermore, publication or dissemination of results does not ensure that conclusions are valid, and consumers of research should examine threats independently. For example, generally accepted conclusions that interventions are effective sometimes are incorrect, as has been the case with D.A.R.E. (Drug Abuse Resistance Education, a program of classroom lessons delivered by police officers) to reduce drug use (e.g., Thombs, 2000).

OVERVIEW OF THE TYPES OF VALIDITY

We will approach Shadish et al.'s (2002) four categories by examining the four major inferences made by the researcher in the anxiety example. Recall that the first question was whether there was a relationship between the in vivo exercises used in this study and scores on the ABC Test. In our example, there was a statistically significant relationship between the independent and dependent variables. Often, one of the major inferences made in interpreting research concerns the existence of a relationship between (or among) the variables in the study. The researcher may conclude that there is a relationship or that there is no relationship. *Statistical conclusion validity* refers to the degree to which the researcher has come to the correct conclusion about this relationship.

The second major inference to be made in interpreting research is an answer to the following question: Given that there is a relationship between the variables, is it a causal relationship? In our anxiety example, the researcher concluded that the statistically significant differences between the anxiety levels for the two groups was due to (i.e., caused by) the addition of the exercises. *Internal validity* refers to the degree of certainty with which one can make statements about the existence of a causal relationship between variables.

The third major type of inference is *construct validity*. Construct validity concerns how well the variables chosen to represent a hypothetical construct actually capture the essence of the hypothetical construct. One of the major issues with construct validity involves confounding—the possibility that what one researcher interprets as a causal relationship between constructs A and B, another researcher might interpret as a causal relationship between A and C, or between D and B. In our example it was presumed that the ABC Anxiety Test used in a contrived situation with a confederate was a suitable measure of the social anxiety of the participant, and that the particular exercises used in this study were truly in vivo exercises appropriate for social interactions. If the operationalizations of the constructs of this study were adequate, then the causality attributed to the independent and dependent variables justifies statements about the causality of the constructs used in the research hypotheses. Thus, construct validity refers to the degree to which the measured variables used in the study represent the hypothesized constructs. In our example, in vivo exercises (in conjunction with cognitive therapy) were the putative cause, and social anxiety was the putative effect.

To be of any value to researchers and practitioners, the causal relationship between the hypothesized constructs must be generalizable to units (typically persons, but not always), treatments, outcomes, and settings other than those in the particular study. In the context of our fictitious example, to what extent can we generalize the use of in vivo behavioral exercises to other socially anxious people? *External validity* refers to the degree to which the causal relationship is generalizable across units, treatments, outcomes, and settings.

THREATS TO STATISTICAL CONCLUSION VALIDITY

In this section we define statistical conclusion validity and delineate nine threats to this type of validity. First, however, we need to examine the role of statistics in counseling research. Although most students study statistics outside the context of design, it is necessary to realize that statistical analysis is just one of many parts of the research process. Typically, a statistical test is used to examine whether there is indeed a relation between the variables in a study. In the anxiety example, most likely a two-group independent t test would be performed.

Traditionally, statistical tests are employed to test two competing hypotheses: the null hypothesis and an alternative hypothesis. Usually, the null hypothesis predicts that there is no relationship between the variables in the study. The alternative hypothesis states that there is some true relationship between the variables (which is typically the relationship that the authors have reason to believe might exist). In the anxiety example, the null hypothesis would be that the mean scores on the ABC Anxiety Test for those who receive in vivo exercises would be equal to the mean scores for those who do not receive the exercises. The alternative hypothesis would be that the mean anxiety scores for those who receive the in vivo exercises would be lower than for those who do not receive this treatment. Rejection of the null hypothesis and acceptance of the alternative hypothesis lends credence to the hypothesis that in vivo experiences add to the efficacy of cognitive therapy.

Statistical hypotheses are stated in terms of what is true for a *population*. When we speak of a true relationship between variables, we mean that generally the relationship exists across all persons in a population, although certainly there will be variability among individuals. The behavioral exercises might be generally helpful, although perhaps slightly less helpful for some persons than for others, or may even be a hindrance for a few. Thus, when we conduct a study on a sample drawn from a population, it may be possible that the results of the analysis for the sample are not indicative of the true relationship between the variables (i.e., in the population). For our example, it is possible that the participants selected to be in the study were unusual in some way and that the results obtained are not indicative of the true relationship.

Statistical tests, which are based in probability theory, are used to indicate whether one should reject the null hypothesis that there is no relationship and accept the alternative that there is a relationship. A statistically significant t test in the anxiety example (say with the p value set at $p < .05$) would indicate that one could comfortably believe that a true relationship exists between the independent and dependent variables. However, it is possible that this conclusion is in error; that is, the null hypothesis of no relationship may be true, even though a statistically significant result was obtained due to, say, sampling error. The significance level of 0.05 indicates, however, that the chances of incorrectly concluding that a true relationship exists are fewer than 5 in 100. Incorrectly concluding that a true relationship exists is called a *Type I error*. Type I errors are pernicious because they result in claims that something is going on when it is not; for example, a Type I error in the anxiety study would perpetuate the belief that in vivo exercises were helpful when they were not.

Another type of error can be made: One can incorrectly conclude that there is no relationship. Suppose the t test in the anxiety example was not statistically significant; in this case, the researcher could not conclude that the independent variable was related to the dependent variable. Nevertheless, there might have been a true relationship between these two variables even though for any of a variety of reasons the researcher did not find it. This type of error is called a *Type II error*. One of the major reasons for Type II errors is that variability in the participants' responses tends to obscure true relationships. This variability, often called *error variance,* can be thought of as static on a radio receiver that obscures the true signal. Even if the true signal is strong, an electrical storm can generate sufficient static that one cannot hear a favorite program. Conditions that create error variance lead to threats to statistical conclusion validity (more on this later).

It is important to realize that one is never totally certain that a statistically significant result indicates that a true relationship exists. Similarly, a nonsignificant result does not absolutely indicate that no relationship exists. Nevertheless, various factors or threats can decrease the confidence with which we conclude that there either is or is not a true relationship between variables.

The statistical testing of null hypotheses is deeply embedded in probability theory and the philosophy of science and remains a source of controversy. Indeed, criticism of null hypothesis statistical testing (NHST) began shortly after Sir Ronald Fisher proposed the procedure, and has continued ever since (Nickerson, 2000; Tryon, 2001). The problem became so acute that the American Psychological Association Task Force on Statistical Inference was convened (Wilkinson & the Task Force on Statistical Inference, 1999) to make recommendations on appropriate procedures. Despite the controversy, the NHST is widely used, and when applied correctly provides information critical to making research inferences (Nickerson; Wilkinson et al.). Nevertheless, it is recommended that other statistical information, such as effect size and confidence intervals, be considered and reported (American Psychological Association, 2001; Wilkinson et al.). Further issues with regard to NHST are beyond the scope of this book, and likely will be discussed in basic statistics courses.

The remainder of this section discusses the various threats to statistical conclusions validity.

Low Statistical Power   Power refers to the probability of correctly deciding that there is a true relationship, if indeed a true relationship exists. Clearly, if there is a true relationship, we want to design a study that is able to detect this relationship. Studies with low power often result in the conclusion that no relationship exists when in fact a true relationship exists. Insufficient power most often results from using too few participants.

For example, in a study with fewer than 10 participants, the probability of obtaining a statistically significant result when the null hypothesis is not true (that is, concluding that there is a relationship when such a relationship exists) will be very small. Power will be discussed in more detail in Chapter 14; here we need only note that inadequate statistical power is a threat to statistical conclusion validity.

Violated Assumptions of Statistical Tests   All statistical tests rely on various assumptions (for example, traditional parametric tests typically rely on the assumption that scores are normally distributed). When the assumptions are violated, the researcher and consumer may be misled about the probabilities of making Type I and Type II errors. For example, if the p level of a statistical test is set at 0.05 and the test is statistically significant (that is, $p < .05$), one commonly believes that the likelihood of incorrectly concluding that there is a true relationship is less than 5%. However, if the assumptions of the test are violated, this probability may be much higher. Thus, the statistical conclusion validity is reduced because of the increased chance of making a Type I or II error. The pernicious aspect of violated assumptions is that it is difficult to determine whether or not there are violations, and, if so, the degree to which the violations affect the results. Although violation of some assumptions carries with it little risk, other violations often create conditions that lead to incorrect conclusions. One of the assumptions of most parametric statistical tests is the independence of observations. If this assumption is violated by ignoring the dependence among clients seeing the same therapist, for example, the probability of falsely concluding that a particular treatment is effective can be dramatically increased (Wampold & Serlin, 2000). We advise you to be aware of the assumptions of statistical tests and the consequences of violating those assumptions.

"FISHING" AND ERROR-RATE PROBLEMS   As previously discussed, when a researcher employs any one statistical analysis there is always a chance of incorrectly concluding that a relationship in fact exists. The probability of making this error is set by the significance level chosen for the test (for example, $p < .05$, or 5 chances in 100). However, the probability of this error escalates dramatically when more than one test is conducted. For example, if 10 statistical tests are conducted, the probability of making at least one Type I error (incorrectly concluding that a relationship exists) is at most 0.40 rather than 0.05 (see Hays, 1988, for a discussion and calculations of experiment wide error rates). The point is this: When a researcher conducts many statistical tests, some are likely to be statistically significant by chance and thus lead to false interpretations, sources of statistical conclusion invalidity. Sometimes researchers engage in "fishing," which is simply conducting many statistical tests on a data set without stating specific hypotheses. This procedure inappropriately capitalizes on chance events and increases the probability of a Type I error occurring. Matching the statistical test to the research hypothesis is preferable (Wampold, Davis, & Good, 1990).

UNRELIABILITY OF MEASURES   Unreliable measures introduce error variance and obscure the true state of affairs, and thus such measures cannot be expected to be related to other measures. For example, think of a bathroom scale that yields a dramatically different weight each time you get on it (that is, the readings are random). It is unlikely that scores obtained from this scale will be related to any other scores (such as caloric intake) in any systematic way. Thus, the unreliability of measures provides another threat to statistical conclusion validity. Reliability and its effects on research outcomes are discussed further in Chapter 13.

RESTRICTION OF RANGE   The restricted range of a variable likely leads to an attenuated relationship with other variables. The restricted range usually occurs because the instrument measuring the variable is not sensitive to the construct being measured at the upper limit (ceiling effects) or at the lower limit (floor effects). For example, suppose that a researcher wants to determine the relationship between the cognitive complexity of counselor trainees and the sophistication of their case conceptualizations, but uses an instrument to measure cognitive complexity on which most trainees score at or near the maximum allowable score; even though there may be a true relationship between cognitive complexity of the trainee and the sophistication of the case conceptualization, it is unlikely that the statistical test will lead to rejection of the null hypothesis. Restriction of range often occurs when an instrument designed to measure pathology is used on a nonclinic population.

UNRELIABILITY OF TREATMENT IMPLEMENTATION   Although a researcher might have carefully developed a particular treatment intervention, it is still possible for treatments to be delivered or implemented in a variety of ways. For example, the in vivo homework exercises in our fictitious study may have been assigned in a variety of ways. One of the group therapists may have given the exercises to the clients in written form at the end of the session with no explanations, whereas another therapist may have explained them and their rationale in detail. These variations tend to lead to uncontrolled variability that obscures the true relationship between the independent and dependent variables. Thus, unreliability of treatment implementation is another threat to statistical conclusion validity. Standardization of treatments is desirable, and is discussed in more detail in Chapter 12.

EXTRANEOUS VARIANCE IN THE EXPERIMENTAL SETTING   Any aspect of the experimental setting that leads to variability in responding will increase the error variance and obscure a true relationship. In the fictitious anxiety study, the situations in which the exercises were practiced were not controlled. Some participants may have completed their exercises in a singles bar, others at work, and still others in the grocery store. The differences in these situations would likely lead to variability in responding, which again increases the error variance and threatens statistical conclusion validity.

HETEROGENEITY OF UNITS   Differences in experimental units can often lead to variability in responding. For example, in our anxiety study, physically attractive participants may have had more success in the exercises than less attractive participants. Thus, differences in attractiveness would have led to variability in responding, adding to the error variance (and again obscuring any true relationship). From this point of view, homogeneous samples (for example, all participants having equal attractiveness) are preferable to heterogeneous samples (participants having various levels of attractiveness). However, the results from homogeneous samples can be appropriately generalized only to populations with similar characteristics (see Chapter 14). To some degree, statistical procedures (such as the analysis of covariance) or some design characteristic (such as matching) can be used to remove variance due to some nuisance factor, such as personal attractiveness in heterogeneous populations (see Porter & Raudenbush, 1987; Wampold & Drew, 1990). The units need not be persons; in studies of school achievement, heterogeneity of schools or teacher effectiveness introduces increased error.

INACCURATE EFFECT SIZE ESTIMATION   There are instances when effects detected in studies will be inaccurately estimated. For example, correlation coefficients, particularly in small samples, can be dramatically affected by outliers, so one unit with extreme scores on both measures will result in a sizable correlation when no true correlation exists. Some statistics are biased in the sense that they consistently overestimate population effects, which is the case for R^2 (the sample value of the proportion of variance accounted for in multiple regression). Reporting R^2, particularly in small samples, provides an inflated sense of the relationship between the independent variables and the outcome variable.

THREATS TO INTERNAL VALIDITY

Internal validity refers to the confidence one can have in inferring a causal relationship among variables while simultaneously eliminating rival hypotheses. Internal validity is concerned with the most basic aspect of research, the relationships among the variables of interest (typically the independent and dependent variables). Thus, internal validity in an experimental study focuses on whether the independent variable is the cause of the dependent variable. In our example, was it the in vivo behavioral exercises that caused the lower anxiety scores in the treatment group, or is there some other explanation for the results? Because one can never know the true state of affairs, internal validity is assessed by the extent to which alternative explanations for the results can be ruled out. The more alternative explanations that can be ruled out, the higher the internal validity. As will become evident, internal validity is directly related to experimental control, such as that achieved through random selection of participants, random assignment to groups or treatments, manipulation of the independent variable, and determination of measurement times. Our discussion of internal validity begins by examining three very basic research designs. We will then discuss in considerable detail nine specific threats to internal validity.

To illustrate internal validity, consider the three designs diagrammed in Figure 5.1. The subscripts for the observations (for example, O_1) are used to indicate the order of different observations. The first design, called a one-shot pretest/posttest design (Campbell & Stanley, 1963), involves observing a sample of participants (O_1), administering some treatment (X), and then observing the participants afterward (O_2). Consider a study designed to test the efficacy of a psychoeducational intervention to teach fifth graders about sexual abuse.

Design 1: One-shot pretest/posttest design	O_1	X	O_2

Design 2: Nonequivalent group posttest-only design		X	O_1
			O_2

Design 3: Randomized posttest-only design	R	X	O_1
	R		O_2

FIGURE 5.1 | THREE POSSIBLE RESEARCH DESIGNS, WHERE O = OBSERVATION, X = TREATMENT, AND R = RANDOM ASSIGNMENT

Suppose that the pretest is a 30-item knowledge test related to sexual abuse (for example, "What should you do if a stranger asks to touch you under your bathing suit?"). The psychoeducational intervention, which consists of puppet shows, plays, discussions, and workbooks, lasts throughout the school year. At the end of the school year the knowledge test is re-administered. We would expect that the posttest scores would be higher than the pretest scores (that is, $O_2 > O_1$). Suppose that this relationship is observed; generally the participants score higher after the psychoeducational program than before it. The question is this: Was the psychoeducational program the cause of the increase in scores on the knowledge test? (Take a few minutes and think of alternative explanations for this increase.)

There are actually many alternative explanations. Perhaps over the course of the school year the participants learned about sexual abuse from their parents, friends, or television. Or perhaps they scored better at the second administration of the test because they had taken the test before and were more comfortable with the format of the questions. Or perhaps their reading ability had improved during the year and they scored better because they understood the questions better. Clearly, there are a number of problems with attributing causality in this example.

One of the problems with the first design is that the performance of the participants who receive the treatment is not compared to the performance of participants who do not receive the treatment. In Design 2 in Figure 5.1, there are two groups of participants; one group receives the treatment and one does not. After the treatment, observations are made. Let's say the psychoeducational program is implemented in Chris Jones's class but not in Dale Wong's class.

If the psychoeducational program increased knowledge, then we would expect the scores in Chris's class (O_1) to be higher than those in Dale's class (that is, $O_1 > O_2$). Again, assuming that this is the case, was the psychoeducational program the cause of this difference? Possibly, but again there are strong alternative explanations for the difference. The most problematic is that it is possible that Chris's class already knew more about sexual abuse before the intervention began. The students may have been placed in Chris's class because it was the accelerated track, or the students may have been placed in Dale's class because they had behavioral/emotional problems. Basically, the problem here is that there is no way of knowing or inferring that the students in the classrooms were comparable before the intervention. (There are other problems as well—for example, Chris may have discussed sexual abuse with his students.)

The best way to make groups comparable is to randomly assign participants to the groups. Although random assignment will be discussed in more detail in subsequent chapters, the principle is that each participant has the same likelihood of being assigned to one group as to the other group. Or, said another way, participants are not assigned in any systematic way that might bias the composition of the groups. (Keep in mind that random assignment most likely will result in some small initial differences between groups. This is sampling error and is accounted for in statistical tests.) Design 3 in Figure 5.1 involves two groups containing participants who were randomly assigned. For example, students were randomly assigned either to a treatment group (they receive the psychoeducational program) or to a group that does not receive treatment (called a no-treatment control group; in this case they might have a study period during the time the other group receives the psychoeducational program). Now, if the expected pattern of scores is obtained ($O_1 > O_2$), it is more difficult to find alternative explanations to the conclusion that the psychoeducational program was responsible for the higher scores. However, there are still some alternative explanations. Perhaps a student in the treatment group had been abused, and this led to a very emotional discussion during the treatment; this event and the ensuing discussion, rather than the content of the psychoeducational program, may well have caused the higher scores for the treatment group.

The anxiety study described at the start of this section is an example of Design 3, which is called a randomized posttest-only design. In this context, one group receives cognitive therapy plus the in vivo behavioral exercises, whereas the other receives only the cognitive therapy. In this way, statistically significant differences can be causally attributed to the addition of the exercises (although there are still some threats to this attribution).

We now discuss the threats to internal validity (also see Shadish et al., 2002). Keep in mind that each of the following is a threat to drawing the conclusion that some variable A causes some variable B.

AMBIGUOUS TEMPORAL PRECEDENCE   In the previous examples, the independent variable was manipulated to determine its effect on the dependent variable.

Even if the threats to the internal validity of the studies can be ruled out, it would appear that the manipulation of the independent variable caused the concomitant change in the dependent variable, and not vice versa. However, the direction is not as clear in designs in which the independent variable is not manipulated. Consider studies in counseling that examine counselor empathy and therapeutic gains in clients; several studies have found a positive relation between these two variables (Mitchell, Bozarth, & Kraft, 1977). Does the empathy of the counselor cause client progress, or does client progress cause the counselor to be more empathic? In other cases, the hypothesized cause clearly precedes the effect in time, but the measurement of the cause is assessed retrospectively. For example, it may be hypothesized that aspects of the parental attachment cause transference in therapy (e.g., Woodhouse, Schlosser, Crook, Ligiero, & Gelso, 2003). Clearly, the temporal precedence is clear; however, if parental attachment is measured concomitantly with the transference, it is not clear that what is measured (i.e., recollections of attachment) precedes the transference in time.

SELECTION   Selection refers to differences between groups that exist before implementation of the treatment. Selection is often a threat when participants are initially chosen for a study based on some group membership—that is, when participants are assigned to a particular treatment or control group because they are part of an existing group. Design 2 is subject to the threat of selection. Recall that in our example, the students in Chris's class may be very different from the students in Dale's class, and therefore observed differences (for example, $O_2 > O_1$) could well be due to these initial differences rather than to the treatment. In the absence of random assignment of participants to groups, selection is always a potentially serious threat to the internal validity of a study.

HISTORY   History refers to an event that transpires during the time when the treatment is administered and may affect the observations. Thus, history refers to any events in the participants' school, work, or home life (for instance, a television program, a newspaper article, a term paper, or the death of a family member). In our example, history is a threat in Design 1 because a television special on sexual abuse may have been aired while the intervention was being administered. There is no way to determine whether it was the television special or the psychoeducational program that resulted in the increase in knowledge.

The primary way to control history is to use two groups (as in Designs 2 and 3) so that the event affects both groups equally (or nearly equally). In our example, the participants in the treatment and control groups would have equal access to the television special, equalizing this threat. (Note that in Design 2, students in one class might stay up later, possibly due to increased homework or some other reason unique to that group, making late night specials more accessible to them than to the other class.) Still, try as the researcher might, it is possible that an event could occur that would affect only one of the groups. The threat that occurs from an event that affects only one of the groups is called local history.

Threats due to history can be reduced in a number of other ways. First, observations on the groups should be made at the same time. For example, in Design 3, O_1 and O_2 should occur at the same time. Delaying observations for one group leaves open the possibility that some important event may occur after one group is tested but before the other is tested, creating a threat due to local history. Second, the shorter the treatment, the less opportunity there is that an event will occur. Third, the participants can be isolated during the treatment, thereby reducing the likelihood that an extraneous event will affect them. This is similar to sequestering a jury; however, this is extremely difficult to accomplish with human participants in naturalistic settings.

MATURATION   Maturation refers to normal developmental changes in participants between the pretest and the posttest that might affect the results. Obviously, studies of physical and mental abilities will be affected by maturation. Design 1 is an example of a study that is particularly vulnerable to the threat of maturation, especially if the time span between O_1 and O_2 is long. For example, if the treatment in a study is a one-year program to increase the physical strength of third graders, gains in strength (that is, $O_2 > O_1$) could be due to maturation instead of to treatment.

Design 3 controls for maturation provided that O_1 and O_2 take place at the same time. The participants in this study design were randomly assigned to groups that therefore were most likely comparable before the study began. It can be expected that participants in each group will mature at the same rate.

REGRESSION   Regression refers to changes in scores due to the fact that generally, participants who score low on the pretest will score higher on the posttest, and participants who score high on the pretest will score lower on the posttest. (For this reason, regression often is referred to as regression toward the mean.) As an example, consider a batting champion in baseball. Obviously, he obtained this title because he is a good hitter. Still, his batting average for a given year is also due in part to serendipity. Perhaps there was a warm spell in his home city in the spring, the player next in the lineup had a good year (and so the opposing team could not pitch around him), he was injury-free, he had more than his share of luck as several balls just eluded the outstretched gloves of fielders, his personal life was stable, and so on. It is unlikely that all these factors will be favorable the next year, and so it is logical to predict that although he likely will have another good year, he will not be the batting champion again. (Indeed, batting champions rarely repeat.)

Similarly, someone who scores low initially is likely to score higher the next time around. Consider the example of a state bar examination. The examinee who scores the lowest during an exam administration is obviously deficient in his or her knowledge. However, because the examination does not perfectly measure knowledge of the law, this score is also due to other factors. The examinee may have been late to the examination (and therefore is more anxious), may have misunderstood some questions, may have missed all questions on which he or she guessed, and so forth. On re-examination, all of these factors are unlikely to be in operation and he or she will do better, although still below average. (Interestingly, the examinee might attribute the gain to better study habits!)

Regression is a problem, especially when an experimenter chooses research participants because of their extreme standing on some variables (such as high levels of depression). If participants are selected based on their extremely low scores, then as a group they can be expected to score higher on the posttest, *regardless of whether or not they have received any treatment*. Again, consider Design 1 in Figure 5.1. Suppose that participants were selected for a study because they fell above a certain cutoff score on a paper-and-pencil test of depression (higher scores indicate greater depression). Upon subsequent testing (that is, at posttest), these participants generally will score lower (less depressed) than they did previously. Therefore, a statistically significant difference from pretest to posttest (that is, $O_1 > O_2$) may be due entirely to statistical regression. Design 3 controls for regression because the participants are randomly assigned (that is, have comparable scores), and thus the regression toward the mean for both groups will be about the same.

ATTRITION   Attrition refers to the effect of participants dropping out of a study. Attrition can be a particularly pernicious threat because it can affect all designs and because its severity is difficult to assess. When participants drop out of a study, the scores that remain at posttest may not be representative. For example, consider Design 1 with participants who are depressed. If the most severely depressed participants drop out, then the observations at posttest will tend to indicate less depression because the most extreme scores are no longer considered. Therefore, the fact that $O_1 > O_2$ could very well be due to the fact that the scores that remain at posttest are unrepresentative. (In this instance, the pretest scores for those who drop out would not be analyzed either, but the discussion illustrates the problems of attrition that ensue.)

When more than one group is involved and the attrition across the groups is not comparable, *differential attrition* is said to exist. Design 3, which has been immune to most of the threats to internal validity so far discussed, is subject to differential attrition. We will consider a few applications of Design 3 to indicate how differential attrition may work. First, consider the psychoeducational example in which the participants were randomly assigned to either a treatment group or a control group. Suppose that five of the participants in the treatment group moved out of the school district, whereas none of the control participants dropped out of the study. If the five participants were representative of the other participants, then their removal would have no effect on the outcome (other than to reduce power, and possibly to make the tests more sensitive to violations of assumptions).

Now consider Design 3 for our fictitious anxiety study. Recall that one group received cognitive therapy plus in vivo exercises, whereas the second group received only cognitive therapy. Because the exercises are anxiety-provoking in their own right, it may well be that the most anxious participants will drop out of the cognitive therapy plus exercises group (treatment group) rather than complete the exercises (a not-uncommon avoidance reaction). Because the participants who drop out of the first group are the most anxious, their attrition will tend to decrease the anxiety scores in this group (that is, decrease O_1) and could be responsible for a significant difference between the groups (that is, $O_1 < O_2$) in favor of the treatment group.

A third application of Design 3 will demonstrate how differential attrition can act against ascertaining that a treatment is effective. Consider a treatment for depression that is effective and provides an immediate palliative effect. Again suppose that the participants are randomly assigned to the treatment condition and to a waiting-list control group (the participants in this group will receive the treatment after the study ends, if it is found to be effective). Because depression is a particularly distressing disorder, the most depressed participants in the control group might be most inclined to drop out of the study and seek treatment elsewhere. If this does in fact occur, the control group scores will reflect a drop in depression because the highest scores have been removed. If this drop due to differential attrition is about the same as the effect of the treatment, then the posttest scores will be about equal (that is, $O_1 = O_2$), even though the treatment was effective!

In short, attrition can often serve as a threat to internal validity. However, to some extent, the effects of differential attrition often can be assessed by administering a pretest. This topic will be discussed in Chapter 7.

TESTING   Testing refers to changes in scores on a test due to taking the test more than once. Participants' scores often improve due to familiarization with the test, recall of items and previous responses, and so forth. For example, participants might be asked to perform anagram tasks both before and after a problem-solving intervention. However, the practice performed on the first anagram task might account for improved performance on the posttest, apart from the effect due to treatment. Testing is a threat in Design 1 because improvement in scores from the pretest to the posttest could be due to taking the test a second time. Effects of testing should always be considered when pretests are given. Testing is not a threat in Designs 2 and 3 because the participants are tested only once in these designs.

INSTRUMENTATION   Instrumentation refers to changes in the measuring device or procedure over the course of a study. One might think that a "test is a test," that its properties cannot change from pretest to posttest. Realize that scores are often obtained from assessments that do not involve tests—for example, observations, interviews, electronic and/or mechanical devices, and so forth. Observations by "objective" coders are known to change or "drift" systematically during the course of a study (Kazdin, 1982). Often raters may change or refine definitions as a result of increased experience with the rating process, thereby changing their rating behavior over time. Electronic devices are subject to changes in weather. Even paper-and-pencil tests are subject to the threat of instrumentation; scoring of the tests may differ systematically from pretest to posttest, especially if the tests are subjectively scored.

ADDITIVE AND INTERACTIVE EFFECTS OF THREATS TO INTERNAL VALIDITY   Many of the threats to internal validity discussed so far can work in concert with each other to affect the results of a study. Consider Design 2 in the psychoeducational example. Suppose that even though the participants were not randomly assigned to Chris's and Dale's classes, they were roughly equivalent on all relevant characteristics (intelligence, previous knowledge, motivation, socioeconomic status, and so forth). Suppose as well that a local television station ran a series about sexual abuse on the late-night news. It would appear that selection is not a threat because of the comparability of the groups, and that history is not a threat because the television series aired when both groups of participants could watch it (assuming that O_1 and O_2 occurred at the same time). However, selection and history could interact; perhaps Dale assigned a great deal of homework and children stayed up late to complete it, and therefore they were awake at the time when this series aired. In this example, the scores in the control group could be improved by the interaction of selection and history, obscuring treatment effects. This interaction could also work in the opposite direction: If for some reason Chris's class included students who stayed up late and watched the series, then it would be difficult to know whether an observed effect for the treatment group was due to the psychoeducational treatment or to the television series.

THREATS TO CONSTRUCT VALIDITY

Construct validity refers to how well the independent and dependent variables represent the constructs they were intended to measure. When there is ambiguity about a construct, a confound is said to exist. More technically, a confound is an alternate construct that cannot be logically or statistically differentiated from a hypothesized construct. Suppose that a researcher hypothesizes that male clients with personal problems prefer female counselors, and male clients are randomly assigned to one of two groups. One group reads a description of a counselor who has a female name and views a photograph of a female counselor; the other group reads the same description, but with a male name and a male photograph. After receiving the materials, each participant indicates his willingness to see the counselor for a personal problem. Suppose that the results indicate that the clients prefer, as predicted, the female counselor (and further suppose that the statistical conclusion validity and the internal validity are adequate). A logical conclusion is that male clients prefer female counselors for personal problems. However, there is an alternative explanation: It may well be that the female in the photograph is more physically attractive than the male counselor. As a result, the willingness to see the female counselor may be due to personal attractiveness rather than to gender.

In this example, the two constructs (physical attractiveness and gender) have been confounded. Construct validity is relevant to both the independent variable and the dependent variable. With regard to the independent variable, the groups should vary along the dimension of interest but should not systematically vary on any other dimension. If the independent variable is meant to operationalize gender (as in our previous example), then the groups should differ on this dimension (which was the case) but should not differ on any other dimensions (such as physical attractiveness). Likewise, the dependent variable or variables should measure what they are intended to measure and should not measure irrelevant factors.

Here, we briefly review the threats to construct validity as described by Shadish et al. (2002), keeping in mind that these threats are discussed in more detail in subsequent chapters, particularly the chapters on independent and dependent variables. These threats cluster into two main groups: construct under-representation and surplus construct irrelevancies. Construct under-representation occurs when we fail to incorporate all of the important aspects of the construct. On the other hand, surplus construct irrelevancies occur when we include irrelevant aspects as part of the construct. Consider an analogy: If we use a fishing net with holes that are too big, some of the fish that we want to catch will get away (construct under-representation). If we use a net with holes that are too small, we will catch a lot of smaller fish that we do not want (surplus construct irrelevancies). In many ways the search for construct validity is like trying to find a net with holes that are just right for catching our target fish.

INADEQUATE EXPLICATION OF CONSTRUCTS   To make a construct operational, one must first have a careful, rational analysis of the construct's important or essential components. A threat to construct validity from inadequate explication of constructs occurs when such an analysis has not taken place. To adequately operationalize a construct, it should be defined clearly. When a construct is referenced by a name but not discussed in detail, it is often difficult to ascertain exactly what is intended. *Spouse abuse* may refer to physical acts with the intent to harm, to any physical acts, to physical and verbal attacks, and so forth. Decisions about the nature of a construct should not be arbitrary; proper definitions are needed so that the research hypotheses follow from theories. Moreover, it is important to define constructs to be consistent with prior research so that conclusions about the construct can accumulate. A field can be choked by the proliferation of similar but slightly distinct constructs; if possible, design research with existing constructs rather than defining new ones.

CONSTRUCT CONFOUNDING   As described earlier, confounding occurs when the operationalization of a construct also inadvertently operationalizes another construct. In the earlier example, gender was confounded with personal attractiveness. Confounding is problematic because it is difficult to design pure operations, and extraneous constructs have a way of surreptitiously weaseling their way into studies.

MONO-OPERATION BIAS   Mono-operation bias refers to problems with single exemplars of a level of independent variable or a single measure of the dependent variable. Mono-operations are problematic because frequently the essence of a construct cannot be captured by a single exemplar or a single measure. Most likely, mono-operations under-represent the construct and contain irrelevancies.

Mono-operations of the independent variable can result when only one exemplar of each treatment is used. For example, in the gender study mentioned earlier, all of the participants in the female-counselor group read the same name and description of the counselor and viewed the same photograph. That is, a single exemplar of a female counselor was used; similarly, a single exemplar of a male counselor was used. Clearly, this operationalization of gender is narrow and thus results are restricted to this particular operationalization, thereby creating a threat to the larger construct of gender. It would have been preferable to have several descriptions, male and female names, and photographs. Including variations of exemplars raises the issue of whether the variations have an effect on the dependent variable; if this is of concern, the experiment can be designed to test the effect of the variations (see Chapter 7).

With regard to the dependent variable, a single measure often will not reflect the construct adequately. The ABC Anxiety Test may reflect social anxiety to some extent, but it will fail to do so perfectly. By adding other measures of social anxiety, the construct is operationalized more completely. The technical bases for the use of multiple dependent measures to operationalize a construct are found in statistics and measurement; these bases are discussed conceptually in Chapter 13. The essential point here is that mono-operation bias presents a threat to construct validity, typically by under-representing a construct.

MONO-METHOD BIAS   As mentioned previously, multiple measures are important in capturing the essence of a construct. However, if all the dependent measures use the same method, there may well be a bias introduced by the method. For example, self-report measures often share a common respondent bias. If a participant responds in a socially desirable way to all self-report instruments, then consistent bias is introduced by this method. If two constructs are measured in the same way (for instance, self-report), the correlation between variables may result from method variance rather than any true correlation between constructs. Another example of mono-method bias pertains to the measurement of depression. Instead of using only self-report measures, a more valid method of operationalizing the construct of depression would be to use a client self-report measure coupled with a therapist and observer measure of depression.

Mono-method bias can also apply to independent variables. Presenting written descriptions, names, and photographs (even multiple exemplars of each) operationalizes gender using one method. The question remains: Would the results be similar if gender were operationalized using a different method (such as videotapes of the counselor)?

CONFOUNDING CONSTRUCTS WITH LEVELS OF CONSTRUCTS   Frequently, constructs that are continuous are operationalized with discrete exemplars. For example, the experience level of the counselor is often an independent variable in treatment studies. Experience is a continuous variable with a wide range. If the experience levels chosen are either at the low end of the continuum (for example, novice counselors, those with one practicum course, and those with a master's degree) or at the high end of the continuum (doctoral-level counselors with 10, 15, or 20 years of experience), then it might be concluded that experience does not affect counseling outcomes. A very different result might be obtained with experience levels that span the continuum. When restricted levels of the construct are chosen, the construct is confounded with levels of the construct.

TREATMENT-SENSITIVE FACTORIAL STRUCTURE   Instrumentation, as discussed earlier, can be problematic with regard to internal validity. There are times, however, when delivery of a treatment affects participants' responses to the treatment separate from the intended effects of the treatment. Occasionally, the treatment will sensitize the participants to aspects of the instrument, which changes the factor structure of the instrument. For example, an instrument measuring depression may be one-dimensional when administered to untreated depressed persons; after treatment, particularly with a psychoeducational component, the clients may now be able to differentiate aspects of their depression related to melancholy, loss of pleasure in activities, eating and sleeping, irrational thoughts, activity level, and so forth, creating a multidimensional instrument. A total score on the depression instrument for the treated subjects may misrepresent the fact that the treatment affects melancholy but not activity level, for instance.

REACTIVE SELF-REPORT CHANGES   Self-report of functioning prior to and after assignment to condition can lead to illusory reports of change. For example, participants wishing to qualify for a treatment in a clinical trial may report increased symptomatology, which quickly dissipates if they are assigned to the treatment condition. On the other hand, participants assigned to a wait-list control may actually report an increase in symptomatology based on the belief that the researchers will not allow them to deteriorate untreated. According to this scenario, the treatment would appear to be efficacious when in fact the superiority of the treatment vis-à-vis the control group was due entirely to reactive self-reports. Posttests can also be reactive to treatments retroactively (see Bracht & Glass, 1968). Clients completing a course of cognitive behavioral treatment who take a depression inventory loaded with items about maladaptive cognitions may respond favorably as they recognize, due to the treatment, that these thoughts are inappropriate, whereas the same retroactive effect may not occur for participants who had received a dynamic or experiential treatment. One solution to this threat is to use instruments administered by objective raters or other nonreactive measures (see Webb, Campbell, Schwartz, & Sechrest, 1966; Webb, Campbell, Schwartz, Sechrest, & Grove, 1981).

REACTIVITY TO THE EXPERIMENTAL SITUATION   Reactivity to the experimental situation occurs when participants respond based on the reaction to aspects of the experimental situation that are incidental to the treatment condition. Sometimes participants attempt to figure out what the researcher wants (sometimes called *hypothesis guessing*) and then attempt to either comply with or rebel against the presumed outcome. One of the most problematic things about hypothesis guessing is that it is very difficult to determine when it occurs, how often it occurs, and the direction and magnitude of its effect. For example, if the participants in the gender study guess that the hypothesis is actually related to their willingness to see a counselor of a specific gender, then they may respond in a certain way to please the researcher, to show that they are open minded and nonsexist, and so forth. Reactivity to the experimental situation is also related to the idea of placebo effects in medicine, which occur to a large extent because of the expectation that the treatment will work. Assignment to the desired or experimental treatment may increase the participant's expectation that the treatment will be effective, which in turn will positively affect the client, creating a treatment effect independent from the actual ingredients of the treatment.

There are some ways to reduce reactivity to the experimental situation, although these solutions are not without their own flaws and problems (Rosnow & Rosenthal, 1997). First, the experimenter can make the purpose of the study ambiguous and obscure any indication that one treatment is expected to produce better outcomes than another. However, this reduces the completeness of informed consent because ethical principles dictate that the purpose of research be explained to participants before they consent to participate (see Chapter 6 for a discussion of these ethical issues). Another action that can be taken is to blind the participants to the treatment so that they are unaware of whether, for instance, they are receiving an active medication or a placebo pill; unfortunately, participants in psychotherapy and medical studies are often able to guess the treatment to which they have been assigned, based on cues (in medicine, for example, by side effects of the active medication) (Greenberg & Fisher, 1997).

EXPERIMENTER EXPECTANCIES   Although experimenters are portrayed as objective scientists, there is evidence that this is not the case. They are often eager to find particular results, and this bias is often communicated to participants in subtle (and sometimes not-so-subtle) ways. For example, if the experimenter is also the counselor in a treatment study, he or she may be overly eager to help the clients to show the effectiveness of his or her valued treatment. When this happens, it is unclear whether the causal element is the treatment or expectation; such uncertainty threatens the construct validity of the study. Experimenter expectancies are discussed in detail in Chapter 16.

NOVELTY AND DISRUPTION EFFECTS   Humans respond to novelty, and it has been noted that this phenomenon might affect how participants in research would behave in novel experimental situations. Innovations create an aura of excitement and expectation that could well influence research participants. For example, when the first selective serotonin reuptake inhibitor (SSRI) fluoxetine (Prozac) was introduced in the 1980s, it was hailed as a miracle treatment and subjects enrolling in clinical trials at that time had a much different sense than those enrolling in clinical trials of later generations of SSRIs. Sometimes, however, novelty can disrupt routines and create deleterious effects. As with many threats to validity, it is difficult to know whether novelty and disruption effects would augment or attenuate the treatment.

COMPENSATORY EQUALIZATION OF TREATMENTS   Most counselors are naturally reluctant to withhold programs from participants in control groups. When personnel directly or indirectly involved in a study provide some type of service to participants in a control group to compensate for their assignment to a group that does not receive treatment, compensatory equalization of treatments is said to exist and might pose a threat to internal validity. In counseling, participants in the control group will often seek services elsewhere (clergy, other counseling services, and so forth). In school settings, administrators, feeling bad for the control group, may provide extraordinary experiences, such as field trips, movies, and so forth. These experiences may well affect the scores for these participants, especially if the dependent variable is nonspecific (for example, self-concept).

COMPENSATORY RIVALRY   Compensatory rivalry refers to efforts by participants in the control group to outperform participants in the treatment group to prove that they are "just as good, if not better." This threat to validity occurs most often when the participants' performance will be publicized and there are consequences of not performing well. To illustrate this threat, suppose that counselors in a mental health center are randomly assigned to a treatment group or a control group. The treatment consists of refresher courses on assessment, diagnosis, and service delivery. Because the counselors find such courses remedial and demeaning, they are determined to demonstrate that they do not need the courses. Therefore, the participants in the control group work extra hard to demonstrate that they are competent in these areas.

RESENTFUL DEMORALIZATION Resentful demoralization is, in some ways, the opposite of compensatory rivalry. Rather than working extra hard to perform, participants in the less desirable treatment group (or in a control group) will often become demoralized, which tends to decrease performance. For example, participants in a study of depression, even if informed that they might be assigned to a control group, may feel more depressed than usual when actually assigned to the control group. Their sense of having little control over the reinforcers in their world is reiterated. The demoralization of the participants in the control group adds to the level of depression of these participants, and therefore differences between scores on the posttest (that is, $O_1 < O_2$) may be due to the demoralization of the control participants rather than to the effectiveness of the treatment.

TREATMENT DIFFUSION   Occasionally, the treatment delivered to one group is unwittingly allowed to spread to other groups. This is particularly likely when the treatment is primarily informational and of much interest. Suppose a study is being conducted on sexual abuse. Because of the relevance of this topic, students in the treatment group may discuss it with students in the control group, thereby effectively delivering the treatment to both groups. Diffusion of treatments makes it difficult to find differences among or between groups, even when the treatment is effective.

THREATS TO EXTERNAL VALIDITY

External validity refers to the generalizability of a study's results. To what group of units (typically persons), settings, treatments, and outcomes do the results of the study apply? Often, external validity is limited to how well the conclusions hold for persons or types of persons who did not participate in the research. However, it is important to understand that we want conclusions to be robust relative to various settings, treatments, and outcomes as well (Shadish et al., 2002).

Traditionally, the external validity of persons has been approached by examining samples from populations. First, a population of persons is defined; second, a random sample is drawn from that population. Based on the results of the research conducted with the obtained sample, conclusions are made about the population. Unfortunately, truly or even approximately random sampling is possible only infrequently. Consider the study with socially anxious participants. It is impossible to randomly sample from the population of all socially anxious individuals in the United States. The concepts of sampling and the inferences that can be drawn in the absence of random sampling are discussed in Chapter 14.

Cook and Campbell (1979) broadened the concept of external validity to include generalization *to* the population and generalization *across* populations. Random sampling from a well-defined population refers to the generalizability *to* the population; however, because true random sampling is infrequently conducted, generalization to the population is difficult. Of greater practical importance is the generalizability of results *across* different populations. Consider the social anxiety example, and suppose that the study finds that cognitive therapy plus exercises is significantly more effective than cognitive therapy alone in reducing social anxiety. (Assume that the statistical conclusion validity, internal validity, and construct validity are adequate to draw valid inferences.) Across which populations are these results generalizable? Do they apply equally to all socially anxious participants? To males and females? To adolescents and adults? To various minority groups? And do the results also apply to participants in various settings (social gatherings, public places), to people of different ages than the participants, to well-being as well as depression, to treatments other than cognitive behavioral therapy (i.e., do exercises augment the effects of process experiential therapy), and so forth?

Generalizability across populations is of particular interest to counseling researchers. Paul (1967) admonished researchers to determine which treatments work with which types of clients in which settings. The intricacies of testing for generalizability across persons, settings, and times are discussed in detail in Chapter 14. As indicated there, generalizability across populations is determined by examining possible interactions between the treatment and various population characteristics. For example, if a statistical interaction occurs between a treatment variable and gender, then the treatment is not equally effective with males and females. Generalization across various kinds of persons, settings, and times is tested by examining statistical interactions between the treatment (or the independent variable) and persons, settings, or times. We will briefly discuss five threats to external validity that serve to limit the generalizability of research results.

INTERACTION OF CAUSAL RELATIONSHIPS WITH UNITS   Interaction of causal relationship with units refers to the generalizability of the conclusions about causation across units. When the unit is persons, the variables relevant to counseling research include such variables as gender, racial or ethnic background, experience level, degree of dysfunction, intelligence, cognitive style, personality, level of acculturation, and sexual orientation, among others. Clearly, there are many choices for populations to be studied; some considerations in choosing populations are discussed in Chapter 14. In short, the external validity of a study is strengthened when the research examines the causal relationship between the independent and dependent variables across different categories of persons.

Units need not be persons. For example, interventions at the school level may involve classrooms as units; the question then is whether the conclusion holds for classrooms in other schools, which may or may not be similar to the school or schools at which the research was conducted.

INTERACTION OF THE CAUSAL RELATIONSHIP OVER TREATMENT VARIATIONS. Interaction of the causal relationship over treatment variations refers to the generalizability of the conclusions across variations of the treatment. Does the treatment have to be given exactly as it was in the clinical trial in order for it to be effective? Treatments in clinical trials are administered by selected therapists, who received supervision and training in the treatment and are required to adhere to the treatment protocol; the question is whether the treatment administered by therapists in the community, who might deviate from the protocol and use techniques from other treatments, is equally effective.

INTERACTION OF THE CAUSAL RELATIONSHIP WITH OUTCOMES   Interaction of the causal relationship with outcomes refers to how well the causal relationship holds for outcomes other than those included in the study. This is an issue that has been a source of contention between proponents of behavior therapies, who utilize behavioral and symptom outcomes, and proponents of dynamic therapies, who utilize more personality and well-being measures. Do the results obtained with one set of measures generalize to outcomes that would be assessed by a different set of measures? A similar debate occurs in schools between those who advocate for narrow achievement outcomes and those who desire a broader net that would include variables related to citizenship, altruism, creativity, general problem-solving skills, and so forth. Often, studies are designed that ignore important constructs, and the research can be criticized because these other constructs might be the most interesting piece of the psychological puzzle. There have been numerous investigations of minority group preference for types of counselors (Coleman, Wampold, & Casali, 1995); however, missing from most of this research are constructs related to counseling outcomes. Does the fact that an Asian-American client *prefers* an Asian-American counselor imply that an Asian American would produce the most desirable outcome in this context? Thus, restriction of the constructs used in a study is a threat to the construct validity of the study.

INTERACTION OF THE CAUSAL RELATIONSHIP WITH SETTINGS   Interaction of the causal relationship with settings refers to how well the causal relationship holds across other settings. For example, how generalizable are results obtained in a university counseling center to a community mental health setting, a hospital setting, or private practice? There are obvious differences among these settings, and there is little reason to believe that results necessarily generalize across these settings. Much research is conducted at counseling centers, perhaps because staff members are motivated, interested, and proactive; however, there are factors that may differentiate this setting from others. Thus, the external validity of a study is strengthened when the relationship between the independent and dependent variables is examined across different settings.

CONTEXT-DEPENDENT MEDIATION   Context-dependent mediation refers to the case where there might be a mediating relationship in one context and not in another. For middle-class European Americans there may be a direct causal relationship between career interests and career choice, whereas for various minority groups and persons of low socioeconomic status, barriers and acculturation might mediate the causal relationship of career interest and career choice. Thus it is important to test not only mean differences among populations, but also relationship differences—constructs unimportant for one group of people may act to mediate many causal relationships in another group.

SUMMARY AND CONCLUSION

In this chapter we discussed four types of validity in considerable detail. Statistical conclusion validity refers to the degree to which a researcher has arrived at the correct conclusion about the relationships among the variables in a research question. Internal validity refers to the degree to which statements can be made about the existence of a causal relationship among the variables. Construct validity refers to the degree to which the variables measured in the study represent the intended constructs. Finally, external validity refers to the degree to which the relationship among the variables is generalizable beyond the study to other units (usually people), settings, treatments, and outcomes. Although one can never establish each of the four types of validity with total certainty, researchers establish estimates of validity by ruling out as many threats to the validity as possible. Most important, different types of designs typically represent trade-offs with regard to the four types of validity.

A wide range of different threats to each of the four types of validity exist. How does one assess the severity of a threat? In some instances, statistical tests can be used to determine whether a threat is problematic. For example, if pretests are administered, differences among participants who drop out of a study can be compared statistically to those among remaining participants. Or external validity can be assessed by examining the statistical interaction between the independent variable and some person, setting, or time variable.

A second way to assess validity is to logically examine the likelihood of a threat's occurrence. In some instances, it is very unlikely that a particular threat is problematic, even in the absence of direct evidence. For example, although maturation may be a threat in some designs, if the treatment lasts only one hour, participants are very unlikely to mature much during that time. Or if the pretest is a commonly used test and the treatment is lengthy, interaction of testing and treatment probably will have little effect on the results. Diffusion of treatments will be impossible if participants are strangers and do not have the opportunity to meet.

It is also possible to reduce threats to validity by building into the study some aspects that control for the threat. Consider the example of the study in which photographs of counselors of both genders were presented to the participants. Recall that personal attractiveness was a potential confound in that study. To control for the confound, the researchers could have judges rate the personal attractiveness of various photographs and then match them so that the personal attractiveness of the photographs was constant across the groups.

In sum, our discussion of validity provides a framework for assessing the types of inferences made in research and the subsequent validity of a study. The fact that many threats were presented indicates that many things can weaken or strengthen any particular study. Keep in mind that no research can be designed that is not subject to threats to validity to some degree, which is in essence the thesis of Gelso's (1979) Bubble Hypothesis. The objective is to design and conduct research in such a way as to minimize the threats and maintain the possibility of obtaining interpretable findings. In this respect, programmatic research is needed because studies can build on each other, and a threat to one study can be ruled out in a future study. In fact, programmatic research on a given topic that examines similar variables over time is essential to creating useful knowledge bases within scientific inquiry in the counseling profession.

STIMULUS QUESTIONS

VALIDITY ISSUES

1. Select two studies in your area of interest.
   a. Identify the major conclusions made by the authors.
   b. Identify three major threats to the validity of these conclusions.
   c. Discuss how these studies could have been designed to better rule out these threats.

2. A researcher is interested in studying racial and ethnic identity. The researcher uses ethnic minorities attending the researcher's university as a sample. What would be some important validity considerations of using this sample?

3. Experimental studies are often criticized on the grounds that, due to the desire to control

extraneous variables and exert experimental control, the results are not applicable to real-world situations. Discuss both sides of this argument (i.e., why experimental studies are useful and why the results are not useful).

4. Search the literature to find several studies bearing on the same question. Identify one study with high internal validity and low external validity and another with low internal validity and high external validity. Discuss how each has handled the tradeoff between internal and external validity. Which study is more informative? Finally, how do the studies compliment each other in terms of building knowledge?

6 CHAPTER | ETHICAL ISSUES IN COUNSELING RESEARCH

Ethics are not simply proper etiquette, but rather "they are expressions of our values and a guide for achieving them" (Diener & Crandall, 1978, p. 14). In essence, "ethics is a generic term for various ways of understanding and examining the moral life" (Beauchamp & Childress, 2001, p. 1). Ethical principles help researchers achieve their goals while avoiding strategies that compromise their values, and ethics help them make decisions when their values are in conflict (Diener & Crandall). We believe that ethics are nothing less than central to the conduct of research. Just as morality is a part of everyday living, ethics are a way of living that permeates the research enterprise. Because of the centrality of ethics in research, this chapter is placed toward the beginning of the book so that ethical reasoning can be integrated into basic design considerations not as an afterthought, but as an intrinsic feature of the research endeavor. Indeed, research suggests that students in counseling training programs regard ethical training as essential for their professional roles (Wilson & Ranft, 1993). To assume that being a counseling researcher involves technical research design skills alone is to have a very incomplete picture. We maintain that it is essential for researchers to be aware of their ethical responsibilities to research participants, co-workers, the profession, and society as a whole.

In this chapter we focus on the investigator's responsibility in two general categories: ethical issues related to scholarly work and ethical issues related to participants. In today's multifaceted world these topics take on a complexity not even imagined several decades ago. It is important to underscore at the outset that ethical issues in research are rarely cut-and-dried, and sometimes one ethical principle will conflict with another to create a tangled and murky dilemma. Our main goals in this chapter are to (1) introduce and sensitize the reader to the ethical issues involved in counseling research; (2) underscore the complexity of real-life ethical dilemmas, which sometimes do not have clear answers; and (3) discuss common strategies and the reasoning process for designing research with ethical rigor.

The first section of this chapter discusses fundamental ethical principles as well as virtue ethics that form the core of our professional values. Specifically, we will discuss the fundamental ethical principles of nonmaleficence, beneficence, autonomy, justice, and fidelity. In addition, we will introduce ethical guidelines that have been provided by the American Psychological Association and the American Counseling Association. Next we introduce the notion of virtue ethics and specifically highlight prudence, integrity, respectfulness, and benevolence. In the second section of the chapter we discuss ethical issues related to scholarly work, specifically (1) execution of the research study, (2) reporting the results, (3) duplicate and piecemeal publication, (4) publication credit, and (5) plagiarism. In the final section we discuss ethical issues pertaining to participants: (1) risks and benefits, (2) informed consent, (3) deception and debriefing, (4) confidentiality and privacy, and (5) special considerations for treatment issues. We end with a brief section on responding to ethical dilemmas.

FUNDAMENTAL ETHICAL PRINCIPLES

To facilitate professionals' decision making with regard to ethics, both the American Counseling Association (ACA) and the American Psychological Association (APA) have developed a set of ethical principles or guidelines: *Code of Ethics,* referred to hereafter as *CE* (ACA, 2005), and *Ethical Principles of Psychologists,* referred to hereafter as *EPP* (APA, 2002), respectively. These principles are presented in Appendixes A and B and will be referred to in the discussion of ethical issues throughout the chapter. It is important to emphasize a qualification by Pedersen (1995) that the interpretation of the ethical principles and the professional ethical codes needs to take cultural values and cultural context into consideration. Implicit in these professional codes of ethics are more general and fundamental ethical principles.

> Because ethical codes may be too broad in some cases and too narrow in others, [the more fundamental] ethical principles both provide a more consistent framework within which cases may be considered and constitute a rationale for the choice of items in the code itself. (Kitchener, 1984, p. 46)

In essence, Kitchener has suggested that the counseling profession move away from the rule-bound conception of ethics to one that focuses on identifying and applying foundational ethical principles in difficult ethical dilemmas. Subsequently, a wide range of training models in counseling psychology have promoted the teaching and application of the foundational ethical principles (see Kitchener & Anderson, 2000). In this chapter we focus on five fundamental ethical principles: nonmaleficence, beneficence, autonomy, justice, and fidelity. In essence, these fundamental ethical principles are central but implied building blocks for the professional codes of the ACA and APA. We briefly discuss these general principles to clarify the essence of ethical issues and facilitate an understanding of professional ethical codes. Readers interested in a fuller discussion of such fundamental ethical principles are directed to Beauchamp and Childress (2001), Diener and Crandall (1978), Drane (1982), Kitchener (1984), and Lindsey (1984).

NONMALEFICENCE

Diener and Crandall, in their book *Ethics in Social and Behavioral Research* (1978), succinctly concluded that "the most basic guideline for social scientists is that subjects not be harmed by participating in research" (p. 17). This central principle has been referred to as the principle of nonmaleficence (above all do no harm; Beauchamp & Childress, 2001). This includes not inflicting intentional harm and avoiding the risk of harming others. Thus, it is the responsibility of the investigator to plan and act thoughtfully and carefully in designing and executing research projects, because harm can occur intentionally or unintentionally. Kitchener (1984) noted that a number of ethicists and psychologists have argued that nonmaleficence should be the paramount ethical principle in applied psychology (Beauchamp & Childress; Brown, 1982; Frankena, 1963; Rosenbaum, 1982; Ross, 1930). Thus, these professionals have argued that if we must choose between harming someone and perhaps helping another person, the strongest obligation would be to avoid harm. Diener and Crandall have argued that nonmaleficence can be superseded only if volunteers knowingly participate and the benefits are of great import.

BENEFICENCE

Beauchamp and Childress (2001) concluded that acting ethically not only involves preventing harm, but also contributes to the health and welfare of others. Doing good for others is beneficence. This central ethical principle is the essence of the goal of counseling—to help people resolve problems that they have been unable to resolve on their own. Moreover, beneficence constitutes the core of the ethical principles advocated by the APA and ACA. In the Preamble to the *EPP* (APA, 2002, p. 4), the Ethics Code "has as its goals the welfare and protection of . . . individuals and groups." Likewise, the first sentence in the Preamble to Ethical Standards (ACA, 2005, p. 3) proclaims that "members are dedicated to the enhancement of human development throughout the lifespan."

Inherent in beneficence is competence. If our value is to help others, particularly those in need who come to rely on our services, then we have an obligation to help others as competently as possible. Such reasoning has a number of implications for service delivery, professional training, and research. With regard to research, Lindsey (1984) noted that the beneficence principle mandates the profession to do effective and significant research to maximally promote the welfare of our constituents. Likewise, White and White (1981) argued that it is our responsibility as a profession to provide all the knowledge and skill we can marshal to benefit our clients.

Another interpretation of beneficence is not only contributing to the welfare of others, but also having an active, altruistic, group/community-oriented approach that "gives back" to the research participants and the community. In fact, the ethical codes have been criticized for emphasizing the prevention of harm rather than the provision of benefits (Casas, Ponterotto, & Gutierrez, 1986; Ponterotto & Casas, 1991). Ponterotto and Casas and Ponterotto and Grieger (in press) pointed out the need for more tangible actions that result not only in positive research outcomes, but also benefits for racial/ethnic minority communities. Such a goal might be achieved by systematically investigating psychosocial problems (for example, substance abuse) as well as psychocultural strengths in minority individuals and communities. In short, an important aspect of beneficence is for researchers to take an active, altruistic approach in order that the results of their research provide benefits to the community under investigation (Ponterotto & Casas; Ponterotto & Grieger).

AUTONOMY

The principle of autonomy centers around the liberty to choose one's own course of action, including freedom of action and freedom of choice (Kitchener, 1984). The principle of autonomy is woven into American political institutions, law, and culture. Not surprisingly, Rokeach (1973) found that Americans ranked individual freedom as one of their most esteemed values. In many ways, autonomy is the cornerstone of subjects' rights to voluntarily participate in psychological research, or conversely to decline to participate. Since the Nuremberg trials after World War II, the principle of autonomy has received increased attention in research. At the center of this attention is the notion of informed consent, or educating potential subjects about a particular research project so that they can make informed decisions about participation.

JUSTICE

The principle of justice implies fairness (Benn, 1967). Because the quantity of services and goods in any society is limited, there are conflicts between people. Thus, a vast array of laws has developed as part of our judicial system for deciding what is fair. In essence, the principle of justice is based on the assumption that people are equals. Thus, as initially suggested by Aristotle, equals should be treated as equals, and unequals should be treated unequally only in proportion to their relevant differences (Beauchamp & Childress, 2001; Benn). Gender and race are not relevant characteristics for deciding access to mental health services, but this is not to suggest that gender and race might not be relevant considerations concerning different treatments. The concept of justice also implies just rewards for one's labor, and ownership of the fruits of one's labor.

FIDELITY

The principle of fidelity implies faithfulness, keeping promises or agreements, and loyalty (Ramsey, 1970). This principle applies directly to voluntary interpersonal relationships, including counselor–client, student–teacher, and researcher–participant. Not fulfilling a contract (by, for example, engaging in deception or breaching confidentiality) is a violation that infringes upon the other individual's choice to enter into a mutually agreed-upon relationship. Issues of fidelity and trustworthiness are central to the helping professions such as counseling. The principle of fidelity is important for the reputation of the profession as well as for individual professionals in their work as counselors, supervisors, consultants, educators, and researchers.

VIRTUE ETHICS

Within the past decade virtue ethics have received increased attention (see, for example, Beauchamp & Childress, 2001; Kitchener & Anderson, 2000; Meara & Day, 2003; Meara, Schmidt, & Day, 1996). The previous section on ethical principles focused on fundamental principles, or what some may refer to as obligations (Meara et al., 1996). By contrast, virtue ethics focuses on ethical ideals to which professionals aspire. But to which ethical ideals should our profession aspire?

Four major virtues have been identified (Meara & Day, 2003; Meara et al., 1996): prudence, integrity, respectfulness, and benevolence. Prudence reflects foresight, appropriate caution, and good judgment. Meara and her colleagues suggested that prudence is the cornerstone virtue for professional psychology and is required for fulfilling the spirit of many of the basic ethical principles. Moreover, Meara et al. maintained that particularly in a multicultural milieu, prudence is especially relevant because "a prudent individual is aware that another's definition of the situation is not necessarily one's own" (p. 40). Integrity refers to a "coherent integration of reasonably stable, justifiable moral values, together with active fidelity to those values in judgment and in action" (Beauchamp & Childress, 1994, p. 473). Thus, integrity is a virtue that involves adherence to a set of values over time. Respectfulness refers to holding another in high esteem, not interfering with another, and in essence regarding individuals or communities in terms they themselves define (Meara & Day; Meara et al.). Such a virtue is, again, especially important in a multicultural society. Benevolence refers to "wanting to do good" and "contributing to the common good" (Meara et al., p. 45).

Clearly, virtue ethics pertain to a wide range of ethical issues involving scholarly research and its participants. Virtue ethics are at the heart of our character as helping professionals. Although they do not prescribe specific behaviors for solving ethical dilemmas, virtue ethics constitute the cornerstones underlying our ethical decisions.

ETHICAL ISSUES RELATED TO SCHOLARLY WORK

The study of human behavior is constantly changing and progressing. This evolution reflects a commitment to "increasing scientific and professional knowledge of behavior and people's understanding of themselves and others" (*EPP,* Preamble, p. 4). One of the basic purposes of scientific endeavors in counseling is to increase our knowledge about topics of value to the counseling profession. This broad and vital goal reflects the fundamental ethical principle of beneficence. In a very simple way, the counseling researcher has a responsibility to provide accurate information about counseling-related phenomena "to improve the condition of individuals, organizations, and society" (*EPP,* Preamble, p. 4) and to support "the worth, dignity, potential, and uniqueness of people within their social and cultural contexts" *(CE,* Preamble, p. 3). It can be argued that accurate information promotes the profession's knowledge bases, and that inaccurate and misleading information may distort or even falsify the profession's knowledge bases. In short, given the role of science within the profession, scientists have the responsibility "to undertake their efforts in a totally honest fashion" (Drew, 1980, pp. 58–59). Although any of a number of factors may tax the typical researcher (for instance, publication pressure or fatigue), it is imperative that the researcher keep in focus the ultimate aim of the scientist—to extend our knowledge bases with accurate, reliable, and thus usable information. If the researcher loses sight of this essential goal, then in our opinion she or he has no business conducting research and may only hinder the profession and the people we try to help.

It is important to note that the goal of providing "accurate information" and extending the profession's "knowledge bases" can sometimes be at odds with promoting the welfare of others and society. Even though it can be argued that research that led to the atomic bomb extended existing knowledge bases and was instrumental for the Allied victory in World War II, it can also be argued that this research did not promote the welfare of many innocent people, because it resulted in the deaths of thousands of people. Seeman (1969) aptly concluded:

> The existence of Hiroshima in man's history demonstrates that knowledge alone is not enough, and that the question "knowledge for what?" must still be asked. If knowledge in psychology is won at the cost of some essential humanness in one person's relationship to another, perhaps the cost is too high. (p. 1028)

Likewise, Jensen (1969, 1985) published research (and there is considerable controversy about whether the data were biased) that has been interpreted as showing that African Americans are intellectually inferior. Clearly, it can be argued that Jensen's writing did not promote the welfare of African Americans.

In short, the essential point is that more information does not necessarily promote human welfare. At a minimum, expanding our knowledge bases raises deeper moral issues about right and wrong (K. S. Kitchener, personal communication, January 2, 1990). Thus, it is imperative to note the complexity, and sometimes the contradictions, in the seemingly straightforward goals of extending knowledge bases and promoting human welfare.

Next we will discuss the implications of the researcher's responsibility to provide accurate information concerning five matters: execution of the research study, reporting the results, duplicate and piecemeal publication, publication credit, and plagiarism.

EXECUTION OF THE RESEARCH STUDY

A study must be properly executed if it is to establish valid knowledge bases and adhere to the fundamental ethical principle of beneficence. The researcher has a responsibility for accurately and reliably planning and conducting the research investigation (CE, G.1). The researcher also has the responsibility for evaluating its ethical acceptability, weighing scientific values and rights of participants, and then conducting all aspects of the study in a careful, deliberate manner that minimizes the possibility that results will be misleading in any way. Thus, to reduce methodological biases and errors, it is essential that researchers have an accurate and sensitive understanding of the target population. Moreover, to enhance both the validity and pragmatic value of the research, consulting with community leaders and agencies is encouraged (Ponterotto & Casas, 1991; Ponterotto & Grieger, in press).

Conducting research typically involves multiple tasks and requires a lot of attention to many details. Typical procedural tasks include contacting participants, arranging experimental conditions, randomly assigning participants to conditions, locating and assembling assessment instruments, administering instruments, coding data, entering the data into a computer, and analyzing the data. Within these major tasks are a myriad of steps and processes, such as collating questionnaires, checking the accuracy of the coded data against the original data set, and checking for data entry errors. In short, many, many tasks confront the researcher in a typical research project, and the researcher is responsible for the accuracy and reliability of carrying out all of them.

Problems can occur if the investigator becomes lax during any phase of executing a study. For example, differential participant biases may be created if participants are not solicited according to a standardized recruitment procedure. (See Chapter 16 for a detailed discussion of such biases.) Or distortion can occur if the researcher does not impress upon all assistants the need for accuracy in matching participants to all of their questionnaire data. Research assistants can be invaluable resources, but they typically need close supervision. Moreover, sometimes it is difficult for research assistants to maintain high levels of performance in extremely difficult or boring tasks, and especially when they do not understand the purpose of the task (or study) or the need for great precision. Drew (1980) noted incidents in which research assistants actually recorded fictitious data rather than conscientiously performing the needed task. Investigators are responsible for the competence of assistants working with them, as well as for the ethical treatment of the research assistants themselves. In short, the researcher needs to maintain constant vigilance over all phases of executing a study to ensure the collection of accurate and reliable data.

REPORTING THE RESULTS

Reporting the results of a study, although seemingly a straightforward task, entails responsibilities and often complexities. The fundamental ethical principles involved are beneficence and nonmaleficence. The investigator has a responsibility to report accurately and prevent misuse of research results (*EPP*, 8.10; *CE*, G.4). This implies that the researcher must honestly report findings and present them in a way that is clear and understandable to readers.

The investigator's task is to present the facts of what happened in the study. Sometimes researchers believe that their data will have greater value if they confirm their hypotheses or support a well-known researcher's theory. It is probably true that most published research reports statistically significant findings. However, it is imperative to note that the researcher is not responsible for whether the data do or do not support a particular theory; perhaps the theory is incorrect. As Carl Rogers once said, "The facts are always friendly," implying that one should not feel bad about data that do not support a given hypothesis (personal communication to P. P. Heppner and L. A. Lee, January 1983). Thus, the job of the investigator is to report the results honestly, regardless of any preconceived notions, predictions, or personal desires.

The researcher also has a responsibility to present proper interpretations of findings. This is especially important when the data may have multiple interpretations (as in qualitative research) or when it is essential to interpret the findings within a cultural context. For example, Ponterotto and Casas (1991) as well as Ponterotto and Grieger (in press) recommended that other researchers verify their interpretations of the findings by involving racial/ethnic minority individuals who have more knowledge of the phenomena under study. Likewise, researchers can ask participants in a qualitative study to verify the accuracy of patterns and conclusions that were drawn from the data (see Chapter 11).

Investigators have a responsibility to discuss the limitations of their data and to qualify their conclusions accordingly. Discussion of limitations is especially important when the research might be "interpreted in such a way as to harm persons in particular groups (e.g., gender, race/ethnicity, national origin, sexual orientation, social class)." Moreover, it is important to explicitly mention "all variables and conditions known to the investigator that may have affected the outcome of a study or the interpretation of data. They describe the extent to which results are applicable for diverse populations" (*CE*, G.4). Sometimes researchers believe that if limitations are discussed, their results will be weakened, perhaps so much as to prevent their publication in a professional journal. It is important to remember that the goal of the researcher is to provide the most accurate information possible about the phenomenon of interest. Specifying the limitations is helpful to the profession, and often to future researchers as well. In our view, if a study's limitations are such that they in fact substantially reduce the probability of publishing the results, then the long-term interests of the profession are probably best served if the results are not published. It is antithetical to the long-term goals of a scientist to publish information that is misleading or to suppress disconfirming data.

The investigator also has a responsibility, after research results are in the public domain, to make original data available to other qualified researchers who may want to inspect them and verify claims (*EPP*, 8.14; *CE*, G.4). This necessitates storage of raw data for some time after a study is published, typically for five years.

Perhaps one of the most serious problems is the intentional fabrication of data. It is clearly unethical to produce fraudulent data (*EPP*, 8.10). There are at least three basic methods of concocting fraudulent data: (1) inventing findings without any actual data collection, (2) tampering with or doctoring actual findings to more closely resemble the desired outcome, and (3) trimming actual findings to delete unwanted or discrepant information (Koocher & Keith-Spiegel, 1998). Tampering with the findings can also include presenting post hoc findings as if they were planned; such fabrication obviously provides misinformation to the profession and serves only to increase confusion and misunderstanding. Unfortunately, numerous instances of fraudulent research have been reported in the scientific community (see Koocher & Keith-Spiegel, pp. 411–412), attracting attention in the general media and even provoking congressional investigations (Broad & Wade, 1982).

Perhaps the most publicized report of fabricating data involves Sir Cyril Burt, a noted British psychologist whose research on identical twins was read and cited internationally. Burt was a well-known scientist who was knighted in 1946 in recognition of his work (Drew, 1980). Burt has been exposed posthumously for publishing implausible and fictitious data that supported his own theory of inherited intelligence. Not only did such fabrications mislead the psychological profession for many years, they also became a major source of embarrassment to the profession.

Clearly, the fabrication of data represents a loss of "scientific responsibility" (Keith-Spiegel & Koocher, 1985, p. 364) and does little to promote human welfare. The goals of science are then trampled in the pursuit of personal rewards and short-term gain. Although a quest for personal recognition and the pressure to publish (the academic publish-or-perish dilemma) may distort a researcher's motivations, probably the most significant inducement pertains to securing grant funds. Researchers who make startling discoveries often are awarded grant funds; grant renewals are contingent upon continued research performance and the breaking of new ground. But sometimes in this pursuit the basic aim of science—extending the knowledge bases of a profession—is lost. Fabrication of data results in especially negative consequences for the counseling profession because most of our research is also aimed at improving psychological services to people in need. Thus, fabrication of data does more than create confusion; it can also reduce the effectiveness of the counseling profession, which affects the lives of real people.

The U.S. federal government has promulgated rules that define fabrication, falsification, or plagiarism as *misconduct*. Furthermore, the rules require institutions to have procedures for investigating and sanctioning the misconduct of scientists they employ (see Department of Health and Human Services, 1989).

DUPLICATE AND PIECEMEAL PUBLICATION

Another issue relates to the duplicate publication of data (*CE*, G.5). Obviously, publishing the same data in different journal articles creates some problems. Duplicate publication may give the impression that there is more information in our knowledge base on a particular topic than is warranted. Suppose that a journal article reports a relationship between a new relaxation training technique and stress management, and that shortly thereafter another article appears in a different journal reporting the same finding—the same relaxation training technique is helpful in reducing stress. The second article appears to replicate the first study, and thus creates the impression that the effect of this new relaxation training technique on stress management is a robust finding. In reality, however, these two articles only represent one data set, and the perception of replication is inaccurate. Moreover, duplicate publications waste valuable resources, including journal space and reviewers' and editors' time. In short, "psychologists do not publish, as original data, data that have been previously published" (*EPP*, 8.13).

A related issue pertains to what is referred to as piecemeal publication. Piecemeal, or fragmented, publication involves publication of several and perhaps slightly different studies from the same data set. Piecemeal publication is not necessarily synonymous with duplicate publication, although it can be. For example, it is possible in piecemeal publication to have one study reporting findings on relationships among depression, hopelessness, and suicidal ideation, while a second study from the same data set reports on relationships among depression, hopelessness, suicidal ideation, and irrational beliefs.

The prohibition of piecemeal publication does not include reanalysis of published data to test a new theory or methodology, although the new article needs to be clearly labeled as such (American Psychological Association, 1994). Likewise, there are times when multiple reports from large longitudinal studies are warranted, especially when the time lag across data collection is significant. Similarly, sometimes multiple reports from a large data set are warranted if the studies are theoretically or conceptually distinct, and thus the data cannot be meaningfully combined into one article. Parsimoniously presenting research is desirable, however, and should be done whenever possible.

It is strongly recommended that authors clearly identify instances of multiple publications from the same data set. Moreover, authors should inform editors of the possibility of multiple publications and preferably provide the relevant articles so that editors can make informed decisions regarding fragmented publication. When in doubt, consult the APA *Publication Manual* (American Psychological Association, 2001), journal editors, and colleagues.

PUBLICATION CREDIT

Researchers have a responsibility to adequately and accurately assign credit for contributions to a project (*EPP*, 8.12; *CE*, G.5). The issues involved with publication credit primarily relate to the fundamental ethical principle of justice. On the one hand, assigning publication credit seems like a straightforward and simple process. People who made minor contributions are acknowledged in a footnote, while those making major contributions are given authorship and listed in order of how much they contributed. In reality, these decisions can be complicated and emotional, primarily because of ambiguity surrounding the term *contribution*. What constitutes minor and major contributions? Some contend that the person who contributed the most time to a project deserves to be first author, while others argue that expertise, or even seniority, should determine author order. At other times it is reasoned that the one who conceived the idea for the study should be the principal or first author. Determining the author order often becomes difficult when the authors were primarily engaged in separate activities, such as writing the manuscript, analyzing the results, collecting the data, designing the study, and supervising the conduct of the study. Assigning publication credit becomes complicated as researchers debate whether all of these contributions are equally important, or whether some contributions should be assigned greater weight than others.

Accurately assigning publication credit is important for several reasons. First and foremost, it is important to publicly acknowledge the contributions of all the people involved in the study—to give credit where credit is due (*EPP*, 8.12; *CE*, G.5). In addition, publication credit is often important in one's professional career, helping one gain entrance into graduate school, obtain professional employment, and earn professional promotion. Moreover, public acknowledgment of one's professional contributions can serve as a "psychic reward" to compensate for the low monetary rewards associated with writing for scholarly outlets (Koocher & Keith-Spiegel, 1998). Sometimes the order of authorship on a publication is important, because the first author is accorded more credit (and responsibility) for the scholarly work than are the other authors. For example, only the first author will receive recognition in citation indices such as the Social Science Citation Index. Clearly, then, determining the order of authorship is relevant to career-related issues.

Ethical Principles of Psychologists and *Ethical Standards* are ambiguous in addressing most of these issues. The *Publication Manual of the American Psychological Association* (2001) provides more direction; major contributions typically include writing the manuscript, formulating the research question or hypotheses, designing the study, organizing and conducting the statistical analysis, and interpreting or writing the results. It is often suggested that "minor contributions" to publications be credited in footnotes. Typically, "minor" professional contributions include such activities as giving editorial feedback, consulting on design or statistical questions, serving as raters or judges, administering an intervention, collecting or entering data, providing extensive clerical services, and generating conceptual ideas relevant to the study (for example, directions for future research). Paid research assistants are remunerated for their contribution. Thus, a common introductory footnote (usually found at the bottom of the first page of a journal article) reads something like: "The authors would like to thank Josephine Computer for statistical assistance and Helen Grammar and Chris Critical for helpful editorial comments." Usually, these contributors went out of their way to help the authors in minor but significant ways. Thus, it is important to publicly recognize these minor contributions. However, the author should receive permission from contributors before thanking them in a footnote. Another type of footnote is a public acknowledgment of a funding source that sponsored the research. A footnote might acknowledge, "This research was supported by a grant received by the first author from the National Institute of Mental Health" (complete with reference to the grant number).

How to distinguish between a minor contributor and a major contributor (an author) and how to determine the order of multiple authors are not clearly specified in *EPP* and *CE*. *EPP* does state that "principal authorship and other publication credits accurately reflect the relative scientific or professional contributions of the individuals involved, regardless of their relative status" (8.12). Spiegel and Keith-Spiegel (1970) surveyed over 700 professionals to examine their opinions about determining authorship. They found modal trends, but not a firm consensus, for the following criteria, in their respective order: (1) generation of hypotheses and design, (2) writing the manuscript, (3) establishing the procedure and collecting the data, and (4) analyzing the data. Contributions tend to be valued according to their scholarly importance, as opposed to the amount of time they required. Moreover, respondents in two studies did not rate professional status as a determining variable (Bridgewater, Bornstein, & Walkenbach, 1981; Spiegel & Keith-Spiegel), which suggests that merit rather than degrees or status is typically a stronger determinant of professional contribution. In short, the list of authors should include those individuals who made a major scholarly contribution to the study in the ways just listed.

The order of authorship (in the case of multiple authorship) typically reflects differential amounts of scholarly contributions; that is, the person who made the greatest scholarly contribution to a project should be the principal or first author, with the others listed in order of their relative contributions. The process of determining authors and order of authorship is very important, perhaps as important as the outcome. Because a great deal of ambiguity enters into deciding authorship, authors may have different opinions about author order. The potential for authors to feel slighted or cheated is greater when author order is autocratically decided by one person, such as the first author. Thus, from our experience, a mutual decision-making process is most desirable, and preferably a consensus model in which those involved discuss these issues.

Sometimes the order of authorship is decided at the conclusion of a study (a post hoc strategy) and just prior to the submission of a manuscript for editorial review to a journal or to a professional convention. The advantage of assigning authorship at this time is that it is possible to assess how much each person actually contributed. The disadvantage is after-the-fact disappointments:

A person might have wanted or expected to be first author but was unaware of either how the order was to be decided or other members' contributions. Or a worse scenario: A person might have thought that his scholarly contribution was sufficient to qualify him as an author, but then learned after the study that his contribution was deemed minor and that he would be acknowledged only in a footnote.

Another strategy (the a priori strategy) is to assign authorship before implementing a study. The advantage here is that as a result of the opportunity to discuss and clarify the relevant issues beforehand, informed decisions and agreements can be made by all participants. The disadvantages to this strategy are that a person might contribute considerably more or less than he or she initially agreed to, or an inexperienced researcher might want to be first or second author without clearly understanding the implications of such an assignment in terms of the tasks and skills needed.

A third strategy is to combine both the post hoc and a priori strategies, discussing author-related issues before the study is conducted, perhaps developing a tentative author order, and then evaluating the accuracy of that initial order after all the tasks have been completed. This strategy offers the benefits of both of the other strategies and minimizes the disadvantages and disappointments.

A final strategy is to assign the order of authorship by chance (for example, by drawing straws). This strategy is sometimes used when it truly seems that each author contributed equally, and it is literally impossible to differentiate among their contributions. It may also seem that any author order would misrepresent the contributions of both the first and last authors. In these situations, authors may use some arbitrary method of assigning the order of authorship. If this strategy is used, an introductory footnote should acknowledge that the author order was determined by chance. Parenthetically, assigning author order by alphabetizing names is not a random process (ask people with names like Zimmer or Zytowski). If chance is to be used as the method of assignment, then drawing straws, pulling numbers from a hat, drawing cards from a deck, or some other random means of assigning order is more desirable.

Winston (1985) has developed a system for analyzing contributions to data-based articles that can facilitate decisions about author order. The system delineates 11 activities common to a research project: (1) conceptualizing and refining research ideas, (2) searching the literature, (3) developing a research design, (4) selecting the instrument, (5) constructing the instrument or designing a questionnaire, (6) selecting statistical analyses, (7) collecting and preparing data, (8) performing statistical analyses, (9) interpreting statistical analyses, (10) drafting manuscripts (first draft, second draft, and so on), and (11) editing the manuscript. Winston suggested that the people involved in the project, as a group and through consensus, assign points for each task. Because some tasks require more or less skill and time than others and vary in importance, the assigned points will be different for different activities; the interested reader might compare his or her assignment of points to those initially specified by Winston. The next step, again through group consensus, is to assign points to each person for each of the 11 activities. Points are then totaled, and the order of authorship is based on the point distribution. This system appears promising not only because it provides more specific criteria for determining author order, but also because it could facilitate communication and make explicit the decision-making process within the research group.

One final note: A very complicated issue pertaining to publication credit involves graduate students' theses and dissertations. Often graduate students feel that because they have contributed a great deal of time, effort, and sometimes money, they have contributed the most to their project. Faculty advisor input might include providing encouragement and technical assistance in designing the study, developing major interpretative contributions, providing funding and other support, and writing major parts of the manuscript. However, it is unclear how much of the faculty advisor's contribution is a part of her or his teaching and training role within the university. There is a real potential for exploiting graduate students if a faculty member has them perform most (if not all) of the research tasks and then claims publication credit, particularly first authorship. *EPP* indicates that "except under exceptional circumstances, a student is listed as principal author on any multiple-authored article that is substantially based on the student's doctoral dissertation" (8.12). Similarly *CE* (G.5) indicates that "For articles that are substantially based on students' course papers, projects, dissertations or theses, and on which students have been the primary contributors, they are listed as principle authors." Keith-Spiegel and Koocher (1985) noted that the number of ethical complaints about this issue has resulted in a policy statement issued by the APA Ethics Committee (1983), which provides detailed guidelines. Whereas the Ethics Committee wrote specifically about dissertations, their guidelines pertain equally well to theses. The guidelines are as follows:

1. Only second authorship is acceptable for the dissertation supervisor.
2. Second authorship may be considered *obligatory* if the supervisor designates the primary variables, makes major interpretative contributions, or provides the database.
3. Second authorship is a courtesy if the supervisor designates the general area of concern or is substantially involved in the development of the design and measurement procedures or substantially contributes to the write-up of the published report.
4. Second authorship is *not* acceptable if the supervisor provides only encouragement, physical facilities, financial support, critiques, or editorial contributions.
5. In all instances, agreements should be reviewed before the writing for publication is undertaken and at the time of submission. If disagreements arise, they should be resolved by a third party using these guidelines.

Plagiarism

Researchers have a responsibility to acknowledge the original contributions of other writers and to clearly distinguish their own original scholarly insights from the work of others (*EPP*, 8.11; *CE*, G.5). Again, these issues revolve primarily around the fundamental ethical principle of justice. Plagiarism can occur in the direct, verbatim copying of another's work, or less explicitly, as in duplicating ideas from others' work without proper citation. Quotation marks and proper citation form should be used when quoting a passage verbatim from another article; paraphrasing sentences from other articles should include a citation to the original work. In both cases of plagiarism, the original author does not receive proper acknowledgment or credit for his or her work. Keith-Spiegel and Koocher (1985) nicely depicted this issue:

> Copying the original work of others without proper permission or citation attribution is often experienced as "psychic robbery" by the victims, producing the same kind of rage expressed by those who arrive home to find the TV set and stereo missing. When plagiarizers reap financial rewards or recognition from passing someone else's words off as their own, the insult is still greater. Readers are also misled and, in a sense, defrauded. Plagiarism and unfair use of previously published material are among the more serious ethical infractions a psychologist can commit. (p. 356)

Plagiarism can occur on several levels. A researcher might omit necessary citations through inattention, perhaps by not being sufficiently careful or conscientious. The plagiarism in such cases is unintentional and due more to oversight. Another level involves the difficulty sometimes encountered in determining what is original in a researcher's ideas. For example, after a researcher has read and written in an area for 20 years, ideas from a variety of sources often blend together in a complex knowledge base. The researcher may one day conceive of what seems like a new insight, and publish it. However, in reality the "insight" had already been published years ago; the researcher simply did not remember the original source. Or, as researchers work together and not only share ideas but also build upon each other's ideas, the ownership of ideas becomes unclear. Sometimes researchers working in slightly different areas may duplicate each other's ideas without being aware of their common work. These types of plagiarism are difficult to control; one needs to be as conscientious as possible while acknowledging that memory lapses can create less-than-ideal conditions.

Another level of plagiarism involves the conscious or intentional exclusion of another person's writing because of petty jealousies or interpersonal competition. Thus, a writer might intentionally fail to cite the relevant work of a particular researcher in part because the writer does not want to publicly acknowledge the researcher's work, but also because the writer would like to have sole credit for an idea or contribution. A final level of plagiarism involves the verbatim copying of another's writing or the duplicating of ideas with the motive of presenting oneself as the original contributor, all the while knowing full well that this is not the case. In these situations the plagiarist has control and has made some deliberate choices.

The point is that acknowledging the contributions of others is basically a matter of fairness and integrity—in essence, of giving credit where credit is due.

Not citing the original author may seem like a rather small issue, but it is really quite important. Imagine that you have worked very hard for two or three years, creating and building a new conceptual model. Naturally, you are very proud of this accomplishment. Then someone publishes a similar model and this person receives the credit for developing this innovative model. Being cited is often meaningful to authors and serves as an important psychic reward. In addition to fairness and integrity, there is also the matter of saluting (in a small way) previous researchers for their accomplishments. From a historical perspective, it is important not only to recognize the authors whose work preceded one's own, but also to recognize where one's work fits into the bigger picture. It is a sad comment on the profession when petty jealousies prevent mutual recognition or even collaboration that might result in important contributions. Keep in mind as well that the federal government considers plagiarism to be misconduct in science, and that employing institutions are required to investigate all cases of suspected plagiarism and provide sanctions where appropriate.

Although not appropriately recognizing an author's contributions is problematic, overcrediting an author can also be an issue, most notably when citing one's own research. For example, overly laudatory reference to one's own "seminal, ground-breaking research that will revolutionize the entire field in the next several years" is inappropriate. It is best to leave these types of judgments to others.

ETHICAL ISSUES RELATED TO PARTICIPANTS

A central issue in all psychological and educational research is the dignity and welfare of the people who participate in the study. The goal of the ethical researcher is to develop a fair, clear, and explicit agreement with participants so that their decision to participate in an experiment is made voluntarily, knowingly, and intelligently (Koocher & Keith-Spiegel, 1998). In this manner, participants are not coerced and make informed decisions about the benefits and risks associated with taking part in a particular experiment. The most fundamental ethical principles implied in the treatment of participants involve nonmaleficence, autonomy, and fidelity.

Historically, the dignity and welfare of those participating in research have not always been of foremost concern. Probably the most notorious example of abuse of participants occurred in the experiments conducted during World War II in Nazi prison camps, where many prisoners died from lethal doses of chemicals and various levels of physical abuse. Physicians conducted research on such topics as effective ways of treating severe frostbite (which involved subjecting individuals to freezing temperatures), infected wounds, and deadly diseases such as malaria and typhus (which involved subjecting individuals to infectious germs) (Stricker, 1982). Fortunately, the Nuremberg trials at the end of World War II, which tried 23 physicians for these research atrocities, served as an initial impetus for guidelines of ethical treatment of research participants. In fact, the Nuremberg Code has been the basis for subsequent ethical principles regarding human subjects in research (Koocher & Keith-Spiegel, 1998). Unfortunately, yet other research tragedies stimulated additional concern and the need for additional regulation.

In 1962, the thalidomide scandal (see Chapter 1) came to public attention because of innumerable gross neonatal deformities. Consequently, the U.S. Food and Drug Administration introduced much stricter regulations for tightly controlled experimentation on drugs and other products (Stricker, 1982). Not long afterward, public attention became focused on a program conducted by a hospital in Brooklyn, where 22 chronically ill patients were injected with cancer cells as part of a study to examine the body's capacity to reject foreign cells. The patients were not informed of their participation. This, and other studies involving excessive shock treatment conditions and subjecting participants to diseases such as syphilis, served to raise public awareness of ethical issues related to informed consent of research participants. Subsequently the issue of informed consent crystallized, and obligations to research participants were made clearer (Stricker).

Diener and Crandall (1978) discussed a number of research studies that have raised concern about ethical issues in research (for example, inducing extreme levels of fear in participants, suppressing disconfirming data, jeopardizing continued employment of participants). As awareness of and sensitivity to the rights of both human and animal participants in psychological and educational research have increased, there have been major changes in the regulation of research.

One of the major changes has been development of the Code of Federal Regulations (rev. March 3, 1983), which implemented Public Law 93-348 (July 12, 1974) establishing institutional review boards (IRBs) and an ethics guidance program to protect human participants in biomedical and behavioral research.

All research projects are subject to federal regulations governing research. Initially, IRBs were established as five-person panels to preview research proposals and weigh potential risks and benefits for all research that sought funding from the Department of Health, Education, and Welfare (now the Department of Health and Human Services, hereafter referred to as DHHS). Although IRBs still serve this function, most institutions now routinely have all research proposals reviewed by a campus IRB (C-IRB) committee of peers at their institution. In essence, the typical C-IRB certifies that projects comply with the regulations and policies set forth by the DHHS regarding the health, welfare, safety, rights, and privileges of human participants. The general procedure is for the investigator to complete and submit to the C-IRB a form that summarizes basic information about the research, including purpose of the study, types of participants needed, informed consent procedures, method of collecting data, and funding sources. Please contact your particularly campus IRB for specific requirements and procedures.

Key issues in evaluating the ethicality of any research project are the risks and benefits involved to the participants, and whether participants have been fully informed about the study so they can make an informed decision to voluntarily participate (informed consent). Given the increased sensitivity to informed consent, documentation of the participant's consent is now required unless specifically waived.

In this section of the chapter we discuss a number of complexities and complications related to using human participants that often arise for the psychological researcher in general, and for the counseling researcher in particular. Assessing potential harm or risk is a difficult and sometimes imprecise process. Because there is some level of risk (even if it is minuscule) in every experiment, how much risk or harm is too much? In some research, deception is needed to adequately investigate a particular construct, and if the full truth were known to a participant, the validity of the experiment might be significantly reduced. Thus, without deception, knowledge of some aspects of human behavior may be inaccessible. But deception conflicts with informed consent and the fundamental principles of autonomy and fidelity. This section focuses on these issues in greater detail as we discuss the issues involved in protecting the dignity and welfare of the people who participate in research investigations. Specifically, we will discuss issues pertaining to risks and benefits, consent, deception and debriefing, confidentiality and privacy, and treatment issues.

RISKS AND BENEFITS

The ethical researcher's goal is to conduct an investigation that creates new knowledge (the beneficence principle) while preserving the dignity and welfare of the participants (the nonmaleficence and autonomy principles). It almost goes without saying that one would not want to harm participants in any way. Particularly for the counseling researcher, the goal is usually to alleviate human suffering; thus harm is antithetical to the immediate and long-term goals of the professional counselor. But harm can be manifested in many ways. The most obvious way involves physical harm, or even death, as in the Nazi "research" during World War II. However, harm can also consist of embarrassment, irritation, anger, physical and emotional distress, loss of self-esteem, exacerbation of stress, delay of treatment, sleep deprivation, loss of respect from others, negative labeling, invasion of privacy, damage to personal dignity, loss of employment, and civil or criminal liabilities. Part of the difficulty in predicting harm is that different people may react to the same experimental condition in very different ways. For example, most clients may feel very comfortable rating their expectations for the counseling they are about to receive; some clients might even enjoy this reflection. However, a few clients might experience distress or embarrassment, or even guilt, by participating in this exercise. Sometimes cross-cultural differences contribute to unintended reactions, which underscores the complexity of this issue. Researchers need to assess harm not only in a general sense, but also with regard to the intended participants' worldview and cultural background.

It is the researcher's responsibility to identify potential sources of risk and eliminate or minimize them to protect potential participants (*EPP*, 8.02; *CE*, G.1).

The professional codes of ethics suggest that the researcher should carefully assess the potential risks of involvement for participants and take precautions to protect participants from physical and mental discomfort, harm, and danger that might occur in a study (*EPP*, 3.04; *CE*, G.1). Implied in these statements is that it is the responsibility of the investigator to reduce risk and prevent harm by detecting and removing any negative consequences associated with a study, to the extent possible.

One of the problems inherent in assessing risk potential is that the task is often subjective, ambiguous, and involves an estimation of probabilities. Typically one does not have prior, empirical, objective data about whether the experimental condition is stressful (and to collect such data would require administering the experiment to participants). Moreover, the type and level of stress that would be harmful is ambiguous and likely varies across cultures and individuals; that is, what is perceived as harmful in one culture may not be perceived as such in another culture. Thus, assessing harm may also involve cross-cultural sensitivity. In short, assessing risk is difficult, if not impossible, to quantify.

Acknowledging the difficulty, ambiguity, and imperfectness of the task, there are at least two main strategies for obtaining approval to conduct a study, typically from an institutional review board. The first strategy involves making a best estimate of the risk/benefit ratio of the study; that is, a comparison should be made of the potential benefits that might accrue from the study relative to the potential risks to participants. This involves a three-step process: (1) assessing risks, (2) assessing benefits, and (3) comparing risks and benefits. For example, a study might be considered ethically acceptable if the potential benefits greatly outweighed the potential risks, or if failure to use the experimental procedures might expose participants to greater harm. Assessing the benefits derived from a particular study, however, is also a difficult and ambiguous task. This assessment is complicated by the question of "benefit for whom?" That is, should participants be the ones to receive the benefit directly, or could it be a larger group, as when a profession's knowledge base is increased. Some may argue that benefits from any single study may be minimal, but that over time programmatic research does increase the profession's knowledge base. Still, balancing individual costs against societal benefits is a difficult task. Moreover, it can be argued that the investigator is at a disadvantage to judge the cost/benefit ratio accurately because he or she may be overly biased regarding the benefit of the study (Diener & Crandall, 1978). In short, in principle the risk/benefit ratio is appealing, but in practice it is difficult to apply. Nonetheless, the risk/benefit ratio is one useful strategy for assessing the ethical issues associated with a particular study.

The second strategy involves several procedures to minimize risk or reduce the probability of harm. Whenever the potential for substantial risk is present, the investigator should search for other possible designs or procedures. The researcher needs to exhaust other possibilities for obtaining the same or similar knowledge by using a slightly different design. A common practice is to consult with colleagues not only to obtain ideas regarding alternative designs or procedures, but also to obtain alternative perspectives in assessing risks and benefits.

Consultation with colleagues is particularly important in planning socially sensitive research or research in which cross-cultural or multicultural issues and investigator bias may be a factor. Researchers have a duty to consult with those knowledgeable about the individuals or groups most likely to be affected (*EPP,* 2.01; *CE,* G.1). Often the researcher's problem solving with regard to ethical issues can be greatly stimulated and facilitated by successively conferring with a wide variety of colleagues. The process of consulting with colleagues has now been formalized at many institutions and agencies, as we indicated earlier, into campus institutional review boards (C-IRBs) or human subject review committees. The C-IRBs serve the extremely valuable function of providing additional perspectives in assessing risk and suggesting possible alternative designs that are not always immediately apparent to the researcher. Even if not technically required to do so, researchers are encouraged to solicit feedback from such committees.

The researcher can also engage in other strategies to minimize risk. We indicated earlier that one of the problems in assessing risks and benefits is the lack of empirical data on which to make informed decisions. Thus, another strategy is to collect some data through safer channels, such as using pilot participants and role playing, to facilitate a more accurate assessment of risks and benefits. For example, the researcher and his or her assistants might role-play the experimental procedures in question (which is often a good idea in general), and perhaps explore alternative procedures. Perhaps colleagues could also be asked to serve as participants to review the procedures and provide feedback on potential risks. Colleagues often can provide very useful feedback because they can discuss their experience as a participant in light of their knowledge of ethical and design issues. Depending on the outcome of such role plays (that is, if the risks do not appear to be substantial), the researcher might take another step by conducting a very small-scale pilot study with two to five participants. In such a pilot, the researcher should not only monitor the experimental procedures very carefully, but also interview participants at length about their experiences and solicit suggestions for alternative procedures. Pilot feedback can be extremely valuable, and its utility should not be downplayed. Likewise, any frequency data from previous studies employing the same procedures may be very useful in assessing the degree of risk; for example, researchers might use a postexperimental evaluation to ask subjects whether they experienced any harm. In short, role plays and pilot projects provide the researcher at least minimal data from which to assess risks and benefits. Additional data can also be obtained by carefully monitoring the actual experiment and even interviewing randomly selected participants both immediately after the experiment and several days later. The researcher should not stop evaluating the potential risks of a study once the study is approved by a C-IRB committee, but rather should remain vigilant by constantly evaluating the risks and benefits as more data about the participants' experiences become available.

Another strategy to minimize risk is to screen participants for a particular study and then select only those participants who have certain characteristics that make them more resistant to the risks involved (or dismiss participants who might be particularly at risk in the study) (Diener & Crandall, 1978). For example, depressed participants with very low self-esteem might be at increased risk if they participated in a protracted study that involved a great deal of interpersonal feedback from other students. In this regard, special populations (such as children, patients from a psychiatric hospital, or prisoners in solitary confinement) merit careful consideration as a group.

In summary, the ethical researcher's goal is to conduct an investigation that creates new knowledge while preserving the dignity and welfare of the participants. A central issue in preserving participants' dignity and welfare is preventing harm. Thus, a major task for the researcher is to carefully assess potential risks and make every attempt to eliminate or minimize such risks. Two strategies were discussed for obtaining approval to conduct a study: (1) attempting to assess and weigh the risk/benefit ratio of the study and (2) using a variety of procedures to evaluate, minimize, or eliminate potential risks. Both strategies should be used in any study involving more than minimal risk. It is important to note, however, that a great deal of ambiguity often enters assessments of costs and risks, particularly in cross-cultural and multicultural situations; the researcher may often experience conflict and struggle with the imperfection of this important task. Consultation is strongly encouraged.

CONSENT

A critical issue in conducting studies involving risk pertains to informed consent. After a researcher has carefully evaluated potential harm and developed the best design to answer his or her question while preserving the participant's dignity and welfare, the researcher is then ready to approach participants with a fair, clear, and explicit agreement about the experiment in question (informed consent). The issue of informed consent revolves around the fundamental ethical principles of autonomy and fidelity. Consent refers to the process of giving participants the opportunity to decide whether or not to participate in a particular research study. This might appear to be a rather simple matter: Simply ask the participant if he or she would like to participate. But a number of factors make obtaining consent a rather complicated process, and a considerable amount of attention has been given to this topic in the past 20 years (see Koocher & Keith-Spiegel, 1998; Schmidt & Meara, 1984).

The professional codes of ethics clearly indicate that the investigator has a responsibility to obtain informed consent from participants (*EPP*, 6.11; *CE*, G.2). The investigator seeks to develop a specific type of relationship with potential participants and thus is ethically bound to establish a clear and fair agreement that clarifies obligations, risks, and responsibilities prior to the study.

Turnbull (1977) discussed consent in this special relationship in terms of three key elements: capacity, information, and voluntariness. *Capacity* refers to a participant's ability to process information and involves two issues: a legal age qualification and ability standards. Minors, people under the age of 18, are not considered to be legally able to make some decisions and thus do not have the needed capacity in these instances. The principle of autonomy creates difficult issues when applied to using children in research (*EPP,* 3.10, 8.02). Ramsey (1970) has argued that because children have a reduced or limited capacity, it is impossible to obtain a fully rational consent from them. Moreover, the child's parent or legal guardian cannot know whether the child, if fully rational, would choose to participate or not. He argued that children should not be used in any research except research from which they would benefit directly. Ramsey's position has been regarded as too extreme (see Cooke, 1982; Powell, 1984), and parents or legal guardians are allowed to give consent. However, federal regulations indicate that a child's assent (defined as an affirmative agreement to participate) is required whenever in the judgment of a C-IRB the child is capable of providing assent, taking into account age, maturity, and psychological state. We encourage counseling researchers to explain to children (and to their parents or guardians), in language they can understand, what they will be asked to do in the course of the research and to secure whenever possible their agreement to participate.

Ability typically refers to mental competence, and thereby protects individuals who may be at risk because of diminished mental capacities. Autonomy is again an issue. If a researcher uses institutionalized adults, then consent must be obtained from parents or legal guardians. We also suggest obtaining assent from adults with diminished capacity if at all possible. In short, a critical element of consent involves the capacity to process information about the merits and drawbacks of participating in a particular study.

The second key element of informed consent pertains to the type of *information* that potential participants are given about a study (*EPP,* 8.04; *CE,* G.2). Participants must be given all of the relevant information about a study so that they can make an informed decision about the merits and liabilities of participating. Turnbull (1977) noted the importance of two issues: the kind of information provided and the process of providing it. Thus, the information given must be complete and presented in understandable, jargon-free language. Drew (1980) referred to these issues as fullness and effectiveness. To satisfy the requirement of fullness, the information presented should contain a description of what the investigation is about and what the participant will be asked to do (such as complete two questionnaires about study habits). This should include a discussion of any type of voice or image recording (*EPP,* 8.03). Moreover, the explanation should include a discussion of possible risks or potential harm involved in the study, as well as a discussion of potential benefits that might accrue from participation. Failure to make full disclosures, as in the case of deception, requires additional safeguards that we will discuss later. Moreover, the information must be understandable to participants given their particular worldview.

The third element of consent is *voluntariness:* assent must be given without any element of explicit or implicit coercion, pressure, or undue enticement

(*EPP*, 8.06). Examples of coercion include requiring students to participate in a study because they are enrolled in a class, living in an institution, part of a therapy group, or seeking individual therapy; publicly humiliating participants if they choose not to participate; paying excessive amounts of money or giving other financial rewards as an inducement to participate; repeatedly contacting clients and soliciting participation; and creating undue social pressure by indicating that all of the other clients have agreed to participate. University courses (such as large introductory psychology classes) sometimes offer bonus credits for or require participation in research studies; in such situations it is essential to offer students viable alternatives to participating in research studies in order to protect their autonomy. Voluntariness can also be a complex issue in a counseling context. For example, situations in which therapists ask their clients to participate may contain elements of undue influence (for example, the therapist is very likable, or the client is vulnerable and wants to be a "good client"). In short, a key aspect of consent is that participants can voluntarily decide on participating free from blatant or subtle extraneous factors that may compel them to participate.

The notion of voluntariness does not end when a potential participant decides to participate in a study; it continues throughout the duration of a study. Thus, participants are typically informed prior to the commencement of a study that they have the right to withdraw from the experiment at any time, and that their initial agreement to participate is not binding. Koocher and Keith-Spiegel (1998) astutely observed that the wise investigator will be alert to signs of discomfort or anxiousness that might influence participants to withdraw, and rather than coerce continued involvement be concerned about the usefulness and validity of data collected under stressful conditions.

In short, an important ethical consideration in recruiting participants in counseling research involves their informed consent. It is important that potential participants have the capacity to process information about the study, have received complete and effective information about the content and procedures of the study, and can decide on the merits of participating voluntarily, without extraneous compelling factors.

As we indicated earlier, documentation of the participant's consent is now common practice. There are a few exceptions; several categories of research are typically considered exempt from these requirements, such as observation of public behavior, the study of anonymous archival data, and certain types of survey and interview procedures. Participants are asked to sign a formal consent form indicating their informed agreement to participate if there is more than what is referred to as a minimal risk (that is, more risk to the participant than he or she would encounter in daily life). Even in studies involving minimal risk to participants, obtaining a signed consent form is advisable to avoid misunderstandings and for the researcher's own protection. It is important to note that cross-cultural issues can also create confusion or misunderstandings that may be relevant during the process of obtaining informed consent, which again reinforces the need for sensitivity to these matters while obtaining consent.

Specifically, the following elements are to be incorporated into a written consent form:

- Name, phone number, and address of the person(s) conducting the study, and whom to contact for additional information or questions; name, phone number, and address of faculty member if the investigator is a student; whom to contact in the event of a research-related injury to the participant
- A statement that the study involves research, along with the title, purpose, and general description of the study
- A description of the procedures, including amount of time involved and any plans for contacting participants at a later time
- A description of any reasonably foreseeable risks or discomforts to the participant
- A description of the benefits to the participant, or to others that can reasonably be expected
- In cases involving treatment or therapy, a statement of appropriate alternative procedures or courses of treatment, if any, that might be advantageous to the participant
- A statement describing the extent to which confidentiality will be maintained
- A statement that the results of the study may be published or reported to government or funding agencies
- A statement indicating that participation is voluntary, and that the participant may discontinue participation at any time without any penalty
- For research involving more than minimal risk, an explanation of whether compensation or medical treatments are available if injury occurs

A sample of a typical consent form for adults is provided as Exhibit A at the end of the chapter, and a sample of a typical consent form for children (note the appropriate language level) is provided as Exhibit B.

Deception and Debriefing

Deception is a topic that has received considerable attention and been the subject of much debate (*EPP*, 8.07; *CE*, G.2). Deception in psychological research refers to misinforming or withholding information from potential participants about the nature of the experiment or the procedures involved in the study. Thus, deception refers to misrepresenting the facts pertaining to a study, through acts of either omission or commission. For instance, an investigator might omit or withhold some information about a study and thus disguise the true nature of the study in some way; or the researcher might purposefully provide false or misleading information, an act of commission, to deceive the participant in some way. Either way, the thorny issues of deception revolve around the fundamental ethical principles of autonomy, fidelity, and, to some extent, nonmaleficence.

It is important to note that there are many types or levels of deception. Perhaps at the simplest and most benign level, the experimenter may accurately describe the study but not disclose all the facts about it, largely because of the tremendous amount of detail involved. Or the experimenter might accurately disclose the nature of the experiment but not reveal the hypotheses so as to not bias the participants. These acts of omission usually do not bother participants. It is typically recognized that an experimenter cannot be completely forthcoming about all aspects of a study (including the researcher's hypothesis or complete descriptions of all experimental conditions); in fact, revealing such information can bias or confound the results of a study (see Chapter 16). Other types of deception, however, mislead the participants in major ways and often lead them to feel "duped" or "had." For example, participants might be told that they failed a problem-solving test (that their score was in the fifth percentile) in order to examine their behavior following failure. In reality, participants probably did not perform so poorly on the test but were merely given bogus feedback. For the most part, the major controversy surrounding deception pertains to those situations in which participants are entirely misled. It is on these instances of deception that we will focus here.

Obviously, the use of deception is antithetical to fully informing potential subjects about the essence of a particular study. The use of deception in psychological research is quite a controversial topic. Schmidt and Meara (1984) reported that in revising the APA Ethical Principles in 1981, a substantial minority of psychologists agreed to forbid the use of any deception. The majority, however, thought that although deception should generally be avoided, important research would be impossible to conduct (and would never be conducted) if deception of all kinds were unethical. For example, sometimes deception is necessary in psychological research to adequately examine certain phenomena, like the process of persuasion. Specifically, in a study of the social influence process in counseling, some participants might very well be predisposed not to change a particular belief or attitude if they were told beforehand that the study was investigating variables related to changing their beliefs. In this case, not using deception would result in a study that did not have much generalizability or resemblance to the attitude change process in counseling.

Schmidt and Meara (1984) noted, however, that deception may have especially troublesome consequences for counseling researchers. A core ingredient of the counseling relationship is perceived counselor trustworthiness; deception would most likely destroy client perceptions of trustworthiness and the working alliance. Thus, because of therapeutic considerations, researchers examining real-life counseling processes must address additional considerations and consequences involving deception. Our view is that researchers should avoid deception whenever possible. In particular, "psychologists do not deceive prospective participants about research that is reasonably expected to cause physical pain or severe emotional distress" (*EPP*, 8.07). Moreover, the use of certain types of deception with oppressed groups is very questionable. Still, we believe there are exceptions in which deception may be allowed. Specifically, when there is little or minimal risk and the benefits from the research are socially significant or directly benefit the participant, deception may be allowed. However, we agree with Lindsey (1984) that "if the risk is significant and subjects are deceived, it is a fundamental violation of the principle of autonomy" (p. 85). In addition, before conducting a study using deception, it is the responsibility of the investigator to have (1) "determined that the use of deceptive techniques is justified by the study's significant prospective scientific, educational, or applied value," and (2) determined that "effective nondeceptive alternative procedures are not feasible" (*EPP*, 8.07). Kazdin (1980) noted two other considerations. First, the aversiveness of the deception itself is an important factor to consider, because there are many types of deception with varying consequences. Some deception does not result in any harm to a participant, whereas other types of deception might result in considerable harm. Second, the researcher must weigh the potential and magnitude of the harmful effects caused by the deception. Thus, the extent or magnitude of the harm is an important consideration. In short, if an investigator decides to use deception, additional responsibilities and safeguards are required to protect the welfare and dignity of research participants, and the researcher must carefully assess the potential consequences and risks to participants. Finally, given the nature of the counseling relationship, deception in real-life counseling with actual clients would rarely seem justifiable.

If deception is justified, the investigator is responsible for informing participants about the nature of the study and removing any misconceptions as soon as is possible within the experiment (*EPP*, 8.07; *CE*, G.2). Providing a sufficient explanation is commonly referred to as debriefing. Moreover, in educational settings, if students are serving as participants to earn research credits and learn about psychological research, debriefing also should emphasize educational issues. Exhibits C and D provide examples of both oral and written debriefings for an analogue study that examined variables affecting laypersons' perceptions of grief reactions. Because this study was conducted with undergraduates who earned extra credit, the debriefing nicely emphasizes educational components. Moreover, the example explains the need for the minimal level of deception used in the analogue study.

It is important to note that the effectiveness of debriefing is unclear and probably varies with each study or experimenter. Moreover, in some cases debriefing can itself create stress or harm. For example, if the researcher preselected two groups of participants who had very high or very low self-concepts, communicating this information may not be well received by some participants. In this regard, Baumrind (1976) identified debriefing as "inflicted insight." In other situations participants may feel angry because they were misled or "duped." Thus, sometimes debriefing adds additional complications and results in delicate situations with which the investigator must contend.

CONFIDENTIALITY AND PRIVACY

Investigators ask participants for a wide array of information, often of such a very personal nature that it could be harmful if publicly released. Often experimenters promise confidentiality to increase the likelihood of honest responses from participants. If a participant agrees to participate confidentially in an experiment, the principles of fidelity, autonomy, and to some extent nonmaleficence suggest that any information that the participant discloses should be protected to safeguard the welfare of the client. The professional codes of ethics clearly indicate that care should be taken to protect the privacy of participants (*EPP*, 6.02; *CE*, G.2).

Maintaining the anonymity or confidentiality of participants is now standard in counseling research. Anonymity exists when there are no identifiers whatsoever on project materials that can link data with individual participants; often researchers assign participants coded designations that appear on their respective questionnaires in lieu of their names. Thus, the participants' responses are anonymous, and even the investigator cannot identify the participants. At other times, investigators collect data and ask for participants' names. Researchers have an obligation to maintain the confidentiality of information obtained in such research. If names are used, typically code numbers will be assigned to participants when the data are transferred to coding sheets, and the original questionnaires containing participants' names will be destroyed. If someone other than the experimenter will have access to data (for example, a research assistant), this should be explained to the participants (and usually is stated in the consent form) along with plans for maintaining confidentiality. In field settings, researchers also should be alert to minimizing the invasiveness of data collection so as to protect the participants' privacy within a social milieu.

Schmidt and Meara (1984) indicated that because confidentiality is central to the counseling relationship, counseling researchers often need to be especially sensitive to maintaining confidentiality, particularly with regard to research conducted in an agency such as a university counseling center. For example, researchers must be sensitive to releasing demographic information that might identify participants in a small therapy group (for example, an eating disorder group or a consciousness-raising group for men over 30); on small college campuses, demographic information about the group composition can easily identify clients. Likewise, research using an intensive single-subject design or an intrasubject design with only a few participants also demands sensitivity to identifying characteristics; typically it is advisable to provide fictitious descriptive information that is similar to the truth if it is necessary to describe a particular client in detail, and to explicitly indicate this in whatever written or oral report is made. Sometimes investigators also communicate to participants how the data will be used. They may also obtain feedback and written approval from clients on written descriptions of the study's results to further reduce any breaches of confidentiality.

Another confidentiality issue arises if researchers want to investigate some aspect of a particular treatment procedure *after* clients have already begun treatment at an agency. Suppose there is an active relaxation training program at a university counseling center, in which students, staff, and faculty are encouraged to participate. Clients enter this program with the usual assurance of confidentiality. Let's say a researcher from the counseling department (outside the agency) is interested in evaluating some aspect of the treatment program and examining the effects of certain individual difference variables (such as coping style) on the relaxation training. Given that the clients have been assured of confidentiality at the outset, it would be a breach of confidentiality at this point to reveal client names to a researcher outside the agency. Some clients might also feel their privacy has been invaded if they were identified to a researcher *in the agency,* because they did not consent to having that person know of their seeking such services. Likewise, if an investigator should conduct a study with a sample of counseling center clients that gave their consent to participate in a study with certain specified procedures, the investigator is limited to accessing only the information or data that the clients consented to disclosing or providing, as opposed to any information in the clients' agency files (see Keith-Spiegel & Koocher, 1985). In short, counseling researchers sometimes have dual responsibilities; they need to be sensitive to confidentiality issues pertaining to research endeavors as well as to confidentiality issues inherent in therapeutic relationships in general.

Confidentiality and privacy issues in research settings can also intersect with a psychologist's duty to protect the welfare of participants and other individuals, thereby creating an ethical dilemma for the researcher. The most notable examples involve participants with homicidal and suicidal intentions that become evident during the course of a research investigation. For example, counseling researchers routinely assess the psychological adjustment of participants in various ways, such as by using the Beck Depression Inventory (BDI) (Beck et al., 1961). In this case, the difficult question concerns what to do when the investigator finds that a participant scored very high on the BDI. Or suppose the researcher is investigating suicidal intentions and in administering the Scale for Suicide Ideation (SSI; Schotte & Clum, 1982) learns that one or more participants scored very high on the SSI. Another ethical dilemma can arise when a participant reveals some information such that the participant or others will be liable for a violation of the law. In short, sometimes the counseling researcher obtains information about participants that either creates considerable concern for the general well-being of particular participants or other individuals, or brings up criminal or civil liabilities.

Concern for the well-being of a particular participant must also be considered in light of the individual's right to privacy. In approaching one participant who had a very high BDI score after a particular investigation, the investigator was curtly informed that the participant "consented to participate in a psychological experiment, not psychotherapy." Some participants may feel embarrassed if attention is called to them within a group setting; obviously, care must be taken to avoid breaching confidentiality to other participants and to being sensitive to the effects of isolating particular individuals.

Concern for the well-being of a particular participant must also be considered relative to the amount of information an investigator has about the participant. Whereas one researcher might have only one data point (a BDI score) that is causing some concern, another researcher might have a much broader array of information (for example, questionnaire data, interview data, information about environmental stressors, knowledge about past suicide attempts) that more strongly suggests considerable reason for concern.

Clearly, the counseling researcher has ethical obligations beyond the research. Moreover, each situation presents a slightly different context and calls for slightly different interventions. The researcher faces a complex decision as he or she weighs the strength of the evidence, the individual's right to privacy, the consequences of approaching a participant with the topic, and the obligation to promote human welfare. Some C-IRBs now require investigators to include in the consent form a statement that indicates that if the participant reveals information that signals danger to the participant or another person, confidentiality may need to be broken. Another strategy is for researchers who collect data of a psychologically sensitive nature to routinely attach to the research questionnaire a statement communicating that it asks questions of a personal nature, and that participants are strongly encouraged to discuss the feelings reflected in the questionnaire, if they so choose. Applicable resources should then be listed, such as the address and phone number of the university counseling center or local mental health center. In addition, verbal announcements can also be made before administering the questionnaire. The following paragraph, developed as part of an introduction to the Scale of Suicide Ideation, is an example of a statement designed to facilitate such an exchange:

> The following questionnaire inquires about a variety of thoughts, feelings, attitudes, and behaviors that are sometimes related to suicide. We are interested in how frequently college students think about suicide. We realize that this is not a rare occurrence. In fact, by some estimates, up to 70% of the population at one time or another contemplate suicide. However, we want you to be aware that counseling services are available to you should your thoughts about suicide cause you some distress. To inquire about counseling, you can contact the Counseling Center [address and phone], or the Psychological Clinic [address and phone]. In the event that your score on this inventory indicates that you are seriously contemplating suicide we will contact you to express our concern and urge you to seek counseling. (Dixon, 1989, p. 42)

TREATMENT ISSUES

In the past, a common strategy among researchers was to use a between-groups design to compare two or more groups of participants; one group received a particular treatment, and instead of the treatment one of the other groups received a placebo or had treatment delayed. Although such designs offer methodological rigor, they can present ethical problems related to withholding treatment from people in need. Clients in a waiting-list or placebo group could be at risk as they continue to struggle under duress. Thus, researchers who are interested in examining questions about comparative treatments often must examine additional ethical issues.

One of the essential issues pertains to the necessity of withholding treatment. In general, if there are treatments that are known to be effective, then withholding them from participants raises serious ethical concerns. However, there is less concern about withholding an intervention of unknown effectiveness. The researcher might examine the need to compare a particular treatment against a no treatment group. The researcher might also consider alternatives, such as comparing the treatment of interest against a well-known treatment.

Or the researcher might examine treatment comparisons in an alternative design, such as a within-subjects design. In short, as with the standards for using deception, researchers must assess potential risk and consider alternative designs to answer treatment questions.

Another consideration is the type of participants involved in the experiment. Kazdin (2003) suggested that volunteer clients solicited from a community setting may be more appropriate for a waiting-list group than are clients from a crisis intervention center. Assessing the risk potential not only involves an assessment of the setting from which participants are drawn, but also consideration of the type and severity of a participant's presenting problem (for instance, depression versus assertiveness).

Kazdin (2003) also suggested that assigning participants to delayed-treatment groups might be more ethically appropriate if the participants initially came from a waiting list, which is in essence delayed treatment. For example, many agencies have waiting lists because service demands are heavier than can be met by the staff. Thus, a treatment study might be conducted by randomly assigning clients from the waiting list to the experimental conditions (treatment and delayed treatment). In such a case, some clients would actually receive treatment earlier than if they had stayed on the agency's waiting list.

Other ethical considerations that merit attention in delayed-treatment conditions include informed consent and ultimately providing treatment. Ethically, participants should be informed before an investigation if there is a possibility that they may be placed in a delayed-treatment group; they then may or may not decide to participate in the study. Moreover, participants in a delayed-treatment group are entitled to treatment after the experiment has concluded, and these participants deserve the same quality of treatment as the experimental group.

In short, counseling researchers who contemplate using placebo or delayed-treatment conditions must carefully examine additional ethical issues. As with the standards for the use of deception, we suggest that researchers assess the potential risks and consider alternative designs as ways of minimizing risks.

RESPONDING TO ETHICAL DILEMMAS

It is important to note that researchers are not likely to be entirely ethical all of the time. In fact, almost all researchers will unknowingly engage in some aspect of research that might infringe upon one of the ethical principles at some time or another. Sometimes an ethical problem may not be foreseen or may be inadequately anticipated, or the researcher may be inexperienced and have an incomplete understanding of the ethical codes. Or because there can be ambiguity in the ethical codes, inexperienced researchers may make questionable decisions. This is not to condone infringements, but rather to acknowledge that oversights and mistakes happen.

Most often, infringements occur due to a lack of sensitivity, knowledge, or experience. We can all help each other by consistently educating each other in our endeavors to conduct our research ethically and to uphold our professional responsibilities. Thus, it is important to talk with each other about ethical issues and dilemmas, particularly when we witness events that make us uncomfortable. From our experience, inexperienced professionals (for example, students, assistant professors) may become paralyzed when they witness what appears to be an ethical infraction and withdraw from the situation. Similarly, people are typically reluctant to raise ethical issues with people in authority positions. Such reservations can be very valid in some situations, but sometimes they are not justified at all. Informal peer monitoring of ethical issues is a powerful mechanism not only to monitor the appropriateness of our behavior, but also to increase our sensitivity and knowledge about ethical issues.

We strongly encourage readers to confront ethical dilemmas, and whenever possible, engage in informal peer monitoring. Typically, it is recommended that concerned individuals review ethical codes, evaluate the evidence (facts versus hearsay), examine their motivations, consult with knowledgeable colleagues, and then discuss the issue with the person or people involved (see Koocher & Keith-Spiegel, 1998, for more details). Another strategy for dealing with people in authority positions is to involve other professionals in authority positions through consultation and problem solving. For more serious or repeated ethical violations, sanctions may be sought from local, state, or national ethics committees (such as state licensing boards or professional organizations such as the ACA or APA), or even the judicial system. The interested reader should consult Koocher & Keith-Spiegel (1998), who provide excellent guidelines for a range of options (and sanctions) in responding to ethical situations. We encourage readers to examine not only the *EPP* and *ES* codes in the appendixes, but also the *Publication Manual of the American Psychological Association* (2001). When in doubt, consult with trusted, knowledgeable colleagues and faculty.

EXHIBIT A
Consent to Serve as a Participant in Research[1]

1. I hereby consent to take part in research directed by Dr. Mary Heppner and Meghan Davidson, and sponsored by the University of Missouri. Dr. Heppner is an Associate Professor and Meghan Davidson is a doctoral student in the Department of Educational and Counseling Psychology. I understand that other persons will assist Dr. Heppner and Meghan Davidson in conducting this research.
2. Further, I understand that:
   a. *Purpose.* The purpose is to study the validity and reliability of a new measure of empathy.
   b. *Requirements.* My part of this research will be to complete a paper and pencil survey designed to measure the way I empathize with others. Surveys will be completed by groups of students in university classrooms.

(Continued)

c. *Time needed.* The total time required will be approximately 25 minutes.

d. *Voluntary participation.* My participation is completely voluntary. Even after I begin participating, I will be free to stop at any time. I have the right to stop after I have started participating, or I have the right to decide not to participate at all in this study. Although the researchers ask that I try to answer every item, I understand that I can skip any item that I simply do not wish to answer. (I do not need to give a reason for skipping any item.) In no case will there be a negative effect for my non-participation or non-completion.

e. *New developments.* I will be told of any new information that develops during the course of this research that might affect my willingness to participate in this study.

f. *Benefits.* I will receive a debriefing sheet that explains more about empathy. General benefits will come for myself and others in the form of an increased scientific understanding of how people relate to and understand other people.

g. *Protections.* I understand that the following precautions have been taken for my protection: (1) no part of the surveys will ask for my name or other identifying information, my responses will remain completely anonymous; (2) no questionnaire asks me to describe specific incidents; (3) I am free to discontinue my participation at any time for any reason; (4) although the researchers would like me to answer every item, I am free to skip any question or item that I find too sensitive or stressful; (5) when the results of this study are published, only aggregate data (for example, group averages) will be reported.

3. My questions about this research have been answered. If I have further questions, I should contact:

Dr. Mary Heppner
16 Hill Hall
HeppnerM@missouri.edu
Department of Educational and Counseling
   Psychology
University of Missouri
Columbia, MO 65211

office phone: (573) 882-8574
email:

Meghan Davidson
16 Hill Hall
Department of Educational and Counseling
   Psychology
University of Missouri

email: mmd75b@mizzou.edu

Institutional Review Board
Jesse Hall
University of Missouri
Columbia, MO 65211

phone: 882-9585

Signature   _____

Date   _____

E X H I B I T   B
Sample Youth Assent Form (Children)[2]

You are invited to participate in a research study conducted by a graduate student at the University of Missouri-Columbia. As a participant, you should read and understand the following statements. Ask any questions before you agree to participate.

1. Goal of the Project: The goal of this research project is to develop a new survey that measures high school students' attitudes about healthy relationships and sexual coercion in dating relationships. It is hoped that this survey will be used in evaluating educational programs about sexual coercion in dating relationships. Please note that you will be asked about information pertaining to your attitudes, beliefs and own personal experiences.

2. Participation Procedure and Guidelines:
  a. You will receive an assent form (this page), get any questions that you might have answered, and then complete the surveys.
  b. The information you provide will be kept **completely anonymous.** That is, your name will not be on any of the forms.
  c. It will take about 30 minutes to complete the surveys.

3. Participation Benefits and Risks:
  a. Your participation in this study does not involve risks that are greater than those you experience in your daily life. You might feel some mild discomfort from reading and responding to some items on the questionnaires. But again, the risk of discomfort is not greater than you might have in class or in other normal activities.
  b. You also might experience some benefits from participating in this project. These benefits might be positive feelings from helping with an important research study.
  c. By filling out the survey, you will be entered into a raffle to win one of fifteen gift certificates to any store in the Columbia Mall.

4. Rights to Refuse or Withdraw: Your participation is VOLUNTARY, and there is no penalty for you not wanting to participate. This means that you are free to stop at any point or to choose not to answer any particular question.

5. Rights as a Participant: You have a right to have any questions about this research project answered. Please direct any questions to the following individuals:

M. Meghan Davidson, M.A.
Department of Educational
& Counseling Psychology
16 Hill Hall
University of Missouri-Columbia
Columbia, MO 65211
(573) 884-4328

Mary J. Heppner, Ph.D.
Department of Educational
& Counseling Psychology
16 Hill Hall
University of Missouri-Columbia
Columbia, MO 65211
(573) 882-8574

For additional information regarding participation in research, please feel free to contact the University of Missouri-Columbia Campus Institutional Review Board office at 882-9585.

6. Agreement to Participate:

Signature_____**Date**_____

E X H I B I T C
Oral Debriefing[3]

That concludes your participation in the study. Thanks so much for your help. Now that you have finished giving your opinion, I can explain more to you about the whole purpose of the study. I could not do so before now without biasing your responses. First, the study is concerned with more than "interviewing styles." We are more interested in impressions of college students about bereaved and depressed persons. Specifically, we wanted to find out both about your personal reactions to someone who is bereaved and also your attitudes about what is normal or pathological grief. We didn't want people to know exactly what we were looking for in advance, because it could have influenced who signed up for the experiment or the answers they gave. We regret that we could not more fully inform you before you participated. We strongly hope you will respect our need to withhold this information and will not discuss this experiment with your fellow classmates.

Some of you received instructions that you were listening to a tape of a middle-aged widow; some were told that she had become widowed three weeks ago and some were told she became widowed two years ago. If you received these instructions, you were in one of the experimental groups. Others received instructions that you were listening to a tape of someone who had lost a job. You were in a control group. In addition, some subjects hear a depressed woman on tape and others hear a nondepressed woman. We will be looking for differences in the answers of these various conditions depending on whether the subjects are male or female.

I want to tell you now that none of you will come back to participate in a further part of the experiment. When you leave today, your participation will end. It was important that you think you might come back, so we could get your reaction about whether you were willing to meet the woman you heard on the tape.

Next, let me explain that this is an analogue experiment. That means that the people you heard on tape were playing parts that were written for them in advance. The purpose of this is so each time a new group hears a particular conversation, it is done exactly the same as the last time a group heard that conversation. This allows for better control of the experiment and helps to eliminate unknown influences on the answers you gave.

I want to thank you for your participation today. Again, it is very important that you do not talk about this experiment with anyone once you leave this room. If people who participate later in the study are aware of its purpose or procedures, their answers may be biased. This would cause us to report misleading results. As we hope our research may some day assist actual bereaved persons, this is a serious problem. Please give others the chance to fairly contribute as you have today.

Does anyone have any questions? [Pause for questions.] I will sign your research cards and you are free to leave. I will stay for a moment in case you have other questions.

If you're having any difficulty dealing with either bereavement or depression, I have the telephone numbers of our University Psychology Clinic and of the Counseling Service, and I will be glad to give them to you when you have finished.

EXHIBIT D
Written Debriefing[4]

This sheet will further explain the purpose of this research project beyond the oral explanation you have already heard. It will outline the independent and dependent variables and research hypotheses. It is crucial that you do not discuss the information on this sheet with any of your friends (who might inadvertently communicate with future participants) or with the experimenter who is present today. She must remain blind (uninformed) concerning the hypotheses in order to avoid influencing the experiment. You may direct any questions to Carol Atwood at 484-1676 (leave a message if no answer). Please sign this sheet as soon as you finish reading it, place it back in the envelope provided, and seal the gummed flap. Thank you very much for your help.

1. Nature of the project: This project would best relate to the major research area of social psychology—attitudes and social perception.
2. Findings of related studies: There is little previous research concerning the layperson's views of what is a healthy versus an unhealthy grief reaction, and whether or not laypersons reject or avoid the bereaved. Vernon (1970) asked participants how they would respond to a recently bereaved person that they knew. Only one-fourth of participants indicated they would spontaneously mention the death; another one-fourth preferred that neither side mention the death at all. Other researchers, such as Lopata (1973) and Glick, Weiss, and Parkes (1974), have indirectly addressed the question by interviewing widows themselves, who frequently reported experiencing strained relationships or the breakup of friendships after the deaths of their husbands.
3. Independent variables: These are the variables in the experiment that the investigator manipulates or controls. There are three independent variables in this project. The first is gender of the participants. We will look for differences in the responses of male and female subjects. Second is the depression condition (whether the woman heard on the tape is depressed or nondepressed). Third is the "bereavement (or widowhood) status"; that is, the woman on the tape is either recently widowed, long-term widowed, or not widowed (loss of a job is mentioned), depending on which written instructions you received.
4. Dependent variables: Used to measure the effects of manipulation of the independent variables. In this project, the dependent variables consisted of the written questionnaire you completed. We want to find out how much you would reject the woman heard on the tape, what your social perceptions of her were, and how pathological you found her to be.
5. Hypotheses: The research questions to be examined in the project. Please do not share this information with today's experimenter.
   A. How do college students' judgments of emotional disturbance compare, based on whether the woman on the tape is recently bereaved, long-term bereaved, or nonbereaved? How do ratings of disturbance differ, depending on whether the woman on the tape sounded depressed or not depressed?
   B. Do college students reject a bereaved person or a nonbereaved person more, and is this rejection affected by whether the woman sounds depressed or not depressed?

(*Continued*)

    C. How does the gender of the participant (male or female) affect participants' responses?

6. Control procedures: Procedures to reduce error or unwanted variance. In this study, random assignment of participants to experimental conditions was used, except that it was not possible to randomly assign participants based on participant gender. Other control procedures used include keeping the experimenter blind to the study hypotheses, not informing participants before the experiment about the true purpose, use of an analogue procedure in which actors were used on the tapes, and use of a control group of participants who listen to the tape of a woman who is neither a widow nor depressed.

I have read the above information concerning the nature of the study, Reactions to Stressful Life Experiences. I agree not to disclose this information either to potential future participants or to the experimenter present today.

Name (Print) _____

Signature _____

Date _____

SUMMARY AND CONCLUSIONS

We have suggested that ethics are central to the conduct of research and, in fact, permeate the entire research enterprise. Broadly speaking, ethics are a "set of guidelines that provide directions for conduct" (Keith-Spiegel & Koocher, 1985, p. xiii). For counselors, research ethics provide direction for interacting with the larger profession, other professionals, and those people who participate in our research. Moreover, how we design and conduct our research reflects our basic values, such as autonomy, fairness, promoting the welfare of others, fidelity, and above all, avoiding harm to others. Sometimes it seems that the business of life overshadows our basic values, as we cut corners to save time. It is essential to keep in mind, however, that the health and longevity of our counseling profession rest on such basic values as honesty and fairness. These values need to be emphasized throughout graduate training in a wide range of situations, and particularly with regard to research. Our values may communicate more about who we are and what we do in our research than any other aspect of our behavior. In essence, "ethical rigor needs to find as central a place of prominence in research as does methodological rigor" (Lindsey, 1984, p. 85). We not only need to "do the right thing," but also to "aspire toward ideals and to develop virtues or traits" (Meara et al., 1996, p. 24) that enable our profession to achieve our moral ideals.

NOTES

1. An earlier version of this consent form was written by Meghan Davidson. At the time this chapter was written for the third edition of the book, Meghan was a doctoral candidate in counseling psychology at the University of Missouri-Columbia.

2. An earlier version of this consent form was written by Meghan Davidson. At the time this chapter was written for the third edition of the book, Meghan was a doctoral candidate in counseling psychology at the University of Missouri-Columbia.

3. An earlier version of this oral debriefing was written by Carol Atwood. At the time this chapter was written for the first edition of the book, Carol was a doctoral student in clinical psychology at the University of Missouri-Columbia.

4. An earlier version of this written debriefing was written by Carol Atwood. At the time this chapter was written for the first edition of the book, Carol was a doctoral student in clinical psychology at the University of Missouri-Columbia.

STIMULUS QUESTIONS

ETHICAL ISSUES IN THE RESEARCH PROCESS

In this chapter, we have maintained that it is essential for researchers to be aware of their ethical responsibilities to research participants, coworkers, the counseling profession, and society as a whole. The purpose of this exercise is to promote additional thinking about ethical issues related to participants and scholarly work. We suggest you reflect on the questions below, write your responses, and then discuss your responses with a peer in the class to further your understanding of ethical issues and responsibilities related to the research process.

1. Why might it be functional to focus on learning the foundational ethical principles rather than just relying on a rule-bound conception of ethics?

2. Explain why it is essential to interpret the findings of any study within the cultural context in which the data were collected. Can you list at least three problems that occur when researchers misinterpret their findings without the appropriate reference to the cultural context?

3. What, in your view, is the most serious consequence of publishing fraudulent data?

4. What do you think Carl Rogers meant when he said "the data are always friendly"?

5. What do you think is the best strategy for determining the author order of a manuscript? Why?

6. In what instances, if any, do you think deception is acceptable in counseling research? In what instances would you definitely not allow deception?

7. Identify two situations where investigators' bias could result in insensitive cross-cultural research.

8. What is the difference between confidentiality and anonymity?

9. Why do you think it is often recommended to talk directly to the relevant people when ethical issues arise?

Major Research Designs

7 CHAPTER | BETWEEN-GROUPS AND WITHIN-SUBJECTS DESIGNS

Many research questions in counseling relate to the very basic question of whether what a counselor is doing is effective; is it really helping people with some aspect of their lives? Whether we work in independent practice, in counseling centers, in school settings, or in academic jobs, we are a profession that helps people in a variety of ways, and we want to know if what we are doing is really having a positive impact. Whether it is a psychoeducational group for teens with eating disorders, a high school classroom intervention aimed at bringing awareness to the discrimination faced by minority group members, or a specific treatment we are using with an individual client, the most basic question we want to answer is: Is the intervention effective? Some of the most rigorous designs we have at our disposal to address such questions are what are called between-groups and within-subjects designs.

In Chapters 3 and 4 we identified the goal of research as isolating relationships among constructs of interest and operationalizing constructs into the independent and dependent variables while simultaneously eliminating sources of bias, contamination, and error. Perhaps the most essential rules of research are expressed by Kerlinger's MAXMINCON principle, in which researchers try to maximize the systematic variance of the variables under study, minimize error variance, and control extraneous variables. Extraneous variables and error variance can mask or obscure the effects of the independent variable on the dependent variable.

In this chapter we will discuss two designs that are often referred to as true experimental designs because of their emphasis on experimental control, minimizing extraneous variables, and internal validity. Even though students sometimes feel intimidated about true experimental designs because of the heavy, ominous meaning that the words sometimes convey, the designs are actually quite straightforward; the label is more ominous than the actual design. The two true experimental designs are commonly labeled between-groups design and within-subjects design.

The between-groups design often adheres to the MAXMINCON principle. Differences between treatments can be maximized by making the treatment (independent variable) stronger or even exaggerated. Thus, researchers will often examine the effects of extreme treatments, such as five counselor disclosures in 50 minutes, or three counselor influence attempts in 15 minutes. Moreover, the between-groups design can be arranged to control extraneous variables and minimize error variance through randomization and experimental control.

The essential feature of between-groups design is the comparison of variables across two or more groups under tightly controlled experimental conditions. In early counseling research, a common comparison group was some type of control group, a group that did not receive one of the active treatments in the study. Over time, differences between or among experimental treatments have been compared. To adequately make comparisons across groups necessitates that the groups do not differ in important ways before the experiment. Thus, initial differences between groups in terms of individual difference variables, demographics, and situational variables must be minimized prior to experimental manipulations to reduce threats to internal validity. Because of the emphasis on comparison and equivalent groups, assignment of participants to groups is a critical consideration in between-groups design. In fact, one of the major identifying features of between-groups design is the random assignment of participants. In short, the between-groups design is a powerful investigative tool, and often the most strongly favored design (Kazdin, 2003, Kerlinger, 1986; Shadish et al., 2002).

The hallmark of the within-subjects design is that it attempts to minimize error variance due to individual variation by having each participant serve as his or her own control because all participants are exposed to all of the treatment conditions. This design, like the between-groups design, is often called a true experimental design because of the random assignment of treatments and manipulation of the independent variable. The random assignment that occurs in the within-subjects design is assignment to a time period in which the treatments are delivered.

For example, perhaps a researcher has located two videos that may be useful for increasing participants' empathy related to issues of poverty and social injustice. In a within-subjects design, all participants would view both videos, but not at the same time. For example, one group of participants would get treatment X_1 (video #1) before X_2 (video #2), whereas the other group would receive the opposite sequence, X_2 before X_1. In within-subjects design, each participant is assigned to either sequence randomly, as a matter of chance. Hence, the comparison in a within-subjects design is between different time periods in which separate treatment conditions are in effect.

BETWEEN-GROUPS DESIGNS

In this section we first discuss some of the historical events affecting the emergence and development of the between-groups design. We then proceed to a discussion of the strengths and weaknesses of three specific between-groups designs. Because the central focus of between-groups designs is to compare treatment groups and control groups, the third section explicitly discusses issues pertaining to control groups. The fourth section discusses more complex designs that contain two or more independent variables, which are called factorial designs. Fifth, we examine a central issue of between-groups design—randomization and participant assignment. The strength of the between-groups design is based on group equivalence before the experimental manipulation, which underscores the importance of participant assignment. As a result of our discussion of participant assignment and especially group equivalence, in the last section we discuss related issues of matching and dependent samples designs.

HISTORICAL OVERVIEW AND PERSPECTIVE

The origins of the group-comparison approach have been related to the discovery and measurement of individual differences and to the development of inferential statistics (Barlow & Hersen, 1984). Adolphe Quetelet, a Belgian astronomer, initially discovered in the nineteenth century that human traits (for example, chest expansion of Scottish soldiers) followed a normal distribution (Gleitman, 1986). Rather than interpreting his findings as indicating that some traits are normally distributed in nature, Quetelet inferred that nature was actually striving to create the "average" person, the ideal. But nature obviously failed, which resulted in errors, or variances, in traits that grouped around the mean in orderly ways. Quetelet found that the traits of the "average" person could be estimated by applying statistical techniques to the errors or differences from the mean. The study of individual differences mushroomed in the early to mid-1900s, notably through the work of psychologists such as Galton, Pearson, Binet, and Cattell.

As traits were being identified and measured, the next logical step was to compare one group of people to another. Various descriptive statistics facilitated such comparisons, although Fisher's work on inferential statistics in the 1930s was one of the most influential statistical advances. Fisher's work not only provided statistical techniques, but also made an important contribution in the realm of making inferences from samples and generalizing the results. As an agronomist, Fisher was interested in generalizing the results obtained from a particular plot of land to many plots of land. Thus, Fisher developed statistical techniques that made it possible to estimate the relevance of data from one small group, or plot, with certain characteristics to the universe having these characteristics. Such developments in sampling theory (that is, making inferences from a sample to a larger population) greatly facilitated the group-comparisons approach within basic psychological research.

By the 1950s, the *zeitgeist* in psychological research was group comparison and statistical estimation (Hersen & Barlow, 1976). Consequently, the between-groups design was also used in counseling during the 1950s and 1960s. For example, between-groups designs were used to examine differences in adjustment changes between students receiving counseling versus a control group (Williams, 1962), as well as in the effects of time limits (limited or unlimited) on adjustment changes (Shlien, Mosak, & Dreikurs, 1962). The group-comparison approach has been and remains extremely popular in counseling and clinical psychology due in part to the advent of managed health care and the continued need to provide empirical support for treatments. Thus, many of the recent clinical trials conducted to identify empirically validated treatments use between-groups designs. For excellent critiques of the research on empirically validated treatments, see Levant, 2004; Norcross, 2001; and Wampold, 2001.

THREE COMMON EXPERIMENTAL BETWEEN-GROUPS DESIGNS

We now discuss the three most commonly identified experimental between-groups designs. To do so, we use the symbolic representation used by Shadish et al. (2002) to depict each of the designs. R indicates random assignment of participants to each of the groups; O indicates an "observation" or point where data are collected as a dependent variable; and X indicates the exposure of a group to an experimental variable, often a treatment intervention of some kind. The purpose of O, in essence, is to measure the effects of X. The subscripts following O and X indicate the sequence of occurrence: O_1 is the first observation, O_2 is the second, and so on.

After describing each of these three designs, we then discuss advantages and disadvantages of each, referring particularly to validity issues. It is important to note that these three designs are most easily conceptualized as using one independent variable. For example, the independent variable may represent two treatment conditions, or contain two levels—treatment and no treatment (that is, control group). After our initial discussion of the three commonly used between-groups designs, we discuss the more complex between-groups designs where two or more independent variables are utilized in what is known as factorial designs.

POSTTEST-ONLY CONTROL GROUP DESIGN   Notationally, the posttest-only control group design is conceptualized as:

$$R \; X \; O_1$$
$$R \quad O_2$$

In its most basic form, this design involves the random assignment of participants to two groups; one of the groups receives exposure to a treatment while the other group serves as a control group, and thus receives no treatment. Both groups receive a posttest, but neither group receives a pretest. The basic purpose of the design is to test the effect of X, the independent variable, on observations of the dependent variable, vis-à-vis O_1 and O_2.

Strengths   The posttest-only control group design controls for most of the threats to internal validity, and thus is a powerful experimental design. For example, history would have affected each group equally because O_1 and O_2 occurred at the same time. Likewise, maturation, instrumentation, testing effects, and regression are controlled in that they are expected to be equally manifested in both the experimental and control groups. For example, if extreme scores were used, the control group would be expected to regress as much as the experimental group.

Both selection and selection-maturation effects are controlled for in that randomization would most likely make the groups comparable on these dimensions before the study. Attrition rates can be examined to determine if differential losses may have occurred across groups, although again randomization would decrease the probability of differential attrition due to preexisting differences in participants.

In many ways the posttest-only control group design is the prototypical experimental design and most closely reflects the characteristics needed to attribute a causal relationship from the independent variable to the dependent variable (Shadish et al., 2002). The difference between O_1 and O_2 reflects the degree to which treated participants are different from untreated participants at the end of the treatment period. Of course, the observed difference needs to be statistically significant (have statistical conclusion validity) to justify a claim that the treatment indeed is effective.

In spite of the simplicity of the posttest-only design, there are some concerns regarding it. The primary concern is that because the dependent variable is examined only at the end of treatment, statements about actual change cannot be made; put another way, there is no evidence to show that the treatment group improved vis-à-vis their level of functioning prior to treatment. However, in our view the level of functioning of treated individuals (at O_1) versus their level of functioning had they not been treated (O_2) is the most important comparison, not the change from before treatment to after treatment. The logic of experimentation does not require that pretreatment levels of functioning be assessed; thus, a pretest is not used.

One of the strengths of the posttest-only control group design, therefore, is that a pretest is unnecessary. Practically speaking, sometimes the repeated testing of participants is bothersome to the participants and expensive to the researcher in terms of time and effort. Furthermore, the absence of pretests removes the need to collect both the pretest and posttest scores, and hence it may be possible to have participants respond anonymously, thereby protecting the confidentiality of responses. Another advantage of the posttest-only control group design is that it eliminates pretest sensitization (which is discussed more fully as a disadvantage to the pretest-posttest control group design).

Weaknesses   The absence of a pretest in this design can present problems, some of which cannot be known before the research is conducted. The arguments for using pretests are presented in the discussion of the pretest-posttest control group design.

Although the posttest-only control group design is generally considered an internally valid experimental design, there are issues pertaining to external validity, namely the interaction of selection and treatment (Shadish et al., 2002). From an internal validity perspective, selection of participants is not a threat because participants are randomly assigned across groups. However, from an external validity perspective, the generalizability of the results of the study to another population is unknown. For example, it is possible that a treatment (for example, a career-planning workshop) is effective but only for the particular sample (for example, returning adults who have a broader set of work experiences). It may very well be that the career-planning workshop is not at all effective for the typical 18-year-old freshman, or it may be that different samples of returning adults (for instance, from a community college versus a four-year university) might also respond very differently to the career-planning workshop. In short, the interaction between the selection of a particular sample and the treatment is an issue that must be tested empirically and considered and acknowledged by the researcher.

Another threat to external validity pertains to reactivity to the experimental situation. That is, participants may react differently, perhaps in biased or socially desirable ways, because they are in an experiment, which again threatens the generalizability of the findings. Because counseling is an applied field, we are especially concerned with external validity, and these and other threats to external validity merit serious consideration.

Finally, a practical issue pertaining to this design is that of timing. To adequately control for history effects, the investigator must conduct the experimental and control sessions simultaneously. Sometimes this requirement places excessive time and energy constraints on the experimenter. Nonetheless, history effects may not be controlled for if the experimenter conducts the two sessions, say, one month apart. The greater the time differential between group administrations, the greater the likelihood of confounding history effects.

An Example   A study aimed at understanding more about how to reduce smoking among women highlights some of the advantages of the posttest-only design. The prevalence of women who smoke has not declined as fast as it has for men, and there is an increase in the proportion of young women smokers (Tobacco Advisory Group of the Royal College of Physicians, 2000). These statistics are particularly concerning given that among the adverse health effects, women who smoke have twice as high a risk of developing cervical cancer (Szarewski & Cuzick, 1998). Hall, Weinman, and Marteau (2004) were interested in promoting women's awareness of the association between smoking and cancer; previous research found that many women do not make a connection between smoking and cervical cancer (Marteau, Rana, & Kubba, 2002). Hall et al. used a between-groups posttest-only design to compare the effectiveness of providing women with a detailed versus minimal explanation of the association between smoking and cervical cancer. Women from England, ages 20–64 years, were randomly assigned to either a minimal explanation leaflet group, a detailed explanation leaflet group, or a no leaflet (control) group. Although the results did not find differential impact across the two types of leaflets, the women who received leaflets (versus no leaflet) reported higher ratings of vulnerability to cervical cancer, had a more coherent explanation of the link between smoking and cervical cancer, and had stronger intentions to stop smoking in the next month. The authors interpreted the results as suggesting that having a coherent or meaningful explanation of the link between an increased vulnerability to a health threat and smoking is a critical component to having a strong intention to change behavior (Hall et al.).

PRETEST-POSTTEST CONTROL GROUP DESIGN   Notationally, the pretest-posttest control group design is conceptualized as:

$$R \ O_1 \ X \ O_2$$
$$R \ O_3 \quad O_4$$

This design involves the random assignment of participants to two (or more) groups, with one group receiving treatment while the other group receives no treatment and thus serves as a control group. Both groups receive a pretest and a posttest. The purpose of the design is to test the effect of the independent variable, X, which is reflected in the differences on the dependent variable, specifically between O_2 and O_4.

Strengths   This design controls for most of the threats to internal validity discussed by Shadish et al. (2002), and in that way it is similar to the posttest-only control group design. The unique strength of this design pertains to the use of the pretest, which allows the researcher to perform various analyses that may be helpful in making valid inferences about the effects of the independent variable.

One of the most important reasons for giving a pretest is that pretest scores can be used to reduce variability in the dependent variable, thereby creating a more powerful statistical test. In essence, such a strategy attempts to minimize error variance in line with the MAXMINCON principle. Much of the variance in any dependent variable is due to individual differences among the participants. Knowledge of the pretest level of functioning allows the researcher to use statistical methods, such as the analysis of covariance, to remove the variance found in the pretest from the variance in the posttests. Such procedures can reduce drastically the number of participants needed to achieve a desired level of statistical power (Porter & Raudenbush, 1987). Of course, the pretest in this case need not be the same measure as the posttest; however, it must be correlated with the posttest to allow a covariance analysis.

Another important reason to give a pretest is that it can be used to help eliminate post hoc threats to internal validity. In this regard, one strategic use of pretests is to compare participants who terminate or drop out to those participants who remain. If more participants terminate from the treatment group than from the control group, then differential attrition is a particularly troublesome threat; however, if pretest scores indicate that those participants who terminated did not differ significantly from those who remained, then concern about differential attrition is reduced.

Pretests can also be used to select or deselect participants. For example, in a study on depression, the researchers may wish to select only those participants who are in the moderately depressed range. For example, if participants report very few symptoms of depression, these participants may not exhibit any change on the dependent variable even though the treatment would have been effective with moderately or even severely depressed participants.

Pretest scores can also be used to describe the participants of a study. For example, it would be important to describe the level of anxiety of undergraduate participants in a study of test anxiety to determine whether the participants were representative of clients who were really affected by test anxiety.

Finally, the pretest-posttest scores allow the researcher to examine the individual performance of specific participants. Kazdin (2003) suggested that in this way, researchers might examine participants who benefited the most versus those who benefited the least from the treatment intervention. Identifying participants in such a fashion, combined with any relevant anecdotal information, may suggest hypotheses for future research. In short, the pretest provides additional information to researchers, and perhaps some clues for future research directions.

Two often-stated advantages of pretests are controversial. The first pertains to comparing posttest scores to pretest scores to determine the degree to which the treatment was beneficial. The problem with making inferences from pretest measures to posttest measures is that there are too many rival hypotheses to infer the degree to which treatment was effective by comparing pretest scores to posttest scores. For this reason, "gain scores" (differences from pretest to posttest) are typically not recommended for statistical analyses. Instead, it is better for researchers to restrict themselves to making inferences only about differences at the posttest, because fewer threats are involved. Parenthetically, statisticians typically recommend using the pretest as a covariate in analyzing the posttest scores (see Huck & McLean, 1975). These techniques adjust or reduce error variance across individuals.

There is a second controversial use of pretest scores. Recall that random assignment was a means of distributing individual differences randomly across the two groups to remove any systematic bias due to selection or assignment. But the groups will not be exactly the same in all aspects; random error, if you will, will often result in some differences between groups. Often there is a tendency to check whether random assignment succeeded—that is, to see whether the groups were indeed comparable. To do so, a researcher might examine as a preliminary analysis the pretest scores to ascertain whether there are significant differences between the groups *before* treatment. However appealing this process is, there are some complex issues that make these comparisons far from straightforward (Wampold & Drew, 1990).

First, how big a difference is necessary to decide whether random assignment failed? For small sample sizes, statistically significant differences between two groups' pretest scores are unlikely to be obtained, but in large samples, it is much more likely that relatively small differences between samples will be statistically significant. Second, pretest scores represent only possible differences on the particular characteristics measured; what about differences in age, gender, intelligence, education, and a host of other variables that were not examined? Third, if a very large number of factors are compared before treatment, by chance some differences will be found.

In short, it is important to note that however appealing it is to check the effectiveness of random assignment in eliminating differences between the groups before the independent variable was introduced, there are a number of complexities that make it difficult to conclude with absolute certainty that the two groups are "equal." Suffice it to say that there are some problems and controversy with this procedure.

Parenthetically, if one wants to ensure that a nuisance factor is evenly distributed across the groups, another alternative is to use a matching procedure. For instance, to equate groups based on intelligence, participants in the treatment and control groups could be matched on intelligence. This process, and its advantages and disadvantages, are discussed in the section on dependent samples designs.

Weaknesses   It is ironic that the unique strength of the pretest-posttest control group design, namely the pretest, is also the main weakness. It is often assumed that pretesting will not sensitize participants to a particular treatment. In the two-group pretest-posttest control group design, the effect of repeatedly administering a test to the treatment group (O_1 to O_2) is the same for the control group (O_3 to O_4). Therefore, the effect of repeated testing is not a threat to internal validity.

However, the pretest may have a potential sensitizing effect pertaining to external validity, and thus generalizing the results from the study to other samples. It is unclear whether any changes found at posttest might be due to the groups' being sensitized by the pretest; that is, it is unclear if the same effect of X on O_2 would be found again without the sensitizing effect of O_1. For example, a pretest questionnaire on attitudes about rape might cue participants not only to reflect on this topic, but also to process information differently in the ensuing treatment, say, an awareness-enhancing workshop about date rape. Although the treatment may or may not have an effect by itself, the interactive effects of the pretest may result in substantially greater changes at posttest. A real problem could result if practitioners implemented the workshop but without the pretest, and thus the treatment had a much weaker treatment effect than they thought they would have. When researchers use the pretest-posttest control group design, they need to be cautious in generalizing the results of the study, and they must discuss this sensitization issue explicitly.

An Example   Schechtman and Pastor (2005) used a between-groups pretest-posttest design to assess the effectiveness of two types of group treatment offered to 200 elementary school children in a center for children with learning disabilities in Israel. More specifically, the authors were interested in whether students would evidence better academic and psychosocial outcomes in either cognitive-behavioral treatment groups or humanistic therapy groups as compared to individual academic assistance alone. Their results suggested that either form of group therapy rather than individual academic assistance resulted in more academic (reading and math), psychological adjustment, and social adjustment gains. Moreover, they also found that the humanistic therapy group resulted in better outcomes than the cognitive behavioral therapy group. The gains were found on all measures pretest to posttest, and most of the differences were also found at a three-month follow-up. The authors interpreted their findings as suggesting that addressing children's general concerns and emotions in and of themselves without focusing on their academic failure may be constructive (Schechtman & Astor).

To examine other examples of the pretest-posttest control group design, see Deffenbacher, Lynch, Oetting, and Kemper (1996), who also employed this design to examine the utility of two different interventions in reducing anger in early adolescence. The results suggested that although both the cognitive-relaxation coping skills and the social skills training interventions were effective in reducing anger in adolescents, the former was more effective in reducing anxiety, depression, shyness, and school-related deviant behavior. Likewise, Schechtman, Gilat, Fos, and Flasher (1996) examined the effects of group therapy (versus a control group) with low-achieving elementary school children; the results indicated that the addition of group therapy resulted in significant gains in academic achievement, self-concept, social acceptance, and locus of control.

SOLOMON FOUR-GROUP DESIGN   When there is a desire to use a pretest but some concern exists about the effect the pretest may have on the participants (such as test-by-treatment interaction), the Solomon four-group design is appropriate. Notationally, this design is conceptualized as follows:

$$R \; O_1 \; X \; O_2$$
$$R \; O_3 \quad\; O_4$$
$$R \quad\; X \; O_5$$
$$R \quad\quad\; O_6$$

This design is a combination of the pretest-posttest control group design (first two groups in the diagram) and the posttest-only control group design (last two groups). The main purpose of this design is to examine potential effects of the pretest, which is one of the main weaknesses or unknowns of the pretest-posttest control group design.

Strengths   In terms of internal validity, this design controls for most threats to internal validity. The Solomon four-group design contains the strengths of both the pretest-posttest control group and the posttest-only control group designs. The unique strength of the Solomon four-group design is that it explicitly examines the potential sensitizing effect of the pretest as it might interact with the treatment (X). The researcher can easily test for pretest sensitization by comparing O_2 to O_5, the only difference between these observations being the pretest prior to the treatment. Thus, this design is useful if the investigator not only wants to test the effect of some treatment, X, but also wants to examine whether the pretest sensitizes participants to the treatment.

Another strength of this design is that it inherently includes a replication test of the treatment intervention. That is, if a significant treatment effect is found when comparing O_2 to O_4, this design allows the researcher to examine whether this treatment effect can be replicated when comparing O_5 versus O_6. If the researcher finds a treatment effect in both cases, the results of the study will be considerably stronger because the treatment has been found to be effective across two trials. In this way, the replication results will enhance the generalizability of the treatment, and thus the external validity of the study.

Weaknesses   The major drawback to using this design is that it costs the investigator a great deal in terms of time, energy, and resources. In essence, the Solomon four-group design contains the two previous designs (pretest-posttest control group and posttest-only control group), which means that the experimenter is almost conducting two investigations. The Solomon four-group design is especially costly if the treatment is a long and rather complex intervention. Such treatments often require considerable effort, such as training therapists (perhaps before each treatment session), preparing training materials, and obtaining financial compensation for therapists. Many times ethical considerations are involved in the intervention, particularly with regard to the control group; an example is withholding treatment from the control group during part or all of the research study. A common option is to offer treatment to control participants after the experiment is over; it is important to plan on this additional cost (that is, additional service delivery for two more groups of participants).

An Example   Our examination of the professional journals revealed that the Solomon four-group design is used infrequently in counseling research. A study by Dixon, Heppner, Petersen, and Ronning (1979) illustrates most of the major elements of the Solomon four-group design. In the mid-1970s the utility of training clients in some sort of problem-solving method was unclear, and there were many unanswered research questions. The investigators wanted to assess the effects of problem-solving training in general, but they also wanted to test the effects of pretesting. Because of the costs involved, the Solomon design was modified and participants were assigned to one of three groups: a pretest-posttest treatment group, a pretest-posttest control group, and a posttest-only control group. Treatment consisted of didactic presentations, group discussions, and directed practice in five hour-and-a-half sessions that were designed for systematic training in five stages of problem solving (problem definition, goal selection, strategy selection, strategy implementation, and evaluation). The investigators used the generation of alternatives, decision-making skill, and participants' perceptions of their problem-solving skills as dependent variables. The results indicated that training did influence the quality of responses, but it did not necessarily increase the number of alternatives. However, the researchers also found that the treatment group differed from the posttest-only control group only; it did not differ from the pretest-posttest control group. These results suggested a practice effect; simply taking the dependent measure twice resulted in the same outcome as the treatment. Subjects participating in the workshop also reported using fewer impulsive behaviors during the problem-solving process than the control participants reported.

The value of the Solomon four-group design in this particular study is rather compelling. By using two control groups, the authors were able to isolate the effects of training as well as the practice effects. Erroneous conclusions might well have been drawn if only a posttest-only control group design or a pretest-posttest control group design had been used.

USE OF CONTROL GROUPS

To this point, the designs discussed have included a control group. The purpose of this arrangement is to compare treated participants with nontreated participants. In this way, the effect of the treatment vis-à-vis no treatment can be determined. However, there are some cases where the use of control groups is not warranted. For instance, it is unethical to withhold treatment from participants who are in need of treatment and who have a condition for which a treatment is known to work. For example, it would be unethical to have a control group of suicidal clients in a study of a new crisis-intervention technique. Furthermore, the research question may not refer to the absence of a treatment. For example, a study by Malkiewich and Merluzzi (1980) examined the relative effectiveness of matching client conceptual level with treatments (desensitization and rational restructuring) differing in structure. To examine this matching question, a control group is not needed; inclusion of a control group, however, would answer the additional question of whether either of these two treatments is more effective than no treatment.

Although some research questions do not call for control groups, the logic of much research dictates the use of a control group. *Control group* refers generically to a class of groups that do not receive any of the active treatments in the study. A *no-treatment control group* does not receive treatment. It should be realized that even though this implies that the researchers do not provide any treatment, participants in such groups often seek treatment elsewhere (see, for example, Frank, 1961; Gurin, Veroff, & Feld, 1960).

Often it is practically and ethically difficult to have a group that does not receive any treatment. However, a viable control condition can be obtained by using a *waiting-list control group*. Typically, participants are randomly assigned to either the treatment condition or the waiting-list control group; at the end of the treatment phase and the posttests, the treatment is made available to the participants in the waiting-list control group. (If more than two treatments were studied, the participants might be given the choice of the available treatments, or the one that proved most effective.) In either the pretest-posttest control group design or the posttest-only control group design, the treatment given to the waiting-list participants is not part of the design but can be analyzed anyway to test the reliability of the results (Kazdin, 2003) or to rule out threats to the validity of quasi-experimental designs (Shadish et al., 2002). One disadvantage of the waiting-list control group is that long-term follow-up of the control participants is lost (because they have by then received treatment). Another disadvantage is that although ultimately the participants in the waiting-list control group receive treatment, the treatment is withheld for some time. (For more details on this topic, see Chapter 18.)

Another type of control group is the *placebo control group*. Participants in a placebo control group are led to believe that they are receiving a viable treatment, even though the services rendered them are nonspecific and supposedly ineffective. For example, in a group counseling outcome study, participants in the placebo condition may be in a discussion group with no active group counseling. The rationale for including a placebo control is that it enables the researcher to separate the specific effects of a treatment from effects due to client expectations, attention, and other nonspecific aspects. Some investigators contend that the major effects of the counseling process are due to nonspecific factors (Frank, 1961; Wampold, 2001); inclusion of a placebo control group allows determination of whether the effects of a treatment are greater than those obtained under conditions that appear to clients to be viable but do not contain the major aspects of the active treatments.

An interesting placebo is the subconscious reconditioning placebo (SRP). Participants are told that the SRP reconditions the subconscious by using subliminal messages, when actually nonsense syllables are presented. Participants believe they are receiving a viable treatment; in fact, SRP has been found to be as effective as other treatments in the areas of smoking cessation (Sipich, Russell, & Tobias, 1974), test anxiety (Russell & Lent, 1982), and speech anxiety (Lent, Russell, & Zamostny, 1981). Of course, inclusion of a no-treatment or a waiting-list control group with a placebo control group strengthens the design considerably because differences between the placebo and no-treatment control groups give an estimate of the strength of effect of nonspecific factors.

A final type of control group is the *matched control group*. Participants in a matched control group are paired in some way with participants in the treatment group. Although the primary purpose of this type of design is to reduce variance due to a matching factor (which will be discussed later in this chapter under dependent group designs), one application of this design is worth mentioning here.

Length of counseling is often a troublesome variable in outcome studies. If the length of treatment is constrained to a given length of time, the treatment may not adequately represent the real way in which the treatment is delivered, reducing the construct validity of the independent variable. However, if the treatment is allowed to vary from one client to another as determined on a case-by-case basis, the timing of the posttest for the control participants is problematic: If the treatment lasts from 7 to 20 weeks and the posttest is administered immediately following termination, when should the posttest be administered to the control participants? The matched control group design solves this problem by administering the posttest to a control participant at the same time the posttest is administered to his or her paired participant in the treatment group, thereby holding time of treatment constant over the treatment and control groups.

FACTORIAL DESIGNS

Factorial designs are used when two or more independent variables are employed simultaneously to study their independent and interactive effects on a dependent variable. It is sometimes cumbersome to relate factorial designs to the three between-groups designs previously discussed; nonetheless, factorial designs are extensions of these earlier designs, namely by the addition of independent variables. Whereas previously we used the notation of Shadish et al. (2002), with factorial designs it is more useful to visualize the design by diagramming the levels of the independent variables into cells. For example, if a study were examining three levels of an independent variable, there would be three cells, diagrammed like this:

The scores on the dependent variables are conceptualized as being placed in each of the cells. If there were 30 participants (10 participants per cell), there would be 10 scores for each dependent variable in each cell.

For example, lets say a researcher were interested in testing the effectiveness of two interventions designed to enhance cross-cultural awareness in high school students. The two interventions (X_1 and X_2) and a no-treatment control are formed. In addition, the researcher is interested in examining whether male and female students might respond differently to the interventions. The study would be considered a 2 (Gender: male and female) $\times$ 3 (X_1, X_2, and control) posttest-only design containing six cells, and could be diagrammed as follows:

Treatments

	X_1	X_2	Control
Males			
Females			

Gender { Males, Females }

Alternately, if there were two independent variables that each had three levels or conditions, this would be considered a 3×3 design and have nine cells.

Strengths   The unique strength or advantage of the factorial design is that it tests the effects of two or more independent variables, and of their interaction with each other on the dependent variable. The factorial design provides more information than the single-independent-variable designs because it simultaneously tests two or more independent variables.

In our hypothetical study, the researcher could examine whether two interventions have an effect on the dependent variables, as well as whether a participant's gender has an effect on the dependent variables. The effect of an independent variable on a dependent variable is often referred to as a main effect. Because of the efficiency of such simultaneous tests in factorial designs, it is not uncommon for researchers to test two, three, or even four independent variables in one study. Usually these added independent variables are person (personality) variables. For example, Kivlighan, Hageseth, Tipton, and McGovern (1981) examined how Holland type (Holland, 1985a, 1987) interacted with treatments that varied in terms of the amount of interpersonal involvement.

More important, factorial designs allow the investigator to examine the interaction of the independent variables. An interaction means that the effect of one of the independent variables depends on the levels of one or more other independent variables. In our hypothetical example, the investigator could examine whether the effects of gender interact with the effects of the two interventions/control. The researcher might find that one of the treatments does not have the same effect on all participants, but instead results in more favorable responses among female participants than among male participants. Thus, factorial designs not only result in more information because they examine the effects of more than one independent variable, but also result in more complex information about the combined effects of the independent variables.

Another advantage of factorial designs is that if the second independent variable added to the design is related to the dependent variable as expected, then the unexplained variance in the dependent variable is reduced. Reducing unexplained variance is again related to Kerlinger's MAXMINCON, which in essence increases the power of the statistical test for analyzing factorial design (for example, in the analysis of variance, the denominator of the F ratio is reduced).

In a way, our fictitious example indicates how the factorial design can provide important qualifications about relationships between variables. The factorial design provides some answers about the conditions under which a treatment may operate, such as the gender of participants, the type of intervention, the age of clients, or the problem-solving style of clients. Whereas the single-variable study most often investigates whether a variable (most notably some treatment) has any effect, the factorial design examines more complex questions that approximate the complexity of real life.

Weaknesses   Although at first one might think the more information, the better, it is important to realize the costs involved as more variables are added to designs. With the addition of variables, the results of the study become more complex and sometimes too complex. In a 2 × 2 design, the researcher would typically examine the main effects of two levels of variable A, the main effects of two levels of variable B, and the interaction of A with B. In a 2 (A) × 2 (B) × 2 (C) design, the investigator would typically examine the main effects of variables for two levels of A, B, and C; the two-way interactions of A with B and B with C; and the three-way interaction among A, B, and C. Complex interactions between three, four, or more independent variables typically are difficult to interpret, and the results of the study may be unclear. Researchers should not add independent variables just to have more than one independent variable; instead, independent variables need to be carefully selected on theoretical and empirical grounds after thought is given to the research questions of interest.

Another disadvantage of the factorial design is the flip side of an advantage: If additional independent variables are added to the design and these variables turn out to be unrelated to the dependent variable, then the power of some statistical test may be reduced. There are also complications regarding the conclusions that can be drawn when the independent variable is a status variable (for example, counselor gender) and is not manipulated. (For more details, see the discussion in Chapter 14.)

An Example   Colorectal cancer is the second leading cause of cancer death in the United States. An estimated 57,100 people in the United States died from colorectal cancer in 2003 (American Cancer Society, 2003). Moreover, African Americans experience higher morbidity and mortality rates from colorectal cancer than do other racial/ethnic groups in the United States. Campbell et al. (2004) conducted a 2 × 2 factorial design to evaluate the effects of two preventive intervention strategies aimed at improving multiple health behaviors among 587 rural African Americans through data collection in 12 North Carolina churches. More specifically, the authors compared a 2 (a tailored print and video group versus a control group) and a 2 (a lay health advisor versus a control) to test the effects of each intervention alone, in combination with each other, and a no-treatment control group. The results revealed that the print and video intervention significantly improved fruit and vegetable consumption, as well as recreational activity, but the lay advisor alone did not result in these significant changes, and the control group did not see significant changes either. Moreover, combining the two interventions did not result in a more effective intervention than the print/video intervention alone. The authors were encouraged by the utility of the professionally developed materials delivered to each person, as opposed to a more diffuse intervention delivered by a nonprofessional.

Participant Assignment

Because the basic purpose of the between-groups design is to make comparisons between participants from different groups, it is critical that the people in the groups do not differ in important ways before the experiment or measurement begins. Participant assignment is also predicated on participant selection, which pertains to external validity. That is, a researcher might satisfactorily assign undergraduate students to one of four group conditions (participant assignment), but the results might not be generalizable to counseling center clients (a participant selection issue).

The intended outcome of assigning people to groups is to eliminate systematic differences across groups before the experiment, so that if any changes are detected in one or more of the groups after the experiment, the change can be attributed to the independent variable. Participants therefore need to be assigned to groups in an unbiased fashion and free from extraneous variables.

The most effective way of ensuring comparable groups is to assign participants to groups randomly, or in such a way that each participant has the same probability of being assigned to each group. Such assignment tends to equalize both known and unknown sources of participant variation across groups, so that extraneous variables will not bias the study.

A number of procedures exist for randomly assigning participants to groups. The most common method is to use a table of random numbers, or a computer program that generates random numbers to determine the order of assigning participants to groups. For example, if a researcher had four groups, participants could be randomly assigned by the order that the numbers 1, 2, 3, and 4 appear consecutively in the random list of numbers (for example, 4, 1, 4, 2, 2, 3, 1, and so on). Numbers other than 1 through 4 would be ignored. In this instance, the first participant would be assigned to group 4, the next to group 1, the third to group 4, and so on. Such a procedure reduces the probability of systematic biases or variations in participants between groups.

Note that random assignment would most likely result in unequal numbers of participants in each of the four groups. For statistical purposes it is better to have equal numbers across groups. To deal with this issue, Kazdin (2003) suggested assigning participants in blocks, or as in the preceding example, in blocks of four participants. Within each block of four participants, the experimenter would simply randomly assign one participant to each of the four groups. This procedure is particularly useful when participants begin the experiment periodically, or at different times.

In counseling research, a researcher will often have a sample identified and available at the beginning of an investigation. For example, a researcher might have 20 people who are available and have expressed an interest in some kind of treatment group, such as assertiveness training or group therapy. In this situation, the investigator knows the total number of participants, their names, and their general characteristics such as age and sex. Underwood (1966) has labeled this type of participant pool as captive. In this situation, random assignment is easily accomplished at one time via a random table, or even by drawing names from a hat. Quite often in counseling research, however, we do not have the entire sample at the outset, but rather must engage in sequential assignment (Underwood). For example, imagine that a researcher is investigating the effect of two types of precounseling information on client expectations of therapy. Most counseling centers have only a few clients beginning therapy each day, which would necessitate randomly assigning clients to the two types of precounseling information each day. In this case, clients can be assigned to either treatment as they enter counseling via some sort of randomization process.

Does randomization *always* result in equivalent groups? Simply put, no. Random assignment refers to a method of assigning participants in a bias-free manner; the method should be considered distinctly different from the outcome or results. Randomization distributes participants along with their similar or unique characteristics, which can be considered extraneous variables, by chance across the researcher's groups. Because randomization distributes by chance, it is possible that by chance some extraneous variable (e.g., sex) will not be distributed equally across groups.

Consider a study conducted on ways to enhance the problem-solving effectiveness of college students (Heppner, Baumgardner, Larson, & Petty, 1988). Participants were randomly assigned to two groups, a treatment group and a delayed-treatment group. Four instruments were used as pretest-posttest measures: the Problem Solving Inventory (PSI; Heppner & Petersen, 1982), the Level of Problem Solving Skills Estimate Form (LPSSEF; Heppner, 1979), the Ways of Coping Scale (WCS; Folkman & Lazarus, 1980), and the Mooney Problem Checklist (MPC; Mooney & Gordon, 1950). Statistical analyses of the pretest measures revealed no significant differences on the PSI, LPSSEF, and WCS; however, the delayed treatment group had significantly lower scores on the MPC. Thus, sampling error can exist even when one uses randomization. Randomization simply ensures that differences in groups are due to sampling error, not to systematic error.

DEPENDENT SAMPLES DESIGNS

Dependent samples designs are a type of between-groups design that are intended to address issues related to some of the problems mentioned previously related to random assignment of participants. Dependent samples designs are based on the assumption that a particular extraneous variable, let's say intelligence or level of psychological functioning, is important to the outcome of the study. Importance in this context can be defined in two ways.

Pairs of Participants	Treatment		Control
1	S_{11}	is matched with	S_{12}
2	S_{21}	is matched with	S_{22}
3	S_{31}	is matched with	S_{32}
—	—		—
—	—		—
—	—		—
N	S_{n1}	is matched with	S_{n2}

TABLE 7.1
ASSIGNMENT
OF PARTICIPANTS
TO TREATMENT
AND CONTROL
GROUPS IN A
DEPENDENT
SAMPLES DESIGN

Note: Paired participants have comparable scores on pretest.

First, the variable may be theoretically important to understanding the phenomenon under investigation. In this case, the variable definitely should be examined fosr its own sake. For example, if intelligence is thought to be an important variable theoretically, then it should be included as an independent variable in a factorial design. In this way the effects of intelligence, as well as the effects of the interaction of intelligence with the treatments (or with other independent variables), can be determined.

Second, if the variable is not interesting for its own sake, it might best be labeled a nuisance variable. Although a nuisance factor is not examined explicitly (that is, by inclusion as an independent variable in a factorial design), it remains an important consideration in the design of an experiment because it could affect the results in unknown ways. For example, pretest level of functioning may not be interesting to the researcher in the sense that the effectiveness of treatment for clients at different levels of psychological functioning is not a burning research question. Nevertheless, it is desirable to have the treatment and control groups comparable on psychological functioning so that psychological functioning does not confound the results. Sometimes a useful way to reduce the effects of a confounding variable is to match participants on the basis of the potentially confounding variable pretest scores and then randomly assign one of the matched participants to the treatment group and the remaining participant to the control group, as illustrated in Table 7.1. As a result, the two samples are dependent. In this way, the researcher can be relatively certain that levels of psychological functioning are comparable across the two groups. More important, if the nuisance factor is related to the dependent variable as expected, then the variance in the nuisance variable can be removed from the variance in the outcome variable, resulting in a more powerful statistical test (Wampold & Drew, 1990). The typical statistical test for this type of design is the dependent samples *t* test (sometimes called the paired *t* test or correlated *t* test).

Essentially, the dependent samples *t* test accomplishes the same purpose as the analysis of covariance—it reduces unexplained variance and yields a more powerful test. The analysis of covariance does not require that participants be matched, and the reduction in unexplained variance is accomplished statistically, by the design of the experiment. The dependent samples design reduces uncertainty by matching comparable participants. Two participants who have high pretest scores are also likely to have high posttest scores; differences in posttest scores for these two matched participants are due presumably to the treatment (and other uncontrolled factors).

Dependent samples can be accomplished in other ways as well. Often natural pairs, such as monozygotic twins, are used. Because monozygotic twins have identical genetic material, using such pairs holds all hereditary factors constant. Other natural pairs include litter mates (not often applicable to counseling researchers), marital partners, siblings, and so forth.

Another means of creating dependent samples is to measure the participant in more than one condition, even though this is difficult to accomplish in the treatment and control conditions. Consider two treatments—say, treatments for increasing the degree to which participants use a computerized career exploration program. Each participant would be exposed to one of the treatments (for example, token reinforcement for use of the system), and then use of the system would be assessed; then the participant would receive the other treatment (for example, social reinforcement for use of the system), and use of the system is again assessed. Of course, the order of the treatments would need to be randomized. In this way, all nuisance factors are controlled because each participant serves as his or her own control. Such a design, called a repeated measures design, contains many of the aspects of the within-subjects design discussed in the next section.

The idea of two dependent samples can be expanded to include more than two groups (for example, two treatment groups and a control group). Typically, the dependency is created by matching or by repeated measures (it is a bit difficult to find enough monozygotic triplets for such a study!). For example, Haupt (1990) was interested in counseling students on religious issues; he had reason to believe that the type of counselor responses to a client's religious statements would affect how the client perceived the counselor's expertness, attractiveness, and trustworthiness. Haupt believed that participants' beliefs about Christianity would most likely affect how participants would react to the counselor responses. In considering assigning participants to one of three group conditions, Haupt decided to ensure group equivalency on this attitudinal variable. Consequently, as he assigned participants to one of the three groups, he first identified three participants who had identical scores on a scale measuring beliefs about Christianity, and then randomly assigned each of these participants to a different group. As a result, participants had identical scores on their beliefs about Christianity across each of the three groups. When more than two participants are matched and assigned to conditions, the design is called a randomized block design. Each group of matched participants is called a block, and the participants within blocks are randomly assigned to conditions. The randomized block design is typically analyzed with a mixed model analysis of variance (see Wampold & Drew, 1990).

In sum, matching is a way to control for a nuisance factor that is believed or known to have an effect on the dependent variable. Dependent sample designs are powerful tools for increasing the power of statistical tests. Properly used, these designs can enable the researcher to accomplish the same purpose with far fewer participants.

One final note: Many times in counseling research, randomly assigning participants to groups is not possible. For example, ethical problems would arise if a researcher tried to randomly assign clients to therapists with different levels of counseling experience, such as beginning practicum, advanced practicum, doctoral-level interns, and senior staff psychologists. If clients were assigned randomly to counselors it is quite likely that a client with complex psychological problems would be assigned to an inexperienced therapist who is ill-equipped to work therapeutically with such a client. In such applied situations, randomization may well introduce more practical problems than it solves experimentally. Sometimes researchers will attempt to show that clients are equivalent (matched) on several dimensions such as age, gender, presenting problem, and personality variables. Matching in such a post hoc fashion can rule out some dimensions in comparing clients, but it is important to realize that many variables, known or unknown, are simply left uncontrolled. Thus, a weakness of such field designs is that unknown variables may confound the relationships among the variables being investigated.

WITHIN-SUBJECTS DESIGNS

The remainder of this chapter examines within-subjects designs. Remember that the hallmark of the within-subjects design is that it attempts to minimize error variance due to individual variation by having each participant serve as his or her own control. Similar to the between-groups design, participants are randomly assigned to groups or treatments, and independent variables are manipulated. The unique feature of the within-subjects design is that all participants are exposed to all of the treatment conditions; random assignment involves assigning people to different sequences of treatment.

In this section we first provide an overview of two types of within-subjects designs: crossovers and Latin Square designs. We then discuss the strengths and limitations of the traditional within-subjects design.

CROSSOVER DESIGNS

Suppose a researcher wanted to compare the effects of two treatments (independent variables)—test interpretation of the Strong Interest Inventory (SII) and work genograms—on a dependent variable, vocational clients' career maturity. The researcher could use the following within-participants design:

$$O_1 \; X_1 \; O_2 \; X_2 \; O_3$$

O_1, O_2, and O_3 represent different observations—in this case, administration of a career maturity inventory (say, the Career Maturity Inventory; Crites, 1978). X_1 represents the test interpretation treatment, and X_2 represents the genogram treatment.

This is called a crossover design; all participants are switched (that is, crossed over) to another experimental condition, usually halfway through the study. Suppose the researcher conducted this study with 20 vocationally un-decided adults as diagrammed. Suppose the researcher found a significantly greater change in career maturity between O_2 and O_3 than between O_1 and O_2 ($p < .01$); could he or she conclude that genograms are better at promot-ing career maturity than test interpretation? This conclusion would be quite tenuous because of the threats to internal validity embedded in this design, such as history (events may have happened to the participants between the administrations), maturation (normal development may have occurred), order effects (that is, perhaps genogram treatments are more effective if they are presented as a second treatment), or sequence effects (that is, perhaps the genogram treatment is effective only if it follows and perhaps adds to an SII test interpretation). In point of fact, a major difficulty in the within-subjects design is the possibility of confounding order or sequence effects. Order ef-fects refers to the possibility that the order (that is, the ordinal position, such as first or third) in which treatments were delivered, rather than the treatment per se, might account for any changes in the development variable. Sequence effects refer to the interaction of the treatments (or experimental conditions) due to their sequential order; that is, treatment X_1 may have a different effect when it follows treatment X_2 than when it precedes treatment X_2.

How might the researcher control these threats to internal validity? One of the primary mechanisms used to control such threats is counterbalancing, which involves "balancing" the order of the conditions. The following is a diagram of a counterbalanced crossover design:

$$R \; O_1 \; X_1 \; O_2 \; X_2 \; O_3$$
$$R \; O_4 \; X_2 \; O_5 \; X_1 \; O_6$$

The R's in the design indicate that participants are randomly assigned to two groups. Again, X_1 and X_2 in the diagram represent the two treatments, and the O's represent the different observation periods. O_1 and O_4 designate a pretesting assessment; O_2 and O_5 represent an assessment at the crossover point, and O_3 and O_6 indicate testing at the end of the experiment. Thus, the groups differ only in the order in which they receive the treatments. In this case, counterbalancing also controls for sequence effects: X_1 precedes X_2 once, and X_2 precedes X_1 once.

It is important to be aware of two issues with regard to counterbalancing. First, the researcher can now use some simple statistical procedures to deter-mine whether the order of the treatment conditions made any difference vis-à-vis the dependent variables. For example, a simple t test can be conducted on O_2 versus O_6 to determine whether treatment X_1 resulted in differential effects depending on whether the treatment was administered first or second. A similar t test can be conducted on O_3 versus O_5 for treatment X_2. These analyses are important not only for the present research, but also so that future researchers can know about order or sequence effects. A second issue is that even if there is an order effect, it can be argued that these effects are "balanced" or equal for both treatments (given the preceding example), and that order effects are therefore controlled.

Stiles, Shapiro, and Firth-Cozens (1988) used a counterbalanced crossover design to examine differences in session evaluation and client postsession mood for an interpersonal-psychodynamic treatment and a cognitive-behavioral treatment. Of the 40 clients studied, 19 were randomly assigned to receive eight sessions of interpersonal-psychodynamic treatment followed by eight sessions of cognitive-behavioral treatment. The remaining 21 clients first received eight sessions of cognitive-behavioral treatment followed by eight sessions of interpersonal-psychodynamic treatment. Session evaluation and postsession mood (both client and counselor ratings) were assessed by having the client, counselor, and external raters fill out a Session Evaluation Questionnaire (Stiles, 1980) for each session. Results revealed that counselors and external raters perceived interpersonal-psychodynamic sessions as significantly more powerful (that is, deep) and more uncomfortable (that is, rough) than cognitive-behavioral sessions. Likewise, clients rated the interpersonal-psychodynamic sessions as significantly more uncomfortable, and their postsession mood was significantly more positive following cognitive-behavioral sessions. Finally, external raters saw counselors' moods as more positive following cognitive-behavioral sessions. It is also important to note that Stiles and colleagues found no evidence for carryover effects (that is, for one treatment affecting the rating of another treatment).

LATIN SQUARE DESIGNS

A second type of within-subjects design is the Latin Square design. As the number of treatments being compared increases, the counterbalancing of treatment order and sequence becomes increasingly complex. The critical issue is ensuring that all treatments are "balanced" or presented in the same ordinal position (that is, first, second, or third) with the same frequency (for example, three times). How should the researcher decide on the order of treatments? Suppose a researcher wanted to compare three treatments (X_1, X_2, and X_3) using a within-subjects design. He or she could randomly assign the order of treatments for each participant. The problem with random assignment is that with a large number of participants, the treatment order normally balances out—that is, an equal number of participants receive the X_1 treatment first, second, and third (likewise for X_2 and X_3). But with a small number of participants, there can be large discrepancies in the distribution of treatments. For example, with 12 participants, suppose that 8 of these participants are randomly assigned to receive treatment X_1 at the first point in the sequence and 4 receive X_2 first, but no one receives X_3 first. Thus, X_2 and X_3 would not be presented first with the same frequency as X_1. This is critical because a number of studies have shown that treatments given first are often more effective (Morrison & Shapiro, 1987).

The researcher can guard against such an imbalance by predetermining a set sequence of treatments that is balanced for order and then randomly assigning clients to a particular order of treatments. A Latin Square is a way of predetermining the order of treatments. The major characteristic of a Latin Square is that each treatment appears in each ordinal position. The following is an example of a Latin Square design for three treatments, X_1, X_2, and X_3.

Group	Order of Treatment		
	1st	2nd	3rd
1	X_1	X_2	X_3
2	X_3	X_1	X_2
3	X_2	X_3	X_1

The one problem with the Latin Square design is that the particular sequence of treatments cannot be controlled (or assessed statistically). In the preceding design, for instance, treatment X_1 never directly follows treatment X_2. Because all possible sequences are not represented in the Latin Square, it is not possible to entirely rule out this type of sequence effect as a rival hypothesis. This problem is usually considered minor, however, compared to order effects.

Hermansson, Webster, and McFarland (1988) used a Latin Square design to examine the effects of deliberate counselor postural lean on levels of communicated empathy, respect, and intensity. They manipulated three levels of the independent variable, postural lean (forward, backward, and counselor's choice). Each counselor conducted three consecutive sessions with a different client. For the first 9 minutes of an 18-minute session, the counselor was seated upright, then for the next 9 minutes each counselor leaned forward, backward, or counselor's choice. The particular order of forward, backward, or choice was determined by the Latin Square. Each counselor was randomly assigned to a particular sequence.

The results of this study suggested a compensatory process between deliberate counselor lean and verbal communication. Specifically, a required forward lean was associated with decreased levels of intensity and empathy, whereas a required backward lean showed a significant increase in the levels of intensity and empathy. There were no significant effects for the choice condition.

STRENGTHS AND LIMITATIONS

We will discuss six issues to depict the strengths and weaknesses of within-subjects design that can affect the appropriateness of a within-subjects design for a particular research question. These six issues are (1) experimental control, (2) statistical power, (3) time, (4) order and sequence effects, (5) measurement considerations, and (6) restriction of certain independent variables.

EXPERIMENTAL CONTROL   The traditional within-subjects design is potentially a powerful design because of its reliance on random assignment of treatments and manipulation of independent variables. The experimenter can often obtain a great deal of experimental control with this design, and the threats to internal validity tend to be low with a counterbalance crossover design. Moreover, the within-subjects design tends to minimize error variance due to normal individual variability by using each participant as his or her own control. The reduction of individual error variance is a noteworthy advantage of the within-subjects design, which merits consideration when the researcher is especially concerned about such error.

STATISTICAL POWER   Because each participant receives all levels of the independent variable, there are typically some advantages from a statistical perspective. In general, a researcher can use half the number of participants in a counterbalanced crossover design and still retain the same statistical power as in the between-subjects design (see Kerlinger, 1986, for a more complete statistical discussion of this matter).

TIME   Although a within-subjects design can use fewer participants to obtain a level of statistical power similar to a between-groups design, the trade-off is that the within-subjects design takes longer to conduct. Consider a research team who want to compare interpersonal and cognitive-behavioral approaches to the treatment of depression. Suppose they recruit 24 depressed clients. If the team chooses to use a between-groups design, they can randomly assign 12 participants to 12 sessions of interpersonal treatment, and the remaining participants to 12 sessions of cognitive-behavioral treatment. In this design, at the end of 12 weeks the research team has implemented the interventions and has collected the data. If the research team instead uses a within-subjects design with only 12 clients—randomly assigning 6 clients to receive 12 sessions of interpersonal therapy followed by 12 sessions of cognitive therapy, and assigning the remaining 6 participants to receive treatment in the reverse order—the team would need 12 more weeks than for the between-groups design to implement the interventions and collect the data. Thus, sometimes an important consideration is the trade-off between the number of participants and the time required. We would encourage researchers, however, not to be too quick to overlook within-subjects designs only because of the time factor.

ORDER AND SEQUENCE EFFECTS   As we indicated earlier, a special problem of the within-subjects design is the effects of order and sequence. Order effects are threats to internal validity. Even when order effects are controlled, as in the counterbalance crossover and Latin Square designs, it is still important to check whether the order of the treatments affected the dependent variable. Sometimes it is assumed that because counterbalancing equalizes any effects due to order, the researcher can ignore such order effects. This strategy, however, does not provide any information about the basic question: Were there any order effects in a particular study? Such information can be useful to future researchers as they design their investigations on a similar topic. Likewise, practitioners may be interested in knowing if the order of treatments makes any difference as they plan to maximize their interventions.

Sequence effects can also create threats to internal validity. In a counterbalanced crossover design, this sequence, or carryover effect, can be statistically examined because all possible sequences are represented in the study. Recall that Stiles and colleagues (1988) examined for and found no sequence effects. However, in the Latin Square design all possible sequences are not represented. Thus, the Latin Square design typically has more threats to internal validity because sequence effects are more difficult to eliminate.

MEASUREMENT CONSIDERATIONS   There are two measurement issues that merit attention when one is considering a within-subjects design: (1) ceiling and floor effects, and (2) equivalency of scale points. *Ceiling and floor effects* refers to problems associated with the upper or lower limits of dependent measures. In essence, the upper or lower limit of a dependent variable may limit the amount of change that can be demonstrated on that variable. Although this can be a problem for any research design, it can be a particular problem for within-subjects designs because they rely on multiple testing, which examines continued increases or decreases in the dependent variable.

Consider Stiles et al. (1988) again, the design of which is diagrammed as follows:

$$R\ O_1\ X_1\ O_2\ X_2\ O_3$$
$$R\ O_4\ X_2\ O_5\ X_1\ O_6$$

Suppose tshat in that study the effect of the two treatments (interpersonal psychodynamic treatment and cognitive-behavioral treatment) on client depression was also assessed. Further suppose that at pretest (O_1 and O_4) all clients had a pretest score of 21 on the Beck Depression Inventory (BDI), and that after the first treatment for both groups of participants, the crossover O_2 and O_5 revealed that all clients had a BDI mean score of 2. Because the BDI score cannot be lower than 0, there is little or no room for the second treatment to show improvement.

There is a related measurement problem in within-subjects designs that involves the equivalency of scale points. For example, is a change in the mean BDI score from 15 to 10 equivalent to a change from 10 to 5? Again, this problem is not atypical of between-groups designs, but these problems are exacerbated by the within-subjects designs. For example, variables involving instructions or participant expectancies may be difficult to reverse at the crossover point.

RESTRICTION OF VARIABLES   A final consideration in the use of within-subjects designs involves the restriction of certain independent variables. It may not be possible to use certain independent variables in a within-subjects design. It is impossible, for example, to induce both the expectation that a given treatment will be effective and then the subsequent expectation that it will not be effective. Or two treatments may be too incompatible with each other. Kazdin (2003) offered as an example the conflicting approaches of systematic desensitization and flooding. It is important for the researcher considering a within-subjects design to closely examine the effects that multiple treatments may have on one another. Given that each participant receives all treatments, the experimenter must assess whether the combination of multiple treatments can be administered realistically and fairly. Finally, variables that involve some personality, demographic, and physical characteristics may not vary within the same participant in a given experiment (Kazdin, 1980). For example, a participant cannot be both a male and female participant, or be a participant from both a rural and an urban community.

It is also important not to dismiss the utility of within-subjects designs if the limitations of these designs initially seem restrictive for a particular study. For example, based on the inherent differences within behavioral and psychodynamic therapy, it could easily be concluded that these two therapy orientations could not be compared within a particular set of participants. However, Stiles and co-workers (1988) did use, quite successfully, a within-subjects design comparing eight sessions each of exploratory (interpersonal-psychodynamic) and prescriptive (cognitive-behavior) therapy. Although worries about treatment contamination may be present or even pervasive among counseling researchers, this study challenges us to fairly evaluate the crossover effect and to be creative in our thinking about within-subjects designs.

SUMMARY AND CONCLUSIONS

There are two types of true experiments: between-groups and within-subjects designs. These are true experiments because in both cases there is random assignment of treatments and manipulation of an independent variable. In between-groups designs, the random assignment allocates participants to treatment conditions to create experimental and control groups. In contrast, in within-subjects designs, all participants are exposed to all treatment conditions. Thus, the overall goal of the within-subjects design is to compare the effects of different treatments on each participant. Both designs lend themselves to Kerlinger's MAXMINCON principle.

In terms of between-groups designs, we discussed the posttest-only control group design, the pretest-posttest control group design, and the Solomon four-group design. These experimental designs are clearly powerful designs, because they can rule out many rival hypotheses. Each design controls for all the common threats to internal validity. A key feature of these designs is the random assignment of participants; randomly assigning participants to groups is a major source of control with regard to internal validity. Kerlinger (1986) concluded that between-groups designs "are the best all-around designs, perhaps the first to be considered when planning the design of a research study" (p. 327). Because control groups are commonly used in these designs, we discussed issues pertaining to different types of control groups, such as no-treatment groups, waiting-list control groups, placebo groups, and matched control groups. Because randomization of participants is a defining characteristic of between-groups design, we also discussed participant assignment, group equivalence, and dependent samples designs.

We also described two traditional within-subjects designs, the crossover and Latin Square designs. Both of these designs make comparisons between two or more groups of participants, but in a different way from the between-groups design. In the crossover design, all participants are switched to another experimental condition, usually halfway through the study. Counterbalancing was introduced within this design as a way of reducing bias due to order effects. The Latin Square design was introduced as a design suitable for research questions that examine more than two levels of the independent variable. We suggested that at least six issues specific to the traditional within-subjects design can affect its utility for examining a particular research question, namely (1) experimental control (particularly with regard to individual participant variation), (2) statistical power, (3) time, (4) order and sequence effects, (5) measurement considerations, and (6) restriction of certain independent variables. In particular, we encouraged researchers to be creative in the application

of traditional within-subjects designs. In short, within-subjects designs offer a powerful means of identifying causal relationships. The advantage of these designs is their ability to reduce both error variance (by using each participant as his or her own control) and the number of participants needed in a particular study. The within-subjects design has a number of strengths, most notably the reduction of participant variability, that ideally suit it for research in counseling. Nonetheless, even a perusal of journals reveals that within-subjects designs have been underused in counseling research. The strengths of the within-subjects designs merit more consideration in our research.

Clearly, the between-groups and within-subjects designs are useful designs for examining research questions of interest to those in the counseling profession. These designs are flexible and can be made applicable to a wide variety of research problems; in fact, the factorial design is widely used in counseling research. However, it is important for the researcher in counseling to evaluate the strengths and limitations of these designs relative to the type of research question being asked and type of participants needed. Given the applied nature of many of our research questions in counseling, the researcher needs to consider carefully a broad range of issues pertaining to external validity to evaluate the utility of the true experimental designs in providing the most-needed information. In addition, many times the random assignment of participants to groups cannot be done because of ethical constraints, such as in a study of the effects of different levels of sexual harassment. We think it is erroneous for students to be taught that the between-groups design is simply "the best"; instead, students should be encouraged to consider the strengths and weaknesses of various designs in relation to different research questions. In other words, the utility of the design needs to be evaluated in the context of the research question, the existing knowledge bases, and internal and external validity issues.

STIMULUS QUESTIONS

BETWEEN-GROUPS AND WITHIN-SUBJECTS DESIGNS

This exercise is designed to promote reflection on between-groups and within-subjects experimental designs. After reading this chapter, write your responses to the following questions. Then discuss your responses with a peer in your class.

1. Talk to faculty and peers about their perceptions of the usefulness of the between-groups and within-subjects design. What advantages and disadvantages first come to mind for them? Is there a pattern in the responses that is reflected when others speak of the disadvantages of between-groups and within-subjects designs?

2. Compare the primary strengths and weaknesses of between-groups and within-subjects designs. Could you argue that one of these designs is better than the other?

3. Identify two topics you could examine with both a between-groups and a within-subjects design. Write four research questions, one between-groups question and one within-subjects question for each topic. After you have written all four research questions, compare and contrast the research questions. What similarities and differences do you see?

4. Make a list of the pros and cons of using a control group. Of all the issues you list, can you pick only one that you believe is the most important methodological issue?

5. In the early days of counseling, more between-groups and within-subjects designs were used. Now it is difficult to find good examples of them in our major journals. Why do you think this trend exists, and what do you think it means for the field of counseling?

QUASI-EXPERIMENTAL AND TIME-SERIES DESIGNS

As discussed in Chapter 7, true experimental designs are very useful in terms of controlling and eliminating many threats to internal validity. One of the hallmarks of a true experimental design is random assignment of subjects to treatments. Random assignment allows the researcher to control many of the threats to internal validity. A true experimental design always includes random assignment of subjects to conditions, manipulation of the independent variable(s), and comparisons between or among groups. For a number of reasons, however, the researcher may not always be able to use a true experimental design. As you were reading Chapter 7, you may have started thinking about your own research areas and perhaps how difficult it might be to achieve this level of experimental control, including randomly assigning participants to groups. Unlike research in the basic sciences, which can be conducted in controlled laboratory settings, much of counseling research happens in natural field settings.

For example, much sexual violence occurs at the high school level, and yet very few prevention interventions have been reported in this setting. Hillenbrand-Gunn, Heppner, Mauch, and Park (2004) were interested in assessing the impact of a sexual assault prevention intervention in a high school setting. But it is difficult to randomly assign students from different classes into treatment and control groups due to the constraints of the schools, which are often present in field research of this nature. Subsequently, they chose a quasi-experimental design to conduct a three-session intervention with intact high school classes that served as the experimental and control conditions. Briefly, the theoretical framework for the study was social norms theory (Berkowitz, 2003), which maintains that the social influence of one's peers is based more on what one thinks his or her peers do and believe (i.e., perceived norms) than on actual behaviors and real beliefs (i.e., actual norms).

The experimental group participated in a three-session intervention on acquaintance rape that incorporated local social norms. The control group attended their classes as usual. As hypothesized, the participants' ratings of their peers were significantly different (worse) from the peers' ratings of themselves at pretest regarding attitudes toward sexual violence. Furthermore, the experimental group participants' ratings of their peers were significantly more accurate following the intervention, indicating they viewed their peers as less supportive of sexual assault. At posttest, the experimental group demonstrated a significant decrease in rape-supportive attitudes, as compared to the control group, and this decrease was maintained at follow-up 4 weeks later. Although additional research is needed, this quasi-experimental study was able to provide very useful information about sexual assault prevention in the high schools, and the generalizability of the findings to other Midwestern urban high school students would be considered high.

In short, it is often difficult to achieve the conditions of the true experimental design in field settings, especially the requirement of random assignment into groups. Because of this difficulty in much applied research, the quasi-experimental design offers more flexibility. Quasi-experimental designs, like true experimental designs, involve the manipulation of one or more in-dependent variables, but not the random assignment of participants to con-ditions. With this flexibility, however, quasi-experimental designs also bring some limitations. For example, Kazdin (2003) noted that some researchers refer to these designs as "queasy-experimental designs" (p. 169) due to their lack of randomization. Nonetheless, with creativity in the use of the designs and appropriate use of controls and statistical procedures, quasi-experimental designs can be very useful for applied researchers.

In this chapter we will first illustrate an early quasi-experimental design that will provide a historical context for this type of design. Then we will discuss some considerations for determining when quasi-experimental designs might be appropriate. We will then focus on the two major classes of quasi-experimental designs, the nonequivalent groups designs and the time-series designs. In nonequivalent groups designs, comparisons are made between participants in nonrandomly formed groups. Specifically, we will discuss three types of uninterruptible designs, four types of interpretable nonequivalent groups designs, and cohort designs, which are a special case within the broad category of nonequivalent groups designs. Then we discuss the time-series designs, which have as their defining feature multiple observations over time.

HISTORICAL PERSPECTIVE AND OVERVIEW

Quasi-experimental designs were used extensively in the 1950s and 1960s to answer one of the most important and confusing questions that psychotherapy and counseling researchers have grappled with: Does counseling work? To answer this question we need to compare clients who have received counseling to clients who have not. The most rigorous (in terms of internal validity) test of the effects of counseling would involve the random assignment of clients to treatment (receiving counseling) and no-treatment control conditions. The random assignment of clients to a no-treatment condition would in effect constitute the withholding of service, which can, of course, raise ethical considerations for the researcher. To avoid this type of ethical dilemma, early counseling researchers attempted to find other groups of participants with whom to compare the effects of counseling.

Many of the early outcome studies in counseling used quasi-experimental designs. For example, Klingelhofer (1954) was interested in examining the effects of academic advisement on the scholastic performance (grade point average) of students placed on academic probation. He compared three groups of students in this study, all of whom were on academic probation. One group received four one-hour counseling sessions, a second group received one one-hour counseling session, and the third group received no counseling interviews. The students who received one or four hours of counseling were randomly assigned to groups. The students in the control group were drawn from students who had been on academic probation during the preceding year. In essence, Klingelhofer's study had elements of both experimental and quasi-experimental designs. The comparison between the students receiving one or four hours of counseling was a true experiment because there was random assignment of participants to treatments, manipulation of the treatment variable, and a between-groups comparison. The comparison between the students who did and did not receive counseling was a quasi-experimental design because the students were not randomly assigned to conditions. This particular type of quasi-experimental design is called a cohort design. The students who had been on probation the year before the study formed one cohort and the students on probation during the experimental year formed a second cohort. Klingelhofer assumed that the students in the two cohorts were similar because the same rules were used to place students on academic probation both years.

The results of this study did not reveal any differences in subsequent grade point average for students counseled for either one or four sessions. There was, however, a significant difference in grade point average between students who had and had not received counseling. Nonetheless, this result must be interpreted with some caution because pretreatment differences between the students in the two cohorts may have existed due either to some unknown selection factor or to different historical events during their year on probation. Despite these possible limitations, Klingelhofer's study of the effectiveness of one widely used counseling intervention represents a typical quasi-experimental study of counseling in the 1950s and 1960s. The designs are still used today, in part because of the restrictions inherent with randomization.

CONSIDERATIONS FOR SELECTING QUASI-EXPERIMENTAL DESIGNS

Under what circumstances would a quasi-experimental as opposed to a true experimental design be appropriate? We will maintain throughout this chapter that selection is a key variable in examining the adequacy and usefulness of a quasi-experimental design. We will discuss four reasons that might lead a researcher to choose a quasi-experimental design: (1) cost, (2) selection issues, (3) ethical considerations, and (4) unavailability of appropriate control groups.

COST

One of the most functional reasons for not conducting a true experimental design is often that of cost. Conducting a true experiment can be quite expensive in terms of time and resources. In true experimental designs, researchers often must pay participants to be part of often two or three treatment groups, along with a control group. Conversely, it is a lot less expensive to evaluate naturally occurring differences in treatment settings, classrooms, or other places where people naturally come together. For example, even in the study of sexual assault prevention provided earlier, if the researchers would have decided to utilize a true experimental design, they would have likely had to obtain a group of 30–40 participants who, after random assignment, would have been willing on their own time to attend a pretest, three intervention sessions, a posttest, and a follow-up one month later. This is a substantial time commitment, and most likely the participants would need to be compensated for their time and involvement. In short, although an experimental design provides a more rigorous design, sometimes the cost is prohibitive. In essence, the researchers may be willing to compromise experimental control in order to conduct the study in the field.

SELECTION OF PARTICIPANTS

The hallmark of experimental designs is randomly assigning participants to various treatment conditions. Ideally, the investigator recruits a pool of participants, and randomly assigns them into the treatment and control groups, which meet at prearranged times. However, a number of issues that arise in field research can make the selection of participants a difficult and complex process. For example, some of the participants might be available to come to a treatment group in the early afternoon, but not in the evening. Such issues of time availability are an important logistical concern in applied research, and often make it more feasible to conduct quasi-experimental investigations within existing group settings such as high school classes, as in the previous example.

In some field settings it would be difficult or even inappropriate to randomly assign participants to an experimental or a control group. For example, an investigator may want to examine the effect of a group session summary (a therapist's written summary of a group session that is mailed to each group member prior to the next session) on session quality and group-member involvement (Yalom, 2005). Group leaders may not agree to randomly assigning clients to groups, because many leaders believe that selecting members to form a compatible mixture is one of the most important decisions a leader makes in order to create an optimal treatment environment in the therapy group. In fact, randomly assigning members may not be what group leaders would consider an effective treatment procedure. The investigator may consequently be restricted to preformed groups. In this case, he or she could use summaries in two preformed groups and not use summaries in two other preformed groups. The researcher could then compare ratings of session quality and member involvement in the groups that did and did not receive the summaries. This design would be a quasi-experimental design because there is manipulation of an independent variable (summary versus no summary) and a between-conditions comparison, but no random assignment of participants to conditions.

However, this example also illustrates some of the drawbacks of quasi-experimental designs. In this case, the members were selected and the groups composed for a reason (perceived compatibility). If the investigator indeed finds a difference between the groups, one possible explanation is the effect of the independent variable (group summaries), but another equally plausible explanation is selection issues pertaining to the group members. Perhaps the group leaders who led the groups that received the summaries were more effective at composing counseling groups. In that case, the differences between the two conditions may reflect differences in clients, not in the experimental manipulation. In short, sometimes it is actually more appropriate to use existing groups because this enhances the generalizability of the results; conversely, whenever an investigator uses previously established groups (classes in schools, wards in a hospital, or therapy groups), he or she must always be aware that these groups were probably established for some reason, and that differences found between them may have more to do with the selection process than with the experimental manipulation.

Selection may also have a more indirect effect by interacting with other variables (Kazdin, 2003). A selection-by-threat interaction effect occurs when the threats to internal validity operate differently across the treatment conditions. For example, in our group summary example, the group leaders may have used very different selection criteria in establishing their groups. The group leaders in the treatment (receiving summaries) condition may have selected only passive-dependent clients for the group (believing that these clients get the most from a group treatment), whereas the leaders in the control condition may have selected clients with various interpersonal styles (believing that a heterogeneous group leads to a better outcome). If passive-dependent clients mature at a faster rate than do clients with other interpersonal styles, then a selection-maturation interaction might account for any observed differences across conditions. Likewise, history, testing, regression, mortality, or other factors may interact with selection to produce differences across conditions (see Chapter 5). In essence, the investigator must often balance the necessity and feasibility of using existing groups in contrast to the inherent biases built into those pre-existing groups.

ETHICAL CONSIDERATIONS

Some studies focus on participants who are in need of immediate services (like counseling or medical assistance). For example, a researcher might be studying a phenomenon that happens infrequently, such as breast cancer. It may take some time to identify a sufficient number of patients that seek help from a particular agency and to randomly assign them to a group. Consequently, it may raise ethical issues to withhold treatment while waiting for more patients to be randomly assigned into groups. The quasi-experimental designs allow for the use of intact groups who may have already come together in a particular setting. Although randomization may not then be possible, other controls can be designed into the study using the methods we will describe in this chapter.

UNAVAILABILITY OF APPROPRIATE CONTROL GROUPS

In other circumstances, a researcher may want to investigate the effects of an intervention or treatment when no appropriate control or comparison group is available. In this situation, the researcher can infer whether the intervention or treatment had an effect by comparing observations made before and after the onset of the intervention, typically in a field setting. Such a design, referred to as a time-series design, requires multiple observations over time and the introduction of a treatment at a specified point in time. In other words, in a time-series design the researcher can and does manipulate one or more independent variables, but there is no random assignment to groups or between-group comparisons.

In short, a number of conditions may suggest that a quasi-experimental design may be the most appropriate design. It should be kept in mind, however, that because the researcher has less control in a quasi-experimental design than in an experimental design, the interpretation of the results of these studies has less certainty. In terms of the MAXMINCON principle, researchers using a quasi-experimental design can both maximize differences in the independent variable(s) and minimize error variance due to measurement issues, just as with true experimental designs. However, because there is no random assignment of participants to treatments, they cannot control all of the various threats to internal validity. We suggest throughout this chapter that the usefulness of quasi-experimental designs for advancing knowledge is directly related to how thoroughly the investigator examines and controls for the selection criteria used in forming the initial groupings.

NONEQUIVALENT GROUPS DESIGNS

In this section we examine a major class of quasi-experimental designs: nonequivalent groups designs. In nonequivalent groups designs, comparisons are made between or among participants in nonrandomly formed groups. These groups are referred to as nonequivalent because participants have generally been assigned to a group prior to the research being conducted. Because of this prior group formation, they may differ on several characteristics before the intervention (Kazdin, 2003). For example, a researcher may want to examine the effects of a videotape that provides precounseling information on subsequent counseling dropout rates. He or she may be able to find a counseling agency that uses such a tape and compare the agency's dropout rate with the dropout rate for an agency that does not use this type of tape. Obviously because the clients at the two agencies may be different on a number of variables that may relate to dropout rate (for example, ethnicity or social class status), the clients in the two agencies represent nonequivalent groups. The usefulness of a nonequivalent groups design is related in part to how much the researcher knows about possible pretreatment differences among participants in the nonequivalent groups.

These types of quasi-experimental designs have also proved beneficial in studying the impact of various training models on counselors in training. For example, in a recent study Crews and her colleagues (2005) used a nonrandom, pretest-posttest design to study the role of counselor personality traits on counseling performance. Counselors in training were given pretesting to determine their level of self-monitoring (on the Skilled Counseling Scale; SCS) and then self-selected into one of two training conditions, an Interpersonal Process Recall (IPR) condition and a Skilled Counseling Training Model (SCTM) condition. The purpose of the study was to determine the impact of two different kinds of training on counselors with differing levels of self-monitoring. The results revealed that there were no statistically significant differences in pretest or posttest scores on the SCS. In addition, both the IPR and SCTM groups improved their scores on the SCS; however, the SCTM group improved significantly more than those counselors in the IPR group.

To examine this design further, we will diagram the nonequivalent groups quasi-experimental designs. The symbol Non R represents the nonrandom assignment of participants to groups. As in the previous chapters, X indicates the independent variable or treatment, and O indicates observations of the dependent variable.

UNINTERPRETABLE NONEQUIVALENT GROUPS DESIGNS

We begin our discussion of nonequivalent groups designs with three designs that are virtually uninterpretable because of multiple threats to internal validity. We describe these designs so that the reader can be aware of their shortcomings and have a basis for their comparison with the more-interpretable nonequivalent groups designs. These three uninterpretable designs are (1) the one-group posttest-only design, (2) the posttest-only nonequivalent design comparing three active treatments, and (3) the one-group pretest-posttest design.

The one-group posttest-only design can be diagrammed as follows:

$$X_1 \; O_1$$

In this design, observations are made of the dependent variable only after participants have undergone some type of treatment. This design is impossible to interpret because there is no way to infer that any type of change has taken place. In addition, the lack of a control group makes it impossible to investigate the presence of maturational or historical processes.

A posttest-only nonequivalent design can be diagrammed as follows:

$$\text{Non R X O}_1$$
$$\text{Non R} \quad \text{O}_2$$

In this design, the two groups are formed in a nonrandom manner. The participants in the first group receive the experimental treatment (X) while the participants in the second group do not receive any treatment. Change is measured by comparing the posttests (O_1 and O_2).

It is important to note that the posttest-only nonequivalent design need not compare a treatment with a control group. Two or more active treatments can be compared using this type of design. The following is a diagram of a posttest-only nonequivalent design comparing three active treatments:

$$\text{Non R X}_1 \text{ O}_1$$
$$\text{Non R X}_2 \text{ O}_2$$
$$\text{Non R X}_3 \text{ O}_3$$

Once again, the groups are formed on a nonrandom basis. Treatments (X_1, X_2, and X_3) are administered to the participants in the three groups, and then posttests (O_1, O_2, and O_3) are used to assess changes.

In essence, the posttest-only nonequivalent designs are especially weak because of the difficulty in attributing results to the intervention. The lack of random assignment of participants to groups allows the possibility that the groups may have differed along any of a number of important dimensions prior to treatment. Typically, students are assigned to classes, patients to wards, clients to groups, and residents to living groups based on some rationale, which suggests that the natural groupings we encounter will differ prior to treatment on a few, or in some cases many, dimensions. Thus, one of the problems with the posttest-only nonequivalent designs is the lack of information about any of the possible differences in the groups that exist before treatment.

Consider the following example. Suppose an investigator wanted to examine the usefulness of an in-class program in alleviating depression in children. He or she might select two classes of sixth graders in a school and then provide one class with the intervention. After one month he or she assesses the students' level of depression. Suppose further that after treatment, the students who received the intervention show less depression. This result may indicate an effect of the treatment, or it may reflect differences between the two classes in their levels of depression before the intervention. Perhaps the principal decided to assign students to classes on the basis of their social skills levels.

Research has documented the relationship between social skills and depression (see, for example, Lewinsohn, Mischel, Chapel, & Barton, 1980). Because there was no pretest, the possible differences in the initial levels of depression were unknown. It is quite possible that the control group actually consisted of students with lower levels of social skills, and subsequently a significantly higher level of depression in the beginning could not be assessed.

The third type of uninterpretable design that we will consider is the one-group pretest-posttest design. This design is diagrammed as follows:

$$O_1 \; X \; O_2$$

In this design, pretest observations (O_1) are recorded, a treatment is administered, and posttest observations are made. This design is better than the one-group posttest-only design because by comparing pretest-posttest observations, we can determine if a change occurred. However, the possible cause of this change is still quite ambiguous. For example, the treatment might be responsible for any observed change, but history (the occurrence of other events between pretest and posttest) might also account for the change. Alternatively, if the intervention or treatment was initiated because of a particular problem (for example, academic probation, as in the Klingelhofer study), then the posttest scores might improve because of statistical regression toward the mean. Another possible explanation for changes in the posttest score is maturation, in which case the change may have nothing to do with the treatment and instead reflects simple growth and development. Without a comparison group, it is impossible to rule out these and other threats to internal validity.

INTERPRETABLE NONEQUIVALENT GROUPS DESIGNS

We will now discuss the interpretable equivalent designs, which include: (1) the pretest-posttest design, (2) the nonequivalent groups design with a proxy pretest measure, (3) the pretest-posttest nonequivalent groups design with additional pretest, and (4) the reversed-treatment pretest-posttest nonequivalent groups design.

A design that is more useful than the four nonequivalent-groups designs above is the interpretable pretest-posttest nonequivalent groups design, which is diagrammed as:

$$\text{Non R } O_1 \; X \; O_2$$
$$\text{Non R } O_3 \quad O_4$$

In this design, participants are nonrandomly assigned to groups and then pretested on the dependent variable. One group then receives the experimental treatment while the other group serves as the comparison (control) group. It is important to note that this design need not involve a treatment–control group comparison; it may involve the comparison of two or more active treatments.

The pretest-posttest nonequivalent groups design is a stronger and more interpretable design than the posttest-only nonequivalent groups design because it allows for an examination of some of the inevitable pretreatment differences. For example, the investigator using such a design can assess the similarity of the participants on the dependent variable(s) of interest, and on other variables that may be related to the dependent variable. It is important for the researcher to remember, however, that pretest equivalence on the dependent variable(s) (and on other assessed variables) does not mean equivalence on all dimensions that might be important to the intended change on the dependent variable. A demonstration of pretest equivalence, however, does increase one's confidence in attributing any observed posttest differences between groups to the experimental manipulation rather than to some selection difference. It is also important to note that usually O_1 and O_3 are not exactly equal. In such instances when $O_1 \neq O_3$, the researcher must decide what is "close enough." One way to decide whether the two groups were equivalent at pretesting is to decide beforehand on a difference that is "too large," such as when $O_1 - O_3$ exceeds one standard deviation of O in a normative population. The researcher can then use a statistical test to see whether $O_1 - O_3$ is greater than this number. If it is not, then the researcher can conclude that the two groups were equivalent (but just on this one particular measure) at pretesting.

In the pretest-posttest nonequivalent groups design, it is unlikely that observed differences between groups can be attributed to factors such as history, maturation, or testing. However, there can be a selection-by-threat interaction that can pose a threat to internal validity. In other words, an event might affect participants in only one group, or it might affect them differently from participants in the other group(s). For example, because of some selection bias, the participants in one group may mature faster or be more likely to encounter some historical event than those in the other group. Like its experimental equivalent, the pretest-posttest nonequivalent groups design may have problems with external validity because participants in the different groups might react to the intervention(s) based on a sensitizing effect of the pretest. Also, participants in one group may react differently to the pretest than participants in the other group(s). However, the possible bias of pretest sensitization is minor compared to the problem of interpreting the results when there has not been a check on pretreatment equivalence.

Sometimes researchers may not want or be able to pretest the participants in the groups in a nonequivalent groups design. This may happen when they are worried about the possible effects of pretest sensitization, or when they are working with archival data and it is no longer possible to administer a pretest. In this case, the researcher may choose to use a nonequivalent groups design with a proxy pretest measure (a proxy pretest that involves administering a similar but nonidentical dependent variable but that will not sensitize the participants to the treatment intervention). This design is diagrammed as follows:

$$\text{Non R } O_{A1} \text{ X } O_{B2}$$
$$\text{Non R } O_{A1} \quad O_{B2}$$

The A and B in this design represent two forms of a test or tests designed to measure similar constructs. In this design, groups are formed nonrandomly and a proxy pretest (O_{A1}) is administered to both groups. Later, one group gets the experimental treatment (X), and then both groups are retested with a different posttest (O_{B2}). The viability of this design depends on the ability of the researcher to find a pretest measure (O_{A1}) that relates conceptually and empirically to the posttest (O_{B2}).

For example, researchers may want to examine a new method of counselor training. They find two training programs willing to participate and institute the new method in one program. At the end of the first year, the researcher administers a paper-and-pencil counseling skills test to all students in the two programs and finds that the students in the treatment program scored higher on this test. However, the researcher is worried about possible pretreatment differences in counseling skill level. Suppose the researcher finds that Graduate Record Exam (GRE) scores (which conveniently all students took before starting graduate school) are correlated ($r = 0.80$) with scores on the paper-and-pencil counseling skills test. (In actuality, the GRE does not predict counseling skills, but suppose it to be the case for this illustration.) In this case, the researcher can use the pretreatment GRE score (O_{A1}) to examine possible pretreatment differences between students in the two programs.

The pretest-posttest nonequivalent groups design can be strengthened by the use of an additional pretest. This design is diagrammed as follows:

$$\text{Non R } O_1 \; O_2 \; X \; O_3$$
$$\text{Non R } O_1 \; O_2 \quad O_3$$

This design is similar to the pretest-posttest nonequivalent groups design except for the addition of a second pretesting to enhance the interpretability of the design. A major threat to the internal validity of a pretest-posttest nonequivalent groups design involves a selection-by-maturation interaction. In other words, the participants in the two groups may be maturing at different rates because of some selection characteristic. The addition of a second pretest allows the researcher to examine this possibility; the difference between O_1 and O_2 for the treatment and control groups can be examined to see if the groups are maturing at different rates and enhances the interpretability of a nonequivalent groups design. A review of the counseling literature, however, suggests that two pretests are rarely, if ever, used. We strongly recommend that researchers contemplating the use of a nonequivalent groups design consider the addition of a second pretest.

We will next discuss the reversed-treatment pretest-posttest nonequivalent groups design, which is also rarely used in counseling research. We include a discussion of this design here because it is one of the stronger nonequivalent groups designs. We hope that an understanding of the strengths of this design will encourage its use in counseling research. The design is diagrammed as follows:

$$\text{Non R } O_1 \; X^+ \; O_2$$
$$\text{Non R } O_1 \; X^- \; O_2$$

In this design, X^+ represents a treatment that is expected to influence the posttest (O_2) in one direction, and X^- represents a treatment that is expected to influence the posttest in the opposite direction.

For example, a researcher may want to test the hypothesis that structure is related to productive group development. Certain schools of therapy contend that ambiguity enhances therapy because lack of structure increases anxiety, and anxiety is necessary for productive work to occur. Other schools contend that anxiety interferes with group work and that structure should be used to lessen the amount of anxiety that group members experience. To test this hypothesis, the researcher could obtain pretest and later posttest measures of the quality of group interactions from two groups of clients. One group of clients could be given explicit information about group procedures; it might be hypothesized that this group would experience less anxiety, and thus manifest lower levels of quality interactions. The other group could be given more ambiguous information; it might be hypothesized that this group would experience more anxiety, and this would manifest in higher levels of quality interactions. Posttest scores could be examined to see if the levels of quality of group interactions moved in the predicted directions. It is hard to imagine that two groups of participants would spontaneously mature in different directions. Thus, this design with such hypotheses would greatly reduce a selection × maturation threat to internal validity.

The main problem with a reversed-treatment design is an ethical one. For example, it is usually unethical to administer a treatment that would cause participants to become more depressed. Thus, this reversal design may not be appropriate for a number of dependent variables. The researcher wanting to use the reversed treatment design must, therefore, display a good deal of thought and creativity.

Shadish et al. (2002) discuss several other nonequivalent groups designs (for example, repeated treatments). Because these designs are so rarely used in counseling research, we believe that a discussion of them is not warranted here. The interested reader is referred to Shadish et al. (2002) for a discussion of the less common designs, as well as an excellent summary of the statistical analysis of nonequivalent groups designs.

AN EXAMPLE OF A NONEQUIVALENT GROUPS DESIGN   Taussig (1987) used a nonequivalent groups design with a proxy pretest to examine the effects of two independent variables, client–counselor ethnicity matching and the time of goal setting (14, 21, 28 days and not at all) on the number of kept, canceled, and broken appointments (the dependent variables). Clients were not randomly assigned to counselors, and the time of goal setting was not randomly specified. In addition, she analyzed possible interactions between these independent variables and client ethnic status and gender. In this study, client–counselor ethnicity match and the time of goal setting were used to form nonequivalent groups. In other words, Taussig hypothesized that client–counselor pairs mismatched on ethnic status would share fewer cultural expectations about counseling and thus would have fewer kept and more canceled and broken appointments than client–counselor pairs matched on ethnic status. She also hypothesized that early goal setting with Mexican-American clients would lead to fewer kept and more canceled and broken appointments than early goal setting with white clients. Taussig reasoned that relationship building would take longer with Mexican-American clients and predicted that early goal setting would disrupt this relationship-building process.

The data for this study were obtained from the archival client records of 70 Mexican-American and 72 white clients seen at a community mental health center. Four pretest proxy variables were used in the design: annual income of the client, client age, client employment status, and goal resetting (number of times goals were set for the client). Each of the proxy variables was related to one or more of the dependent variables: kept, canceled, and broken appointments. Specifically, the proxy pretest variables were used as covariates in an analysis of covariance design. In this manner the author hoped to control several pretreatment differences that could have affected the analysis of counselor–client match and/or time of goal setting. The results of the analysis of covariance showed that none of the dependent variables were related to time of goal setting. However, in terms of the counselor–client ethnicity match, when Mexican-American clients were matched with Spanish-speaking counselors, more kept appointments resulted. Counselor–client ethnicity match, however, was not related to appointments kept for the whites.

The Taussig study is a good example of the use of a nonequivalent groups design. It was certainly less expensive (in time and money) for Taussig to access client records than to go into an agency, randomly assign clients to counselors, and randomly determine duration of goal setting within a particular client–counselor dyad. Her finding that ethnic matching was related to kept appointments but probably not to the timing of goal-setting provided preliminary information for future research. Another strength of the study was the use of proxy pretest variables to look for possible selection differences. The major weakness of the Taussig study involves the possibility of selection effects. We do not know, for instance, why clients were assigned to particular therapists, or why goals were set with some clients within 14 days and never set with other clients. In other words, the conditions examined in the study (client–counselor ethnicity match and timing of goal setting) were formed on some unknown basis that could have affected the results of the study.

COHORT DESIGNS

Cohort designs are a special case of nonequivalent groups designs that utilize adjacent cohort groups that share similar environments. For example, the sixth grade class at a particular school one year is likely to be similar to the sixth grade class the following year. In essence, cohort designs allow researchers to make causal inferences because comparability can often be assumed between adjacent cohorts that do or do not receive a treatment (Shadish et al., 2002). However, the compatibility in a cohort design will never be as high as in an experiment with random assignment. Nonetheless, cohort designs have a relative advantage over other types of nonequivalent groups designs because cohorts are more likely to be similar to each other than in typical nonequivalent groups designs.

It is important for the researcher to have as much knowledge as possible about conditions that could affect the cohorts. Cohort designs are strengthened when the researcher can argue conceptually and empirically that the two cohorts did in fact share similar environments, except of course for the treatment. For example, two successive sixth grade classes at a particular school will likely be similar across two years. However, this would not be the case if, for example, school district lines were redrawn between the two years, or if a new private school opened in the community and attracted many of the wealthier children away from the public school.

Three types of cohort designs have been used in counseling research. The first design, a posttest-only cohort design, is diagrammed as follows:

$$O_1$$
$$-----$$
$$X \; O_2$$

In this design, the broken line indicates that the two groups are successive cohorts and not nonequivalent groups. The O_1 represents a posttest administered to one cohort, whereas the O_2 represents the same posttest administered to the second cohort. It is important to note that the testing occurs at different times because the cohorts follow each other through the system; however, the posttesting occurs at a similar point in each cohort's progression through the institution.

Slate and Jones (1989) used a posttest-only cohort design to test the effect of a new training method for teaching students to score the Wechsler Intelligence Scale for Children-Revised (WISC-R). One cohort of students took the intelligence testing course during the fall semester, the other cohort during the spring semester. The fall cohort received a standard scoring training procedure, whereas the spring cohort received the new training method. The results indicated that students in the spring as opposed to the fall made fewer scoring errors on the WISC-R. Slate and Jones concluded that the new training method was effective. These authors assumed that the students in the fall and spring cohorts were similar prior to training, and buttressed this assumption by examining several possible sources of pretreatment differences. For example, they found that the gender composition was similar across the two cohorts and that the students in the two cohorts had similar GRE scores and grade point averages.

A second type of cohort design, a posttest-only cohort design with partitioned treatments, is diagrammed as follows:

$$O_1$$
$$-----$$
$$X_1 \; O_{2a}$$
$$X_2 \; O_{2b}$$

O_1 is the posttest given to the first cohort, X_1 represents the first level of treatment, X_2 represents the second level of treatment, and O_{2b} is a posttest measure given to all members of the second cohort regardless of level of treatment administered. In essence, the posttest-only cohort designs are strengthened by partitioning the treatment, which involves giving different amounts of the treatment to different groups of participants within a cohort.

In the Slate and Jones (1989) study, suppose that some of the students in the second cohort practiced the new scoring procedure for two hours and that the other students in the cohort practiced it for four hours. Slate and Jones could have analyzed the results separately for these two groups of students. If the students who had practiced for four hours (O_3) committed significantly fewer scoring errors than the students who practiced for two hours (O_2), and if the treatment cohort committed fewer errors than the no-treatment cohort, then the assertion of treatment efficacy would be strengthened. Moreover, the results would provide additional information about the amount of training needed. In short, the posttest-only cohort designs can be useful, particularly relative to the posttest-only nonequivalent groups design. Because clients experience various aspects of counseling treatments in different amounts, we urge researchers to use partitioning as a way of strengthening the internal validity of the posttest-only cohort design in counseling research.

The third cohort design that we will discuss is the pretreatment-posttreatment cohort design, diagrammed as follows:

$$O_1\ O_2$$
$$\text{---------}$$
$$O_3\ X\ O_4$$

The first cohort is pretested (O_1) and posttested (O_2), and then the second cohort is pretested (O_3), treated (X), and posttested (O_4). The main advantage of the pretest-posttest cohort design over the posttest-only cohort design is the increased assurance the pretest provides for asserting that the two cohorts were similar prior to the treatment. In addition, the use of the pretest as a covariate in an analysis of covariance provides a stronger statistical test in general. The main disadvantage of this design is that the pretest can constitute a threat to external validity because of pretest sensitization; that is, taking the pretest itself in some way sensitized the participants and caused their scores at posttest to differ. In most cases the advantages of a pretest to examine pretreatment compatibility across groups outweigh the threat to construct validity.

AN EXAMPLE OF A COHORT DESIGN   Hogg and Deffenbacher (1988) used both an experimental design and a quasi-experimental cohort design in comparing cognitive and interpersonal-process group therapies for treating depression. Depressed students seeking treatment at a university counseling center were screened in an intake interview for (1) presence of nonpsychotic, unipolar depression; (2) absence of major psychopathology; and (3) absence of high suicide lethality. Additionally, prospective participants had to receive a score of 14 or greater on the Beck Depression Inventory (BDI; Beck, Rush, Shaw, & Emery, 1979). Clients meeting these criteria were randomly assigned to cognitive or interpersonal group treatments. A control cohort was formed by selecting clients who met the same screening criteria but who came to the counseling center too late in the fall semester to be assigned to any type of treatment. In essence, the authors used the Christmas break to form a cohort group, assuming that students who came to the counseling center before versus after the break were similar. The participants in the control group received no formal treatment during the break. Participants in the treatment and control groups were administered the BDI, the Minnesota Multiphasic Personality Inventory-Depression scale (MMPI-D; Hathaway & McKinley, 1942), the Automatic Thoughts Questionnaire (ATQ; Hollon & Kendall, 1980), and the Self-Esteem Inventory-Adult Form (SEI; Coopersmith, 1981).

Treatment participants were assessed at pretreatment, mid-treatment (4 weeks), posttreatment (8 weeks), and follow-up (12–14 weeks). Control participants were assessed before the semester break and 8 weeks later, which was equivalent to the pretest and posttest assessment period for the treatment group. Hogg and Deffenbacher (1988) performed initial analyses to assess equivalence across groups prior to treatment. They found no pretreatment differences across groups on the BDI, MMPI-D, ATQ, or SEI scales. A repeated measures (pretesting, posttesting) multivariate analysis of variance, or MANOVA (BDI, MMPI-D, ATQ, and SEI), was used to compare the treatment and control groups. The treatment versus control comparison was not significant. However, a significant change was found for both groups from pretest to posttest; such differences over time are sometimes referred to as time effects. In essence, the findings indicated that participants in both the treatment and control groups significantly decreased depression and distorted cognitions, and increased self-esteem. It is unclear what might have caused this time effect (for example, regression to the mean, maturation, test sensitization, etc.). Perhaps students who are depressed at the end of a semester may also differ significantly from those seeking counseling services at the beginning of a semester. Perhaps the waiting-list students felt considerable relief from depression over the holiday. In short, the potential temporal and participant-selection confounds made the validity of the apparent equivalence between the waiting-list and treatment cohorts highly questionable. For future research, the use of vacation periods as a naturalistic waiting-list condition is not recommended as a solution to the "rigorous methodology versus professional ethics" dilemma inherent in depression research (Hogg & Deffenbacher, 1988, p. 309).

In sum, the Hogg and Deffenbacher (1988) study was well conceived and executed. The authors used the semester break to form a cohort to use as a comparison in addition to the comparison of the two active treatments. They also comprehensively addressed the issue of pretreatment equivalence by comparing treatment and control groups across multiple measures. In retrospect, Hogg and Deffenbacher could have used an additional control group. For instance, they could have recruited nonclients (through a participant pool) who had

BDI scores greater than 14 and who met the criteria for nonpsychotic unipolar depression. These participants could have been tested during the same time frame as the treatment participants. This type of control could have served to test the temporal (Christmas holiday) confound in examining the results.

TIME-SERIES DESIGNS

The defining characteristic of a time-series design is multiple observations over time. These observations can involve the same participant (for instance, the client's ratings of counselor trustworthiness after each counseling session) or similar participants (for example, monthly totals of clients requesting services at a counseling center). In an interrupted time-series design, a treatment is administered at some point in the series of observations. The point at which the treatment takes place is called an interruption of the series. The logic of the interrupted time-series design involves comparing the observations before and after the treatment or interruption. If the treatment has an effect, there should be a difference in the observations before and after the interruption. Although the logic of comparing pre- and postinterruption observations for evidence of difference is simple and straightforward, the statistical analysis can be complex; see Shadish et al. (2002) for more details.

In this section we concentrate on the logical analysis of interrupted time-series designs. (Chapter 9 discusses time series as applied in single-participant designs.) In the next section we describe two time-series designs with the hope of stimulating counseling researchers to consider these designs in planning their research.

SIMPLE INTERRUPTED TIME SERIES

The most basic time-series design is the simple interrupted time series, diagrammed as follows:

$$O_1 \; O_2 \; O_3 \; O_4 \; O_5 \; O_6 \; X \; O_7 \; O_8 \; O_9 \; O_{10} \; O_{11} \; O_{12}$$

Multiple observations occur both before (O_1–O_6) and after (O_7–O_{12}) the treatment (X) is initiated. The diagram shows an equal number of observations before and after the treatment, but this is not a requirement for the design.

The interrupted time-series design has two advantages over the quasi-experimental designs previously described. First, the time-series design allows the researcher to detect maturational changes that may occur prior to treatment initiation. The researcher does this by looking for changes in the pretreatment observations. If found, these maturational changes can be controlled for in a statistical analysis, allowing a more powerful test of the effect of the treatment. The second advantage of the time-series design is that it also allows for the analysis of seasonal trends. Often, data examined by counseling researchers vary systematically over time. For example, more clients seek counseling around holiday periods. It is obviously important to account for this type of systematic variation if a researcher is interested in testing an intervention that affects clients' use of counseling services. The statistical analysis of time-series designs can also control for these types of systematic variations.

Unfortunately, the statistical analysis of interrupted time-series can be quite complicated and require considerable expertise (Crosbie, 1993). One of the main problems in analyzing time-series data is dealing with the problem of autocorrelation. Autocorrelation occurs when each score in a series of scores is more similar to the preceding score than it is to the mean score for the series. When scores are autocorrelated, error variance is deflated and a t test comparing scores from before and after the interruption is artificially inflated. Therefore, researchers have developed sophisticated statistics to deal with the problems of autocorrelation.

In one example of a simple interrupted time-series design, let's say a counseling center director is concerned about the long waiting list of clients that tends to accrue with the typical academic year. She decides to change the center's primary counseling approach to a time-limited model, and also decides to empirically assess the effects of adopting this time-limited model of counseling on the number of clients on the center's waiting list. The center could initiate the time-limited model in September of one year. She could examine the number of clients on the waiting list each month for the preceding three years and the number of clients on the waiting list during the current year. The analysis of this design would require a comparison of the number of clients on the waiting list prior and subsequent to the initiation of the time-limited model.

INTERRUPTED TIME SERIES WITH NONEQUIVALENT DEPENDENT VARIABLES

One of the main threats to the internal validity of a simple interrupted time series design is history. In other words, something other than treatment could affect the researcher's observations. One way to reduce such a threat is to add a second dependent variable. The second time-series design does just that, and is called an interrupted time-series design with nonequivalent dependent variables. This design is diagrammed as follows:

$$O_{A1} \; O_{A2} \; O_{A3} \; O_{A4} \; X \; O_{A5} \; O_{A6} \; O_{A7} \; O_{A8}$$
$$O_{B1} \; O_{B2} \; O_{B3} \; O_{B4} \; X \; O_{B5} \; O_{B6} \; O_{B7} \; O_{B8}$$

In this design, O_A represents one dependent variable and O_B represents a second. Otherwise, the design is identical to the simple interrupted time-series design. If the O_A series shows an interruption at the time of treatment and the O_B series does not, then the internal validity of the treatment effect is enhanced. In other words, it is unlikely (although possible) that history would have an effect on one conceptually related dependent variable but not the other. The important issue in using this design is to select a second dependent variable B that theoretically would be affected by the treatment.

In the simple interrupted time-series design previously described, the researcher could add a second set of observations—for example, the number of clients requesting services each month. If the number of clients on the waiting list

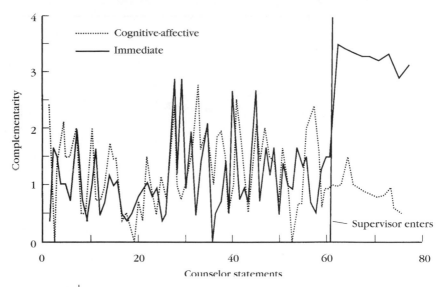

FIGURE 8.1 | COUNSELOR COMPLEMENTARITY BEFORE AND AFTER "LIVE SUPERVISIONS"

(O_A) shows an interruption at the time that the time-limited model was introduced, but the number of clients requesting services (O_B) does not show a similar interruption, then the director can conclude that the initiation of the time-limited model caused a reduction in the waiting list. It is unlikely that history could cause this effect because history would likely also affect the number of clients requesting services.

Kivlighan (1990) used the interrupted time-series analysis with nonequivalent dependent variables to study the effects of live supervision in counselor training. Beginning counselor trainees saw a recruited client for four 50-minute counseling interviews. Advanced counseling doctoral students provided live supervision for the counselor trainees. This supervision involved viewing the counseling interview from behind a one-way mirror, entering the session at some point, commenting on the counseling process, and providing direction for the counselor. The observations in this study consisted of ratings of each of the counselor statements. Trained judges rated each counselor statement on both a cognitive-affective dimension and an immediacy dimension (statements about the client–counselor relationship versus statements outside of the counseling experience). Based on the interpersonal training model used, Kivlighan predicted that after the interruption (the supervisor entering the room), the counselor's statements would be less cognitive and more immediate.

Figure 8.1 shows ratings of statements taken from one counselor–client–supervisor triad during the interview. The supervisor intervened between the 60th and 61st counselor statements. A visual inspection of these graphs suggests that the counselor's statements became more immediate and less cognitive after the

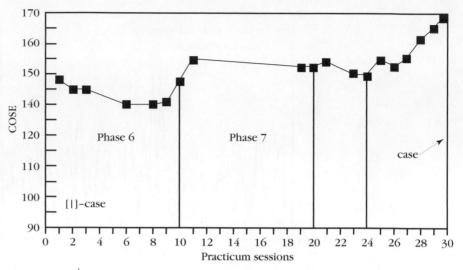

FIGURE 8.2 | GROUP SUPERVISION TIME SERIES FOR "TRAINEE 3"

supervisor's intervention. Based on a statistical analysis of this time series, Kivlighan (1990) concluded that the live supervision interventions influenced the novice counselor to use more affective and immediate statements with clients.

This study illustrates the usefulness of interrupted time-series analysis in studying counseling processes. By using two dependent variables, Kivlighan (1990) strengthened his confidence in the assertion that the observed changes were not due to a history confound. The study could have been further strengthened by replicating this analysis with other counselor–client–supervisor triads, which could enhance the generalizability of the results.

Daus (1995) also used an interrupted time-series design to examine the effects of case presentations on counselor self-efficacy. Case presentation is an integral part of most practicum training experiences, and trainees have identified it as the most meaningful practicum activity (Ravets, 1993). Despite its widespread use and perceived effectiveness, case presentations have not been shown to change either trainees' counseling skills or their perceptions of their counseling skills. To examine the effects of case presentation on counselor self-efficacy, Daus had counselor trainees, enrolled in an individual counseling practicum class, complete the Counseling Self-Estimate Inventory (COSE; Larson et al., 1992) after each class period. The COSE scores were the repeated observations in the time-series analysis. The case presentation served as the interruption in this series of observations. Because the counselor trainees had several case presentations during the semester, each series of observations had several interruptions. Daus's analysis focused on whether counselor self-efficacy changed from pre- to postinterruption (i.e., the case presentation).

The data from Trainee 3 in Figure 8.2 is illustrative of the analysis in the Daus (1995) study. As seen in this figure, COSE scores are plotted along the

y-axis and practicum sessions are plotted along the x-axis. Trainee 3 had her first case presentation during the tenth practicum session. There were six COSE observations (practicum sessions 1, 2, 3, 6, 8, and 9) before this case presentation (interruption) and seven observations (practicum sessions 10, 11, 19, 20, 21, 23, and 24) after the case presentation. The overall omnibus F test for this data was significant (F (2, 10) = 8.30, $p < .01$), indicating that there was an overall change in COSE scores from pre- to postinterruption. Other analyses indicated that the average level of counselor self-efficacy was higher after the case presentation than before it. The significant analysis indicated that the rate of change for counselor self-efficacy was different after the case presentation than before it. Specifically, before the case presentation there was a downward trend in self-efficacy scores, but after the case presentation the scores leveled off. These results suggested that, at least for this one trainee, the case presentation resulted in an overall increase in self-efficacy and also halted a pattern of declining self-efficacy. For a more extended discussion of counselor self-efficacy, see Larson (1998) and Larson and Daniels (1998).

Designs Examining Analysis of Concomitance in Time Series

At times, counseling researchers are interested not just in examining the effect of a treatment in a time series, but whether changes in one variable in the time series cause subsequent changes in another variable in the series. In essence, the researcher observes two dependent variables over time. For instance, do changes in the counselor's level of self-disclosure affect the client's level of self-disclosure? This type of analysis, referred to as an analysis of concomitance in time series, is diagrammed as follows:

$$O_{A1} \; O_{A2} \; O_{A3} \; O_{A4} \; X \; O_{A5} \; O_{A6} \; O_{A7} \; O_{A8}$$
$$O_{B1} \; O_{B2} \; O_{B3} \; O_{B4} \; X \; O_{B5} \; O_{B6} \; O_{B7} \; O_{B8}$$

In essence, the researcher observes two dependent variables over time. In this example, the researcher would check to see whether the counselor's level of self-disclosure adds predictability to the client's level of self-disclosure over and above the predictability obtained from patterns in the client's level of self-disclosure. An introduction to the statistical analysis of concomitance in time series can be found in Cook and Campbell (1979).

An Example of a Time-Series Design in Counseling Research

Kivlighan, Multon, and Patton (1996) used time-series analysis to examine the predictive validity of the Missouri Addressing Resistance Scale (MARS). Twelve adult outpatient clients who completed 20 sessions of planned short-term psychoanalytic counseling provided data for the analysis. One series of observations (series A) consisted of weekly ratings, by trained observers, of the counselor's manner of dealing with client resistances on the Exploring and

Working Through Resistance scales of the MARS. The second series of observations (series B) consisted of weekly ratings, by trained observers, of the level of client resistance using the Resistance Scale (Schuller, Crits-Christoph, & Connoly, 1991). The time-series analysis revealed that for Exploring and Working Through Resistance there was a significant reduction of resistance in later sessions. Specifically, there were significant negative relationships between the Exploring and Working Through Resistance scores and the composite level of client resistance. These results indicated that increases in the therapists' attempts to explore and work through the client's resistance in one session result in fewer manifestations of client resistance in the two subsequent sessions.

SUMMARY AND CONCLUSIONS

We believe that quasi-experimental and time-series designs have a place in contemporary counseling research. They are especially useful in examining relationships in applied settings. It is critically important that counseling psychologists and counselors conduct their research with real clients, workers, and students. Although tightly controlled true experimental designs are highly valuable at some stages of research, many of our most important research questions as applied psychologists dictate our data collection in field settings. Experimental designs are often impossible in these settings for a variety of logistical, methodological, and ethical reasons. Especially for findings from studies that do not use real clinical populations or settings, it is important to have replications in a more applied, real-life setting. Studies using quasi-experimental or time-series designs in real settings could be the final point in a series of investigations.

Because there are inherent problems with the interpretation of the results of quasi-experimental and time-series designs, however, researchers must exercise caution. We strongly recommend against the use of posttest-only nonequivalent groups designs in counseling research. As previously discussed, the absence of any way to assess pretreatment equivalence renders the results from a posttest-only nonequivalent groups design virtually uninterpretable. In addition, when using a pretest-posttest nonequivalent design, we recommend that the researcher attend carefully to how the naturally occurring groups were formed; in applied settings, there is usually some basis on which groupings are made. The more the researcher understands the basis on which the naturally occurring groupings were formed, the better he or she can examine or control for preexisting differences. This can be accomplished by using the selection variable as a covariate in the analysis.

When using the pretest-posttest nonequivalent groups or cohort designs, we recommend that researchers consider using multiple pretest measures or multiple pretesting times to examine pretreatment equivalence. Using multiple measures or measurement periods strengthens the assertion of equivalence of conditions prior to intervention. Also, when using a cohort design the researcher must be vigilant in looking for any differences (other than the experimental manipulation) in what is occurring for participants during the different time periods.

Finally, we believe that counseling researchers have underused time-series designs. These designs can be especially useful in the evaluation of new and innovative programs. Because time-series designs are often used with a single sample from a population, questions concerning their external validity exist. Therefore, researchers should consider replication when they plan their research.

Carefully designed quasi-experiments have the potential for offering critical knowledge of psychological phenomena in naturally occurring settings. Although there are threats to validity inherent in these designs, many of these threats can be controlled by design and statistical techniques.

STIMULUS QUESTIONS

QUASI-EXPERIMENTAL DESIGNS

This exercise is designed to promote reflection on quasi-experimental designs. After reading this chapter, think about your responses to the following questions:

1. Talk to faculty and peers about their perceptions of the usefulness of the quasi-experimental design. What advantages and disadvantages first come to mind for them? Is there a pattern in the type of disadvantages others speak of when they discuss quasi-experimental designs?
2. Why are some quasi-experimental designs uninterpretable? What design elements could make them interpretable?
3. One of the concerns with quasi-experimental designs pertains to using intact groups. What can be done to increase the validity of using intact groups?
4. Identify two research questions you could examine with a quasi-experimental design. What type of quasi-experimental design would you use to examine these questions? Diagram the design using the notation from the chapter.
5. What safeguards would you use to reduce threats to the internal validity of your study?
6. Early in the history of counseling, quasi-experimental designs were used frequently. Now it is more difficult to find good examples of them in the major counseling journals. What factors do you believe have brought about this change?

9 CHAPTER | SINGLE-SUBJECT DESIGNS

Studying the individual to understand more about humanity has been a major interest driving students to study counseling and psychology in general. Understanding ourselves and those close to us can be a fascinating endeavor. For example, what makes one individual experience despair while another remains resilient in similar situations? In the past, applied psychologists have sought such answers about an array of individuals by carefully examining single cases, studying a rare psychological phenomenon, or studying an intensive treatment effect with an individual client. However, methodological issues have plagued the development of a scientific analysis of individuals to the point where the study of just one person has sometimes been regarded as unscientific. Error variance, extraneous variables, and numerous sources of bias—major threats to Kerlinger's MAXMINCON principle—have beset researchers using a single subject.

Consequently, many more studies in our scientific journals rely on studying groups rather than single individuals. The field has conducted many more investigations that produce group averages or means as a way to promote understanding of individual behavior. Single-subject designs are not currently utilized extensively in counseling research. For example, a content analysis of the articles published from 1990 to 2001 in the *Journal of Counseling and Development* (Bangert & Baumberger, 2005) revealed only 1% of the articles (two studies) used a single-subject design. Yet as Kazdin (2003) maintained when making valid inferences about human behavior, "there is nothing inherent to the approach that requires groups . . . findings obtained with groups are not necessarily more generalizable than those obtained with the individual case" (p. 265). Moreover, with the increased availability of different kinds of sophisticated statistical software to analyze single-subject data (e.g., Dennin & Ellis, 2003; Levin & Wampold, 1999), there are more opportunities to examine a variety of issues within the counselor and client domains that have promise to increase understanding of topics of importance to counseling.

A broad range of scholarship has been very loosely labeled under the term single subject designs. These studies have ranged from loosely controlled anecdotal observations to highly stringent and rigorous experimental designs. Although anecdotal, observational studies can be important for heuristic purposes, at times producing useful observations for further hypothesis testing. This chapter will focus on ways to increase the scientific rigor and validity of investigations that study just one individual such that they can be of maximum benefit to the field.

The central thesis of this chapter is that intensive single-subject designs, like other experimental designs, can play an important role in the pursuit of knowledge within the counseling profession. However, important distinctions must be made concerning different types of studies that use a single subject, and concerning the varying amounts of experimental control that are used. This chapter will present a variety of approaches that can be considered single-subject designs. In all cases, single-subject research examines variables that vary within the subject over time. Therefore, single-subject designs involve a longitudinal perspective achieved by repeated observations or measurements of the variable(s). In terms of the type of observations, the data can be quantitative or qualitative. Quantitative data can be categorical, ordinal, interval, or ratio. Qualitative data, in contrast, take the form of text. A critical distinguishing feature among the designs pertains to the operation of the independent variable; it can be either manipulated or simply observed. Single-subject designs can also differ in the goal or focus of the research. The goal of the research can focus on either testing or generating hypotheses; in other words, testing a theory or discovering new information.

We will discuss three categories of single-subject designs in this chapter: (1) uncontrolled case studies, (2) intensive single-subject quantitative designs, and (3) single-subject experimental designs. Briefly, the uncontrolled case study typically does not contain systematic observations, but rather contains many uncontrolled variables. A defining feature of intensive single-subject designs are systematic, repeated, and multiple observations of a client, dyad, or group to identify and compare relationships among variables. Even though both the single-subject experimental and the single-subject intensive quantitative designs share a number of similarities and both use quantitative data, the hallmark and distinguishing feature of the single-subject experimental design is the manipulation of the independent variable. Conversely, in the intensive single-subject quantitative designs the independent variable is observed. Single-subject experimental designs have been conducted almost exclusively within the behavioral and cognitive behavioral tradition, although the theoretical orientation need not be restricted by the type of single-subject design.

The chapter is divided into four major sections. The first section provides a brief historical perspective on the use of single-subject designs within psychology, and particularly within applied psychology. By understanding the historical context, students can better appreciate how this particular design was born and how it has changed as the research methods have become more sophisticated within the field of applied psychology. Second, we differentiate the uncontrolled traditional "case study" from the intensive single-subject design. Unfortunately, there are often misconceptions about single-subject designs, in part based on uncontrolled methodologies, and we want to dispel the myth that all single-subject designs are unscientific and cannot add important information to the counseling literature. It is hoped that this discussion and illustrative examples will not only help students understand important methodological issues in studying individuals, but also promote an understanding of the value and richness of the more rigorous single-subject designs. In the third section, we will focus on single-subject experimental designs (where the independent variable is manipulated). We discuss several defining features of these time-series designs, and then describe and illustrate two different types of designs: AB time series and multiple baselines. In the final section we discuss advantages and limitations of single-subject designs.

A HISTORICAL PERSPECTIVE OF SINGLE-SUBJECT DESIGNS

The study of individual subjects not only has a long history in psychology, but also has played a prominent role in the development of the applied professions. Perhaps the most extensive chronology of the historical sequence of events affecting the development of the single-subject design is to be found in Barlow and Hersen (1984); the interested reader is directed to that source for a more detailed account.

When psychology was initially developing into a science, the first experiments were performed on individual subjects. For example, during an autopsy of a man who had been unable to speak intelligibly, Broca discovered a lesion in the third frontal convolution of the cerebral cortex. The discovery that this area was the speech center of the brain led to the systematic examination of various destroyed brain parts and their relationship to behavior (Barlow & Hersen, 1984). Likewise, Wundt made pioneering advances in perception and sensation by examining specific individuals' introspective experience of light and sound. Ebbinghaus, using a series of repeated measurements, made important advances in learning and memory by examining retention in specific individuals. Both Pavlov's and Skinner's conclusions were gleaned from experiments on single organisms, which subsequently were repeatedly replicated with other organisms. In short, important findings and advances in psychology with wide generalizability have been made from systematic observations of single individuals.

At the beginning of the twentieth century, a number of advances facilitating the examination and comparison of groups of subjects were made. The invention of descriptive and inferential statistics not only facilitated group comparisons, but also emphasized a philosophy of comparing the averages of groups rather than studying individuals. Barlow and Hersen (1984) noted that the pioneering work and philosophy of Fisher on inferential statistics was most likely influenced by the fact that Fisher was an agronomist. He was concerned with the farm plots that on average yielded better crops given certain fertilizers, growing conditions, and so forth; individual plants per se were not the focus. In short, as psychology developed in the middle of the twentieth century, the methods of inquiry were primarily influenced by statistical techniques such as the analysis of variance.

Meanwhile, in the early 1900s the primary, if not sole, methodology for investigating emotional and behavioral problems within the applied fields of psychiatry, counseling, and clinical psychology was the individual case study. Thus, cases such as Breuer's treatment of Anna O. and Freud's Frau Emmy formed the basis of "scientific" observations, which gradually grew into theories of personality and psychotherapy. These studies of therapeutically successful and unsuccessful cases were not tightly controlled investigations from a methodological standpoint. In addition, the typical practitioner was not well trained in the scientific method of critical thinking, and such practitioners extrapolated from the early case studies in fundamentally erroneous ways.

However, as the fields of counseling and clinical psychology developed in the 1940s and 1950s, more and more clinicians became aware of the inadequacies of the uncontrolled case study (Barlow & Hersen, 1984). Greater methodological sophistication led the applied psychologists to operationalize variables, to adopt the model of between-groups comparisons, and to adopt Fisher's methods of statistical analysis. Armed with these new methodological tools, researchers attempted to document the effectiveness of a wide range of therapeutic techniques, as well as the efficacy of therapy itself. These efforts were most likely fueled by the writing of Hans Eysenck, who repeatedly claimed that the profession did not have very compelling evidence for the effectiveness of therapy (Eysenck, 1952, 1961, 1965). In fact, Eysenck claimed that a client's chance of improving was about the same whether he or she entered therapy or was placed on a waiting list (Eysenck, 1952). Eysenck's charges concerning the lack of empirical support for therapy's effectiveness challenged the very existence of the therapeutic professions.

Although it has taken considerable time, researchers have begun to unravel the evidence concerning the efficacy of therapy. Paul (1967) noted that a global measurement of therapeutic effectiveness was inappropriate because of the overwhelming complexity and number of confounding variables. He suggested that investigators instead examine the question, "What treatment, by whom, is most effective for this individual with that specific problem, and under which set of circumstances?" (p. 111). Others noted that clients were erroneously conceptualized as being similar to each other (the uniformity myth; Kiesler, 1966) rather than as individuals with differences that clearly interact with counseling outcomes. Still other investigators noted that the group comparisons masked important variations across clients, specifically that some clients improved but other clients actually became worse (Truax & Carkhuff, 1967; Truax & Wargo, 1966). In short, although group comparison methods and inferential statistics substantially facilitated research on the effects of psychotherapy, researchers quickly encountered a number of confounding variables that underscored the complexity of the therapeutic experience.

In response to the confusion about and the complexity within the therapeutic process, other methodologies have been subsequently proposed and explored, such as naturalistic studies (Kiesler, 1971), process research (Hoch & Zubin, 1964), and a more intensive, experimental single-subject design (Bergin & Strupp, 1970). On the surface it might seem that the applied professions have come full circle, returning to the study of the individual. This is true only in part; there is considerably more methodological sophistication in scientifically studying an individual subject today than there was during the early part of the twentieth century.

THE UNCONTROLLED CASE STUDY VERSUS THE INTENSIVE SINGLE-SUBJECT QUANTITATIVE DESIGN

In this section, we will discuss two types of designs—what might best be described as an uncontrolled "case study" as opposed to an intensive single-subject quantitative design. To begin, we will provide some examples of studies that have been conducted in this area. By reading studies done in applied psychology that utilize both of these approaches, we hope to increase understanding of the range of methods as well as to appreciate the richness of data that can be derived from the more elaborate and intensive designs.

In the past, the prototypical design for studying an individual was the uncontrolled case study. "Case study" here refers to a study that simply consists of the following characteristics: observations of an individual client, dyad, or group made under unsystematic and uncontrolled conditions, often in retrospect. Observations may be unplanned and may consist of "recollections" or intermittent records of statements or behaviors that seem to support a particular hypothesis. The lack of experimental control means that it is difficult to exclude many rival hypotheses that might be plausible in explaining the client's behavior, and thus this type of study provides ambiguous information that is difficult to interpret clearly.

A good example of the traditional case study is provided by Daniels (1976) in his investigation of the effects of thought stopping in treating obsessional thinking. He reported that he found the sequential use of several techniques to be beneficial with clients who wished to control depressing thoughts, obsessive thinking, constant negative rumination, or acute anxiety attacks. The sequential techniques he used consisted of thought stopping (Wolpe, 1969), counting from 10 to 1 (Campbell, 1973), cue-controlled relaxation (Russell & Sipich, 1973), and a modification of covert conditioning. Training consisted of three one-hour sessions to teach the client the various techniques. Daniels reported that these procedures were successful, and that clients responded positively to a "sense of control and immediate success" (p. 131). Although this report may be a useful source of ideas for generating hypotheses for future research, the lack of experimental control makes it difficult to interpret the results unambiguously. Clients may have felt compelled in some way to report success, or perhaps the successful effects were temporary and short-lived, or maybe techniques other than thought stopping were responsible for any client changes.

More recently, investigators have used single subjects in counseling research by examining variables much more systematically, intensively, and rigorously. These studies have been designed to much more closely represent our definition of intensive single-subject quantitative design. As you read the following examples, note that they: (1) are done in a much more systematic fashion than the case study approach; (2) consist of repeated, multiple observations including multimodal assessment of cognitive, behavioral, and affective variables; (3) were conducted by observing a clearly defined variable; (4) used observations that were planned before the beginning of data collection; (5) allowed for the collection of process and outcome data; and (6) involved comparisons of some sort, which is essential for establishing scientific evidence. Later in this chapter we will discuss how these structural issues are included in different ways within AB designs and multiple baseline designs; for now just notice these structural elements as we provide some examples of applied research using an intensive single-subject approach.

Hill, Carter, and O'Farrell (1983) provide an example of an intensive single-subject quantitative design. They observed one client and one therapist over 12 sessions of insight-oriented therapy; measurements consisted of both process and outcome data obtained through subjective and objective means. More specifically, process measures were used to assess verbal behavior, anxiety, and verbal activity level (rated by judges) for both the client (college student) and counselor. In addition, both the client and counselor gave subjective impressions of session effectiveness and significant events for each session. The client and her mother, who was in close contact with the client, also made summary evaluative statements following treatment. Outcome measures, which consisted of the Hopkins Symptom Checklist, Tennessee Self-Concept Scale, Target Complaints, and satisfaction and improvement ratings, were collected immediately after the completion of counseling and at two-month and seven-month follow-ups. The first goal of the study was to describe the process and outcome of the therapeutic treatment; the second was to explore the mechanisms of change within the counseling process. With regard to the second goal, (1) comparisons were made between the best and worst sessions, (2) positive and negative events in each session for both client and counselor were analyzed, and (3) the immediate effects of counselor verbal behavior on client verbal responses were analyzed statistically through sequential analysis.

Outcome measures indicated that treatment was generally positive and resulted in improvement after the 12 sessions. Even though this improvement was maintained at the two-month follow-up, the client seemed to have relapsed at the seven-month follow-up. The process measures suggested that interpretations, direct feedback, Gestalt exercises, and examination of the therapeutic relationship (all within the context of good rapport and support) seemed to be important mechanisms of change. Wampold and Kim (1989) also conducted more sophisticated sequential analyses on the process data and found that the counselor's minimal encourager responses reinforced description responses (storytelling) by the client, and that confrontation did not lead to opening up or greater client experiencing.

The study by Hill and colleagues (1983) nicely illustrates an intensive examination of a single subject within a therapeutic context. A great deal of data were systematically collected from multiple sources (client, counselor, mother, judges) and across time. For example, over 11,000 responses were categorized in examining client and counselor response modes. In addition, the objective and subjective data collected from various perspectives allowed comparisons to be made and subsequent conclusions to be drawn based on the convergence of a wide range of information, rather than on a single data point. It is important to note that the generalizability of the conclusions obtained from this single case is unclear, and that replications are needed. Subsequent research by Hill and her colleagues has resulted in important replications as well as extensions (see Hill, Helms, Spiegel,& Tichenor, 1988; Hill, Helms, Tichenor, et al., 1988; Hill & O'Grady, 1985; O'Farrell, Hill, & Patton, 1986).

Martin, Goodyear, and Newton (1987) provide another good example of an intensive single-subject quantitative design with their study of a supervisory dyad during the course of an academic semester; their strategy merits attention. The authors employed an intensive single-subject quantitative design to compare the "best" and "worst" supervisory sessions as a means of increasing scientific knowledge about the supervisory process. Similar to Hill et al. (1983), this study used multiple measures of process and outcome variables from multiple perspectives (trainee, supervisor, judges). Specifically, information from the supervisor and trainee perspective was obtained by assessing perceptions of themselves, each other, and the supervisory process. Each person (1) evaluated the quality of each session in terms of depth, smoothness, positivity, and arousal; (2) reported expectations about supervision in terms of interpersonal attraction, interpersonal sensitivity, and task orientation; (3) identified and discussed the occurrence of critical incidents within supervision; and (4) maintained a personal log of their reactions within and to supervision on a weekly basis. Two other measures, activity level and the categorization of interactions, were used to allow inferences about the supervisory process by objective judges. All these data were examined by comparing the "best" and "worst" sessions.

Conclusions from this study were based on the convergence of data from the multiple sources and made relative to findings from previous counseling and supervision research. For example, multiple sources of data suggested that the "best" session focused around clarifying the supervisory relationship very early in the semester (second session), a finding that substantiated and extended an earlier conclusion reached by Rabinowitz, Heppner, and Roehlke (1986).

Another conclusion was that substantial differences in activity levels differentiated the "best" from the "worst" session, which is consistent with a pattern noted by Hill et al. (1983), as well as by Friedlander, Thibodeau, and Ward (1985). Methodologically, the important point here is that conclusions and hypotheses that can direct future research were obtained by examining the convergence of data from multiple sources over time from an intensive single-subject quantitative design. Webb, Campbell, Schwartz, and Sechrest (1966) called this convergence from multiple sources and multiple observations "triangulation." They maintained that multiple independent measures can provide a form of cross-validation.

The *Journal of Consulting and Clinical Psychology* devoted a special section to articles illustrating intensive single-subject quantitative research (Jones, 1993); several of the articles used the intensive single-subject quantitative design. In addition, several recent examples of highly rigorous single-subject quantitative designs have been published in leading empirical journals. For example, Honos-Webb, Stiles, and Greenberg (2003) used an intensive single-subject quantitative design to develop a marker-based method for rating assimilation in psychotherapy with a case of one woman who was being treated for depression. In another recent study that will be discussed in greater depth later in this chapter under multiple baseline designs, Dennin and Ellis (2003) tested the application of self-regulation and goal theory to self-supervision using an intensive single-subject quantitative design with process experiential psychotherapy. It is heartening to see the level of scientific rigor and control in theses studies as well as their statistical sophistication in addressing questions of variation in a single subject.

In sum, this section has provided an overview of both a traditional uncontrolled case study as well as intensive single-subject quantitative designs. We provide this contrast so that the reader can begin to understand the range of methods that are possible with investigations of a single participant. We especially want to promote the use of more elaborate and rigorous single-subject designs.

SINGLE-SUBJECT EXPERIMENTAL DESIGNS

Single case experimental designs also examine the relationship between two or more variables typically within one or a few subjects. Clearly, the largest single influence in the development of this design has come from researchers working out of an operant conditioning paradigm, using specific target behaviors and clearly identifiable treatment phases in their research. We will demonstrate however, through the use of case illustrations, that this design need not be restricted to this particular theoretical approach. In this section, we first discuss several common features of single case experimental designs and then describe and illustrate two different types of designs within this category: AB designs and multiple baseline designs.

COMMON FEATURES OF SINGLE-SUBJECT EXPERIMENTAL DESIGNS

Single-subject experimental designs have a number of common features (Drew, 1980; Kazdin, 1980; 2003) including (1) specification of the treatment goal, (2) repeated measurement of the dependent variable over time, (3) treatment phases, and (4) stability of baseline data.

The first common characteristic of single-subject experimental designs involves the specification of treatment goals. Because single-subject experimental designs were initially developed from an operant conditioning paradigm, most studies have specified behavioral goals, often referred to as "targets" or "target behaviors." In essence, target behaviors are the dependent variables of the investigation. The treatment goal can consist of cognitions, affective reactions, behaviors, physiological responses, or personality characteristics. If systems (groups, families, organizations) are used as the subject of the design, then system characteristics (communication patterns, cohesion, involvement) can be designated as treatment goals.

The second defining feature of single-subject experimental designs is the repeated measurement of the dependent variables over time. For example, in a study where the researcher or counselor is trying to help the client engage in less negative self-blaming thoughts, the measurement might occur on a weekly basis, or daily, or even several times a day. Many times this assessment process starts before the initiation of treatment, in which case it is referred to as a baseline assessment. In this example, the baseline would be the number of negative self-blaming thoughts the subject engaged in before the intervention. Because this assessment process is continuous (or nearly continuous), the researcher can examine the patterns in the dependent variable over time. The independent variable is typically a treatment intervention, often referred to as the intervention. It is important to note that the multiple measurement of the single-subject quantitative design is in stark contrast to other research designs that might collect a single data point before and after an intervention.

The third characteristic of single-subject experimental designs is the inclusion of different treatment phases, each representing a different experimental condition. One method of phase specification is to designate a baseline and a treatment phase. Baseline data are collected before treatment initiation and are used both to describe the current state of functioning and to make predictions about subsequent performance. The second method of defining time periods involves the random assignment of different treatments to different time periods (days, sessions). The basic purpose of changing from one phase to another is to demonstrate change due to the onset of the independent variable or intervention.

The stability of baseline data is also an important feature of most single-subject quantitative designs. Change cannot be detected after the onset of an intervention if the baseline data are unstable—that is, are either increasing, decreasing, or lack consistency. Thus, before the researcher can ascribe causality to an intervention, he or she must obtain an accurate and stable assessment of the dependent variable before the introduction of the intervention. This is especially the case when a baseline versus treatment intervention phase comparison is used.

In this section, we will discuss two major types of designs used in single-subject quantitative designs: AB time-series designs and multiple baseline designs. We will start with the AB time-series designs, which have many variations; to illustrate the AB time-series design we will discuss three specific designs: AB, ABAB, and randomized AB.

THE AB DESIGN   The AB design is basically a two-phase experiment; the A phase is a baseline period, and the B phase is an intervention phase. Typically, multiple measurements or observations are taken during each phase. For example, each phase might be six weeks long, with two observations each week. These multiple observations enable the researcher to ascertain first of all if the baseline period is stable, which allows a suitable assessment of the subject before the intervention. If the baseline period is unstable (that is, measurements are accelerating or decelerating), it is often difficult to draw inferences about the effects of the intervention. Multiple observations after the intervention enable a thorough assessment of the effects of the intervention over time. If only one observation per phase were collected, the study would basically be a one-group pretest-posttest design (see Chapter 8), which typically has a number of threats to internal validity. The multiple measurements within an AB design, referred to as a time-series format, provide greater stability over time. The AB design, like the traditional within-subjects design previously discussed, has the subject serve as his or her own control or comparison. Thus, the basic comparison is between the A phase (baseline) and the B phase (intervention) within the same subject. If a researcher measured only the B phase, he or she would have no basis for comparison and would find it impossible to infer any effects due to the intervention.

How does the researcher assess whether change has occurred due to the intervention? As Wampold and Freund (1991) noted, the use of statistical methods to analyze the data generated by single-subject designs is controversial. Rather than employing statistical techniques, researchers plot the raw data on a graph and make inferences from the graph. As you might imagine, such a visual analysis is imprecise and can be unreliable and systematically biased (for example, see DeProspero & Cohen, 1979; Furlong & Wampold, 1982; Wampold & Furlong, 1981a). Consequently, a variety of statistical tests have been proposed for single-subject designs (see Kazdin, 2003; Levine & Wampold, 1999; Wampold & Freund, 1991). The interested reader might examine statistical procedures such as the two standard deviation rule (Gottman, McFall, & Barnett, 1969), the relative frequency procedure (Jayaratne & Levy, 1979), lag analysis (Gottman, 1973, 1979), Markov chain analysis (Lichtenberg & Hummel, 1976; Tracey, 1985), time-series analysis (see, for example, Glass, Willson, & Gottman, 1974), randomization tests (see, for example, Edgington, 1980, 1982, 1987; Wampold & Worsham, 1986), the split middle technique (White, 1974), and the binomial test (Kazdin, 1980). These procedures are meant to increase the validity of the statistical analyses and the observations that can be drawn from this type of data.

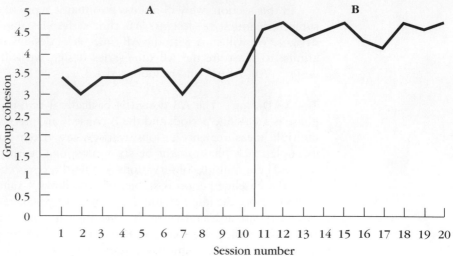

FIGURE 9.1 | AB DESIGN EXAMINING GROUP COHESION (MEASURED ON
A FIVE-POINT LIKERT SCALE, WITH 1 = LOW COHESION,
5 = HIGH COHESION) BY SESSION NUMBER (THE AGENDA-GO-
ROUND EXERCISE WAS INSTITUTED AT SESSION 11)

It may be helpful to see an example of this type of AB design in the area
of group counseling. The famous group therapist Irvine Yalom (1985) has suggested that an agenda-go-round (in which the therapist asks each member at
the beginning of the group session to set an agenda for himself or herself for
that session) can be used to improve group cohesion and member involvement.
A researcher might examine this suggestion by using an AB design. This could
be done by identifying a therapy group, and for the first 10 group sessions
measuring the level of cohesion and member involvement in each session. This
would be the A phase, or baseline. For the next 10 sessions the researcher could
have the group leader use Yalom's agenda-go-round technique and once again
measure cohesion and member involvement for each session. This would be the
B phase, or intervention. The researcher could compare cohesion and member
involvement during the A and B phases to see if the agenda-go-round intervention had an effect. With the rather dramatic changes depicted in the graph
of this design in Figure 9.1, it seems that the agenda-go-round intervention did
have an effect. This type of obvious difference is not always so apparent in
graphic analyses, and thus it is more difficult to ascertain whether the intervention phase actually did have the intended effect.

A problem with this simple AB design is that the researcher cannot eliminate or rule out threats to internal validity from history and maturation as
possible explanations for the results. For instance, going back to the example
of Yalom's technique, most therapy groups increase in cohesion over time,

even without a go-round technique. Thus, although the multiple measurements strengthen this study over the one-group pretest-posttest design, this particular design contains some threats to internal validity. Expansions and refinements of the AB design, including the ABAB design, were developed to circumvent some of these weaknesses.

THE ABAB DESIGN   In contrast to the AB design, which as we have said is basically a two-phase experiment, the ABAB design is a four-phase experiment, and is also frequently referred to as a reversal design. In essence, the ABAB design examines the effect of a treatment (or independent variable) by either presenting or withdrawing the variable during different phases in an attempt to provide unambiguous evidence of the causal effect of the independent variable. The ABAB design starts with a period of baseline data gathering (A_1) and a treatment phase (B_1), and then it returns to a baseline period (A_2) where the intervention is withdrawn, and then finally a second treatment phase (B_2).

The assumption underlying this reversal is that if the independent variable caused the change in the dependent variable in the B_1 phase, then a removal of the independent variable should return the subject to a level similar to the baseline phase. Moreover, if the reversal in fact results in a return to the baseline, then readministering the independent variable at B_2 will serve as a replication, further strengthening the inferred causal relationship. If the behavior at A_2 does not revert to the baseline levels, then a causal relationship between the independent and dependent variables cannot be inferred because other (unknown) variables may have been the causal influence. Thus, in the Yalom agenda-setting example given earlier when describing the AB design, an ABAB design would be collected in the following manner: Ten group sessions in which the researcher collected the baseline cohesion and member involvement data (A_1), followed by 10 sessions in which the group leader implemented the agenda-go-round intervention (with continued data collection) (B_1), followed by another 10 group sessions of data collection without the agenda-go-round intervention (A_2), and then a final 10 sessions with the agenda-go-round intervention reinstituted (B_2). Figure 9.2 presents a graph of data collected from this ABAB design. Because group cohesion increased in both B phases, we can infer that the agenda-go-round exercise caused an improvement in group cohesion.

Let's look at another example of the ABAB design to examine the relationship between therapist behavior and client resistance. This study is also a good illustration of programmatic research that uses both descriptive and experimental designs to study a phenomenon. First, using a descriptive research strategy, Patterson and Forgatch (1985) examined the likelihood of client resistance following various types of counselor behavior (for example, supportive or teaching responses). In essence, they found that client resistance following therapist teaching responses was significantly higher than the clients' baseline resistance. One might guess that this was because the client was feeling talked at or lectured to, and they may have felt resistance as a result. But because this first study was only descriptive, the authors could not infer that therapist teaching caused client resistance. But this question did provide the

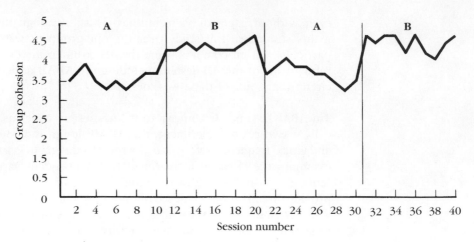

FIGURE 9.2 | AN ABAB DESIGN EXAMINING GROUP COHESION BY SESSION NUMBER (THE AGENDA-GO-ROUND EXERCISE WAS INSTITUTED AT SESSION 11, WITHDRAWN AT SESSION 21, AND REINSTITUTED AT SESSION 31)

researchers with a wonderful question with which to use the ABAB design. Six counselors met with their clients for videotaped sessions. The counselors started with a baseline phase (A_1) in which they interacted with their clients without using teaching interventions; this was followed by a treatment phase (B_1) in which the counselors increased their use of teaching responses. A second baseline phase followed in which the counselors returned to interacting without the teaching responses (A_2). There was then a final treatment phase (B_2) in which the counselors once again increased their use of teaching responses. The results of this ABAB study showed that the counselors did give significantly more teaching responses during the two treatment phases, indicating that the experimental manipulation was successful (such a procedural check is referred to as a manipulation check). More important, the clients were more resistant during the treatment phases (B_1 and B_2). Thus, these data more strongly suggest that therapist teaching behavior caused client resistance.

Although there are many strengths to the ABAB design, it does have three problems that we would like to note. The first problem is a statistical one. Most authors and editors want to report some statistical test that describes the amount of difference between the two phases (A and B; see previous references regarding statistical issues for these designs). When reported, this test is usually a t test or an F test. Both t and F tests, however, assume independent observations, and this is not the case in the ABAB design (Wampold & Freund, 1991). A second problem with the ABAB design is the possible presence of carryover effects (that is, effects from the manipulation at phase B_1 that affect A_2 or B_2). It could be that the effects of the B_1 intervention are irreversible and cannot be withdrawn. For example, if the dependent variable involves learning or skill acquisition (for example, study skills such as test-wiseness), it is difficult to reverse these treatments and return the subject to the A_1 level. Obviously, there are many interventions for which treatments are reversible and carryover effects are not present. However, in some ABAB designs, the interventions are not reversible and carryover effects present problems in drawing inferences and in isolating causal relationships. Finally, there are therapeutic situations in which it is undesirable or unethical to reverse the treatment phase, and both the client and counselor may be reluctant to withdraw an effective treatment. These concerns, among others, have led authors (see Edgington, 1987) to call for the use of randomized single-subject experiments or randomized AB designs.

RANDOMIZED AB DESIGNS   There are many tests of randomization for single-subject designs (see Edgington, 1980, 1987; Wampold & Furlong, 1981b; Wampold & Worsham, 1986). Even though these statistical tests are beyond the scope of this book, we present one example to introduce readers to the design possibilities within randomized AB designs.

The randomized AB design involves two phases that are repeated in a randomized fashion such that the presence of an A or a B phase at any point in time is dependent on random assignment. For example, the randomized AB design for examining the effects of an agenda-go-round exercise on group cohesion and member involvement might look like this:

A A B A B A B B B A B A A B B A B A B A
Session 1 2 3 4 5 6 7 8 9 10 11 12 13 14 15 16 17 18 19 20

In this example, A represents sessions in which the agenda-go-round is not used, and B represents sessions in which this exercise is used. Because the occurrence of A and B phases is random, randomization tests or traditional parametric tests can be used (Edgington, 1980) to compare cohesion and involvement scores for the A and B sessions. This design has a second advantage: It enables the researcher to analyze carryover effects by setting up the following simple 2×2 factorial design.

Phase	Preceded by Phase A	Preceded by Phase B
A	(1) Data from sessions 2, 13	(2) Data from sessions 4, 6, 10, 12, 16, 18, 20
B	(3) Data from sessions 3, 5, 7, 11, 14, 17, 19	(4) Data from sessions 8, 9, 15

Data are assigned to cells based on whether they come from phase A or B and on which phase preceded the phase in question. For example, the first cell in the table contains the data from all phase-A sessions (all sessions without the agenda-go-round) that were preceded by a phase-A session (session without the agenda-go-round). In a like manner, the second cell of the table contains all data from phase-A sessions (without agenda-go-round) that were preceded by a phase-B session (with agenda-go-round). A factorial analysis of variance (ANOVA) using this setup would provide a main effect for phase A versus B, a main effect for preceding phase (preceding A versus preceding B), and an interaction effect for phase × preceding phase. The interaction analysis directly tests for carryover effects.

Some final comments about the AB time-series designs seem warranted. First, although we have discussed and illustrated AB designs as having only two (A and B) phases, this need not be the case. A design could contain three (A, B, and C) or more phases. A three-phase design could compare a baseline phase to two different treatments, or it could compare three different levels of an independent variable. The basic logic of the AB design remains the same no matter how many phases are involved—the researcher is attempting to isolate the effects of the independent variable by examining different levels (or trends) across different phases.

Many times AB designs are not considered with particular research projects because of possible ethical concerns. For instance, one may question whether it is appropriate to withdraw a treatment that seems to be having a positive effect on a client. Although this is an excellent question, it is important to note this is the same dilemma faced by members of the medical profession in the early 1960s in prescribing thalidomide for morning sickness; unfortunately, they decided not to withhold treatment because of the perceived effectiveness of the drug and the results were terrible birth defects. In short, it is important to adequately test the efficacy of our counseling interventions empirically before assuming their effectiveness.

Another concern with AB designs is related to carryover effects of an intervention and the perceived unsuitability of some variables for some theoretical orientations. For example, Gelso (1979) reasoned that one cannot reverse a client's insight (the theoretical effect of an appropriate interpretation), and thus the AB designs would not be well-suited for such content. We believe that the AB designs can be successfully applied to a wider range of topics than is typically acknowledged, although the researcher may need to be creative in adapting the AB designs. Doing so can bring the researcher a wealth of data that are highly useful to the practitioner, in addition to generating important research questions in an area.

MULTIPLE-BASELINE DESIGNS

The second type of single-subject experimental quantitative design that we will discuss is the multiple-baseline design. The essential feature of this design is that data are recorded on more than one dependent variable, or target behavior, simultaneously. Like the AB designs, there is continual collection of data, but in multiple-baseline designs there are two or more data collection baselines on different dependent measures. The basic assumption is that with several dependent measures, one or more of these variables can serve as controls while the intervention is simultaneously applied to one of the dependent measures. But it is important that the intervention is applied to the different dependent measures at different times. If the intervention is truly the causal agent, there should be change on the dependent variable that was targeted by the intervention, but not on the nontargeted dependent variables. Thus, whereas the ABAB design attempts to identify causal relationships by withdrawing the intervention and reversing the change, the multiple-baseline design attempts to determine causality by identifying changes in some but not all of the multiple dependent measures. One of the problems with the multiple-baseline approach is the possible nonindependence of the dependent variables; thus, when the intervention is targeted at one of the dependent variables but all of the dependent variables change, the cause of the change is unclear (more on this later).

There are three different versions of the multiple-baseline design. The first variation involves collecting data on two or more dependent variables in the same individual. For example, a researcher may want to examine the effects of therapeutic homework assignments on the amount of family communication. To use a multiple-baseline design, he or she would have to identify at least two behaviors to measure family communication, perhaps (1) the amount of time after dinner the husband and wife spend talking, and (2) the amount of time after dinner the parents spend talking with the children. Like the AB designs, the multiple-baseline design starts with a period of baseline assessment. In our example, this would involve daily recordings of interaction time between (1) spouses and (2) parents and children. Next, the intervention is targeted at one of these dependent variables; a homework assignment is initiated that is designed to increase inter-spousal communication. The basic assumption in this example is that the second behavior (amount of communication between parents and children) serves as a control for the first behavior (amount of communication between spouses). If the intervention is causally related to inter-spousal communication, there should be a change in the amount of time the husband and wife spend communicating, but not in the amount of time the parents spend communicating with the children. As with AB designs, data are collected on these two behaviors for a specified period of time—say, one week. Finally, a homework assignment can be designed to increase parent–child communication. A change in the amount of time spent in parent–child communication would be expected to occur only after the introduction of this intervention. Sometimes three to five different behaviors are identified and targeted over successive time periods to assess the effects of a particular intervention. Continuation of a stable baseline in the behaviors not targeted for intervention (that is, the controls) indicates the absence of coincidental influences other than the experimental intervention.

The second variation of the multiple-baseline design is to identify the same response across different subjects. Returning to our previous example about agenda setting, a researcher may want to test Yalom's (1985) hypothesis concerning the relationship between the quality of group member agendas and their subsequent involvement in the group. Specifically, Yalom stated that group members will initiate more high-level interactions when the agendas for the group are realistic, interpersonal, and here-and-now oriented. The researcher could begin by making a baseline assessment of each group member's interactions over the first five group sessions. He or she could then begin to train individual group members to set realistic, interpersonal, and here-and-now agendas. Only one group member would be trained at a time, and the initiation of the training with the individual group members would be staggered; the researcher might train a different member every fifth group session. A change in any individual's quality of group participation would be expected to occur contingent on his or her receiving the agenda training, whereas no change would be expected in those not trained. The basic assumption in this example is that individuals can serve as controls when they have not received the intervention. Data collection is continuous, and only those individuals who have received the intervention are expected to change on the dependent measure. A possible source of contamination in this example is that subjects who have not received training might learn how to set effective agendas by observing their peers who have received training.

The third variation of the multiple-baseline design is to identify a given response for one subject but across different situations. As in all illustrations of the multiple-baseline design, a subject can refer to an individual, a group, a classroom, or a larger unit. Suppose a researcher wants to examine the effects of token reinforcement (the independent variables) on a child interacting with peers (the dependent variable). The amount of interaction with peers could be observed both before and after school on the playground, during a baseline period. The researcher could then begin token reinforcement of prosocial interactions only before school. The researcher would then expect to find a change in the amount of interaction with peers in the morning but not in the afternoon. Later the token reinforcement could be done in the afternoon also, and a consequent change in this baseline would then be expected.

Because the logic of the multiple-baseline design requires that the researcher show changes in one assessed behavior while another assessed behavior remains constant, one of the main concerns in using this type of design is the independence of the dependent variables. If there is a relationship between two or more of the behaviors, then a change in one behavior may well lead to a change in the other. If two behaviors show simultaneous change but only one received the independent variable, then it is impossible to rule out threats to internal validity such as history and maturation. Such unintended changes in baselines seriously jeopardize the strength of the multiple-baseline design and typically produce a study with uninterpretable results.

One way to guard against this complication is to carefully assess the independence of the behaviors, perhaps by correlating the baseline behaviors (Christensen, 1980). Another possible solution is the use of several dependent variables; Kazdin and Kopel (1975) recommended using four or more variables. By increasing the number of baselines, the researcher can guard against the possibility that two of the baselines are dependent on each other.

A recent example of using a multiple baseline design was the study mentioned earlier by Dennin and Ellis (2003). Briefly, in this study Dennin and

Ellis studied the use of self-supervision, which is a systematic process in which an individual works independently directing his or her own professional development. Specifically, they were interested in the impact of these different conditions on trainees' actual use of empathy and metaphor in their counseling sessions. They assigned four novice female counselors in training to one of three randomized conditions: (1) self-supervision targeting the use of metaphor first and then empathy, (2) self-supervision targeting empathy and then metaphor, or (3) an attention placebo control condition. The researchers collected data over a series of observations, and monitored both treatments, empathy and metaphor. The researchers obtained a series of observations across an initial baseline phase and subsequent treatment phases that were targeting different behavior. They continued their data collection period for up to 17 counseling sessions, with each treatment starting at a randomly determined point. The results of their study found that self-supervision helped trainees increase their use of metaphor, but did not result in an increase in empathy.

This example notwithstanding, it was striking how few multiple-baseline designs were found in the major counseling journals (Bangert & Baumberger, 2005). This absence is in stark contrast to journals in clinical psychology, and especially the behaviorally oriented journals (for example, *Behavior Therapy, Behavioral Assessment,* and *Journal of Applied Behavior Analysis*). This suggests that this design is being used infrequently in counseling research.

ADVANTAGES AND LIMITATIONS OF SINGLE-SUBJECT DESIGNS

Single-subject designs have a number of advantages and limitations, which we will initially discuss in a rather simple and absolute sense. In weighing these advantages and limitations, it is imperative to distinguish between the uncontrolled case study on the one hand, and both the intensive single-subject quantitative design and the single-subject experimental quantitative design on the other. In our view, much less can be learned from the uncontrolled case study because of the multitude of rival hypotheses. Conversely, the comparisons and control in the intensive single-subject design and single-subject experimental design provide stronger empirical support and thus lend greater utility to the research design. It is also important to note that the advantages and limitations need to be considered relative to the existing scientific knowledge pertaining to a specific question and the previous research methodologies employed in examining that particular research question.

ADVANTAGES OF SINGLE-SUBJECT DESIGNS

Lundervold and Belwood (2000) authored an article titled "The Best Kept Secret in Counseling: Single-Case (N=1) Experimental Designs." They concluded that single-subject designs offer "a scientifically credible means to objectively evaluate practice and conduct clinically relevant research in a practice setting" (p. 92). In this section we discuss some of the strengths and advantages of the single-subject design, specifically as a means of: (1) collecting information and ideas and generating hypotheses about the therapeutic process, (2) testing therapeutic techniques, (3) testing new methodologies, (4) studying individuals and rare phenomena, and (5) providing exemplars and counterinstances.

A MEANS OF COLLECTING INFORMATION AND IDEAS, AND GENERATING HYPOTHESES ABOUT THE THERAPEUTIC PROCESS   Although the traditional between-groups design has been useful in examining outcomes in psychotherapy, a prominent difficulty has been the obscuring of individual variations in group averages. The therapeutic process is complex and highly variable. Clients differ from each other in significant ways; they are not uniform (Kiesler, 1966). Rather, clients process information about themselves, their experiential worlds, and counseling in idiographic ways, and even differently from one time to the next. The same can be said of counselors; therapists not only differ in important ways from each other, but also are different from one time to another. Thus, in the context of the complex and detailed process of therapy, intensive single-subject methodologies in particular are ideally suited for microscopic analyses and for expanding scientific knowledge. In fact, many years ago Bergin and Strupp (1970) maintained that the intensive single-subject design would be one of the primary strategies to clarify the mechanisms of change within the therapeutic process. Intensive single-subject designs have also been recommended for obtaining an in-depth analysis of the therapeutic process (Bergin & Lambert, 1978; Gelso, 1979; Hill et al., 1983; Lundervold & Belwood, 2000; Resnikoff, 1978).

Both the intensive single-subject design and the single-subject experimental design offer unique opportunities to carefully scrutinize aspects of the therapeutic process in depth. Methodologies that use very time-consuming procedures such as interpersonal process recall (Kagan, 1975) or assessing cognitive structures by using an associative network (Martin, 1985) are often impossible when large numbers of subjects are involved. However, these procedures are more feasible when only one or a few clients are involved. In a way, the single-subject design can allow for a more complete description of what happens in counseling and the mechanisms involved in change. The studies mentioned earlier by Hill et al. (1983) and Martin et al. (1987) provided good examples of microscopic analyses of variables involved in the change process. These studies provide important in-depth information that contributes to the scientific knowledge base about counseling and supervision. More specifically, Hill and colleagues (1983) noted that intensive single-subject designs (1) permit a more adequate description of what actually happens between a counselor and client, (2) facilitate more integration of process data with positive or negative outcomes, (3) allow a close examination of the change process in the therapeutic relationship, and (4) allow outcome measures to be tailored to an individual client's problems.

A MEANS OF TESTING THERAPEUTIC TECHNIQUES   Single-subject designs provide a useful means to test the effects of specific therapeutic techniques. The testing of techniques might happen at several levels: (1) the discovery of a new technique, (2) an intentional examination of a relatively new technique, (3) the application of an established technique to a new population or treatment situation, and (4) an in-depth examination of a well-established technique. Occasionally therapists will discover new techniques through a trial-and-error process with individual clients. Breuer's work with Anna O. resulted in the discovery of a "talking cure" or catharsis. In essence, Breuer found through trial and error that some of Anna's symptoms were relieved or disappeared simply by talking about them (Breuer & Freud, 1955). George Kelley, in part out of boredom with the Freudian interpretations, began fabricating "insights" and "preposterous interpretations," and discovered that often clients could change their lives in important ways if they believed these "alternative constructions of the world" (Monte, 1980, p. 434). Likewise, Rogers abandoned the traditional directive and diagnostically oriented therapeutic style after a dismal therapeutic failure in which a client reentered and redirected therapy by initiating a discussion of her troubled marriage. Rogers discovered that "it is the client who knows what hurts, what direction to go, what problems are crucial, and what experiences have been deeply buried" (Rogers, 1961, pp. 11–12). In short, therapists often stumble onto or create new techniques through their therapeutic work with individual clients. The intentional and consistent examination of new techniques within the informal case study, as well as the more formal single-subject design, can yield useful information about the counseling process. Thus, new observations by the therapist might be informally or formally tested with additional clients to further determine the effectiveness and generalizability of the technique.

The single-subject design can also be used effectively to test the application of an established technique with a new problem or a new population. Kazdin (2003) noted that the extension of a given technique to a new problem is really quite common in the literature. For example, systematic desensitization has been found to be applicable to a wide range of phobias or fears, such as fear of heart attacks (Furst & Cooper, 1970) and fear of sharks (Krop & Krause, 1976).

Finally, the single-subject design also lends itself well to an in-depth examination of the effectiveness of a certain technique. For example, a great deal of information could be collected about how a client is processing or reacting to repeated use of a certain technique, such as the Gestalt empty-chair technique, counselor touch, or counselor self-disclosure. Thus, in-depth information could be collected on the use of a specific technique over time.

A MEANS OF TESTING NEW METHODOLOGIES   The single-subject design is especially well suited to testing new research methodologies. This design allows the investigator to "experiment" in a way with a new methodology or procedure. The investigator can determine whether a new methodology provides new or more useful information, or whether some aspect of counseling is better understood in some way.

Several investigations by Jack Martin provide excellent examples of testing new methodologies by using single-subject designs. Martin has conceptualized counseling through a cognitive mediational paradigm (Martin, 1984), in which he maintained the necessity of examining the cognitive processes of clients. Martin suggested that the information contained in a client's cognitive structures, and the organization of that information, would have considerable appeal to researchers of counseling outcomes. Using an information-processing perspective, Martin tested a methodology to assess a client's cognitive structures (Martin, 1985). At the end of each session with a client, fictitiously called Carla, he would ask her to relax and then give the first associations to the following words: problem, Bill (fictitious name for her husband), and Carla. As the client mentioned specific word associations, Martin wrote each on a small square. After Carla had responded to the three memory probes, she was asked to arrange the labels on a laminated board using distance and drawing lines to symbolically depict relationships among the words. Martin found that this procedure produced "an incredible amount of data" (p. 558). The pre- to postcounseling diagrams revealed that Carla had acquired important knowledge about battering (the presenting problem) and her options concerning this particular problem (for example, take advantage of a Women Center's program). Carla's outcomes also reflected important changes in her affective processes, from passive, reactive emotions (such as guilt or shame) to more active emotions (such as hope or anger).

Martin (1985) thus concluded that this particular method of assessing a client's cognitive structures provided very useful data that nicely captured some of the richness and subjective nature of the change process in counseling. Thus, this particular single-subject study provided important information about a new methodological procedure. Given the idiosyncratic nature of the data from this new method, group data would initially be quite overwhelming and not lend itself well to "averaging" across clients. The important point is that the results of Martin's initial study provided empirical support for additional examination of this new methodology.

A MEANS OF STUDYING INDIVIDUALS AND RARE PHENOMENA   A major difficulty noted by many applied researchers and practitioners is the obscuring of individual variations and outcomes when subjects are examined in groups and their data are simply "averaged." In fact, trying to think about the "average" or "typical" client is generally not very useful when developing interventions. Clients are seldom homogeneous or "uniform." By contrast, the single-subject design is particularly well-suited to describing the idiosyncrasies of individual clients, because of its intensive and often microscopic analyses. Thus, the single-subject design can be considered a useful tool for examining change within a single individual. In fact, Bergin and Strupp (1970) proposed that the single-subject design be used as the primary methodology to isolate specific mechanisms of change. The case study approach can provide some information as well, but most often it lacks experimental control, which confounds even tentative conclusions.

The single-subject design also lends itself to more qualitative approaches in studying individuals (see Neimeyer & Resnikoff, 1982; Polkinghorne, 1984).

In this way, the single-subject design can be used to collect data about the "thinking frameworks" of individuals (Edgington, 1987; Neimeyer & Resnikoff) or higher mental processes (Wundt, 1916). Polkinghorne aptly suggested that human action and decision making, which are central to the therapeutic and counseling processes, appear to be related to a "means-end rationality" or mode of processing information. Heppner and Krauskopf (1987) noted similar thinking processes by using an information-processing model to describe client problem solving in a counseling context. The single-subject design may be particularly well suited for gathering information about (1) how clients process information, (2) the thinking steps or means involved in reaching some end or goal (logically or illogically), (3) an individual's plans and intentions (Heppner & Krauskopf; Howard, 1985), and (4) how such plans affect the processing of information and subsequent behavior. The complexity of such information processing, at least initially, may be examined more feasibly via a single-subject design. In short, single-subject designs are useful to study complex phenomena, particularly as counselors use some of the more qualitative approaches in examining higher mental processes.

The single-subject design is particularly useful in studying rare phenomena, such as multiple personality. In addition to rare phenomena, the single-subject design can also be used to study relatively low-frequency occurrences, such as male anorexics and college students under unique situational stress (e.g., Middle Eastern students after 9/11, or aborted grief reactions; see Corazzini, 1980). Although a typical university counseling center usually has a very broad range of clients, it is often difficult to study infrequent occurrences in a group comparison format. It is not usually feasible, or ethical, to withhold treatment until enough of these low-occurrence clients seek counseling to enable random assignment of clients to groups, and so forth. Thus, the single-subject design is useful to investigate various idiosyncrasies or commonalities across clients with similar presenting problems, such as clients with aborted grief reactions.

A MEANS OF PROVIDING EXEMPLARS AND COUNTERINSTANCES The single-subject design can be used to provide exemplars to highlight findings, particularly if these findings run counter to existing beliefs or theories (in which case exemplars become counterinstances). Given that the intensive single-subject and single-subject experimental designs generally provide stronger experimental control, these findings obviously lend themselves better to such highlighting.

More specifically, the findings from a single-subject design can be used to provide data in support of a particular point, argument, or theory. For example, Strupp (1980a, 1980b, 1980c) conducted a series of single-subject studies comparing therapists, each with a successful and unsuccessful case in brief psychodynamic therapy. A wide variety of process and outcome measures were used to examine events related to therapeutic effectiveness. Negative outcomes were related to client characterological problems (as compared to neurotic problems) or counseling countertransference issues. Positive outcomes were related to the client's ability to take advantage of the therapeutic relationship and to work within the therapist's framework. Strupp then used these results to propose that patient variables were more powerful events in assessing therapeutic outcomes, even to the point of overshadowing therapists' attitudes and technical skill.

Kazdin (1980) addressed the problem of symptom substitution stemming primarily from psychoanalytic thinking. The general assumption was that treatment of overt, problematic behavior, rather than treatment of the underlying cause, may result in symptom substitution. However, very early research on specific problematic behaviors such as phobias or bedwetting did not result in the appearance of substitute symptoms (see, for example, Jones, 1956; Meyer, 1957; Yates, 1958). Thus, this early research using primarily uncontrolled case studies cast doubt on the unqualified notion of symptom substitution, suggesting that this phenomenon may be more complex than previously assumed.

In sum, there are many advantages to a well-designed and carefully controlled single-subject design. In essence, the single-subject designs can study important phenomena that other designs are less suited to examine in depth.

LIMITATIONS OF SINGLE-SUBJECT DESIGNS

Although there are a host of limitations to the traditional uncontrolled case study, many of these have been corrected in the two single-subject quantitative designs discussed in the chapter. However, some limitations remain, particularly related to the generalizabilty of the findings.

As traditionally conceived and conducted, the individual case study almost completely lacks experimental control. Many of Cook and Campbell's (1979) threats to internal validity are present, such as history, maturation, testing, selection, and mortality. In addition, many times "data" are collected in unsystematic and even retrospective ways. After working with a particular client for some time, the therapist may reflect back (sometimes months later) to collect his or her "observations" about the case. Such retrospective analyses most likely involve multiple sources of bias and distortion (for example, memory loss, memory distortion, subjective impressions, or selective attention), and blur any temporal succession pertaining to causal relationships. Sometimes the "data" also consist of verbal client self-reports collected by the counselor. If the client believes he or she is doing the counselor a favor by completing a questionnaire, data obtained in such a manner may very well be contaminated or biased, most likely by demand characteristics inherent in the situation. Likewise, data may be collected from the client with instruments of unknown reliability or validity, thereby calling into question the adequacy of the data. In short, any of a number of biases of uncontrolled variables can obscure the relationship between the variables under examination and thus obscure interpretation of the findings. Although it *may* be true that variable x affected variable y in some way, it also may be the case that many other variables created the effect on variable y. The upshot of the uncontrolled case study is that there may be several plausible explanations for the observed effect on variable y, thus limiting the scientific value of the study. The uncontrolled case study is a weak source of "data" and at best is suggestive.

By contrast, the intensive single-subject design and the single-subject experimental design typically involve more systematic observations and experimental control. As such they have less limitations than the traditional case study, but some limitations do remain. A major issue in using single-subject designs is the generalizability of the findings to other individuals or situations. Even if one isolates specific relationships among variables, it is unclear whether the results would generalize to other clients with similar concerns or diagnoses (client generality) or whether a particular technique would work in a different setting (setting generality) (Barlow & Hersen, 1984). Caution must also be used when employing findings from single-subject designs as exemplars or counterinstances. As mentioned previously, in early research relatively uncontrolled case studies were not just overused as exemplars, but also were used as the primary database in the construction of personality theories. Although the generalizability of the findings from single-subject designs must always be questioned, the results can highlight a particular point or cast doubt on previously held beliefs, suggesting that, at a minimum, there are exceptions to the rule or that the rule is somehow incorrect. However, exemplars should not become the only or even primary database relating to a particular phenomenon.

Another disadvantage of the intensive single-subject design is that experimenters may find what they expected to find and overlook information that is contrary to their expectations. For example, subsequent analyses of data from Hill and colleagues (1983) revealed several facets of the interaction between the counselor and client that were undetected by those researchers' analysis (Wampold & Kim, 1989).

SUMMARY AND CONCLUSIONS

The common goal of all counseling research methods is to facilitate an understanding of human behavior. Different methodologies provide different types of data and information about human behavior. Single-subject designs permit an examination of an individual person, dyad, or group. Typically, a practitioner counseling a specific client is less concerned with group averages than with the individual's behavior. It is not sufficient to rely on normative data that suggest a particular intervention strategy works with, say, three out of four clients, and thus simply to rely on probabilities. Single-subject designs, particularly those of an intensive, systematic, or time-series nature, can provide information about the uniqueness of client responses

and counselor interventions. However, researchers must be particularly sensitive to various sources of bias and extraneous variables, as well as cautious about generalizing the results from one individual to other individuals or groups.

In this chapter, we discussed three main types of single-subject design, the uncontrolled case study, the intensive single-subject quantitative design, and the single-subject experimental design. A case study refers to a study that consists simply of observations of an individual, dyad, or group that are made under unsystematic and uncontrolled conditions. The intensive single-subject quantitative design typically involves more experimental control and consists of systematic, repeated, and multiple observations of an individual, dyad, or group under experimental conditions designed to identify and compare relationships among variables. Thus, the comparisons and control in the intensive single-subject quantitative design provide stronger empirical support, and thus give it more utility than the case study.

The single-subject experimental designs also examine the relationship between two or more variables, typically within one or a few subjects, and involve considerable levels of experimental control. These designs are characterized by specific treatment goals, numerous and repeated measurements of the dependent variable, and the inclusion of different phases or periods of time (each representing a different experimental condition such as a baseline phase or an intervention phase). The basic purpose of changing from one phase to another is to demonstrate change, presumably due to the onset of the independent variable or intervention.

Two major types of single-subject experimental designs are the AB time-series designs (AB, ABAB, randomized AB) and multiple-baseline designs. We maintain that the time-series designs are not only appropriate for behavioral researchers, but also can be fruitfully employed within other theoretical orientations.

We firmly believe that both the intensive single-subject quantitative design and the single-subject experimental designs can be powerful methodologies to increase understanding of counseling and the counseling process. These designs can be used for (1) collecting information and ideas, and generating hypotheses about the therapeutic process; (2) testing therapeutic techniques; (3) testing new methodologies; (4) studying individuals and rare phenomena; and (5) providing exemplars and counterinstances. However, limitations imposed by threats to both internal and external validity must be clearly examined and considered. Bergin and Strupp (1970) initially predicted that the single-subject design would be one of the primary strategies used to clarify the process of counseling; this remains to be demonstrated. Nonetheless, because we strongly believe in the potential of this methodology, our first recommendation is to use the more rigorous single-subject designs more frequently in counseling research. These designs can be especially rich in providing more holistic data of both a content and process nature.

A number of the examples cited in this chapter were intentionally drawn from group counseling. One of the main obstacles in group counseling research is sample size. Many times in group counseling research, the variable of interest is a group-level variable such as cohesion. Often, however, researchers use individual scores, such as each subject's attraction to the group, so they can increase the size of the groups in a between-groups design. Researchers could circumvent this sample-size problem by using more single-subject experimental time-series designs. Accordingly, our second recommendation is an increased use of single-subject experimental designs in group (and family) research. This recommendation could also help address a second problem in group research—that most group counseling studies use analogue groups of very short duration. Time-series designs allow the researcher to study the group as an entity and to use real client groups without having to line up a prohibitively large number of subjects.

Our third recommendation is the increased use of randomized designs in AB time-series research. Randomized designs offer additional complexity and flexibility, and enable the researcher to examine for the presence of carry-over effects between treatments. In addition, randomized designs permit the use of powerful parametric statistical analyses. Editors are often reluctant to publish studies that do not have statistical comparisons, and readers rely on these statistical comparisons as a way of comparing studies for AB time-series designs; parametric statistical tests can only be performed appropriately when A and B phases are randomly assigned.

A final methodological consideration in discussing the use of the single-subject methodology is the type of data or knowledge currently available on a particular research question. For example, a considerable number of studies have investigated the therapeutic technique of thought stopping. In 1978, Heppner reviewed the published investigations to determine the clinical efficacy of thought stopping. This body of literature consisted of 22 studies, 20 of which were case studies that lacked experimental control (Heppner, 1978b). Thus, this body of "knowledge" concerning the clinical efficacy of thought stopping was based largely on data collected from a single methodological perspective, a phenomenon that has been called paradigm fixation (Gelso, 1979). The point is that merely ascertaining the advantages and limitations of the single-subject design is not enough; researchers must also weigh these advantages and limitations relative to the applicable existing scientific knowledge base and the types of designs used in past research.

STIMULUS QUESTIONS

SINGLE-SUBJECT DESIGNS

This exercise is designed to help promote reflection on single-subject designs. After reading this chapter, think about your responses to the following questions.

1. Some students have told us that their training programs "do not allow" single-subject designs for a thesis or dissertation. Why do you think that is the case? If you were a person who wanted to conduct an intensive single-subject design for your own thesis or dissertation, what arguments would you use in order to convince your training program of their validity?

2. In the history of counseling, there have been a number of uncontrolled case studies. Now it is more difficult to find examples of these designs in our major journals. What factors do you believe have brought about this change in thinking and the reduced use of the uncontrolled case studies?

3. Think about the topics you feel passionate about in your own scholarly work and practice. Identify three research questions that would lend themselves well to some sort of a single-subject quantitative design. How would you design a study using an intensive single-subject design for this topic?

4. One of the concerns with single-subject design is the issue of generalizability. What can be done to increase the level of external validity or generalizability with such designs?

5. Talk to faculty and peers about their perceptions of the usefulness of the single-subject designs. What advantages and disadvantages first come to mind for them?

$\mathbf{IO}$ CHAPTER | QUANTITATIVE DESCRIPTIVE DESIGNS

Descriptive designs are research strategies that help to define the existence and delineate characteristics of a particular phenomenon. For example, in the counseling profession, we are often interested in the frequency of counseling-related phenomena, like the frequency of eating disorders in college students (see Mintz, O'Halloran, Mulholland, & Schneider, 1997). Such information is very useful for developing both remedial and preventive interventions. Thus, a very important role of our research is to describe the occurrence of phenomena of interest. Similarly, we often want to describe characteristics of particular phenomena, like different dimensions of heterosexual knowledge and attitudes regarding lesbian, gay, and bisexual individuals (see Worthington, Dillon, & Becker-Schutte, 2005). Likewise, we often find it useful to describe the relationship between two or more variables, such as the relationship among ethnic identity, discrimination, and depression in Korean Americans (see Lee, 2005). In short, such descriptive information promotes greater understanding of various phenomena, and this knowledge can then be used to increase the effectiveness of a host of counseling interventions. Thus, descriptive designs are very important and useful research strategies of the counseling profession and consequently are commonly found across counseling journals.

Historically, texts on research design have devoted little attention to descriptive designs. This lack of attention stemmed partially from what we call the "pure science myth," which held that the experimental design paradigm was the "correct" or "best" mode of scientific investigation. Moreover, the received view of science tended to emphasize the testing and verification of theories, as well as comparisons among competing theories. Twenty years ago, Greenberg (1986a) argued that counseling psychology should place greater emphasis on discovery paradigms. He maintained that the empiricist tradition, with its emphasis on the controlled between-groups experiment, was overvalued by counseling researchers. Consequently, too often researchers attempted to manipulate and control variables before enough was known about the phenomenon of interest. Inadequately described phenomena were often subjected to rigid verification, with disappointing results. Before one can test the adequacy of a theory in explaining a phenomenon, one needs a reliable and detailed description of the phenomenon. Clearly, descriptive designs have an important role in the scientific process, which is reflected today in their frequent utilization.

The utility of a descriptive study is directly dependent on the quality of the instruments or assessments used to describe the phenomenon. Moreover, it is impossible to observe all instances of a phenomenon, so instead the researcher carefully studies the phenomenon in a sample drawn from the population of interest. Thus, the reliability and validity of the observations and the generalizability (or external validity) of the sample are two critical issues in descriptive research. At first glance, the MAXMINCON principle that we have emphasized seems antithetical to descriptive research. For example, by exercising experimental control, it might seem that the experimenter would interfere with or change the natural phenomenon he or she was attempting to describe. Indeed, many variables are left uncontrolled in descriptive research, and thus cause-and-effect statements are inappropriate. On the other hand, the investigator can exercise considerable care in making observations so as to minimize measurement errors, which can reduce considerable error variance. Thus, the quality of the observations is the heart of descriptive design. Likewise, the descriptive researcher can exercise experimental control to reduce bias and extraneous variables by using random sampling. Accordingly, in this chapter we emphasize measurement, observation, and sampling as we review the different types of descriptive designs.

The purpose of this chapter is to discuss three major types of quantitative descriptive research: (1) survey or epidemiological research, (2) classification or data reduction research, and (3) correlational research designs. Briefly, research strategies designed to characterize the occurrence of behaviors are commonly known as epidemiological or survey designs. Classification research uses factor and cluster analysis as strategies for categorizing and reducing data, primarily by identifying underlying dimensions or groupings in a set of variables. Research strategies that examine the relationship among or between variables are referred to as correlational designs. This type of design includes studies that use correlational or regression analyses.

SURVEY OR EPIDEMIOLOGICAL RESEARCH DESIGNS

Hackett (1981) observed that survey research is one of the oldest and most widely used research methods in the social sciences. The use of surveys has been traced to ancient Egypt, and surveys were conducted to assess social conditions in England in the eighteenth century (Glock, 1967). Today surveys are commonplace, particularly as public opinion polls and political surveys. Surveys have also been widely employed by counseling researchers. For example, 27 of the 57 data-based articles submitted to a counseling-related journal, *Counselor Education and Supervision,* during July 1991 through June 1992 were survey studies (Fong & Malone, 1994).

The basic aim of survey research is to document the nature or frequency of a particular variable (for instance, the incidence and extent of alcohol use) within a certain population (for example, American college students). Surveys typically use self-reports to identify facts, opinions, attitudes, and behaviors, as well as the relationships among these aspects; data are often collected through questionnaires, mailed surveys, telephone interviews, personal interviews, or online websites. The functions of survey research are to describe, explain, or explore phenomena (Babbie, 1979). Descriptive research provides basic information about a variable or phenomenon (for example, the frequency of rape on college campuses). Explanatory research attempts to identify variables (such as beliefs about women, or beliefs about the acceptability of physical aggression) that might explain the occurrence of a phenomenon (such as rape on college campuses). Exploratory research is often conducted when the researcher wants to learn about a poorly understood phenomenon (for instance, how rapists rationalize rape).

Not surprisingly, descriptive survey research has made important contributions to the counseling profession. For example, in the early years of the counseling profession, the type and frequency of college students' problems were largely unknown. Subsequently, early researchers (see Brotemarkle, 1927; Schneidler & Berdie, 1942) documented the frequency and types of problems that college students experienced. Over the years, many studies have been conducted to assess college students' problems and needs (such studies are therefore called needs assessments; see, for example, Blos, 1946; Carney & Barak, 1976; DeSena, 1966; Koile & Bird, 1956; McKinney, 1945; Rust & Davie, 1961). As college populations have changed over time, needs assessments have been used to document changes in students' problems and needs (see Bishop, 1992; Heppner & Neal, 1983); an excellent strategy to address student needs over time has been longitudinal survey designs, such as a 10-year longitudinal study of the career development needs of college students (Helwig, 2004). Another approach has been to examine the needs of specific student groups, such as adult students (Warchal & Southern, 1986), or more recently, racial/ethnic minority groups or international students. For example, it was found that African-American students on predominately white campuses reported greater social isolation and heightened discomfort with faculty and peers (Neville, Heppner, Ji, & Thye, 2004), as well as more race-related stress (Plummer & Slane, 1996).

Such documentation has had both theoretical and practical significance. On a theoretical level, description of the types of problems encountered by college students has facilitated the formulation and testing of student development theory (see, for example, Chickering, 1969); on a practical level, this information has helped the staffs of college counseling centers to design programs and deliver services appropriate to the needs of students. Parenthetically, this line of research has led to a number of studies that have examined not only the typical problems experienced by students, but also the appropriateness of services delivered by counseling centers (as viewed by students, faculty, and counseling center staff), and ultimately larger issues such as the role and functions of university counseling centers (see the review by Heppner & Neal, 1983).

Other examples of survey research include studies examining the level of distress in psychologists (see, for example, Thoreson, Miller, & Krauskopf, 1989), alcoholism among psychologists (see, for example, Thoreson, Budd, & Krauskopf, 1986), job analysis of psychology internships in counseling center settings (Ross & Altmaier, 1990), career development of college women (Harmon, 1981, 1989), and a survey of professional advocacy efforts of 71 leaders in national, regional, and state credentialing associations in counseling (Myers & Sweeney, 2004).

A common strategy when using survey designs is to compare information across two or more groups. For instance, Koplik and DeVito (1986) compared the problems identified by members of the college classes of 1976 and 1986; this is known as a survey cross-sectional design. Other times a researcher might use a survey longitudinal design and compare, say, students' responses when they were freshmen versus their responses when they were sophomores. Several authors have also examined gender differences in, for example, students' perceptions and reporting of problems (see, for example, Koplik & DeVito; Nagelberg, Pillsbury, & Balzor, 1983) and in academic careers (Thoreson, Kardash, Leuthold, & Morrow, 1990). Comparisons have also been made based on race, year in school, educational level, time of year, type of academic program, and type of service requested. The accumulation of this type of research, particularly for a college population, enables counselors to describe with a high degree of confidence both the types of problems encountered on college campuses and their differential distribution across segments of the student population. In addition, the accumulation of these descriptive findings is instrumental in the process of theory building. For instance, one consistent finding in this body of research is the difference between males and females in the number and types of problems recorded. This finding has led to theoretical speculation about gender differences in problem perception.

Survey research is not limited to documenting the existence of problems within a population. In fact, a wide range of other types of behavior or variables can be described using this type of approach. For example, Hill and O'Grady (1985) were interested in counselor intentions, which they described as the "why" of a counseling intervention. They analyzed the responses of 42 experienced therapists and documented the relative frequency of use of 19 theoretically derived intentions. In addition, they examined the differential use rates of the various intentions as a function of the therapist's theoretical orientation. From these descriptive analyses, Hill and O'Grady were able to construct a profile of intention use for experienced counselors and to identify intentions that characterized various theoretical positions.

Perhaps the most frequent problem with survey research is not with survey methods per se, but rather with the lack of knowledge about conducting sound survey research. A common misperception is that survey research is easy to conduct in general, and that the survey items can be quickly generated in a few hours. For example, Fong (1992, p. 194), in an editorial in *Counselor Education and Supervision*, said, ". . . I have become aware of the large number of survey studies being conducted that are so casually designed that they are invalid and unpublishable." She went on to identify two critical problems with many survey studies:

> Too often, I have reviewed manuscripts that report surveys of a sample that is convenient, not representative, or that represents only a subgroup of the intended population under study. Likewise, I regularly find that the survey instrument was not developed by careful selection of relevant variables or was solely developed by the researcher without any pilot or reliability studies. (Fong, 1992, p. 195)

In a follow-up to her editorial, Fong and Malone (1994) reported on the design and data analysis errors found in survey studies submitted to *Counselor Education and Supervision* from July 1991 through June 1992. Among the 27 survey studies submitted to the journal during this time, Fong and Malone described four types of research design errors as follows:

> (a) absence of or unclear research question to guide data collection and analysis; (b) sample errors such as failure to obtain a sample appropriate to the research questions, inadequate sample, or non-representative sample; (c) instruments, frequently author-made, lacking reliability or inappropriate for the variables being studied; and (d) other methodological problems that prohibited generalization of results, for example, data collection procedures. (Fong & Malone, 1994, pp. 357–358)

In addition, these authors identified two types of data analysis errors: "(a) inappropriate method of data analysis (for example, simple tests when data [are] multivariate)" and (b) piecemeal analysis, "which occurs when the study data is divided so the analysis presented in the manuscript is only a piece of the research" (Fong & Malone, 1994, p. 358).

Fong's writings make a clear statement about the problems associated with survey designs (1992; Fong & Malone, 1994). Researchers considering a survey study should pay particular attention to the issues she raised. Although a well-designed survey can add substantially to our knowledge in a particular area, a poorly designed survey is little more than a waste of time for the researchers and the potential participants.

DESIGN ISSUES IN SURVEYS

At least five major activities are included in the conduct of survey research: (1) matching the survey design to the researcher's questions, (2) defining the sample, (3) developing and/or selecting the survey inventories, (4) selecting and developing a data collection method, and (5) analyzing the data. We previously discussed relevant activities related to matching the survey design to the researcher's question in Chapters 3 and 4, and will discuss to some extent deriving the sample in Chapter 14, selecting inventories in Chapter 13, constructing inventories in Chapter 20, and selecting and developing the data collection method in Chapter 13. These chapters should all be consulted for relevant activities in developing a survey study.

In terms of the actual design of a survey study, unlike true or quasi-experimental designs, the researcher does not form the actual groups a priori. Although groups may be formed for comparison's sake (for example, males versus females), the survey is often given to the entire identified sample. Even when the researcher decides ahead of time to compare, for example, males and females, he or she often finds these participants as they occur in the sample population. However, some surveys purposefully sample from two groups—for example, interns versus practicum students, or clinical psychology programs versus counseling psychology programs. Even when this type of purposeful sampling can be done, the researcher cannot assign participants to be in one group or another as can occur in true experimental or quasi-experimental research. Likewise, in survey designs the researcher does not manipulate an independent variable, and so is not concerned with manipulation checks.

In terms of developing and/or selecting inventories for the survey, we want to emphasize the need to carefully consider the psychometric properties of existing inventories (see Chapter 13). Perhaps most important are the procedures for developing new survey items. It is a major misconception that developing new survey items is quick and easy. Readers are encouraged to consult Chapter 20 on scale construction, because many of those myths and procedures apply to survey construction, most notably myths about scale construction, convenience samples, and cultural issues, as well as steps in developing scales or surveys such as writing items, performing content analysis, and piloting items.

Perhaps the most frequent way of collecting data in survey research is through self-report questionnaires, particularly mailed or online questionnaires. The primary advantage of such surveys is the ease of data collection, particularly when the sample covers a wide geographic area (in which case it would be difficult to collect on-site data). One of the biggest potential disadvantages is the difficulty of getting participants to respond and return the completed questionnaires. For example, often the return rate from a first mailing is only 30%, which raises questions about the external validity of the results. Was there some reason why the majority of the participants did not respond? Would their responses be different from those of the 30% who responded? It is doubtful that one could safely generalize from a 30% return rate of a sample to the target population. Because the return rate is such a critical issue in mail surveys, researchers usually try to make it easy both to complete the questionnaire (by keeping it short) and to return it (by including a stamped, addressed return envelope). Two sets of reminder letters or postcards are also usually sent. Typically a follow-up letter is sent about two or three weeks after the initial mailing, and subsequently two or three weeks later as a final follow-up. Researchers commonly report obtaining around a

30% to 40% return rate from an initial mailing, and approximately 20% and 10% returns from the two successive follow-ups. Although some published survey research is based on less than a 40% return rate, some researchers recommend at least a 50% return rate as an "adequate" basis for findings (Baddie, 2001); others recommend at least 80% to 90% (Kerlinger, 1986).

A more recent method of data collection is through an online website. The advantage of such a data collection method is that a broad range of individuals in the target population, from whatever location within the United States or beyond, can complete the questionnaire. Consequently, a researcher can often obtain larger data sets, especially with restricted populations, than through more traditional data collection methods. Conversely, it is difficult to ascertain the representativeness of those participants who complete the survey.

Whatever method the researcher uses to collect data, the final step entails data analysis. A critical starting point for data analysis is checking the adequacy of the sample. This involves checking how closely the sample resembles the general population along a number of important dimensions. For instance, is the proportion of male and female (or racial/ethnic minorities and whites, or young and old) respondents in the sample similar to the proportions in the general population? Another especially important type of check when using mail or online questionnaires is a comparison of respondents and nonrespondents. For example, when using a college population, do respondents and nonrespondents differ in sex, year in school, major, grade point average, or the like? Only after this type of sample adequacy checking has been done should the data be analyzed and interpreted.

Survey research with diverse populations can present some unique challenges. Ponterotto and Casas (1991) discussed three issues that counseling researchers should consider when using a survey design with culturally, linguistically, and/or economically diverse groups. The first issue concerns how to tailor the survey to the particular group under study: Do the respondents understand the questions in the way that the researchers intended? Are any items offensive to people in the group the researcher wants to survey? Do potential respondents understand how to respond to the format? According to Ponterotto and Casas, these questions can be addressed by examining the language and format of potential questions in a pretest conducted on a pilot sample that is representative of the target population. These authors suggest that the survey be pilot-tested on a sample that represents about 5% of the target sample. When the pilot test is administered, the respondents should be interviewed to make sure that the questions asked were meaningful, clear, and appropriate for the purpose of the survey.

The second issue raised by Ponterotto and Casas (1991) involves research with participants who do not speak standard English. In this case, the researcher must translate potential questions into the participants' native language. Unfortunately, this translation process is neither straightforward nor simple (see Chapter 20, as well as Mallinckrodt & Wang, 2004). Briefly, we will highlight two issues here: translation/back translation and decentering. In back translation, a bilingual person first translates the original questions into the new language; once this translation is complete, another bilingual person translates the translated questions back into English. Any discrepancies between the original and the back-translated versions of the questions are identified and corrected. The process of translation and back translation is then repeated until the back-translated version matches the original version. However, it is important to note that even though the words of a question can be correctly translated and back translated, this does not mean that the meaning of the words are the same in both languages. Decentering attempts to address the issue of comparable functional and cultural meaning. In decentering, the researcher attempts to ensure that no specific language is the "center" of attention. This decentering is accomplished by having bilingual judges examine both versions of the survey and compare the functional and cultural equivalence of the questions.

The third issue to be addressed involves the distribution and collection of the survey. As noted by Ponterotto and Casas (1991), some socioeconomic and/or cultural groups may not trust researchers who are connected with the white middle-class establishment. This suggests that obtaining an adequate response rate may be a larger problem with these groups of participants. According to Ponterotto and Casas, it is important to be able to ascertain the reason for a low response rate. These authors recommend that the researcher attempt to interview a random subsample of respondents and nonrespondents. In particular, the researcher should attempt to determine the characteristics that distinguish the respondent and nonrespondent groups.

AN EXAMPLE OF SURVEY RESEARCH

Good, Thoreson, and Shaughnessy (1995) were interested in documenting the incidence of professional impairment for counseling psychologists. Their specific research questions were as follows:

> (a) What is the prevalence of past and current substance use reported by counseling psychologists? (b) Are counseling psychologists aware of colleagues with substance abuse problems? If yes, are they complying with APA ethical principles by taking appropriate action? and (c) What is the psychological functioning (i.e., personal and professional life satisfaction, work-related stress, and psychological distress) of counseling psychologists? (p. 707)

The first two questions called for an examination of the occurrence or frequency of these specified events and were measured with two author-constructed scales. To address the third research question, the authors chose three constructs based on their review of the current literature. The three constructs were measured with validated inventories, including the Satisfaction with Life Scale (Diener, Emmons, Larsen, & Griffen, 1985), the Work Related Strain Inventory (Revicki, May, & Whitley, 1990), and the Brief Symptom Inventory (Derogatis, 1992).

The authors wanted to generalize their results to the population of counseling psychologists. Accordingly, a sample of counseling psychologists was obtained by randomly selecting 1,000 members (500 men and 500 women) of Division 17 (the Society of Counseling Psychology) of the American Psychological Association. These 1,000 potential participants were sent the Division 17 Health Practices Survey via the U.S. Postal Service. In an attempt to increase the response rate to the survey, Good, Thoreson, & Shaughnessy (1995) sent a second copy of the survey to potential participants two weeks after the initial mailing, and then sent a reminder postcard to each potential participant one week after the second mailing.

Of the 405 surveys returned, 12 were incomplete or unusable. This represented a 39% return rate. The final sample, based on returned surveys, was 55% female and 45% male, with an average age of 48.2 years. The sample consisted of predominantly married respondents (71%), with single (14%), divorced (13%), and widows/widowers (3%) making up the rest of the sample. In addition, the sample was predominantly white (94%); the remainder of the sample was black/African American, 2%; Asian/Asian American, 2%; Hispanic/Hispanic American, 1%; and other, 1%.

One particularly strong aspect of Good, Thoreson, and Shaughnessy's (1995) study was their attempt to check the representativeness of their sample. They accomplished this check by comparing selected demographic characteristics of their sample's participants to those same demographic characteristics for members of Division 17 as a whole. For example, there was a similar percentage of degree type in the sample (Ph.D., 82%; Ed.D., 14%; and master's degree, 3%) and in the membership of Division 17 (Ph.D., 78%; Ed.D., 17%; and master's degree, 5%). Good and colleagues concluded that their sample was representative of Division 17 because the demographic characteristics of the sample closely matched those of Division 17.

As to the first research question—What is the prevalence of past and current substance use reported by counseling psychologists?—the authors' results revealed that 19.7% of the sample reported "almost daily/daily" *previous* use of alcohol, and 16.4% of the counseling psychologists surveyed indicated "almost daily/daily" *current* use of alcohol. Usage rates were also reported for cigarettes, marijuana, tranquilizers, hallucinogens, stimulants, opiates, cocaine, and sedatives.

In response to the second research question—Are counseling psychologists aware of colleagues with substance abuse problems?—the researchers found that 40% of the sample knew at least one female psychologist and 62% knew at least one male psychologist who had substance abuse problems in the past. However, only 19% of the respondents reported that they had confronted a colleague about his or her substance problem. The most frequently cited reasons for not confronting the colleague about her or his substance abuse problem were: (1) knew of subtle changes but lacked tangible evidence of negative impact (53%), (2) did not see it as detrimental to their job performance (42%), and (3) thought it would do no good (39%).

To determine the relationship between substance use and psychological functioning (the third research question), the authors initially created an index of substance use by summing the reported levels of use. This substance use composite was correlated with the measures of psychological functioning. Good and colleagues (1995) used a Bonferroni correction to guard against the increased risk of Type I error that results from examining multiple correlations (28 correlation coefficients were obtained in this analysis). The Bonferroni correction was obtained by dividing the study-wide alpha level ($p < .05$) by the number of pairwise correlations (28). This resulted in an adjusted alpha level of $p < .001$. Using the corrected alpha level, none of the correlations between current levels of substance use and the measures of psychological functioning (personal satisfaction, professional satisfaction, work-related strain, and the Global Severity Index of the Brief Symptom Inventory) were significant.

The study by Good, Thoreson, and Shaughnessy (1995) is exemplary in many ways. The authors carefully defined the research questions and used the existing research literature to select measures of the central constructs. The use of their tailor-made questionnaires in conjunction with previously constructed questionnaires having known psychometric characteristics strengthened the design. In addition, the authors examined the internal consistency of the previous and current substance use scale calculated from their author-constructed measure. They were also cognizant of possible problems with statistical conclusion validity. To assure that fishing/error rate problems did not contaminate the relationship between substance use and psychological functioning, they used the Bonferroni method to apply a more stringent alpha level to identify statistically significant correlations. Although it is important to be concerned with alpha inflation, readers should also note that the Bonferroni method is an extremely conservative approach for dealing with this issue; it drastically reduces the power to detect true differences if they do exist. Finally, the authors used multiple measures to assess psychological functioning, thereby increasing the construct validity of putative causes and effects. An additional strength of the study involves the sampling procedure. Although the response rate was relatively low (only 39%), the comparison of the sample's demographic characteristics to those of Division 17 members strengthened the contention that the sample was indeed representative of the target population. Thus, the data from this descriptive study provide new and useful information about substance use among counseling psychologists and the confrontation of impaired colleagues, about both of which we know relatively little. These findings have immediate implications for professional training of counseling professionals.

CLASSIFICATION OR DATA REDUCTION RESEARCH DESIGNS

Often in counseling research it is necessary to reduce or simplify data to only a few variables by developing categories, subgroups, or factors—in general, some sort of classification system. Frequently, a taxonomic system not only simplifies a data set, but also can have important theoretical implications. In chemistry, for example, the periodic table provides a means of classifying elements and also describes underlying dimensions of atomic structure (protons, electrons, and neutrons). The establishment of reliable and valid categorical and dimensional systems likewise can advance the counseling profession.

In fact, all sciences start from commonly accepted bases of description and classification. Two commonly used classification strategies are factor analysis and cluster analysis. Both of these procedures describe data sets by reducing or categorizing the data into simpler underlying structures or subgroups. Specifically, factor and cluster analyses assume that there are a small number of "latent variables" or constructs that account for the relationships among the many variables examined. We will define and discuss these two techniques, provide an overview of the steps involved in using them, and examine illustrations from contemporary counseling research.

Factor Analysis

Factor analysis is a class of multivariate statistical methods whose primary purpose is data reduction and summarization (Hair, Anderson, & Tatham, 1987; Hair & Black, 2000; Fabrigar, Wegener, MacCallum, & Strahan, 1999). This statistical technique is often used in developing and validating assessment inventories. For example, a researcher might carefully develop a 50-item questionnaire to measure beliefs about social justice and social advocacy. Factor analysis could be used to identify how the 50 items could be grouped together in theoretically meaningful categories, with the end product being five distinct factors consisting of 30 items. In essence, factor analysis examines the interrelationships among a large number of items (or variables) and condenses (summarizes) that information into a smaller set of common underlying dimensions or factors. These dimensions or factors presumably correspond to underlying psychological constructs. Thus, the fundamental aim of factor analysis is to search for underlying psychological constructs seen in the common dimensions that underlie the original items or variables (Hair et al., 1987).

There are two major types of factor analysis: exploratory and confirmatory. In exploratory factor analysis, the researcher examines a set of data to determine underlying dimensions, without any a priori specification of the number or content of these constructs. In confirmatory factor analysis, the researcher first identifies (either theoretically or through previous research) the number of dimensions he or she expects to find along with the items in the data set that will correlate with (or "load on") each dimension. In essence, the researcher has an existing model of the factor structure. The researcher then examines how well the model fits the actual relationships observed in a new set of data. The analysis can either confirm (hence the name) or disconfirm the researcher's model.

As an example of exploratory factor analysis, suppose a researcher has observed over a 10-year period that for some adult clients, changing careers is a difficult process. The researcher begins to wonder what distinguishes the people who have difficulty from those who do not. After considerable reflection, more observation, and a review of the professional literature, she develops a 100-item questionnaire that assesses barriers associated with changing careers.

Such an instrument has not existed before because at this time little is known about barriers to changing careers. But answering a 100-item questionnaire is time consuming, and there is a lack of empirical support for putting the items into subgroups or scales; consequently, the researcher can only compute a total score of barriers, or look at individual barrier items. Thus, factor analysis can be a useful statistical tool to condense these 100 items by putting them into factors that group items that correlate with each other. In this way, the researcher can use empirical methods to group items. For example, let's say the researcher would find through exploratory factor analysis that there are three main types of career barriers, reflecting (1) career myths, (2) self-efficacy, and (3) attributional styles. The researcher could then summarize a client's career barriers into these three types and provide scores for each of these factors. For example, a client might score exceptionally high on career myths, which would suggest that interventions are especially needed on this dimension. Moreover, the three factors provide theoretical extensions of the topic of career barriers or of the career planning process in general. In sum, factor analysis analyzes a large number of items (or variables) and condenses or summarizes them into common or underlying dimensions. Parenthetically, interested readers could follow up on this not-so-hypothetical example of career transition barriers by reading Heppner, Multon, and Johnston (1994).

Factor analysis has been used frequently in the counseling literature in scale construction (see Chapter 20). For example, this technique has been used to describe dimensions of vocational interest (Fouad, Cudeck, & Hansen, 1984), supervisory styles (Worthington & Stern, 1985), expectancies about counseling (Tinsley, Workman, & Kass, 1980), perceptions of counselors (Barak & LaCrosse, 1975), religious commitment (Worthington, 2004), and counselor self-efficacy in working with gay, lesbian, and bisexual clients (Dillon & Worthington, 2003). Thus, for instance, in examining client expectations about counseling, Tinsley et al. (1980) found four factors that account for a large portion of the variance in clients' expectations: personal commitment, facilitative conditions, counselor expertise, and nurturance. Likewise, Phillips, Friedlander, Pazienza, and Kost (1985) described three dimensions of decision-making styles: rational, intuitive, and dependent. These examples nicely illustrate how factor analysis can identify dimensions to further understanding of relevant constructs for the counseling profession.

Although factor analysis is frequently used, many readers of the counseling literature may not be aware of the many complexities and decision points in conducting a factor analysis. In fact, factor analysis is a multivariate statistical method that involves a number of decision points for the researcher, which sometimes entails rather complex procedures with specialized vocabulary. Many of these decision points are beyond the scope of this text; a wide variety of more detailed resources are available for further consultation to aid decisions about which variables will serve as the basic data (see, for example, Dawis, 1987; Kline, 2005; Patten, 2001; Pett, Lackey, & Sullivan, 2003; Thompson, 2004). We will, however, provide a brief overview of some of the major decision points.

Typically, the researcher will develop his or her own questionnaire, the items of which constitute the variables. A great deal of time, planning, and reflection are needed to develop quality items (see Chapter 20). For example, first the researcher must decide what type of factor analysis to use in analyzing the data. The choice of factor analysis type involves assumptions about the treatment of item variance; in Chapter 20 we discuss the different options, and follow Kline's (2005) recommendation of utilizing common factor analysis. Second, the researcher must decide how many factors exist in a set of data. Although specific criteria can be used to suggest how many factors may exist (e.g., a scree test), many times deciding on the number of factors involves examination of several different factor solutions to identify the most meaningful factor structure. It is important to understand that this is not a clear-cut process, and two researchers looking at the same data might decide that a different number of factors exist. A third decision point involves the method of rotation. The solution from a factor analysis must be rotated to distribute the variance across the factors; the researcher has a choice of orthogonal or oblique rotations, which typically has important implications for the interpretation of the underlying constructs. After the researcher decides upon a factor solution, the researcher needs to name the factors. To do this, he or she examines all of the items that make up a factor and attempts to choose a name that captures the conceptual meaning inherent in the items. Obviously, this naming process is subjective, and researchers examining the same set of items may propose different names for the same factor. In short, you should also be aware of the subjective nature of the factor naming process when examining the report of a factor analysis.

EXAMPLES OF FACTOR ANALYSIS   Tinsley, Roth, and Lease (1989) used both confirmatory and exploratory factor analysis to examine the dimensions that define group leadership. The main purpose of this study was to attempt to confirm a four-factor model of group leadership originally described by Lieberman, Yalom, and Miles (1973). In a classic study of group leadership, Lieberman and colleagues found that leader, member, and observer ratings of leadership converged on a four-factor structure of leadership. They labeled these factors emotional stimulation, caring, meaning attribution, and executive functioning. The researchers wanted to determine whether group leaders' self-ratings, obtained from a large number of these leaders, would confirm this four-factor structure.

The study used both survey and factor analysis methods. These authors randomly selected 500 members of the Association for Specialists in Group Work and mailed them survey questionnaires. Usable responses were returned by 200 of the 500 identified group leaders. The survey instrument contained 130 items, 5 items measuring each of the 26 leader characteristics studied by Lieberman et al. (1973). Twenty-six scale scores (one score for each of the 26 leader characteristics) were calculated for each participant. These scale scores were used as the data for the factor analysis. Tinsley et al. (1989) first used confirmatory factor analysis to ascertain whether the 26 scales would result in the four factors described by Lieberman et al. They found that only 8 of the 26 scales loaded on (or scored highest on) the factor that they theoretically should have loaded on. Tinsley et al. concluded that their analysis failed to confirm the factor model proposed by Lieberman et al.

Because of this failure to confirm, Tinsley et al. (1989) then used exploratory factor analysis to determine how many and what dimensions accounted for self-rating of leadership. The authors examined 8-, 9-, and 10-factor solutions before adopting an 8-factor solution that they believed best explained the data. Next, Tinsley et al. examined the scales that correlated with each factor and determined a name for the underlying construct that these items represented. For example, the scales managing/limit setting, mirroring command stimulation, cognizing, charismatic leader, and model all loaded on (were a part of) the first factor. Tinsley et al. named the underlying construct "cognitive direction." In a similar manner they examined the scales that loaded on the other factors and derived names for the underlying constructs. The constructs they named were affective direction, nurturant attractiveness, group functioning, verbal stimulation, charismatic expert, individual functioning, and nonverbal exercises.

Tinsley et al. (1989) concluded that the four factors identified by Lieberman et al. (1973) could not adequately account for the self-rating of leadership obtained in their sample. In fact, eight factors were used to account for the obtained self-ratings. Tinsley et al. also concluded that group leadership is more complicated and multifaceted than the Lieberman et al. model would suggest.

The Tinsley et al. (1989) study is an excellent example of the use of factor analysis. It is exemplary because the researchers explicitly delineated for readers the basis for their choice of the number of factors and for naming the factors. In this way, readers are invited to make their own judgments about the critical choices made by the researchers.

Exploratory factor analysis was also used to identify underlying dimensions of a new inventory, an Ethnocultural Empathy Scale. Wang et al. (2003) noted that as the United States is increasing in racial/ethnic diversity, there are also "reoccurring conflicts among racial and ethnic groups, from the Rodney King beating to hate crimes that resulted from the tragedies of September 11, 2001" (p. 221). They suggested that more than tolerance is needed, specifically "more understanding, awareness, and acceptance of individuals from different racial and ethnic backgrounds" (p. 221). The main purpose of the authors of this study (who were six graduate students in counseling psychology at the time) was to develop a measure of cultural empathy. To generate scale items they first conducted a comprehensive literature search on empathy and ethnocultural theory; from this literature, they delineated three domains of empathy: intellectual empathy, empathetic emotions, and communicative empathy. After operationalizing these constructs, they then generated 71 items, with each item needing to have a primary focus on one of the three domains of empathy. The authors then had three judges match each item to one of the three categories; this process led to the authors deleting nine items and revising six others. It is important to note that the authors spent a great deal of time not only generating items, but also obtaining some face validity for the items from independent judges.

Data were obtained from 323 undergraduate students, who completed not only the Scale of Ethnocultural Empathy (SEE), but also a demographic form and a measure of social desirability. For the exploratory factor analysis, they made the following decisions: (1) They began with a principle-components analysis. (2) Based on a scree test and eigenvalues above 1.0, they selected a four-factor solution with oblique rotation; the four-factor solution was chosen because it yielded strong psychometric properties as well as being conceptually meaningful. (3) The four factors were named empathetic feeling and expression, empathetic perspective taking, acceptance of cultural differences, and empathetic awareness. The authors also found that the SEE total and four factors were not strongly associated with social desirability, which provided an important estimate of discriminate validity.

The authors conducted a second study to examine the stability of the SEE factor structure, as well as to examine other validity estimates of the SEE. In this study, Wang et al. (2003) used data from an additional 364 undergraduate students and conducted a confirmatory factor analysis (CFA). The results of the CFA provided empirical support for the initial four-factor model, but also found support for a second-order hierarchical model, which suggested not only evidence for the four distinct factors, but also a general ethnocultural empathy factor as reflected in the total SEE score. Moreover, the results of this study also provided estimates of concurrent validity with other empathy scales, which is a very useful research strategy in the initial phases of scale construction. Finally, a third study was conducted with another 51 undergraduate students who completed the SEE on two administrations two weeks apart; the results indicated that the SEE has acceptable test-retest reliability (rs = 0.64–0.86).

In sum, Wang et al. (2003) conducted an excellent study to develop a new scale. It provides a very good example of using exploratory factor analysis to first identify four underlying dimensions for a new scale on ethnocultural empathy, and then to use confirmatory factor analysis to test the stability of that four-factor model in another sample.

CLUSTER ANALYSIS

Often in counseling we would like to be able to identify natural groupings or subtypes of people, such as clients or counselors. Cluster analysis is frequently used to put people into subgroups, which is quite functional for examining individual differences in counseling research. For example, students who are undecided about their choice of career might be undecided for very different reasons. Some students might lack the necessary career information whereas others may experience a great deal of anxiety in making career decisions. Indeed, when researchers have utilized cluster analysis to address this issue, they have found that there are multiple subtypes of career indecision at both the high school (Larson & Majors, 1998; Multon, Heppner, & Lapan, 1995) and college levels (Chartrand et al., 1994; Kelly & Pulver, 2003; Larson,

Heppner, Ham, & Dugan, 1988; Lucas & Epperson, 1990). Brown and Krane (2000) analyzed these cluster analytic studies and concluded that at least three types of individuals have been identified consistently on career indecision subtypes:

> (1) those who seem just to need additional occupation information and help with occupational exploration, (2) those whose career-choice problems are primarily anxiety-related, and (3) those who are more severely impaired clients who present with a constellation of problems revolving around anxiety, poor vocational identity development, high perceived needs for occupational information, and low feelings of efficacy around their abilities to solve problems and make career decisions. (p. 757)

A recent cluster analytic study utilizing 278 actual career clients found support for Brown and Krane's (2000) observation of these three clusters (Multon, Wood, Heppner, & Gysbers, in press). In addition, the researchers also found a cluster of psychologically healthy adults who did not seem to be experiencing many career problems, but were perhaps the type of proactive individuals who availed themselves of resources to affirm choices they had already made. In terms of practice, the results of these cluster analytic studies suggest that it may be very useful to design different career planning interventions to address the specific needs of these distinctly different subgroups of clients.

In essence, cluster analysis is a multivariate statistical method that reduces data by identifying and then classifying similar entities into subgroups (Hair et al., 1987; Hair & Black, 2000). Borgen and Barnett (1987) noted three primary purposes for cluster analysis: exploration (to find a certain structure or set of groupings), confirmation (to test an existing classification, perhaps based on theory), and simplification (to reduce a complex data set into a simpler structure). Cluster analysis can be used to categorize objects (e.g., counselor statements), people (e.g., counseling center clients), or variables (e.g., items on a test) (Borgen & Barnett). In terms of identifying types of people, Megargee and Bohn (1979) used cluster analysis to develop a typology of criminal offenders based on Minnesota Multiphasic Personality Inventory (MMPI) profiles, whereas Rojewski (1994) used the Career Decision Scale (Osipow, Carney, Winer, Yanico, & Koschier, 1976) to identify three types of career-indecisive adolescents. Hill and O'Grady (1985) used cluster analysis of variables to develop a classification of counselor intentions. Their 19 therapist intentions were collapsed into four categories: assessment, therapeutic work, nonspecific factors, and problems. Using a similar analysis, Hill, Helms, Spiegel, and Tichenor (1988) found five clusters of client reactions. As an example of clustering other objects, Wampold and White (1985) used cluster analysis to analyze research themes in counseling psychology. Examining common citations among 27 articles published during 1982, they concluded that the social influence model was a common underlying theme in the 27 articles. In essence, cluster analysis classifies objects, variables, or persons so that each object is very similar to others in its cluster. Thus, within each cluster, the objects are homogeneous; however, there is considerable heterogeneity among clusters (Hair et al., 1987; Hair & Black, 2000).

PERFORMING A CLUSTER ANALYSIS   As with factor analysis, many of the processes involved in cluster analysis are beyond the scope of this text. Interested readers should consult the following references for more details: Aldenderfer and Blashfield, 1984; Blashfield, 1984; Borgen and Barnett, 1987; Borgen and Weiss, 1971; Hair et al., 1987; Hair and Black, 2000; and Lorr, 1983. Perhaps one of the most critical decisions is to select the appropriate instruments. This decision assumes added importance in cluster analysis because the instruments are the tools for measuring the similarity between objects. Objects can be determined to be similar only in the ways in which they are measured. To use the flashlight analogy again, a flashlight will provide light only in the direction in which it is pointed. After data are collected, the researcher proceeds to the statistical procedures involved in cluster analysis.

Two other major decision points in cluster analysis are similar to those involved in factor analysis. The cluster analysis procedure produces a number of possible cluster solutions. The researcher must decide on the best solution for the data set. Fewer guidelines are available in cluster analysis than in factor analysis for making this decision, so the number of clusters retained is a subjective decision. Once this decision has been made, the researcher makes decisions to name the clusters. To do this, he or she examines the items or individuals that make up a cluster and identifies an underlying commonality or construct. Obviously, this naming process is subjective, and disagreement about the meaning or interpretation of the cluster can occur. In sum, cluster analysis can be a very powerful data reduction technique. Different measures and categorizing techniques often result in different clusters, and thus the researcher must often be cautious and tentative.

THREE EXAMPLES OF CLUSTER ANALYSIS   Elliott (1985) provides an example of a study using cluster analysis to categorize objects, specifically a taxonomy of helpful and nonhelpful events in brief counseling. Such a system could help researchers describe the counseling process with greater consistency as well as facilitate training. First, clients were asked to describe the most helpful and least helpful events in a counseling session. Twenty-four student clients identified 86 helpful and 70 nonhelpful counselor responses. Next, 34 judges sorted the descriptions of events into categories. The judges were instructed to create 3 to 12 categories for classifying these descriptions. Similarity was calculated by tabulating the number of judges who put each pair of events into the same category. Finally, these sorts were combined and cluster-analyzed. Elliott used two clustering methods (average linkage and maximum linkage) to cluster the data. These methods yielded high levels of agreement. The analysis identified eight kinds of helpful events, which were grouped into two higher-order super clusters. One super cluster, the task super cluster, contained four categories: problem perspective, problem solution, problem clarification, and focusing awareness. The other super cluster, the interpersonal super cluster, contained another four clusters: understanding, client involvement, reassurance, and personal contact. The six clusters of nonhelpful events were misperception, negative counselor reaction, unwanted responsibility, repetition, misdirection, and unwanted thoughts.

This study is a good example of using two methods of cluster analysis (average and maximum linkage) to examine the stability of the derived clusters. Elliott (1985) also validated the derived clusters by examining their relationship to counselor response modes. For example, Elliott found that paraphrases were usually followed by focusing awareness but not by unwanted thoughts. Moreover, he found that particular sets of following responses were nicely described by the derived categories. The major weakness of Elliott's study involves the sampling procedure; because he used undergraduates recruited from a psychology class in the research, it is unclear whether their responses are generalizable to a client population. This study could have been strengthened by replicating the cluster structure with actual clients. Despite this weakness in sample selection, Elliott's study is a good example of a carefully designed cluster analysis study.

The second example of cluster analysis involves the categorization of people, specifically counseling center clients. Heppner, Kivlighan, et al. (1994) were interested in using presenting problems to describe the types of clients seeking help at a university counseling center. As these authors noted, counseling researchers have traditionally been interested in describing the types of problems that confront college students. Such research, however, has generally tabulated only the frequency of occurrence for various types of problems. Heppner, Kivlighan, et al. wanted to move beyond the general description of presenting problems to developing an empirically derived classification system of college students' presenting problems at a university counseling center. Because clients present with multiple problems, simple frequency counts do not adequately describe their concerns. Heppner, Kivlighan, and colleagues therefore derived eight problem categories from a computerized assessment program (CASPER; see McCullough & Farrell, 1983): (1) global distress rating, (2) chemical problems, (3) suicide problems, (4) thought problems, (5) physical problems, (6) interpersonal problems, (7) mood problems, and (8) leisure activities. These eight problem categories were used as the clustering variables (using Ward's method of cluster analysis) to analyze the data.

Based on this information, the authors chose to evaluate a 12-cluster solution. It is important to note that the clients within a cluster had similar profiles on the CASPER dimensions examined. However, three clusters were dropped because they contained fewer than eight clients, leaving a nine-cluster solution. Heppner, Kivlighan, et al. (1994) examined the mean problems ratings when naming the clusters. For example, the clients in Cluster 6 reported the highest number of days experiencing physical problems, while the other seven problem categories were all in the low to moderate reporting range. Because these clients were almost exclusively reporting physical concerns, the authors named this cluster of clients severe somatic concerns. The names for the other eight client clusters were (1) severe general distress, (2) high general distress, (3) interpersonal concerns, moderate distress, (4) interpersonal concerns, low distress, (5) moderate physical, mood, interpersonal concerns, (6) moderate somatic concerns, (7) chemical concerns, moderate distress, and (8) situational adjustment, unassessed concerns.

The stability of the identified cluster solution was assessed by randomly dividing the sample into two groups and rerunning the cluster analysis. The nine-cluster solution was replicated in the two subsamples. To validate the cluster solution, the authors used demographic variables that were external to the clustering process; specifically, they examined how the clusters of clients differed in terms of client (1) age, (2) gender, (3) race, (4) use of medication, (5) relatives with alcohol problems, and (6) relatives with mental illness. For example, the clients in the severe somatic concerns cluster had greater medication use than did the clients in the other clusters.

The Heppner, Kivlighan, et al. (1994) study provides a good example of clustering people for several reasons. First, they used a reliable and valid problem identification system to obtain the clustering variables. Both the participants-to-variable ratio and the participants-to-cluster ratio were large, suggesting that the obtained clusters were less of a function of chance findings. Heppner, Kivlighan, et al. replicated the cluster solution through a split sample procedure. Finally, the authors used a relatively large number of variables not used in the clustering procedure to validate the cluster solution. In terms of limitations of this study, the CASPER problem list may not have represented the scope of problems encountered at a university counseling center. For example, career and academic concerns were not represented among the problems assessed in CASPER. Second, several researchers have attempted to validate their cluster solutions by analyzing their data with a different clustering method. The authors could have further examined the stability of their cluster solution by using an alternate clustering method (e.g., average link clustering).

A third example of a cluster analysis focuses on clustering different subtypes of perfectionists. The construct of perfectionism has received considerable attention in the literature in part due to the Almost Perfect Scale (APS; see Slaney, Rice, Mobley, Trippi, & Ashby, 2001). Grzegorek, Slaney, Franze, and Rice (2004) sought to replicate a previous cluster analytic study that found three clusters: adaptive, maladaptive, and nonperfectionistic. In addition, the authors sought to further examine the relationships between the clusters and other constructs that were predicted based on the conceptualization of perfectionism.

The participants were 273 undergraduate students who completed not only the revised APS, but also measures of self-esteem, depression, and GPA. The authors first used a hierarchical cluster analysis using Ward's linkage method, and found results similar to the previously identified three-cluster solution: adaptive, maladaptive, and nonperfectionistic. In addition, Grzegorek et al. (2004) found similar percentages of participants who fell into each category. The authors then performed a nonhierarchical cluster analysis, which further supported the three-cluster solution. Moreover, the results also indicated, as expected, that maladaptive perfectionists had higher scores on self-criticism, and conversely adaptive perfectionists reported higher self-esteem.

The Grzegorek et al. (2004) study is a good example of using two methods of cluster analysis to test the stability of the results across different cluster analysis methods. Moreover, the study also illustrates the utility of testing conceptually driven hypotheses based on the conceptualization of the clusters, which also provide estimates of construct validity for the perfectionism scale. Generalizations to actual clients, however, are difficult given the nonclinical, undergraduate sample.

EX POST FACTO DESIGNS

Many independent variables of interest to counseling researchers cannot be manipulated. For instance, gender, personality type, treatment success (versus failure), and race are important and interesting variables, but they cannot be manipulated. Designs that use these types of variables are called ex post facto designs. The name literally means "after the fact." In other words, the investigation or research takes place after the groups or conditions have been formed.

In many ways, ex post facto designs resemble the posttest-only quasi-experimental design described in Chapter 8. The experimenter selects an appropriate independent variable (male versus female) and then observes differences in a dependent variable (counseling skills). For instance, do male and female therapists differ in client-perceived empathy? Ex post facto designs often have multiple variables or use factorial designs; for instance, an investigator can simultaneously examine the effect of both counselor race and gender on client-perceived empathy. These more complex designs, however, share the same strengths and limitations as the simpler two-level designs.

Like quasi-experimental designs, ex post facto designs present a number of problems in interpreting results. One of these problems is the role of chance in the findings. Especially if the researcher examines a large number of variables, it is likely that he or she will find some significant results by chance. For instance, a researcher who seeks to distinguish between continuing clients and those clients who do not continue in therapy may give a number of instruments (50 variables in all) to clients as they come to an agency, and then subsequently compare the continuers and noncontinuers on these 50 variables. Suppose the researcher finds differences between continuing and noncontinuing clients on five variables: How important are these findings? Are they a reflection of real differences or chance? Probability theory would suggest that *if* there were in reality no differences between the continuers and noncontinuers, and *if* the alpha level was set at $p < .05$, it would be expected by chance alone that 2.5 of the 50 correlations would be statistically significant. Thus, the researcher knowing these probabilities is in a difficult position to identify which of the five statistically significant differences are real or chance differences. In short, ex post facto designs that examine many variables can capitalize on chance, and the researcher may be misled into erroneous conclusions based on chance findings.

AN EXAMPLE OF AN EX POST FACTO DESIGN

Gade, Fuqua, and Hurlburt (1988) were interested in the relationship between Holland personality type and satisfaction with the educational setting in high schools that represented three different models of education (residential schools, provincially controlled schools that were predominantly Native American, and tribally controlled schools). Students were classified (not assigned) as a particular Holland type on the Self- Directed Search (Holland, 1985b). Satisfaction with the educational environment was measured by the Teacher Approval and Educational Acceptance scales of the Survey of Study Habits and Attitudes (Brown & Holtzman, 1967).

Two 6 (Holland code) × 2 (gender) analyses of variance (ANOVAs) were used to examine differences in teacher approval and educational acceptance. Gade et al. (1988) found significant main effects for Holland code on teacher approval and educational acceptance, and for gender on educational acceptance. There was no Holland code by gender interactions for either satisfaction variable. In terms of specific Holland codes, investigative and social students had higher school satisfaction than realistic students.

This study is a good example of ex post facto research. The hypotheses were theoretically derived, and tested presumably after the relationship between the variables had already happened. Specifically, the researchers hypothesized (based on Holland's notion of congruence) that there would be a specific difference in school satisfaction for different Holland types, and then tested this hypothesis "after the fact." A strength of the study was the selection of students from different types of schools. Because of sample heterogeneity, it is unlikely that the obtained results were caused by some characteristic of students in one particular sample.

This study also illustrates some of the weaknesses of ex post facto research. The examination of gender differences in school satisfaction was not based on theory. The authors never offered a theoretical explanation for why males and females might differ in school satisfaction, or why this was an important variable to address. Also, there was no theoretical discussion of possible Holland code by gender interactions. In keeping with this lack of theoretical discussion of gender differences, the authors noted only in passing the significant gender difference found on the Educational Acceptance scale.

CORRELATIONAL RESEARCH DESIGNS

What is the relationship between job congruence and satisfaction with one's job (see, for example, Gottfredson & Holland, 1990)? What is the relationship between a person's self-efficacy expectations and his or her choice of career options (see Betz & Hackett, 1981, 1987; Lapan, Boggs, & Morrill, 1989)? These are questions that can be addressed by correlational designs.

Correlational designs are used to examine the relationships between two or more variables. A simple correlational design examines the relationship between two variables (for instance, depression and social skills), and then uses a statistical analysis (typically a Pearson product moment correlation) to describe their relationship. The correlation coefficient, or r, provides an index of the degree of linear relationship between the variables. Suppose that as one variable (x) increases, so do the scores on the second variable (y); then x and y vary together, or covary, and have a "strong positive relationship." If x scores do not vary with y scores, we typically say there is not a relationship between x and y. The correlation coefficient between two scores can range from +1.00 (a very strong positive relationship) to −1.00 (a very strong negative relationship). The amount of variance that is shared between two variables is the square of the correlation. Thus, the correlation between x and y might be +.5, which means that the amount of variance shared between these two variables is 25% ($.5^2$). Sometimes in the past (see Cook & Campbell, 1979) these designs were also referred to as passive because the researcher neither actively forms groups or conditions through random or nonrandom assignment, nor actively manipulates an independent variable.

For example, Hoffman and Weiss (1987) were interested in the relationship between individual psychological separation from parents and healthy adjustment. They developed an inventory of common problems to reflect healthy adjustment, and correlated this measure with scores from another inventory that measured four aspects of psychological separation. Two hundred sixty-seven white college students completed the two self-report inventories. Hoffman and Weiss found that students with greater conflictual dependence with their mothers or fathers reported more problems ($r = .43$ and .42, respectively). Because the results are correlational, however, the direction of the relationship between conflictual dependence and reported problems cannot be determined; that is, conflictual dependence may cause more emotional problems, or having more problems may lead to greater conflictual dependence on parents. Or it is also possible that a third variable may cause both conflictual dependence and emotional problems. In short, the correlational design Hoffman and Weiss used allowed them to describe the degree of relationship between two variables—individual psychological separation and psychological adjustment.

Studies employing a correlational design have been used to describe relationships among a wide variety of variables of interest to counseling researchers. A study by Nocita and Stiles (1986) is a particularly noteworthy example of the use of a simple correlational design. These authors wanted to assess the relationship between a client's level of introversion and his or her perception of counseling sessions. The client's level of introversion was assessed by the Social Introversion scale of the MMPI. At the conclusion of each counseling session, clients also filled out a Session Evaluation Questionnaire (Stiles, 1980), which assessed the client's perception of session depth and smoothness and his or her feelings of positivity and arousal. Nocita and Stiles correlated the client's social introversion score with each of his or her scores on the four Session Evaluation Questionnaire scales. Introverted clients saw the counseling session as less smooth and felt less positive after the session than the more extraverted clients. The noteworthy and unusual aspect of this study is that the correlational results were replicated with two different client samples. As with all correlational designs, however, this type of analysis does not allow for causal explanation. This type of replication provides useful information and suggests that the results may generalize to other client samples.

We also want to mention a more sophisticated development in the use of correlational designs. Cole, Lazarick, and Howard (1987) maintained that most of the correlational (as well as the experimental) research in counseling has underestimated the relationships among the variables examined because researchers tend to examine only manifest variables—that is, derived scores, usually from an inventory, that are presumed to reflect a person's standing on a construct or latent variable. However, because manifest variables (for example, the score on the Beck Depression Inventory) contain measurement error, the relationship between two manifest variables is a function of their relationship and the reliability of the measures. Cole et al. described a better method for determining the relationship between the constructs that the manifest variables are presumed to measure.

Cole et al. (1987) proposed that the constructs of interest must be assessed by multiple methods, and that confirmatory factor analysis be used to examine the relationship between the constructs, or latent variables. For example, Cole et al. were interested in assessing the relationship between depression and social skills. A simple correlational design would examine the correlation between scores from one depression inventory and one social skills inventory. The authors, however, assessed each of the constructs from four perspectives: self-report (e.g., Beck Depression Inventory and Survey of Heterosexual Interactions), as well as behavioral ratings, interviews, and ratings from significant others. Cole et al. found an average cross-trait correlation of –.25 across the four measures of depression and social skills. When confirmatory factor analysis was used to estimate the relationship between the constructs of depression and social skills, a –.85 correlation was found. Rather than accounting for only 6% of the variance in depression using a Pearson product moment correlation ($-.25^2$), social skills accounted for approximately 72% ($-.85^2$) of this variance using confirmatory factor analysis.

In short, Cole et al. (1987) suggested an important methodological issue with the use of latent as opposed to manifest variables in the analysis of correlational designs. Suffice it to say that although simple correlational designs provide useful information, more sophisticated analyses that use latent variables may likely provide better estimates of the correlational relationships. But again, note that this type of analysis does not allow for causal explanation. Although simple correlational designs have been used throughout the history of counseling research, they have not been used as frequently since the mid-1980s.

MULTIPLE REGRESSION

Whereas a correlation identifies the relationship between two variables, most often researchers are interested in describing the relationships among more than two variables. For example, one might ask: If we know the correlation between x and y, would it not be more powerful to include variables a, b, and c (along with x) to study y? Indeed, in many cases it is, and thus multiple regression has become increasingly popular in the counseling literature. We will briefly focus on multiple regression here as a way of increasing our ability to describe the relationships among multiple variables. (For more details, see Cohen & Cohen, 1983; Hair et al., 1987; Hair & Black, 2000; Pedhazur, 1982; and Wampold & Freund, 1987.)

Multiple regression is a statistical method for studying the separate and collective contributions of one or more predictor variables to the variation of a dependent variable (Wampold & Freund, 1987). In essence, multiple regression can be used to describe how multiple predictor variables are related to a single "dependent" (criterion) variable. Thus, researchers frequently refer to predicting the criterion variable and discuss the extent to which they can accurately predict the criterion. The relationship between a "dependent" variable and a set of multiple "independent" variables is expressed as the multiple correlation coefficient R, which is a measure of how well the predictor scores correspond to the actual scores of dependent variables. The square of the multiple correlation coefficient (R^2) is the proportion of variance in the dependent variable explained by the independent variables. The word *explained* here does not necessarily imply a causal relationship, but rather an association of the dependent variable with variability in the predictor variables (Wampold & Freund).

There are three basic methods for entering predictor variables in regression equations: simultaneous, stepwise, and hierarchical regression. Because each method serves slightly different purposes and outcomes, it is important for the researcher to be familiar with the strengths and weaknesses of each method (see Wampold & Freund, 1987, for an overview). In *simultaneous regression,* all of the predictor variables are entered concurrently (simultaneously) into the regression equation. Simultaneous regression is most often used when there is no basis for entering any particular predictor variable before any other predictor variable, and the researcher wants to determine the amount of variance each predictor variable *uniquely* contributes to the prediction of the criterion variable (after the common varience among the predictor variables has been removed). For instance, Parham and Helms (1985b) examined the relationship between African-American racial identity attitudes and self-esteem. Four racial identity attitudes were simultaneously entered in a regression equation to predict self-esteem; the authors found a multiple R of .36 for the analysis. Thus, racial identity accounted for about 13% of the variance ($.36^2$) in the African-American participant's self-esteem. Examination of the specific racial identity attitudes revealed that African-American students in the pre-encounter stage of racial identity formation had lower self-esteem than students in the immersion stage of identity formation.

Asner-Self and Marotta (2005) also used simultaneous regressions to examine the predictors of psychological distress in 68 Central American immigrants who had been exposed to war-related trauma. The authors noted that one of the fastest growing immigrant groups in the United States was people from wartorn Central America. (Marotto & Garcia, 2003). The authors were particularly interested in examining whether developmental indices related to mistrust, identity confusion, and isolation would predict symptoms such as depression, anxiety, and posttraumatic stress (PTS). Although a randomized sampling procedure is preferable, it is difficult to recruit people from this and other immigrant groups for a number of reasons, such as difficulties involving legal status and a host of cross-cultural fears. Therefore, volunteers were recruited via flyers and snowball sampling (Asner-Self & Marotta). The authors used the three developmental indices (mistrust, identity confusion, and isolation) in three simultaneous regressions to determine which if any developmental indices would predict each of the indices of psychological distress (de-pression, anxiety, and PTS).

The results revealed that the three developmental indices predicted 32–51% of the variance in the three distress variables. However, the three predictors were not all equally effective in predicting distress. Although both mistrust and identity confusion were associated with participants' depressive symptoms, only identity confusion was a significant (unique) predictor of anxiety and PTS. Thus, the authors concluded "the more these Central Americans' sense of identity was in flux, the more likely they were to feel depressed and anxious or to report symptoms related to PTS" (p. 165). This study illustrates how simultaneous regressions can identify which variable (in this case the three developmental indices) contributes the most unique variance in predicting three separate criterion variables. This study also nicely illustrates the need for counselors to be cognizant not only of identity confusion for immigrant groups such as those examined in this study, but also the need to engage in culturally sensitive interventions (Asner-Self & Marotta, 2005).

In *stepwise regression,* the regression model first enters the predictor variable with the highest correlation with the criterion variable. The next variable that is entered is the one that results in the largest increase in R^2. This procedure is repeated until adding variables does not result in a statistically significant increase in R^2. Thus, a stepwise procedure identifies which variables contribute the most variance in the equation, and in what order. Cohen and Cohen (1983) recommended that stepwise regression be used only when the research goal is to understand the total explanatory power of many variables.

Kivlighan and Shapiro (1987) used a stepwise regression to predict who would benefit from a self-help career counseling program. This type of prediction was important because previous studies had shown that self-help and counselor-directed career interventions had equivalent effects (Krivatsky & Magoon, 1976). Scores for the six Holland types (realistic, investigative, artistic, social, enterprising, and conventional) were used as predictor variables. The criterion variable was change in vocational identity (Holland, Daiger, & Power, 1980). The conventional and investigative scores entered the stepwise regression as statistically significant predictors.

Participant scores on the two variables accounted for 25% (adjusted R^2) of the variance in outcome. Adjusted R^2, sometimes referred to as the adjustment for shrinkage, is calculated in relation to the study's sample size; it is an estimate of what the R^2 would be if the study were replicated with several different samples. Kivlighan and Shapiro's (1987) study is also noteworthy because they used an analysis of covariance to remove the variance in the dependent variable attributable to pretest scores. The pretreatment vocational identity scores were regressed on the posttreatment vocational identity scores.

The residuals (the variance in the posttreatment scores that could not be accounted for by the pretreatment scores) from this regression were used as the dependent variable in the stepwise regression. In this manner, the researchers were able to examine how much the Holland scores could accurately predict *change* in vocational identity from a pretest period to a posttest period.

In *hierarchical regression,* the researcher specifies the order of entry of the predictor variables based on some rationale (for example, research relevance, causal priority, or theoretical grounds). Lent, Brown, and Lankin (1987) were interested in examining the relationships among self-efficacy, interest congruence, consequential thinking, and various career and academic behaviors. One behavior of interest was academic grade point average. In the first step of the regression analysis, a measure of composite ability (high school rank, Preliminary Scholastic Aptitude Test) was entered first to control for the effects of previous academic performance. Next, the three theoretically derived variables (self-efficacy, interest congruence, and consequential thinking) were entered in a sequential manner. In predicting career indecision, the multiple R for composite ability was .34. When interest congruence was added, the multiple R increased to .44 ($F = 9.62$, $p < .01$). This result indicated that interest congruence added additional predictive variance beyond that accounted for by composite ability. By using a hierarchical model in which composite ability was entered first, Lent and colleagues were able to perform a more stringent test of the relationship between interest congruence and career indecision.

In evaluating the usefulness of multiple regression, it is always important to remember that the results of these types of analyses are based on correlational data. Multiple regression designs use terminology from experimental designs (*dependent variable* and *independent variables*); we prefer the terms *criterion* and *predictor*. Moreover, even though the variables may be referred to as independent and dependent variables, it is important to note that the results obtained are relational, not causal. Likewise, it is important to note that the choice of a criterion variable and of predictor variables is always arbitrary. In other words, prediction is not causality, and thus causal statements are not appropriate with these designs. Multiple regression is suited to describing and predicting the relationship between two or more variables, and is especially useful in examining the incremental as well as total explanatory power of many variables (Hair et al., 1987). Perhaps the main caveats for researchers pertain to inadequate sample sizes (see Wampold & Freund, 1987) and spurious results due to methodological procedures.

TESTING FOR MODERATION AND MEDIATION   As we indicated earlier in this chapter, it is useful to understand when one variable is correlated with a second variable, such as knowing that the client's rating of the working alliance is related to counseling outcomes. However, many times there are more complex relationships among variables that are important for counselors to understand. These more complex relationships not only enhance counselors' understanding, but also advance counseling research and theory. Examining moderating and mediating effects among variables are two common research strategies for understanding more complex relationships among variables (Frazier, Tix, & Barron, 2004).

Mediation and moderation are often confused by psychological researchers, and it is important to distinguish between them (see Baron & Kenny, 1986; Frazier et al., 2004). We will first discuss moderator variables, and then later discuss mediator variables.

"Questions involving moderators address 'when' or 'for whom' a variable most strongly predicts or causes an outcome variable" (Frazier et al., 2004, p. 116). In essence, a moderator is a variable that affects the direction and/or strength of the relationship between a predictor (independent variable) and a criterion (dependent variable) (Baron & Kenny, 1986). In other words, a moderator changes the relationship between the predictor and criterion variables, and in essence is an interaction between the predictor and moderator variables to predict the criterion. Thus a moderator is "nothing more than an interaction" (Frazier et al., p. 116).

A classic example of a moderator relationship is the stress buffering hypothesis that has been prominent in social support research. According to this model, social support is predicted to moderate the relationship between negative life events (e.g., death of a spouse) and depression. In this example, negative life events is the predictor variable, social support is the moderator, and depression is the criterion variable. Negative life events are theoretically related to depression. However, social support changes this relationship. For people with low levels of social support, the more negative life events a person experiences, the higher her or his levels of depression. However, with higher levels of social support, the relationship between negative life events and depression is altered; when a person has more social support, negative life events do not necessarily result in higher levels of depression. Thus, there is an interaction between negative life events and social support in predicting levels of depression. This example nicely illustrates "for whom" negative life events are associated with higher levels of depression (those with low levels of social support).

Moderators can be either categorical (e.g., sex) or continuous (e.g., amount of social support). The appropriate statistical analysis for testing for moderating effects depends on the categorical or continuous nature of both the moderator variable and the predictor variable. For a more in-depth discussion of the statistical issues involved in testing for moderation effects, see Baron and Kenny (1986) and Frazier et al. (2004).

As an example of these analytic procedures, we describe the statistical approach used when both the predictor and moderator variables are continuous. When both variables are continuous, the potential moderator effect is tested in a hierarchical regression. In the first step of the regression, both the predictor and moderator variables are entered into the regression equation predicting the criterion variable. This first step produces an R^2 representing the amount of variance in the criterion variable that is explained by the predictor and moderator variables in combination. In the second step of the regression, the multiplicative product or interaction (predictor × moderator) is entered into the regression equation. After this second step, a new R^2 is obtained; it represents the amount of variance in the criterion variable that is explained by the combination of the predictor variable, the moderator variable, and their interaction. The difference between the R^2 obtained in the first step of the regression and the R^2 obtained in the second step is the amount of variance in the criterion variable that is predicted by the interaction of the moderator. If the difference between the R^2 values from the first and second steps of the regression is significant, then there is a moderation effect. For more statistical and design details, see Frazier et al. (2004).

Previous research has indicated a relationship between perceived ethnic discrimination and psychological distress (Thompson & Neville, 1999). However, Lee (2005) wanted to know which individuals were least affected by perceived ethnic discrimination (i.e., for whom). Specifically, Lee noted that "racial and ethnic minorities in the United States demonstrate a remarkable ability to sustain well being, adapt to situations, and succeed in life despite persistent discrimination in society" (p. 36). He was particularly interested in examining ways in which two cultural resources (ethnic identity and other-group orientation) might differentially moderate or protect against discrimination in predicting psychological adjustment (specifically depression, social connectedness, and self-esteem). Thus, Lee used three separate hierarchical regression analyses for testing the moderation effect on the three criterion adjustment indices. The predictor variable was discrimination. The moderators were the two cultural resources (ethnic identity and other-group orientation), and psychological adjustment (depression, social connectedness, and self-esteem) was the criterion. Lee first entered ethnic identity, other-group orientation, and discrimination; then as a second step he entered the interactions between ethnic identity × discrimination as well as the other-group orientation × discrimination to determine whether there was a moderation effect above and beyond the first step. The results suggested that only one aspect of ethnic identity (specifically ethnic pride) moderated the effects of discrimination on depression and social connectedness, but not on self-esteem. Lee found that Korean Americans with high ethnic pride reported fewer depressive symptoms and high social connectedness when perceived discrimination was low. When the perceived discrimination was high, however, the depressive symptoms increased and social connectedness decreased. Thus, as perceived discrimination increases, the buffering effects of ethnic pride diminish (Lee).

This study nicely illustrates how the interaction between two variables (in this case cultural resources and discrimination) can be examined to predict criterion variables (in this case, psychological adjustment indices). Moreover, the results illustrate the importance of examining not only first-order individual relationships between the predictors (i.e., cultural resources, discrimination) and the criterion variables, but also the interaction among the predictors. Finally, the study also illustrates the utility of using more complex regression analyses to identify the specific mechanisms that moderate the negative effects of perceived discrimination, which has direct implications for remedial and preventive interventions with Korean Americans.

FIGURE 10.1
A MEDIATIONAL
MODEL (MODIFIED
FROM BARON AND
KENNY, 1986)

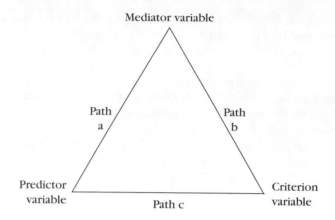

We will now focus on mediating variables. A mediating variable establishes "how" or "why" one variable predicts or causes a criterion variable (Frazier et al., 2004). That is, a mediator is a variable that explains the relationship between a predictor and the criterion (Baron & Kenny, 1986); more specifically, the mediator is the mechanism through which the predictor influences the criterion variable (Frazier et al.). This type of research strategy helps counselors to identify the underlying mechanisms that may be important to target in counseling interventions. Psychological processes are often hypothesized to mediate the relationship between environmental events and psychological distress.

Ellis's (1962) ABC paradigm is a classic example of a mediational model. In this paradigm, A stands for the activating event, B stands for the individual's beliefs, and C denotes the consequence, usually a behavioral or emotional response. Ellis maintained that a person's underlying beliefs explain the relationship between the event and the consequence.

Figure 10.1 is a modified representation of the path model for mediation presented in Baron and Kenny (1986). This path model depicts three paths or relationships among the three variables. Path a depicts the relationship between the predictor variable and the mediator variable; path b rep-resents the relationship between the mediator variable and the criterion variable; and path c depicts the relationship between the predictor variable and the criterion variable. In order to demonstrate that a variable is a mediator, four conditions must be met: (1) path c, the relationship between the predictor variable and the criterion variable, must be statistically significant; (2) path a, the relationship between the predictor variable and the mediator variable, must be significant, (3) path b, the relationship between the mediator variable and the criterion variable, must be statistically significant; and (4) path c, the relationship between the predictor and criterion (that was previously significant) is now significantly reduced when the mediator is added to the model. If path c does not differ from zero when the mediator is added to the model, the strongest demonstration of mediation occurs; this is called a complete mediator. If path c remains significantly greater than zero after the mediator is added to the model, the mediating variable is called a partial mediator. To test for mediation, Baron and Kenny recommend that a series of regression models be conducted to test the four conditions listed. (For more statistical and design details, see Frazier et al., 2004.)

We will examine several research examples to illustrate mediating variables in the counseling literature. For example, there is growing empirical evidence of an association between prejudice and discrimination and greater levels of psychological distress with several previously marginalized groups such as African Americans, white women, and lesbian, gay, and bisexual individuals (e.g., Corning, 2002; Moradi & Subich, 2003; Waldo, 1999). However, Moradi and Hasan (2004) noted that there has been a dearth of evidence examining the prejudice stress–distress link with Arab Americans, a group that has been experiencing increasing discrimination. Based on theory and some previous findings, they hypothesized that personal control mediates the relationship between perceived discrimination and both self-esteem and psychological distress in Arab Americans. Their results indicated a relationship between perceived discrimination and psychological distress ($r = .32$). Moreover, they found that a sense of personal control partially mediated perceived discrimination and psychological distress, and fully mediated the relationship with self-esteem. Thus, the loss of control seems to play an important role in underlying the perceived discrimination events leading to decreased self-esteem and increased psychological distress for Arab Americans.

In another example, Wei, Vogel, Ku, and Zakalik (2005) were interested in whether different types of affect regulation might mediate the relationships between attachment styles and psychological distress. More specifically, based on theory and previous research, they hypothesized that: (1) the association between attachment anxiety and negative mood or interpersonal problems would be mediated by emotional reactivity (i.e., overreacting to negative feelings) and (2) the association between attachment avoidance and negative mood or interpersonal problems would be mediated by emotional cut-off (i.e., suppressing their negative feelings). Their results supported both hypotheses, and also supported growing evidence suggesting that the link between attachment and distress is not simply a direct relationship, but one involving mediating psychological processes (e.g., Wei, Heppner, & Mallinckrodt, 2003). The results of this study suggest that the anxiety and avoidant attachment styles prefer to use different affect regulation strategies. This study suggests that practitioners can help individuals with anxiety and avoidant attachment styles by recognizing the temporary and long-term positive benefits of using their specific maladaptive affect regulation strategies.

Parenthetically, Moradi and Hasan (2004) used path analysis whereas Wei et al. (2005) used a statistical analysis called structural equation modeling, which allowed them to simultaneously examine the direct and indirect effects required for mediational models. Note that in both studies, the authors provide figures depicting the relationships among the hypothesized variables. (See both articles for more details, as well as Heppner & Heppner, 2004, for more detailed explanations of how to write a results section when using structural equation modeling.)

SUMMARY AND CONCLUSIONS

As Greenberg (1986a) asserted, the goal of science is to describe, explain, and predict; thus, descriptive designs play an important role in describing the existence and establishing the characteristics of a particular phenomenon. As we maintained in Chapter 1, the value of a design is not inherent to the design; rather, the value of a design depends on the state of knowledge in a particular area and the specific questions being addressed. Descriptive designs play a unique and very important function in the process of scientific exploration, especially in the early phases of investigating a phenomenon. With these designs, in contrast to experimental designs, a researcher can quickly and relatively easily describe possible relationships among variables. Descriptive studies can rule out the existence of causal relationships—if no correlation exists between variables, there can be no causal relationship. In addition, descriptive studies can suggest possible causal connections among variables that can be examined in a subsequent experimental design.

This chapter has illustrated a number of descriptive designs, all of which describe variables by making systematic observations, summarizing information, reducing or categorizing information, or providing information about basic relationships among variables. Throughout the chapter we have emphasized that both the reliability and the validity of the variables examined are critical issues in descriptive research and directly affect the internal and external validity of the research.

Survey designs allow the researcher to describe the occurrence and frequency of variables of interest. In these designs the researcher is interested in quantitatively describing the occurrence of a variable in a population. The usefulness of the research results depends to a large extent on the measurements used and the adequacy of the sampling techniques. Researchers should make efforts to use or develop psychometrically sound instruments, choose appropriate sampling techniques, maximize return rates, and include checks between both (1) returners and nonreturners and (2) characteristics of the sample and parameters of the population.

Classification is also an important descriptive step in the scientific endeavor. Factor analysis and cluster analysis are statistical methodologies that can aid in this process. The factors derived from factor analysis, as well as the clusters found in cluster analysis, depend on the instruments used and the characteristics of the sample. Therefore, instrument selection and sampling are again important considerations in using these techniques. Factor and cluster solutions should be replicated on separate samples to assure validity. It is also important to validate clusters and factors by linking them with other variables. Finally, it is important to note that both of these procedures involve many decision points, and experts often disagree on criteria for decision making. Thus, the particular methodology or analysis used often affects the results, which suggests the need for further validation.

In descriptive designs, the researcher can examine the relationships between two or more variables. The adequacy of these designs is greatly influenced by the reliability of the measures used in operationalizing the variables of interest. Also, the size of the relationship obtained depends to some extent on the sample size; thus, many multiple regression studies include an adjustment for shrinkage to control for sample size. We hope that more researchers will use latent variables to reduce variance when assessing relationships between variables. As for other descriptive designs, sampling considerations and methodological strategies are extremely important in interpreting the results of multiple regression studies. We encourage researchers to use random sampling and/or to replicate their results when using descriptive designs.

Descriptive designs can be used to examine complex relations among variables. Regression analyses allow researchers to examine the effect of multiple predictor variables on a criterion variable. Moreover, regression analyses can be used to examine more complex relations concerning moderation and mediation among variables. Increasingly, counseling researchers are using moderation and mediation analyses to examine complex theoretical models. The same cautions that apply to simple passive designs also apply to the more complex designs.

We would like to offer three suggestions for counseling researchers considering a descriptive design. First, descriptive research should be undertaken from a strong theoretical grounding. Researchers would do well to avoid questions such as, How do these sets of variables relate? How do these groups differ? Rather, theory should be used to inform the research in the determination of the variables examined. Second, descriptive designs are strengthened when they contain differential predictions. For example, theory may indicate that a variable (realistic Holland code) might be positively related to one variable (lack of accidents), not related to another (weight), and negatively related to a third (school satisfaction). A study is strengthened when these patterns of relationships are predicted and assessed. Specifically, we recommend

that researchers consider examining multiple relationships, especially ones that are predicted to show results in opposite directions. Our third recommendation is that researchers pay particular attention to sample characteristics. For instance, Gade et al. (1988) purposefully selected a varied sample in an attempt to eliminate any chance results based on sample characteristics. Researchers may want to select samples in which various demographic or psychological characteristics are held constant. For example, researchers wanting to compare "good" versus "poor" counseling sessions in terms of type of therapist response used may want to select only sessions that are temporally close. This type of selection would lessen the chance that the results were influenced by the stage of therapy.

The designs described in this chapter can be important building blocks in the scientific process. Based on a careful analysis of the current state of knowledge in a given area, the researcher can choose a design that will lead to a progressively better understanding of the content area. When chosen wisely, the descriptive designs can serve the important function of describing phenomena of interest in counseling research.

STIMULUS QUESTIONS

QUESTIONS TO TEST YOUR KNOWLEDGE ABOUT QUANTITATIVE DESCRIPTIVE DESIGNS

The purpose of this exercise is to test your understanding of some key issues regarding descriptive designs. Write down your answers to the following questions, and then discuss your responses with a peer in your class.

1. What is the difference between a mediating variable and a moderating variable?
2. There are three main types of regression; what are they and how do they differ?
3. Cluster analyses and factor analyses have some similarities and some differences; please describe.

4. In which situations do you use an exploratory factor analysis and in which do you use a confirmatory factor analysis?
5. List three advantages of survey research.
6. The strength of descriptive research is that it allows us to describe phenomena. When might it be possible to use theory to guide the descriptive study, and when is it more helpful not to use theory?

II CHAPTER | QUALITATIVE RESEARCH

Yu-Wei Wang

A central concept of the research designs discussed in previous chapters is that psychological constructs can be measured at the individual level and that understanding can be obtained by averaging these measurements over many persons. The participants respond to questions that in turn yield numbers that the researcher uses to form an understanding that is applicable to others. Participants may be subjected to various treatments or other manipulations, may complete inventories or instruments, and may interact with the researcher; all such actions, however, are used in the service of examining the relationship among the constructs assessed. Although we can learn much about counseling from the quantitative measurement of persons involved in the endeavor, as counselors well understand, the individual meaning that people attribute to their activities and experiences are critically important.

Qualitative research involves understanding the complexity of people's lives by examining individual perspectives in context. Qualitative research methodology is a radically different way to approach knowing and understanding. The following is part of a narrative given by Janie (pseudonym), a woman who was interviewed by the researcher, Lawless, at a women's shelter in Missouri. Janie described her childhood of living with her abused and depressed mother and her alcoholic father who moved their family away from civilization.

> There was a time when I heard the gun go off in the basement of my home. . . .
> She didn't have a vehicle. She never had any money. He wouldn't let her have any money, and if she didn't have money, of course, she didn't have a way to go spend it, because she didn't have a vehicle, you know, she just didn't have any friends. [Crying] One time she just lost it. She went into a nervous breakdown. . . .

One day, and this just brings tears to my eyes to say, one day I remember I was a young teenager, about thirteen. My dad was working all the time, doing drugs, was an alcoholic, and my mom went through the same abuse I went through [with my husband], with my dad. She had a loaded .357 Magnum lying on the table and I walked in and she says, "See this gun?" I was scared to death of what she was going to do. She says, "I'm going to pick it up as soon as you walk out the door, and I'm going to shoot myself, unless you can give me ten reasons not to." And me being only thirteen, I had to give her ten reasons why. And that was a hard thing for me to do. (Lawless, 2001, p. 97)

Qualitative methodology emphasizes the importance of context in helping us understand a phenomenon of interest. Imagine how you would interpret Janie's coping mechanisms and relationship patterns as well as the impact of the past trauma on her life if you also knew the following facts from the interview with her: Janie had to raise her own sister because later her father left and her mother was hospitalized for depression. Janie "impulsively got pregnant" at the age of 15. She talked about "how quickly her young husband became abusive," and how like her father, her husband "moved their mobile home ever farther out into the country, isolating her more and more." Despite all of the hardship that Janie encountered while growing up with a depressed mother and raising her sister on her own, she reported having "a very happy childhood overall" and a "very, very close" relationship with her mother. By the end of the interview, Janie described her mother as "a good woman," who "just did everything in the world to please anybody" (Lawless, 2001, pp. 96–97).

The researcher (Lawless) conducted face-to-face interviews with numerous female survivors of violence. She invites the readers to compare the narrative data generated through these interviews with data obtained from quantitative measures that include questions like: "1. Overall, how upset were you by this experience—extremely upset, somewhat upset, not very upset, or not at all upset? 2. Looking back on it now, how much effect would you say this experience(s) has had on your life—a *great* effect, *some* effect, *a little* effect, or *no* effect?" (Russell, 1986, p. 138, as cited in Lawless, 2001).

The comparisons explicate the sharp differences in the type, range, and depth of the data generated through qualitative and quantitative methodologies. Janie's first-person account provided in-depth information about her lived experiences as a domestic violence survivor. Her narratives revealed the complex and inextricably intertwined relationships between life events, personal development, cognitive appraisals, psychological adjustment, and human resilience. Qualitative methodology stresses the process in which individuals create and give meanings to their social experience and lived realities. In contrast, quantitative methodology paints a broad picture of the relationship among the constructs assessed through generating and averaging nomothetic data over a relatively large number of participants.

This chapter will provide a discussion of qualitative research methods and designs. First, the definition of qualitative research and key myths and facts about qualitative research will be presented. Next, we will briefly review the philosophical foundations of qualitative research and the reasons why it is important to attend to these underlying paradigms. Furthermore, three strategies of qualitative inquiry (i.e., grounded theory, phenomenology, and consensual qualitative research) will be illustrated with exemplar studies. The primary tasks in qualitative research (ways to gather and analyze data) will be presented. Finally, the criteria that may be used for evaluating the rigor of qualitative methodology will be briefly described.

WHAT IS QUALITATIVE RESEARCH?

Qualitative research is employed in various disciplines (e.g., anthropology, education, nursing, sociology, and psychology) with numerous strategies of inquiry (e.g., ethnography, grounded theory, discourse analysis). Students often feel confused about and overwhelmed by the variation of terminology as well as the philosophical and procedural diversity of qualitative research. For this reason, we will delineate several common myths and basic facts about the nature of qualitative research in the following sections.

DEFINING QUALITATIVE RESEARCH

A generic definition of qualitative research is provided by Denzin and Lincoln (2000) as follows:

> Qualitative research is a situated activity that locates the observer in the world. It consists of a set of interpretive, material practices that make the world visible. These practices transform the world. They turn the world into a series of representations, including field notes, interviews, conversations, photographs, recordings, and memos to the self. At this level, qualitative research involves an interpretive, naturalistic approach to the world. This means that qualitative researchers study things in their natural settings, attempting to make sense of, or to interpret, phenomena in terms of the meanings people bring to them.
>
> Qualitative research involves the studied use and collection of a variety of empirical materials—case study; personal experience; introspection; life story; interview; artifacts; cultural texts and productions; observational, historical, interactional, and visual texts—that describe routine and meanings in individuals' lives. Accordingly, qualitative researchers deploy a wide range of interconnected interpretive methods, hoping always to get a better understanding of the subject matter at hand. It is understood, however, that each practice makes the world visible in a different way. Hence, there is frequently a commitment to using more than one interpretive practice in any study. (pp. 3–4)

In other words, qualitative researchers are devoted to understanding the specifics of particular cases and embedding their research findings in an ever-changing world. Influenced by the interpretivist-constructivist tradition, qualitative researchers believe that objective reality can never be fully understood or discovered, and there are many possible ways of looking at realities. Qualitative researchers are interested in capturing the individual's point of view through the use of multiple strategies such as interviews and observations (emic and idiographic perspectives), instead of deploying etic and nomothetic approaches that emphasize the goal of discovering and describing universal principles by quantifying the observed phenomena. Qualitative researchers choose from a variety of research tools in accordance with their research questions and contexts to better understand the phenomenon of interest (Nelson, Treichler, & Grossberg, 1992), rather than verifying or falsifying an a priori hypothesis through experimental designs and statistical analysis. They value rich descriptions of the phenomenon under analysis and attempt to represent an individual's lived experience through writing and interpretations.

Similarly to quantitative research, the questions that qualitative researchers ask their participants and the methods that they utilize to observe certain phenomena are all "filtered" through the researchers' lenses of knowledge, language, values, and worldviews. Denzin and Lincoln (1998) described qualitative research as "an interactive process" shaped by the researcher's "personal history, biography, gender, social class, race and ethnicity, and those of the people in the settings" (p. 4). Qualitative researchers acknowledge ("bracket") their assumptions about the study by taking field notes, writing reflexive journals, and informing the readers as to what their "filters" are. The lived experiences of the research participants are what qualitative researchers focus on, and the researchers are the instruments in this discovery process who hold their expectations and hunches about the phenomenon under study in abeyance (Rennie, 2000).

The discovery orientation of the qualitative approach helps to focus on the context where the phenomenon is situated and make the findings more applicable for people's everyday lives in various cultures. Qualitative inquiry allows researchers to study the local interactions in counseling settings and their meanings for counselors and clients. For these reasons, qualitative inquiry is particularly appropriate for multicultural/cross-cultural research (see Morrow, Rakhasha, & Castañeda, 2001) as well as process and outcome research (see McLeod, 2001). In fact, it has gained increasing popularity among researchers in different parts of the world, such as Asia (e.g., Kim & Cho, 2005) and Europe (e.g., Forum Qualitative Sozialforschung).

MYTHS AND FACTS ABOUT QUALITATIVE RESEARCH

Due to insufficient understanding of the definition and characteristics of qualitative research, there are several common myths about this form of inquiry. First, many students equate "qualitative data" with "qualitative research," thereby holding a mistaken belief that qualitative research consists only of asking people open-ended questions and analyzing participants' answers. Second, some people think that there is only one kind of qualitative methodology and are unaware that there are a variety of methods in qualitative research, such as phenomenology and narratology. Third, some people believe that qualitative research should be used only in areas where we do not have enough information to do quantitative studies; this perspective overlooks how qualitative research can add to the depth and breadth of our understanding about certain phenomena. Finally, some students choose to adopt a qualitative approach because they feel uncomfortable with statistics or believe that it is easier to conduct a qualitative inquiry than a quantitative one. These students ignore the fact that conducting qualitative research actually requires rigorous efforts and introspection; the researcher listens to other people's stories and retells the stories in a way that she or he understands them or even reconstructs the story with the participants.

Creswell (1998) indicated that qualitative researchers should be willing to: (1) "commit to extensive time in the field"; (2) "engage in the complex, time-consuming process of data analysis—the ambitious task of sorting through large amounts of data and reducing them to a few themes or categories"; (3) "write long passages, because the evidence must substantiate claims and the writer needs to show multiple perspectives"; and (4) "participate in a form of social and human science research that does not have firm guidelines or specific procedures and is evolving and changing constantly" (pp. 16–17). Although qualitative procedures may not be as clearly delineated as quantitative procedures, researchers must acquire highly specialized knowledge and demonstrate rigorous endeavors, as will be made evident in the remaining parts of this chapter.

Students are encouraged to reflect on the following factors before deciding to conduct a qualitative study: (1) the fit between the research question and qualitative methodology; (2) the extent of their knowledge on the fundamental paradigms and methods of qualitative inquiry and the level of skills gained from appropriate coursework and research apprenticeship; (3) whether they have adequate support from advisors and/or research mentors who are knowledgeable about qualitative methodology; (4) the existing knowledge bases and types of research designs previously used; and (5) their readiness to conduct a rigorous, qualitative investigation. These elements are worthy of considerable reflection. In the subsequent sections of this chapter, we will explore some of the essential components of qualitative research.

PHILOSOPHICAL FOUNDATIONS

In Chapter 1, we contrasted four paradigms that bear on the research process. Readers are encouraged to review that chapter again to be familiar with the philosophical foundations of scientific inquiry.

Overall, quantitative research is aligned with two of the paradigms—constructivism and critical theory. In general, all qualitative paradigms assume relativist ontology (there are multiple realities that are socially and individually constructed) and transactional epistemology (the knower and the known are inextricably intertwined), as well as dialogic/interpretive methodology (Guba & Lincoln, 1998). It is crucial to understand these underlying paradigms so that they match the researcher's own personal values, beliefs, and personality, as well as personal and mental models (Morrow et al., 2001). Also, the research approach adopted should be appropriate for answering research questions within the context of existing knowledge. As introduced later in this chapter, there are many different strategies of inquiry in qualitative research; each inquiry has somewhat different philosophical underpinnings (see Ponterotto, 2005b, for an excellent discussion about locating the strategies of inquiry within research paradigms). Therefore, understanding the basic tenets and philosophical foundations of qualitative research will help students select a particular paradigm and strategy of inquiry that may best address a particular area of inquiry.

Readers who are interested in advancing their knowledge about the philosophical underpinnings of these paradigms can find excellent introductions and discussions in the *Handbook of Qualitative Research* (e.g., Lincoln & Guba, 2000; Schwandt, 2000), the *Handbook of Counseling Psychology* (Morrow & Smith, 2000), the *Handbook of Multicultural Counseling* (Morrow et al., 2001), and the special issue on qualitative research in the *Journal of Counseling Psychology* (e.g., Ponterotto, 2005b). Next, we will shift our focus to qualitative research methods and design issues.

STRATEGIES OF INQUIRY

Each qualitative strategy of inquiry is connected to specific paradigms and research designs. Researchers should be clear about the differences among various strategies of inquiry in order to make informed decisions regarding what qualitative approaches to use and when to use them (Creswell, 1998), and subsequently to design their studies according to the guidelines of a particular chosen strategy. The rationale of using a specific paradigm and strategy of inquiry should be presented and the relationship between the paradigms/strategies of inquiry and purposes/research questions of the studies should be explicated in the final write-up.

It is worth mentioning that great confusion may arise at this stage because a variety of strategies of inquiry exist across various disciplines. For example, Strauss and Corbin (1990), who are in the field of sociology and nursing, grouped qualitative strategies of inquiry into five categories (grounded theory, phenomenology, life history, ethnography, and conversational analysis); conversely, Moustakas (1994), who is in the field of psychology, listed six qualitative traditions (grounded theory, hermeneutics, empirical phenomenological research, ethnography, heuristic research, and transcendental phenomenology). Narrative studies provides another example of this diversity: According to Hoshmand (2005), "narratology is a term historically used to refer to the study of narratives in the literary field, though other disciplines in the humanities (such as history) and the social sciences (such as cultural studies) also are associated with the study of narratives"(p. 178). Hoshmand further clarified that she used the term *narratology* "as a way of distinguishing a mode of qualitative inquiry and data analysis that is informed by narrative theory," differing from "other qualitative research that involves narrative data but not a narrative perspective per se" (p. 178).

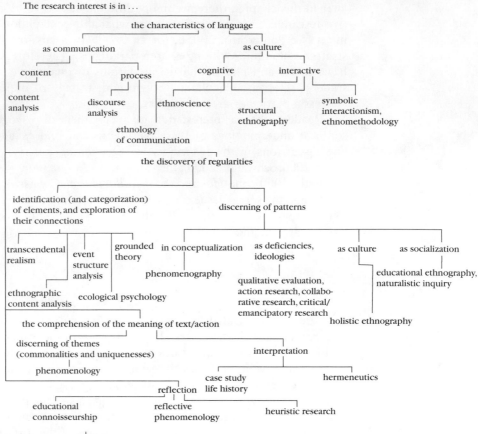

FIGURE 11.1 | AN OVERVIEW OF QUALITATIVE RESEARCH TYPES
(REPRINTED FROM TESCH, 1990, BY PERMISSION)

Each of these numerous types of qualitative research has distinct purposes
and methods. Figure 11.1, borrowed from Tesch (1990), provides a schematic
diagram for various types of research depending on the research interest.
The primary categories in this hierarchy, which are based on the interest
of the research, focus on (1) the characteristics of language, (2) the discovery
of regularities, (3) the comprehension of the meaning of text or action, or
(4) reflection.

Due to space limitations, we selected three strategies of inquiry to present
in this chapter based on their potential utility in counseling research: grounded
theory, phenomenology, and consensual qualitative research. We will briefly
describe these three strategies of inquiry along with exemplar studies. Note that
the studies cited in this chapter are good examples of qualitative research but
are not the "only correct" way to conduct qualitative research. These three
types of strategies are mentioned to provide a flavor of the variations possible;

readers interested in a particular approach will need to explore the specific methodological literature for that type. Also, students who use these strategies of inquiry for theses or dissertations may also examine the illustrations and examples of writing different sections of qualitative studies in Wang, Heppner, and Heppner (2004a, 2004b).

GROUNDED THEORY

This section first provides the definition and purpose of the grounded theory approach. Then, its primary features—(1) constant comparative method, (2) memo writing, (3) theoretical sampling, and (4) the emerging theory that is grounded in data—will be discussed and elucidated with exemplar studies.

The grounded theory approach was developed by Glaser and Strauss (1967) in an attempt to challenge the dominant trend of "excessive reliance on the quantitative testing of hypotheses derived from a small number of grant (totalizing) theories, typically through numerical survey and other statistical approaches" (Henwood & Pidgeon, 2003, p. 132). According to Charmaz (2000),

> Grounded theory methods consist of systematic inductive guidelines for collecting and analyzing data to build middle-range theoretical frameworks that explain the collected data. Throughout the research process, grounded theorists develop analytic interpretations of their data to focus further data collection, which they use in turn to inform and refine their developing theoretical analyses. (p. 509)

The grounded theory approach is rooted in sociology and the tradition of symbolic interactionism. It is appropriate for studying "the local interactions and meanings as related to the social context in which they actually occur," and therefore is particularly attractive to psychologists (Pidgeon, 1996, p. 75). In fact, the grounded theory methods have gained increasing popularity among researchers across various disciplines over the past two decades (see Fassinger, 2005; Rennie, Watson, & Monteiro, 2002) and has been named "the most influential paradigm for qualitative research in the social sciences today" (Denzin, 1997, as cited in Patton, 2002, p. 487).

Grounded theory has been associated with seemingly opposing philosophical views—"realism (by claiming to directly reflect the 'data')" and "constructivism (inherent to the approach of symbolic interactionism)" (Henwood & Pidgeon, 2003, p. 134). Related to this epistemological tension, grounded theorists have been advocating competing approaches to data analysis and interpretations. For example, Strauss and Corbin (1990, 1998) promote the use of open coding, axial coding, and selective coding in specifying the properties and dimensions of categories and organizing the emerging theory in a conditional matrix that contains the antecedents, context, intervening conditions, and consequences of core categories. Glaser (1992) stresses the importance of constant comparative method and theoretical memoing in generating a theoretical model. Rennie (2000) presents the grounded theory method as methodical hermeneutics (i.e., a methodological approach that "involves the interplay between induction and abduction conducted reflexively") (p. 494). Recently, the constructivist version of grounded theory also has been advocated by several grounded theorists (e.g., Charmaz, 2000; Henwood & Pidgeon, 2003), which emphasizes the interpretive process of a grounded theory study.

Novice researchers often are perplexed by these divergent perspectives. Readers should consult the key literature listed earlier for more information about specific grounded theory methods. Nonetheless, there are some commonalities across these various grounded theory methods, which will be described in the following sections.

CONSTANT COMPARATIVE METHOD   The constant comparative method, the hallmark of grounded theory research, consists of four stages: (1) comparing incidents applicable to each category, (2) integrating categories and their properties, (3) delimiting the theory, and (4) writing the theory (Glaser & Strauss, 1967). It is worth noting that although one stage leads to another, some earlier stages will continue operating simultaneously until the termination of the data analysis.

Glaser and Strauss (1967) developed the constant comparative method to generate "many categories, properties, and hypotheses about general problems" and to formulate a theory that is grounded in the data, instead of "[ascertaining] either the universality or the proof of suggested causes or other properties" (p. 104). Specifically, the following procedure is suggested for generating categories and properties: (1) assign codes to segments of the text (meaning units) in the initial open coding phase; (2) sort these codes into clusters according to their shared meanings; (3) convert the meaning of each cluster into a category; and (4) discontinue the sorting of the codes when no new category emerges (i.e., categorization has reached saturation) (Rennie, 2000).

Pidgeon and Henwood (1996) emphasized the importance of documenting this analytical process fully while conducting grounded theory research, which helps to track the procedures and helps the researchers become aware of their implicit, a priori assumptions. Pidgeon and Henwood described the analytic process using the flow chart shown in Figure 11.2.

Consistent with the depiction in Figure 11.2, this data collection and analytic procedure was described as a "zigzag" process by Creswell (1998), "out to the field to gather information, analyze the data, back to the field to gather more information, analyze the data, and so forth" (p. 57). In other words, data collection and data analysis are not discrete stages in grounded theory research. This method sets grounded theory apart from content/thematic analysis, which employs reliability and validity as criteria and uses "the counting of instances within a predefined set of mutually exclusive and jointly exhaustive categories" (see Pidgeon, 1996, p. 78).

MEMO WRITING   It is essential to keep memos during the process of conducting the constant comparative method. Memo writing is defined as a process to record "hunches; comments on new samples to be checked out; explanations

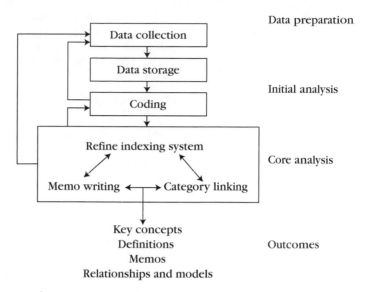

FIGURE 11.2 | THE GROUNDED THEORY APPROACH (REPRINTED FROM
PIDGEON & HENWOOD, 1996, BY PERMISSION)

of modifications to categories; emerging theoretical reflections; and links to
the literature" (Pidgeon & Henwood, 1996, p. 95). Charmaz (2000) indicated,

> Memo writing is the intermediate step between coding and the first draft of the
> completed analysis. . . . It can help us to define leads for collecting data—both for
> further initial coding and later theoretical sampling. Through memo writing, we
> elaborate processes, assumptions, and actions that are subsumed under our
> codes." (p. 517)

Pidgeon and Henwood (1996) also warned that researchers should "write a
memo as soon as the thought has occurred, for, if left unrecorded, it is likely
to be forgotten" (p. 95). In sum, memo writing is a vital technique for
grounded theorists. It not only serves as an instrumental mechanism for the
constant comparative practice, but also facilitates the theoretical sampling and
theory development processes that will be described in the following sections.

THEORETICAL SAMPLING   The data sources of grounded theory research could
include a combination of data types (e.g., archival/textual materials, participant observation, autobiographies, and journals). Among all of these options,
however, interviews with the participants are a primary data source (Pidgeon
& Henwood, 1996).

Theoretical sampling characterizes the ongoing analytic process in the
field and is a theory-driven method of sampling. Theoretical sampling helps
researchers target new data that would facilitate the emergence of theory after
the initial analysis of the data at hand. It is used by grounded theorists to

> select a sample of individuals to study based on their contribution to the development of the theory. Often, this process begins with a homogeneous sample of individuals who are similar, and, as the data collection proceeds and the categories emerge, the researcher turns to a heterogeneous sample to see under what conditions the categories hold true. (Creswell, 1998, p. 243)

Therefore, theoretical sampling differs from the sampling method used in quantitative research, in which researchers are expected to obtain a representative sample in order to enhance generalizability of the research finding. "Theoretical saturation" occurs when "the new data fit into the categories already devised" (Charmaz, 2000, p. 520) and it indicates the ending of the data collection process.

THEORY IS GROUNDED IN THE DATA   Grounded theorists argued that theories should be derived from the data. Unlike quantitative researchers, grounded theorists neither test an existing theory nor try to fit their data into preconceived concepts. Instead, all of the theoretical concepts should be derived from the data analysis and account for the variation in the studied phenomenon, thereby allowing the theoretical framework to emerge through the aforementioned constant comparative practice, memo writing, and theoretical sampling processes (Charmaz, 2000).

EXEMPLAR STUDY   We will use a grounded theory study conducted by Morrow and Smith (1995) as an example to illustrate the grounded theory method. This study aims at understanding the survival experience of women survivors of childhood sexual abuse and representing their coping processes in a theoretical framework that emerged from the data. The authors explicitly discussed the reasons for choosing a qualitative methodology and grounded theory approach for the purpose of their study.

> As Hoshmand (1989) noted, qualitative research strategies are particularly appropriate to address meanings and perspectives of participants. In addition, she suggested that naturalistic methods offer the researcher access to deep-structural processes. . . . The primary method of investigating those realities was grounded theory (Glaser & Strauss, 1967), a qualitative research method designed to aid in the systematic collection and analysis of data and the construction of a theoretical model. . . . Chosen to clarify participants' understandings of their abuse experiences, the methods used involved (a) developing codes, categories, and themes inductively rather than imposing predetermined classifications on the data (Glaser, 1978), (b) generating working hypotheses or assertions (Erickson, 1986) from the data, and (c) analyzing narratives of participants' experiences of abuse, survival, and coping. (pp. 24–25)

Participants for this study included 11 childhood sexual abuse survivors with a wide age range (25 to 72 years old) and diverse racial/ethnic backgrounds, sexual orientations, and educational levels; three of the participants also reported physical disabilities. Morrow and Smith (1995) provided a detailed description of the participants' backgrounds (including brief abuse histories and counseling experiences). These "thick descriptions" (a qualitative tactic that will be further explained later in this chapter) provide the readers an understanding of the context of the phenomenon. The authors also did a nice job of describing the participant recruitment process: Letters that detailed the research's purpose and process were sent to therapists with expertise in working with sexual abuse survivors; these therapists were asked to give the research announcement to those clients "who might benefit from or be interested in participating in the study" (p. 25).

Morrow and Smith (1995) clearly identified their sampling criterion: participants' "self-identification as an abuse survivor" based on the constructivist approach (i.e., "[accepting] the stories of participants at face value as their phenomenological realities") (p. 25). The authors utilized a variety of data sources, including: (1) semi-structured, 60- to 90-minute, in-depth interviews with individual participants; (2) a 10-week focus group with 7 of the 11 research participants that emphasized the survivors' coping experiences and thoughts on the emerging categories from the initial data analyses; (3) documentary evidence such as participants' journals and artistic productions; and (4) Morrow's self-reflective and analytic memos, which consisted of the researcher's reflections and assumptions about the data. The interviews were transcribed verbatim, and "the data corpus consisted of over 2,000 pages of transcriptions, field notes, and documents shared by participants" (p. 25).

Following Strauss and Corbin's (1990) suggestions, the authors conducted open coding, axial coding, and selective coding on the data, and "the language of the participants guided the development of code and category labels, which were identified with short descriptors, known as *in vivo codes,* for survival and coping strategies" (Morrow & Smith, 1995, p. 26). Subsequently, the authors generated a theoretical framework for the surviving and coping process experienced by those childhood sexual abuse survivors. Figure 11.3 shows the theoretical model derived from the data analysis.

The authors provided a rich description of the model, which serves as an overall illustration of the phenomenon under study. They also elucidated the categories in the model with quotes from the participants. For example, the following is the description of a "Phenomena" category:

> [P]articipants experienced what was termed *helplessness, powerlessness, and lack of control.* Lauren provided an exemplar of the second category, illustrating the pervasiveness of her perpetrator's power:
>
> > He stands there. A silhouette at first and then his face and body come into view. He is small, but the backlighting intensifies his figure and he seems huge, like a prison guard. He is not always there but it feels like he might as well be. When he's not there, I search the distance for him and he appears. He seems to be standing there for hours. As if he's saying, you are weak, I am in control.
>
> Not only did Lauren experience powerlessness during her abuse, but her lack of control invaded her dreams and her moments alone. (pp. 27–28)

Furthermore, the authors demonstrated that the analytic process is not only sequential, but also recursive, which is the spirit of the constant comparative

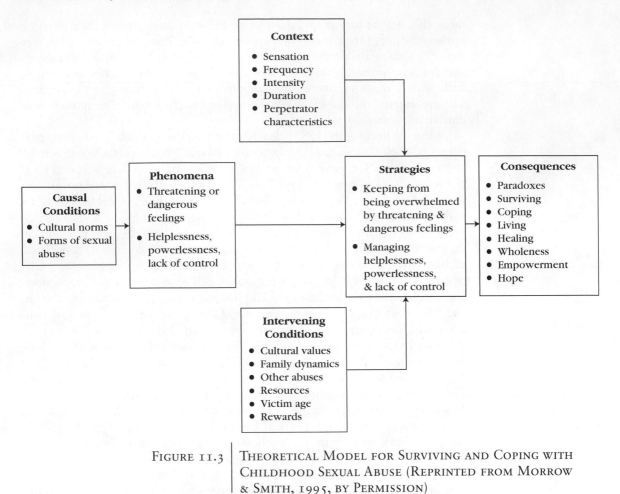

FIGURE 11.3 | THEORETICAL MODEL FOR SURVIVING AND COPING WITH CHILDHOOD SEXUAL ABUSE (REPRINTED FROM MORROW & SMITH, 1995, BY PERMISSION)

method and theoretical sampling. They described how the researcher's memos facilitated this process:

> Meghan foreshadowed one of these phenomena the first night of the group, when she said, "To keep from feeling my feelings, I have become a very skilled helper of other people." Throughout the data, others echoed her words. The analytic moment in which this category emerged is illustrated in the following analytic memo written by Morrow (in vivo codes are in italics):

>> I'm reading a higher level of abstraction. Is the overarching category *protection from feelings*? Many categories are subsumed under it: One *talks* to get out the *stories*; the *feelings* are less intense. Fake orgasm (*sex*) because you don't have any physical feelings. *Art* was used to deal with *feelings*, express *anger*, *release* the pressure of the *feelings*, use *chemicals* to deal with *feelings* (and a whole complex interaction here) . . .

> Existing and emergent codes and categories were compared and contrasted with this category; the category was modified to accommodate the data, producing the

phenomenon that was labeled *being overwhelmed by threatening or dangerous feelings*—feelings that participants described as subjectively threatening or dangerous. (p. 27)

Morrow and Smith (1995) also explicitly explained the rigor of their method: triangulating multiple data sources (i.e., interviews, focus groups, documents, memos), immersing in the data (the entire data collection period lasted over 16 months), member check (participants were invited to verify data analysis results and revise the emergent theoretical model), and peer debriefing (Morrow invited other qualitative researchers to review the analysis, her writing, and the "audit trail that outlined the research process and evolution of codes, categories and theory" [p. 26]).

Other exemplar grounded theory studies include Rennie and his colleagues' research on psychotherapy (Rennie, 1994a, 1994b, 1994c; Watson & Rennie, 1994) and Fassinger and her colleagues' studies on career development of highly achieving Black and White American women (Richie et al., 1997) and highly achieving women with disabilities (Noonan et al., 2004). Interested readers may also find the researchers' own thoughts about their investigation process in their articles on the grounded theory methods (e.g., Fassinger, 2005; Rennie, 1996).

PHENOMENOLOGY

The purpose of phenomenology is "to produce an exhaustive description of the phenomena of everyday experience, thus arriving at an understanding of the essential structures of the 'thing itself', the phenomenon" (McLeod, 2001, p. 38). In the following paragraphs, the historical development of the phenomenological approach and its major principles will be introduced along with exemplar studies.

Phenomenology has its roots in the work of Edmund Husserl on phenomenological philosophy. Since then, many individuals (e.g., Giorgi, Moustakas, Polkinghorne) in the social science field have followed its tenets and transferred Husserl's work from philosophy to psychological or sociological research. Over the past decades, different approaches to phenomenology were developed (e.g., empirical/psychological phenomenology, hermeneutic phenomenology, existential phenomenology, social phenomenology, reflective/transcendental phenomenology, and dialogical phenomenology). (For a review, see Creswell, 1998.) McLeod (2001) provided an overview of the three branches of "new" phenomenological traditions that evolved from Husserlian phenomenological principles: (1) "the Duquesne school of empirical phenomenology" developed by Giorgi and his colleagues in North America; (2) "the method of 'conceptual encounter' developed by Rivera" who was influenced by the Duquesne school and "the German social psychologist Lewin"; and (3) "the existential-phenomenological investigations" of "the Scottish psychiatrist Laing and his colleagues" at the Tavistock Institute for Human Relations in England (pp. 40–48). Interested readers are referred to McLeod for a comparison between the original phenomenological philosophy developed by Husserl and the "new" phenomenological traditions advocated by psychological researchers.

Also, a recent review of the phenomenological movement in psychology and a comparison between phenomenological research and other qualitative methods can be found in Wertz (2005).

In spite of the existence of multiple phenomenological approaches, phenomenological researchers follow some general guidelines in developing plans for their studies. These guidelines were summarized by Creswell (1998) into five areas: (1) philosophical perspectives and epoché, (2) research question and lived experiences, (3) criterion-based sampling, (4) phenomenological data analysis, and (5) essential, invariant structure (or essence) of the lived experience. These five dimensions of the guidelines are key concepts of the phenomenological approach and will be illustrated below with an exemplar study.

PHILOSOPHICAL PERSPECTIVES AND EPOCHÉ   First and foremost, researchers who intend to adopt the phenomenological approach should have a thorough understanding of the underlying philosophy because its philosophical assumptions greatly influence the formulation of research questions and inquiry techniques (Creswell, 1998; McLeod, 2001). Because there are various phenomenological traditions, as mentioned earlier, the philosophical perspectives embraced by the researchers should be specified in the final write-up. Furthermore, before conducting a phenomenological study, researchers should "bracket" (i.e., set aside) their assumptions and judgments about the phenomenon, and these presuppositions should be documented. This strategy was termed *epoché* by Husserl. Phenomenological researchers use epoché to bracket and question all of their assumptions, hoping to reveal new and meaningful understanding that transcends the extant knowledge about a particular phenomenon (McLeod, 2001).

RESEARCH QUESTIONS AND LIVED EXPERIENCES   The key subject matter studied by phenomenological researchers is "the lived world" of human beings (i.e., "the life-world manifests itself as a structural whole that is socially shared and yet apprehended by individuals through their own perspectives") (Wertz, 2005, p. 169). A phenomenological study aims to "fill in the gap" between "knowledge and reality that requires qualitative knowledge, that is, an understanding of what occurs" (Wertz, 2005, p. 170). The research questions for a phenomenological study are developed in order to understand the everyday lived experiences of individuals and to explore what those experiences mean to them (Creswell, 1998). Data are typically generated through written or verbal responses of the research participants to "a descriptive task with instructions" or an open-ended interview (Wertz, 2005, p. 171). The research questions guide the development of the descriptive task or specific interview questions. Long interviews are often utilized to generate in-depth dialogues between the researcher and the participant about a specific phenomenon. Wertz suggested that the best type of data for phenomenological researchers is "concretely described psychology life," which helps to further our understanding about a given phenomenon beyond "any previous knowledge or preconceptions" (p. 171).

CRITERION-BASED SAMPLING   Criterion-based sampling is often used in a phenomenological study to select participants who meet the following criteria: (1) they experienced the phenomenon under study, and (2) they can articulate their lived experiences (Creswell, 1998). Similar to the grounded theory approach, there is no absolute number of participants needed for a phenomenological study. Yet, in assessing the adequacy of the sample size, the following criteria were proposed by Wertz (2005): "deliberation and critical reflection considering the research problem, the life-world position of the participant(s), the quality of the data, and the value of emergent findings with regard to research goals" (p. 171).

PHENOMENOLOGICAL ANALYSIS   Husserl developed the procedure of *intentional analysis,* which "begins with a situation just as it has been experienced—with all its various meanings—and reflectively explicated the experiential processes through which the situation is lived," thereby producing "knowledge of human situations, their meaning, and the processes that generate those meanings" (Wertz, 2005, p. 169). The intentional analysis is carried out through the use of epoché and an *empathic* understanding of the participants' lived experiences. In the analytic process, the researcher constantly "focuses on relations between different parts of the situation and the psychological processes that subtend it while attempting to gain explicit knowledge of how each constituent contributes to the organization of the structure as a whole" (Wertz, 2005, p. 172). Yet, phenomenological researchers who follow the different traditions mentioned earlier have proposed different analytic techniques (McLeod, 2001). Researchers need to decide which tradition to follow when conducting their analyses and clearly state the steps of the analytic method in their research methodology section.

ESSENCE OF THE EXPERIENCES   Husserl advocated the use of the *intuition of essence* or *eidetic reduction* to understand the essence of the phenomenon under study and to achieve *psychological reduction.* For this purpose, he developed a procedure, *free imaginative variation,* which "starts with a concrete example of the phenomenon of which one wishes to grasp the essence and imaginatively varies it in every possible way in order to distinguish essential features from those that are accidental or incidental" (Wertz, 2005, p. 168). The exhaustive descriptions of the phenomenon of interest are subsequently constructed through extracting the significant statements, formulating meanings, and clustering themes of the original data (Creswell, 1998). The exhaustive descriptions could provide the readers an understanding of the essence of the lived experiences and represent a unifying structure of a phenomenon.

EXEMPLAR STUDY   A study conducted by Teixeira and Gomes (2000) in Brazil will be used as an example of phenomenological studies. Their research aimed to understand the career trajectories of Brazilians who have chosen to change careers at least once in the past. The authors indicated that past research has not focused on the process of self-initiated career change, and most studies used quantitative methodology. The phenomenological approach was used for this study because it allowed the researchers to understand the meanings that participants ascribed to their autonomous career change in a specific context.

Teixeira and Gomes (2000) explicitly described the criterion they used to select participants: All of the participants would have experienced at least one self-initiated career change. Specifically, the participants were chosen "who had left one career for which they had received a university training for another that also required advanced training, such that the change had been voluntary (criteria for time spent in the careers were not established)" (p. 81). A "thick" (detailed) description of the participants (e.g., their first and current careers) was provided in the article.

The authors utilized interviews as the data collection method for this study. They started the interviews with a broad question, "I should like you to tell me about your career choices," and left it open-ended for the participants to freely discuss their career trajectories. Interviews were conducted with seven participants (four women and three men; age range from 32 to 42 years), audio taped, and subsequently transcribed. Locations (i.e., participants' home or work settings) and the actual lengths (i.e., one to two and a half hours) of the interviews were described in their manuscript.

Teixeira and Gomes (2000) followed the Duquesne school of empirical phenomenology tradition and explicitly delineated the phenomenological analytic approach utilized in their study:

> The analytical procedures observed the methodological recommendations of Giorgi (1997) and Lanigan (1988) in the following way: transcriptions and successive readings of the material, search and demarcation of significant units within each interview, verification of cross units among interviews, and definition of the main themes. The relations between parts and whole were worked out by the preparation of a synthesis for each narrative. The confront [sic] between these syntheses and their constitutive themes were the base for the phenomenological description. Throughout this process, the researchers' prior knowledge of the subject was set to one side, thereby avoiding interferences from anticipated qualitative judgments (phenomenological *epoché*). The analysis rigorously observed the three steps of phenomenological method (description, reduction, interpretation) as indicated below. Excerpts taken from the interviews were used as illustrative evidence of the researcher' phenomenological understanding. (p. 82)

The authors concluded that their analysis yielded five essential themes that "comprise a general structure of the experiences described by the interviewees, although the limits, contents and scope of each theme may vary from case to case according to personal circumstances" (p. 82). Following the methodological recommendations of prominent phenomenological researchers, Teixeira and Gomes (2000) defined each theme (which they called a "moment") and subsequently identified the interviewees' accounts that "specify the affective, cognitive and conative limits of the experience that participants lived through in relation to each of the selected themes" (p. 82). The authors then provided a rich description of the themes with the participants' narratives. Following is the description of one of the five themes ("moments").

Moment 5: Evaluating the change and present situation

The participants evaluated their professional careers, including their present situations, in a positive way. The evaluation was accompanied by a feeling of having matured and of personal transformation. Career change was generally associated with personal changes, for example the feeling of being less tied down and capable of making changes in other spheres of life (S2: ". . . after I took this decision I feel much more given to change, just as I had changed"; S4: ". . . I think that all that I had gone through made me succeed in not being so tied up with things . . . I am much more . . . much lighter") or yet as a transformation in the personal outlook, ceasing to like working to a "prepared formula" (S5).

Career change was also seen as a personal search for interpersonal development, self-determination and, most importantly, increased self-esteem (S7; ". . . it is something that makes me feel good, I like to hear people say that I am a doctor, I feel proud of what I am"). Yet others viewed their professional trajectory as an opportunity for steady development of their personality and of their capacities and interests, integrating all the professional experience they had (S3, S1).

S1: "So I made it . . . made use of knowledge, right, built up through a piece of my life in all the areas that I worked in, and I'm still reaping the benefit today. . . ."

The contrast with these positive evaluations on career changes, in which those interviewed considered themselves more mature and in the process of re-engagement in a profession, is given by S6. She still claims to have adolescent doubts about future career, just as she is on the point of finishing a course in Visual Arts (her professional interest abandoned in adolescence).

S6: "I think that basically I didn't change . . . I think I still . . . I'm 36 now, and I still feel I have those adolescent doubts. . . . 'What am I going to be in the future?' . . . I have the feeling that I'm still looking for something . . . [Can you see how you will be, I don't know, ten, fifteen years from now?] No . . . no, I can't, I can't, for me it's all far too hazy." (p. 87)

After summarizing and illustrating each theme that emerged from the data analyses, Teixeira and Gomes (2000) presented the essential structure (phenomenological reduction) of the phenomenon under study. They used the reduction to illustrate the characteristics of the phenomenon of career change. The complete description is approximately three pages long; below is its summary:

In summary, career change can be defined as a broad process of change in the relationship between the participants and their work. The change begins with the awareness of feelings of dissatisfaction with their career, leading the participants to ask questions of themselves and what they do. The questioning of career emerges in the consciousness as a figure whose background is the other roles lived by the participants in their daily lives. Personal plans are redefined and new priorities established, enabling the career to acquire a different meaning in this new context. Thus the search for a new career is also a search for a new way for the participants to express themselves in the world, which can lead them—although not necessarily—to feelings of greater self-determination and personal satisfaction. (p. 90)

In addition to the phenomenological reduction, Teixeira and Gomes also presented their interpretations of the phenomenon, which focus on "the possible meanings of these changes and of the career change itself" as follows (p. 91).

> In general, the statements analyzed in this study suggest that career change can result from a career choice which we could call immature at adolescence. Immaturity is understood as a decision taken without the necessary exploration of alternatives which would allow the subjects to build up a clear occupational self-understanding and to make choices compatible with their interests and the conception that they have of themselves (Super, 1963; Super, Savickas, & Super, 1996).
>
> But the histories presented by those interviewed also shows [sic] us that the choice made at adolescence is not something definitive. Above all it is a continuing process that reaffirms itself through practice of the profession or which provides experiences leading to new choices. Rather than being a fundamental error, as one of those interviewed called it, an inappropriate choice at adolescence can also be a way leading to deeper knowledge of oneself, and to personal and even professional changes. . . . This interpretation, moreover, is in contrast with the idea that adolescents (or anyone else) have to make the correct choice of profession, and that this choice must be retained for the rest of their lives (Wrightsman, 1994), indecision or change of profession being regarded almost as mental disorder requiring treatment (Krumboltz, 1992). This search for the correct profession illustrates a concept widespread in society that identity (professional, in this case) is something that is relatively ready within individuals, static and immutable, therefore requiring only to be "discovered" for the best choice of career to be selected. . . .
>
> The meaning of change, therefore, is revealed in the plan through which the subjects decide to take account of their lives. From this standpoint, we can propose a new interpretation of what those interviewed named maturity: it is the capacity to make choices (their own) and to make plans, professional plans. When speaking of their own or authentic choices, this is not to say that unconscious factors or social or economic pressures may not exist which override the choice in some form. It is intended to emphasize, however, the active nature that the subjects can have in constructing their history, even though they may not have full control or knowledge of their motives. (pp. 91–92)

The rich and exhaustive descriptions about the seven Brazilians' experiences with voluntary career change in Teixeira and Gomes (2000) extended previous career theories and provided new knowledge about a phenomenon that was understudied. The authors' detailed illustrations of the method, analysis results, and their reasoning help the reader understand how their interpretations were derived from the data. More exemplars of phenomenological studies can be found in Wertz (2005), McLeod (2001), and the *Journal of Phenomenological Psychology*.

CONSENSUAL QUALITATIVE RESEARCH

In this section, we will briefly introduce a relatively newly developed strategy of inquiry, consensual qualitative research (CQR), followed by a discussion of exemplar studies. CQR is a systematic way of examining the representativeness of results across cases through the process of reaching consensus among multiple researchers.

Hill, Thompson, and Williams (1997) developed CQR based on the grounded theory (Glaser & Strauss, 1967; Strauss & Corbin, 1990), comprehensive process analysis (Elliott, 1989), and phenomenological approaches (Giorgi, 1970, 1985, as cited in Hill et al., 1997), as well as feminist theories (e.g., Fine, 1992; Harding, 1991, as cited in Hill et al., 1997). There are many common premises and differences between the CQR and these other qualitative approaches (see Hill et al.; Hoshmand, 1997 for a review). Yet, as Hoshmand noted, the initial guidelines for CQR (Hill et al., 1997) "did not articulate the implicit philosophical perspective on which the communal processes of CQR are based" (p. 601). For these reasons, CQR has been described as a "generic" qualitative approach (McLeod, 2001, p. 147). Recently, Hill and her colleagues (2005) and Ponterotto (2005b) attempted to locate the philosophical stance of this method in order to link the gaps among the ontology, epistemology, and methodology for CQR.

The primary components of CQR include gathering data through interviews and open-ended questions, describing the phenomenon of interest using words (not numbers), using a criterion-based sampling method, and understanding the parts of the experiences in the context of the whole. Usually a small number of cases (8 to 15) are studied. A primary team of three to five researchers independently and inductively analyze narratives of participants' experiences and then form consensus on ways to interpret the data. Through this process, multiple perspectives are included in the data analytic decisions. Also, domains and core ideas (abstracts) are identified from the data. Categories are developed by cross-analyzing the consistencies in the core ideas within domains; the terms—*general, typical, variant,* and *rare*—are used to characterize the occurrence rate of the categories. One or two auditors examine the consensual judgments on the domains, core ideas, and categories in order to ensure that important data were not overlooked (Hill et al., 1997; Hill et al., 2005).

The following key elements of CQR will be illustrated in greater details: (1) researchers, researcher biases, and training of the research team; (2) participant selection; (3) interview (data collection) and transcription; and (4) data analytic procedure.

RESEARCHERS, RESEARCHER BIASES, AND TRAINING OF THE RESEARCH TEAM   Hill and colleagues (1997) stress the importance of clearly describing the researchers because the data analyses of the CQR rely on the consensual process of the research team members. Although the composition and the dynamics of the team are essential, there is no absolute correct type of team composition (e.g., faculty members, senior practitioners, graduate or undergraduate students). Researchers need to clearly consider the various possibilities of the team composition and be very careful in selecting the team members, considering possible power differences among the group members, types of expertise, and the level of commitment needed from each team member. Before the data collection and analytic process begin, researchers receive appropriate training in conducting interviews and data analyses. It is also crucial that the researchers bracket (i.e., set aside) their biases and the information gained from the literature so that data can be approached from a fresh perspective and allowed to "speak" for themselves.

PARTICIPANT SELECTION   CQR adopts the criterion-based sampling method (Goetz & LeCompte, 1984, as cited in Hill et al., 1997), for which the criteria of selecting the participants should be clearly stated. This method ensures that the participants have had some depth of experiences with the phenomenon of interest and can provide meaningful information for the purpose of the study. Usually, 8 to 15 cases are studied intensively when using CQR because (1) this sample size, albeit small, usually provides a sufficient number of cases for the researchers to examine variability and consistencies across cases; and (2) additional cases typically add minimal new information (Hill et al., 1997). However, the sample size should also be determined by the homogeneity of the sample and the amount of data collected (e.g., length of the interviews) from each participant (Hill et al., 2005).

INTERVIEW (DATA COLLECTION) AND TRANSCRIPTION   An interview protocol can be developed based on literature review, conversations with the population of interest, and researchers' personal reflections (Hill et al., 2005). Pilot interviews are conducted to evaluate the adequacy of the interview protocol (at least two pilot interviews are recommended by Hill and colleagues). The actual interviews could be conducted over the phone or face to face. Previous CQR researchers also have used survey (open-ended questions) or email format to collect data (see Hill et al., 2005).

Immediately following the interviews, the interviewer(s) should record memos (e.g., impression of the interviewee, comments about the flow of the session) that later may be used to facilitate data analysis. Once the interview is completed, it should be transcribed verbatim with identifying information omitted and unnecessary nonlanguage utterances ("um," "ah") and fillers ("you know") deleted. Copies of the transcripts could also be reviewed by the interviewees for additions, corrections, or clarifications. This step is called "member check," and it enhances the credibility and trustworthiness of the data (Lincoln & Guba, 1985).

DATA ANALYTIC PROCEDURE   Hill and colleagues (1997) delineated the step-by-step data analytic procedure and divided it into the following sequential stages: (1) identify domains, (2) summarize core ideas, (3) construct categories from the cross-analysis, (4) audit the analysis results, (5) check the stability of the results, and (6) chart the findings. Specifically, these procedures were summarized in the update article about the CQR method as follows:

> Domains (i.e., topics used to group or cluster data) are used to segment interview data. Core ideas (i.e., summaries of the data that capture the essence of what was said in fewer words and with greater clarity) are used to abstract the interview

data within domains. Finally, a cross-analysis is used to construct common themes across participants (i.e., developing categories that describe the common themes reflected in the core ideas within domains across cases). . . . The auditor . . . provides detailed feedback at each stage of the analysis process (e.g., creating domains, constructing core ideas, creating the cross-analysis). . . . For a stability check . . . after the domains and core ideas were completed for all of the cases, at least two cases be withheld from the initial cross-analysis and then used as a check to determine whether all of the data for these cases fit into the existing categories and whether the designations of the general, typical, and variant changed substantially with the addition of the two new cases. . . . Hill et al. (1997) recommended charting the results to depict visually the relationships among categories across domains, particularly for data representing sequences of events. (Hill et al., 2005, pp. 200–202)

EXEMPLAR STUDIES   Recently, Hill and her colleagues reviewed 27 published studies utilizing the CQR method (Hill et al., 2005). Interested readers can find their recommendations for using CQR in Table 11.1 and numerous exemplar studies in their article, such as several multicultural studies (e.g., Kim, Brenner, Liang, & Asay, 2003; Kasturirangan & Williams, 2003) and psychotherapy research by Hill and colleagues (e.g., Hayes et al., 1998; Knox, Hess, Petersen, & Hill, 1997; Knox, Hess, Williams, & Hill, 2003). Next, we will use the research conducted by Juntunen and colleagues (2001) as a CQR example.

The study aims at understanding the meaning and relevant concept of career or career development for a group of American Indians (Juntunen et al., 2001). The authors interviewed 18 American Indians, mostly from one Northern Plains state, with varying ages (21–59 years old), genders (11 female and 7 male), educational levels (from 10th grade to some graduate work), occupations, and tribal affiliations. The sample included college students who self-identified as American Indian recruited through a university's Native American Programs Center, and their friends or partners, as well as attendees of two local powwows. Also, the authors divided the participants into two groups according to their educational levels because later data analyses revealed differences between participants who attended college and those who did not; a detailed description of each subsample was provided in the Participants section of their article.

A semi-structured interview protocol was developed for the purpose of the study by the primary researcher and two consultants who are American Indian scholars. The protocol was piloted with two American Indians and subsequently modified based on the results of the pilot interviews. CQR researchers use pilot interviews to examine the appropriateness and relevance of the interview questions from the participant's perspective and to uncover any important concepts that are unexpected by the researchers. The research team members were trained to conduct the face-to-face interviews using the protocol. The interview procedure was presented in great detail and examples of interview questions were provided. Interviews were subsequently transcribed verbatim and each transcript was checked for accuracy.

TABLE 11.1 | RECOMMENDATIONS FOR USING CQR

Consideration	Recommendation
Consensus process	1. Researchers should openly discuss their feelings and disagreements. 2. When there are disagreements among the researchers about the interviews, everyone should listen to the tape of the interview.
Biases	1. Report demographics and feelings/reactions to topic in the Methods section. 2. Discuss the influence of biases in the Limitations section. 3. Openly discuss biases among the research team throughout the process. 4. Journal reviewers need to be aware that biases are a natural part of any research, including CQR.
The research team	1. Either set or rotating primary teams are acceptable. 2. All team members must become deeply immersed in all of the data. 3. At least 3 people should comprise the primary team. 4. The educational level of team members should match the abstractness of the topic. 5. Team members with more designated power should not claim "expert status." 6. Power issues should be addressed openly. 7. Rotate the order of who talks first to reduce undue influence.
Training team members	1. Prior to training, read Hill et al., (1997), the present article, and exemplar studies. 2. Consult with an expert if having difficulty learning the method. 3. Describe training procedures in the Methods section.
Sample	1. Randomly select participants from a carefully identified homogeneous population. 2. Choose participants who are very knowledgeable about the phenomenon. 3. Recruit 8 to 15 participants if 1 to 2 interviews are used.
Interviews	1. Review the literature and talk to experts to develop the interview protocol. 2. Include about 8–10 scripted open-ended questions per hour. 3. Allow for follow-up probes to learn more about the individual's experience. 4. Conduct several pilot interviews to aid in revising the interview protocol. 5. Train new interviewers. 6. Ideally, each interviewee should be interviewed at least twice.
Data collection	1. Match the data collection format to the data desired and the needs of the study. 2. Record reactions to interviews; review tape before subsequent interviews.
Domains	1. Develop the domains from the transcripts or a "start list." 2. The entire primary team codes the data into domains in the first several cases; the remaining coding can be done by 1 researcher and reviewed by the team.

TABLE 11.1 | RECOMMENDATIONS FOR USING CQR (*Continued*)

Consideration	Recommendation
Core ideas	1. Use the participant's words; avoid interpretive analysis. 2. The entire primary team develops the core ideas for the first several cases; the remaining core ideas can be done by 1 researcher and reviewed by the team, or the entire primary team can work together to code the domains and construct the core ideas.
Cross-analysis	1. Use frequency labels to characterize data: *General* applies to all or all but 1 case; *typical* applies to more than half up to the cutoff for general; *variant* applies to 2 cases up to the cutoff for typical. When more than 15 cases are included, *rare* applies to 2–3 cases. Findings applying to single cases are placed in a miscellaneous category and not included in results/tables. 2. When comparing subsamples, results are *different* if they vary by at least 2 frequency categories (e.g., general vs. variant). 3. Continually refer to the raw data in making interpretations. 4. Continue revising the cross-analyses until elegant and parsimonious. 5. If there are mostly variant or rare categories or a lot of miscellaneous items, revise the cross-analysis (e.g., combine categories, subdivide the sample, or collect more data). 6. Get feedback from others about the cross-analysis.
Auditing	1. Either internal or external auditors are appropriate for the domains and core ideas, but at least 1 external auditor is desirable for the cross-analysis. 2. For inexperienced researchers, it is helpful for the auditor to examine revisions until he or she is confident that the data are characterized accurately. 3. Auditors should also be involved in reviewing the interview protocol.
Stability check	The stability check (i.e., holding out 2 cases from the initial cross-analysis), as proposed by Hill et al., (1997), can be eliminated, but other evidence of trustworthiness should be presented.
Charting the results	Charting or other visual approaches for depicting findings (e.g., "webs" or organizational diagrams of categories) could be helpful.
Writing the results and discussion section	1. At least the general and typical categories should be fully described in the Results section, although all categories in the cross-analysis should be included in a table. 2. Either quotes or core ideas can be used to illustrate the results. 3. Case examples are useful for illustrating results across domains. 4. In the Discussion section, pull together results in a meaningful way and develop theory.
Participant's review	Give transcripts of interviews and write-up of results to participants.

Note: CQR = consensual qualitative research.

Source: Reprinted from Hill et al., 2005, by permission.

TABLE 11.2 | CATEGORIES WITHIN THE DOMAINS OF MEANING OF CAREER AND SUCCESS IS A COLLECTIVE EXPERIENCE (REPRINTED FROM JUNTUNEN ET AL., 2001, BY PERMISSION)

Domain	Category	Frequency
Meaning of career	Lifelong endeavor	Typical
	Pursuit of a chosen goal	Typical
	Promoting American Indian traditions	Variant
Success is a collective experience	Contribute to well-being of others	Typical
	(a) American Indian community or tribe	Typical
	(b) Family members	Typical
	(c) The next generation	Typical
	Personal satisfaction	Variant
	Material gain	Variant
	Explicit rejection of material gain as an indicator of success	Variant

The authors clearly portrayed the backgrounds and experiences of the researchers composing the CQR analysis team. They also took specific steps to decrease the effects of researchers' assumptions on the data analysis results and to monitor the group dynamics (e.g., documenting and discussing their assumptions about potential findings in the early phase of the analysis process, audio taping the analysis team meetings, and then reviewing these tapes to ensure that each team member was equally involved in the analysis process).

Following the CQR guidelines, researchers coded the data independently and convened to form consensus on the domains, core ideas, and categories through cross-analyses. One auditor reviewed the work of the data analysis team and the auditor's feedback was subsequently discussed and incorporated into the final results by the team members. As mentioned earlier, the initial cross-analysis results revealed major differences in the career journey of participants with postsecondary education and those without. Therefore, the authors reexamined the domains and core ideas for each group separately. Although all of the domains remained unchanged, the categories within certain domains (i.e., *supportive factors, obstacles,* and *living in two worlds*) varied remarkably. Findings from this study were charted and summarized in Tables 11.2 and 11.3.

Overall, participants articulated their own definitions of career and success. In particular, participants with different educational backgrounds reported differences in the support for and obstacles in their career development processes and the diverse struggles related to living in two distinct cultures. Categories, which emerged from the data, were discussed and illustrated with direct quotes from participants. Following is the description of one of the domains with categories that vary across the two subsamples (i.e., *living in two worlds*).

TABLE 11.3 | CATEGORIES WITHIN THE DOMAINS OF SUPPORTIVE FACTORS, OBSTACLES, AND LIVING IN TWO WORLDS, BY EDUCATIONAL LEVEL (REPRINTED FROM JUNTUNEN ET AL., 2001, BY PERMISSION)

| Domain | Secondary Education Participants | | Postsecondary Education Participants | |
	Category	Frequency	Category	Frequency
Supportive factors	High value on education	General	Family influences	Typical
			(a) Family Support	Typical
			(b) Being a provider	Variant
			Sobriety	Typical
Obstacles	Lack of family support	Typical	Discrimination	Typical
			Alienation from tribal community	Variant
			Restrictions of reservation	Variant
Living in two worlds	Two distinct and distant worlds	Typical	Moving between two worlds	Typical
			Creating holistic third world	Variant

Six of the seven participants with a high school education viewed the Native and White cultures as quite distinct. In the words of one woman, "Those [White] people are way different from us . . . they don't understand a lot of our ways" (Participant 3). Another participant felt the need to adjust her own behavior to be effective outside of the reservation. She stated, "We have to live like Whites when we're out there" (Participant 6). This woman also noted that during the times she had lived off the reservation, she frequently needed "a powwow fix" as a way to stay connected to the Indian community. . . .

The experience of living in two worlds was dramatically different for the college group. Rather than seeing the two worlds as distinct and distant, the respondents who had attended college described the concept in two ways: moving between two worlds (a typical category) and finding a holistic, third world (a variant category). . . .

The process of moving between two worlds was often described as difficult, both emotionally and cognitively. A tribal elder remembers her experience in the college classroom, several hundred miles from her home reservation:

> You always have to do twice as much . . . because you have to process everything you think, reprocess it back into a thinking that you know [doesn't] fit with your thinking to make it right for the school. . . . Back when I applied to law school . . . they said 'You got to stop being Indian and you got to get through these 3 years of school' . . . anyway, you can't do that. You can't take that piece of you and set it aside. (Participant 13)

However, not all of the participants who moved between two worlds found the experience difficult. . . . People who sought a holistic, third world spoke of the desire to appreciate their own culture yet integrate those pieces of the majority culture that they accepted. Some respondents viewed this as a personal internal choice, which can be made whether one lived on or off the reservation.

Another woman spoke of her experience of two worlds as an evolution into a third world, which she has created from those aspects that are most important to her from each world.

> I've lived in those two worlds and there's also even a middle world. I mean, you have the Native, the non-Native and you have a middle world that I have experienced and it's a very personal, personal world where you gather, it seems like you gather from both worlds, and create, you know, a happy medium for yourself. I have two children that have lived with me on the reservation and off the reservation and I like it that way. I like them to be able to know both worlds. Because it just opens so much more range of experiences. (Participant 11)

> However, creating that third world does not mean that the original experience of her Native world is diminished in any way. "There's no leaving the Native American world. That comes along. When it's your core being, you can't leave it. I wouldn't want to leave it . . . I'm Indian to the core" (Participant 11). (Juntunen et al., 2001, pp. 281–282)

CQR researchers often use quotes from the interviews or core ideas to illustrate each category. As Hill and colleagues (2005) suggested, visual representations of the results in tables, diagrams, or figures also help the readers understand the relationships among categories. Finally, narrative case examples may provide a holistic picture of the findings. Examples of case descriptions can be found in the articles written by Williams and colleagues (1998) and Ladany and colleagues (1997).

PRIMARY TASKS IN QUALITATIVE RESEARCH

To this point, we have discussed the paradigms that form the philosophical bases of qualitative research as well as various strategies of inquiry. Regardless of the type of research paradigms and strategies utilized, the researcher must (1) gather data, and (2) analyze and present the data, two topics we will explore in depth next.

GATHERING DATA

Although there are many ways to collect data in qualitative research, we discuss three primary sources here: observations, interviews, and existing materials. Wolcott (1992) refers to these sources in the active voice as *experiencing, enquiring,* and *examining,* respectively, which provides a glimpse of the qualitative researcher's state of mind in these three activities.

MAKING OBSERVATIONS
The Nature of Observations   Observations are obtained by a trained observer who is present and involved in the phenomenon of interest and who makes

reports of his or her observations. There are several advantages of observations in qualitative research. First, because observers can experience firsthand the transactions among persons in the field, they need not rely on retrospective reports of the participants, which could be clouded by the participants' involvement in the situation. In the vernacular, observations take place "where the action is." Second, by being close to the phenomenon, observers can feel, as well as understand, the situation. The emotion present in any situation is likely to be attenuated as time passes; the oft-spoken expression "You had to be there [to understand]" aptly summarizes this advantage of observations. Moreover, informants may not be willing or able to talk about sensitive material, may not be aware of important events, or may consider important transactions to be routine. Third, deep involvement in the process over time will allow researchers to develop conceptualizations that can be examined subsequently. In contrast to quantitative research, investigators will not have a conjecture a priori that will be confirmed or disconfirmed; qualitative researchers may, over the course of the study, come to identify themes based on the observations of the participants and to relate those themes to each other, but such themes and their relations grow out of observation. This inductive process is the basis of some methods of qualitative research, such as grounded theory.

Qualitative observers traditionally have followed the dictum of nonintervention (Adler & Adler, 1994), which holds that the observer does not influence the phenomenon, but acts as a recorder of events. The observer neither asks the participants questions, nor poses problems to be solved, nor suggests solutions to dilemmas. The stream of life goes on in exactly the way that it would had the observer not been present, although qualitative researchers are aware that observers can have an effect on the observed.

Degree of Involvement of Observers   Observers can be described by their degree of involvement in the context being observed. Traditionally, the involvement of the observer has been described as ranging from complete observer, to observer-as-participant, to participant-as-observer, to complete participant (Gold, 1958).

The complete observer is entirely outside the context and would most likely be undetected by the participants. Observing public behaviors in a park by sitting on a bench would fit this category. The observer-as-participant is known to the participants, but is clearly identified as a researcher and does not cross over to membership in the group being observed or to friendship. In his observations of chemistry laboratories, Wampold and colleagues (1995) were observers-as-participants. Their presence in the laboratories during work hours was clearly recognized by the chemists, but the observers did not interact with the chemists during these periods.

Either of these two observational stances (namely, complete observer or observer-as-participant) could be used in quantitative research; the data would be transformed to numbers that indicate the degree of presence of some construct. For example, observations in a park might be used to quantify parental engagement, which could be defined as minutes spent by parent and child in face-to-face interaction. In psychotherapy research, behavior often is classified into one of many codes, with the goal of relating the degree to which the coded behaviors occurred with some other construct. As we will discuss further, even when the observer in qualitative research is not involved with the participants, the observations are not used to quantify some preconceived construct, but instead are used to gain a better understanding of the naturalistic context.

In modern conceptualizations of qualitative research, the unique contribution of participants-as-observers is their insider perspective: As participants-as-observers, they can experience what the other participants are experiencing, gaining an understanding of the context in ways that nonparticipant observers cannot. Participants-as-observers sometimes fill roles within the group, although "without fully committing themselves to members' values and goals" (Adler & Adler, 1994, p. 380). Many studies of schools have involved participants-as-observers who, in roles such as teachers or coaches (see, for example, Adler & Adler, 1991), become important people in the lives of the participants.

The final observational role is the complete participant, in which the investigator is a full-fledged member of the group before the research begins. Memoirs are examples of qualitative products created by complete participants in an activity. In an example from psychotherapy, Freud took the role of complete participant in his description of his cases. The degree to which one becomes a participant obviously depends on the phenomenon being studied. As Patton (1987) noted, one cannot become chemically addicted in order to become a participant in drug treatment programs, although one could be involved in such programs in ancillary ways (for example, as a staff member).

Whatever the role of the observer, the "challenge is to combine participation and observation so as to become capable of understanding the experience as an insider while describing the experience for outsiders" (Patton, 1987, p. 75). The tension between participant and observer is ever present and again emphasizes the necessity of research teams, which can process this tension and use it to produce an informative product.

Methods of Observations   Obtaining data through observations involves several steps. In the first step, the observer must select the phenomenon and its setting. Care must be taken in making this selection. At times this selection will be made opportunistically—because the setting is available and accessible. At other times the researcher may be invited to observe because the group values or desires a consultation by the researcher, which is the case in qualitative program evaluation. It is important that the setting be appropriate given the goals of the investigation. In quantitative research, the important consideration is the representativeness of the sample, whereas in qualitative research, greater emphasis is put on selecting settings strategically so that the data are meaningful. For example, instead of choosing a representative (that is, average) therapist to study intensively, a qualitative researcher may be more interested in studying therapists identified as successful, powerful, charismatic, or even unsuccessful. Patton (1990) provides a useful typology of sampling, including the purpose of various procedures.

The second step involves training investigators to be skilled and careful observers. Observers must be trained to attend to detail, to separate the mundane from the important, to write highly descriptive field notes, to be sufficiently knowledgeable to make sense of the context, and to be open to reconciling observations with those of other research team members. Consider a study of a K–12, urban school that primarily serves African-American students and consistently produces high achievement in their graduates (Pressley, Raphael, Gallagher, & DiBella, 2004). The researchers observed classroom interactions (e.g., teachers' instructional styles, students' responses to teachers' instruction, artifacts displayed in the classrooms) and nonclassroom activities (e.g., lunch hour in the cafeteria, conversations between the teachers/principal and students/parents in the hallway). The knowledge and skills in teaching, learning, and qualitative method facilitated the observers' teamwork in recording detailed field notes, sifting through a large amount of data, and sorting out the factors that contributed to the success of the school.

The third step is to gain access to the context being studied. Gaining access, of course, varies greatly, depending on the people being studied. Observing public behavior involves no special arrangements other than finding a suitable vantage point, but studying secret societies, especially those engaged in illegal or undesirable behavior, will be nearly impossible because these groups are unlikely to give their informed consent to participate in a study. Fortunately, most foci of qualitative research in counseling involve groups that are amenable to being observed. Often, trust is the key to gaining entrée to a group. If its formal leader is trusted, then his or her support can be sufficient for acceptance and cooperation from the group. However, if the leader's personal influence is tenuous and relations strained, then the recommendation to accept the researcher may be counterproductive and the observations undermined.

The fourth step involves deciding the time and duration of observations. At the outset, the observations are relatively unfocused and the researcher is getting the "lay of the land," and thus the duration of observation is as important as the time of the observation. Generally, observations should be taken at various times so as not to miss something particular to a certain time. For example, a study of work climate should involve observations from all shifts and during various days of the week. Clearly, the focus of the study should guide the researcher; for example, a researcher interested in how people from various disciplines negotiate their roles in multidisciplinary settings will want to observe instances in which the disciplines work together (for example, in staff meetings or multidisciplinary work groups). As the research progresses, the data will suggest ways that the observers can focus their attention. In the study of chemistry groups, Wampold and colleagues (1995) found that instances of conflict demonstrated how the array of chemists' social skills guided their actions, and consequently observations were arranged during times when conflicts were more likely (for example, during transitions from one research team to another on an expensive apparatus).

The fifth and final step is to collect the data. Most frequently observational data are the researcher's field notes (memos) taken during or immediately after the observations. Field notes are descriptions of everything relevant to understanding the phenomenon. Because relevance is not always clear in the beginning, initially field notes are likely to contain everything that happened. The novice observer will feel overwhelmed, but it should be recognized that almost anything missed will be repeated over and over again. As the observations become more focused, so will the field notes. For example, if it is observed that one group is superior in multidisciplinary work, the observations may be focused on how this is established as new members join the group; the field notes would similarly be focused on the process of transmitting power to incoming persons.

Field notes should contain basic descriptions of the setting—time, physical setting, persons present, the purpose of activity, and so forth—as well as complete descriptions of the interactions among the participants. Patton (1987) provides a good contrast between vague, generalized notes and detailed, concrete notes:

> Vague: The new client was uneasy waiting for her intake interview. Detailed: At first the client sat very stiffly on the chair next to the receptionist's desk. She picked up a magazine and let the pages flutter through her fingers very quickly without really looking at any of the pages. She set the magazine down, looked at her watch, pulled her skirt down, and picked up the magazine again. This time she didn't look at the magazine. She set it back down, took out a cigarette and began smoking. She would watch the receptionist out of the corner of her eye, and then look down at the magazine, and back up at the two or three other people waiting in the room. Her eyes moved from people to the magazine to the cigarette to the people to the magazine in rapid succession. She avoided eye contact. When her name was finally called she jumped like she was startled. (p. 93)

The latter description is more complete and involves little inference on the part of the observer, whereas the vague description both involves the inference that the client was uneasy and lacks data to enable confirmation of this inference at a later time. People's conversations should be recorded as close to verbatim as possible. Audiotapes can be used to supplement field notes if possible. Field notes should contain the observer's interpretations of events, but these interpretations should be so labeled to distinguish them from descriptions. Field notes might also contain working hypotheses, suggestions for interviewers, and so forth.

Undoubtedly, observations and field notes are influenced by the personal constructions of the observers. Multiple observers cross-checking their descriptions and their interpretations are vital for the integrity of observations, because trained observers may see a situation very differently. Acknowledging and honoring these perspectives is part and parcel of qualitative research.

Conducting Interviews

Types of Interviews   Qualitative researchers are interested in using interviews to make sense of people's actions in naturalistic settings. The language used by respondents is a powerful means to accomplish this goal. Basically, the interview is a face-to-face or indirect (for example, telephone) interaction between the investigator and one or more participants in which the investigator asks the respondents questions in order to obtain information.

Interviews can be classified into three types: structured interviews, unstructured interviews, and group interviews (Fontana & Frey, 2000). In a structured interview, the questions and the order in which they are asked are determined a priori. Moreover, responses are classified into categories or are quantified according to some protocol that also is developed a priori. The interviewer develops rapport with the respondent but takes a neutral stance in that he or she does not show either approval or disapproval of responses and does not follow up on unusual, interesting, or uninformative responses. The advantage of structured interviews is that they are standardized across respondents and minimize variations. However, they have limited usefulness in qualitative research because they (1) shape data to conform to structures that emanated from the investigator's previously held beliefs about the phenomenon, (2) use a standard language across respondents (rather than questions customized to the language of particular respondents), and (3) restrict affective components of responses (Fontana & Frey, 1994). Although technically not an interview, the questions can be printed and administered to participants, which is similar to a questionnaire except that the responses are not constrained in any way.

On the other end of the continuum, unstructured interviews provide latitude to explore the responses of participants and to adapt questions for respondents. Qualitative researchers often use unstructured interviews to collect data, and the responses would not be quantified. The type of question asked in qualitative research is shaped by the type of research conducted; thus, ethnographers approach this endeavor differently from grounded theorists, for example. Because the questions are not determined a priori, the interviewer has great latitude to explore the phenomenon and ask probing questions to get a more complete description. The respondents are encouraged to use their own language to describe their experiences; however, the interviewers must take care not to shape the responses by covertly reinforcing certain types of responses (for example, following up only on responses that fit the researchers' assumptions). As Polkinghorne (2005) suggested, "although the produced account is affected by the researcher, it is important that the participant remain the author of the description" (p. 143). Also, in the case when more than one researcher is conducting interviews, interviewers need to discuss how each person's personal styles may influence the participants' responses and subsequent analytic results. Furthermore, it should be noted that that data from unstructured interviews take a lot more time to collect and organize. Researchers usually need to do follow-up interviews because new insights about the phenomenon (and thus, additional questions) may emerge as more participants are interviewed.

Most of the interviews used in counseling research span the structured/unstructured continuum. Researchers often use semi-structured interviews to provide some consistency across interviews but also allow the respondents to have ample opportunity for offering richer responses. The challenge of utilizing the semi-structured format lies in the decision of how much structure should be imposed on the interview process. For an example of a relatively unstructured interview, consider Rennie's (1994b) study of clients' deference in psychotherapy, in which clients viewed a videotape of a recent counseling session (a variation of Interpersonal Process Recall; Kagan, 1975) and stopped the tape when they were experiencing something interesting or significant. The interviewer then "conducted a nondirective inquiry into the recalled experience" (Rennie, 1994b, p. 429), creating a description of the client's perceptions of the therapy in the client's own language without imposing predetermined categories for understanding these descriptions. As an example of a more structured approach, Frontman and Kunkel (1994), who also wanted to access clients' reactions to therapy, asked clients immediately after a session (rather than being stimulated by a videotape) to respond to the following probe: "As if you were making a personal journal entry, write what you felt was successful about the session" (p. 493). Because this probe was responded to in writing, no follow-up questions were used. Although the probe for this study was standardized, no preconceived categories were used to make sense of the responses, so that the conclusions were grounded in the data and not structured by the investigators' prior understanding of the phenomenon.

A third type of interview is the group interview, in which more than one person is interviewed simultaneously. Madriz (2000) describes a focus group as "a collective rather than an individualistic research method that focuses on the multivocality of participants' attitudes, experiences, and beliefs" (p. 836). Particularly exciting possibilities exist for focus groups, a modality that evolved from marketing research related to reactions to products, advertisements, and services. (For a brief history of the development of the focus group method, see Morgan, 1988, or Madriz, 2000.) In marketing research, the members of a focus group are strangers, but applications to qualitative research suggest possibilities for using intact groups, such as the staff of a mental health clinic. The goal of a focus group is to obtain the participants' opinions, not to reach a consensus or reconcile opposing views; the expression of different opinions is informative. Typically, the participants in a focus group are relatively homogeneous and are asked to reflect on a particular issue. The economy of using group interviews is self-evident, but a less obvious advantage of the group format is the interaction among the respondents, which can provide richer information as various members of the group provide more details, disagree on points, and reconcile differences of opinions. Having participants respond in a social context is thought to provide honest and responsible comments. However, the interviewer needs to ensure that minority opinions are allowed expression, given the natural tendency for such opinions to be suppressed (Madriz, 2000). A good illustration of this method has been provided by O'Neill, Small, and Strachan (1999) who used focus groups to explore the employment issues facing people with HIV/AIDS.

Methods of Interviewing   Counselors are well trained in the art of asking questions, and there are many similarities between the counseling interview

TABLE 11.4
TYPES OF
QUALITATIVE
INTERVIEW
QUESTIONS

Type	Examples
Background	Tell me about your background.
	How long have you been with the agency?
Behavioral	If I had been with you during a typical day, what would I observe you doing?
	What do you usually do when this situation happens?
Opinion or belief	What is your opinion about the recent decision to use untrained assistants?
	What do you believe is the best way to provide service to these clients?
Feeling questions	How do you feel about the decision to reduce the number of counselors in the agency?
Knowledge questions	How do you know when to terminate?
	How do clients get assigned to counselors?
Sensory questions	Describe for me the waiting room at your counselor's office.
	When you go to the principal's office after being tardy, what do you see?
Experiential	What is it like to be a counselor at this agency?
	Describe for me your experience of being in counseling for the first time.

Source: Adapted from Patton, 1987.

and the qualitative research interview. However, note that "research interviewing has different goals and requires different skills" (Polkinghorne, 2005, p. 143). Although the goals of qualitative interviewing will depend on the type of qualitative research conducted, a generic goal is to understand the experience of the participant; therapeutic actions should be avoided. Table 11.4, a typology of questions suitable for qualitative research, provides some examples of questions aimed at gaining understanding at various levels.

We now briefly examine the various steps in conducting qualitative interviews, adapted from Fontana and Frey (2000). The first step is to gain entrée to the setting in a way similar to gaining entrée for observations. Wampold et al. (1995) were able to gain access to two chemistry groups by first obtaining the support of the laboratory leader. Although all the members subsequently agreed to be observed, several declined to be interviewed because of the time it took away from their work.

The second step involves preparing to understand the language and the culture of the interviewees. A qualitative investigator strives to have participants express their experiences in their own language. To achieve that goal, the questions should be understandable and nonoffensive to participants. Also, the interviewer must instantly understand what the interviewee means by various idioms and expressions so that appropriate follow-up questions can be asked. This knowledge is acquired from previous experience and preparation and is accumulated over the course of the interviews. Moreover, knowledge of language and culture is needed to make sense of the interviews in the data analysis phase, which is described in the next section.

The third step is to make a decision about self-presentation. Whereas quantitative researchers present themselves as objective scientists, qualitative researchers can choose among various self-presentations. For example, a researcher might present herself to abused women as a feminist as well as a researcher. Basically, the issue here is the degree to which the researchers should share of themselves and how it would affect the participants' willingness to share their stories or personal accounts.

The fourth step is to identify the interviewees. The central concept in this step is *key informants*, people whose perceptions are particularly important for understanding the context being studied. Of course, the key informants will likely be unknown to the investigator initially, but as knowledge is gained their identity will emerge. Key informants are often those who have a different experience than the norm, who are willing to divulge sensitive information, who are formal or natural leaders, and so forth. Moreover, key informants may not be directly involved in the phenomenon being studied. For example, the support staff in a mental health clinic could provide important information relative to counseling at the agency, even though they neither deliver nor receive treatment. In quantitative research the emphasis is on representative samples, but in qualitative research the goal is to obtain a depth of understanding, and thus the choice of interviewees is a crucial process.

The fifth step is to establish rapport with each interviewee, a process that is beneficial for two reasons. First, rapport leads to trust, which in turn leads to honest and descriptive responses. Second, an empathic stance enables the interviewer to better understand the interviewee's responses. Interviewers must take care, however, that the natural affinity that goes hand in hand with empathy does not cloud their assessment of the situation.

The sixth and final step is to decide how the interview data will be collected. If done unobtrusively, interviews should be recorded and subsequently transcribed for analysis. In any case, field notes should be taken. (Note that the comments regarding field notes for observations apply here as well.) Important information is contained in the nonverbal responses of the interviewees, and in the setting and its surroundings. Therefore, certain critical data may be missing when interviews are conducted over the phone or via email.

It should be noted that interviewing is the predominant mode of obtaining data in qualitative research in counseling psychology, and it is deemed one of the most difficult and advanced techniques to master (Fassinger, 2005; Hill et al., 2005; Polkinghorne, 2005). Therefore, neophyte qualitative researchers are encouraged to hone their skills in this area. Kvale (1996) and Douglas (1985) discuss qualitative interviewing in depth. In particular, the procedures for conducting focus group interviews can be found in Greenbaum (1998) and Vaughn, Schumm, and Sinagub (1996).

USING EXISTING MATERIALS   Existing materials are written text and artifacts, which can often inform qualitative research in ways that observations and interviews cannot; such materials are essential to any historical study for which observations are impossible. As always, the goal is to use this material to provide a richer understanding of the phenomena being examined.

Written documents are of two types, official records and personal documents (Lincoln & Guba, 1985). Official documents include government reports, licenses, contracts, diplomas, and so forth. Personal documents include diaries, letters, email, literature, field notes, and so forth. Artifacts include material and electronic traces, such as buildings, art, posters, nontextual computer files—essentially any disturbance of the natural environment created by people.

One type of existing material has assumed primacy in qualitative research in counseling: the counseling interview (see, for example, Elliott et al., 1994; Thompson & Jenal, 1994), either represented as a verbal record (that is, a tape recording) or as text (that is, a transcript). In such studies, interpretations are made of the records of counseling. For example, Friedlander, Heatherington, Johnson, and Showron (1994) examined family therapy sessions to understand how sustaining engagement was important to change.

Of the three sources of qualitative data discussed in this chapter (observations, interviews, and existing materials), existing materials present the most issues, even though such materials can be particularly valuable. The difficulty with existing materials involves the interpretation of the text or artifacts, particularly when the analyses of existing materials and use of other methods (e.g., observations or interviews) yield different or even opposing results. Hodder (1994) gives several examples of discrepancies between material traces and people's reports of their activities (e.g., report of alcohol use versus number of beer bottles found in garbage).

ANALYZING AND PRESENTING DATA

As is the case for the collection of data, the analysis and presentation of qualitative data depend on the particular qualitative strategy of inquiry utilized. Here we discuss three generic means to analyze data and present results: thick description, themes and relationships, and interpretation. For more detail, see Wolcott (1994), who presented a thorough discussion of these methods, including lengthy examples.

THICK DESCRIPTION   Thick description is the most basic means of presenting qualitative data. Essentially, a thick description is an unadulterated and thorough presentation of the data. The researcher may write some introductory and transitory material, but principally the presentation consists of lengthy excerpts from interviews, field notes, and existing materials (text and/or descriptions of artifacts).

The consumers of thick descriptions have the raw data, which for the most part have not been altered by the investigator. In this way, "the data speak for themselves" and provide a rich account of what happened. Of course, the process of observing, interviewing, collecting materials, and deciding what to describe filters what is available to consumers. Still, even though the understanding achieved by readers of a thick description is affected by the research process, thick descriptions are closer to the phenomenon being studied than are any other means, qualitative or quantitative.

Despite the primary advantage that the data are minimally filtered, there are numerous disadvantages to using thick descriptions. True descriptions are too lengthy for journal articles, and many important thick descriptions languish as lengthy dissertations or unpublished reports. Another disadvantage is that the thick descriptions may be unfocused and uninteresting: "Readers are likely to get the idea that the researcher has been unable to sort out (or unwilling to throw away) data and has simply passed the task along. . . . [D]ata that do not 'speak' to the person who gathered and reported them are not likely to strike up a conversation with subsequent readers either" (Wolcott, 1994, pp. 13–14). It is hoped that the story, as told by the participants or as observed by the investigator, will be fascinating enough to hold the interest of readers.

Rarely are qualitative investigators able to present all data verbatim in a thick description, and thus they must use various strategies to present a condensed but still relatively complete description. As discussed earlier in this chapter, the methods of condensing and presenting the data vary in accordance with the strategies of inquiry adopted. Regardless, the investigator has the critical task of deciding what must go, and there are few guidelines. Crucial decisions about data should be made through a process that acknowledges the investigators' suppositions. Moreover, the process involved in examining these suppositions and making sense of the data in the context of these suppositions should be a prominent part of the presentation so that readers can understand how the descriptions were distilled to a reasonable length.

THEMES AND RELATIONSHIPS   Themes are recurrent patterns in data that represent a concept, whereas relationships are the interconnections among the themes. Through development of themes and relationships, the essence of a phenomenon is revealed. Extracting themes and establishing relationships are the essence of the three strategies of inquiry discussed earlier (i.e., grounded theory, phenomenology, and CQR). Essentially, the relationships of themes constitute the theory or the structure of the phenomenon, which is grounded in (is inductively developed from) the data.

The first step in this process is to generate codes for various themes that are intrinsic to the phenomenon being studied. Often tentative codes are first generated from initial observations or field notes on a word-by-word, sentence-by-sentence, or paragraph-by-paragraph reading of the text, and are then written directly on the transcripts. These codes name various patterns. For example, in a grounded theory study of psychotherapy, Watson and Rennie (1994) developed the code "reflective self-examination" to describe clients' observations of themselves that were "spurred by the questions they posed about their behavior, their feelings, and their interactions with the world" (p. 503).

As the investigator progresses through the data, the explanatory power of the various codes becomes apparent. The codes are revised and refined until a clear theme is developed. When the theme is relatively robust, the investigator reexamines the data to understand how the theme functions with the phenomenon (e.g., what is the context needed to give rise to the phenomenon?). In the Watson and Rennie (1994) study, the authors answered these questions by presenting the complex relationship among themes:

> The analysis of clients' subjective experiences during the exploration of problematic reactions provided access to the internal operations that clients engaged in to effect changes in their behavior. The model of the clients' experiences during the event highlights two important foci of clients' attention and activity during the session: client operations and session momentum. When engaged in the former, clients alternated between two primary activities: symbolic representation of their experience and reflective self-examination. . . . These two processes, together with therapists' operations, are related to clients' making new realizations and engaging in activities to alter their behavior. (p. 506)

The model of themes and their relationships provides an emerging grounded theory. As the model is developed, the investigator returns to existing data or collects additional data to test crucial aspects of the model. In their study of chemistry groups, Wampold et al. (1995) had a tentative model that described the chemists' avoidance of social interaction involving encoding and decoding emotion. Given that strong affect is intrinsic to conflictual situations, they returned to observe the chemists during conflict in order to understand more fully the interplay between the chemists' expression and understanding of emotion and their social interactions. The point is that the themes and relationships model should always be considered emergent and should guide further collection of data.

INTERPRETATION   Interpretation, as described by Wolcott (1994), is aimed at extracting meaning and identifying context. Rather than providing a theory of a specific phenomenon by relating themes, interpretation addresses more global issues, such as "What is the role of race and ethnicity in American society?" and "How do cultural factors affect conceptions of mental health and treatment?" Wolcott noted that "at the interpretive extreme, a researcher-as-writer may seem merely to swoop down into the field for a descriptive morsel or two and then retreat once again to the lofty heights of theory or speculation" (p. 11) and that interpretation "is well suited to mark a threshold in thinking and writing at which the researcher transcends factual data and cautious analyses and begins to probe into what is to be made of them" (p. 36). Clearly, novice researchers need to acquire more training and experiences in order to master these types of higher level skills.

TRUSTWORTHINESS OF QUALITATIVE RESEARCH

Finally, we will briefly discuss the criteria used by qualitative researchers to evaluate the rigor or trustworthiness of a qualitative research design. Some researchers have argued for alternative ways to evaluate the rigor of data collection and analytic procedure in qualitative research (Pidgeon, 1996). For example, compared to the criteria used by quantitative researchers for evaluating a quantitative study (e.g., internal validity, external validity/generalizability, reliability, and objectivity), a different set of criteria (i.e., credibility, transferability, dependability, and confirmability) were proposed by Lincoln and Guba (1985) to evaluate the scientific worth of qualitative research. Many qualitative researchers have since followed Lincoln and Guba's recommendations. Several guidelines also have been published by other qualitative researchers (see Cobb & Hagemaster, 1987; Elder & Miller, 1995; Elliott, Fischer, & Rennie, 1999; Morrow, 2005). Interested readers should refer to these publications for more details.

SUMMARY AND CONCLUSIONS

In this chapter we discussed the definition and underlying paradigms of qualitative research. The key myths and facts regarding qualitative methodology were also explored. Occasionally, we have encountered students who have undertaken qualitative research under the misguided notion that qualitative research is easier or less technical than quantitative research. Rigorous qualitative research certainly is different from quantitative research, but selecting this approach will lead to disappointment if the primary motivation is the avoidance of work or numbers. Qualitative research is time consuming and thought provoking. Be prepared to stay up late thinking about the meaning of field notes or transcripts, attempting to make sense of intrinsically ambiguous data, and writing, writing, writing.

This chapter has only scratched the surface of qualitative research. Volumes have been written about this subject, and one could devote all of one's energy to learning about only one particular strategy of qualitative inquiry. We have sought to provide the reader an appreciation of qualitative research, an overview of the various strategies of inquiry, general methods, guidelines for evaluating the rigor of qualitative research design, and references for those who want to pursue the topic in greater depth (also see Ponterotto, 2005a, for books and journals with a qualitative research focus). In addition, helpful examples of theses and dissertations that utilized various strategies of inquiry can be found in Wang, Heppner, and Heppner (2004a, 2004b).

Finally, we recommend that students seek out ongoing qualitative research teams and volunteer to participate. As suggested by McLeod (2001), we believe that the *personal qualities* of qualitative researchers (e.g., integrity, perseverance, and willingness and ability to struggle with ambiguity), rather than the *methodology* per se, have a greater impact on the potential contribution of the studies. The experiences encountered when conducting a qualitative research apprenticeship with veteran qualitative researchers not only can hone a person's methodological skills, but also can help to facilitate the development of these notable personal qualities.

STIMULUS QUESTIONS

ANALYZING THREE QUALITATIVE STUDIES

The following exercises are designed to help readers become familiar with the qualitative methodology and various strategies of inquiry.

1. Identify three published articles that utilized grounded theory, phenomenology, or consensual qualitative research approach in the following journals: *Grounded Theory Review, Journal of Phenomenological Psychology,* and *Journal of Counseling Psychology.* Review these three articles and respond to the following questions for each of the three articles:
   a. How did the authors situate their study in a particular paradigm (philosophical tradition)?
   b. How did the paradigm selected by the authors fit the conclusion of the literature review, the research question(s), the intended purpose(s), and the strategy of inquiry?
   c. Which strategy of inquiry was adopted? Write down the corresponding data collection method and analytic procedure utilized by the authors.

   d. How did the authors provide a "thick description" of the participants, the context, and their own perspectives about the phenomenon under investigation?
   e. How did the authors present their findings and their interpretations of the results?
   f. What methods did the authors utilize to establish the trustworthiness of their research?

2. After responding to the previous questions for all three articles, compare and contrast your answers. Then, select a topic of interest and a strategy of inquiry that may help to answer your research questions. Design a study using this particular strategy. Locate and read a number of publications that would help you gain more knowledge about this type of qualitative approach. Write down the appropriate paradigm, research method and design, analytic procedure, and expected outcomes.

Methodological Issues

12 CHAPTER | DESIGNING AND EVALUATING THE INDEPENDENT VARIABLE

One of the primary goals of the research endeavor is to establish a causal relationship between the independent and dependent variables. After a researcher has identified a research question, he or she takes the critical step of selecting or designing these variables. This chapter focuses on issues pertaining to independent variables, while Chapter 13 focuses on dependent variables.

Selection, design, and evaluation of the independent variable are crucial in establishing and interpreting causal relations in a study. If the independent variable is poorly designed, the researcher's effort will be unrewarding—either the expected effect will not be found or the results will be ambiguous or meaningless. Poorly designed independent variables create unwanted bias and extraneous variables, which are clear threats to Kerlinger's MAXMINCON principle.

This chapter discusses four issues related to the development and selection of independent variables. The first section discusses operationalizing the independent variable. But even when a researcher has carefully designed an independent variable, there is no assurance that the experimental manipulation will achieve its purpose, and thus the second section describes methods to check or verify the manipulation of the independent variable, often called manipulation checks. The third section focuses on interpreting the results of a study, whether the manipulation of the independent variable was successful or unsuccessful.

Thus, the first section focuses on issues pertaining to the independent variable that are relevant before an experiment begins, the second section on issues during an experiment, and the third section on issues after an experiment has been conducted. In the final section of the chapter we discuss independent variables that are not amenable to manipulation, which we define as status variables.

OPERATIONALIZING THE INDEPENDENT VARIABLE

Before an experiment begins, four concerns with regard to operationalizing the independent variable are particularly important to the researcher: (1) determining the conditions or levels of the independent variable, (2) adequately reflecting the constructs designated as the cause in the research question, (3) limiting differences between conditions, and (4) establishing the salience of differences in conditions.

DETERMINING CONDITIONS

In counseling research, the typical independent variable consists of several conditions. In the between-groups designs discussed in Chapter 7, the emphasis is on independent variables with two conditions: treatment and no treatment (that is, a control group). However, an independent variable can contain any number of conditions.

A treatment study can examine three treatments as well as a no-treatment condition (that is, four conditions in all). Or a treatment group may be contrasted with a placebo control group and a no-treatment control group (that is, a total of three conditions). Of course, the independent variable is not restricted to psychological treatments; in a study of preferences for counselors, European-American or Mexican-American counselors (two conditions) would constitute an appropriate independent variable (see, for example, Ponce & Atkinson, 1989). In this chapter, independent variables are discussed generally; Chapter 18 contains a presentation of treatment outcome designs in which the independent variable is used to establish the efficacy of treatments (that is, at least one of the conditions is a treatment).

Two notes need to be made about our discussion of conditions. First, we use the term *conditions* to indicate the groups that constitute the independent variable. However, *levels of the independent variable, groups, categories,* and *treatments* are other interchangeable terms that are used in the discussion of research design. In this context, *treatments* refers generically to conditions, and not to psychological interventions. Second, we have conceptualized the independent variable as a categorical variable—that is, each discrete category (level, condition, group, or treatment) is different. The independent variable need not be restricted to categories. Classical regression designs involve quantitative independent variables; in that case, the conditions reflect different amounts of something (see Wampold & Drew, 1990). For instance, in a drug study, the independent variable could consist of different dosage levels (for example, no drug, 2 cc, 4 cc, and 6 cc) or, in a psychotherapy treatment study, the independent variable might be the amount of homework assigned.

Because true quantitative independent variables are used infrequently in counseling research, they will not be emphasized here. However, later in this chapter we discuss status variables, and these variables are often quantitative.

The most important point is that, in experimental designs, the conditions of the independent variable are determined by the researcher. This determination is often referred to as the experimental manipulation, because the researcher essentially manipulates the independent variable to determine what effect it has on the dependent variable. In this way, the independent variable is related to the cause, and the dependent variable is related to the effect.

ADEQUATELY REFLECTING THE CONSTRUCTS OF INTEREST

It is important that the independent variable be designed to reflect the construct or constructs designated as causal in the research question. That is to say, the independent variable should be adequately defined or operationalized (see Chapter 3). If the causal construct is inadequately operationalized, alternative explanations for the results can be offered; these alternatives are potential confounds. In this chapter we indicate how problems associated with potential confounds can be minimized or eliminated.

To illustrate the importance of adequately reflecting the construct designated as causal, consider a study conducted by Malkiewich and Merluzzi (1980) to test the client–treatment matching model. The research hypothesis stipulated that high conceptual level thinkers would benefit from relatively unstructured counseling, whereas low conceptual level thinkers would benefit from relatively structured counseling. In this study, the structure of the counseling was one of the independent variables, and it was operationalized by including three conditions of the independent variable: a desensitization condition, a rational restructuring condition, and a control group. The desensitization group represented high structure, and the rational restructuring group, low structure. In this study, the expected interaction effect was not detected; one primary explanation for this null result was that the independent variable did not provide good exemplars of structured and unstructured counseling. It is unclear whether these two groups adequately represented differing structures, because both interventions are rather structured. This restricted range resulted in the threat of confounding levels of a construct with the construct, which is a threat to construct validity. To provide a better test of the independent variable (structure of counseling), it might have been useful to provide a type of counseling that is more clearly unstructured, thus providing a greater range of counseling structure. For example, client-centered counseling (which is often characterized as unstructured) could have been used to represent low structure.

Often constructs represented by an independent variable are operationalized by selected various exemplars, as illustrated by the Malkiewich and Merluzzi (1980) study, or by using various stimuli (sometimes called stimulus sampling). Generally, there are two considerations when selecting exemplars or stimuli. First, variability among the stimuli increases the generalizability of the results. This principle can be understood by examining the case where only one stimulus or exemplar is used. Suppose that a researcher is interested in the effects of self-disclosure on counseling process and decides that, in order to standardize the independent study, every counselor should use exactly the same self-disclosure. When the researcher concludes that self-disclosure affects the counseling process, the study is open to the criticism that the result is restricted to the idiosyncratic nature of the self-disclosure used in the study. It would be advisable for this researcher to have the counselor use a variety of self-disclosures, as was the case in a study of self-disclosure discussed later in this chapter (Kim, Hill, et al., 2003). An additional example of the failure to address the issue of stimulus sampling is Burkard and Knox's (2004) study of the effects of counselor color blindness on empathy. Each respondent received a vignette that varied on two dimensions: client race (European American or African American) and causal attribution (discrimination or depression). However, all respondents in a particular cell of this design (e.g., those who received the European-American client with the causal attribution of discrimination vignette) received the same vignette. Thus, the result that therapist level of color blindness was inversely related to capacity for empathy may have been specific to the particular vignettes used in this study; the study would have been improved by using several variations of each vignette.

The second issue is that the exemplars and stimuli should be representative of the universe of such exemplars and stimuli as they exist in the natural world. This idea stems from the work of Egon Brunswick, and is sometimes referred to as ecological validity (see Dhami, Hertwig, & Hoffrage, 2004). Again, there is a tension, this time between experimental control and ecological considerations. To the extent that the self-disclosures were similar to self-disclosures typically used in counseling and were delivered in the therapeutic context (i.e., in an actual case rather than in a one-session analogue), the conclusions would be more generalizable to actual counseling situations. However, this increase in generalizability results in a threat to internal validity, because one is less able to attribute differences to isolated differences in the independent variable. Illustrating this tension, Dhami et al. demonstrated that many conclusions about cognitive decision tasks obtained in laboratory studies do not hold in studies that attended to issues of representativeness of actual decision tasks. In Chapter 17, the topic of analogue research will be covered more fully.

Limiting Differences Between Conditions

The conditions selected for the independent variable should differ only along the dimension of interest. If the conditions are allowed to differ on other dimensions, the additional dimensions become confounds. To illustrate this principle, consider the previously mentioned study of perceived credibility of European-American and Mexican-American counselors as a function of counseling style and acculturation (Ponce & Atkinson, 1989). Although several independent variables were considered in a factorial design in this study, we focus here on the independent variable related to ethnicity of the counselor. Although there are many possible ways to operationalize ethnicity of the counselor, in this study ethnicity was manipulated by showing the participants photographs of the counselor and by using written introductions. In one condition, participants saw a photograph of a Mexican-American counselor, and the introduction used surnames and birthplaces that reflected Mexican-American ethnicity (for example, *Chavez* and *Mexico,* respectively). In the other condition, participants saw a photograph of a European-American counselor, and the introduction used surnames and birthplaces that reflected European-American ethnicity (for example, *Sanders* and *Canada,* respectively). Clearly, this arrangement operationalizes ethnicity of the counselor; the question is whether the two conditions differed on any other dimension. Because Ponce and Atkinson chose to use photographs, there exists the possibility that the Mexican-American and European-American counselors in the photographs also differed in personal attractiveness, which would provide an alternative explanation for the results pertaining to this independent variable. That is, higher ratings given to Mexican-American counselors by the Mexican-American participants may be due to either the counselor's ethnicity or personal attractiveness. Fortunately, Ponce and Atkinson were aware of this potential confound and controlled for it by ensuring that the counselors in the photographs were comparable with regard to personal attractiveness (and with regard to age, another possible confound).

As in the stimulus sampling methods described above, before research is conducted, potential confounds should be considered. It is not always possible to eliminate confounds, but identifying them before the study begins can enable the researcher to add features that minimize such confounds (for example, with manipulation checks, which are discussed later in this chapter). It is distressing to discover a major confound after the data are collected when some prior thought could have led to a modification of the study that ruled it out.

Often a researcher finds it necessary to argue logically that a confound has a low probability of occurring. Personal attractiveness seems to be an important variable in the counselor credibility literature (see Corrigan, Dell, Lewis, & Schmidt, 1980), so taking steps to rule it out was important in the Ponce and Atkinson (1989) study. However, Ponce and Atkinson did not rule out the possibility that the results of the study were caused by anti-Canadian sentiment due to the then-current difficulty of negotiating a trade agreement between Canada and the United States. Although this explanation cannot be ruled out by the design of the experiment, there is no evidence that political relations with the mother country of a counselor either affects or does not affect credibility. As noted in Chapter 5, the plausibility of a threat is critical when examining the validity of a conclusion.

Some troublesome confounds are unique to treatment studies; one of them is the counselor. Ruling out counselor confounds could be accomplished by holding the counselors constant across treatments; that is, the same counselors would administer all treatments. However, some counselors may be more skilled with one treatment than with another, or counselors may have some allegiance to one treatment or the other, and so forth. Hence, the superiority of a treatment may not be due to the treatment at all, but instead to the skill or allegiance of the counselor.

One alternative is to have experts in a particular treatment administer it, but this strategy introduces possible confounds related to experience, training, and so forth. Another possibility is to select relatively untrained counselors (for example, graduate students in counseling), randomly assign them to treatments, and then give them equal training in their respective treatments. Of course, this reduces the external validity of the study because the results are then generalizable only to inexperienced therapists. Once again, Gelso's (1979) bubble appears—there is no perfect solution to the counselor confound problem. Counselor or therapist effects are discussed further in Chapter 18.

ESTABLISHING THE SALIENCE OF DIFFERENCES IN CONDITIONS

The difference between the conditions on the desired dimension should be salient—that is, noticeable—to the participants. For example, Ponce and Atkinson (1989) could have used only the surname and birthplace of the counselor to operationalize ethnicity, which would have eliminated the personal attractiveness confound and made the research simpler. However, they included the photograph to increase the salience of ethnicity because without it, it would have been easy for the participants to read the half-page introduction (which focused more on the client) without attending to the counselor's surname and birthplace.

Although it appears that salience on the important dimension of the independent variable is vital to a study's validity, there are dangers when the salience is too great. If the participants can infer the research hypothesis from the study's procedures then there is the possibility that responses will be biased. Transparent salience creates a situation in which the participant may react to the experimental situation (as opposed to the intended manipulation), a threat to construct validity mentioned in Chapter 5. Often the inference about the hypothesis is based on the research's stated (to the participant) purpose and various procedures, as well as on the salience of the experimental manipulation. Presumably, participants who guess the research hypothesis tend to respond in ways that please the researcher and thus confirm the research hypothesis.

Reactivity to the experimental situation might have been a threat to the counselor credibility study discussed above (Ponce & Atkinson, 1989). Two Mexican-American researchers asked for Mexican-American volunteers from college classes. As the salience of differences in ethnicity was further increased by including photographs, the participants in the condition in which the counselor was Mexican American may have guessed that the hypothesis involved ethnicity of the counselor and therefore raised (subconsciously) their credibility ratings to please the Mexican-American researchers. Ponce and Atkinson attempted to minimize this by disguising the exact purpose of the research, although generally there are constraints on the degree to which deception can be used in research, as we discussed in Chapter 6.

In sum, conditions of independent variables should vary on the intended dimension but not on other dimensions, and the intended dimension should reflect the research question of interest. Furthermore, differences between experimental conditions on the intended dimension should be salient, but not transparent; participants within a condition should be aware of the critical component of the condition but should not be able to infer the research hypothesis. Of course, making decisions between salience and transparency is difficult, and is one of the skills that experienced researchers acquire.

MANIPULATION CHECKS

Even when great care has been taken to define and operationalize the independent variable, there is no assurance that the experimental manipulation will achieve its purpose. It is possible for the researcher to misjudge the salience of the independent variable. To verify that a manipulation has been adequately designed, it is often advisable to check the characteristics of the manipulation. The goal of manipulation checks is to show one or more of the following: (1) that conditions vary on the intended dimension, (2) that conditions do not vary on other dimensions, and (3) that treatments are implemented in the intended fashion.

To determine whether the conditions vary on the intended dimension, judgments of characteristics related to the dimension should differ across conditions. This determination can be made in a number of ways. First, inquiries can be made of the participants themselves. For example, Jones and Gelso (1988), in a study of the effects of the style of interpretation, manipulated style by having participants listen to audiotapes of a counseling session. In one condition, the counselor's interpretations were tentatively phrased and ended with a question, and in the other condition the counselor's interpretations were decisively phrased. The manipulation check was accomplished by having participants rate on a seven-point scale whether the counselor's comments were phrased tentatively or decisively, and whether they were in the form of questions or statements. As anticipated, there were significant differences between the conditions on both of the seven-point scales, providing evidence that the manipulation was indeed salient to the participants.

Another means to assess differences on the intended dimension is to have independent raters (persons other than the participants or the experimenters) judge the experimental materials. These independent raters could be either naïve individuals (those untrained in counseling) or experts. In the ethnicity-of-counselor study discussed previously, Ponce and Atkinson (1989) also varied counselor style (directive versus nondirective). Graduate students in counseling psychology rated the dialogue of the sessions, and the intended differences in directiveness were found, lending support for the adequacy of the independent variable.

Independent raters and the participants can also be used to establish that the conditions do not vary on dimensions other than the intended one. Recall that Ponce and Atkinson's (1980) use of photographs of the counselors introduced a possible confound related to the counselors' personal attractiveness. To control for this threat, undergraduates rated the attractiveness of several

European Americans and Mexican Americans in photographs, and the photographs used in the study were matched on the dimension of personal attractiveness. Parr and Neimeyer (1994), in a study of vocational differentiation, manipulated the personal relevance of occupations by having the participants circle either 12 occupations that were relevant to the respondent, 12 occupations that were irrelevant to the respondent, or 6 relevant and 6 irrelevant occupations, and subsequently giving them information about the 12 occupations they had circled. Later, the participants rated the occupations, and these ratings were used to check whether relevant occupations received more positive ratings than did irrelevant occupations, which they did.

A laudatory study that featured the various considerations relative to the independent variable discussed earlier was conducted by Kim, Hill, et al. (2003). The authors investigated whether counselor self-disclosure and Asian-American client cultural values affected the counseling process. In this study, counselor self-disclosure was manipulated by forming two conditions, one in which counselors did not self-disclose and another in which they did. After counselors received training in self-disclosure, clients were randomly assigned to counselors and counselor–client dyads were assigned to conditions; that is, counselors were told to self-disclose to some clients and to refrain from self-disclosing to other clients. Clearly, this is a manipulation that needs to be checked to determine the following: (1) Did counselors follow the directions to self-disclose and to refrain from self disclosing? (2) Were the sessions comparable with the exception of the self-disclosure? and (3) Were the self-disclosures salient to the clients? With regard to disclosure, observers were used to record each self-disclosure, and it was found that the sessions in the self-disclosure condition contained many self-disclosures ($M = 6.39$ per session) whereas the sessions in the no self-disclosure condition contained few ($M = 0.13$). Furthermore, the sessions for the two conditions did not differ in terms of client ratings of session quality, therapeutic relationship, counselor credibility, and counselor empathy. Finally, to check for salience, clients were asked to rate the degree to which the counselor self-disclosed; it was found that clients in the self-disclosure condition reported more counselor self-disclosure than did clients in the control condition. Moreover, Kim et al. allowed counselors to use several types of disclosures and tested the effects of the various types, thus ensuring that the conclusions were not restricted to one type of disclosure. Kim et al. carefully designed the independent variable and built in ways to assess critical aspects of the manipulation—fortunately, the checks demonstrated that the manipulation was successful.

Credibility of treatment is a potential confound in treatment studies. Thus, demonstrating empirically that credibility does not differ across conditions improves the validity of a treatment study. Deffenbacher, Thwaites, Wallace, and Oetting (1994), in a study of anger reduction, compared three treatments: inductive social skills training, skill assembly social skills training, and cognitive-relaxation coping skills. To test for treatment integrity, the subjects in each of the treatment groups completed a therapist evaluation questionnaire and a treatment evaluation questionnaire (Deffenbacher & Stark, 1992;

Hazaleus & Deffenbacher, 1986); the researchers found that these ratings were comparable across the three treatments.

In treatment studies it is important that the treatments be delivered to participants in the intended fashion. When the saliency of a manipulation is in doubt, checks provide a means of verifying the researcher's claim that the conditions differ on the intended dimension only. Whether or not manipulation checks are worth the extra time and effort required to implement them is a determination that can be made only in the context of a particular research study. Further issues related to manipulation checks are discussed in Chapter 18.

INTERPRETING RESULTS

The purpose of an experimental design is to establish a causal relationship between the independent and dependent variables. Thus far we have discussed topics related to design of the independent variable and to checking on the manipulation. Equally important is interpreting the results of an experiment, which provide much of the information upon which inferences are based. In this section we discuss various problems in interpreting statistically significant and statistically nonsignificant results with regard to the independent variable.

STATISTICALLY SIGNIFICANT RESULTS

Statistical significance indicates that the results for each of the conditions are sufficiently different, and consequently the null hypothesis of no differences is rejected. That is to say, there appears to be a true difference among conditions. For example, in a comparative treatment study, a statistically significant result indicates that some treatments were more effective than others, and thus the omnibus null hypothesis of no differences among treatments is rejected.

Although it might appear that statistically significant results are easy to interpret, there is much room for confusion. As we discussed earlier, the results may be due to a confound; that is, there may be another explanation for the results other than the intended one. In a treatment study, the experience of the therapist may be a confound. Even though the researcher attempts to design independent variables in such a way that there are few plausible confounds, no experiment is perfect, and several confounds may remain. Although manipulation checks can be used to rule out remaining alternatives, checks can also introduce confusion.

One of the most confusing instances occurs when the manipulation check fails to indicate that the conditions varied on the intended dimension, yet statistically significant differences on the dependent variable were found. This outcome is ambiguous because there are at least three explanations for the results. First, the results of the check may have been misleading; the failure to find that the conditions varied may be due to Type II error, inadequate measures, or poor procedures. A second explanation for a failed manipulation check but observed differences on the dependent variable may be related to the presence of a confound: The manipulation check was accurate (that is, the conditions did not vary on the intended dimension), but the conditions varied on some other dimension. Even if the researcher checked other dimensions and found no differences, it is not possible to check all confounds. A third possibility is that the statistically significant results were in error (that is, Type I error). Clearly, statistically significant results in the presence of failed manipulation checks are difficult to interpret.

It would seem that the best situation is when the results are statistically significant and the manipulation check shows that the conditions differed on the desired dimension. But even here ambiguities may exist. A manipulation check can be reactive, and thus significant results may be due to the demand characteristics of checking the manipulation and not to the independent variable. More specifically, asking the participants about the experimental manipulation may have sensitized them to many aspects of the study, and their responses on the dependent measures may have been due to this sensitization. For example, asking participants whether the counselor's comments were phrased tentatively or decisively (see, for example, Jones & Gelso, 1988) might cause the participants to review the preceding session critically and retrospectively change their opinion of the counselor.

To minimize reactivity, the researcher should consider administering the check after the dependent measure (of course, then the check may be influenced by the dependent measure), making the check indirect rather than transparent, and using unobtrusive measures (see Chapter 13). It is worth repeating that successfully checking the manipulation to determine that the conditions varied on the intended dimension does not rule out confounds, for it is entirely possible that the conditions varied on other dimensions as well. Nevertheless, interpretation is least ambiguous when the check was successful and the expected differences among conditions were found.

STATISTICALLY NONSIGNIFICANT RESULTS

From a philosophy of science perspective, null results are very informative. Nevertheless, nonsignificant results can be due to a number of factors other than the lack of a true effect, including inadequate statistical power, insensitive instruments, violated assumptions of statistical tests, careless procedures, and bias. We can also add poorly designed independent variables to this list. As discussed earlier, Malkiewich and Merluzzi's (1980) failure to detect the expected interaction in the client–treatment matching model may have been due to an inadequately designed independent variable. Showing that the experimental manipulation successfully differentiated the conditions increases the importance of nonsignificant findings; that is, if the conditions were indeed found to be distinct as expected but the results did not produce the expected pattern, then evidence begins to accumulate that the hypothesized causal relationship is not present. Jones and Gelso's (1988) study of interpretations in counseling did not produce the expected interaction between client type and interpretation style; without the manipulation check it would have been easy to attribute the null results to lack of salience of differences in conditions (different interpretation styles). Although Jones and Gelso discussed many possible explanations for their nonsignificant findings, the manipulation check strengthened the possibility that counseling outcomes are not dependent on the interaction of client type and interpretation style, as had been thought.

Nonsignificant findings can also accompany unsuccessful manipulation checks, as occurs when the check indicates that the conditions did not differ on the intended dimension, and the expected differences on the dependent variable are not found. This circumstance suggests the distinct possibility that poor design of the independent variable was responsible for the nonsignificant findings; consequently, the importance of the null findings for the field of counseling is mitigated.

STATUS VARIABLES

In this chapter we have emphasized the fact that the nature of the independent variable is determined by the researcher. By designing the independent variable in some particular way, the researcher attempts to examine its effect on the dependent variable. We have used the word *manipulation* to characterize this deliberate process. As mentioned previously, a study may contain more than one independent variable, in which case the effects of independent variables are typically examined in a factorial design, as discussed in Chapter 7. For example, Ponce and Atkinson (1989) manipulated both counselor ethnicity (European American or Mexican American) and counselor style (directive and nondirective) in a 2×2 factorial design.

Counseling researchers are often interested in variables that are not amenable to manipulation, due either to ethical constraints or to logical impossibilities. It is not ethically permissible to assign participants to a spouse abuse condition, nor is it possible to assign participants to a gender condition. We define all participant-related variables that cannot be assigned as *status variables*. Examples include personality variables (for example, locus of control), socioeconomic variables (such as education), gender, and ethnicity. Although many researchers label these variables as independent variables, the distinction between status variables and independent variables is critical to understanding the types of conclusions that can be drawn from these two types of variables.

Independent variables are manipulated and the effect on the dependent variable is subsequently assessed; if everything goes well, a *causal relationship* is established. In contrast, status variables cannot be manipulated, and statistical tests involving them detect *associations*. For example, Vredenburg, O'Brien, and Krames (1988) classified college students as either depressed or nondepressed; depressed students vis-à-vis nondepressed students were less assertive, had less control over their depressions, had lower degrees of instrumentality and persistence, and had a higher degree of dysfunctional attitudes. Because Vredenburg et al. were not able to randomly assign participants to levels of depression (that is, manipulate the independent variable), it would not be proper to assert that depression caused any of the personality variables. The causal relation could be in the opposite direction; for example, dysfunctional attitudes may be the cause of depression for college students. Or a third variable (for example, some biochemical dysfunction) could be the cause of both depression and the personality variables.

An important point must be made about the statistical analysis of status variables: Even though the analysis of status variables is often identical to that of independent variables, it is more difficult to make causal inferences because status variables are not manipulated (Shadish et al., 2002). It is the design, not the analysis, that determines the inferential status of the study (Cohen, 1968; Wampold & Freund, 1987). For example, Vredenburg et al. (1988) conducted analyses of variance with two groups (depressed and nondepressed); because depression was not manipulated, it cannot be said that depression was the cause of differences in the dependent variables.

It is not unusual to include both independent variables and status variables in the same study. Kim, Hill, et al. (2003) included adherence to Asian cultural values as a status variable as well as the manipulated self-disclosure independent variable. Frequently, research hypotheses are directed toward an interaction of an independent variable with a status variable; studies that address the question of which treatments work best with which clients are of this type. Two studies discussed in this chapter are examples: Malkiewich and Merluzzi (1980) examined the interaction of the conceptual level of the client (a status variable) with the structure of the counseling (an independent variable), and Jones and Gelso (1988) predicted an interaction between client type (a status variable) and counselor style (an independent variable). When interpreting the results of studies with multiple variables, one needs to keep clearly in mind the distinction between independent and status variables, particularly with reference to causal inferences.

We do not make the distinction between independent variables and status variables so that one type can be considered first class and the other inferior. The important point is that independent variables are manipulated so that causal inferences can be made directly. This is not to say that causality can never be attributed to some status variables. However, inferences in this case are made in a much different (and more difficult) manner. Consider the research on smoking and health. Smoking behavior cannot be ethically manipulated; for example, participants cannot be assigned to smoking and nonsmoking conditions. Even though there is little ambiguity about the fact that smoking is the cause of a number of diseases (Holland, 1986), this causal relationship was established by animal studies, epidemiological surveys, cross-cultural studies, retrospective comparisons, and the like. Because smoking cannot be an independent variable, the American Tobacco Institute is correct when it states that there has not been *one* study that has established scientifically that smoking is the cause of any disease; however, the causal relation has been firmly established over *many* studies. The first step in this process was to establish that a relationship exists between smoking and disease; then, alternative explanations were ruled out. Cook and Campbell (1979) provide a good discussion of the problems with attributing causality in field settings. We return to status variables in the context of sampling in Chapter 14.

Finally, it should be noted that some argue that any variable that cannot logically be manipulated cannot be the cause of any effect (Holland, 1986). For example, because it is not possible to assign gender to participants, gender cannot be a cause. According to this position, differences in rates of depression for men and women are not caused by gender; rather, differences in depression are associated with gender. Cultural or biological factors may be potential causes of this difference because, at least logically, they can be manipulated (even though it may not be practical to make such manipulations).

Confusing interpretations of studies are sometimes made because independent and status variables are not differentiated. A perusal of research articles in counseling demonstrates that status variables are often called independent variables. Nomenclature is not the issue here; there is little harm when the term *independent variable* is used inclusively. However, attributing causality without justification is an error that should be avoided assiduously. Causality is the strongest claim that can be made about relations between constructs, and one should always carefully examine the basis of causal attributions.

SUMMARY AND CONCLUSIONS

If causal attributions about the relation between constructs in counseling research are to be made correctly, the independent variable must be adequately designed. As we discussed in Chapters 3 and 4, the first step in this process is to state the research question clearly so that the manipulation of the independent variable can adequately operationalize the cause of an effect. Once the critical dimension has been identified, the researcher must design the independent variable such that the conditions vary on the intended dimension, but not on other dimensions. When the conditions vary on a dimension other than the intended dimension, a confound is said to exist, and it is not possible to ascertain whether the construct of interest or the confound is the cause of an effect. Furthermore, the intended differences among the conditions of the independent variable must be salient, so that they have an effect on participants, but not so vivid as to become transparent to participants, in which case their responses may be affected. If the independent variable does indeed vary on the intended dimension and is salient to the participants,

then between-group variance is maximized. Furthermore, avoiding confounds gives the researcher more control. Clearly, the independent variable is a critical component of Kerlinger's MAXMINCON principle.

To demonstrate that the experimental manipulation accomplishes what the researcher intended, it is often advisable to check the manipulation. The goal of manipulation checks is to show that the conditions vary on the intended dimension, that the conditions do not vary on other dimensions, and/or that treatments are implemented in the intended fashion. Manipulation checks typically are made by having either participants in the experiment or independent raters judge various aspects of the conditions of the independent variable. However, even when manipulation checks are used, the results of an experiment can be confusing. For example, ambiguity results when statistically significant differences are found among groups on the dependent variable but the manipulation check reveals that the conditions did not vary on the intended dimension. When the manipulation check is successful and there are statistically significant differences on the dependent variable, causal attributions are most plausible, although the researcher needs to make sure that the manipulation check was not reactive.

In many counseling studies, status variables are included in the design and analysis. Status variables are variables that cannot be manipulated by the researcher, such as personality variables, socioeconomic variables, gender, and ethnicity. Although the analysis of status variables may be identical to the analysis of true independent variables, the inferences that can be made are much different. When status variables are used, statistical tests detect associations rather than causal relations.

Clearly, design of the independent variable is a critical step in research. It is not unusual for researchers to have confidence in their manipulations only to discover after the data have been collected that a threatening confound was present. It is best always to be one's own greatest critic, and attempt to think of every possible problem with the independent variable before a study is conducted.

STIMULUS QUESTIONS

METHODOLOGICAL ISSUES

1. Find three studies in your area of interest. For each study, identify the independent variable. For each independent variable, state the various levels of the independent variable and indicate whether they are experimentally manipulated or are status variables.

2. Suppose a researcher is interested in editorial reactions to manuscripts on oppositional defiant children, where the research manuscripts differ on the basis of the ethnicity of the children (European American versus African American) and the attribution for the cause of the children's difficulties (external, such as poor family conditions, versus internal, such as poor impulse control). Describe how you would design a study to operationalize the independent variable.

3. Find a study in which a manipulation check was successfully used and one in which the failure to use a manipulation check led to a major threat to validity of the conclusions. Describe how the use of the manipulation check improved the validity in the first study. For the second study, design a manipulation check that could have been used.

4. Suppose a researcher compared the efficacy of two treatments for depression and found that one treatment was superior to another. Discuss possible threats to this conclusion that could result from the manner in which the independent variable was designed.

13 CHAPTER | DESIGNING OR CHOOSING THE DEPENDENT VARIABLE

The basic purpose of the dependent variable (sometimes called the dependent measure) is to measure the construct that is hypothesized to be the effect (referred to as the effect construct; see Chapter 5). Thus, selecting or designing dependent variables and the methods of data collection vis-à-vis the dependent variables are critical activities for the researcher. Typically, one subsection of the methods section of a journal article is entitled "Dependent Variables" or "Dependent Measures" and contains a brief description of and some psychometric information about the dependent variables used in the study. Only infrequently, however, is a rationale given for the choice of dependent variables: Why were these particular variables included and others excluded?

Extreme caution must be exercised in this process because the choice of dependent variables can be critical to the merits of the research. For example, a mother's report may be used to assess her children's behavior, but her ratings of her children's behavior may be affected more by her own psychopathology than by the children's actual behavior (Webster-Stratton, 1988). Likewise, the reported outcome of psychotherapy and counseling differs depending on whether the effects are judged by clients, therapists, or independent raters (Orlinsky, Grawe, & Parks, 1994). Investigations with poorly chosen or poorly designed dependent variables will at best be uninformative or uninterpretable and at worst be erroneous and misleading. Conversely, creatively designing a set of dependent variables might reveal new information that adds greatly to the knowledge base in a particular area.

In the first half of this chapter we discuss considerations in choosing or designing dependent variables. The essential issue is selecting dependent variables that are adequate operationalizations of the effect constructs in the research question of interest. In the second half of the chapter we discuss methods of data collection vis-à-vis dependent variables. In that section we classify and discuss seven nonexclusive methods of data collection that are useful in counseling research. The essential point is that because each method of data collection has different advantages and disadvantages, the task of the informed researcher is to collect data in a method that provides the type of information most relevant to the research question.

OPERATIONALIZING THE DEPENDENT VARIABLE

Choosing or designing dependent variables that are adequate operationalizations of the effect constructs in the research question is a critical step in research. The dependent variables must be designed or chosen to reflect the constructs embodied in the research question. This section focuses on three issues related to the design and/or selection of dependent variables. First, we examine the psychometric properties of the variables; we discuss reliability and validity as considerations in understanding the degree to which a construct is properly operationalized. Second, because the researcher must take care to ensure that the dependent variables do not react with the treatment in some way, we briefly discuss the role of reactivity of the dependent variable within the experimental context. Third, we discuss several procedural issues that can potentially affect participants' responses to the dependent variable, such as total administration time of dependent variables, order of presentation, and the reading level of the instruments.

A clear research question is critical to the proper choice or design of a dependent variable, as we emphasized in Chapter 3. It is important that the dependent variables be designed to reflect the construct designated as the effect or outcome of the independent variable. For example, in a treatment study of anxiety, it should be mentioned whether the treatment is expected to affect state anxiety, trait anxiety, or both (see, for example, Smith & Nye, 1989). If the target construct is not easily differentiated from related constructs, the research question (and related discussion) should explicitly indicate how it differs. Once the relations among constructs are hypothesized and the constructs differentiated from each other, the researcher's task is to choose or design dependent variables that appropriately operationalize the construct that is expected to change as a function of manipulation of the independent variable.

PSYCHOMETRIC ISSUES

One important question about the operationalization of a construct involves the psychometric properties of the dependent variable. Researchers need to know to what extent the dependent variables they select to operationalize a construct are reliable and valid. If the estimates of reliability and validity are poor, then the operationalization of the construct is likely to be inadequate. Although entire volumes have been devoted to psychometrics, we will review the rudiments nontechnically here because they are critical to understanding the degree to which a construct is properly operationalized, and how this affects the validity of research. The skilled researcher needs to have a strong background in psychometrics and broad knowledge of the psychometric properties of the dependent variables used in a study.

RELIABILITY   To be informative, scores on the dependent measure need to vary among a study's participants. If everyone obtained the same score on a measure, nothing can be learned about the individuals; however, when participants' scores are different, we begin to learn something about how the participants differ. It is hoped that differences between two scores are due to true differences in the level of the characteristic of interest; that is, variance in scores should reflect variance in the respondents. Unfortunately, the variance among scores may also be due to various types of error. To understand reliability, we must understand that the variances in scores obtained in any context are due to several factors.

The first vital factor accounting for variance in scores is related to the central construct being measured. In test theory, we say that for each individual a true score exists that reflects the actual level of the construct of interest. The degree to which obtained scores reflect the true scores for individuals is the reliability of the scores. More technically, reliability is the variance in scores that is due to true differences among the individuals. If an instrument produces generally reliable scores, then participants who possess more of a given construct will obtain higher scores on the variable (or lower, depending on how the variable is scaled). For example, on a scale designed to measure depression, a participant with a high score on the scale presumably is in fact truly depressed. Nevertheless, as we will see, some of the variance in most scores obtained from instruments is due to factors other than differences in the true scores.

Typically, the reliability coefficient of scores for variable X is denoted by the symbol r_{xx}. A coefficient of r_{xx} that equals 0.80 indicates that 80% of the variance in the scores is due to true differences, and that 20% is due to other factors. (Note that this coefficient is not squared to obtain variance accounted for, as is the case for a Pearson correlation coefficient.)

With regard to reliability, we first examine several sources of error in measurements: random response error, specific error, transient error, inter-rater disagreement, scoring and recording errors, and compounding. Then we discuss how to interpret reliability estimates and how to estimate reliability (that is, the variance due to true scores). Finally, we discuss how reliability affects the relationship among measured variables.

Random Response Error   There is often some error in any response that a participant makes. The most obvious example of these errors occurs in response to written items in a paper-and-pencil instrument, but random response error occurs in measurements of all kinds. One participant may read the word "ever" as "never" and respond accordingly; another participant may be distracted by a noise during testing and mark a response to the wrong item; a third participant might forget which end of the scale is "disagree" and which is "agree"; and so forth.

Although later in the text we discuss ways to calculate error due to random responses, a few important points need to be made here. First, the assessment of almost all meaningful characteristics of individuals and situations contains random response error. Simply asking participants "Are you male or female?" produces a random response error rate of about 5% (that is, it has a reliability of coefficient of 0.95; Campbell, Converse, Miller, & Stokes, 1990). With regard to measuring more ambiguous characteristics than gender or age, performance tests (such as intelligence tests) typically have the lowest random response error rates (namely, reliabilities in the neighborhood of 0.90). Measurements of other characteristics, such as personality traits or therapist skill level, generally have larger random response error rates.

A second point is that instruments typically contain many items measuring the same trait so that a single random response will not unduly affect the total score. Given items of the same quality, instruments with more items will be more reliable than instruments with fewer items. Consider a 15-item scale with reliability of 0.84. It can be shown mathematically (with the Spearman-Brown formula) that randomly selecting seven items to compose the scale would produce a reliability of 0.70. Extrapolating further, a one-item scale would have a reliability of 0.25, a value that is typical of a single-item scale (see Schmidt & Hunter, 1996, scenario 1, for an elaboration of this example). The point is that whenever anything is measured using a single item, one must assume that the reliability of this measurement is catastrophically low (with some exceptions, such as gender and age).

Although researchers are aware of this problem, occasionally they believe some phenomenon to be so straightforward that a single item is sufficient. For example, it is all too common to see global evaluations of satisfaction, such as "On a scale of 1 to 100, how satisfied were you with this experience?" In such cases, researchers pay dearly in terms of low reliabilities.

Specific Error   Specific error is error produced by something unique to the instrument that is different than what the researcher intended. For example, in an instrument designed to measure depression, the questions may be phrased in such a way that participants are well aware that responses to the questions vary in degree of social desirability; in such cases, participants' responses are determined to some extent by the degree to which they wish to appear socially desirable (a legitimate construct in itself), as well as to the degree to which they are depressed. Specific error is a confound because scores on this instrument measure both depression and social desirability.

Transient Error   Transient errors occur when a researcher is measuring a stable trait at a single point in time or in response to a single stimulus in such a way that the conditions at that time or with the particular stimulus affect the measurement of the trait. Consider the measurement of depression, the manifestation of which can be affected by transient mood states: A depressed college student's responses to a depression inventory, for example, would be affected by receiving a failing grade on an examination in the hour preceding the assessment; other participants' responses would be similarly affected by moods created by recent events.

Transient errors can be induced by administering tests in a particular order. For example, an instrument used to assess anxiety may in fact create in participants an anxious mood, which in turn would affect scores on a subsequent instrument, producing artifactual scores on the second instrument. These transient effects create error that is unrelated to true scores.

A related problem is particularly problematic in counseling research. Suppose that one were interested in the assessment of the cultural competence of a beginning counselor, and such a determination is made by the novice counselor's responses to only one client. Idiosyncrasies of the client and of the novice counselor's relationship with this client will affect the assessed level of skill, creating unreliability in the assessment of cultural competence.

Inter-rater Disagreement   In counseling research, raters are often used to obtain assessments. Consider a study of the antisocial behavior of school children involving naturalistic observations of the children's conduct in the school setting. Although raters of the children's conduct would be trained to adhere to some coding system, some of the variance in the observers' rating may be due to the observer rather than the behavior (e.g., some raters are more sensitive to negative behaviors). If ratings reflect the actual behavior and not idiosyncrasies of the observer, then we would expect the observers' ratings to agree. In any observational study, adequate agreement among raters is required. For example, Melby, Hoyt, and Bryant (2003) demonstrated that rater race may account for significant variance in rater bias. Furthermore, race-related bias may not decrease with training. The authors suggest these findings may indicate that certain interpretations of target behavior are culturally mediated.

It should be noted that inter-rater agreement is necessary, but not sufficient, for reliable assessments. If the observers rate an individual's behavior at a single time, then transient error remains problematic. Schmidt and Hunter (1996) described a study (McDaniel, Whetzel, Schmidt, & Maurer, 1994) that found that the correlation between raters of a common job interview was 0.81, but the correlation between raters of the same applicant in different interviews was only 0.52, demonstrating the magnitude of transient error. Specific error may also occur because the rating system is sensitive to some construct other than the targeted construct. For example, raters in the antisocial behavior example who are sensitive to personal appearance may rate unkempt participants as more antisocial, regardless of behavior, which would then add error variance to antisocial ratings. Moreover, observers can agree and still be off the mark. Continuing the antisocial behavior example, several observers may initially be sensitive to every antisocial behavior (as when a student bumps into another student intentionally), but as they are exposed to more egregious behavior (students striking other students or threatening others with weapons) they may become desensitized to and consequently ignore less objectionable behavior, all the while maintaining rater agreement. This is called *observer drift*.

Scoring and Recording Errors   Errors in assessment can be created by researchers through scoring and recording errors, which are any errors created in any way by manipulating the data in the process from scoring a protocol to preparing the data for statistical analysis. These errors, which function as random response error (and technically could be classified as such) obscure true score variance. Outliers in data may result from such errors. Researchers are encouraged to treat their data carefully to minimize such errors, although scoring and recording errors are usually minor in comparison to the previously discussed errors.

Compounding Errors   The errors we have mentioned can be compounded to form an assessment with abysmal reliability. Consider the worst-case scenario: Several observers, each observing one participant, rate some characteristic only a single time in response to a single stimulus using a one-item, pencil-and-paper rating instrument, and then record the response, which later will be entered into the computer. This is exactly the case when a practicum instructor is asked to rate, on a scale of 1 to 100, the skill level of a practicum student with a particular client in a particular session. This operationalization of counseling skill introduces many sources of error. First, there is unknown variance among the practicum instructors. They likely have very different implicit criteria that underlie their judgment of skill; inter-rater reliability is unknown and indeterminate because multiple raters of the same participant were not used. Second, only a single, ambiguous item was used to assess the construct. Third, the skill level displayed in a single session is subject to transient errors due to the characteristics of the client, to the presence of particular factors that affect the success of the session (for example, the mood of student and client), and to other factors. Finally, opportunities for scoring and recording errors were not minimized. Although we are unlikely to encounter a case this extreme, awareness of the various sources of error can help researchers avoid the problems discussed here. In this example, it would have been much better to have more than one rater rate all of the students, over several sessions with several clients, using an instrument that contained multiple items related to skill that was scored via computer.

Interpreting Reliability Estimates   Determining the reliability of a research instrument involves many considerations. First, any reliability coefficient is an estimate of the true reliability, in the same way that a mean of a sample is an estimate of the population mean. Later in this section we describe various methods for calculating reliability coefficients, but it should be kept in mind that these coefficients are estimates that vary across samples. Second, reliability reflects variance due to true scores, but it does not indicate what the true scores are measuring. A set of scores that are reliable may be measuring something quite different than what was postulated; for example, a personality measure may be measuring social desirability rather than the targeted construct. Developers of scales often attach names to them that indicate some construct (for example, the ABC Scale of Social Skills), but adequate reliability does not establish that the instrument actually measures that construct (in this instance, social skills). It is validity, which will be discussed later in this chapter, that is concerned with whether the construct being measured is the construct of interest. A third point is that reliability is based on the scores and not on the instrument from which they were derived. The scores have certain properties that are derived from the characteristics of the instrument. A vital consequence of this distinction is that reliability estimates are restricted to the types of participants on whom, and the conditions under which, the psychometric study was conducted.

An instrument may perform adequately for one type of participant but not for another type, or under one set of conditions but not under others. For example, an anxiety measure that yields adequate reliability estimates with undergraduates when administered in a classroom may be completely useless for measuring the anxiety of agoraphobics in a laboratory setting. Put another way, the instrument may be very sensitive to midrange differences in anxiety but insensitive at the upper range. This is called a *ceiling effect*; all the agoraphobics may have scored at or near the maximum, and thus their scores were not reflective of true differences in anxiety. Of course, this problem may also be manifest at the bottom of the range, creating a *floor effect*. Reliability is also dependent on characteristics of the participants, such as reading ability and age. An instrument may yield adequate reliability for college students but not for high school dropouts because of random error created by the latter's difficulty in reading the items. Moreover, instruments may contain items that have different meanings to different cultures, and it should not be assumed that reliability estimates are transferable. Ponterotto and Casas (1991) found that only 25% of counseling instruments used in multicultural counseling research were developed psychometrically for ethnic minority populations. The implication of this discussion is that researchers should choose instruments that are sensitive in the range of scores anticipated and the type of participants used in the study. Such a choice requires a careful reading of the psychometric studies conducted on various instruments. Alternatively, the reliability of the scores actually obtained in a study could be estimated; typically this is impractical because large numbers of participants are needed for such studies (typically in excess of 300; Nunnally, 1978) and because reliability estimates are affected by mean differences obtained for the various conditions of the independent variable. How high should reliability be? Some sources indicate that reliability estimates in excess of 0.80 are sufficient. Certainly, all things being equal, the instrument that yielded the highest reliability in the desired range should be chosen over other instruments. However, all things are rarely equal, and choices must be made.

Other factors need to be considered, including validity, time required to complete the instrument, and costs (topics to be discussed later in this chapter).

Thus, in instances when a construct is elusive, reliability of 0.70 may be adequate. Keep in mind, however, that reliability of 0.70 means that 30% of the variance of the scores on the dependent variable is due to error. Certainly, reliability indexes below 0.50 contain serious psychometric problems that limit the utility of the instrument.

Calculating Estimates of Reliability   There are many ways to estimate the reliability of scores, each of which is sensitive to one or more of the errors previously discussed. The various coefficients will be briefly discussed here; for additional detail the reader is referred to psychometric texts. If the various items of an instrument are measuring the same construct, then scores on the items will tend to covary; that is, someone who has a high level of the construct (for example, is anxious) will tend to answer all the items in one direction (assuming the items are all keyed in the same direction), whereas someone who has a low level of the construct (for example, is not anxious) will tend to answer all the items in the other direction. *Internal consistency* refers to the homogeneity of the items. When scores for the various items are highly intercorrelated, internal consistency is high. Consequently, if the test is internally consistent, then the score derived from one half of the items will be highly correlated with the score derived from the other half of the items. This correlation (corrected for the fact that it is derived from tests half as long) is called the split-half reliability coefficient. Because this coefficient is dependent on the particular split, a better estimate is derived using the formula for the coefficient alpha, which is equal to the mean of all the possible split-half coefficients. One occasionally sees reliability estimated with the Kuder-Richardson 20 formula, which is a special case of coefficient alpha used when items are scored dichotomously (that is, when each item has two possible outcomes, such as correct and incorrect). Although measures of internal consistency are widely used, they are not sensitive to specific and transient errors. For example, a measure of extroversion may reflect (to some degree) transient mood states, or a measure of counseling skill may be specific to a particular client. Scores on extroversion or counseling skill may be internally consistent but contain variance due to extraneous specific or transitory sources.

Indexes that take into account measurements taken at different times or made in response to different stimuli are sensitive to transient effects. The most common such index is the test-retest correlation. If a construct is expected to remain stable over a period of time, and if the instrument is not subject to transient or random response errors, then test-retest correlations should be high. If internal consistency is high but the test-retest coefficient is relatively low and the construct is expected to be stable over that period of time, then the scores reflect transient effects. A similar index can be used to assess transient effects due to different stimuli. If a measure of counseling skill is internally consistent with one client, but the correlation of the skill measure with two different clients is low, then one can conclude that the skill measure is not adequate to measure general counseling competence because it is measuring something related to specific clients. Of course, test-retest coefficients are inappropriate if the construct being measured is not expected to remain constant.

One problem with the test-retest coefficient is that it overestimates reliability because it is not sensitive to specific error. If something unique is measured by an instrument, then this unique characteristic would be measured on the second administration of this instrument as well. One way to address this problem is to use parallel forms at the two times. Correlations between parallel forms of an instrument at two different times (or in response to two different stimuli) help identify random response, specific, and transient errors. If ratings are used, indexes of inter-rater agreement are necessary. Essentially, multiple raters are needed so that their level of agreement can be calculated.

Although there are many ways to measure inter-rater agreement, most methods simply index agreement between the raters and do not take into account random response, specific, or transient errors, as discussed previously. Even if raters are responding randomly, they will agree occasionally merely by chance, and consequently any measure of inter-rater agreement should be corrected for chance agreements.

Effects of Unreliability on Relationships among Variables   We have made much of the fact that instruments should yield reliable measures in order to be useful in counseling research. We now illustrate, through some examples, the pernicious effects of unreliability. Consider two constructs, A and B, and two measures of the constructs, X and Y, respectively. Suppose that all of the sources of error (internal inconsistency, transient errors, and so forth) for these two constructs are equal to about 30%; that is, $r_{xx} = 0.70$ and $r_{yy} = 0.70$. Now suppose that the researcher claims that the two constructs are distinct because X and Y are highly, but not perfectly, correlated—say, $r_{xy} = 0.70$. In this example, the researcher is claiming that two constructs exist, and that interpretations can be made about those constructs from the variables X and Y. But it should be kept in mind that the correlation of 0.70 is the correlation of the measures X and Y, not the correlation of the constructs A and B. Because the error in each of the measures cannot be systematically related (that is, it is random error), the obtained correlation of the measures is less than the correlation of the constructs, and we say that the correlation of the constructs has been attenuated by the unreliability of the measures.

Classical test theory provides a formula for correcting for the attenuation:

$$r_{AB} = r_{xy} / \sqrt{r_{xx}\, r_{yy}}$$

Put into words, the correlation between the constructs is equal to the obtained correlation between the measures divided by the square root of the product of the reliabilities of the measures. In our present example, the correlation between the constructs would be

$$r_{AB} = 0.70 / \sqrt{(0.70)(0.70)} = 1.00$$

That is, the correlation between the constructs is perfect, and the only differences between the scores on X and Y are due to random error—any interpretations involving two distinct constructs would be in error.

The point of this example is that even if two constructs are perfectly correlated, the obtained correlation will be dramatically attenuated by unreliability. (Note that we have not discussed the effect of sampling error, which could also dramatically affect the obtained correlation.) This is not an artificial example; many subscales of instruments are correlated in the neighborhood of 0.70, with reliabilities in the neighborhood of 0.70, suggesting that these subscales are measuring the same construct, rather than distinct constructs (see, for example, Atkinson & Wampold, 1982).

Now consider the following example, which illustrates how unreliability can make it almost impossible to obtain expected results in a study. Suppose that a researcher is interested in the relation between the skills of counselors in training and counseling outcome. The generic skill of the beginning counselors is rated by the practicum instructor on a single-item scale anchored by "Very skilled—top 5% of all practicum students" and "Very unskilled—lowest 5% of all practicum students." Suppose that a single measure of outcome was used—for example, a measure of depression. Now also suppose that the researcher is very fortunate to sample all of the students in a large program, say $n = 30$. What are the chances that the researcher will detect a true relationship between skill and outcome? As we will see, the probability is low. As we discussed earlier, the reliability of skill ratings, especially on a single-item instrument, is probably extremely low; for this example, suppose that the reliability of such ratings is generously assigned a value of 0.50. Suppose also that the measure of depression is fairly reliable—say, $r_{yy} = 0.80$. Furthermore, suppose that about 20% of the variance in outcome is due to the skill of the counselor (a reasonable estimate, given that variance in outcome is also due to initial severity, treatment administered, motivation for therapy, social support of client, and so forth). If 20% of the variance in outcome is due to skill, then the population correlation between the constructs of skill and outcome would be 0.45 (that is, variance accounted for is the square of the correlation coefficient). However, this correlation is attenuated by the unreliability of the measures of the constructs; using the attenuation formula, the correlation is reduced to 0.28. The power to detect a population correlation of 0.28 with 30 participants is about 0.35; that is, the probability of rejecting the null hypothesis of no relationship between skills and outcome is 0.35 when the true correlation is 0.28. Said another way, about 65% of the times this study would be executed, the researcher would conclude that there was no relationship between therapist skill and outcome, despite the fact that the true relationship between skill and outcome is strong! This is obviously a disturbing result, because it will likely be concluded that the skills of practicum students are unrelated to outcome, when this is not the case. In Chapter 5 we discussed threats to the statistical conclusion validity of a study due to unreliability of measures and low power; this is a graphic illustration of these effects. The central point here is that the obtained relation between measures of constructs may be very different than the true relationship between constructs, due to the unreliability of measures. When any statistical relation is represented, one must be very clear about whether one is discussing variables (measures of constructs) or constructs.

Although the preceding example involved correlations, the same principles apply to experimental designs. The reliability of the dependent variable, and the degree to which the independent variable faithfully and saliently represents the intended differences between conditions, attenuates the size of the effect and reduces the power of the statistical test of differences among groups. Any conclusion that a treatment resulted in no differences in outcome may be due to the low power resulting from unreliability.

VALIDITY   Of the many types of validity, the most important type for research purposes is *construct validity*—the degree to which the scores reflect the desired construct rather than some other construct. Clearly, unreliable scores cannot have construct validity because they are due mostly to random error. Nevertheless, as mentioned previously, reliable scores may reflect one or more constructs other than the one specified. Specifically, scores may be quite reliable but lack construct validity. Determining construct validity, although complicated and indirect, is vital to the integrity of a study.

One way to establish construct validity is to examine the relation between scores on the instrument and scores on other instruments intended to measure the same and other constructs. Clearly, there should be a high correlation between instruments that measure the same construct. If these expected correlations are found, then *convergent validity* is said to exist. Measures of different constructs should not be highly correlated, although a moderate correlation can be tolerated and may even be expected. Nevertheless, the correlation of measures of different constructs should be smaller than correlations of measures of the same construct; if this pattern is found, *discriminant validity* is said to exist.

Exploratory Factor Analysis and the Use of Subscales of an Instrument   Construct validity can be established through a statistical procedure called factor analysis (Tinsley & Tinsley, 1987), a data reduction procedure that examines the factors that underlie a set of variables. If the set of variables is the scores on a variety of tests, then factor analysis can be used to detect a small number of factors that account for the variance in the scores. Variables that measure the same construct will be grouped together in the sense that they will correlate highly (load on) a single factor. The factors are then interpreted as constructs.

Sometimes factor analysis is used to develop scales. This strategy involves factor-analyzing items rather than variables. A set of items is subjected to a factor analysis, items are segregated by their loadings on factors, descriptors are assigned to factors, and subscale scores are calculated based on the segregation (for example, the score for the subscale that corresponds to Factor 1 is formed by summing the scores for those items that load on Factor 1).

Generally, this is not a procedure that produces satisfactory results. There are three problems: (1) The method is atheoretical and may lead to factors that have little psychological basis and are driven by the data; (2) even if the factor analysis uses a method that produces independent factors, the subscale scores likely will be highly correlated, because items load to some degree on all factors; and (3) the reliability of single items is low, and thus the results of factor analyses are often unstable, in which case cross-validations are necessary.

An improvement on the exploratory factor analytic strategy is to develop items specifically to measure factors of a construct. This strategy was used to develop one of the most widely used counseling instruments, the Counselor Rating Form (CRF; Barak & LaCrosse, 1975). The CRF is a 36-item scale designed to measure three characteristics of the counselor related to the social influence the counselor possesses vis-à-vis the client: trustworthiness, attractiveness, and expertness. Each item contains an adjective and its opposite (for example, logical/illogical), and respondents rate their perception of the counselor on a seven-point scale with regard to these adjectives (1 = logical, 7 = illogical). Subscale scores for trustworthiness, attractiveness, and expertness are determined by summing the scores for the items within each subscale. There are 12 items for trustworthiness, 12 items for attractiveness, and 12 items for expertness.

Although factor analyses of the CRF (see Heppner & Claiborn, 1989) have verified the existence of three factors (that is, the 12 items loaded on the expected factors), the correlation among the factors was high (generally in the range of 0.60 to 0.80), suggesting that one general factor may be operating. This general factor, labeled the "good guy" factor (Ponterotto & Furlong, 1985), suggests that responses to the CRF are due primarily to a general opinion about the counselor. Based on a revision of the CRF called the Counselor Rating Form—Short (CRFS; Corrigan & Schmidt, 1983), Tracey, Glidden, and Kokotovic (1988) showed the pervasiveness of the general evaluation factor using a variation of confirmatory factor analysis. Moreover, in a study of premature termination, Kokotovic and Tracey (1987) found that continuers and dropouts differed in the degree to which they rated their counselors as trustworthy and expert, but when the effects of general satisfaction (measured on a different instrument) were controlled, the three CRF scales poorly discriminated continuers from dropouts.

The preceding discussion of the CRF and its subscales raises an issue: whether one should use the total score of an instrument or its subscale scores. The choice is exclusive; that is, one should never use both the total score and one or more of the subscale scores in the same analysis, because they are linearly dependent and will result in nonexistent or meaningless solutions in statistical analyses. The decision to use subscale scores or total scores is primarily related to the hypotheses of the study, but it is partially related to psychometrics as well. If the hypotheses of the study reference the general construct (for example, global evaluation of the counselor), then one should either use the total score or combine the subscale scores, rather than performing analyses on each separate subscale. Trying to interpret results for the subscales in the

FIGURE 13.1
USE OF
MULTIPLE
VARIABLES TO
OPERATIONALIZE
A CONSTRUCT

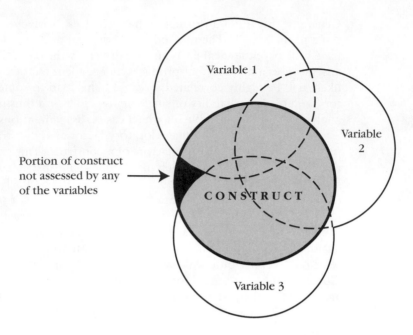

Portion of construct
not assessed by any ⟶
of the variables

absence of hypotheses about the subscales will result in ambiguity when some of the subscales lead to statistically significant results but others do not (see Wampold, Davis, & Good, 1990). However, if the hypotheses specify relationships for the constructs of the various subscales, then one should analyze the subscales separately (Huberty & Morris, 1989). For example, Wampold et al. (1995) hypothesized that social-coping skills would vary as a function of Holland type, whereas problem-focused social skills would not; consequently they analyzed the social-coping skills subscales of the Social Skills Inventory (Riggio, 1989) separately from the problem-focused social skills subscales, rather than using a total social skills score. Finally, subscale scores should never be used if there is not persuasive evidence that they are measuring distinct constructs, a point on which we will elaborate subsequently.

Multiple Measures of a Construct to Improve Construct Validity   The use of multiple dependent variables is often recommended (Shadish, Cook, & Campbell, 2002; Kazdin, 2003). No one variable can adequately operationalize a construct because, as was discussed previously, some of the variance in this variable is due to other constructs (specific variance) and some is due to error. Using several variables can more adequately represent the construct because one variable will be sensitive to aspects of the construct absent in other variables. The overlap of these variables reflects the essence of the construct, as represented in Figure 13.1.

Another reason for including multiple measures is the expectation that different constructs produce different outcomes. For example, McNamara and

Horan (1986) investigated how behavioral and cognitive treatments affected behavioral and cognitive manifestations of depression. The cognitive battery contained the Automatic Thoughts Questionnaire, the Cognitive Scale, and the Recalled Cognitions exercises. The behavioral battery included the Pleasant Events Schedule, the Behavioral Scale, and Observer-Evaluated Social Skills ratings. They found that the cognitive treatments clearly reduced cognitive manifestations of depression with some generalization to behavioral measures, whereas the behavioral treatments appeared to have little effect on either the cognitive or the behavioral measures.

Multiple measures of constructs can also be used to avoid the attenuation of correlations between constructs and can account for method variance. The next two sections discuss the intricacies involved in using multiple measures to form latent variables, which represent constructs better than any single variable can.

Calculating Correlations Between Constructs Unattenuated By Unreliability
We have discussed how unreliability attenuates measures of association, such as correlations. Multiple measures of a construct can be used to detect relationships among constructs that are untainted by unreliability. We now show how structural equation modeling can be used to detect the true relationships among constructs. Structural equation modeling is a statistical method that examines the relationship among constructs (sometimes called latent variables or traits) by using several observed measures to operationalize the construct (see Bollen, 1989; Fassinger, 1987; Hoyle, 1995; Loehlin, 1992; Mueller, 1996). The statistical method is complex, and only a conceptual presentation is included here.

The example we consider here is provided by Cole (1987) from data collected on two important constructs—depression and anxiety—by Tanaka-Matsumi and Kameoka (1986). Tanaka-Matsumi and Kameoka administered three commonly used measures of depression and six commonly used measures of anxiety; the correlations among these measures are presented in Table 13.1. Several observations can be made from this table. First, it appears that the measures of the same construct are moderately high, showing some convergent validity (correlations for depression measures ranged from 0.54 to 0.68, and correlations for the anxiety measures ranged from 0.32 to 0.79). The constructs of anxiety and depression seem to be related because the obtained correlations among measures of depression and anxiety ranged from 0.33 to 0.74. However, we must keep in mind that all the correlations in this table are attenuated by unreliability. Structural equation modeling provides a means of estimating the correlation of the constructs of depression and anxiety, taking this unreliability into account.

The results of the structural equation modeling are presented in Figure 13.2. First note the arrows from the ellipse "Depression" to ZungD, BDI, and DACL (observed variables in rectangles), which indicate that the construct (or latent variable) of depression loads on these three instruments. This is akin to factor loadings in exploratory factor analysis; here the loadings

TABLE 13.1
CORRELATIONS
OF DEPRESSION
AND ANXIETY
MEASURES*

	Depression				Anxiety				
	ZungD	BDI	DACL	ZungA	SAI	TAI	MAS	EHE	EHS
ZungD	1.00								
BDI	0.68	1.00							
DACL	0.54	0.60	1.00						
ZungA	0.71	0.67	0.48	1.00					
SAI	0.61	0.60	0.66	0.60	1.00				
TAI	0.74	0.73	0.61	0.69	0.66	1.00			
MAS	0.67	0.71	0.50	0.72	0.53	0.79	1.00		
EHE	0.39	0.42	0.33	0.47	0.37	0.48	0.49	1.00	
EHS	0.40	0.40	0.36	0.41	0.32	0.53	0.52	0.60	1.00

*ZungD = Zung Self-Rating Depression Scale; BDI = Beck Depression Inventory; DACL = Depression Adjective Checklist; ZungA = Zung State Anxiety Measure; SAI = State Anxiety Inventory; TAI = Trait Anxiety Inventory; MAS = Manifest Anxiety Scale; EHE = Endler-Hunt Examination Anxiety; EHS = Endler-Hunt Speech Anxiety.

Source: Tanaka-Matsumi, J., & Kameoka, V. A., (1986). Reliabilities and concurrent validities of popular self-report measures of depression, anxiety, and social desirability *Journal of Consulting and Clinical Psychology, 54,* 328–333.

FIGURE 13.2
MULTIPLE
MEASURES OF
DEPRESSION
AND ANXIETY

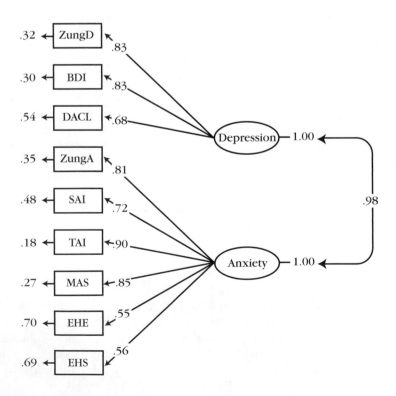

are 0.83, 0.83, and 0.68, respectively. The latent variable "Depression" is a statistical entity representing the construct operationalized by the three measures of depression. This latent variable represents the construct depression measured without error, because in a sense it is the variance that the three measures have in common, excluding specific or error variance. This procedure statistically accomplished what is pictured in Figure 13.1 (that is, it uses the common variance among measures to produce a variable that represents the construct). Similarly, the construct of anxiety (the ellipse "Anxiety") is the statistically developed measurement of the construct of anxiety from the six observed measures, with factor loadings ranging from 0.55 to 0.90.

The correlation of the constructs of depression and anxiety is then estimated from the latent variables of anxiety and depression. The curved double arrow between "Depression" and "Anxiety" represents this correlation, which was calculated to be 0.98. This says that the estimate of the correlation of the constructs of depression and anxiety, as measured by the three measures of depression and the six measures of anxiety, is 0.98. This correlation is not attenuated by unreliability. The conclusion here is that, at least as measured by these commonly used instruments, the constructs of depression and anxiety are not distinct. If these nine measures were used in an outcome study, it would only make sense to talk about the effect of treatment on the aggregate of the measures because it has been shown that the constructs operationalized are not distinct. It would not make sense to talk about the relative effectiveness of one treatment on one of the constructs but not the other (for example, to say that Treatment A is more appropriate for the treatment of depression) regardless of the pattern of results on the individual measures, a pattern that is surely random (that is, is due to error). It would be even more problematic to perform individual tests on the nine measures and make conclusions about individual measures, as this example has shown that they are measuring the same construct. Moreover, conducting nine statistical tests dramatically increases the probability of obtaining a statistically significant result by chance alone (that is, it inflates the alpha level). With nine variables, the probability of obtaining at least one significant result by chance is approximately 0.40, dramatically higher than is desired to make valid conclusions (see Hays, 1988).

Although it has been shown that latent variables can be used to calculate correlations that are not attenuated by unreliability, these correlations may be inflated by the fact that measures use the same method of data collection. In the next section we show how this method variance can be removed.

Removing Method Variance   In the previous example, all of the measures of anxiety and depression were pencil-and-paper measures. As discussed in Chapter 5, construct validity is dependent on assessments using different methods. It may well be that something in these instruments affects participants' responses but is unrelated to either depression or anxiety. One possibility is trait negativity, a general tendency to evaluate self negatively on all dimensions; these respondents would appear to be more depressed and more anxious than is truly the case. Still another possibility is a transient mood state that might

	Trait A			Trait B		
	Method 1	Method 2	Method 3	Method 1	Method 2	Method 3
	A1	A2	A3	B1	B2	B3
A1	1.00					
A2	0.64	1.00				
A3	0.57	0.60	1.00			
B1	0.72	0.54	0.46	1.00		
B2	0.39	0.78	0.46	0.56	1.00	
B3	0.35	0.43	0.75	0.54	0.55	1.00

affect responses to the instruments. Students attending the testing session just after receiving grades on their mid-term may experience transient feelings induced by the results of the exam. Because only one method was used, these possibilities are likely to affect responses to all instruments similarly, increasing the correlations among them. Variance common to all measures using the same method is called method variance. Method variance inflates relationships among variables; that is, the relationship between two measures is due not only to a conceptual relationship in the constructs of interest, but also to a relationship in how the constructs were measured. Whereas unreliability attenuates correlations, method variance inflates correlations, as the following example demonstrates.

Table 13.2 displays a multitrait-multimethod correlation matrix in which two traits, A and B, are measured with three different methods, forming six measured variables, A1, A2, and A3 (Trait A measured using the three methods) and B1, B2, and B3 (Trait B measured using the three methods). In this fabricated example, the correlations correspond to the convergent and discriminant validity presented in Table 13.1. The correlations of the same trait with different methods are relatively high (0.57 to 0.64 for Trait A and 0.54 to 0.56 for Trait B), and the correlations between different traits using different methods are relatively low (0.35 to 0.54). However, as described earlier, correlations of different traits using the same method are inflated by method variance and are high (0.72 to 0.78). Furthermore, all the correlations are attenuated by unreliability. From this matrix, we want to estimate the correlation between traits A and B to determine whether they are independent, related but distinct, or essentially the same. To this end, we again use structural equation modeling.

The first structural equation model, shown in Figure 13.3, examines the correlation of the latent traits in the same manner as we did for depression and anxiety. It appears that both Trait A and Trait B are measured well because the loadings on the observed variables are high, suggesting convergent validity. (Structural equation modeling provides model fit indexes that

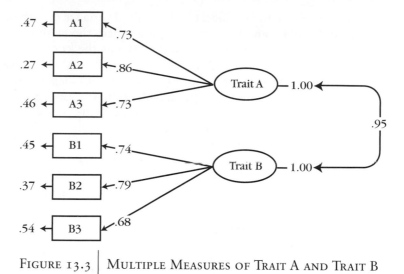

FIGURE 13.3 | MULTIPLE MEASURES OF TRAIT A AND TRAIT B

assess the adequacy of measurement. Although not discussed here, these fit indexes should be examined to determine whether the constructs are being measured well.) Moreover, the two traits are highly correlated (namely, 0.95), indicating that Trait A and Trait B likely are not distinct.

It should be kept in mind, however, that the three correlations that estimate the relationship between different traits measured with the same method were inflated by method variance. Structural equation modeling can reflect this method variance by calculating correlations of the same method across traits, shown by the two-headed arrows in Figure 13.4. Essentially, paths have

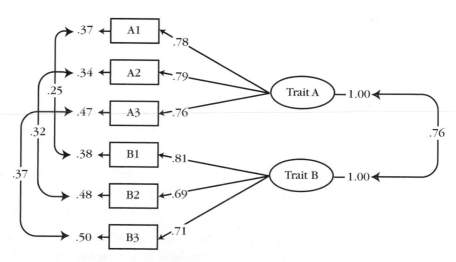

FIGURE 13.4 | MULTIPLE MEASURES OF TRAIT A AND TRAIT B ACCOUNTING FOR METHOD VARIANCE (CORRELATED ERRORS)

been added to the model to take method variance into account. The correlations 0.25, 0.32, and 0.37 in the figure reflect the method variance for methods 1, 2, and 3, respectively. As expected, the correlation between the traits dropped from 0.95 to 0.76 when the method variance was modeled, indicating that the traits are distinct, although not independent.

Method variance appears often in counseling research when various aspects of counseling are rated from the same perspective. For example, if the supervisor rates both cultural competence of the counselor and therapeutic progress of the client, then the correlation between the cultural competence and outcome is influenced in part by the rating perspective. If the supervisor has a generally favorable attitude toward the counselor, then that supervisor will tend to rate all aspects of the counselor and the client as positive.

Multiple Measures—Final Considerations   The previous sections can be summarized by the following six points:

1. A single operation (that is, a single scale or instrument) will almost always poorly represent a construct.
2. The correlation between two constructs is attenuated by unreliability.
3. Unreliability always makes it more difficult to detect true effects (should any be present) because of reduced statistical power.
4. The correlation between two measures using the same method is inflated by method variance.
5. If possible, multiple measures using multiple methods should be used to operationalize a construct.
6. Typically, interpretations of relationships should be made at the construct level, for seldom are we interested in the measures per se. Cognizance of the effects of unreliability and method variance is critical for drawing proper conclusions.

Generalizability   In our discussion of construct validity, we noted that, as is the case for reliability, validity is a property of the scores and not of the instruments. In addition, the degree to which variables produce scores that adequately reflect a construct depends on the type of participants used in the study. The relationships demonstrated by structural equation modeling, such as those shown in Figures 13.2 through 13.4, are generalizable only to persons similar to those used to collect the data. As noted earlier, Ponterotto and Casas (1991) analyzed the multicultural research in counseling journals and found that only 25% of the instruments used in those studies were developed using racial and ethnic minority populations. The construct validity of the 75% developed with other groups (primarily middle-class European Americans) is questionable (see Ponterotto, 1988b). Ponterotto and Casas concluded that the lack of minority-based instrumentation was one of the greatest limitations of the multicultural research they reviewed. Although more minority-based instruments are now available, the assumption of generalizability across groups continues to be a major issue in this area (see Chapter 15).

REACTIVITY

The dependent variable should be sensitive to some characteristic of the participant, but the assessment process itself should not affect the characteristic directly; that is, the dependent measure should indicate how the participant functions normally. Sometimes, something about obtaining scores on the dependent measure alters the situation so that "false" readings are obtained. Variables that affect the characteristics of the participants they are intended to measure are said to be *reactive*. For example, a test-anxious participant may report increased anxiety on a self-report instrument because completing the instrument is like taking a test; an aggressive child may display less aggressive behavior when being observed by an adult than at other times; a person may smoke less when asked to record the number of cigarettes smoked; a counseling trainee may demonstrate more culturally sensitive behaviors because he or she is aware of being observed. Clearly, the reactive nature of dependent variables must be considered in designing research; again, knowledge of the substantive area is vital. Later in this chapter we discuss unobtrusive measures, which are designed to be nonreactive.

PROCEDURAL CONSIDERATIONS

A number of procedural issues must be considered when selecting or designing the dependent variable. Often, the time involved with the assessment is critical to the success of the study. Participants will be reluctant to volunteer for studies that demand a long time to complete forms and instruments, or if they do volunteer they may respond carelessly to items (increasing error variance), especially toward the end of a long assessment period. As mentioned previously, the readability of instruments is critical to their psychometric performance. Any instrument administered should be checked to ensure that participants can adequately read the materials. Often the manuals of published tests contain references to the reading level required. Alternatively, the researcher can use one of the relatively easy-to-use methods for determining readability (see Klare, 1974–1975).

The order of the administration of instruments can have an effect on responses; one instrument may sensitize or otherwise influence responses on another instrument. An instrument that draws attention to a participant's own pathology (for example, the Minnesota Multiphasic Personality Inventory) may well affect how the participant rates other measures (for example, the counselor on the CRF). Order is also important when the same instrument is administered repeatedly. Performance at a given time may be due to previous responding (a testing effect) rather than to the amount of the characteristic. For instance, on an intelligence test, participants may acquire knowledge about specific questions or tasks (such as picture completion) that improves performance, even though intelligence remains unchanged.

When repeated measures are used in a study, use of alternative forms is desirable if testing effects are anticipated. Alternative forms enable the researcher to give a pretest and a posttest without having to use the identical instrument.

Students often ask questions about what to include when describing the psychometric properties of an inventory for something like a Methods section of their thesis, dissertation, or journal article. Although all of the above conceptual issues are essential considerations in the design of research, when describing the psychometric properties of a particular instrument that will be used, authors typically provide a description of the inventory, roughly in the following order:

1. Description of measure itself
   a. Instrument name
   b. Acronym
   c. Author(s)
   d. Key references
   e. A brief description of the construct the instrument measures
   f. Self-report, behavioral observation, interview, or Internet
   g. Number of items and examples of items
   h. Type of items (e.g., Likert items)
   i. Factors or subscales, and their definitions
   j. Indication of the direction of scoring, and what a high score means
2. Validity estimates
   a. Convergent and discriminant validity
   b. Samples on which measure was validated
3. Reliability estimates
   a. Cronbach's alpha coefficients
   b. Test-retest (if applicable)
   c. Reliability is a property of the scores resulting from a particular administration of a test, so researchers should report reliability estimates for the current data set.

Readers are encouraged to consult Heppner and Heppner (2004) for specific written examples of instruments.

METHODS OF DATA COLLECTION

Given that the basic purpose of the dependent variable is to measure the effect or outcome of the independent variable, an essential aspect of any discussion of dependent variables involves collecting data vis-à-vis the dependent variable. To this point we have emphasized the use of instruments in data collection. Nevertheless, there are a number of other methods to collect data relevant to the dependent variable. For the purposes of this text, we discuss seven nonexclusive methods of data collection that are relevant in counseling: (1) self-reports, (2) ratings of other persons and events, (3) behavioral observations, (4) physiological indexes, (5) interviews, (6) projective techniques, and (7) unobtrusive measures.

There are other ways to categorize methods; for instance, measures can be divided into objective versus subjective methods. Whenever relevant, these other methods of classification are discussed. Note also that these seven data collection methods may sometimes overlap; the interview method also is a form of self-report, and ratings of other people are sometimes behavioral measures. The main point is that there is a broad range of data collection methods, each of which has its respective advantages and disadvantages. Finally, each method of data collection should be evaluated in terms of its congruence with the research question, psychometric properties, relation to other methods used in the study, reactivity, and so forth.

SELF-REPORTS

In self-report measures, the participant assesses the degree to which some characteristic is present or to which some behavior has occurred. The self-report may be accomplished by responding to items in an inventory, completing a log, or keeping a journal. In any case, the sine qua non of self-reports is that participants themselves make the observation or report. Generally, the assumption is made that the report accurately reflects the true state of affairs—that participants respond honestly and accurately. In this section we discuss advantages, disadvantages, types of inventories, and scoring formats for self-report inventories.

ADVANTAGES OF SELF-REPORTS   Although they take many forms, self-reports have some general advantages that make them the most popular assessment device in counseling research. First, they are relatively easy to administer. Most self-report inventories, tests, or questionnaires used in counseling research can be administered to a group of participants, providing economy of time. Even when administered individually, self-report measures typically do not require special expertise on the part of the administrator; for example, receptionists can give clients inventories to be completed at the end of a session (see, for example, Kokotovic & Tracey, 1987). Similarly, most self-report inventories are relatively simple to use and require little training of the participant.

Another advantage of self-reports is that they can be used to access phenomena that otherwise would be extremely difficult or impossible to measure. Self-reports can assess private cognitions and feelings, behavior in private settings (for example, sexual behavior), and future plans. In addition, participants can be asked to report about cognitions, feelings, and behaviors in hypothetical situations. Consider the following examples. Counselors could be asked to report how they would respond to a sexual advance by a client or trainees might be asked to respond how they would react to a culturally insensitive remark made by a supervisor, both situations that would be unethical to arrange experimentally.

Self-reports also are advantageous because they are compatible with phenomenological views of counseling and psychotherapy. According to the phenomenological perspective, the thoughts and feelings of a client are of paramount importance, and self-reports of such constructs as happiness, marital satisfaction, and anxiety are more important than other indicants of these constructs, such as therapist ratings of client change, behavioral observations, physiological measures, or other measures that use a locus other than the self. For example, even though anxiety can be assessed physiologically, the distress caused by anxiety states is the debilitating factor for clients, and their self-report of anxiety is essential to understanding this phenomenon.

DISADVANTAGES OF SELF-REPORTS   The most obvious, and the most troublesome, disadvantage of self-reports is that they are vulnerable to distortions (intentional or unintentional) by the participant. For a variety of reasons, the participant may consciously or unconsciously respond in a way that yields a score that reflects a response bias rather than the construct being measured. For example, participants may guess the hypothesis of the study and respond (1) in a way that they think will confirm the researcher's conjecture, (2) in a manner that makes them look good, (3) in a way that makes them appear more distressed than is truly the case in order to receive promised services, or (4) in a socially desirable way. Some inventories are constructed to minimize such distortions. For example, the Minnesota Multiphasic Personality Inventory-2 (MMPI-2) contains four scales to assess the attitude of the participant. Two scales (L and K) measure whether the participant is trying to look better than is actually the case, one scale (F) measures deviate response sets, and one scale (the "?" scale) indicates the number of questions unanswered, which may indicate the participant's resistance to the test, confusion, or insufficient time to complete the test (Graham, 1990). To avoid participant bias, the Edwards Personality Preference Schedule is constructed so that the two choices for each item are equivalent with regard to social desirability (Sax, 1989).

Another disadvantage of self-report measures is that the participant may not be aware of the characteristic being measured. For example, a test-anxious participant may deny that he or she is anxious and attribute poor performance to inadequate preparation. Self-report measures must assume that participants have sufficient insight into their experience such that they are able to convey information about it to others through conscious terms. Metaphorically, if the whole of a participant's experience is a stage, this would be equivalent to restricting examination to the area lit by the spotlight.

A final disadvantage of self-report measures is the flip side of the advantage related to the congruence between a phenomenological perspective and self-reports: Self-reports are less valued by some other theoretical perspectives. For example, self-reports tend to be of minimal importance to staunch behaviorists. In spite of the disadvantages of self-reports, a listing of the dependent variables used in counseling research clearly indicates that the self-report is the most frequently used dependent measure.

SPECIAL CASE: INTERNET DATA COLLECTION   The increasing ubiquity of Internet access for many individuals has led to the Internet being an increasingly viable research tool. The use of self-report scales adapted for online data collection may facilitate the investigation of research questions that might have previously been logistically unfeasible or impractical (e.g., obtaining self-report data from a geographically diverse sample of counselors in training) and may have a number of other pragmatic advantages (e.g., reductions in missing data, reduced errors; see Stanton, 1998). The use of Internet technology provides an easy way for respondents to complete surveys, which presumably increases response rates. An additional practical advantage of Internet data collection is that data may be directly imported into a statistical software package, rather than being entered by hand (Strickland et al., 2003).

In addition to a number of technical and confidentiality issues that must be addressed before research can begin (for further description of these issues see, for example, Strickland et al., 2003), the disadvantages of self-report measurement may be exacerbated in the context of Internet data collection. The first and most obvious disadvantage is that research utilizing online data collection is necessarily restricted to participants with access to computers. This may or may not be an important consideration depending on the research question (e.g., most counselor trainees will likely have access to the Internet), but should nevertheless be considered (e.g., potential participants from low socioeconomic status backgrounds and without access to a computer will be selected against, thus biasing the sample). Researchers should recall that results cannot be generalized beyond the sample studied. In this case, the interpretation of most web-based studies should be limited to those individuals with computer access who would be able to complete the study online (Stanton, 1998; Strickland et al., 2003).

In terms of validity and reliability, the main question the researcher must contend with is whether the Internet is an appropriate vehicle for collecting the data of interest. As we have noted earlier, reliability estimates are a product of the setting and the manner in which an instrument is used (not the instrument itself). Therefore, it cannot be assumed that simply because a paper-and-pencil self-report measure demonstrated adequate psychometric properties previously that it will do so in an Internet modality. The change to electronic administration introduces another source of variability and increases the need for researchers who utilize traditional paper-and-pencil tests in a web-based format to report the psychometric properties of the current administration (Strickland et al., 2003).

RATINGS OF OTHER PERSONS AND EVENTS

Counseling research often relies on ratings made of other persons or of events. The procedures here are similar to those for self-reports, except that respondents rate characteristics of the participant or the event. Often the respondents are experts, and their judgment is assumed to reflect accurately characteristics of the person or event. For example, in treatment studies, the therapist or a significant other could rate the degree of dysfunction or improvement of a client. A perusal of the literature in counseling reveals that direct rating of participants is seldom used. However, many studies derive variables from ratings of events, particularly counseling sessions. For example, the Session Evaluation Questionnaire (SEQ; Stiles, 1980) is designed to measure the depth and smoothness of counseling sessions (see, for example, Stiles, Shapiro, & Firth Cozens, 1988).

Ratings of other persons and events share many of the advantages of self-reports, particularly their ease of administration and flexibility. When raters are experts, their judgments are particularly valuable because they are made with a rich background and deep understanding. Experienced counselors' judgments take into account years of experience with many types of clients. Another advantage is that many rating scales (for example, the SEQ) have proven psychometric properties under various conditions.

The primary problem with ratings of other persons and events is that the ratings may be systematically biased. This is especially a problem when the raters are aware of the hypotheses and cognizant of the conditions to which participants belong. If counselors are raters who also are involved in the experimental treatment, they may rate the progress of clients higher because they have an interest in the outcome of the study. If at all possible, raters should be blind to as many factors of the experiment as possible.

When raters are used to make judgments about events, the ratings can reflect characteristics of the rater as well as those of the event. When the participants (counselors and clients) judge the depth and smoothness of interviews on the SEQ, they are actually reporting their perceptions of the interview, and in that respect their ratings are self-reports. Thus, when interpreting ratings of events (or of other persons, for that matter), researchers must be careful to separate the variance due to differences in the event from the variance due to the raters themselves.

One strategy to examine the variance due to raters is to use neutral or multiple observers, and then test for differences across raters. For example, Hill, Carter, and O'Farrell (1983) compared observers' ratings as well as the counselor's and the client's ratings of counseling sessions.

Another problem with ratings is that because they often are relatively general, it is not possible to determine what led to them. In the SEQ, raters respond to the stem "The session was" on seven-point scales anchored by adjectives such as "bad/good," "dangerous/safe," and "difficult/easy." However, it is unknown which aspects of a session lead to a rater's responding with "difficult" as opposed to "easy."

An imaginative way to use ratings of events is to have participants respond to a stimulus and rate their responses in some way. Tracey, Hays, Malone, and Herman (1988) used the Therapist Response Questionnaire to obtain counselors' reactions to various client statements. The counselors indicated how they would normally respond, and then these responses were rated on eight dimensions: dominance versus submission, approach versus avoidance, focus on cognition versus affect, immediacy, breadth versus specificity, the extent to which the counselor met the client's demand, verbosity, and confrontation. In this way, Tracey et al. were able to obtain a set of counselor responses to various client statements and then obtain additional dimensional ratings on those counselor responses, which allowed for greater precision and interpretability of the ratings.

BEHAVIORAL OBSERVATIONS

Behavioral measures are derived from observations of overt behavior, most typically by a trained observer. Behavioral psychology has emphasized the importance of overt behavior and deemphasized intrapsychic phenomena. Accordingly, observing and recording behavior is the key component of applied behavior analyses. (See the *Journal of Applied Behavior Analysis* for examples of this type of research.) Essentially, behavioral observations are the same as ratings of other persons or events, except that behavioral measures focus on overt, observable behavior and presumably do not rely on inferences by raters.

As is the case with other modalities of assessment, behavioral assessment encompasses a wide variety of methods (Barlow, 1981; Mash & Terdal, 1988). Generally, behavioral assessment requires an operational definition of the behaviors of interest, direct observation of participants' behavior, recording of occurrences of the targeted behavior, and some presentation or summarization of the data.

The general advantages of behavioral observations are that they are direct and objective measures. Although there can be systematic biases in the observation and recording of overt behavior, behavioral measurements are not typically as subject to the personal biases inherent in self-reports. Another advantage of behavioral measures is that participants can be assessed in various environments. Studies have repeatedly shown that behavior is situation-specific; behavioral measures can be used to assess functioning in several situations. Finally, for many dysfunctions the behavior itself is problematic (for example, stuttering, social skills deficits, sexual dysfunction, physical avoidance, substance abuse) and thus warrants specific attention.

Among the disadvantages of behavioral observations is the fact that problems and concerns of clients frequently do not center around readily observable behavior. Marital satisfaction is a construct that is difficult to operationalize behaviorally (although there are many behavioral correlates of marital satisfaction). The central question, as with any operationalization, is whether the behavior chosen reflects the construct of interest. Another disadvantage of behavioral observations is related to representativeness.

A presumption of behavioral assessment is that the behavior sampled is representative of behavior at other times. However, for a number of reasons, this may not be the case. For instance, nonrepresentativeness can occur when behavior is recorded at fixed but unusual times (for example, classroom behavior on Friday afternoons). In addition, the reactivity that results when participants are aware that they are being observed leads to observations that may not be representative.

Issues related to reliability are problematic for behavioral assessment. An observer's decision that a particular behavior occurred may be idiosyncratic to that observer. In the context of behavioral assessment, these reliability issues are judged by calculating indexes of agreement; that is, how well do observers agree about the occurrence of targeted behavior? As was the case for traditional assessment, inter-observer agreement is a complex topic (see Suen, 1988).

Even if overt behavior is of paramount importance, it may not be possible or practicable to observe the behavior. Observation of sexual behavior, for instance, is typically precluded. Other behaviors are difficult to observe and are sometimes assessed in contrived situations. In counseling research, the behavior of a counselor often is assessed using confederate clients who appear to manifest some type of problem. Of course, the representativeness of behavior in contrived situations must be considered.

Behavioral observations have been used successfully in counseling and supervision process research. In the usual paradigm, the interactions between counselor and client (or supervisor and trainee) are recorded and coded as a stream of behaviors. A number of coding systems have been developed or adapted for this use (see, for example, Friedlander, Siegel, & Brenock, 1989; Hill et al., 1983; Hill & O'Grady, 1985; Holloway, Freund, Gardner, Nelson, & Walker, 1989; see also Chapter 19). The sequence of behaviors is used to derive measures that can be used to characterize the nature of the counseling or supervision interaction. The simplest measure is the frequency of behaviors. For example, Hill et al. (1983) used the frequency of counselor behaviors to discriminate the best from the worst sessions in a case study of 11 sessions. Simple frequencies, however, are not sensitive to the probabilistic relation between behaviors. More sophisticated methods can be used to ascertain whether the frequency of a behavior of one participant (for example, the client) increases the likelihood of some behavior in another participant (for example, the counselor). Using such methods, Wampold and Kim (1989) showed that the counselor in the Hill et al. study was reinforcing the storytelling behavior of the client. However, methods that look at sequential dependencies are not without their problems or their critics (for example, compare the results of Hill et al., 1983, with Wampold & Kim, 1989; see also Howard, 1983; Lichtenberg & Heck, 1983, 1986; Wampold, 1986a).

PHYSIOLOGICAL INDEXES

Biological responses of participants can often be used to infer psychological states. Many psychological phenomena have physiological correlates that can be used as dependent variables. In fact, physiological responses often can be thought of as direct measures of a construct. For example, whereas self-reports of anxiety can be biased by a number of factors, measures of physiological arousal can be made directly and can be presumed to be free of bias. However, although physiological arousal is a focus in the theoretical conceptualization of anxiety, the relation between physiological states and psychological phenomena is not as straightforward as was anticipated in the early years of this research. Moreover, physiological measures are expensive, require special expertise, may be reactive, and may be subject to error due to a number of mechanical and electronic factors (such as electrical interference). As a result, physiological measures are infrequently used in counseling research.

However, the proliferation of increasingly sophisticated physiological measurement techniques holds great promise for counseling psychology and may be an area of increasing focus for the next generation of counseling researchers. For example, numerous researchers have begun to investigate the neurobiological correlates of psychotherapy response (e.g., Goldapple, Segal, & Garson, 2004). Counseling psychologists are well positioned to bring a level of expertise in regards to measuring counseling process and outcome that has been lacking in these studies thus far.

INTERVIEWS

Interviews are a straightforward means of obtaining information from participants. In Chapter 11 we discussed using interviews in qualitative research. Essentially, the process of using interviews to obtain data on a dependent variable is similar, except that the goal is to quantify some construct. In everyday life, interviewing is a pervasive activity; we simply ask people to supply information. Interviews typically involve an interpersonal interaction between the interviewer and the interviewee or participant. Kerlinger (1986) advocated using personal interviews because of the greater control and depth of information that can be obtained. The depth of information most often results from carefully planning and developing the interview schedule.

Personal interviews allow flexibility in questionnaire design; the interviewer can provide explanations (and thus reduce participant confusion), make decisions during the interview about the adequacy of a particular response (and probe if necessary), and evaluate the motivation of the participant. The flexibility of the personal interview can be a real advantage if the topic is complex and if participants are unaware of their psychological processes; interviewer probing can then be extremely beneficial and add considerable depth to the information obtained. Babbie (2001) also observed that personal interviews that are properly executed typically achieve a completion rate of at least 80–85% of the participants targeted. Even though interviews rely on the self-report of the participant, the human interaction with the interviewer provides another facet to the self-report. In short, the interviewer can also make observations about the participant, which is an additional data source (Babbie, 1979).

Interviews, however, are costly in terms of money and time. If the topics are sensitive (for instance, sexual behavior), then participants may be more reluctant to divulge information than if they were allowed to respond to an anonymous questionnaire. Interviewers must be recruited and trained. It is also important in quantitative research to standardize procedures across interviews to avoid introducing confounding variables due to different interviewer behavior or biases.

Often considerable training is needed to standardize procedures (general greeting, introduction of the interview schedule, methods of recording exact responses, manner of asking questions, responses to participants' questions, handling of unusual participant behavior, and termination of the interview). Thus, interviewer training is another task for the experimenter (see Babbie, 1979, for more details regarding interviewer behavior and training).

The telephone interview consists of a trained interviewer asking a participant a series of questions over the telephone. This method is usually quick and inexpensive (financially), unless long-distance calls are involved. Babbie (1979) recommends that the interview be kept short—10–15 minutes. Such brevity, however, often limits the depth of information obtained. Moreover, the telephone method reduces the amount of evaluative information that the interviewer can observe about the participant. As with other personal interviews, an interview schedule must be developed, but an additional consideration is the generally lower responsiveness of telephone participants.

PROJECTIVE TECHNIQUES

The rationale behind projective techniques is that participants' responses to ambiguous stimuli will reveal some facet of their personality. The Thematic Apperception Test (which uses ambiguous drawings) and the Rorschach (which uses inkblots) are probably the two most well-known projective tests. However, a wide variety of possibilities exist, including drawing pictures, writing essays, completing sentences, playing with dolls, associating words, and so forth. The assumption is that because the method is indirect, participants will not censor themselves. In turn, participants' responses are indirect measures and need to be interpreted in some way. Scoring of projective tests is typically subjective, although there are some very objective systems for scoring them, such as the Exner system for scoring Rorschach responses (Exner, 1974).

Historically, projective techniques have been associated with psychodynamic approaches to understanding human behavior. As the popularity of psychodynamic approaches has decreased, however, so has the use of projective techniques. One of the most troublesome aspects of these techniques is that their scoring is subject to systematic biases that tend to confirm preconceived (but incorrect) conceptions about people (see, for example, Chapman & Chapman, 1969). Furthermore, the connection between underlying personality characteristics and overt behavior is tenuous.

In spite of their disadvantages, some forms of projective techniques have made useful contributions to several areas of counseling research. For instance, one of the conspicuous themes in counseling research involves the matching of environmental structure with conceptual level (Holloway & Wampold, 1986). The conceptual level theory states that high-conceptual thinkers will perform best in low-structured environments, whereas low-conceptual thinkers will perform best in high-structured environments. Studies in this area typically have used the Paragraph Completion Method (PCM; Hunt, Butler, Noy, & Rosser, 1978) to measure conceptual level. The PCM asks participants to respond to six sentence stems; scores are based on the cognitive complexity of the responses.

UNOBTRUSIVE MEASURES

To eliminate reactivity, it is often possible to collect data on participants without their awareness of this process. Measures used in such a way that participants are unaware of the assessment procedure, known as unobtrusive measures, have been described in some detail by Webb, Campbell, Schwartz, and Sechrest (1999). It may be possible to observe participants without their knowledge in naturalistic settings, to observe participants in contrived situations (for example, with a confederate), to collect data from archives or other sources (such as school records), or to examine physical traces (such as garbage or graffiti). Most psychologists are extremely interested in sources of unobtrusive data. How often do people observe others in public and make interpretations of their behavior?

Of course, the most conspicuous advantage of unobtrusive measures is that they are by definition nonreactive. Because participants are not aware that data are being collected, they do not alter their responses. Furthermore, unobtrusive measures are often very accurate. Grade point averages obtained from the registrar will be more accurate than those obtained from participants' self-reports. Still, there are a number of limitations to unobtrusive measures. Certain types of unobtrusive measures are unethical. For instance, disclosure of personal information by public agencies without the participant's permission is forbidden. Another limitation is that unobtrusive measures are often difficult and/or expensive to obtain. In addition, once the data are obtained, interpretation or classification is often needed; a study of graffiti might involve classifying the graffiti as sexual, drug related, violent, and so forth.

Although use of unobtrusive measures is not widespread in counseling research, the literature contains a number of studies that have used such measures. Heesacker, Elliott, and Howe (1988), in a study relating Holland code to job satisfaction and productivity, assessed a number of variables unobtrusively. Productivity data were obtained through the payroll office by multiplying the units produced by the value of the unit; absenteeism rates were obtained from the payroll office; data on injuries on the job were obtained from examining health insurance claims; and demographic information was gleaned from employment applications. Zane (1989) observed participants in a contrived situation; in a study of placebo procedures, male participants interacted in a waiting room with a person they thought was another participant but who actually was a female confederate. The interaction between the participant and the confederate was surreptitiously videotaped, and subsequently rated and coded for indicators of social skills and social anxiety (such as talk time, facial gaze, and smiles).

SUMMARY AND CONCLUSIONS

The basic purpose of the dependent variable is to measure the effect or outcome of the manipulation of the independent variable. We discussed several issues that relate to operationalizing the construct that represents the effect of some cause.

Once the construct has been defined, the psychometric properties of the dependent variable vis-à-vis the construct should be established. Reliability and validity are the primary psychometric considerations. *Reliability* refers to the proportion of variance in the dependent variable that is due to true differences among participants.

The remaining variance is error. To be useful, a dependent variable must have adequate reliability.

Although there are several types of validity, the one most germane to research design is *construct validity*, the degree to which scores reflect the desired construct rather than some other construct. Establishing construct validity is complicated and indirect, but nevertheless vital to the integrity of a study. Construct validity can be investigated in a number of ways, including recent applications of structural equation modeling. Commonly, a single dependent variable is unable to adequately operationalize a construct; multiple dependent variables are often recommended. The hope is that each variable reflects some aspect of the construct of interest, and that together they measure the essence of the construct. In any study, the researcher must be cognizant of both the attenuation of true relationships due to unreliability and the inflation of true relationships due to method variance. However, the dependent variables are designed or chosen such that they do not react with the treatment.

There are many methods of collecting data related to dependent variables, each of which has its advantages and disadvantages. The most widely used measure in counseling research is the self-report. The *sine qua non* of the self-report is that each participant makes his or her own observations or reports. The advantages of self-reports are that they are relatively easy to administer, can access areas that otherwise would be impossible or difficult to measure (such as sexual behavior), and are compatible with phenomenological views of counseling. The most conspicuous problem with self-reports is that they are vulnerable to distortions by the participant. However, participants may not be consciously aware of the construct being measured, and self-reports are incompatible with several theoretical approaches to counseling (for example, behavioral approaches). Self-report instruments may either be published, by professional publishers or in the literature, or tailor made for a specific study, and they can be written in a number of formats.

Less frequently used dependent measures include ratings of other persons and events, behavioral measures, physiological indexes, interviews, projective techniques, and unobtrusive measures. Ratings of other persons and events are useful because experts or participants can be used to judge important aspects of counseling, such as the counseling interview itself. Behavioral measures reflect overt behavior and thus are not subject to the distortions that can plague self-reports and ratings of other persons and events; furthermore, they are compatible with behavioral approaches to counseling, even though they may be incompatible with other approaches (such as psychodynamic approaches). Physiological responses can be used to infer psychological states because many psychological phenomena (for example, anxiety) have physiological correlates; however, due to lack of reliability, significant expense, and other problems, physiological indexes are infrequently used in counseling research. Interviews are advantageous because much information can be obtained quickly and because the interviewer can pose follow-up questions, but they are relatively expensive, depend on the skill of the interviewer, and can be biased. Projective techniques, which use ambiguous stimuli to reveal some facet of personality, can be useful to uncover unconscious aspects of the personality. Unobtrusive measures are designed to eliminate reactivity because the participant is unaware that any measurement is being conducted.

Given the multitude of data collection methods, the task of the informed researcher is to collect data with a method that provides the type of information that is most relevant to the research question.

Obviously, the selection of the dependent variable and the method of data collection require considerable forethought and examination of the research literature. Moreover, these tasks often require creative thinking to tailor measurements to the constructs of interest. Unfortunately, sometimes researchers spend very little time in selecting dependent variables, and weak and disappointing findings often result. We firmly believe that careful deliberation and consultation with colleagues can greatly facilitate the selection of dependent variables and enhance the overall quality of research in counseling.

STIMULUS QUESTIONS

The Dependent Variable

1. Randomly select four recent counseling research articles. Classify the dependent measures according to the method of data collection (self-report, ratings of others or events, behavioral observation, physiological indices, interviews, projectives, or unobtrusive measures). Discuss the adequacy of the method used to capture the nature of the construct in question.

2. Select a commonly used measure in your area of interest. Research the development and validation of the measure and discuss the adequacy of the measure for the purpose it was intended.

3. As discussed in this chapter, the nature of the sample on which a measure was normed is important. Consider measures commonly used in outcome research (e.g., the Beck Depression Inventory, the Brief Symptom Inventory, the Outcome Questionnaire) and characterize the samples on which the measure was normed and validated.

4. Suppose a researcher is interested in the construct of cultural competence and wishes to avoid self-report measures. Indicate how the researcher could use raters for this purpose. What issues would be considered?

14 CHAPTER | POPULATION ISSUES

The numerous complexities involved in selecting participants and generalizing the results based on the data collected from those participants constitute what we call *population issues*. Perhaps the one question we are most frequently asked by student researchers is, "How many participants do I need?" Less frequently asked but perhaps more crucial are questions related to how applicable the results of a study are to other contexts. For example, do the results of a treatment study apply to the types of clients seen in mental health agencies? Does a study of marital satisfaction provide information that is valid for various ethnic/racial groups? Is the use of undergraduates appropriate for a particular study? These and many related questions can be answered only when we understand population issues.

This chapter focuses on the ways in which population issues impinge on the design and interpretation of research in counseling. Key population issues for successful research in counseling include (1) what types of participants to use, (2) how many participants to study, (3) how to treat different types of participants in the design and analysis, and (4) to what extent the results are generalizable.

Selecting participants for a study typically involves selecting samples from a population of interest. Because the rationale for using samples from a population is based on sampling theory, we discuss this subject first. Then we address practical issues in selecting participants including (1) defining the target population, (2) creating a participant pool, (3) selecting participants,

(4) establishing the validity of research in the absence of random selection, and (5) determining the number of participants. Finally, we examine the relationship of external validity and population issues by considering factorial designs involving factors related to person or status variables.

SAMPLING THEORY

Selecting participants for a study typically involves selecting samples from a population of interest. For example, it would be too cumbersome for an investigator interested in homophobia to interview all Americans about homophobia, so instead the investigator selects a sample of participants that presumably reflects the American population as a whole. For example, Barrett and McWhirter (2002) conducted an analogue study of how client sexual orientation and counselor-trainee homophobia and gender influence perceptions of clients. The researchers solicited responses from a sample of counseling graduate students so that they might be able to make conclusions about counseling students in general. However, as will be described below, a number of practical concerns lead one to question whether this was accomplished in this and other related studies.

Sampling theory provides the foundation for understanding the process and the implications of selecting participants for a particular study. We briefly discuss sampling theory and elucidate some of the real life restrictions and subsequent problems that investigators encounter. The essence of sampling theory involves selecting samples that reflect larger or total populations. We typically think of a population as a well-defined set of people, such as college students seeking help at a counseling center, depressed adolescents, or counselors-in-training, but technically a population is a set of observations. Put another way, it is the observations (or scores) of the people, rather than the people themselves, that constitute the population. The important aspect of populations, whether viewed as people or observations, is that conclusions reached from the research sample should apply to the population. By necessity, counseling research is conducted with a limited number of participants; the results for these particular participants alone are rarely of primary interest. The object of most research is to generalize from the observations of these study participants to some larger population; that is, some inference is made about the population based on a small number of observations.

The concept of population, however, is elusive. Some populations are quite real. For example, consider a population that includes the cumulative grade point averages of all college students enrolled as of January 3, 2005, and who have completed at least one term of college. The grade point averages (that is, the observations) exist and can be obtained from student records. The size of the population in this instance is fixed and finite, although quite large. Other populations are more ambiguous. For example, examination of depression in college students might involve a population that includes scores on the Beck Depression Inventory (BDI; Beck, Ward, Mendelson, Mock, & Erbaugh, 1961) for all college students enrolled as of January 3, 2005.

Clearly, not every college student has taken the BDI, so in some sense this is a hypothetical population. Nevertheless, it is not difficult to imagine having each of these students take the BDI; the population would consist of all these scores. However, it probably would be unwise to limit the population to students enrolled as of January 3, 2005, because to be useful the results of the study should be applicable to students enrolled at different times. A truly hypothetical population might involve college students enrolled both currently (at the time of the research) and in the future. This hypothetical population is infinite.

Clearly, some problems arise when generalizing to infinite hypothetical populations, some of whose scores exist in the future; however, it is just as clear that limiting conclusions to populations in existence only at a given time restricts the generalizability (and practical utility for that matter) of the results.

Inferences about populations are made on the basis of samples selected from populations. Technically, a sample is a subset of the population; that is, the observations in the sample are taken from the set of observations that constitute the population. This process is called sampling. Again, inferences about the population of observations are made from the observations of the sample; the validity of the inferences about the population depend on how well the sample in fact represents the population. Representativeness is a complex concept that requires further explanation.

Certainly, selecting 20 males at an Ivy League college and recording their scores on the BDI would poorly represent the population of BDI scores for all college students nationally. Samples that systematically differ from the population in some way are said to be *biased*. More technically, a biased sample is a sample selected in such a way that all observations in the population do not have an equal chance of being selected. In the example of male Ivy Leaguers, the sample is biased because female students do not have the same chance of being selected as males (that is, the probability of selecting a female is zero), and students in non-Ivy League colleges do not have the same chance of being selected as students in the Ivy League. However, as we shall describe, sample bias often operates in much more subtle ways than the above.

Samples that are not biased are random samples—that is, samples in which each observation in the population has an equal chance of being selected. Logistically, random samples can be selected by assigning each observation a consecutive number (1, 2, 3 . . .) and then choosing the observations by selecting numbers from a random numbers table or by using a computer-assisted random numbers generator. To randomly select a sample of size 20 from all college students, each student could be assigned an eight-digit number, a computer could be used to generate 20 eight-digit random numbers, and the BDI scores for the students whose numbers were generated would compose the sample. Clearly, this would be a laborious process (and could never realistically be accomplished), but it illustrates the ideal that researchers seek to approach when utilizing random selection.

Although random selection eliminates systematic bias, there is no guarantee that a random sample will be representative of the population. For example, even though it is highly unlikely, the random selection process just described *could* yield a sample of 20 male Ivy League students! To understand representativeness, and to comprehend how inferences from samples to populations are made, we now discuss some basic principles of sampling theory. Consider a population that has a mean of 100 (that is, the mean of the observations in the population is 100). Typically, this is denoted by writing $\mu = 100$; the Greek symbol μ (mu) indicates a population parameter. A researcher selects a random sample of 25; if the obtained mean M of the 25 observations is close to 100 (say $M = 103.04$), then in one sense the sample is representative. If the mean of the 25 observations is far from 100 (say $M = 91.64$), then it could be said that the sample is not representative.

This all seems logical; however, the situation in the real world is that the population parameter is unknown to the researcher, and the researcher selects only one sample. Therefore, it is unclear how representative any given sample in fact is. Fortunately, statistical theory helps us here by allowing calculation of the probability that an obtained mean is some arbitrary (but acceptable) distance from a specified population value (more about this later in the chapter). It should be noted that larger samples are likely to be more representative of the population than smaller samples (more about this later as well).

We now integrate our previous discussion of random assignment from Chapters 5 and 7 with random selection in the context of a particular design (see Wampold & Drew, 1990, for a similar but more technical discussion of these issues). Consider the case of a posttest-only control-group design (as discussed in Chapter 7); let's say the researcher is testing the efficacy of an innovative treatment. Two populations are of interest here: the population of individuals who have received the innovative treatment, and the population of individuals who have received no treatment. Suppose that 30 participants are randomly selected from a well-defined population; the researcher does not know how well the sample represents the population, only that there are no systematic biases in the sample because the participants were selected randomly. The next step is to randomly assign the 30 participants to the two groups (15 in each). Participants in the treatment group are administered the treatment, and at some subsequent time both the treatment and the control participants are tested. At this point something crucial should be noticed: The 15 observations for the treated group are considered to be randomly selected from a hypothetical population of observations of individuals in the population *who have received the treatment*. Think of it this way: All people in the well-defined population are eligible to be treated; hypothetically, all of these people could receive the treatment and subsequently be tested. The 15 observations (that is, the posttest scores) in the treatment group are considered to be randomly selected from the hypothetical population of posttest scores for all persons as if they had been treated. The 15 observations in the control group are considered to be randomly selected from the hypothetical population of posttest scores for persons who have not been treated. These concepts are illustrated in Figure 14.1. These are fundamental assumptions under which the majority of clinical research (both medical and psychological) rest. However, there is sufficient evidence to believe that the samples often utilized in both clinical

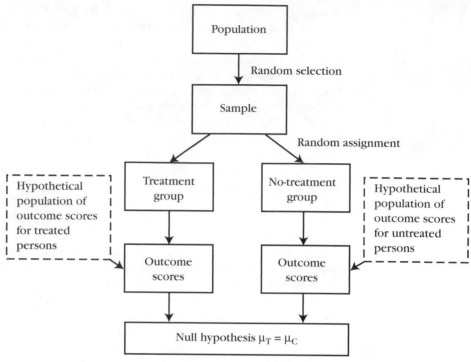

FIGURE 14.1 | HOW SAMPLING IS CONCEPTUALIZED FOR A HYPOTHETICAL
POSTTEST-ONLY CONTROL-GROUP DESIGN

trials and psychological research in general are not entirely representative of populations to which the results are often generalized.

Next, we discuss a crucial point about experimental design and the tests of statistical hypotheses. The null hypothesis in the above case is that the population mean for all individuals who hypothetically could be treated is equal to the population mean for all individuals who are untreated, symbolically expressed as $\mu_T - \mu_C = 0$. An appropriate alternative hypothesis (assuming higher scores indicate a higher level of functioning) is that the population mean for all individuals who hypothetically could be treated is greater than the population mean for all individuals who are untreated: $\mu_T > \mu_C$. If the statistical test (here a two-group independent t test) is statistically significant, then the null hypothesis is rejected in favor of the alternative. Because statistical hypotheses are written in terms of population parameters, the researcher— by deciding to reject the null hypothesis and accept the alternative—is making an inference about the *population of observations* based on the sample scores. In this example, if the null hypothesis is rejected in favor of the alternative hypothesis (based on, say, a statistically significant t test), then the researcher concludes that the mean of scores of treated persons is in general higher than the mean of scores of untreated persons. However, this conclusion could be incorrect because the samples might not have been representative.

Perhaps the 15 participants assigned to the treatment condition were initially superior in some way(s) to the other persons in the population. (Of course, this cannot be determined with this design.) Perhaps certain subsets of the population were not adequately represented in the sample (as it is often the case that racial and ethnic minorities are under-represented in psychological research). When researchers generalize the results of studies to such groups, they must assume there are no systematic differences in the variables of interest between the two groups, an assumption that is often tenuous at best. Nevertheless, protection against this possibility is expressed as the alpha level, the probability of falsely rejecting the null hypothesis. When alpha is set at, say, 0.05, the probability that the null hypothesis is rejected when it really is true is less than or equal to 0.05. Because alpha conventionally is set at low levels (for example, 0.05 or 0.01), the probability that significant results are due to unrepresentative samples is small. Remember this central point: Rejection of a null hypothesis does not mean that the null hypothesis is false; it means that the obtained results would be very unusual if the null had been true, and thus the decision is made to reject the null. However, there is still the small possibility that the null is true, and that sampling error (that is, Type I error) was responsible for the obtained results.

Even though we have just emphasized the importance of random selection from a population, we must point out that random selection is almost always an impossibility in applied research. A perusal of journals in counseling convincingly demonstrates that random selection is seldom used. For all practical purposes, it is not possible to select participants for a treatment study from across the country; researchers are fortunate to be able to afford to select clients locally. Even when random selection is pragmatically feasible (for example, a survey of members of Division 17 of the American Psychological Association [APA]), not all persons selected will choose to participate, creating a bias. For example, in the study of homophobia in counseling trainees described earlier, the response rate for counselors was 36% (162/435), calling into serious question the representativeness of the studied sample. Researchers might generate numerous hypotheses concerning how the participants who returned questionnaires differed in important ways from those who did not. In the next section we discuss procedures for conducting research without random selection, and the attendant problems involved.

PRACTICAL CONSIDERATIONS IN SELECTING PARTICIPANTS

If true random sampling were possible, the researcher would define the target population, identify all people in the population, and randomly select from that group of people. But as we have noted, this process is not practical except in the most contrived contexts. In this section we explore the practical issues in participant selection by discussing the following topics: (1) defining the target population, (2) creating a participant pool, (3) selecting participants, (4) establishing validity in the absence of random selection, and (5) determining the number of participants.

DEFINING THE TARGET POPULATION

The first step in the selection of participants is to define the target population, or the population to which the investigator wants to generalize. Although technically *population* refers to a set of observations, the population is typically defined in terms of the characteristics of people. Researchers must carefully consider many different characteristics in this definition, because ultimately these characteristics define the group to which the study's results will be generalized.

Defining characteristics may include diagnostic category, gender, ethnicity, age, presenting problem, marital status, and socioeconomic status, among others. For example, Mahalik and Kivlighan (1988) limited participants in a study of self-help procedures for depression to undergraduates who were mildly depressed (had a score of 10 or greater on the Beck Depression Inventory), had indicated an interest in participating in a self-help program for mood control, and were not receiving psychotherapy.

One important issue in defining the target population is deciding how heterogeneous the population should be. Heterogeneous populations are desirable because they contain a wide variety of characteristics to which the results of the study may be generalizable; conversely, homogeneous populations limit the degree to which the results are generalizable. By limiting the population to undergraduates, Mahalik and Kivlighan (1988) restricted the degree to which the results are generalizable; the study does not shed light on the efficacy of self-help procedures with other groups, such as unemployed laborers. Nevertheless, there are problems with heterogeneous populations as well. For one thing, it is unclear how the results of a study apply to various subgroups of a heterogeneous population (a topic that we revisit in a later section); furthermore, by their very nature, heterogeneous populations show much variability in responding, such that the error variance is greater than it would be for homogeneous populations, creating less powerful statistical tests. Again, as is the case with most decisions in research design, determining a study's optimal degree of population heterogeneity depends on the nature of the problem being investigated. In terms of Kerlinger's MAXMINCON principle, this is a trade-off between minimizing within-group variance and controlling extraneous variables.

As a practical example of this phenomenon consider two examples. The findings of the Treatment of Depression Collaborative Research Protocol (TDCRP), a large National Institute of Mental Health (NIMH)-funded treatment trial, have heavily influenced treatment decision making in the United States (Elkin, Shea, & Watkins, 1989). In addition, the Task Force for the Promotion and Dissemination of Psychological Procedures (TFPDPP) has generated a list of empirically supported treatments (ESTs) that it argues should be used by all practicing psychologists (TFPDPP, 1995). However, both of these examples base their findings on predominately European-American, middle-class samples. The generalizability of these findings to non-European-American, non-middle-class samples is highly suspect.

CREATING A PARTICIPANT POOL

After defining the target population, the researcher needs to identify a group of people who both fit this definition and are accessible; this group is called the participant pool. Suppose that the target population is defined as university counseling center clients. Clearly it is impossible to identify all such clients, so the participant pool is often limited to possible participants in the researcher's vicinity.

The participant pool might consist of counseling center clients at the researcher's university, a not uncommon practice (see, for example, Tracey, Glidden, & Kokotovic, 1988). However, restricting the participant pool to a subset of all possible participants introduces various kinds of bias—in this case, those related to geography, including socioeconomic factors, ethnicity, and values. In the Tracey et al. study, the participants were clients at a "large mid-western university counseling center." Are the results of this study applicable to clients at counseling centers at a small mid-western college, an Ivy League university, or a university in Southern California? Restricting the participant pool restricts the population, and so technically the results of the Tracey et al. study are generalizable only to clients at that particular mid-western university counseling center.

There is no empirical way to determine whether restricting a particular participant pool limits the generalizability of a study, other than by investigating the potential participants excluded from the participant pool. Clearly, this is not a feasible solution, because if those participants were accessible to the researcher, they would have been included in the study in the first place. Therefore, the researcher needs evidence to support the contention that restricting the participant pool does not affect the results. Background knowledge and prior research are crucial in making the decision to restrict the participant pool. For example, the physiological responses to physical stress would not be expected to vary from one area of the country to another, whereas attitudes toward abortion very well might. Of course, restriction of participant pools is not based on geographical criteria alone; often participants are recruited from local mental health agencies, undergraduate participant pools, school districts, and so forth.

In one sense, all participant pools are restricted. Because it is required that research participants take part voluntarily, all participant pools are restricted to participants who satisfy the definition of the target population and volunteer to participate. A bias is introduced here because volunteer participants have been found to be quite different from nonvolunteers. As an illustration, researchers have found that volunteers are better educated, have a higher need for social approval, are more intelligent, are less authoritarian, appear to be better adjusted, and seek more stimulation than nonvolunteers (Rosenthal & Rosnow, 1969).

Another complicating factor in composing participant pools is that because the presence or magnitude of characteristics contained in the definition of the target population may not be readily apparent, testing may be required. For example, in Mahalik and Kivlighan's (1988) study of depressed undergraduates, it was necessary to assess the level of depression of every potential participant. Over 800 students were given the Beck Depression Inventory to identify those who were at least mildly depressed.

SELECTING PARTICIPANTS

The next step is to determine those participants in the participant pool who will participate in the study. Ideally, participants are randomly selected from the participant pool. For example, if the participant pool comprised students seeking help at a counseling center at a particular university, then the researcher could assign each such student a number and, with the aid of a random numbers table or a computer-assisted random numbers generator, randomly select the participants for the experiment. However, even this process can be pragmatically troublesome. Often the researcher needs all participants to be at the same stage of counseling, but if there are not enough qualified clients, the researcher may solicit participants as they become available. For example, Tracey, Glidden, and Kokotovic (1988) had university counseling center clients evaluate their counselor immediately after the intake session. To obtain a sufficient sample, the researchers asked all clients who presented themselves at the center to participate in the study; in all, 192 of 430 clients agreed to participate and completed the study. Thus, in this study, random selection from a participant pool did not occur because all available participants were used.

ESTABLISHING VALIDITY IN THE ABSENCE OF RANDOM SELECTION

Even though random selection has historically been considered an element critical to generalizing the results of a study sample to a larger population (Serlin, 1987), random selection does not typify research in counseling. Nevertheless, available samples may be "good enough for our purpose" (Kruskal & Mosteller, 1979, p. 259). The "good enough" principle stipulates that nonrandom samples can have characteristics such that generalization to a certain population is reasonable. Accordingly, when samples are obtained by some means other than random sampling, "valid inference can be made to a hypothetical population resembling the sample" (Serlin, p. 300). In this way, generalization is made rationally rather than statistically.

However, making rationally based generalizations requires care. As Serlin (1987) indicated, generalizations of this type should be theory driven; he cited two areas of counseling research to illustrate this point. First, the social influence model of change in counseling (Strong, 1968) relies on a credible counselor and an involved client, and thus research with undergraduate psychology majors who are not involved clients has theoretical shortcomings. Similarly, a sample of upper-middle-class European Americans used to demonstrate the efficacy of a particular treatment may not be "good enough" to reach conclusions about how the intervention may work for clients from varying demographic backgrounds. For example, Williams and Chambless (1994) have presented data that suggest exposure-based treatment of agoraphobia may be less effective for African Americans than European Americans. By contrast, in other areas of counseling research, undergraduates may constitute a sufficient sample from which to make valid inferences. Second, the conceptual-level matching model (Holloway & Wampold, 1986) has implications for the training of beginning counselors; accordingly, participants who are relatively naive with regard to counseling skills are necessary, and thus psychology undergraduates, given their interest in behavior and lack of training in counseling, are perfectly appropriate, even desirable participants. In this case, undergraduates are "good enough," but they are not "good enough" for studies of the social influence model. In reference to Barrett and McWhirter's (2002) study of homophobia cited earlier, although the sample may not sufficiently represent the general population of counselors, it may be "good enough" in that results demonstrate that homophobic attitudes have an effect on a counselor trainee sample that is willing to participate in such research (wherein one might theoretically expect homophobia to be somewhat less prominent).

Thus, in the absence of random sampling, researchers must take great care in identifying the characteristics of study participants. The burden of proof is on the researcher to establish that the characteristics of participants are such that generalizations to a relevant hypothetical population are valid. The current vogue in counseling research is to eschew studies with limited generalizability in lieu of field studies with actual clients. Accordingly, for studies investigating anxiety (including treatment studies), clients seeking treatment for anxiety are favored over mildly anxious undergraduates who had not presented themselves for counseling.

Of course, recruiting clients seeking treatment is more difficult than recruiting undergraduates. Researchers must take special care when making generalizations about differences between groups defined by categorical status variables. To understand these difficulties, consider first a true experimental design in which a treatment is compared to a control group. In such a design, questions about the cause of any differences found between the treatment and control groups are internal validity questions; if the study is well designed (specifically, if the subjects are randomly assigned), then the effects are relatively unambiguously attributed to the treatment.

The generalizability of the results is an external validity issue. Consider, for example, a study in which Kiselica, Baker, Thomas, and Reedy (1994) compared stress-inoculation training to a control group to test the efficacy of this treatment on anxiety, stress, and academic performance of adolescents. Using "48 White students from a public high school in a rural community with a population of approximately 7,000," they found that the stress-inoculation training reduced anxiety and stress vis-à-vis the control group. Because this was a well-designed study, the effects could be attributed to the treatment. However, because the participant characteristics were narrowly defined, the efficacy of stress-inoculation for adolescents with other characteristics (for example, minority populations in urban schools) is unknown. Nevertheless, this study makes an important contribution because it demonstrates, at least in one context, that the treatment works; future researchers should examine generalizability.

Now consider a hypothetical status study whose purpose is to compare the anxiety, stress, and academic performance in two samples—European-American and African-American adolescents. Suppose that samples of European-American and African-American students were obtained from a school to which the European-American students were transported from suburban areas, and that significant differences were found between the groups in levels of anxiety, stress, and achievement. Because there was no random assignment, the two populations might well have differed on many characteristics other than ethnicity, such as socioeconomic status (SES), family status, parental involvement and supervision, community crime rates, and so forth. Consequently, it would be difficult to attribute the differences in dependent variables to ethnicity, and therefore the sampling method causes a problem for both internal and external validity. It might well be that the differences between the two groups of students were due to the characteristics mentioned, and had the researchers selected samples that held these factors constant (which would be extremely difficult), the differences would not have been present. The point here is that when status variables are used, internal as well as external validity problems arise, whereas if a study involves a true independent variable, only external validity is problematic.

Because the generalizability of results relies on the characteristics of the participants, researchers must carefully document the important characteristics of the sample. Given that race and ethnicity are always important considerations in generalizability for studies in the United States, Ponterotto and Casas (1991) made the following recommendation:

> Knowing simply the ethnic make-up and mean ages of one's sample is insufficient in assessing result generalizability. Describe the sample fully: mean and median age; educational level (and in immigrant groups, where the education was received); socioeconomic status; gender; preferred language and level of acculturation in immigrant samples; the level of racial identity development; geographic region of the study, and any other sample characteristics you believe your reader would consider when interpreting the results. As a rule of thumb, the more accurately you can describe your sample, the more accurate you can be in determining the generalizability of your results. (p. 107)

The National Institutes of Health's (NIH) guidelines on the inclusion of subpopulations recognize the importance of gender and race/ethnicity as critical status variables in research:

> It is the policy of NIH that women and members of minority groups and their subpopulations must be included in all NIH-supported biomedical and behavioral research projects involving human subjects, unless a clear and compelling rationale and justification establishes to the satisfaction of the relevant Institute/Center Director that inclusion is inappropriate with respect to the health of the subjects or the purpose of the research. Exclusion under other circumstances may be made by the Director, NIH, on the recommendation of an Institute/Center Director based on a compelling rationale and justification. Cost is not an acceptable reason

for exclusion except when the study would duplicate data from other sources. . . . Under this statute, when a . . . clinical trial is proposed, evidence must be reviewed to show whether or not clinically important gender or race/ethnicity differences in the intervention effects are to be expected. (NIH, 1994, p. 14509)

Admittedly, recruiting appropriate samples of racial and ethnic groups can often be difficult. Suggestions have been given for the recruitment and retention of American Indians and Alaska Natives (Norton & Manson, 1996), African Americans (Thompson, Neighbors, Munday, & Jackson, 1996), Latinos (Miranda, Azocar, Organista, Muñoz, & Lieberman, 1996), and other ethnic minorities (Areán & Gallagher-Thompson, 1996).

DETERMINING THE NUMBER OF PARTICIPANTS

The number of participants used in a study is important because as the number of participants increases, so does the probability that the sample is representative of the population. The question "How many participants?" is intimately involved with the concept of statistical power. Recall that power is the probability of rejecting the null hypothesis when the alternative is true, or the likelihood of detecting an effect when the effect is truly present. Even given a treatment that is effective, a study comparing the treatment group to a control group will not necessarily result in a statistically significant finding— it is entirely possible that even though an effect exists (the alternative hypothesis is true), the obtained test statistic is not sufficiently large to reach significance (that is, the null hypothesis is not rejected). Generally, the greater the power, the better the study (although after we discuss factors that lead to increased power, we will present a caveat to this general rule).

Power is dependent on (1) the particular statistical test used, (2) the alpha level, (3) the directionality of the statistical test, (4) the size of the effect, and (5) the number of participants. Even though an in-depth discussion of these factors involves statistics more than design, an elementary understanding of statistics is required before the important question "How many participants?" can be answered (see Cohen, 1988; Kraemer & Thiemann, 1987; and Wampold & Drew, 1990, for more complete discussions).

Before power can be determined, the researcher must select a statistical test. For a given situation, often a variety of statistical tests will do the job. For example, for a design with two treatment groups and a control group, the most frequently used test is an analysis of variance. However, nonparametric alternatives exist; in this case, the Kruskall-Wallis test would be appropriate. The relative power of different alternative tests varies, and this topic is beyond the scope of this book (see, for example, Bradley, 1968). The point is that power must be calculated for each specific statistical test.

Another factor that affects power is the alpha level. If a researcher sets alpha conservatively, say at 0.01, then it is more difficult to reject the null hypothesis, and power is decreased. So in being careful not to falsely reject the null hypothesis (in setting alpha small), the researcher sacrifices power.

The directionality of the test also affects power. If a two-tailed (that is, nondirectional) test is used, the researcher reserves the option of rejecting the null hypothesis in either direction. This is helpful when a researcher is interested in results in both directions and/or is unclear about the direction. For instance, when comparing two treatments, knowing whether Treatment A or Treatment B is superior is important; however, keeping options open in both directions costs the researcher power because it is more difficult to detect effects in this case than when one direction or the other is specified. One-tailed (directional) tests are more powerful when the effect is in the expected direction. For example, when testing the efficacy of a treatment vis-à-vis a control group, it makes sense to test only whether the treatment is more effective than no treatment (one is rarely interested in knowing whether the treatment is less effective than no treatment). By specifying the direction (that the treatment is superior to no treatment), the researcher increases the power of the statistical test.

The most difficult factor to specify in any determination of power is the size of the true effect. When a treatment is extraordinarily effective, the effect of the treatment is relatively easy to detect, and thus power is high. For example, if a treatment of depression reduces self-deprecating statements from an average of 20 per hour to zero, achieving a statistically significant finding will be easy. However, if the reduction is from an average of 20 self-deprecating statements to 18, then detecting this small change will be difficult. Specifying the size of the effect before the study is conducted is problematic—if one knew the effect size for any experiment beforehand, there would be no need to conduct the study. Nevertheless, the effect size must be stipulated before the number of participants can be determined. The effect size can be stipulated in a number of ways. First, prior research in relevant areas often provides clues about the size of effects. For instance, if the effect of cognitive-behavioral treatments of test anxiety is known to be a certain size, it is reasonable to expect that the effect of a cognitive-behavioral treatment of performance anxiety would be approximately the same size. Haase, Waechter, and Solomon (1982) surveyed the effect sizes obtained in the counseling psychology research in general, although it is unclear how applicable these results are to specific areas within the field. A second way to stipulate effect size is to specify the effect size considered to have practical or clinical significance. For example, in a treatment study involving a treatment group and a control group, the researcher might want to stipulate the percentage of those treated that exceeds the mean of those untreated. Using normal distributions, it can be shown that an effect size of 1.00 indicates that at the end of treatment, 84% of the treatment group functioned better than the mean of the control group (assuming normality); an effect size of 1.5 indicates that 93% functioned better than the mean of the control group; an effect size of 2.0 indicates that 98% functioned better than the mean of the control group. Translation of effect size into indexes of clinical improvement allows the researcher to gauge how large the effect must be to have clinical significance. Finally, based on a number of considerations, Cohen (1988) classified effects into three categories: small, medium, and large. This scheme makes it possible for a researcher to determine the number of participants needed to detect each of these three effect sizes. Of course, the researcher must still stipulate which of the three sizes of effects the study should detect. Furthermore, Cohen's determination of effect size is arbitrary and cannot apply equally well to all areas of social and behavioral research. Nevertheless, in the absence of other guiding lights, stipulation of a "medium"-sized effect has guided many a researcher.

The last determination needed before deciding how many participants to use in an experiment is the level of power desired. Power of 0.80 has become the accepted standard (although, again, this level is arbitrary). A level of power of 0.80 refers to a probability level; that is, 80% of the time the stipulated effect size will be detected (i.e., the test will be statistically significant). It also means that there is a 20% chance that no statistically significant results will be found when the effect in fact exists!

Once the researcher has selected the statistical test to be used, chosen whether to use a one-tailed or two-tailed test, set alpha, stipulated a desirable level of power, and determined the effect size to be detected, he or she can ascertain the number of participants needed to obtain the stipulated level of power.

Typically this is accomplished by using tables, such as those provided by Cohen (1988) or Kraemer and Thiemann (1987). Cohen provided extensive examples, but his format uses different tables for different tests. By using approximations, Kraemer and Thiemann were able to reduce the complexity of the process of determining the number of participants needed. Perhaps the simplest way to make this important determination is to use computer programs designed for this purpose (see, for example, Borenstein & Cohen, 1988).

Some caveats are needed about determining sample size. First, all of the procedures presume that the assumptions of the chosen statistical test are met. When assumptions are violated, power is typically decreased, so beware. Second, even though one often hears rules of thumb about sample sizes—10 participants for each variable in a multiple regression, 15 participants to a cell in a factorial design, and so forth—be warned that such rules are almost always misleading, as Table 14.1, an abbreviated power table for multiple regression, shows. In some instances fewer than 10 participants per variable are needed, and in other instances many more than 10 are needed. Third, the general rule that the more participants for an experiment, the better, is also misleading. Certainly, the researcher wants to have a sufficient number of participants to have a reasonable opportunity (say 80%) to detect an effect of a specified size. However, using too many participants raises the possibility that a very small effect size can be detected (see Meehl, 1978, for an excellent discussion of this issue). Although small effects can be interesting, they often mislead the researcher into believing that something important has occurred when in fact only a trivial finding has been obtained. Given a large enough sample, a researcher might find a significant (although meaningless) correlation between, say, hours of television watched and shoe size. An interesting exercise might be to obtain the World Values Survey (*n* > 200,000) available from www.worldvaluessurvey.org and attempt to find two variables that are not significantly related. For example, in a regression problem, a statistically significant finding

TABLE 14.1
NUMBER OF
PARTICIPANTS
NEEDED TO
ACHIEVE VARIOUS
LEVELS OF POWER
($\alpha = .05$)

		Number of independent variables							
		K = 3				K = 6			
R^2	Power = .30	.50	.70	.90	.30	.50	.70	.90
.10	34	56	83	132	47	74	107	164
.30	11	17	25	37	17	24	33	45
.50	7	10	13	18	11	14	18	24

Note: R^2 is the minimum value of the proportion of variance accounted for.

Source: "Use of multiple regression in counseling psychology research: A flexible data-analytic strategy" by B. E. Wampold and R. D. Freund in *Journal of Counseling Psychology, 34,* p. 378. Copyright 1987 by the American Psychological Association. Reprinted by permission.

with a large number of participants that accounts for only 2% of the variance in the dependent variable will likely add little to our understanding of psychological processes. Because statistical significance can be obtained for trivial effects, it is often recommended that researchers report effect size and power in addition to significance levels (Fagley, 1985; Folger, 1989; Shadish, Cook, & Campbell, 2002).

EXTERNAL VALIDITY AND POPULATION ISSUES

Recall that external validity refers to the generalizability of findings across persons (for example, adolescents, college students, African Americans, gay men), settings (for example, university counseling center, in-patient hospital setting, mental health center), or times (for example, 1960s, 1990s). The most direct way to increase the external validity of findings is to build into the design variables that represent persons, settings, or times. Because issues related to the generalizability of findings across persons are the most relevant to counseling researchers, we next illustrate these issues and indicate how they might also extend to settings or times. We first describe how population issues can be incorporated into factorial designs, and then we discuss several general considerations of studying external validity in factorial designs. It is important to note that even though factorial designs are discussed here, they are not the only designs that can examine population issues.

USE OF FACTORIAL DESIGNS TO STUDY EXTERNAL VALIDITY

To determine how results apply to various groups of persons, a status variable related to persons can be added to the design to create a factorial design (discussed in Chapter 7). Consider a factorial design with one independent variable (with three levels) and a status variable related to persons (with two levels):

Independent variable

	I	II	III
Persons I			
II			

To make this strategy more clear, consider the three levels of the independent variable to be three treatments, and the two levels of the status variable related to persons to be gender. Interpretation of the main effects and the interaction effects of this factorial design will illustrate how it establishes the generality of the results across persons.

Treatments

	Treatment A	Treatment B	Treatment C
Gender Males			
Females			

Suppose that it was found that there was no treatment effect; that is, there was insufficient evidence to establish that one treatment was more effective than any other. External validity involves answering the question of whether this result applies equally to males and females. It may well be that there was no main effect for gender as well (e.g., no effect of gender across treatments). However, the presence of an interaction (e.g., does the effect of a particular treatment vary depending on the gender of a client?) effect most clearly addresses issues related to external validity. For example, Treatment A may have been most effective with males, whereas Treatment C may have been most effective with females, indicating that the results are not generalizable across gender. Clearly, considerations of person variables can be vital to the proper understanding of research results. Parenthetically, both gender and racial/ethnic variables are receiving increased attention in the counseling literature (interested readers could examine Arredondo et al., 1996; Betz & Fitzgerald, 1993; Cook, 1990; Cournoyer & Mahalik, 1995; Fouad, 2002; Fouad & Mohler, 2004; Good, Gilbert, & Scher, 1990; Good et al., 1995; Heppner, 1995; Kim & Atkinson, 2002; Melby, Hoyt, & Bryant, 2003; Mintz & O'Neil, 1990; Ponterotto, 1988b; Ponterotto, Rieger, Barrett, & Sparks, 1994; Richardson & Johnson, 1984; Scher & Good, 1990; Williams & Chambless, 1994).

The general principle to be gleaned from this discussion is that when external validity is examined within a design (by including person as a status variable), it is the interaction effect that is most interesting. An interaction effect indicates that the levels of the independent variable interact with the person variable to produce different outcomes. Researchers with a background in educational research will recognize this phenomenon as essentially that of aptitude-treatment interactions.

Some theories in counseling are expressed in terms of interactions between independent variables and person variables, as illustrated by the cognitive complexity model (Miller, 1981). According to this model, low conceptual level thinkers benefit from a more structured environment, whereas high conceptual level thinkers benefit from a less structured environment. In this model, conceptual level is a person variable, and structure of the environment is an independent variable that is manipulated by the researcher. Holloway and Wampold (1986) conducted a meta-analysis of studies investigating this hypothesis and found that the expected interaction effect appears to be operating. Results indicated a main effect for environmental structure (participants generally performed better in structured environments) and a (small) main effect for conceptual level (high conceptual level participants generally performed better). However, these conclusions were mitigated by the interaction between environmental structure and conceptual level. According to these results, one should provide more-structured environments to low conceptual level thinkers, whereas high conceptual level thinkers appeared to do about equally well regardless of structure.

Researchers have also offered such models in multicultural research. For example, Kim and Atkinson (2002) found that Asian volunteer career counseling clients who demonstrated traditionally Asian cultural values found counselors who demonstrated these values in session to be more empathic and credible. The authors concluded that this finding supports the social influence theory of counseling, which holds that both attitudes and group membership similarity promote positive counseling interactions. Accordingly, it may be important for career counselors to assess the value systems of Asian clients (and for that matter all clients) before engaging in the counseling process.

Thus far we have discussed external validity in terms of a factorial design, with emphasis on the interaction effect. However, examination of interaction effects is not limited to factorial designs (and concomitant analyses of variance). For example, regression analysis also accommodates interaction effects nicely, and thus, external validity is related to the interaction of independent and person variables, regardless of the analysis.

CONSIDERATIONS IN EXAMINING GENERALIZABILITY ACROSS POPULATIONS

Although the factorial design approach to external validity seems straightforward, there are some issues concerning group differences that need consideration. One important and difficult to resolve issue is the choice of variables related to persons, settings, or times. Furthermore, the researcher cannot know whether an interaction effect crucial to external validity would occur with other unexamined person, setting, or time variables. Selecting variables related to external validity is tricky business.

The problem is exacerbated by the fact that literally hundreds of such variables might be included in the design, including gender, ethnicity, race, age, level of dysfunction, intelligence, personality types, and type of clinic. Most of these variables are status variables, for which, as we have seen, sampling becomes intimately involved in both internal and external validity. Moreover, some of the most important status variables are not clearly defined. For example, although race is an important aspect of American society, psychologists have yet to agree on a definition of this construct (Yee, Fairchild, Weizmann, & Wyatt, 1993). Finally, even if the variables can be well defined and measured, related constructs may be more important. For example, gender and ethnicity appear often in counseling research, but it is possible that sex-role orientation is more critical than biological gender, or that level of acculturation and/or racial identity is more critical than ethnicity. Many psychologists have offered these alternatives to simplistic notions of race and ethnicity, and researchers are engaged in a significant and productive debate regarding the use of various cultural instruments in counseling research (see, for example, Casas, 2005; Delgado-Romero, Galván, & Maschino, 2005; Neville & Carter, 2005; Ponterotto & Grieger, in press; Sabnani & Ponterotto, 1992; Spanierman & Poteat, 2005). At this juncture, we invoke the usual refrain: Knowledge of the substantive area should inform the choice of variables related to external validity. If prior research or theory—or for that matter, common sense—indicates that gender is an important variable, add it to the design. Alternatively, it is unwise to include variables when there is no compelling reason for their inclusion.

The field of counseling has placed much emphasis on understanding the role of race/ethnicity/culture on counseling and psychological functioning; researchers are encouraged to investigate this area, for race/ethnicity/culture factors are ubiquitous. Whether or not a given study is directly focused on race/ethnicity/culture, the influence of these factors on behavior and on the research endeavor should be understood (see Alvidrez, Azocar, & Miranda, 1996; Areán & Gallagher-Thompson, 1996; Atkinson & Lowe, 1995; Beutler, Brown, Cruthers, Booker, & Seabrook, 1996; Coleman, Wampold, & Casali, 1995; Hohmann & Parron, 1996; Leong, Wagner, & Tata, 1995; Miranda et al., 1996; Norton & Manson, 1996; Ponterotto & Casas, 1991; Ponterotto & Grieger, in press; Rowe, Vazsonyi, & Flannery, 1994; Thompson et al., 1994; Yee et al., 1993).

We have alluded to the problems inherent in comparing two groups formed from differences on a categorical status variable (for example, African-American and European-American groups). Because the issues involved in examining group differences are so important, we explore them again, in a slightly different way. A previous example involved differences between African-American and European-American adolescents in terms of stress, anxiety, and achievement. The goal of such a study was to identify mean differences between the two populations (for example, are the mean levels of anxiety for the two groups different?). One of the most persistent but controversial findings in psychology involves just such a comparison—namely, the group differences found on traditional tests of intelligence.

The research design point that we want to make is that simply identifying group differences on some variable is of limited usefulness; ultimately, the goal of research is understanding, and research could be profitably used to explore observed differences among groups.

When differences between groups are found, a vital question arises: Are the processes that lead to these differences the same for both groups? Suppose there are two groups, A and B, that reliably show differences in some construct, say antisocial behavior (Group A > Group B). A critical piece of the puzzle is to determine whether the factors that lead to antisocial behavior in the two groups are the same. Given that we know inadequate parental supervision to be a key causal construct in antisocial behavior, the question could be expressed as follows: "Is the rate of antisocial behavior in Group A higher because there is less adequate supervision, or because there is some other variable that uniquely influences behavior in Group A but not Group B?" In a comprehensive reanalysis of several large data sets, Rowe, Vazsonyi, and Flannery (1994) found racial similarity in developmental processes related to achievement and behavior; that is, they found that the variables that predicted achievement and behavior were common across groups, and that no variables were uniquely important to specific racial groups.

Clearly, then, if a researcher is going to examine group differences, an understanding of the processes that lead to those differences is paramount to making sense of the results. Basically, if an examination across populations reveals that the causal factors are similar, then the efficacy of interventions would be similar; if causal factors are not similar, then group-specific interventions would be needed. As is becoming clear, such research is needed to establish the efficacy of culture-specific educational and psychological interventions.

As an example of systematic examination of group differences, Fouad (2002) has investigated the cross-cultural validity of the Strong Interest Inventory and the RIASEC model of career interests, demonstrating basic support for similarity of interests and structure of interests. Although these findings have made important contributions to our understanding of career interests across cultures, they do not comment on the processes through which interests may have developed cross-culturally.

As an example of unique processes in different groups, Eugster and Wampold (1996) found that the factors that predicted global evaluation of a counseling session were different for the counselor and the client. Although clients and therapists had some factors in common, the researchers found that clients' global evaluation of a session was positively related to their perceptions of therapist interpersonal style and of the real relationship, whereas therapists' evaluations were positively related to their perceived expertness and negatively related to perceptions of the real relationship. These differences were verified by statistically testing the differences in regression equations. The goal of this research was not to determine whether there were mean differences between client and therapist evaluation of sessions, but to determine whether the factors that form the bases of these evaluations were different.

The statistical and methodological issues involved in testing common versus unique processes are complex. Eugster and Wampold (1996) examined the equivalence of regressions to test for unique processes. Rowe, Vazsonyi, and Flannery (1994) present a particularly cogent explanation of research issues related to testing models involving the hypothesis that psychological processes differ among groups.

Another, although subtle, issue related to group differences involves the proportions of participants assigned when status variables are included in a factorial design. It is desirable in a factorial design to have equal numbers of participants in each cell; in this way, main and interaction effects are independent (provided the assumptions of the analysis of variance are met; see Wampold & Drew, 1990). Accordingly, equal numbers of participants of each type should be selected (recruited). For instance, equal numbers of males and females should be selected and then randomly assigned to the three treatments. For research on gender, this presents no problems; however, when the base rates of various person variables are different, conceptual (as well as statistical) problems occur. For example, selecting equal numbers of Native Americans and European Americans for a study results in a sample that is not representative of the general population (that is, it is biased toward inclusion of Native Americans). This is problematic because the results are peculiar to the manner in which the sample was obtained. For example, correlations are affected by the proportions of types of participants included (see Cohen & Cohen, 1983).

This is a complex issue and is beyond the scope of this text, but a simple example will illustrate the problem. If one were conducting a study to examine how various types of political television commercials affected voting preferences of European Americans and Native Americans, equal numbers of these persons would be selected. The design of the experiment might involve exposing participants to various types of commercials and then measuring their attitudes. The results of this study might be theoretically interesting and applicable to real political campaigns. However, if one were polling to determine the expected outcome of an election, one would not want to bias the sample by having equal numbers of Native Americans and European Americans in the sample. Generally, experimental studies that examine theoretical phenomena or treatment efficacy should have equal numbers of participants. However, for studies that examine relations between variables in society, participants should be selected so that the proportions of the various person variables reflect the proportions in the population.

The factorial design approach to external validity also has philosophical implications for various classes of persons. Typically, studies are either conducted on predominantly majority samples (for example, European Americans) or include person variables that contrast a majority sample with a minority sample (for example, European Americans versus African Americans). The latter design includes the assumption that European Americans are somehow the norm, and that all other groups are to be contrasted with them (see Delgado-Romero,

Galván, & Maschino, 2005; Heppner, Casas, Carter, & Stone, 2000; Ponterotto, 1988b). It is also assumed that each of these groups is homogeneous. African Americans comprise a diverse population, and typically such diversity (in, for example, level of acculturation, racial identity, and generational status; again, see Delgado-Romero, Galván, & Maschino, 2005; Heppner et al., 2000; Ponterotto, 1988b) must be considered in research designs. Furthermore, there are phenomena that may be culture-specific and for which it is not optimal or even sensible to use a design that contrasts various groups. For instance, the reasons for the underutilization of mental health clinics by ethnic minorities, which is a major concern to providers of service, may best be understood by examining intra-ethnic processes rather than ethnic differences.

External validity is often established using multiple studies. For example, single-participant designs preclude the inclusion of person variables because only one or a few participants are used. Therefore, researchers use a strategy called systematic replication (Barlow & Hersen, 1984), which involves replicating an experiment while varying a single element. By systematically varying the one element over time, the researcher can identify its effects. For example, a single-participant design that establishes the efficacy of social reinforcement in the attenuation of off-task behavior with students in a primarily European-American urban school might be replicated in a rural school with a European-American student body, in an urban school with a Hispanic student body, and so forth.

The idea of systematic replication can apply to group studies as well. For example, interaction effects might be identified by two studies that differed only insofar as one had female participants and the other had male participants. However, there are disadvantages of such a strategy. True replication is difficult to accomplish, and thus the differences between two studies may be due to factors other than different types of participants. Furthermore, examination of external validity in one study allows direct estimation of the size of the interaction effect, a procedure that is precluded in the systematic replication strategy.

SUMMARY AND CONCLUSIONS

Population issues affect the design and interpretation of research in counseling. A critical issue in the development of a study is the selection of a sample of participants from a broader target population. Considerable care is needed to (1) define the target population (or the population to which the investigator wishes to generalize), and (2) select participants that fit the definition of the target population.

Theoretically, the generalizability of the results is established by randomly selecting a sample from a population. Because of the practical constraints on most counseling research, sampling is rarely achieved through true random selection. Instead, researchers often use nonrandom samples that have similar relevant characteristics to a target population, and then rationally argue that the results apply to a population with the same characteristics. Finally, a critical issue in selecting participants is determining how many participants are needed to adequately test the relationships among the study's constructs of interest. The number of participants needed for any study pertains to statistical power, or the probability of rejecting the null hypothesis when the alternative hypothesis is actually true.

With regard to estimating statistical power (and thus the number of participants needed), we discussed (1) the particular statistical test used, (2) alpha level, (3) directionality of the statistical test, and (4) effect size. Thus, investigators must make a number of decisions in selecting participants for a study. Typically, researchers are interested in generalizing the results of a particular study to a larger population of individuals, which is the essence of external validity. External validity also relates to the generalizability of findings across persons, settings, or times. We suggested that the most direct means to increase the external validity of findings is to build into the design factors that represent relevant persons, settings, or times. In this way, external validity can be investigated by examining the interaction of the independent variable and a variable related to persons, settings, or times.

Because counseling is an applied profession designed to help a broad array of individuals in various settings across different times, external validity is very important. Far too often, convenience samples consisting of predominantly European-American undergraduate participants are used in counseling research. We strongly encourage efforts to broaden the external validity of research in counseling in order to develop the more extensive databases that are needed in the counseling profession.

STIMULUS QUESTIONS

EXERCISES ON POPULATION ISSUES

1. A researcher is considering the relative efficacy of two treatments for depression. What population issues are important when considering the interpretation of the results?
2. Discuss the differences between random selection and random assignment. How are these concepts related to the validity of a study?
3. Select a recent issue of a counseling journal. Describe the samples used in the research in the issue and rate the adequacy of the samples vis-à-vis the purpose of the research.
4. Suppose that you are designing a study to test theoretical propositions related to career development. Discuss issues related to the definition of the population and recruitment of participants.

15 CHAPTER | CONCEPTUAL AND METHODOLOGICAL ISSUES RELATED TO MULTICULTURAL RESEARCH

Kevin Cokley and Germine H. Awad

One of the distinguishing characteristics of counseling research in recent years is the increasing emphasis on multiculturalism. Indeed, just as counselors need to be culturally competent in providing mental health services to an increasingly diverse clientele, they also must be equipped to conduct and critically evaluate research in terms of its responsiveness to and treatment of cultural issues.

How to conceptualize multiculturalism has been an ongoing debate in the literature. Some argue for a broad definition of multiculturalism that would include, but not be limited to, race, ethnicity, gender, sexual orientation, religion, socioeconomic status, disability, and other social identities that are marginalized or otherwise sources of differences among people (e.g., Fukuyama, 1990; Robinson & Howard-Hamilton, 2000; Sue & Sue, 2003); others argue for a narrow approach that focuses on race, primarily because a broad definition of multiculturalism often serves to obscure or avoid focusing on difficult issues of race (e.g., Carter, 1995; Helms, 1994; Helms & Cook, 1999; Locke, 1991). Others have opted to use both a narrow approach (Atkinson, 2004) and a broad approach (Atkinson & Hackett, 2004). Thus, the first order of business must be to establish an operational definition of multiculturalism, and by extension multicultural research. All human differences are certainly important and worthy of research; however, for pragmatic reasons, we have chosen to define multicultural research as any research that has as its primary purpose the examination of psychological processes and phenomena among racial and ethnic groups. This definition is consistent with the research that is most often published in the *Journal of Multicultural Counseling and Development* and the *Cultural Diversity and Ethnic Minority Psychology* journal, and is also consistent with multicultural research that is published in counseling-oriented journals (e.g., *Journal of Counseling Psychology, Journal of Counseling and Development*).

This chapter will discuss conceptual and methodological issues related to multicultural research. The first section discusses defining and operationalizing race, ethnicity, and culture. The important issue to understand is that these terms are hard to define, and are often used loosely and interchangeably, making efforts to scientifically study them very challenging. The second section focuses on theoretical considerations in conducting multicultural research, and the third section focuses on methodological challenges, with an emphasis on validity issues.

OPERATIONALIZING RACE, ETHNICITY, AND CULTURE

Central concepts to all multicultural research are race, ethnicity, and culture. Their definitions and meanings are critically important to multicultural research because variations of psychological phenomena often exist between groups of people identified racially, ethnically, and culturally. Before any meaningful interpretations regarding these concepts can take place, the researcher must have a clear definition of what the concepts actually mean. As has been noted by Betancourt and Lopez (1993), particularly problematic is that these concepts are unclearly defined and understood from a psychological perspective.

RACE

Race has been defined as a "... presumed classification of all human groups on the basis of visible physical traits or phenotype and behavioral differences" (Carter, 1995, p. 15), "... a sociopolitical designation in which individuals are assigned to a particular racial group based on presumed biological or visible characteristics such as skin color, physical features, and in some cases, language" (Carter, 1995, p. 15), and "... an inbreeding, geographically isolated population that differs in distinguishable physical traits from other members of the species" (Zuckerman, 1990, p. 1297). Most definitions of race include a biological component, where the assumption is that people can be divided into groups defined by similar physical features and behavioral tendencies. These groups are generally classified as Mongoloid, Caucasoid, and Negroid, where Mongoloid is defined as anyone whose ancestors were born in East Asia, Caucasoid is defined as anyone whose ancestors were born in Europe, and Negroid is defined as anyone whose ancestors were born in sub-Saharan Africa (Rushton, 2000).

However, it has been documented that the creation of racial taxonomies has occurred in a distinctly unscientific manner (Gould, 1994), and there does not exist any agreed upon racial classification system. There are no physical traits that are inherently and exclusively found in combination with other physical traits (e.g., "black" skin is not always linked with full lips; "white skin" is not always linked with straight hair, etc.). Most social scientists agree that race is not a biological reality, but rather a social construct used to divide people and perpetuate power relations and social inequities. Several researchers have discussed at length the problematic nature of race as a biological reality (Atkinson, 2004; Betancourt & Lopez, 1993; Helms & Cook, 1999; Zuckerman, 1990). Race is often described as a social construct because there are real social consequences of being perceived to be a part of an identifiable racial group. These consequences include being the targets of prejudice and discrimination, which have long-term quality of life and mental health implications.

ETHNICITY

Similar to race, there has not always been agreement or consistency on the definition of ethnicity or ethnic group. Carter (1995) defined ethnic group as "one's national origin, religious affiliation, or other type of socially or geographically defined group" (p. 13). Betancourt and Lopez (1993) defined ethnicity as ". . . groups that are characterized in terms of a common nationality, culture, or language" (p. 7), while Helms and Cook (1999) characterized ethnicity as a euphemism for race, and defined ethnicity as ". . . the national, regional, or tribal origins of one's oldest remembered ancestors and the customs, traditions, and rituals (i.e., subjective culture) handed down by these ancestors . . ." (p. 19). Phinney (1996) used the term *ethnicity* to encompass race, and indicates that ethnicity refers to broad groups of people on the basis of culture of origin and race. There are also broad and narrow interpretations of ethnicity. When ethnicity is characterized as sharing cultural characteristics and physical features, the broad interpretation of ethnicity is being used. This interpretation of ethnicity is similar to the way in which race is discussed (Atkinson, 2004). When ethnicity is restricted to cultural characteristics and differences, the narrow interpretation of ethnicity is being used (Atkinson). From our perspective, a broad interpretation of ethnicity is problematic because it primarily relies on physically distinguishable features as markers of ethnic group membership, and minimizes the psychological and cultural processes believed to play a critical role in ethnic group membership. Thus, in this chapter we will use a narrow interpretation of ethnicity.

CULTURE

Culture is perhaps the most difficult of the three terms to define because there are well over 100 different definitions of culture found in various psychological, anthropological, and sociological literatures. Although the definitions overlap in many instances, it is important to note that there are some important differences. These differences often depend on whether the scholar is defining culture psychologically, anthropologically, or sociologically. The scientific study of culture is the domain of anthropologists, who focus on objective culture (e.g., the human-made part of the environment such as buildings, roads, homes, tools, etc.) (Herskovits, 1955) and subjective culture (e.g., values, beliefs, attitudes,

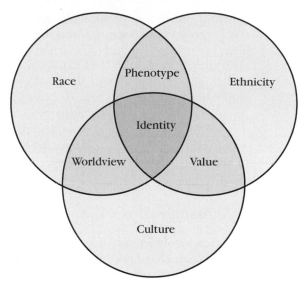

FIGURE 15.1 | RACE, ETHNICITY, AND CULTURE

© 2004 Kevin Cokley, Ph.D., kcokley@siu.edu. Created using the online Create-A-Venn system at www.venndiagram.com.

role definitions, etc.) (Triandis, 1972). Subjective culture falls within the interests of counselors and psychologists. Helms and Cook (1999), using a psychological definition, defined culture as ". . . the values, beliefs, language, rituals, traditions, and other behaviors that are passed from one generation to another within any social group . . ." (p. 24). Matsumoto (2000), also using a psychological definition, defined culture as

> a dynamic system of rules, explicit and implicit, established by groups in order to ensure their survival, involving attitudes, values, beliefs, norms, and behaviors, shared by a group but harbored differently by each specific unit within the group, communicated across generations, relatively stable but with the potential to change across time. (p. 24)

Similar to ethnicity, culture has both broad and narrow interpretations. Broadly interpreted, culture encompasses any socially definable group with its own set of values, norms, and behaviors. Thus, culture would include but not be limited to ethnic groups; men and women; gays, lesbians, bisexuals, and transgendered individuals; religions; disabled individuals; and socioeconomic statuses. Narrowly interpreted, culture encompasses countries (e.g., United States, Egypt), and even more narrowly interpreted, culture refers to specific ethnic groups (e.g., African Americans, Mexican Americans). In this chapter, we will utilize a narrow interpretation of culture to refer to specific ethnic groups (e.g., African Americans).

The interchangeable use and overlap of these concepts can be very confusing. Figure 15.1 illustrates the shared and unshared variance of these concepts.

When phenotype, or physical characteristics, becomes the primary marker of ethnic group status, race and ethnicity share variance. In other words, they are being used interchangeably. When race and culture overlap, a racial worldview is created that involves classifying human groups as exclusive, ranking these human groups as superior or inferior, linking physical features with psychological qualities, and believing that the psychological qualities are inheritable, unalterable, and ordained by God (Smedley, 1999). When subjective culture (e.g., values, beliefs, attitudes, norms, behaviors) is the focus, ethnicity and culture overlap. The combination of race, ethnicity, and culture intersects to contribute to group identity.

THEORETICAL CONSIDERATIONS

Research involving race, ethnicity, or culture goes by many names (e.g., cross-cultural research, ethnic minority research, multicultural research). Cross-cultural research is interested in determining which aspects of behavior are culture-specific (i.e., emic) and which aspects of behavior are universal across cultures (i.e., etic) (Matsumoto, 1994). Multicultural research is interested in examining emics and etics of ethnic minority and majority groups living within one country (e.g., African Americans and European Americans living in the United States). Typically, cross-cultural researchers are interested in examining behaviors between two or more countries. For example, Stipek (1998) found that Chinese people feel more ashamed for behavior related to family members than do Americans, and also feel more pride for an affiliated other's achievement than do Americans. Studies like this are published in the *Journal of Cross-Cultural Psychology*, which is devoted to publishing cross-cultural research studies; however, in some instances, multicultural research is also published. For example, Ayalon and Young (2003) found group differences in depressive symptomatology among African Americans and European Americans, with African Americans reporting less pessimism, dissatisfaction, self-blame, and suicidal ideation relative to European Americans. In another example, Okazaki and Kallivayalil (2002) found that cultural norms about depression were not related to depressive symptoms in European Americans, but were related in Asian Americans.

THEORY-DRIVEN VERSUS DESCRIPTIVE RESEARCH

There is nothing so practical as a good theory.
—Kurt Lewin, father of modern social psychology

Kurt Lewin is best known for his field theory, which proposes that human behavior is the result of both the person's characteristics and the environment or social situation that a person finds him- or herself in, as represented by the symbolic terms $B = f(P, E)$, where B = behavior, P = personality, and E = environment.

Lewin's often-quoted statement about theory is the driving force behind theory-driven research. Although multicultural and cross-cultural research continues to become increasingly popular, a lingering criticism is that much of the research is atheoretical and primarily descriptive (Betancourt & Lopez, 1993; Fisher & Moradi, 2001). Betancourt and Lopez make the following observations about multicultural/ethnic minority research:

> Ethnic minority research shares conceptual problems similar to those of cross-cultural psychology. Direct measures of cultural elements are frequently not included, yet cultural factors are assumed to underlie ethnic group differences. Furthermore, ethnic minority research often lacks sufficient attention to psychological theory. It appears that investigators of ethnicity are more inclined toward description than testing theoretically derived hypotheses. (p. 634)

Although these criticisms are in part valid, researchers who are critical of multicultural/ethnic minority research must consider two issues. The first issue is the sociohistorical context within which ethnic minority research developed. Early research pathologized ethnic minorities, operating out of a genetically deficient model whereby racial and ethnic minorities were considered to be inferior (Sue & Sue, 2003). Eventually this model was challenged by "well-meaning social scientists" (Sue & Sue, p. 55) and replaced with the "culturally deficient model," which assumed that the problems of racial and ethnic minorities could be attributed to being culturally deprived of middle-class culture. This model was limited in that it perpetuated the "myth of minority inferiority" (Sue & Sue, p. 56). The current zeitgeist emphasizes a culturally diverse model, in which it is not necessary for racial and ethnic groups to be compared with European Americans as the standard, but rather they are understood on their own cultural terms in and of themselves.

Multicultural research was born essentially out of the necessity to conduct research on ethnic minority populations that was not pathologically oriented or deficit driven. In many ways, its initial purpose was solely to refute the negative nature of much of the early research conducted on racial and ethnic minority populations. To that end, much of the research has been characterized by providing descriptive information about racial and ethnic minority populations, and describing in nonpathological terms how they differ from European Americans.

The second issue to consider is the level of existing knowledge on a particular research topic. Some topics have been heavily researched, such as the counseling process (see Chapter 19). Other topics, especially with racial/ethnic minority populations, have not been researched extensively, and thus there is presently a considerably smaller knowledge base. As suggested in Chapter 4, sometimes atheoretical, descriptive research can be very informative for topics where there is a small knowledge base.

Descriptive research is concerned with simply describing phenomena. Tools of descriptive research include the use of descriptive and inferential statistics. Descriptive statistics refer to data that are summarized (e.g., means, medians, standard deviations, percentages). For instance, calculating a mean and standard deviation on scores from the Beck Depression Inventory for

Mexican Americans and European Americans would be an example of using descriptive statistics. Inferential statistics refers to data where one can use statistics to draw inferences or conclusions. For instance, using a t test to compare the scores on the Beck Depression Inventory between Mexican Americans and European Americans to determine if the groups are significantly different in their levels of depression would be an example of using inferential statistics. It should be emphasized that both descriptive statistics and inferential statistics can be used in descriptive research.

Most beginning stages of a research program rely on descriptive research. A phenomenon is observed, or is otherwise believed to exist, and consequently is thoroughly described. (See Chapter 4 for more details.) For instance, let's say that someone is interested in studying rates of depression among ethnic minority college students, and let's say little empirical evidence is available about this topic. After much observation and repeated data collection, the researcher finds this general trend: Native-American students typically report the highest rates of depression, followed by African-American students, then Latino students, with Asian-American students reporting, on average, the lowest rates of depression. The researcher finds that numerous research studies have been published that document this general trend, and it has come to be expected by researchers interested in this topic. In essence, the phenomenon has been thoroughly described and documented.

At this point in the research program, the researcher is now interested in more than simply documenting and describing the differences. The researcher is interested in *why* these differences exist. In order for the researcher to answer this question, she or he must (1) possess basic knowledge and theory about the nature of depression; (2) possess knowledge and theory about the stress and adjustment issues faced by college students, especially ethnic minority college students; (3) possess knowledge about the history and culture of the ethnic minority groups of interest; and (4) have an empirical and theoretical understanding of how stress, college adjustment, minority issues, history, and cultural issues all interact to influence the rates of depression among the different ethnic minority groups. In short, the researcher must be informed by the previous empirical literature and existing theory, and must now hypothesize as to why the differences exist. A theory is "a system of interrelated ideas used to explain a set of observations" (Weiten, 1998, p. 23). If the researcher used a cognitive theory to understand the cause of depression, she or he might hypothesize that the ethnic differences in depression are a result of differential social experiences with students, professors, and other individuals (e.g., campus police), which result in different cognitive appraisals of the environment.

DISTAL VERSUS PROXIMAL EXPLANATIONS

An important function of research is to identify causes of human behavior (see Chapter 1). Here we want to highlight an important distinction between distal and proximal explanations in multicultural research. Going back to our earlier example with Mexican Americans and European Americans, let's say that Mexican Americans had significantly higher scores on the Beck Depression Inventory than European Americans, and we are interested in why that difference exists. As previously mentioned, ethnic minority research has been criticized for being primarily descriptive in nature. Research that is descriptive in nature usually relies on distal factors to explain differences in behavior. The word *distal* means farthest from the point of origin. Distal factors are factors that, in and of themselves, do not directly explain observed phenomena. They are often not psychological in nature, but rather, they tend to be demographic. For example, when researchers collect data, they usually incorporate demographic information. The demographic information will usually include information about race and/or ethnicity, sex, socioeconomic status, age, and so on. When researchers analyze their data, descriptive statistics are usually the first set of analyses conducted. It is common to compute the mean scores on the variables or constructs of interest, and then, using inferential statistics, compare demographic groups to see whether there are statistically significant differences. When differences are found, researchers often attribute the differences to the demographic variables themselves. Continuing with our earlier example, the difference in depression scores between Mexican Americans and European Americans is attributed to *cultural differences*. The researchers relied on the self-reported ethnic categorization of the participants as a necessary and sufficient explanation for the observed differences. However, as Phinney (1996) reminds us, ethnic categorization is problematic because of its imprecise and arbitrary nature. Ethnic categories can vary over time and context, such that an individual can identify with one ethnic group in a certain context and identify with another ethnic group in a different context. Furthermore, even if the researchers were 100% certain that the individuals in the study categorized themselves in a way that was consistent with societal norms, attributing the differences to ethnic status is insufficient. Phinney stated that ethnic categories, or ethnicity, has psychological dimensions. She says that ethnicity can be thought of as culture, identity, or minority status, with each dimension having a specific psychological impact.

As ethnic minority research starts to mature, it begins to move away from purely descriptive research and reliance on distal explanations to more theoretically driven research with proximal explanations. The word *proximal* means situated nearest the point of origin. Proximal factors are ones that more directly and parsimoniously explain observed phenomena. Unlike distal factors, proximal factors are usually more psychological in nature. In our example, ethnic identity, as a psychological dimension of ethnicity, is a proximal factor that could be hypothesized to account for the differences in depression between Mexican Americans and European Americans. Using the scientific method, we would test this hypothesis against other plausible or rival hypotheses. We may find that ethnic identity does not account for the differences in depression, and instead, the answer may lie with the importance of familial roles in the lives of both groups. We may discover that a disproportionate number of Mexican-American students are first generation college students, and that leaving home and going to college far away from their

TABLE 15.1
PROXIMAL
AND DISTAL
EXPLANATIONS
FOR GROUP
DIFFERENCES

Proximal Explanations	Distal Explanations
Racial identity	Race
Ethnic identity	Ethnicity
Worldview	Culture
Acculturation	Sex
Values	Age
Communication patterns	Socioeconomic status*
Spirituality/religiosity	Education
Individualism/collectivism	Generation status
Independence/interdependence	Year in school
Familial roles	Major

*If used simply as a demographic, categorical variable (e.g., low, middle, high), socioeconomic status is a distal explanation. However, socioeconomic status may also be used as a proximal explanation if race and ethnicity differences are observed, and these differences can best be explained because of differences in socioeconomic status.

families is causing not only higher rates of depression, but also guilt because of the desire to want to work and financially help the family. Thus, it can be seen that although the distal factor of ethnicity is not sufficient to explain why differences in depression exist between the two groups, a proximal factor related to familial roles provides the specific reason for the difference. A list of variables that serve as proximal or distal explanations for observed phenomena is provided in Table 15.1.

MODERATOR AND MEDIATOR VARIABLES

In Chapter 10, moderator and mediator variables were discussed. Recall that moderators are variables that affect the direction and/or strength of the relationship between a predictor (independent variable) and a criterion (dependent variable). Moderators are usually involved in questions addressing "when" or "for whom" a variable most strongly causes or predicts an outcome variable (Frazier, Tix, & Barron, 2004). Moderators are either categorical (e.g., race, ethnicity, sex) or continuous (e.g., income, amount of depression) (Baron & Kenny, 1986). In Table 15.1, many of the variables that are distal in nature can also be considered as moderators. When the researcher moves beyond using distal variables like race and ethnicity in descriptive fashion, and specifies how the variable changes the direction or strength of the relation between a predictor and an outcome, the distal variable is being used as a moderator. For example, Cokley (2003a) reported that African-American students were significantly higher in self-esteem than European-American students. In this instance, Cokley was using ethnicity in a descriptive, distal fashion.

Later, Cokley (2003b) reported that the relationship between grade point average (i.e., predictor) and self-esteem (i.e., outcome) differed by ethnic group. He found that for European-American students, grade point average significantly predicted self-esteem; however, for African-American students, grade point average did not predict self-esteem. In this instance, Cokley was using ethnicity as a moderator variable, because ethnicity moderated the relationship between grade point average and self-esteem.

Recall that mediators are variables that account for or explain the relationship between a predictor (independent variable) and criterion (dependent variable). Mediators are usually involved in establishing "how" or "why" a predictor variable causes or predicts a criterion variable (Baron & Kenny, 1986; Frazier et al., 2004). Mediators are usually psychological in nature (Baron & Kenny). In Table 15.1, many of the variables that are proximal in nature can also be considered as mediators. For example, Lee (2003) reported that discrimination was negatively correlated with psychological well-being and positively correlated with distress. He hypothesized that ethnic identity mediated the effects of discrimination. However, contrary to his hypothesis, ethnic identity did not mediate the effects of discrimination.

Regarding our earlier point about the importance of conducting theoretically driven research, we want to emphasize the point that when multicultural researchers are able to consistently identify when and under what conditions a variable predicts or causes another variable, the level of understanding about a particular multicultural topic will be evident. Similarly, when multicultural researchers are able to consistently explain how and why variables like ethnic identity and acculturation explain relationships between predictors and criterions, multicultural research on a particular topic will be seen as reaching a high level of understanding.

METHODOLOGICAL CONSIDERATIONS

The comparison of groups—whether they are different ethnic groups; males and females; low, middle, or high socioeconomic status; high achievers or low achievers; or clinical or nonclinical samples—is an inherently interesting research endeavor. As mentioned previously, any differences found in comparisons of ethnic groups should be explained by proximal factors. However, before conducting comparisons using ethnic groups, a clear theoretically driven rationale should guide the decision to compare ethnic minority and majority groups.

COMPARATIVE RESEARCH FRAMEWORK

Whites or Europeans are no longer the standard by which the psychology of people is judged.

—Daudi Ajani Ya Azibo

Thus far, the discussion of multicultural research has been, ironically, politically neutral. This book has focused on the role that science and research play in counseling, and this chapter has continued that theme relative to conducting multicultural research. However, we are reminded that science is neither apolitical nor neutral (Guthrie, 1998). This is perhaps most evident when research involves ethnic minority populations, in which case the generalizability of the findings tends to be questioned more than research involving predominantly white populations (Sue, 1999). Azibo (1988) shared a vivid example from his own experiences interviewing for a faculty position. After presenting two colloquia where he presented empirical studies using culturally specific instruments normed on African Americans, he was asked the question, "Why didn't you use a white control group?" In the ensuing dialogue, Azibo replied by asking what he would be controlling for, to which there was no reply.

In Chapter 14, the problems in comparing two groups formed from differences on a categorical status variable (i.e., distal variable) were briefly discussed. It was pointed out that examining group differences requires an understanding of the processes that lead to the differences. However, Azibo (1988) argues that comparing two different ethnic groups, especially when the comparison involves an ethnic minority group with European Americans, is only appropriate when "racial" groups are equated on all relevant variables, especially culture. He states that it is not appropriate to compare "racial" groups when they are not equated on any relevant variable. In those instances, he says that differences should only be described and reported, not interpreted. Finally, he says that whenever psychological constructs are used in research, culture will always be relevant. Azibo's stance is, admittedly, extreme. Taken to its logical conclusion, it would almost never be appropriate to do any comparisons of ethnic groups when they are not equivalent. Finding ethnic groups that are equivalent on all relevant variables is virtually impossible, because researchers obviously cannot control for differences in history and differential experiences with prejudice and discrimination, which will influence the thoughts, beliefs, attitudes, and behaviors of ethnic groups. Although we do not endorse the position of equating ethnic groups on *all* relevant variables because of pragmatic reasons, we recognize the dangers and limitations of interpreting group differences when relevant cultural variables have not been controlled or measured.

The comparative research framework has been criticized because of the history of ethnic minority groups being compared to European Americans as a "norm group." Today such comparisons are not viewed as necessary because we believe it is useful to study various groups in and of themselves. We need to expand our knowledge base across groups without necessarily comparing them.

CULTURE AND VALIDITY

As our society becomes more diverse, researchers must adjust their methods and develop new ways to accurately investigate social phenomena with different cultures. Because culture is an essential source of human behavior, a researcher must ensure that the research design is amenable to finding behavioral determinants that may be due to culture. Some validity issues become more crucial when culture is considered in research. Some scholars contend that an additional category of validity, namely cultural validity, should be added to the list of discussed validities in research (Quintana, Troyano, & Taylor, 2001). In an effort to increase awareness of multicultural issues in research, the addition of such a term to denote a separate validity only further marginalizes concerns of culture in research. The issues that are subsumed under the characterization of cultural validity (e.g., construct operationalization, selection issues) are already part of the extant discussion on validity. Instead of creating a new term to denote the importance of culture on validity, a paradigm shift toward the acceptance of culture as a part of everyday life and as a result a part of everyday human behavior needs to occur.

Chapter 5 presented the types of and threats to the four categories of validity outlined by Shadish et al. (2002). Although these four types of validity are for the most part exhaustive of general validity concerns in research design, we will highlight some important aspects of these four types of validity that should be considered when incorporating culture into research.

THREATS TO STATISTICAL CONCLUSION VALIDITY   Recall that statistical conclusion validity refers to the degree a relationship between variables in a study does or does not exist. As Quintana, Troyano, and Taylor (2001) have noted, multicultural research is not any more susceptible to statistical conclusion validity threats than any other type of research. The main concerns that arise involve having enough power to detect an effect—a problem that is critical when there are relatively fewer individuals of a certain cultural or minority group (which is not uncommon in many communities) to allow for valid conclusions. Furthermore, the issue of unreliability of measures becomes salient when a measure that has been previously normed on a group different than the one being investigated is used to ascertain relationships among variables of interest. These measures are more susceptible to error variance and may mask true relationships among study variables.

THREATS TO INTERNAL VALIDITY   As defined in Chapter 5, internal validity refers to the extent that a researcher may infer a causal relationship among variables in a given study. A study is said to have adequate internal validity when the presence of possible rival hypotheses is ruled out. When plausible rival hypotheses are not ruled out, threats to internal validity arise. Several of these threats are made more salient when conducting multicultural research. One of these threats is local history. As an illustration, consider the following example. Suppose an individual was conducting a large-scale, two-week diversity training designed to increase awareness and understanding of cultural groups on campus. A pretest measure was given before the implementation of the intervention and a posttest was planned after the workshop series was completed. Imagine that the majority of the participants in the workshop were whites, blacks, and Latinos. Suppose that while this intervention was in progress, an incident occurred where on a Friday night, black college students were seemingly targeted by university police and told that their house parties must end. Imagine that one black male house tenant argued with the officer and refused to send individuals home, citing that there was a white fraternity on their street that was also having a party but was not told to send its guests home. As a response to the apparent anger displayed by the black male student, the officer became alarmed and decided to use mace to subdue the student. Although the incident was not publicized in the school newspaper, the news spread like wildfire to all the black students and faculty at the university. It appeared that many of the white and Latino students were unaware that this incident occurred. When the diversity training intervention was completed and the posttest was given, scores significantly decreased for the black students, indicating a decrease in awareness, knowledge, and acceptance of other groups, whereas scores for whites and Latinos increased, indicating the opposite finding. The researcher, unaware of any of the events that occurred, may conclude that the intervention did not work for blacks but was successful for Latinos and whites. In this case, the threat of local history or selection × history interaction occurred and led to invalid conclusions by the researcher. Strategies for dealing with such issues will be discussed later in the chapter.

Another threat that may have occurred in the previous example is attrition. Suppose that instead of staying in the study, the black students were so upset with what had happened that they refused to participate in the research, and as a result dropped out of the study. This threat would also lead to invalid conclusions about the intervention due to the altered composition of participants at the posttest.

Some interventions that are performed with immigrant populations or individuals for whom English is not their first language are especially susceptible to internal validity threats. If individuals are tested more than once during the implementation of an intervention, there is a possibility of testing threats. This holds true for individuals who may not understand all the items on a test and because of increased exposure to the measure actually begin to understand the language used on the pre- or posttests. Therefore, the change in score at the intervention may be due to increased levels of acculturation as opposed to the effectiveness of the intervention.

Similarly, level of acculturation may also introduce maturation threats to internal validity. Let us suppose, for example, that an intervention was implemented with immigrant women that was designed to prevent domestic violence. Part of the intervention included assertiveness training and education about domestic violence laws in the United States. The intervention was part of a three-year longitudinal study assessing several factors related to personal relationships; every six months participants were contacted and asked to complete a series of measures. At almost every data collection time, scores on assertiveness and knowledge of domestic violence laws increased. Researchers concluded that the intervention was successful in increasing knowledge and level of assertiveness among participants. What the researchers have not considered is that as the length of the participant's residence in the United States increased, their level of acculturation also increased. Some women may have come from more patriarchal societies where domestic violence is more common and laws to protect women from abuse are nonexistent or not enforced. As they continued to live in and learn about the culture in the United States, they learned that what may have been more acceptable in their former countries of residence is not customary in the United States.

One of the most pernicious threats to internal validity is selection. Selection is particularly threatening to multicultural research in that studies using a comparative framework analyze data based on group membership. Sometimes individuals are chosen on the basis of their membership in a cultural or minority group and other times analysis is conducted post-hoc (after the fact with no theoretically based hypotheses) after the researcher realizes that he or she has enough participants from each group to conduct analyses. One reason that selection threats are dangerous to internal validity is that one cannot randomly assign race or ethnicity; therefore, selection biases are inherent in these types of studies. Another reason is that race or group membership is used as a proxy for numerous cultural variables. As discussed earlier, differences found among cultural groups are erroneously attributed to group membership as opposed to more proximal variables that may actually be responsible for differences (e.g., socioeconomic status, acculturation). As stated in Chapter 5, selection biases may also interact with other threats to internal validity to impact results of a study.

THREATS TO EXTERNAL VALIDITY Recall that external validity refers to the generalizability of a study across people, settings, and times. As Quintana et al. (2001) have contended, multicultural studies have significantly contributed to the understanding of external validity in mainstream psychological research, finding that theories developed for white middle-class populations are not necessarily appropriate for culturally different groups.

Scholars have noted the limited generalizability of traditional psychological research that tends to use college students (Quintana et al., 2001; Sue, 1999). As noted in Chapter 5, it is rare to find studies that obtain a random sample of a specified population to draw inferences about psychological phenomena. The more common use of external validity in counseling research involves the generalization *across* populations instead of *to* populations. With regards to multicultural research, a common research question involves the extent to which psychological phenomena are generalizable across populations.

In any research study, there is often a trade-off between internal validity and external validity. Usually when a study is said to have strong external validity, the internal validity of the study may be compromised due to the increase of extraneous variables leading to plausible rival hypotheses. In other words, there is an increase in internal validity threats. The internal validity of psychological research appears to be disproportionately given more weight than external validity in psychological journals (Sue, 1999). Although inferences about generalizability are sometimes made to include conclusions about populations not explicitly examined in a particular study, reviewers of psychological research are sometimes less critical toward obvious external validity violations (e.g., not including individuals from diverse backgrounds in the study sample) (Sue), or the issue is relegated to future research suggestions.

What we believe is more important with regards to external validity is to explicitly define the researcher's population, time, and setting of interest. These aspects of external validity should be chosen with the research question in mind. If a researcher wants to know the extent that a certain counseling technique is applicable to individuals who experience depression, then the sample must be heterogeneous to allow for valid conclusions about different populations. Therefore, the researcher should include individuals whose differences (e.g., ethnicity, socioeconomic status, gender) reflect their population of interest. For multicultural research, given that some psychological phenomena operate differently based on cultural group membership, it may be inappropriate to combine participants together into one "representative" population. Assuming that different cultural groups were equally represented numerically in a study, critical differences between these populations may be obscured and as a result increase the error variance in the study. Error variance may be random, but some of the error that occurs is systematic, meaning that a variable has not been accounted for. When cultural group differences are not accounted for in a study, a selection by treatment threat may have occurred.

THREATS TO CONSTRUCT VALIDITY   Construct validity refers to the extent study variables (e.g., independent and dependent variables) represent the constructs they are purported to measure. One of the most important issues in multicultural research is that the constructs being studied are appropriate for use with the cultural group(s) of interest. Because many of the measures used in mainstream psychology were created for and normed on white, European-American, middle class populations, the importance of construct validity becomes salient in multicultural research. When a construct is not adequately operationalized, study conclusions are at best dubious. What is problematic is when a construct is operationalized using a definition found adequate with majority group populations, but is not interpreted the same way for groups that are culturally different from the majority. Take, for example, the idea of self. In Western, individualistic cultures the self is seen as a bounded, independent entity consisting of needs, abilities, motives, and rights; however, in collectivistic cultures, the self is seen as an unbounded, interdependent entity socialized to fit in and be a part of a group (Matsumoto, 2000). Traditional self-esteem measures in Western cultures are typically operationalized with an individualistic notion of the self. Giving these measures to more collectivist populations, who possess a more collectivist notion of self (e.g., the self extends beyond the individual), would be inappropriate and lead to unsound conclusions.

In terms of construct validity, a measure is considered biased if it measures different traits for whites and minorities or measures the same attribute with differing levels of accuracy for minority and majority groups (Reynolds, C. R., 1982). Factor analysis can be used to determine whether minority and majority groups exhibit the same underlying factor structure for a given construct

(Reynolds, C. R., 1982; Tabachnick & Fidell, 1996; Valencia & Suzuki, 2001). This procedure identifies the degree that clusters of test items or clusters of subsets of psychological test items correlate with one another, and in turn can provide some indication that individuals are conceptualizing the meaning of item subsets in similar or different ways (Tabachnick & Fidell). Furthermore, if the factor structure differs between groups then the test does not demonstrate construct validity, and thus is biased.

Although factor analysis is a useful tool for tapping into construct validity, it should not be used as the only method for determining construct validity. Furthermore, the replicability of factor structure across groups is not sufficient evidence of measurement invariance and instrument equivalence (Byrne & Watkins, 2003; also see Chapter 20). Byrne and Watkins contended "even though a factor structure may yield a similar pattern when tested within each of two or more groups, such findings represent no guarantee that the instrument will operate equivalently across these groups" (p. 156), that is, with the same meaning across groups. Furthermore, for any given measure there are sources of error that sometimes can be identified, but most times are not. For example, a measure may not cover all the important aspects of a construct across different cultural groups, and thus result in construct under-representativeness (Shadish et al., 2002) for some groups. Therefore, due to possible imperfections in a given measure, one cannot fully assess construct validity; one can only hope to strengthen it.

SUGGESTIONS FOR CONDUCTING MORE CULTURALLY COMPETENT RESEARCH STUDIES

One of the longest ongoing debates relating to research methods is the use of quantitative versus qualitative research designs. In recent years, there has been a movement toward the use of mixed method approaches for investigating social phenomena. Mixed methods refer to the conjunctive use of both qualitative and quantitative data analysis strategies (Greene, Caracelli, & Graham, 1989). Although the use of quantitative methods allows researchers to gather large amounts of data in a relatively short period of time, qualitative data provide rich and detailed information that is often difficult to collect in survey formats. Researchers who value descriptive and inferential statistics may sometimes discredit the usefulness of qualitative methods; however, by using different sources and methods in the design, implementation, and evaluation of research, a researcher can build on the strength of each type of data collection and minimize the weakness of any single approach (Greene et al.).

There are several benefits to using mixed method designs. First, the validity of results can be strengthened by using more than one method to study the same phenomenon (triangulation). Including multiple methods and multiple instruments to assess constructs of interest will help reduce mono-method and mono-operation bias, respectively. Combining two methods (i.e., qualitative and quantitative methods) increases the researcher's understanding of findings in a study. Mixed method approaches may also lead researchers to modify or expand the research design to more appropriately study the population of interest. Including a qualitative segment to quantitative research may, for example, prevent or help clarify instrumentation issues with particular multicultural groups.

Flaskerud and Nyamathi (2000) provide a good example using mixed methods in their longitudinal research study conducted over a six-year period, which focused on HIV education, counseling, and antibody testing with low-income Latina women. Flaskerud and Nyamathi used both focus groups and surveys to study needle use and other health-related variables. Results of the survey revealed an increase in needle utilization but low levels of intravenous drug use. To clarify this finding, focus groups were conducted to address the discrepancy. The focus groups revealed that participants in the study were using needles to inject prescription medications brought in from Mexico. This finding prompted the research program to continue to provide a program demonstrating needle and syringe cleaning with bleach. In this case, mixed methods helped clarify a finding and saved a useful program.

An additional method of increasing multicultural competence in research is the involvement of multiple stakeholders or diverse samples. Involving members of the target population or stakeholder group in the design, implementation, and evaluation stages of the research project can help researchers gain valuable insight on how to approach the question of interest with multicultural sensitivity and relevance. In the case of Flaskerud and Nyamathi's (2000) longitudinal research study with Latina women, community members were involved in all steps of the research study. Participants and researchers worked together as equals with respect for each other's expertise and contribution (Flaskerud & Nyamathi). The researcher and potential targets of the study developed the questions of interest collaboratively. This design method considers the cultural and political context of the research. Also, for this particular study the inclusion of community members as research partners lessened the power and social status differentials between researchers and participants and made it easier for participants to be forthcoming about sensitive issues. As a result, the threat of evaluation apprehension in regards to construct validity was lessened. The researcher assistants who were hired for this particular study were also Spanish-speaking Latina women. Inclusion of community members as researchers enhanced the quality and the relevance of the research questions and interventions.

A final way to increase the level of multicultural competence in a study is to pilot test all protocols and instruments. This is important for all research, but is especially crucial when the researcher is not familiar with all the cultural groups in the participant pool. At the piloting stage, researchers can preempt any fatal flaws and make the necessary changes to ensure that conclusions made in the study are valid. It may not be clear as to whether the wording or conceptualization of a construct or instrument makes sense for the population of interest. Piloting provides opportunities to investigate such issues by allowing participants to provide feedback.

SUMMARY AND CONCLUSIONS

In an ideal world, there would not be a need for a chapter on multicultural research. All methodologically sound and scientifically rigorous research should be attendant to the issues raised in this chapter. However, we live in a less than perfect world, and researchers are subject to the same biases (intentional and unintentional) and myopic mindsets as exist in the society in which they live. Scholars, scientists, and researchers have never been consistent in their definitions of race, ethnicity, and culture. A basic premise of all psychological research is that the constructs used are operationally defined. Race, ethnicity, and culture, although traditionally the province of anthropology and sociology, are indeed psychological in nature. These constructs constitute an important part of the subjective, phenomenological world of the observer and the observed.

The convenience of having samples, especially college samples, with diverse ethnic groups often results in post hoc analyses based on the comparative research paradigm. The problem with this approach is that it is primarily descriptive and atheoretical, reflecting little thought of the underlying causal relationships. Researchers who employ this approach unwittingly perpetuate the marginalization of multicultural research. The early stages of ethnic minority research, as in other areas of research, necessarily are predominated by descriptive research that was not often guided by established psychological theories and principles. Multicultural researchers have rightfully been critical of traditional psychological theories and principles that were primarily created using European-American and often middle-class people, thereby raising serious questions about the external validity of the findings to other groups. However, both etic and emic approaches are important, because by virtue of our shared humanity we all experience the full range of human emotions (e.g., happiness, love, sadness, depression, anxiety, anger, jealousy, confidence). However, the expression and manifestation of these emotions are often filtered through cultural lenses that are not always well understood.

In studies with an explicitly multicultural focus, it is critically important that proximal rather than distal variables be used to explain observed differences in behavior. The use of moderational and mediational analyses reflects theoretical and methodological sophistication, and will be most beneficial in advancing the state of affairs of multicultural research on particular topics.

Finally, we provided examples of validity issues and threats that may occur in multicultural research. Using mixed methods, including stakeholders, and piloting measures and protocols may help reduce threats to validity. The main purpose of addressing validity in psychological research is to ensure that a study's conclusions are valid. Multicultural researchers are often driven by concerns about validity, and at their best will reflexively critique their work to ensure that state of the art science is being conducted that generates valid psychological insights relevant to culturally diverse groups of people.

STIMULUS QUESTIONS

AN INTEGRATION EXERCISE

The purpose of this exercise is to promote integration and utilization of the material presented in Chapter 15. Students should respond to each question, and then discuss their responses with a peer.

1. Why is it problematic to use the terms race, ethnicity, and culture interchangeably?
2. What is the difference between distal and proximal explanations for behavior in multicultural research?

3. A researcher hypothesizes that there are racial differences in intelligence test scores. What issues would the researcher need to address, and what evidence would need to be presented, in order to provide support for the hypothesis?

4. What are the advantages and disadvantages of conducting multicultural research that is primarily descriptive versus theoretically driven?

5. What are the advantages and disadvantages of adding cultural validity as an additional category of validity in research?

6. What are some ways individuals can conduct more culturally competent research studies?

7. Think of a situation where the validities discussed in this chapter would be at odds for a person trying to conduct culturally competent research (i.e., increasing one type of validity at the expense of another type of validity).

INVESTIGATOR, EXPERIMENTER, AND PARTICIPANT BIAS

When a researcher designs a study, he or she seeks to examine the relationships among specified variables. One of the most crucial tasks that confronts the researcher is to control the extraneous variables or reduce the error variance (serious threats to Kerlinger's MAXMINCON principle) that may influence the relationships among the study's experimental variables of interest. Most often, when the extraneous variables or sources of measurement error are known, they are relatively easy to control; the problem is that in designing most studies, it is difficult, if not impossible, to identify all of the possible extraneous variables and error variance.

The purpose of this chapter is to identify potential sources of bias in participants, investigators, and experimenters of particular relevance to researchers in counseling. By the term *bias*, we mean the systematic introduction of extraneous variables that may distort or disguise the relationships among the experimental variables. Whereas *error variance* (or "noise" or "static") refers to variance due to random events, *bias* refers to the creation of differential effects between groups or subgroups of participants due to some systematic kinds of errors.

In this chapter, *investigator* refers to the person who designs the study, and *experimenter* refers to the person who executes the investigation. The first section of this chapter examines investigator and experimenter bias, particularly with regard to (1) experimenter attributes, (2) investigator and experimenter expectancies, and (3) experimental procedures. The second section of this chapter examines participant bias, particularly with regard to (1) demand characteristics, (2) participant characteristics, and (3) introspective abilities. Throughout both sections we use examples from previous research efforts to clarify different types of bias. Moreover, in discussing the various sources of bias, we also discuss some strategies for controlling or minimizing these variables.

INVESTIGATOR AND EXPERIMENTER BIAS

In an ideal world, an investigator is an objective, unbiased seeker of truth who engages in a systematic, scientific enterprise and is able to remain an impartial, passive observer throughout. In this way, the researcher does not contaminate the research in any way, but rather is an unbiased observer of some phenomenon, and subsequently a reporter of the truth. We might even assume that:

> All experimenters [investigators] are created equal; that they have been endowed by their graduate training with certain interchangeable properties; that among these properties are the anonymity and impersonality which allow them to elicit from the same participant identical data which they then identically observe and record. Just as inches were once supposed to adhere in tables regardless of the identity of the measuring instrument, so needs, motives, traits, IQs, anxieties, and attitudes were supposed to adhere in patients and participants and to emerge uncontaminated by the identity and attitude of the examiner or experimenter. (Friedman, 1967, pp. 3–4)

We know, however, that investigators do not conduct research in such an unbiased manner. Moreover, we know that experimenters who execute investigations may consciously or unconsciously affect the results of their studies. Instead, researchers sometimes have opinions, beliefs, and values that unconsciously (or even consciously) compromise their objectivity, sometimes in very subtle ways. Likewise, researchers' values and cultural biases are inherent in their assumptions concerning participants, research hypotheses, data analysis strategies, and conclusions. Thus, culturally encapsulated researchers may unknowingly make a number of decisions that might introduce a number of systematic biases in their research. In essence, it is important for investigators and experimenters to be cognizant of their cultural stereotypes and preconceived notions, particularly with cultural groups that are less familiar to the individual. For example, Erickson and Al-Timimi (2001) suggest that because Arab Americans are one of the most misunderstood ethnic groups in the United States, certain biases may be elicited.

The story of Clever Hans nicely illustrates the effects of subtle experimental bias. Hans was a horse around the turn of the twentieth century that reliably computed various arithmetic problems, identified musical intervals, and had a working knowledge of German. His owner, Herr Wilhelm von Osten, would ask Hans all kinds of questions; Hans would tap numbers out with his hoof or gesture with his head toward objects. Hans passed a number of tests with various local citizens and professionals, much to everyone's amazement—until, that is, a young psychologist, Oskar Pfungst, came along. Pfungst discovered that Hans could reliably answer questions (that is, nine times out of ten) only when the interrogator knew the correct answers, but his performance dropped to one out of ten if the interrogator was ignorant of the answer. As it turned out, Hans had not learned math, or music, or the German language, but rather had learned to read subtle cues in the interrogator's posture, breathing, and facial expressions (Pfungst, 1911). Research in the 1980s revealed that laboratory animals can learn to read a wide variety of subtle behavioral cues in trainers that give away the intended answer.

In short, investigators and experimenters can be the source of extraneous variables and error variance that may very well bias the results of a study. We next discuss three major types of bias: experimenter attributes, investigator and experimenter expectancies, and experimental procedures. In addition, we offer some strategies for reducing such biases.

EXPERIMENTER ATTRIBUTES

Experimenter attributes are primarily biological and interpersonal characteristics of the experimenter that may cause differential responses in participants. Examples include the experimenter's age, gender, race/ethnicity, physical appearance, and interpersonal style. For example, some participants might respond more honestly to a female researcher investigating sexual harassment than to a male. Likewise, an experimenter of age 50 might inhibit younger participants but facilitate disclosure for older participants. In another case, the experimenter's interpersonal style (say, unfriendly and dominant) might interact with the independent variable (for example, expertness cues) such that some participants feel uncomfortable or even threatened during the experiment. Race and ethnicity can also influence bias in a study's results if a participant has preconceptions or stereotypes about the experimenter's racial or ethnic group. Another potential biasing characteristic pertains to previous contact between the experimenter and participants. Some participants may feel that having some prior knowledge about an experimenter would make it easier for them to respond, whereas others may feel much less likely to disclose personal information.

In short, a wide range of experimenter characteristics might influence some or all participants to respond differentially in a particular experiment, thereby confounding its results. In fact, several writers (see, for example, Christensen, 1980; Kazdin, 1980) have reported empirical investigations that document that experimenter characteristics can affect responses given by participants on various tasks, such as self-report inventories, projective tests, laboratory tasks, and measures of intelligence (see, for example, Barber, 1976; Johnson, 1976; Masling, 1966; Rumenik, Capasso, & Hendrick, 1977). For example, one study found some African-American clients tend to rate white counselors as less proficient and credible (Watkins & Terrell, 1988).

In short, experimenter attributes create threats to validity. Consider the following example, which raises questions about construct validity. Imagine an investigator (Professor Kay Tharsis) who has reason to believe that a psychodynamic, insight-oriented therapy group would be more effective in treating bulimic clients than a cognitive-behavioral therapy group. The good professor designs a study in which two bright, advanced graduate students act as experimenters to conduct the group therapies, each lasting 10 weeks. Each student conducts one of the treatment groups. Suppose a broad array of extraneous participant variables are controlled (for example, age, sex, and personality dynamics), the treatments are carefully matched, and random assignment of clients is used. Imagine further that the results clearly favor the psychodynamic treatment group on a broad array of dependent variables (such as self-report, behavioral indexes, and therapist observations). Nonetheless, in this example the results of the treatment groups cannot be separated from the different experimenter attributes and their potential biases. In reality, it may be that the two therapists' attributes did not affect clients differentially, but we have no way of determining whether this is the case. Thus, if different experimenters are used to administer different treatments, it may be difficult to determine whether the results are due to the different treatments, the different experimenters, or an interaction between the two.

Experimenter attributes can also threaten the external validity or generalizability of a study by interacting in some way with the independent variable. For example, it could be that the results of a study would generalize only to therapists with certain characteristics, such as androgynous men, feminist therapists, or African-American therapists. Imagine the following modifications to the fictitious example just mentioned. Suppose that Professor Kay Tharsis seeks out and uses two female therapists in their thirties with excellent interpersonal skills to co-lead both groups. Within the psychodynamic, insight-oriented treatment, a major therapeutic intervention involves the use of the therapeutic relationship to provide interpersonal feedback and promote awareness of each client's interpersonal style and intrapersonal dynamics (see Yalom, 1985, for such a therapeutic orientation). Again imagine that the insight-oriented therapy clearly results in the more favorable outcomes. Would these obtained results generalize to other female therapists who may not have excellent interpersonal skills, or to male therapists? Even though this is obviously an empirical question, it is useful because it highlights how experimenter attributes might interact with independent variables and possibly limit the generalizability of specific findings.

Among the many strategies that investigators can use to reduce the possible effects of experimenter attributes are the following:

- *Avoid using a single experimenter* for different levels of the independent variable if at all possible, because this clearly confounds the study's construct validity with experimenter attributes. Whenever possible, use two or more experimenters for each level of the independent variable.
- If two or more experimenters are used for each level of the independent variable, statistically *analyze the data for differences across experimenters* to determine whether any differences could be related to experimenter attributes such as gender. Often this is done as a preliminary data analysis

to rule out possible confounding variables related to experimenter attributes. For example, McCarthy, Shaw, and Schmeck (1986) were interested in studying whether stylistic differences in client information processing (shallow versus deep processors) would be related to their verbal behaviors during counseling sessions. They used two counselors, each of whom saw half of the participants across all of the conditions. Before doing their main data analysis, they did a preliminary analysis to determine whether there were any main effects or interactions due to the counselors on the dependent variables. No differences were found, suggesting that the counselors did not differentially affect the dependent variables. Thus, the authors were able to rule out differences due to different experimenters and to proceed with their main statistical analyses.

- Because there are currently so many unknowns concerning the effects of experimenter attributes, it would be useful for investigators to *specify the characteristics of therapists used in treatment interventions*. Perhaps over time patterns pertaining to certain therapist characteristics might emerge, such as interpersonal style. Kazdin (1980) suggested that investigators analyze their data for experimenter characteristics (gender), which might provide a useful knowledge base over time. One review of two major counseling journals revealed that at the time, more authors analyzed their results for gender differences than they did a decade earlier (Lee, Heppner, Gagliardi, & Lee, 1987).

- Authors should explicitly *examine the generalizability of their data in terms of experimenter attributes,* and qualify the conclusions in their discussions accordingly. For example, if researchers used only male therapists, then the discussion of the results should focus on male therapists, and not on therapists in general. Gender is a particularly important variable in counseling research. For now, suffice it to note that Lee et al. (1987) found that authors still tended to overgeneralize their results in terms of gender, although less than they did a decade earlier.

INVESTIGATOR AND EXPERIMENTER EXPECTANCIES

Investigator and experimenter expectancies are beliefs and desires about either how the participant should perform or how the study should turn out. Kazdin (1980) noted that the effect of these expectancies has been referred to as an "unintentional expectancy effect," because even though the investigator and experimenter may not intentionally try to influence the participant, they actually do so unconsciously through a range of verbal and nonverbal behaviors (such as head nods, smiles, glances, or subtle comments). Such bias obviously introduces confounding variables, as illustrated in the Clever Hans story.

Robert Rosenthal, one of the first to investigate this topic in the early 1960s, found that investigator and experimenter expectancies directly influenced how participants performed (see Rosenthal, 1966). Subsequent research indicated that investigator and experimenter bias can influence participants in a wide variety of contexts, such as learning studies, ability studies, psychophysical studies, reaction time studies, inkblot test studies, structured laboratory studies, and person perception studies (see Rosenthal, 1966). Although some writers have argued that the effect of experimenter bias has been overstated (Barber, 1976; Barber & Silver, 1968), it is generally concluded that investigators and experimenters can and do influence participant responses (Barber; Christensen, 1980).

Expectancies can be positive or negative and occur in many different ways. Investigator and experimenter bias can affect participants or clients at any stage of an investigation, such as during participant recruitment, during data collection, or after treatment interventions. For example, an exuberant experimenter (serving as a therapist) may subtly or not-so-subtly promote the effectiveness of one intervention over others. This form of bias is operative when an investigator's enthusiasm for a new treatment intervention (that perhaps he or she has developed) gets communicated to the experimenter, who then might consciously or unconsciously be too enthusiastic in conducting the therapeutic role within a study.

Sometimes the desire to be effective even leads experimenters serving as therapists to break protocol and engage in activities outside of normal therapeutic or experimental procedures. For example, in one study that examined the counseling process, a relatively inexperienced therapist was found engaging in a friendly conversation with the client immediately after the counseling session, during which time the client was completing forms evaluating the counseling session and the counselor! This type of interaction could certainly influence participants to give more favorable responses.

Investigator and experimenter bias also can influence clients in a negative way. For example, if an experimenter is not very motivated or interested in conducting a study, the lack of enthusiasm can very well affect client recruitment and willingness to participate. Halfhearted efforts by experimenters can result in halfhearted responses by clients. Biases resulting from lack of experimenter motivation can be a particular problem with doctoral dissertations, notably when the author asks a friend to assume total responsibility for certain aspects of a study (such as recruitment, data collection, or monitoring data flow); even most "good friends" will not be as motivated as the researcher, especially as problems arise and frustrations mount. Sometimes inexperienced investigators feel shy or guilty about asking clients to participate in a study, but telling clients three or four times in an apologetic tone that they do not have to participate is not especially persuasive. Another probable source of bias can arise during the administration of inventories to participants or clients; a busy counseling center receptionist, for example, might be tired at the end of each working day, given the added demands of the research, and verbally or nonverbally convey impatience to the final clients.

In summary, there are many opportunities for investigator and experimenter bias to contaminate the results of a study. Experimenter and investigator expectancies can bias participants whenever anyone involved in conducting the study interacts with participants, can bias the results to favor one treatment over another, or can affect the generalizability of findings. Thus, experimenter and investigator expectancies can affect both construct and external validity in similar ways to those discussed with respect to experimenter attributes.

Some strategies to lessen the effects of investigator and experimenter expectancies include the following:

- Perhaps the most common strategy to offset experimenter biases is to *keep experimenters "blind"* as to the purpose of the study. Thus, for example, an investigator who is comparing the effectiveness of two treatment approaches would not communicate to the experimenters serving as therapists the specific purposes and hypotheses of the study, thereby reducing the probability that the therapists will unintentionally influence participants in the hypothesized direction. In fact, the investigator may want to keep anyone involved in the study who has contact with participants (for example, receptionists, therapists, or assistants who collect data from participants) blind as to the specific purpose of the study.

- Because keeping various personnel blind is more difficult in some studies than others, the investigator may need to *resort to a partial-blind strategy*. For example, it would be very difficult to keep therapists blind as they administer a cognitive-behavioral group treatment for bulimics that will be compared with a placebo nondirective discussion group. In such cases, the investigator might try to keep the therapists as blind as possible, and especially with regard to the specific hypotheses and variables involved in the study. Another strategy is to restrict the amount of contact the partial-blind therapists have with participants; therapists might administer the treatments only and not be involved in participant selection, data collection, and debriefing. In short, even when one can achieve only a partial-blind situation, the goal is to keep the experimental personnel as blind as possible to the purpose of the study.

- Because experimenter expectancies can affect participant responses, another strategy is for investigators to *assess the accuracy of experimenter expectancies*. For instance, an investigator may assess whether experimenters correctly surmise the purpose of the study, or even the general hypotheses. If experimenters have accurately pieced together the purpose of the investigation, the potential bias from experimenter expectancies is generally much higher than if the experimenters have not adequately discerned the nature of the study. Although experimenters might still bias participants in subtle ways even when kept blind about the purpose of a study, the probability that participants will be biased toward the hypotheses is reduced. In short, assessing experimenter expectancies allows for both an evaluation of the degree to which experimenters have been kept blind and an assessment of the accuracy of their expectancies.

- *Use strategies for decreasing negative experimenter bias due to halfhearted efforts.* Investigators should be wary of recruiting "friends" to assume total responsibility for various aspects of a study, especially if the investigator is physically removed from the location of the study. Given our experience, which suggests that no one will do the same quality of work as the researcher most directly affected, investigators should try to avoid conducting a study in absentia; if it is absolutely impossible to avoid such a predicament, researchers should regularly converse with their collaborators and make repeated on-site visits.

EXPERIMENTAL PROCEDURES

Once investigators have carefully developed a study, operationalized constructs, identified variables, and controlled as many extraneous variables as possible, they usually attempt to conduct the experimental procedure in a constant and consistent manner. A typical study involves a wide range of experimental procedures—recruiting participants, greeting participants, obtaining informed consent, administering instructions, providing a rationale, administering interventions, recording observations, reminding participants about returning questionnaires, interviewing participants, administering questionnaires, and debriefing; imprecision or inconsistencies in the manner in which the experimental procedures are conducted can therefore be a major source of bias and contamination. Procedural imprecision occurs when the activities, tasks, and instructions of an experiment are not specifically defined. As a result, experimenters might treat participants differently because they are unclear exactly how to conduct the experiment in specific situations. Thus, experimenters introduce bias (or error variance, if it occurs randomly) into an experiment due to variability in experimental procedures.

If, for example, an investigator wants to study the effects of training residence hall staff to be career resource specialists, then the training given to the staff should be clearly specified, and the specific ways the staff are to interact with students on their hall floors should be clearly delineated as well. Are the staff supposed to actually dispense career information? If so, what kind of information? Should they make referrals to the career center? If so, to anyone in particular? Should they administer career assessment inventories? If so, which ones? Should they engage in actual counseling sessions with students? If so, are there any guidelines for topics and number of sessions? Should they promote information-gathering activities? If so, what kind? This example indicates only some of the ways residence hall staff acting as career resource specialists might behave. If the investigator does not specifically delineate what the staff should and should not do, it is very likely that a wide variability in activities will occur across the different residence hall staff members. Moreover, the lack of delineation of staff responsibilities increases the probability of systematic staff biases, such as preferential treatment for brighter students, for same-gender or opposite-gender students, or for students who come from families of higher socioeconomic status.

Likewise, investigator and experimenter biases pertaining to biological sex, race, ethnicity, sexual orientation, age, and physical disability might inadvertently affect participants' responses, either negatively or positively. For example, a male investigator who is insensitive to gender issues and makes sexist comments might systematically bias the recruitment of participants.

In another case, racial bias can influence the interaction and communication between the experimenter and participants (see Dovidio, Gaertner, Kawakami, & Hodson, 2002). In short, any of a number of culturally insensitive behaviors, comments, instructions, or procedures by investigators and experimenters might bias participants' responses.

Even if an investigator has carefully specified the procedures for a particular study, variability across experimenters can occur for a number of reasons, of which we discuss three: fatigue, experimenter drift, and noncompliance. An experimenter who becomes fatigued over time, resulting in different performances across participants, can be a particular problem if experimenters engage in an intensive activity, such as interviewing several participants or clients in a short period of time. An experimenter may also gradually and unconsciously alter his or her performance over time (experimenter drift); this is of special concern if an experimenter is involved in repetitive tasks over time. Or an experimenter may fail to comply with the exact experimental procedures over time, perhaps because of a lack of awareness of the importance of some procedures. For example, toward the end of a data collection process in one study, an experimenter began to estimate a timed task to "about the nearest minute," obviously an imprecise procedure! In another study designed to compare the effects of two therapists, a researcher was chagrined to find one counselor complying with the normal 50-minute sessions while the other counselor, trying very hard to do well, conducted therapy sessions for as long as 70 minutes each! In short, even when procedures are carefully specified, experimenter variability can still occur.

At least three problems are associated with procedural imprecision. First, as suggested in the preceding example, experimenters most likely vary among themselves in addition to introducing systematic biases over time. Thus, not only is there a good chance that each residence hall staff member would engage in quite different activities in the role of career resource specialist, it also is likely that they would act differently from one student to another, thereby adding a confounding variable to the study.

Second, if the procedures are unclear, the investigator does not know what actually occurred. It may be unclear whether the independent variable was administered consistently, or whether other variables might have intervened (recall the discussions of construct validity in Chapter 5 and independent variables in Chapter 12). If significant results are found, it is not clear whether they are to be attributed to the independent variable or to other variables. Or if a participant responds negatively in a survey, it is unknown as to whether this is the participant's true response or if he or she responded negatively due to frustration, such as completing the survey in a loud environment. In short, if investigators do not know what was done in an experiment, their conclusions are confounded, and it is difficult, if not impossible, to discuss the study's results with much precision.

A third problem of procedural imprecision pertains to the statistical issue of introducing error variance or "noise" into the data due to experimenter variability. Statistically speaking, the variability due to the experimenter increases the within-group variability, making it more difficult to find an effect due to the independent variable (assuming such an effect actually exists). Thus, the independent variable must be more potent to offset the increased within-group variability due to experimenter differences.

Given the applied nature of much of our research, procedural imprecision is a particular problem in counseling. For many experiments, the procedural details of a study can be specified and followed. For example, Feldman, Strong, and Danser (1982) were interested in comparing the effects of paradoxical and nonparadoxical interpretation and directives on depressed clients. The authors trained master's-level counselors over the course of 10 hours to integrate a series of paradoxical and nonparadoxical interpretations and directives into a basic counseling interview. In this case, the interpretations and directives were uniform within different treatment conditions. At the end of training, counselors were able to integrate the interpretative and directive statements verbatim at certain points within the counseling interview. However, because other counseling interventions that entail several individuals or therapy sessions are more difficult to control, the amount of consistency that can be achieved across counselors depends a great deal on the type of experimental manipulations involved in the study.

The following strategies can be useful in reducing bias due to experimental procedures:

- Perhaps the most basic strategy is to *carefully describe and make explicit the experimental procedures* involved in a particular study. Putting the procedures in writing both organizes the investigator's thoughts and communicates precise procedures for personnel involved in conducting the study. If experimenters are to make specific statements, it is important that they be delivered verbatim and smoothly. Especially for complex or extended therapeutic interventions, it is often useful to write detailed training manuals that identify and document the specific interventions of treatment; for example, see O'Neil and Roberts Carroll (1987) for a detailed description of a six-day gender-role conflict workshop (cited in O'Neil & Roberts Carroll, 1988). Such manuals are helpful both in training experimenters and for communicating to other investigators the content of a particular intervention.

- In another common strategy, investigators *attempt to standardize the procedures* through some type of structure or even automation. For example, an investigator interested in studying the effects of counselor self-disclosure might encounter some difficulties in examining similar types of self-disclosures from different therapists across different clients. However, video or audio recordings portraying counselor self-disclosures can be developed and shown to participants, so that each participant sees or hears identical counselor self-disclosures (see Dowd & Boroto, 1982, for such an example). Another common example of standardization is to develop a structured interview so that experimenters ask the same questions in the same order using exactly the same words. For example, Josephson and

Fong-Beyette (1987) developed a structured interview to identify specific behaviors and characteristics of counselors that were correlated with adult female clients' disclosure of incest during counseling. The structured interview consisted of a list of questions, asked in a particular sequence, in four general areas: demographic questions, questions pertaining to the incest experience and its perceived effects on the participants, questions about counseling experiences during childhood, and questions about all counseling experiences since age 18. Other examples of standardization include formulating verbatim statements for experimenters or receptionists, providing participants written instructions for completing tasks or inventories, developing a specific order for participants to complete instruments, and using structured forms to facilitate the observation and recording of data. The intent of all these examples is to enhance consistency throughout various aspects of a study by standardizing or providing structure for various procedures.

- Given that misunderstandings and different assumptions can lead to important differences in experimenter procedures (for example, duration of counseling sessions), it can be useful to *reiterate basic experimental procedures with all personnel,* before a study begins and at various times throughout the study.

- Investigators can often improve standardization if they *train experimenters.* Such training includes specific instructions to experimenters about their experimental tasks and interventions, as well as role-playing, feedback, and skill-acquisition exercises. One way to standardize experimenter behavior is to carefully train experimenters to behave exactly in the manner desired. If at all possible, all experimenters should be trained simultaneously to ensure they will receive identical information. Training typically involves attention to and suggested guidelines for anticipated procedural problems or participants' reactions. Ideally, experimenters will have consistent responses to difficult questions (for example, "How did you get my name?") or ways of responding to infrequent but difficult situations (such as strong negative emotional reactions of clients, including crying or pleas for additional help).

- Another strategy for reducing problems related to experimenter procedures is to *maintain close contact with all the personnel involved with the study.* Close monitoring of experimenters' experiences with their assigned tasks, especially when the research is just getting under way, often reveals unexpected problems that may require small changes in the protocol or procedures. In addition, actively encouraging experimenters to report problems, ask questions, and identify errors leads to useful feedback and opens lines of communication. It is particularly important that the investigator be present to closely monitor all stages of a study, so that, for example, all standardized instructions for completing instruments be conducted in the way the investigator intended. Whereas novice investigators may erroneously believe that they can sit back and relax once the experiment starts, veteran researchers spend a considerable amount of time vigilantly monitoring and troubleshooting to ascertain whether the study is proceeding as planned.

- Investigators have developed various strategies that *check experimenters' performance and combat experimental fatigue.* Most of these strategies are in essence manipulation checks (discussed in Chapter 11). For example, Kazdin (1980) reported on the use of confederate participants to check on the experimenter. The confederates were randomly assigned to the various experimental conditions and provided feedback to the investigator about the adequacy of the experimenter's performance. Sometimes merely informing experimenters that confederate participants will be used is enough incentive to maintain performance standards. Likewise, researchers can use audio recordings or direct observations of structured interviews or counseling sessions to evaluate experimenters' performance. For example, when Hogg and Deffenbacher (1988) compared cognitive and interpersonal-process group therapy in the treatment of depression, as a check on the adequacy of the experimental manipulation they trained undergraduates to identify components of cognitive or behavioral treatments. After the undergraduates listened to the therapy sessions, they were highly proficient (96%) in correctly identifying the type of treatment. Hogg and Deffenbacher concluded that because raters who did not know the details of the experiment were able to discriminate audiotapes of different types of treatment with accuracy and certainty, the therapists were reliably following treatment guidelines. Another strategy is to discuss the potential problem of experimenter fatigue with the experimenters and then enlist their help in finding solutions to this problem.
- As a general strategy, it is a good idea to *have researchers participate in a wide range of diversity training activities* to enhance their awareness, sensitivity, and skills pertaining to a wide range of diverse issues, such as racism, sexism, and homophobia (see Fassinger & Richie, 1997; Pedersen, 1988, 1994; Pedersen, Draguns, Lonner, & Trimble, in press; Ponterotto, Casas, Suzuki, & Alexander, 1995, 2001; Ponterotto & Grieger, in press; Ponterotto & Pedersen, 1993; Ridley, 1995; Ridley, Mendoza, & Kanitz, 1994; Sue, 2003).

PARTICIPANT BIAS

Returning again to our ideal world, the perfect participant is an honest, naive person who comes to an experiment without any preconceived notions, willingly accepts instructions, and is motivated to respond in as truthful and helpful a way as possible (Christensen, 1980). Such participants would not be afraid to be seen in a negative light and would be willing to disclose personal information concerning their innermost secrets. Likewise, within counseling, ideal clients would openly discuss their experiences in counseling, the problems they have been unable to solve on their own, the reasons they chose to enter counseling, their perceptions of their counselor, and the ways in which they have changed. Moreover, ideal participants would be aware of both their subjective experiences and the world around them, and thus they could reliably describe their internal and external worlds.

Unfortunately, we know that participants often come to psychological experiments with preconceived notions, sometimes even resenting their participation in a research study (Argyris, 1968; Gustav, 1962). For example, some research suggests that racial and ethnic minorities prefer counselors who are members of their cultural group (see Coleman, Wampold, & Casali, 1995). As Christensen (1980) observed, participants entering a psychological experiment are not passive organisms just waiting to respond to the independent variable; instead they bring with them a host of opinions, preferences, fears, motivations, abilities, and psychological defenses that may or may not affect how they respond in different experiments.

We discuss three major sources of participant bias—demand characteristics, participant characteristics, and participants' abilities to report their experiences—and again we offer some strategies for guarding against such confounding variables.

DEMAND CHARACTERISTICS

One major source of participant bias pertains to what is commonly referred to as demand characteristics, which are cues within an experiment that may influence participants to respond in a particular way apart from the independent variable. Demand characteristics may or may not be consistent with an experimenter's expectancies; they often include events other than the experimenter's expectancies. Examples of demand characteristics include instructions on a personal problems questionnaire that give the impression that most college students do not have personal problems, a receptionist's nonverbal behaviors that seem intended to make potential participants feel guilty if they do not complete a questionnaire, or an experimenter's apologetic nonverbal cues toward participants in the control group.

Demand characteristics are typically subtle influences or pressures, although sometimes they are not so subtle. For example, in one study of client preferences, clients coming to a counseling center were asked very leading questions, such as "What kind of counselor do you expect to see, expert or inexpert?" Not surprisingly, the results of this study revealed most clients preferred expert counselors, although it is unlikely that counselor expertness would have been consistently cited by clients if a more general question were used. Demand characteristics can occur at any point during an experiment, such as in recruiting participants, during interactions with any personnel involved with the experiment, during the completion of inventories or experimental tasks, and in debriefing.

Demand characteristics operating within a particular study are often difficult to identify. Even though investigators' intentions are to be objective and conduct a rigorous study, they may be unaware that the specific instructions on an inventory might influence some participants to withhold personal information.

Likewise, very minor comments in recruiting participants may mask the effects of the independent variable. For example, consider the story of a group of researchers interested in the effects of breaches of confidentiality on participants' perceptions of counselor trustworthiness. In the pilot study, the researchers were shocked to find that blatant breaches of confidentiality within a counseling analogue did not seem to affect how participants rated the counselor on trustworthiness. For example, even if the counselor began an interview by commenting on the previous participant, saying something like, "Did you see that person who just left? Boy, he has some serious problems!" the second participant still rated the counselor as quite trustworthy. Close examination of all of the experimental procedures revealed that when participants were initially contacted, they were asked if they would be willing to participate in a counseling study in which they would talk with a "highly competent professional counselor, a person who is well liked and has a very positive reputation with students on campus." Additional piloting of participants revealed that omitting this emphasis on prestige in the introduction resulted in more accurate perceptions of the counselor's behaviors. In sum, demand characteristics operating on participants are often subtle and unintentional.

PARTICIPANT CHARACTERISTICS

Not all participants respond in the same way to different experimental tasks and procedures. Some participants may respond more than others to subtle cues or pressures. A broad range of participant characteristics may affect how participants respond not only to demand characteristics, but also on a broader level to the experimental situation. We now briefly discuss five participant characteristics that may bias participants' responses: self-presentation style, motivation level, intellectual skills, psychological defenses, and worldview.

SELF-PRESENTATION STYLE   Christensen (1980) has suggested that a consistent theme among participant motives in psychological experiments is positive self-presentation, a desire to present themselves in a positive light. Some participants may begin to feel threatened if they believe their performance is inadequate or their responses are "wrong"; other participants may be reluctant to disclose negative information about themselves or others, especially if they feel that the investigator will be able to connect their responses to their name in some way (see Kelly & Achter, 1995; Kelly, Kahn, & Coulter, 1996; Kelly, McKillap, & Neimeyer, 1991). For example, a young researcher debriefing doctoral trainees in a supervision study was shocked when one of the participants acknowledged that he did not dare report his true perceptions because he "just was not sure" who would see his responses.

Likewise, participants may feel compelled to respond in socially desirable ways, such as reporting positive outcomes from counseling or liking their therapist. Social desirability is sometimes a difficult issue when investigating topics that require socially undesirable responses, such as premature termination of counseling. Former clients may feel reticent to report negative perceptions of the counselor, particularly if they believe that their comments will be disclosed to or cause trouble for the counselor.

Participants with a strong desire to present themselves in a positive manner may be more susceptible to being influenced by demand characteristics. Christensen (1980) has argued that such participants use available demand characteristics to identify the types of responses that make them appear most positively. In short, participants who want to present themselves well may try, either consciously or unconsciously, to be the "good participant" and respond in a way they believe is consistent with the experimenter's desires or wishes. Interested readers might examine Friedlander and Schwartz (1985) for a theory of self-presentation in counseling.

MOTIVATION LEVEL   The participant's motivation level can also be a source of bias. Sometimes participants in psychological experiments really do not want at some level to put forth much energy in the study. For a variety of reasons, participants might feel apprehensive about the experimental conditions, apathetic about the experimental tasks, angry about being in a control group, or simply tired. As a result, participants may fail to appear for a scheduled appointment, give halfhearted responses or, worse yet, give random responses.

Some clients in counseling research may be motivated to "help" their counselor. Thus, in studies that evaluate some aspect of the counselor, clients who feel very grateful or even indebted to the therapist may be motivated to give glowing responses to "help" their counselor.

INTELLECTUAL SKILLS   Sometimes bias is introduced into a study because participants do not have adequate intellectual skills, such as reading or writing ability. One investigator at a Midwestern college was surprised to learn from interviews that some of the participants had difficulty reading the assessment inventories; this was after she had collected data on three self-report inventories! Another investigator gave four self-report inventories, commonly used with college students, to rural Midwestern farmers and learned that such intellectual activities constituted a very demanding task for this group, who required considerably more time to complete the forms. Yet another investigator found that a group of inpatient alcoholics experienced a great deal of difficulty in completing a commonly used instrument on college campuses; after defining many words in the items, he learned that the average reading level for this group was below the sixth grade. In short, the intellectual skills of the participants can bias the results of a study and thus require some consideration.

PSYCHOLOGICAL DEFENSES   Sometimes bias is introduced into a study because of some participants' psychological defenses. For example, even though some men feel sexually aroused when viewing a violent rape film, it is difficult for most of them to admit such sexual arousal even to themselves, much less to others. Thus, some participants may feel threatened by their responses to certain material and may deny or repress their true feelings.

At other times some participants may feel defensive or paranoid about revealing their feelings or thoughts about sensitive topics (for example, sexual orientation, race relations, or feelings of inadequacy or embarrassment). Likewise, participants such as prison inmates may be suspicious of any experimenter and withhold or temper their responses because of perceived danger. In short, bias may be introduced into a study because participants perceive some real or imaginary threat, which consciously or unconsciously tempers their responses.

WORLDVIEW   Sometimes bias can be introduced into a study because of the worldview of the participants. Worldview pertains to a complex constellation of beliefs, values, and assumptions about people, relationships, nature, time, and activities in our world (Ibrahim & Kahn, 1987; Ibrahim & Owen, 1994); in essence, worldview represents the lens through which we view the world (Ivey, Ivey, & Simek-Morgan, 1997). As such, the participants' beliefs, values, and assumptions constitute a certain way of perceiving events, a productivity or bias (also see Ibrahim, Roysircar-Sodowsky, & Ohnishi, 2001). The participants' worldview may sometimes affect the results of a study. For example, there is some research that suggests that racial/ethnic minorities initially prefer counselors who are members of their cultural group (e.g., Coleman, Wampold, & Casali, 1995). Watkins and Terrell (1988) found that some African-American clients tend to rate white counselors as less proficient and credible.

PARTICIPANTS' ABILITY TO REPORT THEIR EXPERIENCES

A topic with a great deal of relevance for counselors is clients' ability to accurately report their internal experiences. (This discussion extends the previous discussion in Chapter 13 on self-report inventories.) Nisbett and Wilson (1977) examined a broad array of data to determine participants' ability to reliably report their cognitive processes. In general, their analyses suggested that participants provide more accurate reports when causal stimuli and plausible causes for responses are salient. In addition, participants more accurately report (1) historical facts, (2) the focus of their attention, (3) current sensations, and (4) knowledge of their plans, evaluations, and emotions. However, a considerable amount of data suggest that participants have greater difficulty describing their mental processes when the situation is ambiguous, such as when participants are unaware of the stimuli that trigger their cognitive responses.

An early experiment conducted by Maier (1931) nicely depicts participants' inability to connect causal elements in ambiguous situations. Maier used the "string problem," in which participants were given the goal of holding two cords (one in each hand) hanging some 10 feet apart from the ceiling of a room that also contained various objects. Some of the participants, after some trial and error, would tie an object onto one of the cords, swing it like a pendulum, walk over and grab the other cord with one hand, and catch the swinging cord with the other hand. Voilà, the solution! If participants were unsuccessful in finding a solution, Maier, who had been wandering around the room, would walk by the cords and swing one of them into motion. Some of these participants then would subsequently pick up some object, tie it to the end of the cord, swing the cord like a pendulum, and shortly thereafter solve the problem. But when Maier asked these participants how they had arrived at the solution, he got answers such as "It just dawned on me" or "I just realized the cord would swing if I fastened a weight to it." In short, most of Maier's participants could not accurately report the causal events involved in their cognitive and affective processing. More recent research in experimental information processing also suggests that participants have difficulty explaining the causal chain of events in their cognitive processes, particularly with the passage of time (Ericsson & Simon, 1984).

Even though Nisbett and Wilson's (1977) work has been the subject of some debate, their observations should be carefully considered when counseling researchers attempt to examine clients' cognitive processes, especially within the often-ambiguous situation we call counseling. For example, why clients changed or what influenced them to change in the course of counseling may be a very difficult question for them to answer accurately and reliably. Likewise, as one researcher learned, asking clients how they decided to seek help at a counseling center resulted in a very broad range of responses—some of them incomprehensible! In short, counseling researchers in particular must carefully consider the type of information that can be accurately and reliably obtained about clients' mental processes, particularly retrospectively. Researchers may well ask clients to tell them more than the clients can know, and thus clients may provide misleading self-reports.

STRATEGIES FOR REDUCING PARTICIPANT BIAS

Investigators can use several strategies to reduce participant bias:

- Perhaps the most commonly used strategy to reduce participant bias due to the "good participant" role is to *keep participants blind or naive to the real purpose of the study,* which makes it more difficult for participants to consciously or unconsciously conform in ways similar to the predicted hypotheses. Participants are kept blind by withholding information not only about the hypotheses of the study, but sometimes even about the purpose of the study as well. Thus, participants involved in a study might be asked in some unspecified manner to complete an inventory about their perceptions of a college career center. When both participants and the experimenter are kept blind, as discussed in the previous section, the study is called *double blind*. Because the double-blind procedure tends to reduce both experimenter and participant bias, it is often recommended in counseling research.
- To reduce bias due to participants' desire to present themselves in a positive light, a general strategy is to *reduce the threat associated with the experiment.* Thus, instructions on a questionnaire may explicitly state that "there are

no right or wrong answers" and that "this inventory is not a test." The actual title of an inventory might also be altered if it is found to arouse anxiety or introduce demand characteristics. In addition, some researchers attempt to reduce threat by explicitly normalizing typical participant fears. For example, in a study of the coping process, participants might be told that it is normal to have unresolved personal problems, and that in fact "everyone has them."

- Several procedures can be used to *increase participants' honesty and reduce participants' fears about confidentiality.* First and foremost, researchers often make honest and direct statements about their desire or need to obtain honest responses to increase the profession's understanding of a phenomenon. In addition, researchers typically communicate to participants that their responses will be strictly confidential, and then they explain the mechanisms for safeguarding confidentiality (for example, coding). Moreover, in research using groups of participants, it is often helpful for participants to know that the researcher is interested in how whole groups of participants respond to the items, rather than specific individuals. Sometimes participants are asked to omit their name from their questionnaires, thereby maintaining anonymity. To ensure confidentiality when a researcher needs to collect data on several occasions and then compare a given participant's responses over time, participants can be asked to supply a code name in lieu of their actual name, or to generate an alias or develop a code based on some combination of numbers related to their birth dates, age, social security number, or the like (see Kandel, 1973).

- Often researchers will *make appeals to participants to increase their motivation level.* For example, participants can be briefly told the importance of the research and its possible outcomes (for example, honest responses to the questionnaires will clarify changes or growth within supervision, or learning about one's experience as an Asian American will provide information about potential ethnic-related stressors). In exchange, researchers sometimes promise to mail participants the results of the study, particularly if the study is of a survey nature.

- Sometimes researchers concerned about demand characteristics and participant bias *conduct a postexperimental inquiry.* As per our discussion in Chapter 14, after the experiment the experimenter assesses potential participant bias by asking participants questions about their understanding of the purpose of the experiment, about their beliefs concerning how the experimenter wanted them to respond, and about any problems they encountered. Such a postexperimental inquiry might consist of a brief questionnaire (with perhaps follow-up inquiries of those participants who identified the true purpose of a study or those who felt pressured in some way) or be conducted via direct interviewing. Because direct interviewing can introduce demand characteristics in and of itself, it may best be done by someone who has not previously interacted with the participants. Even though there is considerable value in postexperimental inquiries, they have their limits: If participants have been biased by some demand characteristic but are totally unaware of any such influence, postexperimental inquiry will not reveal such participant bias.

- In addition to withholding information about the purpose of a study, a researcher can *reduce participant bias through disguise or deception*. The purpose of a study can be disguised by giving participants information that leads them to believe that a particular study is investigating some other research topic. Such strategies, however, carry important ethical considerations (see Chapter 6). For example, participants about to take part in an attitude-change study might be told that they are being asked to evaluate whether the university should institute final oral exams for all undergraduates. Likewise, a study involving client perceptions of counselors might be framed in terms of evaluating the adequacy of the counseling center's service delivery. In short, another strategy to reduce participant bias is to provide information that disguises a study's true purpose.

- In counseling research that uses undergraduate students who participate to fulfill a class requirement, lack of student motivation or apathy can be a serious source of bias. One strategy to counter this bias is to *perform "spot checks" on participants' performance*. For example, a question can be inserted in the middle of a questionnaire asking participants to "Leave this item blank" or "Mark 'strongly agree'"; participants who do not follow such simple instructions are eliminated from the study.

- With regard to intellectual skills, researchers can and should *evaluate the reading level of all instruments* used in a study and match them to the sample. Typically, such information about the sample can be obtained from personnel in the corresponding agencies or from colleagues familiar with the participants of interest.

- Researchers in counseling must *be attentive to participants' ability to report their cognitive and affective processes*. One strategy is to develop questionnaires based on cognitive processes that are most readily accessible to participants. Another is providing participants additional information to facilitate accurate reporting of the more ambiguous cognitive and affective processes, such as by enabling video or audio replay or by using Interpersonal Process Recall (Kagan, 1975).

SUMMARY AND CONCLUSIONS

This chapter identified potential sources of bias in participants, experimenters, and investigators that might disguise or cloud the relationships between the experimental variables of interest; such biases are major threats to Kerlinger's MAXMINCON principle. The more uncontrolled are the conditions of an experiment, the more various biases are likely to create more error variance or extraneous variables. More error variance makes it more difficult to identify systematic variance due to the independent variables in question; the introduction of extraneous variables makes it difficult to isolate the variables responsible for change. Thus, participant, experimenter, and investigator biases introduce extraneous variables that may distort or disguise the relationships among the experimental variables.

This chapter discussed investigator and experimenter biases that may well affect the results of a study. We discussed three major types of experimenter bias: experimenter attributes, investigator and experimenter expectancies, and experimental procedures. We also discussed three major sources of participant bias—demand characteristics, participant characteristics, and participants' abilities to report their experiences—and described several strategies for controlling or minimizing such biases.

Participant, investigator, and experimenter biases represent serious problems for the counseling researcher. These sources of bias can quickly reduce the results of many long hours spent developing and conducting a study into a pile of meaningless information. The veteran researcher remains vigilant of various sources of bias and constantly monitors the study to detect any biases that might have crept in. Bias is a particularly important issue for counseling researchers because much of our research is conducted in applied settings, where fewer experimental controls are available and thus more sources of bias are potentially operative.

Because minimizing and eliminating bias is a matter of degree, and because the researcher is often uncertain whether various sources of bias are operative, it is useful to qualify the results of one's research (typically done in the discussion section) concerning the possible sources of bias that might have been operative. An increasingly commonplace research strategy is for investigators to statistically test for the existence of various biases and confounds in a series of preliminary analyses. Hogg and Deffenbacher (1988) provide a good example of using such preliminary analyses. Such statistical procedures are recommended, as are frank discussions of other possible sources of bias that were untested.

STIMULUS QUESTIONS

REFLECTIONS ON BIAS

It is often very difficult to clearly identify the myriad of biases that threaten the validity of a study. The purpose of this exercise is to reflect on a wide range of biases with the goal of becoming more aware and sensitive to biases that threaten the validity of a study.

1. Briefly discuss how your values and beliefs could result in cultural biases.
2. Are there particular topics in which your values and beliefs could result in cultural biases?
3. In considering your research interests, which of your personal attributes could cause differential responses in participants?
4. List four ways you could most significantly reduce biases related to the experimental procedures in the type of research topics you are considering.
5. Identify potential demand characteristics in the research topics you are considering.
6. Discuss how the participants' worldviews might create some confounding biases in the type of research topics you are considering.
7. In what ways could participants' need for self-presentation, or saving face, affect the results of your research?
8. Discuss the most important things you have learned about investigator, experimenter, and participant bias in scholarly research.

Analogue Research

This chapter focuses on analogue research in counseling, which is defined as research that is conducted under conditions that resemble or approximate the therapeutic situation. In an effort to follow Kerlinger's MAXMINCON principle, some investigators have sought to reduce bias and extraneous variables by creating tightly controlled conditions that approximate the counseling context. Not surprisingly, analogue research has historically been at the heart of the debate on naturalistic versus experimental approaches to research. Bordin aptly depicted the debate in 1965:

> A . . . decision in research strategy is whether to choose the naturalistic or experimental path. This is a familiar controversy with established clichés, e.g., "Only when we bring phenomena under precise control as in the laboratory can true knowledge be gained," versus "Of what use is precision when it is obtained by reduction to the trivial?" A frozen posture is not helpful to psychology or any other scientific discipline. (p. 493)

The first section of this chapter provides a brief historical overview of the use of analogue methodology in counseling; the second section provides examples of recent analogue studies. The third and fourth sections discuss the advantages and disadvantages of this particular methodology. The fifth section proposes that the external validity of analogue research be evaluated by examining variables that depict real-life counseling, most notably those related to the counselor, the client, and the counseling process. The sixth section maintains that the ultimate utility of analogue methodology must be evaluated within the context of current knowledge bases and existing research methodologies used in a particular topic area. The use of analogue methodology in social influence research in counseling is analyzed to demonstrate this point.

HISTORICAL OVERVIEW

Real-life counseling is a tremendously complex process. Clients differ, therapists differ, and counseling is such a highly interactive, emotionally charged, and complex communication process that it is difficult to describe, much less investigate. Over 30 years ago such complexity led Heller (1971) to conclude that the counseling interview, "while an excellent source of research hypotheses, is a poor context for isolating factors responsible for behavior change. The varied complexity of the therapeutic interaction and the inability to specify and control therapeutic operations make it difficult to obtain reliable information concerning exact agents of change" (p. 127). Heller, a strong believer in the scientific method and its use of experimental control, contended that part of the solution to investigating and understanding the complexity within counseling was to exercise the experimental control offered in what he called laboratory research: "The purpose of clinical laboratory research is to determine what factors produce change, under what conditions they operate best, and how they should be combined to produce an effective therapeutic package" (Heller, p. 127).

Basically, a counseling analogue is an experimental simulation of some aspect of the counseling process involving manipulation of some aspects of the counselor, the client, and/or the counseling process. In the past, analogues have been referred to as "miniature therapy" (Goldstein, Heller, & Sechrest, 1966) or as a "simplification strategy" (Bordin, 1965).

Keet (1948) has been credited with one of the first uses of the analogue methodology in psychotherapy research (see, for example, Bordin, 1965; Heller, 1971; Kushner, 1978). Keet used volunteer participants and examined the efficacy of expressive (reflective) versus interpretative therapeutic statements in overcoming previously identified memory blocks on word association tasks. Interpretative statements were found to be more effective. It is interesting to note that even though subsequent research did not replicate Keet's findings (Grummon & Butler, 1953; Merrill, 1952), Bordin observed that "so great is the attractiveness of control and simplification as a research strategy that this failure [to replicate] only spurred further efforts in this direction" (p. 494). In general, however, the use of analogue research has been a relatively recent development within counseling research, a phenomenon Heller attributed to the fact that analogues are rather foreign to psychotherapy because knowledge in the clinical fields has normally been accumulated in the more naturalistic tradition (as, for example, in the case studies of Freud). Munley (1974) attributed the slow emergence of the analogue to the reluctance of counselors to accept a contrived and highly controlled methodology that might well be too artificial and unrealistic.

Bordin (1965) wrote one of the earliest theoretical critiques of "simplification" (analogue methodology) in counseling research. He appears to have been keenly aware of the strengths and limitations of this methodology. Although the experimental control afforded by the analogue was quickly recognized, some researchers expressed concern about the generalizability or external validity of the results (see, for example, Lewin, 1951; Rappaport, 1960). Bordin acknowledged that the criticisms of "simplification" research related primarily to its oversimplification of the phenomenon of interest; to counteract such problems, he proposed three rules for achieving "acceptable simplifications":

1. Start from and keep in central focus the natural phenomenon that aroused the researcher's curiosity.
2. The degree to which a researcher can safely depart from the relevant naturalistic setting is proportional to the amount already known about the phenomenon in question.
3. If not based on prior knowledge, simplification should be accompanied by empirical investigations of the naturalistic phenomenon it simulates.

Researchers initially used analogue methodology in two general lines of research (Heller, 1971). One line of research involved an analysis of therapies to "find their most potent ingredients and the conditions under which each is optimized" (Heller, pp. 148–149); this approach included analogue studies of systematic desensitization, Rogerian facilitative conditions, and free association.

The second major approach examined the communication process, particularly in terms of the social influence process. This line of research was sparked by the applications of social psychology to counseling, particularly the work of Goldstein, Heller, and Sechrest (1966) and Strong (1968). The late 1960s and early 1970s saw a flurry of analogue studies, primarily examining the effects of counselors' behavior on client perceptions of the counselors' expertness, attractiveness, and trustworthiness. Social influence research "continued unabated" (Borgen, 1984) until the mid-1980s and has been the focus of most of the analogue research in counseling.

There are several different types of analogue studies. In reviewing the counseling analogue research methods used in the *Journal of Counseling Psychology*, Munley (1974) categorized the analogue studies into five categories: (1) audiovisual counseling studies, with counselor behavior as the dependent variable; (2) audiovisual counseling studies, with client behavior as the dependent variable; (3) quasi-counseling interview studies, with client behavior as the dependent variable; (4) quasi-counseling interview studies, with counselor behavior as the dependent variable; and (5) experimental tasks not directly resembling a counseling interview. To date, the types of analogues that investigators have used are quite broad, ranging from highly artificial recorded simulations to very realistic live simulations involving multiple sessions.

Despite Bordin's (1965) earlier proposal for "acceptable simplifications," debate over the utility of analogue methodology has persisted. A number of theoretical critiques have addressed the utility of the analogue methodology (see, for example, Gelso, 1979; Heller, 1971; Kazdin, 1978, 1980, 2003; Strong, 1971).

At the center of the controversy is the questionable generalizability of analogue findings. Goldman (1978) summed up the criticisms best by claiming that the "venerated laboratory experiment has been highly overrated as a way to gain understanding of human behavior as it exists in real life. . . . [T]he laboratory has become so 'pure' that it has little or nothing to say about how people function in real life" (p. 8).

Before entering into this debate ourselves, we first provide some recent examples of analogue studies, and then discuss in greater detail the advantages and disadvantages of analogue methodology.

EXAMPLES OF RECENT ANALOGUE STUDIES

We will describe three analogue studies to provide more details about how this methodology has been used more recently by investigators. The first study, by Hayes and Erkis (2000), utilized eight vignettes to present different client scenarios to psychologists in the American Psychological Association (APA). The second study, by Mohr, Israel, and Sedlacek (2001), used a fictitious intake report to obtain clinical responses from counselors in training. The third study, by Kim and Atkinson (2003), employed counselor trainees to deliver two types of counselor cultural value expressions to university students with career concerns who volunteered to participate in the study.

Hayes and Erkis (2000) studied the components of therapists' reactions as the dependent variable in a case description of a client with HIV infection. Specifically, the independent variables were therapist homophobia, client sexual orientation, and the source of client HIV infection; the dependent variables were counselor reactions to clients, namely empathy; attributions of client responsibility for their HIV infection and solving problems; willingness to work with the client; and an assessment of client functioning. In order to manipulate client sexual orientation and source of client HIV infection, eight vignettes (two sexual orientations × four sources of HIV infection) were developed. The vignettes described a male client who was gay or heterosexual, and whose HIV infection source was sexual contact, a blood transfusion, intravenous drug use, or unspecified. They described their vignette as follows:

> The independent variables were manipulated through the use of clinical vignettes adapted from the *Diagnostic and Statistical Manual of Mental Disorders* (4th ed.: DSM-IV) Case Book (Spitzer, Gibbon, Skodol, Williams, & Frist, 1994). Each vignette was approximately 400 words long and described a 35 year-old client, Marvin, who recently discovered that he was HIV positive and was seeking psychological services because of anxiety stemming from recurrent thoughts about dying, becoming disfigured, and losing his independence. He hoped that therapy would "help reduce stress" and "help my immune system fight off AIDS." In the vignettes, the client alluded to feeling fulfilled in his long standing relationship with his romantic partner (Dave or Mary) and either did not indicate how he became HIV infected or mentioned one of three sources: sex, intravenous drug use, or a blood transfusion. (Hayes & Erkis, 2000, p.73)

Hayes and Erkis (2000) gathered the data from 425 psychologists who were licensed, practicing therapists and members of the APA. Participants received a packet in which they were randomly assigned to one of the eight vignettes, and scales measuring homophobia and the dependent variables. They found that therapist homophobia and the source of HIV infection predicted therapist attributions of client responsibility for problem cause. In addition, they found that when therapists were more homophobic, when the client was gay, and when the client's source of HIV infection was other than drugs, the therapists responded with less empathy, attributed less responsibility to the client for solving his problems, assessed the client's functioning to be worse, and were less willing to work with the client.

Mohr et al. (2001) investigated the influence of counselors' attitudes toward bisexuality on counselors' clinical responses to a fictitious intake report. Specifically, the independent variable was the counselor's attitude toward bisexuality and the dependent variables were reactions to the client, anticipated reactions to the bisexual client, and psychosocial functioning.

Unlike Hayes and Erkis's (2000) study, in which two independent variables were manipulated using eight vignettes, Mohr and his colleagues used one fictitious intake report about a bisexual woman, which was used as a stimulus for each counselor's assessment and response to the client. They summarized the vignette as follows:

> . . . a two-paragraph fictional scenario summarizing a clinical intake session with a client named Alice, who was a 20-year-old White bisexual woman. . . . In the scenario, which was set in a university counseling center, the presenting problems included (a) difficulty making a career choice, (b) grief over the end of a 2-year romantic relationship with a woman, (c) a boyfriend who was having difficulty accepting the client's bisexuality. Thus, the predominant clinical issues involved issues with career indecision, negotiating emotional boundaries with parents, and romantic relationships. (Mohr et al., 2001, p. 213)

The data were gathered from 97 counselor trainees in master and doctoral programs. The authors found that attitudes regarding bisexuality were related to counselors' clinical judgments and reactions. Counselors who had a negative attitude toward bisexuality assessed the function of clients to be low, anticipated biased and judgmental responses to the client, and were more likely to have negative reactions to the client.

Kim and Atkinson (2002) investigated the effect of client adherence to Asian cultural values, counselor expression of cultural values, and counselor ethnicity on the career counseling process among Asian-American college students. They used a quasi-counseling interview, and the sessions were conducted by trained counselors with students who were recruited for this study but had real career issues. A $2 \times 2 \times 2$ factorial design was used with two levels of client adherence to Asian cultural values (low and high), two levels of counselor expressions of cultural values (Asian cultural values and U.S. cultural values), and two levels of counselor ethnicity (Asian American and European American). Client-perceived counselor effectiveness, counselor empathetic understanding, physical attractiveness, and session evaluation were measured as dependent variables. Five Asian-American and seven European-American counselors were trained to express Asian and U.S. values. Before the counseling session, students were asked to complete the Asian Value Scale and assessed the level of their adherence to Asian cultural values (low and high) using the median score in previous research.

> The counselor began the session by providing a brief description of the trait factor theory of career counseling (e.g. "I believe that a career choice is best made when you have a clear understanding about your ability and limitations, as well as the requirements for success in various careers. So, how about if we begin by you telling me a little bit about yourself?"). The counselor then helped the client explore and gain a better understanding of the requirements and conditions for success, advantages and disadvantages about compensation, and future opportunities in the types of careers in which the client was interested. At various points during this process, the counselor raised career-related contextual issues, such as family expectations and salary needs, in which either Asian or U.S. values were expressed to the client. For example, in terms of family expectations, counselors assigned to the Asian values condition were trained to say the following (the Asian cultural value reflected in each sentence is identified in brackets): "I believe that your family should help you decide what career you will pursue, particularly when you are just beginning your adulthood [Collectivism]. I also believe that it is important for you to consider your parents' needs when deciding on the type of career to enter [Filial Piety]. So what do you think will make your parents happy [Filial Piety]?" In contrast, counselors assigned to the U.S. values condition were trained to say the following (the U.S. cultural value reflected in each sentence is identified in brackets): "I believe that you should decide what you will pursue, particularly when you are just beginning your adulthood [Individualism]. I also believe that it is important for you to consider your needs when deciding on the type of career to enter [Duty to Satisfy Personal Needs]. So what do you think will make you happy [Duty to Satisfy Personal Needs]?" At the end of the session, the counselor gave the client a referral to the university career services center and encouraged the student to obtain further career counseling. (Kim & Atkinson, 2002, p. 7)

Asian-American clients evaluated the session with the European-American counselor to be more positive and arousing. However, Asian-American clients who had high adherence to Asian culture evaluated the Asian-American counselor as being more credible and empathetic, whereas Asian-American clients who had low adherence to Asian culture evaluated the European-American counselor as more empathetic.

ADVANTAGES OF ANALOGUE RESEARCH

The hallmark of analogue research is control of the experimental situation, primarily by eliminating extraneous variables, controlling confounding variables, and manipulating specified levels of an independent variable. In a counseling situation, many variables pertain to the client and counselor (for example, personality variables, coping skills, manner of processing information, expectations, and demographic variables), to the counseling process (for example, counselor interventions and client reactions and disclosures), and to the particular situation (for example, room decor and arrangement, cost of therapy, and reasons for seeking help). In analogue designs, variables extraneous to the particular research problem can be eliminated or controlled. For example, participants easily can be randomly assigned to treatment conditions, thereby reducing confounds from participant variability. Participants also can be selected based on a particular variable (such as locus of control or level of depression), which can be either held constant across treatment conditions or varied to create levels of an independent variable. Therapists' theoretical orientation and interview behaviors can be controlled or even standardized across conditions. In short, analogue research allows for a great deal of situational control by enabling the researcher to manipulate one or more independent variables, to eliminate or hold extraneous variables constant, and to use random assignment.

Along with providing situational control, analogue methodology has the advantage of enabling the experimenter to achieve a high degree of specificity in the operational definitions of a variable. For example, level of counselor self-disclosure could be manipulated to enable examination of, say, three distinct levels of self-disclosure (no self-disclosure, 5 self-disclosures per session, 10 self-disclosures per session). In this sense, analogue methodology often offers greater precision—not only in terms of the variables under examination, but also in terms of experimental procedures.

Such increased specificity is a major advantage in isolating specific events or processes in the complex activity that is counseling. Thus, within a laboratory analogue it is possible to isolate and examine the effects of rather small events, including self-involving counselor disclosures, specific counselor introductions, the counselor's professional titles, and the client's perceptions of the counselor (see Andersen & Anderson, 1985; Strong & Dixon, 1971).

Another advantage of analogue methodology is often the reduction of practical and ethical obstacles in experimentally examining some aspect of the counseling process. Many times, real-world constraints such as financial limits and unavailability of participants can be substantially reduced by using client surrogates in an analogue design (see, for example, Dixon & Claiborn, 1981). Given that real-life counseling involves clients with real-life problems, stresses, and anxieties, experimental procedures such as randomly assigning clients to placebo groups or to waiting-list control groups can cause problems. Or certain experimental manipulations, such as varying the type of counselor feedback or type of counselor self-disclosure, may pose serious ethical dilemmas when clients with real problems are involved. Creating a situation analogous to counseling or using transcripts, audiotapes, or videotapes of counseling interactions sidesteps ethical problems with manipulations, especially with clients under some kind of duress.

DISADVANTAGES OF ANALOGUE RESEARCH

The major concern about or disadvantage of analogue research pertains to the generalizability of the research findings, or external validity. External validity is of special importance to members of the counseling profession because the primary focus of our work is on real-life, applied counseling with actual clients.

Sometimes the strengths of analogue methodology—experimental control and internal validity—result in rather artificial circumstances. The investigation may be very high in experimental precision but examine events under such artificial and contrived conditions that they no longer resemble actual counseling situations. It can even become unclear whether the research is in fact investigating the counseling process, or instead variables that are so abstract and removed from actual practice that they are irrelevant to real-life counseling. Thus, the most serious concern pertains to whether the results of a particular study can be generalized to actual counseling practice. The power of the experimental controls may result in the loss of external validity, or as Bordin (1965) stated, "oversimplification."

The limitations of analogue methodology often lead to discussions about the relative importance of internal versus external validity. The inexperienced student wants to know which is more important, or which should be the focus of initial research in an area. Although there are reasons to emphasize either internal validity or external validity in undeveloped research areas (see, for example, Gelso, 1979; Kerlinger, 1986), we contend that both internal and external validity are needed in all research areas, and that the knowledge accumulated on any one topic should result from research that balances internal and external validity. Given that knowledge on any topic will accrue over time, the issue of which type of validity to examine first is often less important than the larger issue of overall balance.

VARIABLES TO CONSIDER IN EVALUATING THE GENERALIZABILITY OF ANALOGUE STUDIES

The basic question concerning analogue research is: To what extent does a particular laboratory experiment resemble actual counseling circumstances? One way to evaluate the external validity of analogue methodology is to consider some of the variables that describe the situation of interest—namely, real-life counseling. Several writers have attempted to provide some criteria for evaluating the relevance of analogue methodologies to the practice of counseling (for example, Kazdin, 1980; Strong & Matross, 1973). We propose that the external validity of analogue research can be evaluated in part by examining the resemblance of the analogue variables to those in real-life counseling. Any given study might vary on these variables and resemble the actual counseling situation to various degrees.

Table 17.1 depicts several variables pertaining to the client, the counselor, and the counseling process; each of these variables can be evaluated as having either relatively high, moderate, or low degrees of resemblance to real-life counseling. Rarely are all of the variables relevant for a given study. If, for example, a study focuses primarily on counselor behavior, then evaluating counselor variables would likely be more important to consider than, say, client variables. For

TABLE 17.1 | EVALUATING THE GENERALIZABILITY OF ANALOGUE METHODOLOGIES TO REAL-LIFE COUNSELING

Variables	Relatively High Degree of Resemblance	Moderate Degree of Resemblance	Relatively Low Degree of Resemblance
Client			
Expectations of change	Client expects treatment and change	Person expects experimental treatment	Participant expects course credit or to learn about psychology
Motivation and distress level	Client is distressed enough to seek help at a treatment center	Person is distressed enough to seek relevant academic experiences and psychological experiments	Participant is not distressed and does not seek help; participant has ulterior motivation (such as course credit) other than seeking psychological help and change
Selection of treatment	Client often chooses therapists or type of treatment	Person selects relevant psychological experiments providing treatment	Participant is assigned to treatments and therapists/interviewers
Presenting problem	Real-life problem typically seen in counseling	Hypothetical problems	None, or some experimental task(s)
Knowledge of problem	Relevant and current concern; high level of information processing and knowledge	Relevant but not pressing concern; moderate level of information processing and knowledge	Irrelevant or new issue; low level of information processing and knowledge
Counselor			
Counselor expectations	Client change	Moderate expectation of client change	Successful role play or interview
Role credibility	High status; appearance is role congruent	Moderate level of status	Absence of status cues; role incongruent
Knowledge bases	Broad range of knowledge about assessments, personality and counseling theories, and the counseling process	Moderate levels of knowledge about assessments, personality and counseling theories, and the counseling process	Low level of knowledge about assessments, personality and counseling theories, and the counseling process
Counseling skill	High levels of procedural skills within the counseling process	Moderate levels of procedural skills within the counseling process	Low levels of procedural skills within the counseling process
Motivation level	Highly motivated to provide therapeutic relationship and facilitate change	Moderately motivated to provide therapy; possibly some motivation for experimental change	Not motivated to provide therapy; primary goal is to conduct an interview
Experience level	10 years +	3rd-year doctoral student	1st-year M.A. student

(Continued)

TABLE 17.1 | EVALUATING THE GENERALIZABILITY OF ANALOGUE METHODOLOGIES TO REAL-LIFE COUNSELING (*Continued*)

Variables	Relatively High Degree of Resemblance	Moderate Degree of Resemblance	Relatively Low Degree of Resemblance
Counseling process and setting			
Assessment	Client is carefully diagnosed and goals established	Person may be assessed to determine congruence with treatment goals	Participant is not assessed; goals for specific individual lacking
Interventions	Specifically targeted to client's presenting problems	Relevant to person's problem	Not relevant to participant's concerns or problems
Duration	Several normal-length therapy sessions over time	A few normal-length sessions	A single brief (10 minutes or so) session
Interpersonal interchange	Counselor and client interact and exchange information	Counselor and client/participant interact on restricted topic or in some defined manner	Participant views counseling scenario but does not interact with a counselor
Client reactions	Client processes the counseling experience and reacts in some way to the relevant information	Person reacts to restricted topic or semirelevant topic	Participant views counseling scenario and responds hypothetically
Client change or outcome	Client changes or is different in some way because of the counseling interchange	Person may change in some way, providing the treatment is successful	Participant does not change in any way because the counseling scenario was not personally relevant
Environment	Professional treatment center	Facility that may not offer regular treatment services	Laboratory setting or classroom

research purposes, it may be useful to increase the specificity of these evaluations by developing Likert-type items to assess each variable. Here we use three rather general categories (low, moderate, and high) for each variable primarily to illustrate varying degrees of resemblance on each dimension. Moreover, variables listed in the table were developed through rational means; empirical research may well identify new variables or rule out some of the variables in this table.

CLIENT VARIABLES

A number of variables pertaining to clients or participants directly relate to the generalizability of research findings to actual counseling practice. We now discuss several client variables that illustrate important aspects of clients seeking counseling and then relate these variables to evaluating the generalizability of a particular study.

In most actual counseling situations, clients experience personal problems that they have been unable to resolve (Fretz, 1982). These personal problems typically cause anxiety and distress of some sort, as people find themselves "failing" where they want to "succeed" in some way. As people cope with their "current concerns" (Klinger, 1971), they typically engage in a wide range of cognitive, affective, and behavioral trial-and-error processes (Heppner & Krauskopf, 1987). Because these clients typically have thought about their problem and tried a number of possible solutions, they have compiled some kind of knowledge base (whether accurate or inaccurate) pertaining to this problem. After unsuccessful problem solving and the accompanying distress, a person might seek a wide variety of resources for assistance (see Wills, 1987, for a review of client help-seeking) and may even end up at a counseling center or some kind of treatment facility. Most important, people seeking psychological help have expectations about being treated. They often choose a certain therapist based on a recommendation or reputation, and they are motivated to change in some way. In short, typically clients seeking psychological help enter therapy (1) with expectations about change; (2) with expectations about the therapist and treatment; (3) under distress, and thus in a motivated state; (4) with the intention of discussing specific problematic situations; and (5) with a range of information or knowledge about their particular problems. Although there may well be other variables that depict other aspects of clients seeking help, we recommend that researchers evaluating the relevance of analogue methodology begin by considering client variables.

Table 17.1 lists these five client variables and what might constitute relatively high, moderate, and low degrees of resemblance of each to real-life counseling. A relatively high degree of resemblance for client expectations might, for example, entail a client expecting treatment and change, as opposed to a participant simply expecting course credit (low degree of resemblance). Also related to client expectations is the way in which treatment is selected. Clients often choose a type of treatment or therapist based on their presenting problem or a counselor's reputation (high resemblance), rather than being assigned to particular treatments and therapists/interviewers (low resemblance). Distress and motivation levels may also be polarized; a client is distressed enough to seek help at a treatment center (high resemblance), whereas a participant is part of a convenient or captive participant pool and merely seeks course credit (low resemblance) rather than seeking psychological help and change. Perhaps most important, actual clients have both "current concerns" or real problems and a high level of information processing and knowledge about that problem (high resemblance); conversely, participants assigned to a potentially irrelevant task have relatively low knowledge levels about the task and thus represent low resemblance to real-life counseling.

The main point is that several client variables might be considered in evaluating the generalizability of particular analogue methodologies within counseling. Strong and Matross (1973) facetiously referred to typical participants in social influence investigations as "client surrogates." This rather good phrase underscores participant substitution and its many implications, all of which commonly occur in most analogue studies. If an experimenter designs a study in which the participants do not closely resemble actual clients, then the generalizability of the findings to actual clients comes under question.

COUNSELOR VARIABLES

A number of variables pertaining to counselors or interviewers also directly relate to the generalizability of analogue research findings to actual counseling practice. In the ideal therapeutic counseling relationship, the counselor is experienced and has a broad range of knowledge about assessments, personality and counseling theories, and the counseling process in general. In addition, the therapist has high levels of procedural skill—the interpersonal and counseling skills required to in fact be therapeutic with a client. The therapist also is highly motivated to provide a therapeutic relationship, as reflected in establishing Rogerian conditions such as empathy and unconditional positive regard, or perhaps through other ways of establishing a strong working alliance. Thus, the therapist approaches counseling with the expectation that the therapy will be successful, and that the client will change in some desired way(s). Finally, the therapist appears to be a credible professional, an expert and trustworthy person who can provide therapeutic assistance.

Table 17.1 suggests relatively high, moderate, and low degrees of resemblance of six counselor variables to actual counselors. For example, high degrees of resemblance characterize therapists possessing a broad range of relevant knowledge about counseling and high levels of procedural skill. Such counselors have a considerable amount of counseling experience. By contrast, relatively low resemblance to actual therapists characterizes interviewers or inexperienced counselors who lack both essential knowledge about counseling and the skills to actually do counseling. The other variables can also be polarized, so that people resemble actual therapists when they (1) are highly motivated to provide a therapeutic relationship and facilitate change, (2) expect counseling to be successful and the client to change, and (3) appear credible and congruent within a therapeutic role. Conversely, a person having a relatively low resemblance to actual therapists may be characterized as not intending to provide a therapeutic and caring relationship, but rather being motivated solely to conduct an interview. Moreover, often the interviewer reflects an absence of status and credibility cues.

In some previous research in counseling, the therapist variables under examination did not closely resemble the role or behaviors of a typical therapist; several examples are apparent within what is referred to as the social or interpersonal influence area in counseling (see Corrigan, Dell, Lewis, & Schmidt, 1980; Heppner & Claiborn, 1989; Heppner & Dixon, 1981). In the past, researchers have manipulated a broad range of cues associated with perceived counselor expertness, attractiveness, and trustworthiness. One goal of much of this research has been to identify behaviors and cues that enhance the counselor's credibility and subsequent ability to affect the client. A common research strategy has been to examine extreme levels of an independent variable to ascertain whether that particular variable has an effect on client perceptions of the counselor, but all too often the therapist variables have not resembled the role of a typical therapist closely enough.

For example, in attempting to lower the perceived expertness of an interviewer, participants have been told, "We had originally scheduled Dr. _____ to talk with you, but unfortunately he notified us that he wouldn't be able to make it today. In his place we have Mr. _____, a student who unfortunately has had no interviewing experience and has been given only a brief explanation of the purpose of this study. We think he should work out all right, though. Now, if you would step this way . . ." (Strong & Schmidt, 1970, p. 82).

Likewise, in some cases the procedural skills of interviewers have been manipulated to produce interviewer behaviors that do not closely resemble those of actual therapists. For example, a counselor portraying an unattractive role "ignored the interviewee when he entered the office, did not smile at him, did not look beyond a few cold glances, leaned away from him, and portrayed disinterest, coldness, and boredom" (Schmidt & Strong, 1971, p. 349). Gelso (1979) referred to such procedures as "experimental deck stacking" and raised questions about the utility of research on such atypical therapist behaviors. In short, although a considerable amount of information was obtained about events contributing to clients' perceptions of counselor credibility, the generalizability of some of this knowledge to actual counseling practice is questionable because of the relatively low resemblance of the events to actual therapist behaviors.

Note that the focus here is on the extent to which a person in a therapeutic role resembles an experienced therapist in terms of knowledge, skill, and expectations. Trainees—perhaps beginning-level practicum students counseling their first actual client—may at best only poorly resemble an actual therapist, and thus, it is important not to confuse a trainee with a therapist just because they both counsel an actual client seeking psychological help at a treatment center. In sum, to evaluate the generalizability of analogue research to actual counseling practice, it is important to consider several variables pertaining to therapists, notably their knowledge bases, skills, expectations, and role credibility.

COUNSELING PROCESS AND SETTING

We must also consider a set of variables related to the counseling process when evaluating the external validity of analogue research. In a real-life counseling situation, the counselor and client typically meet for a number of sessions, often once per week, extending over several weeks. Typically, the client and his or her presenting problem are carefully diagnosed, and treatment goals as well as intervention strategies are tailored specifically to this particular client.

Most important, the counselor and client freely interact and exchange a wealth of information. The client is not a tabula rasa, but instead assimilates the new information into his or her existing conceptual framework and reacts in some way (see Hill, Helms, Spiegel, & Tichenor, 1988, for a taxonomy of client reactions). In a positive counseling situation, the client changes in some desirable manner, such as learning new behaviors; altering beliefs, attitudes, or feelings; and adapting to environmental demands more effectively. The environmental context for the therapeutic situation is typically a professional treatment center of some sort, a university counseling center, or a community mental health center.

Table 17.1 provides examples of relatively high, moderate, and low degrees of resemblance of seven counseling process variables to actual counseling practice. In terms of assessment and interventions, high resemblance characterizes those situations in which the client is carefully diagnosed and interventions are specifically targeted to the client's problems. Low resemblance involves a lack of assessment, as well as interventions that are not relevant to a participant's concerns or problems. Analogues that resemble the actual therapy process involve multiple 50-minute sessions extended over several weeks (as opposed to one-shot, 10-minute counseling scenarios). In addition, analogues that resemble actual counseling include rather extended interactions between the counselor and client during which a broad range of information is exchanged, as distinct from analogues that do not include live interactions between counselor and client. The analogue also can be evaluated in terms of how much and what kind of information the client processes; high resemblance entails the client's processing the counseling experience repeatedly over time, whereas low resemblance entails the participant's responding to counseling scenarios in a hypothetical and often irrelevant manner. The analogue might also be evaluated in terms of therapeutic outcomes: Did the client change in some desired way? High resemblance involves change of personally relevant behaviors, thoughts, or feelings, whereas low resemblance entails a lack of change on the part of the participant, most likely because the counseling scenario was not personally relevant. Finally, the analogue can be evaluated in terms of the environment or context of the counseling situation. Analogues involving a high resemblance to actual practice take place in a professional environment, such as a treatment or counseling center, whereas an experimental laboratory setting or classroom offers relatively low resemblance.

CREATING ANALOGUE STUDIES THAT MORE CLOSELY RESEMBLE REAL LIFE

We would like to provide another example of an analogue study that addresses several concerns related to client and counselor variables, as well as the counseling process and setting. A study by Chang (1994) provides an excellent example of a study that used an analogue design with interview conditions similar to actual counseling. In keeping with true experimental design, Chang randomly selected 80 women from 127 respondents to campus advertisements soliciting volunteers to participate in a weight control study. The women were subsequently interviewed for one session by four male counselors in the context of a weight-control clinic to examine the effects of (1) the types of questions asked and (2) the types of feedback on dependent variables related to behavioral compliance. In essence, Chang utilized a 2 (type of question: positive or negative) by 2 (type of interviewer feedback: positive or neutral) matrix on a variety of behavioral compliance measures, including weight loss.

It is important to note that Chang (1994) trained the interviewers for approximately 20 hours in order for the interviewers to consistently implement their roles across the four conditions; in addition, he held regular meetings with the interviewers to review procedures throughout the study. Another strength of the study was the variety of behavioral measures used by Chang for a two-week period: recording all food consumed, limiting meals to 20 minutes, meditation ("the more the better"), making lists of good and bad foods, returning the weekly recordings, actual weight loss, returning for a second visit, and punctuality for the return visit.

The results revealed that the type of question asked did not affect the participants' behavioral compliance. However, positive (as opposed to neutral) feedback resulted in the women being more behaviorally compliant to the interviewer's requests, such as returning the weekly reports, spending more days meditating, constructing more lists of good and bad foods, returning for a second interview at a higher rate, and losing more weight. In short, positive feedback from the counselor (i.e., agreement with the client, praise for being honest, and support for disclosures and encouragement for effort) significantly affected the participants' behavior after one interview session.

This analogue study is particularly noteworthy in that the experimental conditions were imbedded in an actual counseling setting (i.e., a weight loss clinic), used motivated participants with actual weight loss concerns, provided extensive training to increase accuracy and adherence in delivering the counselors' roles or independent variables, and employed a broad range of indicators of behavioral compliance for their dependent variable. Although, as Chang (1994) cautioned, the generalizability of the study to extended counseling sessions is unclear, the strengths of this type of analogue study create a more useful analogue design.

EVALUATING ANALOGUE UTILITY
WITHIN AN EXISTING KNOWLEDGE BASE

A common goal in counseling—to facilitate change in clients—implies that the counselor can favorably affect the client to alter specific thoughts, attitudes, and behaviors. The process of one person influencing the actions, attitudes, or feelings of another has been labeled the interpersonal or social influence process and has been considered by some the "central core of social psychology" (Zimbardo & Ebbesen, 1970, p. iii). Initially, research in social psychology established the importance of several variables in promoting attitude change: source characteristics (such as perceived expertness or trustworthiness), message variables (such as message discrepancy or incongruity), and recipient characteristics (such as locus of control or authoritarianism). Subsequent research has indicated that the attitude change process is more complex, and different persuasion routes have been proposed and empirically substantiated (Petty & Cacioppo, 1981).

Strong (1968) initially conceptualized counseling as an interpersonal or social influence process, as he explicitly integrated social psychological concepts into counseling. Since 1968, considerable research has been conducted on interpersonal influence variables in counseling. Investigators have examined a wide range of variables affecting counselor power, or the counselor's ability to influence a client (see Corrigan et al., 1980; Dorn, 1986; Heppner & Claiborn, 1989; Heppner & Dixon, 1981; Heppner & Frazier, 1992; Strong, Welsh, Corcoran, & Hoyt, 1992).

Analogue methodology has been used in a very high proportion of published studies of interpersonal influence. Aware of the advantages and disadvantages of the analogue methodology, Strong (1971) proposed five criteria or "boundary conditions" that, if met, would increase the external validity or generalizability of analogue methodology: (1) Counseling takes the form of a conversation between or among persons; (2) status differences between or among interactants constrain the conversation; (3) the duration of contact between interactants in counseling varies and at times is extended; (4) many clients are motivated to change; and (5) many clients are psychologically distressed and are heavily invested in the behaviors they seek to change.

Although other criteria could be used, Heppner and Dixon (1981) used these five conditions to assess the external validity of investigations of the interpersonal influence process in counseling. The third condition (extended duration) was operationally defined as two sessions. Heppner and Dixon reviewed 51 studies that examined events associated with perceived expertness, attractiveness, and trustworthiness; 29 (57%) did not meet any of the boundary conditions, 16 met only the first two conditions, 5 fulfilled three conditions, and 1 met four conditions.

Heppner and Claiborn (1989) did a similar analysis of the interpersonal influence literature in counseling between 1981 and 1989; 37 of the 56 studies reviewed (66%) did not meet any of the boundary conditions. These studies presented the counseling situation to participants via written, audiotaped, or videotaped materials, which can be considered noninterview analogues. Moreover, these noninterview studies contained an average of only about 12 minutes of stimulus material, which suggests that this research is based on minimal information and initial impressions. Thus, a majority of the interpersonal influence research examined by Heppner and Claiborn consists of data collected in situations of questionable generalizability (that is, none of Strong's boundary conditions were met). In addition, only 12 minutes of stimulus material constitutes an extremely small sample of counseling. Twenty-nine percent of the studies (16 of 56) met three or more boundary conditions, compared to about 12% in the Heppner and Dixon (1981) review. Further analysis of these investigations revealed that seven studies were conducted with counseling center clients during actual counseling. Thus, there appears to be some progress in examining the social influence process under conditions more similar to actual counseling situations; still, relatively little research has examined the influence process in a real-life counseling context over time.

Clearly, utility of a particular methodology—in this case, analogue methodology—is contingent upon previous research and the accumulated knowledge bases. There is no doubt that the analogue methodology is powerful and useful. However, when it is by far the most frequently used methodology, the resultant body of knowledge becomes unbalanced and tends to emphasize one methodological approach to the exclusion of others. In short, the utility of the knowledge obtained from the analogue methodology diminishes if this methodology far outweighs other methodologies in a particular research area. Gelso (1979) discussed this issue in terms of paradigm fixation. In addition, when the analogues used are very dissimilar to the actual counseling experience, additional questions are raised about the generalizability of the results.

The question then becomes: Can additional research using the analogue method significantly increase our knowledge base about the influence process in counseling? Although the analogue can still play a powerful role in acquiring knowledge about counseling, additional analogue studies of social influence that do not meet any of Strong's boundary conditions are unlikely to add substantially to our knowledge base at this time, and their value in the area of social influence will remain doubtful given the generalizability issues. (See Heppner & Claiborn, 1989; Heppner & Frazier, 1992; Hoyt, 1992; and Strong et al., 1992, for recommendations regarding future research directions in this area.)

Conversely, Ponterotto and Casas (1991) expressed concern that a majority of multicultural research has used analogue designs. However, when they analyzed several counseling journals over a six-year period in the late 1980s, they found that only 12.5% of the published multicultural research in these journals was analogue research. They concluded that analogue research was not being overutilized in multicultural research.

In sum, the utility of any given methodology in a particular topic area must be evaluated within the context of existing knowledge bases and prior research methodologies. Studies that consistently use the same methodology create a knowledge base that is vulnerable with regard to the particular disadvantage of that methodology. Moreover, when the overwhelming majority of research in an area derives from the same methodology, the strength and utility of the knowledge base is unclear.

SUMMARY AND CONCLUSIONS

As Munley (1974) has noted, there are several different types of analogue research, including audiovisual and quasi-counseling interviews. Without a doubt, the analogue methodology can be and often is powerful and useful. In terms of Kerlinger's MAXMINCON principle, analogue research typically allows for a great deal of experimental control to manipulate one or more independent variables, eliminate or hold extraneous variables constant, and use random assignment.

The major question surrounding analogue methodology in counseling research pertains to the external validity of the results; sometimes analogue methodology examines circumstances so far removed from actual counseling practice that the research becomes oversimplified and artificial. We propose that the external validity of analogue research can be evaluated in part by examining variables that depict real-life counseling in three categories: (1) the client, (2) the counselor, and (3) the counseling process and setting.

We suggest that analogues fall on a continuum from low to high resemblance to the counseling situation. Given the sparsity of empirical research, the relationship between analogues with various degrees of resemblance to actual counseling is unclear. Investigations that have examined the comparability of analogue studies and more applied research have produced mixed results (see, for example, Elliott, 1979; Helms, 1976, 1978; Kushner, 1978). Clearly, more research is needed.

Nonetheless, as Kerlinger (1986) has indicated, the temptation to incorrectly interpret the results of analogue (laboratory) research as they apply to real-life phenomena is great. When an investigator obtains highly statistically significant results in the laboratory, it is tempting to assume that these results would also be applicable to actual counseling practice. As a general rule, *it is questionable to generalize beyond the conditions or population used in a given study.* Thus, if an investigator is primarily interested in generalizing about clients, counselors, and/or the counseling process, then the analogue methodology must be evaluated with those particular conditions or populations in mind. Depending on the degree of resemblance to actual counseling practice, the investigator may be able to conclude that the analogue results apply to actual counseling. Again, as a general rule, *relationships found under laboratory conditions must be tested again in the context to which we wish to generalize— typically, actual counseling.*

But does this mean that all analogues should closely resemble the conditions of actual counseling practice? We believe not. In our opinion, a considerable amount of information can be obtained about counseling from tightly controlled analogue studies that do not closely resemble actual counseling. This may well be the case early in a line of research, when relatively little is known about certain variables. For example, researchers have collected a substantial amount of knowledge from tightly controlled analogue studies about events that affect clients' perceptions of counselor expertness, attractiveness, and trustworthiness (see reviews by Corrigan et al., 1980; Heppner & Claiborn, 1989; Heppner & Dixon, 1981).

The extent to which an investigator emphasizes external validity, and perhaps sacrifices internal validity when examining events in counseling, depends on the knowledge base that currently exists in that particular line of research. One argument states that if relatively little is empirically known, the researcher should avoid sacrificing internal validity (see Kerlinger, 1986). This reasoning emphasizes the role of internal validity in making scientific advancement. Another argument holds that the powerful analogue methodology can be used to refine knowledge obtained from less internally valid field situations (see Gelso, 1979). In this way, the strength of the analogue (precision and experimental control) can be taken full advantage of, and the results may be more readily interpreted within the existing base of knowledge collected in the field. Both lines of reasoning have merit and pertain to a central theme of this book— namely, that the strengths or weaknesses of any particular methodology for a specific research area are related to the existing knowledge base and prior research methods used in that area. In line with Bordin's (1965) recommendation, we suggest that analogue research be combined with empirical investigations conducted in a field setting to create knowledge bases that emphasize both internal and external validity.

STIMULUS QUESTIONS

ANALYZING ANALOGUE STUDIES

This exercise is designed to give you practice in analyzing an analogue study, weighing the advantages and limitations of this research method. We suggest that you pair yourself with a colleague in your class, respond to the following questions individually, and then compare your responses with your colleague. Pick one of the three recent examples of analogue studies in the second section of this chapter; copy and read that article, and then answer the following questions.

1. One of the advantages of an analogue study is control of the experimental situation. In the study you chose, what independent variable(s) was (were) manipulated by researchers? What extraneous variables were eliminated? Was random assignment used in any way?

2. Another advantage of an analogue study is a high degree of specificity in the operational definition of the dependent variables. What was the operational definition of the dependent variables in this study?

3. What were the main advantages of using an analogue methodology for this study?

4. In order to make the analogue study similar to actual counseling, what did researchers do in this study?

5. What would be some of the possible practical and ethical obstacles that the researchers might well have encountered if they would have tried to examine the same or similar research questions in an actual counseling situation?

6. Strong (1971) suggested five "boundary conditions" that would increase the external validity or generalizability of analogue studies. Discuss the study in terms of these five criteria.

7. The major disadvantage of analogue studies is the threats to external validity related to the artificial circumstances of the study. In your view, what factors were the most serious threats to the external validity of the study?

8. Discuss the main conclusions from the study relative to the limitations of the study. What do you believe can be concluded from this study?

18 CHAPTER | OUTCOME RESEARCH: STRATEGIES AND METHODOLOGICAL ISSUES

Does counseling really work? Is therapy effective? Can couples assessment and feedback improve relationships? Is cognitive-relaxation coping skills training more effective than social skills training in reducing anger expression of early adolescents? Can the addition of brief group therapy to an academic assistance program improve the academic and social functioning of low-achieving elementary school students? Does helping group clients set realistic, interpersonal, and here-and-now agendas enhance group participation and client outcome? These and many similar research questions are questions about counseling outcome.

Typically outcome research attempts to address the question of counseling efficacy by comparing a treatment group to a control group or by comparing different treatments. Outcome research—which is not a category of research designs per se, but rather a specific focus within counseling research—is predominantly conducted using true experimental or quasi-experimental designs. The counseling researcher must address a number of methodological issues, which constitute the major focus of this chapter.

By way of introduction to outcome research, we initially discuss how outcome questions have captivated counseling researchers since the beginning of the profession. In addition, we briefly examine how methodological critiques of outcome research have occupied a central role in researchers' thinking about evaluating counseling. Next we describe the different types of strategies used to conduct outcome research and provide recent examples of each of these strategies. The subsequent section focuses on four methodological issues in outcome research: (1) selecting the appropriate comparison group (i.e., inclusion and exclusion criteria), (2) assessing treatment integrity, (3) measuring outcomes and change, and (4) therapist effects. Additionally, throughout the chapter we summarize literature that questions some of the fundamental assumptions underlying counseling outcome research.

EARLY OUTCOME RESEARCH IN COUNSELING

At the beginning of research in counseling it was evident that outcome research was prominent and valued. Indeed, the first article in the first issue of the *Journal of Counseling Psychology* (Forgy & Black, 1954) was a three-year follow-up assessment of 100 Stanford students counseled with either "client-centered permissive counseling procedures and materials" or "highly structured counselor-centered procedures" (p. 1). In the original study, the 100 students were counseled by one of three counselors, each of whom used each counseling method (i.e., therapists were crossed with treatment; see the issues involved with therapist effects that are discussed in the section on methodological issues). At the end of treatment, satisfaction data suggested that the students were more satisfied with the client-centered procedures. However, at the follow-up, Forgy and Black found no differences in client satisfaction between the type of counseling (client-centered versus counselor-centered) or among the counselors. They did detect, however, a significant interaction between counselor and type of treatment: One of the three counselors had more satisfied clients when he used the counselor-centered methods, whereas the other two counselors had more satisfied clients when they used the client-centered methods.

In another early study, Rogers (1954) was interested in comparing two different counseling techniques: a "test-centered" and a "self-evaluation" method of test interpretation. The major differences in the two methods were the amount of client participation in the interview and the relative concentration on nontest data. Rogers conducted all the test interpretation interviews, alternating between the two methods of test interpretation. The outcome measure in this study was a "self-understanding score," which represented the match between the student's self-assessment and the counselor's assessment of the student. Rogers used an integrity check to assess whether the two types of test interpretation interviews were conducted properly. Specifically, he and a second counselor listened to audiotapes of 20 sessions (10 tapes from each method of test interpretation) and classified each discussion unit (a counselor–client exchange regarding a given topic). Based on these tape ratings, Rogers concluded that the "test-centered" and "self-evaluation" methods had the expected differences in session content and process. An analysis of changes in self-understanding revealed that both methods of test interpretation led to increases in self-understanding, but no difference in overall counseling effectiveness. Rogers did, however, identify an interaction between students' level of intelligence and the type of test interpretation used: More-intelligent students had gains in self-understanding with either method of test interpretation, whereas less intelligent students showed gains in self-understanding only when the "self-evaluation" method of test interpretation was used.

By today's standards, the outcome measures and statistical analyses used in Forgy and Black (1954) and Rogers (1954) are rather primitive. Still, a clear continuity is evident between the questions and research design strategies used in 1954 and today. Researchers remain interested in testing the efficacy of treatments. As well, the results of these and the other early studies foreshadowed predominant patterns of results with regard to the small or nonexistent differences in outcomes among different treatment types (Wampold, 2001) and the presence of differences among therapists (Crits-Christoph et al., 1991; Wampold). Early outcome researchers attended to many important methodological issues, including assessing how faithfully the proposed treatments were delivered and assessing therapist effects and their influence on outcomes. In addition, the differential effects of the type of test interpretation session for clients with different levels of intelligence is an example of client characteristics that moderate treatment outcome, a reminder that treatment effectiveness may not be uniform (what Kiesler, 1966, referred to as the uniformity myth).

Treatment effectiveness has received a tremendous amount of attention in the past 40 years (for a partial listing, see Bergin & Garfield, 1971, 1994; Garfield, 1993; Garfield & Bergin, 1978, 1986; Gurman & Razin, 1977; Hollon, 1996; Howard, Moras, Brill, Martinovich, & Lutz, 1996; Jacobson & Christensen, 1996; Lambert, 2004; Lambert & Bergin, 1993; Lambert, Christensen, & Dejulio, 1983; Rachman & Wilson, 1980; Strupp & Howard, 1993; Vandenbos, 1996; Wampold, 2001). Clearly, determining the effectiveness of the treatments counselors use is fundamental to the field as, after all, counseling is most centrally involved with the delivery of services to people— logically, counseling researchers are charged with ensuring that such services are indeed benefiting these people.

It was not always accepted that counseling and psychotherapy were effective. One of the most important challenges came from Hans Eysenck (1952, 1960, 1969), who asserted that little empirical evidence supported the effectiveness of psychotherapy. Eysenck's critique influenced a number of researchers to examine the outcome question; over the years, more and more knowledge has been created using ever more sophisticated research methodologies. In a landmark study, Smith and Glass (1977) published a meta-analytic review of all controlled research in counseling and psychotherapy that, although controversial at the time, established that counseling and psychotherapy interventions were remarkably effective (see Smith, Glass, & Miller, 1980; Wampold, 2001).

It is important not only to know that treatments work, but also to answer Gordon Paul's (1967) important question: "What treatment, by whom, is most effective for this individual with that specific problem, under which set of circumstances, and how does it come about?" (p. 111; see also Kiesler, 1966). Other researchers, suggesting that much valuable information is lost when researchers only test pre- to postchange, have argued for the need to examine important events from session to session and within sessions. (See Chapter 19 for more details on counseling process research.)

STRATEGIES FOR CONDUCTING OUTCOME RESEARCH

In this chapter, seven types of outcome research strategies are discussed: (1) the treatment package strategy, (2) the dismantling strategy, (3) the constructive strategy, (4) the parametric strategy, (5) the comparative outcome strategy, (6) the common factor control group design, and (7) the moderation design. We now describe each strategy and provide an illustrative example from the counseling literature.

THE TREATMENT PACKAGE STRATEGY

The most fundamental question that outcome research can address is whether a treatment or intervention has an effect. One example is: Does treatment with Dialectical Behavior Therapy (DBT; Salsman & Linehan, 2006) lead to a decrease in self-injurious behavior in individuals diagnosed with borderline personality disorder (BPD)? In one study on this subject, researchers randomized 50 females diagnosed with BPD to an inpatient DBT treatment program or to a wait-list/community referral control. Results indicated that DBT led to significant decreases in a majority of clinically relevant variables including self-harm relative to the wait-list/community treatment control (Bohus et al., 2004).

This type of effectiveness question is addressed by the *treatment package strategy,* in which the researcher compares a treatment, in its entirety, to some control condition, usually a condition where the participants do not receive any treatment (e.g., a no-treatment or wait-list control). In this way, the following question can be answered: Is the treatment more efficacious than no treatment? In such a design, ideally, the only difference between the two conditions is the treatment—one group of participants receives the treatment and the other does not, so that differences found at the end of the study can be attributed to the treatment. This difference is the treatment effect.

We now discuss the logic of the no-treatment control and the design of the control group in more detail. The basics of this design were introduced in Chapter 4. Randomly assigning clients to the two groups, treatment and control, assures that the groups are comparable in all respects; that is, any differences for any variable (e.g., initial severity of the disorder, age, ethnicity, or ego strength), measured or not, that exist before treatment are due to chance and not any systematic factor. In order to estimate how effective the treatment is, the objective is to compare the difference in mental health status (i.e., the dependent variable) between those who received treatment and those who did not. Therefore, the typical strategy in treatment package studies is to administer the treatment to one group and to provide no intervention to the other group.

The assumption is that any differences between the groups at the end of the study were due to treatment.

There are several issues inherent in this design. One is that it is assumed that a difference in the groups at the end of treatment, should a difference be found, was due to the efficacy of the treatment. However, as discussed often in this book, such a difference may be due to chance. This is, of course, a problem encountered in any experimental design and one that is addressed by the statistical test. That is, one sets an alpha level that is tolerable; for example, if alpha was set at 0.05, then the probability of falsely claiming that the treatment works (i.e., rejecting the null hypothesis) would be less than 5 out of 100.

A second issue relates to the assumption that mental health status at the end of treatment of the no-treatment control group is truly representative of how clients would fare without treatment. If the treatment is for a mental disorder (e.g., depression), then a no-treatment group is intended to represent the natural history of the disorder (i.e., the course of the disorder without any intervention). An issue here is that the experimental situation attenuates the validity of this assumption. Suppose that the study is examining a treatment for depression, and those who are enrolled in the study are eager to avail themselves of the latest treatment. Some clients, when notified that they have been assigned to the no-treatment group, will become demoralized: "Story of my life—I never have any good luck. Even when I enroll in a study I get the short end of the stick." Other clients may seek treatment elsewhere. In these ways, the status of the control group clients might not represent how they would have fared had they never heard of and enrolled in the experimental protocol.

A third issue is an ethical one. If viable treatments are available for a particular disorder, then withholding a treatment from control group clients is problematic. One solution is to promise that, should the treatment being studied be found to be effective, it will be made available to the clients at the end of the study. Typically, novel treatments being studied are not generally available, and clients in the control group are informed that they are being placed on a waiting list for the treatment, in which case the control condition is labeled "wait-list control group." However, the mental health status of those on the wait lists should be monitored so if serious sequelae of the disorder should arise, such as suicidal behavior of depressed clients, appropriate action can be taken. The benefits to society that accrue from comparing a treatment to a no-treatment control group should always be weighed against the risks of withholding treatment. However, it could be argued that until a treatment for a disorder has been established as effective, not providing a treatment does not disadvantage a client.

The Dismantling Strategy

If several research studies have shown that a treatment package is effective, a researcher may want to determine which components of the multi-component intervention are necessary and which are superfluous. In other words, the outcome question is: What are the active/effective components of the treatment?

This design attempts to take apart the treatments to identify the critical components, and thus aptly has been labeled as a "dismantling" study. In a study using the dismantling strategy, the researcher compares the treatment package to the treatment package with one or more of the critical components removed.

Perhaps the best example of a dismantling study is Jacobson et al.'s (1996) study of cognitive therapy (CT) (Beck, Rush, Shaw, & Emery, 1979). Although Beck et al. are explicit in their claim that the alteration of core cognitive schemas drives the effectiveness of CT, the treatment contains numerous components that may be responsible for treatment efficacy. If the hypothesis is that alteration of core schemas is crucial to the effectiveness of CT, then the full package of CT should be significantly more effective than a treatment without the purported critical components. In order to test the mechanisms involved in the efficacy of CT, Jacobson et al. used a three-group pretest-posttest experimental design. The first treatment contained the full package of CT (i.e., containing all its components). The second treatment contained both the behavioral activation (BA) and automatic thought components of CT, but no therapeutic actions related to altering core schemas. The third treatment contained only the BA component (i.e., no therapeutic actions related to reducing automatic thoughts or changing core schemas). All therapists were well trained and adhered to treatment protocols (see the section on methodological issues in this chapter for a discussion of adherence in outcome research). Despite an admitted researcher bias toward CT, results indicated no differences in the efficacy of the three treatments at termination or at 6-month follow-up, suggesting that the cognitive components are not critical for the success of cognitive therapy for depression (see Wampold, 2001).

THE CONSTRUCTIVE STRATEGY

The constructive strategy is used to determine whether adding some component to treatment already demonstrably shown to be effective adds to the benefits of the treatment. Research examining whether a particular component, when added to an established intervention, enhances treatment effectiveness is considered the *constructive strategy* (Kazdin, 1995). In the prototypic constructive design, one group of participants receives the standard treatment regime and another group of participants receives the adjunctive component in addition to the standard treatment.

For example, Foa and Rauch (2004) compared exposure therapy (ET) to exposure therapy plus cognitive restructuring (ETC) in the treatment of female assault survivors with chronic posttraumatic stress disorder (PTSD). This study was designed to test the hypothesis that the addition of a cognitive component would augment the efficacy of exposure procedures. The researchers also measured trauma-related thoughts (as measured by the Post-Traumatic Cognitions Inventory (PTCI); Foa, Ehlers, Clark, Tolin, & Orsillo, 1999), hypothesizing that ETC would have a more pronounced impact on this measure than ET alone. Although the decrease of trauma-related thoughts was related to symptom improvement, no treatment differences were observed on this measure.

The Parametric Strategy

In using the parametric strategy, counseling researchers try to identify changes in *treatment parameters* that are related to the effectiveness of a treatment. The term *parameter* refers to the quantities of aspects contained in a treatment rather than whether or not a component of treatment is present. For example, a parametric study of homework assignments would attempt to identify the optimal number of homework assignments, whereas a component design (e.g., a dismantling design) would attempt to determine whether homework was necessary or not. Thus, a study using the parametric strategy compares two or more treatments that differ in the quantity of the component.

Turner, Valtierra, Talken, Miller, and DeAnda (1996) provide an interesting example of a parametric strategy, in which they hypothesized that 50-minute counseling sessions would be more effective than 30-minute counseling sessions. The authors used a two-group pretest-posttest design to test their hypothesis. The 94 college students who came to the counseling center and volunteered to participate in the study were randomly assigned to receive either eight 50-minute sessions or eight 30-minute sessions. A 2 (treatment group; 50-minute session versus 30-minute session) $\times$ 2 (time; pretest versus posttest) repeated measures analysis of variance (ANOVA) was used to analyze data from the College Adjustment Scales (Anton & Reed, 1991). The analysis of the College Adjustment Scales data revealed a significant main effect for time, but no significant main effect for treatment and no significant interaction effect for treatment time. The analysis of separate Client Satisfaction Questionnaire (Attkisson & Zwick, 1982) data also revealed no significant effect for treatment group. Turner et al. (1996) concluded that their study "found weekly 30-minute sessions to be as effective as 50-minute sessions when using a brief therapy model with young adult, college students" (p. 231).

The Common Factor Control Group

One of the issues inherent in the treatment package design is that it is not possible, if it is found that the treatment is effective, to determine which components of the study are responsible for the benefits. The dismantling, constructive, and parametric strategies are designed to shed some light on this important issue. However, these strategies are designed to isolate one or a few critical components that might be related to positive outcomes attained by clients. One of the debates in psychotherapy is whether the benefits produced by treatment are due to the specific ingredients in treatments or whether the benefits are due to the factors common to all treatments. For example, are the benefits of cognitive-behavioral treatment for depression due to the therapist's specific strategies to reduce irrational thoughts and change core schemas (specific ingredients) or are they due to the relationship with an empathic healer, the provision of a treatment rationale, agreement about tasks and goals, and other factors common to all or most treatments intended to be therapeutic? Modern medicine faces a similar issue in attempts to demonstrate that the active ingredients of a medication are responsible for the benefits and not hope, expectation, or other psychological factors. In medicine, the effects of the psychological factors are often called placebo effects.

The "gold standard" for establishing the efficacy of drugs is to compare a pill with active ingredients to a placebo (sugar) pill in a randomized double-blinded design. Double blind refers to the conditions that render both the recipient of the pill and the administrator of the pill "blind" to whether it is the pill with the active medication or a pill with inert ingredients (i.e., the placebo). (Actually, the best design is a triple blind in which evaluators are also blind to treatment administered.) To maintain the blind, the active medication and the placebo must be indistinguishable so that no cues are given to the patient or the administrator that the pill is active or a placebo. If the design is successful, any superiority of the drug over and above the placebo is due to the effects of the active ingredients and not due to hope, expectation, or receipt of an explanation. In this case, the "specificity" of the drug is established because the benefits of the drug are due, in part, to the specific ingredients. Medical researchers are not interested in whether the placebo pill is superior to no treatment (i.e., the existence of a placebo effect) (see Wampold, Minami, Tierney, Baskin, & Bhati, 2005).

In 1956, Rosenthal and Frank suggested that psychotherapy borrow the randomized placebo control group design for the study of psychotherapy to control for the factors that are common to all treatments, such as the relationship. The logic of the placebo control group in psychotherapy is that it contains all these common factors but none of the specific factors of the treatment. For example, if the researcher was testing a cognitive-behavioral treatment for a particular disorder, the placebo control would have no ingredients related to cognitive-behavioral treatments (such as behavioral activation, reality testing, changing core schemas, and so forth) but would likely involve a compassionate and caring therapist who responded empathically to the client (Wampold, 2001; Wampold et al., 2005). Often these control groups are referred to as "alternative treatments," "supportive counseling," or "common-factor controls," the latter to indicate that they control for the common factors; the term *placebo control* is no longer typically used in psychotherapy research.

There are a number of problems with common factor control groups (see Wampold, 2001; Wampold et al., 2005), as will be illustrated by the examples presented below. Foremost is that they cannot be employed in a double-blind design. The therapists providing the treatment are always aware of whether they are providing the "real" treatment or the "sham" treatment (the term *sham* is often used in medical studies to denote the placebo). Moreover, some of the common factors are not present in such a control group. For example, the provision of a cogent rationale is common to all treatments but is typically absent in common factor controls (see Wampold, 2001). Nevertheless, the common factor control group design is often used in psychotherapy research.

In one such study, Markowitz, Kocsis, Bleiberg, Christos, and Sacks (2005) compared the effect of interpersonal psychotherapy (IPT), Sertraline, and brief supportive psychotherapy (BSP) in the treatment of individuals diagnosed with dysthymia, a disorder that has been traditionally understudied. Although a nonspecific control, the authors indicated that BSP was by no means a nontreatment because therapists were well trained and motivated. Results did not support the superiority of IPT over BSP in reducing depressive symptoms. The authors indicated that their control treatment may have been "too active" and that well-trained therapists with a motivated supervisor who performed BSP may have obscured any treatment differences. In retrospect, Markowitz and colleagues contend that in this case BSP may be considered an active treatment. This example illustrates the numerous difficulties involved in interpreting results from common factors control group designs (see Baskin, Tierney, Minami, & Wampold, 2003).

The Comparative Outcome Strategy

The comparative outcome strategy is used to determine the relative effectiveness of two or more treatments. Sometimes the strategy can be used to identify which of two established treatments is more effective. Other times it can be used to determine whether a new treatment, which is perhaps less costly or complex, is as effective as an established treatment. Essentially, the design involves comparing two or more treatments that are intended to be therapeutic for a particular disorder. Of course, the researchers may also choose to include another type of control group, such as a no-treatment control group. In this latter case, two research questions would be addressed: (1) which of the treatments intended to be therapeutic is superior, and (2) are the treatments superior to no treatment? It should be emphasized, however, that a no-treatment control group is not needed to answer the first of these two questions. Again, a central principle of outcome research is that the question to be answered determines which groups are chosen to constitute the independent variable.

Care must be taken to ensure that the comparison between the treatments of a comparative outcome study is fair. For example, if one treatment lasts 12 sessions and the other treatment lasts only 6 sessions, the dose of treatment becomes a confound. It is relatively easy to think of numerous potential confounds, but perhaps the most important one is the skill and allegiance of the therapist. It has been shown that the allegiance of the researcher to a particular treatment has a large effect on the outcome of the study (Luborsky et al., 1999; Wampold, 2001).

Although the causes of researcher allegiance effects are difficult to discern, there is some evidence to suggest that it is because the therapist's allegiance to and enthusiasm for the treatment being advocated by the researcher are greater than for the alternative treatment (Wampold, 2001). It is also important that the therapists delivering the various treatments are equally skilled (this issue is considered in more detail when therapist issues are discussed in the section on methodological issues). In any event, care must be taken to ensure that the comparison is fair. The fact that researcher allegiance is such a strong predictor of the effects produced in such designs is *prima fascie* evidence for bias in the design of comparative outcome studies.

In a recent comparative design, Markowitz et al. (1998) compared the effectiveness of interpersonal psychotherapy (IPT), cognitive behavioral therapy (CBT), Imiprimine, and brief supportive psychotherapy (BSP) in the treatment of HIV patients with depressive symptoms. In order to encourage treatment fidelity, each treatment team was led by a team leader who encouraged uniformity and therapist morale. All therapists were well trained and technically adherent. In this trial, results indicated that IPT was superior in decreasing depressive symptoms relative to CBT and BSP. The authors state that IPT may be superior to CBT in treating HIV patients because IPT therapists attempt to link mood symptoms to life events, a rationale that may be particularly compelling for this population. This conclusion has to be considered, however, in light of the fact that the authors had an allegiance to IPT.

THE MODERATION DESIGN

In the designs considered to this point, the independent variable has consisted of various treatments and controls. Accordingly, conclusions are restricted to statements about the treatments vis-à-vis the types of clients being treated. However, these designs do not address the question raised by Paul (1969) about which treatments work with which types of clients. In the moderation design, the researcher attempts to answer this question by examining the relative effectiveness of treatments for various types of clients, settings, or contexts. For example, Beutler, Molieri, and Talebi (2002) contend that resistant clients do better with unstructured treatments, whereas nonresistant clients do better with structured treatments. Such contentions suggest factorial designs and interaction effects (see Chapter 7). In this case, treatment (structured versus unstructured) is crossed with resistance (high versus low, or left as a continuous variable).

Hembree, Street, Riggs, and Foa (2004) provide an example of a study that used this strategy. Hembree and colleagues examined predictors of response in 73 female assault victims diagnosed with chronic PTSD. The researchers hypothesized that certain trauma-related variables (e.g., childhood trauma, trauma severity, type of assault) would predict response to CBT for PTSD. Results indicated that a history of childhood trauma resulted in greater PTSD severity posttreatment. The authors concluded that prior experience of trauma interferes with the ability to process and cope with later traumatic experiences.

METHODOLOGICAL ISSUES IN CONDUCTING OUTCOME RESEARCH

In this section we will discuss four methodological issues that researchers undertaking an outcome study must address: (1) inclusion and exclusion criteria, (2) assessing treatment integrity, (3) measurement of change, and (4) consideration of therapist effects.

INCLUSION AND EXCLUSION CRITERIA

One decision that must be made in outcome research is related to the inclusion and exclusion criteria relative to the participants of the study. Of course, inclusion and exclusion criteria should be determined, to the extent possible, by the research question. However, there will also be pragmatic, ethical, and design issues to be considered; many of the issues here have been discussed in Chapter 6, but will briefly be discussed here as they pertain particularly to outcome research.

We illustrate inclusion and exclusion criteria by considering a researcher who has developed a new treatment for adults with depression. Logically, the nature of the research dictates that participants be adults with depression. The researcher could operationalize this in various ways: DSM diagnosis of, say, major depressive disorder or score above a cut point on a depression inventory. Certain types of patients may also be excluded so that the conclusions are made with regard to depressed patients and not patients with other disorders (i.e., rule out co-morbidities). For example, such trials typically exclude clients with psychosis, substance abuse, and certain personality disorders (e.g., Elkin, Shea, & Watkins, 1989; Jacobson et al., 1996). Moreover, clients concurrently taking psychotropic medication are also excluded so as not to confound psychotherapy and drug effects. For ethical, clinical, and research purposes, suicidal clients are often excluded. These exclusionary criteria result in fewer threats to validity, but at the expense of generalizability; that is, the clients seen in a trial with fairly stringent inclusion and exclusion criteria may not be similar to the population of depressed clients. (For a discussion of the representativeness of clients in clinical trials, see Norcross, Beutler, & Levant, 2006; Westen, Novotny, & Thompson-Brenner, 2004; see also Chapter 4).

Clearly, the researcher wants to balance the validity of conclusions with regard to whether differences noted among groups are due to treatment (internal validity) with the representativeness of the sample to patients seen in practice (external validity). This is an example of the tension between various types of validity; such tensions are inherent in the design of research in applied psychology, as discussed elsewhere in this book.

ASSESSING TREATMENT INTEGRITY: ADHERENCE, COMPETENCE, AND DIFFERENTIATION

As discussed in Chapter 12, one of the components of construct validity is that the independent variable be properly defined, specified, and operationalized. In treatment studies, the independent variable is constituted by the various treatment conditions and control groups that are employed by the researcher. In the various designs discussed in the previous section, issues relative to the validity of the control group were discussed. However, it is important to ensure that that the treatment delivered to clients in the treatment conditions is a valid representation of the treatment purported to be studied. If the treatments arc not valid representations of the purported treatment being studied, then the validity of the study could be criticized (i.e., a lack of efficacy could be due to the treatment itself or to a failure to implement the treatment competently).

For example, Snyder and Wills (1989) compared insight-oriented marital therapy (IOMT) with behavioral marital therapy (BMT). The authors found that both treatments resulted in positive relationship and intrapersonal variables and that the two treatments were equally effective. However, at three-year follow-up it was found that there were significantly fewer divorces in the IOMT condition (Snyder, Wills, & Grady-Fletcher, 1991). Jacobson (1991) criticized the study because he contended that BMT was inadequately delivered: "The data suggest that BMT was practiced with insufficient attention to nonspecifics" (p. 143). If this is the case, the results are difficult to interpret.

There are several steps to developing and deploying an adequately valid treatment, including (1) specifying the treatment, (2) training the therapists to adequately deliver the treatment, and (3) checking whether the treatment was delivered as intended. The degree to which these steps are completed successfully is often referred to as *treatment integrity* or *treatment fidelity.*

One of the advances related to specifying the treatment has been the development of treatment manuals. A treatment manual, according to Luborsky and Barber (1993), contains three components: (1) a description of the principles and techniques that characterize the particular treatment, (2) detailed examples of how and when to apply these principles and techniques, and (3) a scale to determine how closely a specific session or treatment conforms (adherence measure) to the principles and techniques described in the manual. Luborsky and Barber traced the advent of treatment manuals to Kelerman and Neu's (1976) unpublished manual describing an interpersonal approach for treating depression; the best known manual is the *Cognitive Behavioral Treatment of Depression* (Beck, Rush, Shaw, & Emery, 1979). The treatment manuals developed to date involve far more precise specification of the experimental treatment. Still, treatment manuals in and of themselves do not guarantee that the treatment in any particular study is delivered as the researcher intended. *Adherence measures* attempt to assess the degree of match between the intended treatment (as described in the manual) and the treatment actually delivered in a study. Although at least rudimentary treatment manuals have existed for some 30 years, in the late 1980s researchers began to develop adherence measures that are associated with specific treatment manuals (see Waltz et al., 1993). One adherence measure that has been used in several counseling studies is Butler, Henry, and Strupp's (1992) Vanderbilt Therapeutic Strategies Scale. Developed to measure adherence to Strupp and Binder's (1984) treatment manual, *Psychotherapy in a New Key,* the Vanderbilt Therapeutic Strategies Scale consists of two scales, labeled Psychodynamic Interviewing Style (with 12 items) and Time-Limited Dynamic Psychotherapy (TLDP) Specific Strategies (with 9 items). Trained observers typically watch a videotape or listen to an audiotape of a counseling session and then use the Vanderbilt Therapeutic Strategies Scale to indicate the degree to which each of the 21 items was descriptive of what the therapist had observed.

By using scales like the Vanderbilt Therapeutic Strategies Scale, researchers can begin to obtain an assessment of how well the treatment implemented in a study matches the treatment described in the manual. Measuring adherence, however, is not completely straightforward. One unresolved issue concerns who should perform the ratings of adherence. Some authors propose that ratings of adherence are best done by experienced clinicians who are "experts" in the treatment model being rated (see, for example, Luborsky & Barber, 1993); other authors contend that clients can use treatment adherence measures to report on counselor session behavior (see, for example, Iberg, 1991); still others maintain that the counselor's supervisor is in the best position to assess adherence (see, for example, DeRubeis, Hollon, Evans, & Bemis, 1982); and finally some claim trained lay persons (e.g., undergraduates) can accomplish the task (Waltz, Addis, Koerner, & Jacobson, 1993). In any event, researchers will need to design procedures to ensure that therapists are delivering the treatments as intended by the manual.

It is probably not sufficient to rate adherence without also examining the quality of treatment implementation. Counselors may follow all of the principles outlined in the manual and perform all of the associated techniques, but they might not apply the principles and techniques skillfully. Waltz et al. (1993; see also Barber & Crits-Christoph, 1996) use the term *competence* to refer to the skillful application of principles and techniques to such things as the correctness and appropriate timing of an interpretation or the correct identification of cognitive distortions.

Barber and Crits-Christoph (1996) maintain that measures designed to capture counselor adherence have often confounded adherence to the principles and techniques described in the manual with the competent implementation of these techniques. To address the confounding of adherence and competence, Barber and Crits-Christoph developed a measure of both adherence and competence designed to accompany Luborsky's (1984) manualized expressive-supportive approach. Their research showed that adherence and competence were related, but not identical, constructs (adherence and competence had 25% overlapping variance). In a subsequent study using this measure, Barber, Crits-Christoph, and Luborsky (1996) found that competence showed a stronger relationship to treatment outcome than did adherence. However, Shaw et al. (1999) showed that competence and adherence are not independent and that adherence to a protocol may suppress the relationship between competence and outcome (see also Wampold, 2001, for an explanation of this relationship). Further, Barber et al. (2006) found that adherence was related to outcome only when the alliance was weak, in which case a moderate degree of adherence to the protocol was superior to either a low or high degree of adherence.

As with adherence, it is not absolutely clear who should determine the competence of the counselor. The conventional wisdom is that only experienced clinicians who are experts in a particular treatment can accurately rate how competently that treatment was delivered (Waltz et al., 1993). Barber and Crits-Christoph (1996) followed this conventional wisdom when rating competence in supportive-expressive counseling. At least one study, however, asked clients to rate their counselor's competence on three dimensions: facilitating interventions, detracting style, and detracting effect (Thompson & Hill, 1993). Moreover, Thompson and Hill found that the use of facilitating interventions was related to session depth and treatment satisfaction, detracting style was related to treatment satisfaction, and detracting effect was related to symptom change and treatment satisfaction. At present, both expert-judged (Barber, Crits-Christoph, & Luborsky, 1996) and client-judged (Thompson & Hill) competence have been shown to relate to aspects of counseling outcome. Generally, however, the relationship between competence, as rated by either clients or experts, and outcome has been weak, casting doubt on whether competence, defined in this way, is an important construct in outcome research (Wampold, 2001). The issue of competence is discussed below in the section on therapist effects, where it is suggested that competence should be defined by the outcomes obtained by therapists.

When conducting a comparative outcome study, the researcher should establish not only that the therapists adhered to the manual and competently delivered the treatment, but also that the treatments delivered were noticeably different (Kazdin, 1996; Waltz et al., 1993; Wampold, 2001). Kazdin defined *differentiation* as "whether two or more treatments differed from each other along critical dimensions that are central to their execution" (p. 416). If, for example, a researcher wanted to compare the relative effectiveness of Strupp and Binder's (1984) Time-Limited Dynamic Psychotherapy (TLDP) and Beck et al.'s (1979) cognitive therapy for the treatment of depression, she or he must show that the two treatments, as delivered, differed along the critical dimensions that distinguish the two theories. Specifically, the TLDP manual and the associated Vanderbilt Therapeutic Strategies Scale specify that the counselor identifying a maladaptive interpersonal cycle is a critical component of the model. Therefore, the researcher should expect the counselors who use the TLDP model to rate high on this component of the Vanderbilt Therapeutic Strategies Scale; conversely, the counselors who use the cognitive therapy model would be expected to rate low on this component of the Vanderbilt Therapeutic Strategies Scale.

This example suggests that differentiation can often be assessed by applying the adherence scales from two different approaches to treatments from both approaches. To demonstrate differentiation, a treatment session must rate highly on its treatment adherence measure and have low ratings on the adherence measure from the other treatment (see Waltz et al., 1993).

To summarize, the assessment of treatment integrity involves a complex and multidimensional process. First, the treatment must be explicitly specified in a treatment manual so that counselors can know how to deliver the treatment and so that future researchers can replicate the treatment. Next, the researcher must demonstrate that the treatment as delivered adhered to the specifications of the manual and was delivered in a competent manner. Finally, in comparative outcome, dismantling, constructive, or parametric studies the researcher must also show that the treatments compared differed along the crucial dimensions studied.

As with many areas of counseling research, the assessment of treatment integrity is not without controversy. For example, Wampold (1997, 2001) has offered several criticisms of the standardization of treatments through treatment manuals. First, he argued that the quest to standardize treatments may distract researchers' attention away from more important areas of research focus, and that the effects of treatment type pale when compared to therapist effects (see the following discussion of therapist effects). By attempting to standardize treatments (and, by consequence, therapists), researchers may be getting rid of the most potent source of outcome effects (therapist differences). Second, Wampold noted that adherence to treatment manuals is inconsistently related to treatment outcome. In fact, some studies suggest that training counselors to adhere to a treatment manual may inhibit some areas of their functioning (e.g., Henry, Strupp, Butler, Schacht, & Binder, 1993; Shaw et al., 1999). In short, although the assessment of treatment integrity is crucial, many methodological issues remain unresolved.

Measuring Change

As noted by Francis et al. (1991), measuring and analyzing change plays a central role in many areas of study, but especially when trying to identify counseling outcomes. There is a voluminous literature dealing with the measurement of change (see, for example, Keller, 2004; Willett, 1997; Willett & Sayer, 1994). Although we cannot review this entire literature here, three areas have particular relevance to counseling researchers: (1) clinical versus statistical significance, (2) hypothesis testing, and (3) growth curve analysis. In the following subsections we discuss how each of these issues relates to the conduct of counseling outcome research.

Clinical versus Statistical Significance   A number of authors have argued that statistical significance is not a good indicator of treatment effectiveness. Lambert and Hill (1994) asserted that a well-designed outcome study can achieve statistically significant differences between treatment groups without producing real-life differences in enhanced functioning. For example, even though a date rape prevention program may result in a small but statistically significant decrease in rape myth acceptance when compared to a no-treatment control group, it is not clear that this small change makes any difference in the likelihood that one of the program's participants will commit a date rape. To address these types of practical issues, Jacobson, Follette, and Revenstorf (1984) and Jacobson and Truax (1991) introduced methods for calculating clinical significance.

As defined by Jacobson and Truax (1991), *clinical significance* is the degree to which an individual client improves after treatment. Two criteria are used to define improvement or recovery for a particular client. First, to be labeled as recovered, a participant's posttest score on a particular measure (for example, Inventory of Interpersonal Problems) must fall within a functional (as opposed to a dysfunctional) distribution of scores, given that the participant's pretest score on the particular measure fell within a dysfunctional distribution of scores. The second criterion for determining improvement is labeled the *reliable change index,* in which the pretest to posttest difference observed for a client is greater than the change that would be expected due to chance alone. The formula used to calculate the reliable change index is:

$$(\text{Pretest} - \text{Posttest})/\text{Standard Error of Measurement}$$

A score greater than 1 on this index indicates that there was more change from pretest to posttest than the measurement error in the instrument. Using these criteria, an individual participant in a treatment study is considered to have improved if her or his posttest score is in the functional distribution and her or his reliable change index is greater than 1. In a study calculating clinical significance for a treatment group versus control group design, the researcher would compare the percentage of participants in the treatment group who had improved versus the percentage of participants in the control group who had improved.

Paivio and Greenberg (1995) used the two criteria proposed by Jacobson and Truax (1991) when examining the effects of "the empty chair" on resolving "unfinished business." Thirty-four clients completed either 12 weeks of counseling using the empty-chair technique or an attention-placebo minimal treatment condition. Although several measures in the outcome battery were used in this research, only the SCL-90-R (Derogatis, 1983) and the Inventory of Interpersonal Problems (Horowitz, Rosenberg, Baer, Ureno, & Villasenor, 1988) were used in calculating clinically significant change. Paivio and Greenberg averaged the SCL-90-R and the Inventory of Interpersonal Problems scores in their calculation of clinically significant change. Using normative information, Paivio and Greenberg determined that before treatment, 44% of their clients in both experimental conditions were in the functional distribution of SCL-90-R and Inventory of Interpersonal Problems scores. After treatment, however, 89% of the clients receiving 12 weeks of counseling using the empty-chair technique were in the functional distribution, whereas only 59% of the clients in the attention-placebo minimal treatment condition were in this distribution. The improvement rate for the counseling using the empty-chair technique was 45% (89% at posttest – 44% at pretest), whereas the improvement rate for the attention-placebo minimal treatment condition was only 15% (59% at posttest – 44% at pretest). In terms of the reliable change index, 73% of the clients in the counseling using the empty-chair technique had a reliable change index greater than 1, but only 10% of the clients in the attention-placebo minimal treatment condition had reliable change indexes greater than 1. These results led Paivio and Greenberg to conclude that the counseling using the empty-chair technique resulted in clinically significant changes in client unfinished business.

Tingey, Lambert, Burlingame, and Hansen (1996) presented an extension of Jacobson and colleagues' method for calculating clinically significant change.

At the heart of this new method is an expanded definition: Tingey et al. defined clinically significant change as "movement from one socially relevant sample to another based on the impact factor selected, rather than (moving) from a 'dysfunctional' to a 'functional' distribution as proposed by Jacobson and Revenstorf (1988)" (p. 111). Tingey et al. proposed that multiple samples be used to form a continuum, and that a client's pretest-posttest movement (or lack of movement) along this continuum be used to identify clinically significant change.

According to Tingey et al. (1996), five steps are involved in establishing such a continuum:

> 1) selecting a specifying factor that is defined by a reliable outcome instrument; 2) identifying an impact factor (a behavior relevant to society that covaries with different levels of the specifying factor); 3) determining the statistical distinctiveness of these socially relevant samples; 4) calculating RCI's (Reliable Change Indices) for all possible sample pairs; and 5) calculating cutoff points between adjacent sample pairs along the continuum. (Tingey et al., 1996, p. 114)

For example, for step 1, Tingey et al. used the SCL-90-R (Derogatis, 1983) as the specifying factor. According to these authors, one important factor related to the SCL-90-R is the type of psychological treatment a person receives, because more symptomatic clients generally receive more intensive treatment (e.g., inpatient versus outpatient services). Consequently, for step 2 they identified four samples of people who differed in the intensity of psychological treatment they were receiving: (1) asymptomatic (a specially collected healthy sample), (2) mildly symptomatic (unscreened community adults), (3) moderately symptomatic (people receiving outpatient counseling), and (4) severely symptomatic (people receiving inpatient counseling). Next, for step 3, Tingey et al. utilized t and d tests to ascertain whether the four identified samples were in fact distinct. In this example, their tests showed the four samples to be distinct. RCIs were calculated for the 10 possible pairs of samples (step 4). Finally, the authors established cut points and confidence intervals for each pair of adjacent samples (step 5); these cutoff points represent the point at which a score is more likely to be in one distribution as opposed to the adjacent distribution.

One of the most exciting features of Tingey et al.'s (1996) approach is that any researcher who uses the SCL-90-R as a pretest-posttest measure can use the information provided in the article to calculate the amount of clinically significant change for each individual client in her or his study. In addition, clinicians can use the information to ascertain whether their clients are making clinically significant change. To illustrate the usefulness of Tingey et al.'s calculations, Figure 18.1 both illustrates the cutoff points identified in the article and plots the pretest-posttest changes for two clients involved in the Missouri Psychoanalytic Psychotherapy Research Project (Patton, Kivlighan, & Multon, 1997). In this project, community clients seen for 20 sessions of psychoanalytically oriented counseling were given an extensive battery of tests prior to and upon completion of counseling; one of these measures was the

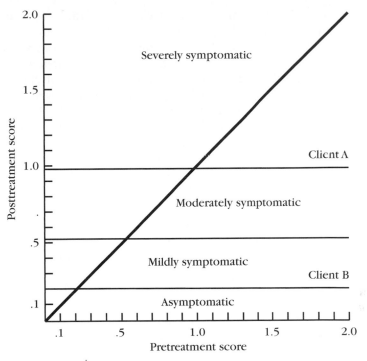

FIGURE 18.1 | CUT-OFFS BETWEEN THE NORMATIVE SAMPLES (HORIZONTAL LINES). DIAGONAL REPRESENTS POINT OF NO PRE- AND POST-TREATMENT CHANGE

SCL-90-R. As can be seen in the figure, Client A made a substantial and clinically significant improvement, as indicated by movement from the severely symptomatic distribution at pretest to the asymptomatic distribution at posttest. By contrast, Client B, who both began and ended treatment in the moderately symptomatic range, exhibited no clinically significant change.

Lambert and his colleagues (Condon & Lambert, 1994; Grundy & Lambert, 1994b; Seggar & Lambert, 1994) have used this method of defining clinical significance with several other well-validated psychometric instruments (State-Trait Anxiety Inventory, Auchenbach Child Behavior Checklist, and Beck Depression Inventory). However, an attempt to define clinically significant change groups for the Hamilton Rating Scale for Depression was unsuccessful because the authors could not find appropriate samples (Grundy & Lambert, 1994a). Even though the method described by Tingey et al. (1996) is an exciting extension of Jacobson et al.'s (1984) methodology, for the most part the instruments used are not commonly used in counseling outcome research. It would be interesting to examine this method with instruments such as the Career Beliefs Inventory (Krumboltz, 1991) or the Rosenberg Self Esteem Scale (Rosenberg, 1965).

The idea of calculating clinically significant change is very appealing. Clearly, counseling researchers would like to know that their treatment interventions are making a real difference. Even though it would be very useful if the profession had a specified standard for determining the clinical significance of a study's results, the measurement of clinical significance has not been widely embraced by counseling researchers. Few studies published in counseling-related journals have yet provided calculations of statistically significant change, perhaps because this method is not without psychometric problems. In order to determine whether a score is in a functional or a dysfunctional distribution, the researcher must have good psychometric information about a test. At the very least, the test must have been administered to one population clinically defined as dysfunctional, and to another clinically defined as normal. For more sophisticated analyses of clinical change, several different population groups must be identified. For example, Tingey et al. (1996) identified four different samples (asymptomatic, and mildly, moderately, and severely disturbed on the SCL-90-R) in their analysis of clinically significant change.

Unfortunately, for many measures used in psychotherapy outcome research, this type of normative data is not readily available. Even when a measure has been used with different samples, the adequacy of the sampling procedure is often questionable.

Therefore, a great deal of additional psychometric work must be done before the assessment of clinical significance can become a standard practice in most counseling outcome studies. Nonetheless, we contend that calculations of the clinical significance of change should be used more widely than currently occurs in counseling research. For example, the population of students that seeks help at a career counseling center is probably more undecided about a career than a population of students in general; although not labeled as dysfunctional, the career center population is one normative group that could be used in a study examining the clinical significance of a career exploration intervention.

MEASURING OUTCOMES AND CHANGE   Measuring outcome and estimating change over the course of therapy involve tricky issues that statisticians and methodologists have struggled to address. Often, strategic choices make little difference, but there are instances when adoption of a certain statistical model can drastically influence the conclusions that are made about psychotherapy (see, e.g., Elkin, Falconnier, Martinovich, & Mahoney, 2006; Kim, Wampold, & Bolt, 2006; Wampold & Bolt, 2006, for an example of debates about models and the conclusions they produce). Thus, great care must be taken in choosing statistical models, and the researcher should be familiar enough with the data to ensure that results are indeed reflections of the data and not artifacts from inappropriate statistical models. In this section, we briefly review several options.

The simplest method, and a logically defensible one, of measuring the outcome of any of the designs discussed in this chapter is to use only the posttest measure and perform some type of analysis of variance on these measures to test the omnibus hypothesis that the groups vary on the posttest. If clients were randomly assigned to treatment groups and/or controls, and the experiment was well designed in other respects, then differences among groups at the posttest are due either to the treatment or to random sources (i.e., error variance). The analysis of variance results in a test of the null hypothesis that is valid. If the null is rejected, and, say, it is concluded that Treatment A is superior to Treatment B and alpha was set at 0.05, then there are less than 5 chances out of 100 that differences as large as those observed were due to chance. In a no treatment comparison, if client outcomes at posttest of Treatment A are found to exceed the outcomes of clients receiving no treatment (e.g., a wait-list control) at the 0.05 level, then it can be concluded that Treatment A provides some benefits to the clients vis-à-vis the natural course of the disorder.

Using posttest scores often raises the (uninformed) objection that it is impossible to know whether patients improved over the course of therapy. The superiority of Treatment A over a no-treatment control group may be due to the fact that the clients in Treatment A, as a group, displayed no change (posttest scores would have been equal to the pretest scores, had they been assessed) but that those in the no-treatment group deteriorated. Some would claim that the posttest-only design cannot detect this pattern of results and thus one cannot determine whether Treatment A actually helped clients. Two points need to be made here. First, the question being tested is not whether clients improve with Treatment A, but whether clients receiving treatment are better off than patients who do not receive treatment (i.e., compared to the natural course of the disorder without treatment). It may well be that clients with this disorder would deteriorate without treatment and that treatment is successful because it prevents deterioration. The second point is that interpretation of pre- to posttest scores, had they been collected, is difficult because they are subject to many threats, including maturation, history, and regression toward the mean (see Chapter 5). Observed client improvement from pre- to posttest may be due entirely to regression artifacts because their scores were initially severe. Consequently, care must always be taken when attributing pre- to posttest changes to the treatment. Indeed, this is the very reason that no-treatment controls are used—it is the comparison of treatment to the natural history controls that permits inferences about the effects of a treatment.

Notwithstanding the discussion about not logically needing a pretest score, there are several reasons for collecting a pretest score (again, see Chapter 7). First, the pretest score is often used to make decisions about inclusion (i.e., is the score above the cutoff for this disorder). Second, the pretest score is typically correlated with the posttest score (i.e., much of the variance in the final score of any participant is accounted for by the pretest score), and thus the pretest score can be used in a way that increases the power of the statistical test by reducing unexplained variance (i.e., error variance). Third, despite the problems with interpreting pre- to posttest scores, as a descriptive statistic, it can be useful to have an indication of the progress of clients. For these reasons, outcome studies typically involve collection of pretest scores.

The pretest score can be used in several ways for the analysis of data obtained in outcome studies. First, the pretest score can be used as a covariate in an analysis of covariance. Second, change scores can be calculated and an analysis of variance conducted on the change score. Third, the pretest score can be used to calculate a residualized change score. A description of the statistical theory that forms the bases of these three methods and the relative advantages and disadvantages of the methods is beyond the scope of this text (see Keller, 2004; Willett, 1997; Willett & Sayer, 1994).

The most stringent method with which to measure client progress in any intervention is to collect data over time. Measuring client functioning solely at pretest and posttest restricts knowledge of client functioning to two points—at the beginning of therapy and at the end of therapy. More sophisticated methods, often called growth curve modeling, can be used to investigate therapeutic effects if multiple measurements across the course of therapy are collected. For example, Doss, Thum, Sevier, Atkins, and Christensen (2005) were interested in the mechanisms of change that lead to response in two forms of couple's therapy (traditional vs. integrative couple's therapy). In order to do so they assessed both measures of relationship satisfaction, communication, behavioral change, and emotional acceptance four times throughout the course of therapy. The authors found that change in relationship satisfaction during the first half of both therapies was related to both emotional acceptance and behavior change, but that during the second half of treatment acceptance remained important while changes in behavior became less critical.

Statistical methods that use multiple measurements are able to estimate the rate and nature of change rather than simply estimating the amount of change, increase the power of statistical tests, handle missing data points, and model other important aspects of therapy (such as therapist effects—see the following section). However, these methods are complicated and can obscure relatively obvious conclusions. Interested readers should consult Raudenbush and Bryk (2002) and Snijders and Bosker (1999).

THERAPIST EFFECTS   Recently, Wampold and Bhati (2004) examined the history of psychotherapy and clinical trials and noted that many important aspects of psychotherapy have been omitted in current theory and research. One of the important omissions is the therapist. Because the randomized control group design was originally used in the fields of education, agriculture, and medicine, the provider of service was thought to be unimportant. Education was interested in which programs were effective; relatively unimportant were the teachers, primarily women, who were thought to be interchangeable. Agriculture was focused on fertilizers, seed varieties, and irrigation and not on the farmer. Finally, medicine, attempting to distance itself from charismatic healers such as Mesmer, emphasized the potency of medicines and purposefully ignored physician effects. Psychotherapy research, borrowing the randomized design, similarly ignored the provider of service—that is, the therapists. Indeed, apparently there are no clinical trials of psychotherapy that have considered therapist effects in the primary analyses of the data (Wampold & Bhati, 2004).

Unfortunately, ignoring therapists (or groups in group-based treatments; see Baldwin, Murray, & Shadish, 2005) has deleterious effects on conclusions that are made in outcome research (see Wampold, 2001, for an extensive discussion of these issues).

The essential issue with regard to therapist effects is that it seems reasonable to believe that therapists vary in the outcomes they attain with clients. That is to say, some therapists may consistently produce better outcomes with their clients than do others. Indeed, it appears that this is true. Based on re-analyses of existing data sets and analyses of outcomes in practice settings, it appears that between 5% and 8% of the variance in outcomes is due to therapists (Kim, Wampold, & Bolt, 2006; Wampold, 2001; Wampold & Brown, 2005), which when compared to other sources of variability in outcomes, including what treatment the client receives, is extraordinarily large (e.g., the particular treatment that is administered accounts for less than 1%; Wampold, 2001). This variability also appears to extend to psychiatrists in pharmacotherapy trials (McKay, Imel, & Wampold, 2006). Therapist variability suggests a new definition of competence: Competent therapists are therapists who produce better than average outcomes. This definition stands in contrast to that discussed earlier, which involved ratings of competence by observers.

There are two reasons to examine therapist effects in any study of counseling interventions. The first reason is rather obvious—therapist effects are interesting and informative in their own right. If much of the variability in outcomes in a study is explained by differences among therapists, then it can be concluded that the therapist is an important factor—this is particularly interesting when therapist effects are much larger than treatment effects and as large as any other effects, such as the alliance (see Norcross, Beutler, & Levant, 2006; see also Chapter 5). The second reason to examine therapist effects in any treatment study is that ignoring therapist effects inflates estimates of treatment effects (Wampold, 2001; Wampold & Serlin, 2000). Essentially, in analysis of variance, the estimate of between group variability is due in part to therapist effects as well as treatment effects (see Wampold & Serlin). Conceptually this makes sense—if therapists indeed are an important determinant of outcomes, then the choice of therapists for a treatment in a particular study will determine, in part, the outcomes produced. Suppose that therapists are randomly selected to administer Treatment A and Treatment B and suppose, by chance, that the therapists chosen to deliver Treatment A were superior to those chosen to deliver Treatment B; then it will appear that Treatment A is superior to Treatment B even if the two treatments are equally effective. This is not an easy phenomenon to grasp (similar in that respect to regression toward the mean) but it is extremely important. If therapist effects are present and ignored, then the likelihood that a researcher will falsely conclude that a treatment is more effective than another is relatively large, and any estimate of treatment differences will be inflated. The size of those errors are presented and discussed by Wampold and Serlin (2000).

In comparative treatment studies, two designs are possible: crossed and nested. In the crossed design, therapists deliver all treatments. The crossed design has the advantage that the general skill of the therapist is balanced. However, problems arise if the therapists have more allegiance to or skill in delivering one of the treatments. In the nested design, therapists deliver one of the treatments only (i.e., the therapists are nested within treatment). Ideally, the therapists delivering a particular treatment would have allegiance to and skill in delivering the respective treatment and allegiance and skill would be balanced. A commendable effort to balance allegiance and skill was shown by Watson et al. (2003), who compared cognitive behavioral treatment and process experiential treatment for depression. The therapists for each treatment were adherents to their respective treatment and then were trained by internationally recognized experts in this treatment.

Appropriately including therapists in the design and analysis of outcome research is more complex than simply ignoring therapists. However, the extra effort is needed to correctly estimate treatment effects, and it has the potential to detect therapist effects should they exist. Generally it is recommended that therapists be considered a random factor in the model; that is, therapists are assumed to be randomly selected from the population of therapists. Of course this is rarely done, but the issues are comparable to the ones created by the fact that we do not randomly select study participants from a population of participants (see Chapter 8 and Serlin, Wampold, & Levin, 2003). In the nested design, the analysis would be a mixed model in which the treatments are considered to be fixed (i.e., not drawn from a population of treatments) and the therapists are a random factor (Wampold & Serlin, 2000). In a balanced design, the analysis would be a relatively simple mixed model analysis of variance; when the number of clients per therapist and the number of therapists per treatment varies, it is recommended that a multilevel model (sometimes called a hierarchical linear model) analysis be conducted (Raudenbush & Bryk, 2002; Snijders & Bosker, 1999).

SUMMARY AND CONCLUSIONS

Counseling researchers often address questions related to counseling outcome. This chapter described several different strategies for addressing outcome questions and provided counseling examples for each. Each strategy answers a different research question; researchers are advised to select the strategy that is appropriate to the goals of the investigation. In addition, a number of methodological issues important for researchers planning a counseling outcome study were discussed. These issues, which involve inclusion and exclusion criteria, treatment integrity, measuring outcomes and change, and therapist effects, have to be considered so that valid conclusions are made from outcome research.

A chapter on outcome research was included in this book because of its importance in answering questions that are central to the field of counseling: Are the interventions we use more effective than no treatment? Are some treatments more effective than other treatments? Are some treatments more effective with certain clients under certain circumstances? Are the benefits of treatments due to the specific therapeutic ingredients? Although there are complex issues involved in outcome research, such research must be undertaken and undertaken well to answer these questions.

STIMULUS QUESTIONS

THREE EXERCISES TO ENHANCE STUDENTS' UNDERSTANDING OF OUTCOME RESEARCH

1. Suppose that you have developed a new treatment for a particular disorder or problem. Discuss how you would design a series of outcome studies to establish that this treatment is the treatment of choice. What steps would need to be taken before the first study was undertaken? What precautions would need to be instituted to protect the research from threats to validity?

2. Find three outcome studies. Describe the design of each and classify them into one of the types of outcome research discussed in this chapter. Discuss the degree to which each study handled the issues presented in this chapter appropriately.

3. Find several outcome studies and discuss how allegiance was handled in each study.

DESIGN ISSUES RELATED TO COUNSELING PROCESS RESEARCH

Every therapist, regardless of level of experience, has reflected on what happens in the course of therapy. Beginning therapists often ask supervisors about ways of establishing a working alliance, how to confront clients, or how to use various counseling interventions, such as the Gestalt empty chair technique. Is it OK to touch the client? Does touching a client help or hinder the counseling process? After considerable experience, therapists realize that all clients are not alike, and that it is important to consider, for example, how to establish a working alliance with very different clients. All these counseling topics reflect on aspects of the counseling process in some way and have been the focus of considerable research. This type of counseling research is often considered to be "relevant," "meaningful," and "useful" as the researcher finds "what works" in therapy. Such research can be exciting, as the researcher discovers relationships among variables related to the counseling process.

This chapter provides a general introduction to counseling process research and then discusses issues pertaining to some of the major design issues related to counseling process research. Process research is not a category of research design per se; rather, it is a specific area of focus within counseling research. Moreover, a variety of research designs are used to conduct process research, including descriptive, intensive single-subject, within-subjects, and between-subjects designs.

There are three major sections to this chapter. In the first section we define process research in general terms; then we provide a brief overview of

The second process study published in Volume 1 of *JCP* involved an examination of counselor directiveness. Danskin and Robinson (1954) examined counselor directiveness by rating the amount of "lead" in a counselor statement. They defined "lead" as (1) "the extent to which the content of the counselor's remark seems to be ahead of the content of the client's last remark," and (2) "the degree of pressure or definiteness in the counselor's remark that is apparently used to bring about client acceptance of the expressed idea" (p. 79).

Danskin and Robinson's (1954) major finding was that counselor lead was related to the type of problem being discussed. They found that the counselor used more leading statements with clients who had a "skills" problem than with clients who had an "adjustment" problem. This focus on counselor lead bears some similarity to Tracey's research, which examined control in individual counseling (see, for example, Tracey & Ray, 1984).

A third study (Berg, 1954) examined differences between two groups of clients (those whose presenting problems either were or were not sexually related) in nonverbal behavior displayed during counseling interviews. Based on psychoanalytic theory, Berg tabulated the following classes of gestures, which were thought to represent sexual symbolism: rotating and sliding, clasping or wrapping, insertion, pressing, and licking and biting. Although the categories of coding nonverbal behavior seem quite different today, there is still a continuity of this line of research (see, for example, Hill & Stephany, 1990). Berg found, contrary to his hypothesis, that both groups of clients made a relatively high number of sexually suggestive gestures. Thus, the content or the presenting concern bore little relationship to the type or number of nonverbal gestures exhibited.

There are important differences between these early studies and more recent process research. Two of the most striking differences involve the emphasis on content in the counseling interview and the link between process and outcome. In two of the studies from Volume 1 of *JCP*, the content of the counseling interview was an important defining variable. As mentioned earlier, Dipboye (1954) categorized segments of counseling interviews as representing one of six content categories. Likewise, Danskin and Robinson (1954) used four categories to classify the content of their counseling interviews. Such emphasis on content is representative of the focus that content received in much of the early research, but content has been almost completely neglected in more recent process research (see reviews by Highlen & Hill, 1984; Hill, 1982; Parloff, Waskow, & Wolfe, 1978).

A second point of discontinuity concerns the process–outcome link. Early counseling research tended to focus solely on either client outcome or counseling process; none of the early studies reviewed attempted to link the process variables with some measure of outcome. For example, Danskin and Robinson (1954) did not know whether more-leading interviews were more productive than less-leading interviews in addressing skill problems. Within the last 25 years, however, studies have emphasized linking process to outcome (see Highlen & Hill, 1984; Holloway, Wampold, & Nelson, 1990; Orlinsky & Howard, 1978; Orlinsky et al., 1994, 2004; Wampold & Kim, 1989).

For example, Wampold and Kim related patterns of client interaction to evaluations of sessions made by counselor, client, and observers.

Two conceptual systems established in early process research remain subjects of current research. F. P. Robinson's book *Principles and Procedures in Student Counseling* (1950) had a seminal influence on early process research. In addition to his emphasis on session content, Robinson also devised a system of classifying counseling behavior based on the concept of counselor roles and subroles. This concept is still the basis for category systems used to classify counselor actions. The second conceptual system that influenced early process research was T. Leary's (1957) system of interpersonal diagnosis. Unlike Robinson's ideas, which led to the classification of counselor behavior in terms of actions or response modes, Leary's system classified counselor behavior in terms of its interpersonal style. W. J. Mueller (1969) used the Leary system to study the manifestation of transference and countertransference in counseling interviews. Researchers continue to apply Leary's system in examining client and counselor interpersonal style (see, for example, Strong et al., 1988).

Even though several studies conducted in the 1950s could be classified as counseling process research, Carl Rogers's (1957) formulation of the necessary and sufficient conditions for positive therapeutic change probably served as the major stimulus for much of the process research in the 1960s and 1970s (Toukmanian & Rennie, 1992). Rogers identified what he believed to be the core therapeutic conditions, which in essence were largely process variables, such as therapist empathy and unconditional positive regard. The large volume of process and outcome research that followed empirically tested Rogers's postulations. Although the research initially supported Rogers's ideas, subsequent research revealed that the effective elements of therapeutic change are more complex than he first postulated (see reviews by Orlinsky & Howard, 1978; Orlinsky et al., 1994, 2004; Parloff et al., 1978).

SOME CURRENT RESEARCH FINDINGS

The individual counseling process literature is vast. Orlinsky et al. (1994) counted more than 2,300 process and outcome studies from 1950 to 1992. Moreover, over half of these studies appeared in the literature in the final 7 years of that time frame. Process research has continued to flourish since 1992. In a subsequent review, Orlinsky et al. (2004) found an additional 279 new studies. Detailed reviews of the counseling process literature can be found in Orlinsky and Howard (1978) and Orlinsky et al. (1994, 2004). To date, the research evidence suggests a strong relationship between the following process variables and positive therapeutic outcomes: the overall quality of the therapeutic relationship, therapist skill, client cooperation versus resistance, client openness versus defensiveness, and treatment duration (Orlinsky et al., 1994, 2004).

Counseling process research has also been expanded to incorporate race and cultural factors, and has been applied to contexts other than individual counseling (see Zane, Hall, Sue, Young, & Nunez, 2004). Even though theorists have suggested for some time that race and cultural factors affect the dynamics of the counseling process (e.g., Helms, 1990; Sue & Sue, 1990; Vontress, 1970), relatively few empirical studies have been conducted on racial and cultural factors in the therapy process (Helms, 1994). Some early research suggested that black clients report lower levels of rapport with white counselors than with black counselors (see Atkinson, 1983), although subsequent research suggested that other variables, such as attention to cultural issues, similar values, attitudes, and personalities, also are important variables affecting client reactions (e.g., Atkinson & Lowe, 1995; Thompson, Worthington, & Atkinson, 1994; Zane et al., 2004). Ridley, Mendoza, Kanitz, Angermeier, and Zenk (1994) provided an excellent conceptualization integrating race and cultural factors (particularly cultural sensitivity) into the counseling process by focusing on the cognitive schema of counselors. Some useful resources for beginning process researchers interested in racial and cultural factors in counseling are Chapter 15 as well as Atkinson and Lowe; Grieger and Ponterotto (1995); Leong, Wagner, and Tata (1995); Ponterotto and Casas (1991); Ponterotto, Fuertes, and Chen (2000); Ponterotto and Grieger, in press; Ridley et al. (1994); Sue, Zane, and Young (1994); Thompson et al. (1994); and Zane et al. Clearly, race and cultural factors are important topics in process research and merit additional attention.

Although process research in psychotherapy has a long history and much has been learned about process variables that contribute to effective outcome, the specialty of career counseling has not had a focus on the examination of process variables. As Swanson (1995) commented: "Although we know a great deal about the effectiveness of career interventions in general, we know considerably less about career counseling specifically, and further, we know almost nothing about the career counseling process" (p. 217). M. Heppner and Heppner (2003) published a research agenda for career counseling process research in which they identify 10 avenues for future investigations in this area. In the article they review some of the areas that have led to the richest information in psychotherapy process research and discuss possible applications to career counseling.

When process research has been conducted in the area of career counseling, researchers have discovered both similarities and differences with psychotherapy processes. For example Kirschner, Hoffman, and Hill (1994) found that, similar to psychotherapy research, when counselors used challenge and in-sight it was most helpful. Other research indicates that psychotherapy and ca-reer counseling verbal responses were similar and tended to be active, directive, and focused on problem solving (Nagel, Hoffman, & Hill, 1995). Conversely, in their career counseling study, Multon, Ellis-Kalton, M. Heppner, and Gysbers (2003) found that self-disclosure, which has been found to be helpful to building the relationship in psychotherapy, was actually negatively related to the working alliance. On closer examination it appears it might be the type of self-disclosure used that accounted for these contrasting findings.

Similarities and contrasts have also been found between career counseling and psychotherapy process research regarding the importance of the working alliance. In psychotherapy process research more than 26% of the outcome variance can be accounted for by the working alliance, making it a highly important variable for successful psychotherapy. Some studies in the career area have found that career clients also perceive the alliance to be important (M. Heppner & Hendricks, 1995); when counselors provided support, it was viewed as one of the most helpful client intentions (Kirschner et al., 1994), and the quality of the counseling relationship was the same in both career and personal counseling (Lewis, 2001). However, other studies have indicated that although the working alliance did grow stronger over the course of counseling, that growth was either unrelated to outcome or when it did account for outcome variance, the amount of variance accounted for was much smaller (1–12%) than in psychotherapy (M. Heppner, Multon, Gysbers, Ellis, & Zook, 1998).

Thus, the area of career counseling process research is one that has great potential for future research. The few studies that have been conducted indicated both similarities and differences with psychotherapy process research. Understanding not only that change has happened, but also how change occurs will help practitioners target interventions for particular clients.

DESIGN ISSUES IN PROCESS RESEARCH

It is important to reiterate that process research is not a category of research design. One does not speak of using a counseling process design because process research is a specific area of focus within counseling research.

Many of the methodological considerations pertaining to the selection of the research topic (see Chapter 3), independent or predictor variables (Chapter 12), dependent or criterion variables (Chapter 13), population issues (Chapter 14), multicultural competence issues (Chapter 15), and experimenter/participant bias (Chapter 16) apply to conducting counseling process research. Before 1980, the most common methodologies used in process research were experimental analogues and descriptive. However, between 1984 and 1998, the methodologies expanded to include discovery-oriented, task analysis, and qualitative approaches (Hill & Williams, 2000). As the qualitative methods have evolved and gained greater acceptance in counseling psychology, more process studies have appeared in counseling journals (Hill & Lambert, 2004). (See Chapter 11 for more details on various qualitative methods.)

In this section we highlight several methodological and measurement issues of relevance to researchers interested in conducting counseling process research. We start by discussing the initial development of the research question(s) and hypotheses. We then focus on several major methodological issues that typically face the process researcher: What to study and in what context? What to measure? Whose perspective? How much to measure? How to code and analyze the process data?

Although counseling process research can be very exciting, it can also be tedious, and the number of methodological details and the volume of data can be overwhelming. It is not uncommon for beginning students to change research topics after beginning a process study. Beginning researchers may have the misperception that because process research can be relevant and exciting, it will also be easy. The many details and the complexity can translate into more opportunities for problems to arise. Hill (1992) recommended that beginning process researchers become apprentices to an experienced process researcher to facilitate learning the methodological skills needed to conduct process research. Being a part of a research team is another way of making the demands more manageable while learning about the complexity of the methodological issues.

Getting Started: What to Study and in What Context?

One of the first steps is to choose the general topic or focus of the process research (see Chapter 3). Hill (1982) has underscored the importance of developing a good research question and hypothesis:

> This has been a particularly difficult problem in the process area, perhaps because of the overwhelming nature of the multitude of variables in counseling which can be examined. What seems to have happened in the past is that researchers have responded with a flight into detail, creating an obsessive's nightmare for themselves and their readers. Researchers tend to painstakingly describe, categorize, and develop measures but rarely are these put into a context of what they mean for counseling or theory. Further, there has been a tendency to study easy variables that can be measured reliably because of clear operational definitions rather than those which might have more clinical relevance. (Hill, 1982, p. 10)

Thus, given the complexity of the counseling process, it is important to clearly identify a specific research question(s) and subsequent hypotheses. It is common for researchers to develop research ideas as they engage in actual counseling, perhaps by reviewing a tape of a counseling session, or in discussions with a supervisor or supervisee. It is critical to go well beyond the initial identification of the idea and to spend considerable time reviewing relevant literature (see Chapter 3). Hill (1992) recommended "writing a complete proposal of the research project including the data analyses, even if it is not a thesis or dissertation" (p. 90) at this early stage; although such a process may seem tedious, the act of writing typically facilitates the process of identifying the topic, operationalizing variables, and thinking through procedural details.

An equally important issue pertains to the context or setting in which the study is to be conducted; typically, researchers decide to what degree the study will be conducted in a naturalistic setting or in an analogue setting (see Hill, 1982, 1992). This issue basically concerns the levels of internal and external validity that the researcher deems most important to best answer the relevant research questions. If the researcher wants a great deal of internal validity (and typically to be able to manipulate one or more independent variables), an analogue setting might be advisable (see Chapter 17). However, if external validity (or generalizability) is very important, then a study conducted in more of a naturalistic setting may be advisable. The decision between an analogue and a naturalistic setting is not a categorical either/or decision, but rather one that involves a continuum. Some analogue designs emphasize internal validity more than others (see Chapter 17), and some naturalistic designs incorporate analogue methods to create quasi-naturalistic settings (see Chapter 8). In the final analysis, the decision regarding the type of context or setting is thus a matter of the degree to which the research will be conducted in a context that maximizes either internal or external validity.

Another key design issue is whether to use a quantitative or qualitative approach (see Chapters 10 and 11). It is critical to carefully contemplate both the type of research questions of interest and the type of data that will best answer those questions at this time. For example, despite an abundant literature on reducing client resistance, there has been very little research on either willingness to work through interpersonal difficulties in family therapy or a family's level of engagement/disengagement. Because of the lack of empirical data, Friedlander et al. (1994) used a qualitative, discovery-oriented approach to examine events related to successful, sustained engagement in family therapy. Moreover, they were able to develop a conceptual model of successful, sustained engagement based on their qualitative analysis. Researchers are encouraged not to dichotomize their research approach as either quantitative or qualitative, but to integrate these approaches into their research to provide the most informative data possible (see, for example, Cummings, Martin, Halberg, & Slemon, 1992).

What to Measure?

Once a general research topic has been identified, a subsequent issue concerns the aspect of the counseling process to examine. At the most basic level, researchers must decide whether they want to examine aspects of the individual participants' behaviors or aspects of the developing relationship or system. Process research focuses on either a participant (counselor or client), the relationship, or some combination thereof. Indeed, some of the most common activities examined in process research are therapist techniques, client behaviors, and the therapeutic interaction. In group and family counseling, the clients are obviously multiple individuals, and the counselor dimension often involves a measurement of the activities of co-counselors. In individual counseling, the relationship involves how the client and counselor work together. In group and family process research, this relationship dimension is usually referred to as the group (cohesion, norms) or family (closeness, involvement) process. We will discuss issues pertaining to what to measure specifically with regard to individual participants and the client–counselor relationship.

Suppose that a researcher, Dr. B. Famous, decides to conduct a process study that examines the counselor's behavior. But there are many counselor behaviors: what the counselor said, how the counselor said it (for example, emphatically or angrily), how often the counselor said it, when the counselor said it, and so on. So the insightful Dr. Famous knows it is necessary to consider specific types of counselor behaviors that might be examined. Elliott's

(1991) four focal points of the communication process—content (what is said), action (what is done), style (how it is said or done), and quality (how well it is said or done)—could be used to clarify the focus of the Famous study of "counselor behaviors." Likewise, Hill's (1991) classification scheme (described earlier in this chapter) could be used to think about "what type of behaviors" Dr. Famous might want to examine.

Suppose as well that Dr. Famous was especially keenly interested in counselor intentions; how might she measure that? One strategy might be to make some type of measurement after each counselor statement, but such a measurement would involve many "microscopic" assessments for each interview hour. Another strategy might be to ask counselors to reflect on their overall intentions during a counseling session, which would be a more global type of assessment.

In essence, process researchers must decide at what level they are going to measure the aspects of the process. Greenberg (1986a) suggested that three levels of analysis be used in examining the counseling process: speech acts, episodes, and the relationship. In counseling process research, *speech acts* refers to the microanalysis of statement-by-statement transactions, *episodes* refers to a coherent thematic section of counseling, and the *relationship* refers to the ongoing counselor–client relationship over multiple sessions. Greenberg nicely elucidated the need to examine the notion of different levels of measurement within process research, from the microscopic (statement-by-statement) to the more global or general. He also suggested that process measurements be context-sensitive, such as within a relationship. Interested readers wanting to learn more about past research that has examined different levels of analysis might read reviews of the process literature, such as Hill and Williams (2000) and Hill and Lambert (2004).

WHOSE PERSPECTIVE?

Another major question that process researchers must address is: From whose perspective should the counseling process be evaluated? A considerable amount of evidence suggests that client, counselor, and observer perspectives on the counseling process may offer quite diverse views of what happens in counseling (see Eugster & Wampold, 1996; Lambert, DeJulio, & Stein, 1978; Wampold & Poulin, 1992). For example, Dill-Standifond, Stiles, and Rorer (1988) found that clients and counselors had very different views of session impact (in terms of depth, smoothness, positivity, and arousal).

In part, differences and similarities across perspectives may be related to the type of rating used. For example, Lambert et al. (1978) found only minimal relationships among ratings of facilitative conditions across the three perspectives. Likewise, Gurman (1977) found that client ratings of empathy were positively related to therapy outcome, but ratings from outside observers were not related to outcome. Other research reveals little difference between, for example, client and counselor perspectives on the rating of therapist behavior (Carkhuff & Burstein, 1970). Eugster and Wampold (1996) found that regression equations predicting session evaluation from process variables were significantly different for clients and therapists. Likewise, supervisors and supervisees typically differ when asked to rate the frequency of various supervisor behaviors (see, for example, Heppner & Roehlke, 1984).

Different relationships among the three perspectives have been found in research that has examined the working alliance. For example, a study by Tichenor and Hill (1989) suggested that clients, counselors, and observers have different views of the working relationship (correlations among the three perspectives averaged $r = -.02$). Other research, however, found that both client and counselor (Horvath & Greenberg, 1989) and observer (Marmar, Marziali, Horowitz, & Weiss, 1986) ratings of the working alliance are related to client outcome, suggesting that even though different perspectives of the working alliance may measure different constructs, each of them is important.

Less discrepancy among raters from the three perspectives may occur when concrete and observable behaviors are assessed. The more subjective the process variable is (especially if the assessment pertains to the raters' perceptions of conditions), the greater the difference among various raters is likely to be. When researchers want to examine more subjective process variables, they should obtain ratings from multiple perspectives. In this way, researchers can empirically examine the degree of relationship among the perspectives on the particular variable of interest and determine if the different perspectives add useful information. Put another way, the combination of client, counselor, and observer perspectives on, say, the working alliance may be a better predictor of counseling outcome than any single perspective.

Clearly, research reveals differences in the ratings obtained from counselors, clients, or outside observers. Moreover, the correlation among the three perspectives on various measures is often minimal (Hill & Lambert, 2004; Lambert & Hill, 1994). Thus, the decision from whose perspective to assess the counseling process has major effects on the results of and the conclusions that can be drawn from a study. We encourage researchers to think carefully about the different perspectives when they are developing their research questions. Some research topics might dictate the perspective the researcher decides to examine. For example, a great deal of attention has been focused on the nature of client memories of child sexual abuse and the manner in which therapy is related to the retrieval of those memories (see, for example, Enns et al., 1995). Because the research literature provides very little information about either the actual experience of clients in psychotherapy or any factors related to memory retrieval, Phelps, Friedlander, and Enns (1997) conducted a qualitative study from the client's perspective that examined how the psychotherapeutic process was associated with the retrieval of sexual abuse memories.

How Much to Measure?

If you were doing a process study, would it be sufficient to collect data from one session, or should you collect from multiple sessions? If you are using measures that assess statement-by-statement variables (for example, counselor intentions), should you collect data from the whole counseling session, or perhaps from only the first (or last) 15 minutes of the session? Although it seems desirable to collect a lot of data from multiple sessions, which would increase the external validity or generalizability of the findings, such a strategy quickly results in an overwhelming amount of data. Hill et al. (1983) for example, analyzed over 11,000 responses from one intensive single-subject study; another study that examined data from only three group counseling sessions had 5,833 adjacent turns in the group communication to categorize (Friedlander, Thibodeau, Nichols, Tucker, & Snyder, 1985). Process researchers must decide how much of a session or how many sessions to use in their analyses. Even though little empirical evidence pertains to this issue, we briefly discuss sampling and its role in counseling process research.

Friedlander and colleagues (1988) empirically examined the issue of how much to measure. Specifically, they asked: (1) What fraction of an interview, if any, best represents the entire interview? and (2) At what point in the interview should this "best" sample be drawn? Friedlander et al. decided that the answer to these questions depended on the researcher's purpose. If the researcher was interested in group data, such as the process across several different counseling–client dyads, then fairly small segments of sessions (as little as 10%) were reasonable representations of an entire session. For a group design, the point in the interview at which the researcher drew the sample did not seem to matter. Friedlander et al. did recommend, however, that a "mini-generalizability" study be routinely conducted when using a group design; that is, a subsample of the data should be analyzed to ascertain that the use of small segments is appropriate in that particular case. On the other hand, Friedlander et al. recommended that entire sessions be used when an intensive single-subject strategy is used; their data suggested that sampling of single-subject data leads to enormous differences in the conclusions.

Additional data suggest that clients from different diagnosis groups show different patterns of experiencing the counseling process; for example, one study found that neurotic clients showed an upward trend in experiencing during a counseling session, whereas schizophrenics showed a saw-toothed pattern (Kiesler, Klein, & Mathieu, 1965). Other data suggest that patterns of client responding change over the course of many sessions (see, for example, Kiesler, 1971). Likewise, some data suggest that counselors change their behavior across counseling sessions (see, for example, Hill & O'Grady, 1985; Mintz & Luborsky, 1971). These studies underscore potential differences across clients and counselors over time.

Thus, the question of whether to use sample session segments seems to depend on the type of research question and the nature of the design. Certainly, investigators must be alert to individual differences across clients, particularly across very different diagnostic groups. Moreover, some differences in counselor behavior seem likely over time. Accordingly, researchers might choose to include both individual differences and time intervals in their research questions. If these variables are not desired in the research questions, then the researcher could decide to control these variables to reduce potential confounds.

Apart from the individual differences and time intervals, segments of as little as 10% of the session will likely yield acceptable results with group designs, whereas with single-subject designs it is best to use an entire session without sampling. Clearly, the issue of how much to measure is relatively unexplored and needs additional empirical research. Sampling and its effects on external validity merit serious attention in counseling process research.

HOW TO CODE AND ANALYZE THE PROCESS DATA?

Suppose that in carefully designing a process study you have identified specific variables within several focused research questions that interest you. You have also deliberated on what to measure and from whose perspective, and you have decided how much to measure. Now another major issue looms—how to analyze the process data. Although it is tempting to wait until you have collected the data, we strongly recommend that you think carefully about how you will analyze the data before they are collected. As researchers think through various issues related to data analysis, they may realize that more participants are needed, or that the data need to be collected more frequently. Thus, it is important to think through the issues related to data analysis while designing a process study.

The data analysis might involve a wide range of activities, depending on the nature of the data (see Hill & Lambert, 2004). Qualitative data might require nonparametric statistics, or perhaps categorizing data in the form of events by independent judges (see Chapter 11). Quantitative data might involve a range of statistical procedures, such as analysis of variance and correlations, or more complex designs such as sequential analysis. Because you typically have a lot of data (maybe even over 11,000 data points!), the data will need to be summarized or reduced in a way that still allows appropriate analysis. Although this book is not a book on data analysis, we will briefly discuss two data analysis issues pertinent to counseling process research: use of nonparticipant judges in rating data, and statistical strategies to analyze quantitative data.

USE OF NONPARTICIPANT JUDGES IN RATING DATA   It is quite common in process research to have nonparticipant observers "judge the presence, intensity, and frequency of certain events" (Lambert & Hill, 1994, p. 99). However, how can the researcher be sure that a judge's ratings are accurate or reliable? Perhaps a judge's ratings involve personal bias and have little to do with the observed event. Thus, a major issue pertains to the reliability and validity of observers' judgments.

Hill (1992) and Lambert and Hill (1994) have written extensively on issues pertaining to the use of nonparticipant judges. Among the major issues are the number of judges, rater selection, rater bias, rater errors, rater training, assigning judges to data, maintaining morale among judges, rater drift, debriefing of judges, and data aggregation. We now briefly examine some of these issues (see Lambert & Hill for more details).

Researchers typically use more than one rater to assure some reliability and validity of the ratings. The recommended number of raters ranges from 2 (the most common number) to 10 (Mahrer, Paterson, Theriault, Roessler, & Quenneville, 1986). Lambert and Hill (1994) recommended that the number of judges be linked to the difficulty of the rating task: The higher the reliability expected, the fewer judges are needed, whereas if lower reliability is expected, pooling ratings from several judges increases the probability of getting closer to the "true" score. Because the skills of the raters can have a major effect on the results of a study (Lambert & Hill), it behooves the researcher to carefully select skillful raters. But what constitutes a "skillful" rater? Although empirical evidence is lacking, previous researchers have selected raters based on levels of clinical experience, intelligence, theoretical sophistication, interpersonal skills, motivation for the specific project, attentiveness to detail, dependability, trustworthiness, and a sense of ethics (see, for example, Hill, 1982; Lambert & Hill; Mercer & Loesch, 1979; Moras & Hill, 1991).

Raters are "two-legged meters" (Lambert & Hill, 1994, p. 99) who are asked to interpret and make judgments on observed events. As such, judges bring biases to the rating task and are subject to the broad range of inference errors that humans often make (Gambrill, 1990). Thus, to reduce "error" created by the judges, researchers typically provide raters training concerning description of the rating system, discussion of sample items, rating of sample items, and monitoring of rater drift over the course of the rating task. To ensure that all judges receive exactly the same training, all judges should be trained together in one group.

In the first step, the rater must be introduced to the rating system. This step often includes a discussion of the theory base from which the rating system is derived, as well as a description of the specific system. Introduction to the rating system is enhanced by the use of manuals describing examples of expert ratings. Next, the rater uses the rating system on a set of sample items. This aspect of the training is often enhanced if each rater does the ratings independently and if raters are given the whole range of events to be rated so they can become familiar with all points of the ratings scales. Once these ratings are made, the raters discuss the ratings they made and the reasons for them. This step is enhanced if "expert" ratings of the sample items are available so trainees can compare their ratings to those of the experts. Discussion can help judges refine their knowledge of the rating system and make finer distinctions in their ratings. The previous two steps (rating sample items and discussing the ratings) continue until a specified level of agreement exists among the raters. Suppose that after the judges rate the first set of sample items (but before the general discussion of the items) the experimenter calculates the inter-rater reliability between two raters and finds that the level of agreement is .50. (That is, the judges agreed in their ratings only half the time.) Typically, this rate of agreement is considered to be too low. Rather than allowing the judges to proceed to rate all of the responses (and hope their inter-rater reliability goes up!), the experimenter would typically discuss the items and then provide another sample test. Although the "acceptable" level of inter-rater agreement depends on the difficulty of the rating task, .80 is generally considered acceptable.

After an acceptable level of inter-rater reliability is obtained, the judges begin the actual rating task. It is essential that judges do their ratings totally independent of each other. If each judge does not rate all of the data, then judges should be randomly assigned to various rating tasks to reduce potential error due to any particular judge. Even though judges typically begin the rating task conscientiously, the accuracy of their judgments might decline over time due to fatigue or repetition, or their understanding of the anchor points on rating scales might change. This phenomenon is called rater drift. Marmar (1990) recommended recalibration sessions during the rating task to maintain fidelity to the original training standards. Similarly, Elliott (1988) has recommended "the care and feeding of raters"—that is, listening to raters, reinforcing them, and if possible, removing administrative or procedural problems that make the rating task more cumbersome. The "care" of raters is a very important process that requires close monitoring.

At the end of the rating, the experimenter calculates the inter-rater reliability of all ratings. In some ways this is an assessment of the rater training program. Hill (1982) stated that researchers should calculate both inter- and intra-rater reliability. Intra-rater reliability assesses whether an individual rater makes consistent ratings over time, whereas inter-rater reliability assesses the amount of agreement among raters. (See Tinsley and Weiss, 1975, for methods of calculating inter- and intra-rater reliability.) Once rating has concluded, the experimenter can debrief judges concerning the specific purpose and hypotheses of the study. To ascertain whether the judges were indeed "blind" to the nature of the study (see Chapter 16), the experimenter can first ask judges to relate their ideas about the purpose of the study.

It is appropriate here to introduce the issue of training participants to make certain ratings at the time of data collection. For example, Martin, Martin, and Slemon (1989) found that counselors used different categories of the Hill and O'Grady (1985) Intentions List to record nominally similar descriptions of their intentions. The authors' solution to this problem was to ask therapists to give verbal descriptions of their intentions and then have raters classify these descriptions. This solution is very expensive in terms of time and effort. An alternative approach might be to train the counselors/raters in the use of the intention system. Although providing people training in introspection has a long history in psychology (Wundt, 1904), it is rarely used in modern process research. In this case, counselors could be trained to use the Intentions List by first learning to classify a series of intention statements to a specified level of accuracy. Only after they reached this level on the practice statements would they start to rate their own intentions. Rater drift could be assessed by administering additional series of intention statements to be rated throughout the study.

STATISTICAL STRATEGIES TO ANALYZE QUANTITATIVE DATA   An important trend in process research has been a move toward studies that explicitly examine the link between counseling process and outcome. This trend has raised important questions about statistically analyzing process data. Traditionally, process has been linked to outcome using a correlational strategy. If, for example, a researcher found a significant positive relationship between counselors' use of interpretation and session depth, then he or she could infer that interpretation was an important process element. Unfortunately, correlational designs cannot enable the researcher to identify causal relationships (whether counselor interpretations caused session depth).

A second example of a correlational design (an ex post facto design) involves comparisons across successfully and unsuccessfully treated cases. In this instance the researcher would examine whether the frequency of a response (for example, open-ended questions) differed across the two kinds of cases. Again, more frequent occurrence of open-ended questions in the successful cases may or may not mean that counselors who use more open-ended questions will be more successful.

Thus, correlational designs in counseling process research, although helpful, have limited utility. In fact, Gottman and Markman (1978) are quite critical of these types of correlational designs in process research. They argued instead for analyses that examine the direct effect of counselor behavior on subsequent client behavior. Stiles (1988) also observed that counselors often use a behavior more frequently not because it is working well, but because it is not working well. For instance, a counselor might offer a lot of interpretations because the client is being "resistant" and is rejecting the interpretations. This situation would cause a higher number of counselor interpretations and likely a low rating for session depth. Thus, the correlation between these two variables alone presents rather misleading information.

An alternative way of examining the relationship between counselor behavior and client response is sequential analysis, a set of statistical techniques that examine the mutual influence of counselor and client behaviors. For example, sequential analysis can be used to examine the likelihood of a client response (for example, self-disclosure) given a prior counselor response (for example, interpretation). At a more sophisticated level, sequential analyses can examine issues such as control and power (that is, is the counselor's response made more predictable by knowing the client's preceding response, or vice versa?). Excellent descriptions of these types of analyses can be found in Bakeman and Gottman (1986), Claiborn and Lichtenberg (1989), Gottman and Roy (1990), and Wampold (1995).

A study by Wampold and Kim (1989) illustrates the power of sequential analysis in examining counseling process. Wampold and Kim reanalyzed data from Hill, Carter, and O'Farrell's (1983) study using an intensive single-subject design across 12 counseling sessions. The process variables used in this study were Hill's counselor and client verbal response category systems. Categories for counselor responses included minimal encouragement, silence, approval-reassurance, information, direct guidance, closed question, open question, restatement, reflection, interpretation, confrontation, nonverbal referent, self-disclosure, and other. Client categories included simple response, requests, description, experiencing, insight, discussion of plans, discussion of client–counselor relationship, silence, and other.

The purpose of the study was to examine the reciprocal influence of counselor and client behaviors. We highlight only a couple of findings here to describe the utility of sequential analysis. First, analyses revealed what Wampold and Kim (1989) called two "circuits" between client and counselor behaviors. One circuit was from client description to counselor minimal encouragement back to client description. A second circuit involved client description to counselor confrontation. In addition, Wampold and Kim tested the first circuit for dominance; the dominant member of the dyad was defined as the one with the most influence. For the client description–counselor minimal encouragement–client description circuit, the client was dominant. In other words, the counselor's behavior was more predictable from the client's behavior than the other way around. Wampold and Kim concluded that sequential analysis allowed them to document several important aspects of client and counselor interactions that had been undetected in the correlational and descriptive analysis used by Hill et al. (1983).

Later in this chapter we make a distinction between micro and macro processes. For now, we define micro processes as those that usually occur at the level of the counseling turn (that is, counselor and client statements in a counseling session). The counselor and client verbal response mode categories examined by Wampold and Kim (1989) are examples of micro processes. Macro processes occur over longer periods of time (for example, adherence ratings, or ratings of how closely a particular session conforms to a treatment manual). In counseling process research, the types of sequential analyses recommended by Gottman and Markman (1978) have been used almost exclusively with micro-process data. Only recently have counseling researchers used time-series analyses with macro-process (session level) data.

One example of the use of time-series analysis with macro-level data is Patton, Kivlighan, and Multon's (1997) study of time-limited psychoanalytic counseling. Through factor analysis, Patton et al. identified four aspects of session-level psychoanalytic counseling process: (1) psychoanalytic technique, (2) client resistance, (3) working alliance, and (4) client transference. These authors were interested in the possible mutual influence of these four aspects of the counseling process across 20 sessions of time-limited treatment.

To examine the possible mutual influence of the four aspects of psychoanalytic counseling process, Patton et al. (1997) used a time-series analysis. According to Gottman and Markman (1978), some questions can be answered only at the intrasubject level; examples include "How does a particular therapist's behavior affect the client?" (p. 28) and the related question, "How does a particular client's behavior affect the therapist?" (p. 28). Although time-series analysis is a sophisticated method for answering this type of within-subjects question, unfortunately few time-series analyses have been applied to counseling/psychotherapy research. According to Jones et al. (1993), in time-series analysis the researcher attempts to infer a causal relationship between observations constituting one series of data points (for example, psychoanalytic techniques) and observations of a second series (for example, client resistance). In other words, the issue is whether series A (psychoanalytic techniques) can predict series B (client resistance).

In the terminology of time-series analysis, the relationship between two series is the *cross-correlation function*. However, spuriously large cross-correlation coefficients can be found when two time series have large auto-correlations (correlations of a time series with itself). Therefore, time-series analysis involves two steps. In the first step, each individual time series is examined for the presence of nonstationary trends, which involves plotting and examining the autocorrelation function (ACF) and the partial autocorrelation function (PACF). If the ACF or PACF plots indicate significant or partial autocorrelations for an individual time series, the series is made stationary by transforming it. (One method of doing so is to use differencing, which controls for trends in the data.) Once the identified series are made stationary, these transformed series are then cross-correlated at various lags. The cross-correlation coefficients from this second step are examined for the presence of significant lead/lag relationships. If a significant lead/lag relationship is identified, then the leading variable is considered a potential "cause" of the lagging variable. If the only significant cross-correlation coefficient is for zero lag, then no presumption about the causal direction of the relationships is possible.

The complete results of Patton et al. (1997) are beyond the scope of this discussion; however, they did find significant cross-correlation functions (CCF) between psychoanalytic technique and client resistance. In examining a cross-correlation analysis, a positive lag means that the counseling process scale indicated first (in this case, psychoanalytic techniques) leads the counseling process scale indicated second (in this case, client resistance). A negative lag means that the counseling process scale indicated second (in this case, client resistance) leads the counseling process scale indicated first (in this case, psychoanalytic techniques). As is the case for a correlation coefficient, the sign of the CCF denotes the direction of the relationship, whereas the absolute value of the CCF indicates the magnitude of the relationship.

In short, Patton et al. (1997) found that the CCFs for the psychoanalytic technique–client resistance relationship were significant at lag 1 (−.57) and at lag 2 (−.54). This pattern of CCFs suggested that the counselor's relatively higher use of psychoanalytic techniques in a particular session led to lower levels of client resistance during the two subsequent counseling sessions. The Patton et al. study illustrates the promising results when time-series analysis is applied to session-level data. We hope counseling process researchers will apply these time-series techniques to macro-process data with the same level of enthusiasm that has accompanied their use with micro-process data.

Another critical statistical issue that confronts many counseling process researchers involves the analysis of process variables collected over time. In the past, there has not been a practical and powerful method for the statistical analysis of repeated measures types of counseling process data. To represent this type of data, process researchers have either (1) used nonstatistical graphical methods coupled with visual inspection, or (2) arbitrarily divided data points into predetermined phases (for example, early, middle, and late periods) and used repeated measures analysis of variance or repeated measures multivariate analysis of variance. As discussed by Willett, Ayoub, and Robinson (1991) and Francis, Fletcher, Stuebing, Davidson, and Thompson (1991), these methods have proven problematic from both a logical and a statistical perspective. Growth modeling, also known as growth curve analysis, offers a powerful alternative method for analyzing repeated measures types of counseling process data. In the first step of growth curve analysis, a theoretical or heuristic growth model (for example, linear or quadratic curve) is fit both to the data from an individual counseling dyad or a counseling group and to the sample of dyads or groups as a whole. The parameters from these initial models are then used in the second step of the modeling process as outcomes (that is, dependent variables) onto which other variables are regressed. For example, if a linear growth model is used in group counseling research, each group will have (1) an intercept term that represents that group's process score (for example, level of cohesion) at a particular time, and (2) a slope term that represents the linear change in the group's process score (for example, cohesion) over time.

Growth modeling has typically been applied to outcome data. Kivlighan and Shaughnessy (1995) and Kivlighan and Lilly (1997) are two examples of studies that have used growth modeling with counseling process data. In the Kivlighan and Lilly study, hierarchical linear modeling (HLM) was used to estimate growth curves from group climate data. Based on the theory of hierarchical linear models developed by Bryk and Raudenbush (1992), growth modeling was used in a two-level analysis to estimate growth curves from the within-group, group climate data and to relate the growth parameters from this within-group analysis to the between-group variable of "group success."

Conceptually, HLM involves a two-stage analysis. In the first or unconditional model, the growth trajectory of each individual group is modeled or characterized by a unique set of parameters. This set of parameters, which is assumed to vary randomly, is then used in the second or conditional model as dependent variables in a series of regressions. Arnold (1992) has summarized this analytic technique by describing HLM as "regressions of regressions" (p. 61).

Hierarchical linear modeling differs from trend analysis in analysis of variance (ANOVA) or multivariate analysis of variance (MANOVA) in that individuals (as opposed to group means) are being modeled; that is, in trend analysis, individual variance is subsumed under the error term. Variance in the individual growth parameters (that is, across groups) can then be plotted against correlates of change. This type of analysis allows for "a different set of research questions" (Francis et al., 1991, p. 31) than is found in more traditional research (that is, based on group means only). For a detailed discussion of the statistical aspects of hierarchical linear models, see Arnold (1992), Bryk and Raudenbush (1992), Francis et al., and Raudenbush and Chan (1993).

Kivlighan and Lilly (1997) investigated how the shape or function of group climate growth patterns were related to the amount of participant-rated benefit from the group experience. HLM analyses were run three times, once for each of the three aspects of group climate (engaged, conflict, and avoiding). Examination of the relationship between group climate ratings and group benefit proceeded through a series of model-building steps.

Several specific findings related group climate to outcome. For example, a quadratic, high-low-high pattern of engaged (cohesion) development was related to increased member benefit. In addition, the pattern of engaged development was more predictive of member benefit than was the absolute level of engaged feeling. In fact, the pattern of group climate development consistently accounted for more of the variance in member benefit than did the absolute level of the group climate dimension. This suggests that pattern over time is an important dimension of counseling process. We believe that growth modeling provides a powerful methodology for counseling researchers interested in examining repeated measures types of data. Also see Kivlighan, Coleman, and Anderson (2000) for examples of growth modeling in group counseling.

REPRESENTATIVE EXAMPLES OF INSTRUMENTS USED IN COUNSELING PROCESS RESEARCH

A multitude of measures have been used in counseling process and outcome research. For a review of some of the most widely used measures, interested readers can consult Greenberg and Pinsof (1986); Hill and Lambert (2004); Hill and Williams (2000); Kiesler (1973); Lambert and Hill (1994); Lambert and Ogles (2004); Ogles, Lambert, and Fields (2002); and Russell (1987). This section provides representative examples of some commonly used instruments used to assess different aspects of counseling process research. To provide some structure and organization for our discussion, we developed a categorization scheme (see Table 19.1). Basically, we used Hill's (1992) seven aspects of the counseling process and added an evaluative dimension (quality) from Elliott's (1991) classification scheme. We then used Greenberg's (1986a) notion of different levels of measurement to create two levels of analysis, a micro (statement-by-statement) level and a macro (or global) level. Together, these two dimensions form a 2 × 8 matrix; each of the cells contains one or more appropriate instruments. In the pages that follow we briefly discuss instruments in each of the 16 cells, as well as other representative instruments and research, to provide concrete examples of counseling process measures. Moreover, for each cell we discuss instruments that could be used to assess either the counselor's or client's perspective.

ANCILLARY BEHAVIORS, MICRO LEVEL

Ancillary behaviors are the nonverbal behaviors displayed by counseling participants. At the micro level, these ancillary behaviors are nonverbal behaviors connected to particular speech units (for example, sentences or client–counselor turns at speaking). Ancillary behaviors are important because they

TABLE 19.1
INSTRUMENTS
REPRESENTATIVE
OF THE
COUNSELING
PROCESS BY
LEVEL OF
MEASUREMENT

	Level of Measurement	
Counseling Process	Micro	Global
Ancillary behaviors	Client Vocal Quality (Rice & Kerr, 1986)	Arousal Scale (Burgoon, Kelly, Newton, & Keeley-Dyreson, 1989)
Verbal behaviors	Hill Counselor Verbal Response Modes Category System (Hill, 1985)	Supervision Questionaire (Worthington & Roehlke, 1979)
Covert behaviors	Thought-Listing Form (Heppner et al., 1992)	Brief Structured Recall (Elliott & Shapiro, 1988); Session Evaluation Questionnaire (Stiles & Snow, 1984)
		Comprehensive Scale of Psychotherapy Session Constructs (Eugster & Wampold, 1996)
Content	Hill Interaction Matrix (Hill, 1965)	Discussion Units (Dipboye, 1954)
Strategies	Counselor Intentions List (Hill & O'Grady, 1985)	Therapist Session Intentions (Stiles et al., 1996)
	Client Reactions System (Hill et al., 1988)	
Interpersonal manner	Interpersonal Communication Rating Scale (Strong et al., 1988)	Check List of Interpersonal Transactions (Kiesler, 1984)
Therapeutic relationship	Categories of Semantic Cohesion Analysis (Friedlander et al., 1985)	Working Alliance Inventory (Horvath & Greenberg, 1989)
Quality	Client Experiencing Scale (Klein, Mathieu-Coughlan, & Kiesler, 1986)	Penn Adherence and Competence Scale for Supportive-Expressive Therapy (Barber & Crits-Christoph, 1996)

carry communicative value. For example, researchers estimate that as much as 60% of the communication that takes place in groups takes place on the nonverbal level (Kleinke, 1986). Kiesler (1988) called nonverbal behavior the language of relationship and emotion.

Researchers assess ancillary behaviors because, unlike speech acts, they are often out of the counseling participants' awareness and therefore out of their conscious control. This lack of conscious control suggests that nonverbal behaviors may provide a more sensitive indicator of client or counselor emotional state than self-report measures. In line with this assumption, Mohr, Shoham-Salomon, Engle, and Beutler (1991) found that nonverbal behaviors provided a more accurate assessment of client arousal than did verbal reports.

Two classes of nonverbal behaviors have interested counseling process researchers. Vocalics involve the voice qualities of the interactants; examples are voice tone or rate of speech. Kinesics are body movements such as facial expressions and gestures. Counseling researchers have measured both kinesics and vocalics in their process studies.

Rice and Kerr's (1986) Client Vocal Quality (CVQ) measure is probably the most widely used vocalic index. The CVQ rater uses auditory cues to categorize client or counselor statements into one of four categories: (1) focused, (2) external, (3) limited, and (4) emotional. The focused category describes an inner-directed exploratory voice quality. An outer-directed, lecturing type of voice quality is considered external. The emotional category is used when the voice "breaks its normal platform and expresses emotions." Finally, a low-energy, wary type of voice is classified as limited. The four CVQ categories are mutually exclusive, so any individual speech act can have only one vocal quality rating. Rice and Kerr have shown that the CVQ has good reliability. In addition, CVQ ratings have been shown to predict productive engagement in both client-centered and Gestalt counseling; even though the CVQ system has mainly been used to rate client speech, it could equally apply to counselor speech.

Greenberg and Foerster (1996) used the CVQ in their task analysis of the process of resolving unfinished business. Task analysis is a specific approach to process research that incorporates eight steps, as outlined by Greenberg and Newman (1996): (1) explicating the implicit cognitive map of expert clinicians; (2) describing the therapeutic task and the context in which this task exists; (3) verifying that the task is therapeutically significant; (4) constructing rational models of successful task performance; (5) empirically describing cases of actual task performance; (6) revising the rational model by comparing the rationally derived and empirically derived task performances; (7) validating the task model by comparing successful and unsuccessful performances; and (8) relating process to outcome.

In the Greenberg and Foerster (1996) study, the CVQ was a critical component of the verification phase of the task analysis paradigm. The focus of this study was the use of the Gestalt empty-chair dialogue to resolve unfinished business, defined as lingering bad feelings toward a significant other. Fourteen counselors provided 46 audiotaped counseling sessions containing empty-chair dialogues. Eleven "resolved" and 11 "unresolved" sessions were identified through client, counselor, and judge ratings on a five-point resolution scale. Once these 22 sessions had been identified, clinical judges selected 2-minute sections from each tape for CVQ rating by a second set of judges. Greenberg and Foerster found that the client dialogue was more focused and emotional in the "resolved" sessions than in the "unresolved" sessions. According to the authors, the CVQ data confirmed that both (1) the intense expression of feelings (that is, higher proportion of emotional responses in the resolved group) and (2) the presence of self-affirmation, self-assertion, or understanding of the other (that is, higher proportion of focused responses in the resolved group) were associated with the successful resolution of unfinished business.

Counseling process researchers have also used micro-level ratings of kinesics. Merten, Anstadt, Ullrich, Krause, and Buchheim (1996) studied the affective/emotional exchange between counselors and clients during counseling sessions. According to these authors, emotional exchanges happen at a micromomentary level. Merten et al. sought to study this process of moment-to-moment emotional exchange by coding the facial expressions of emotion.

Friesen and Ekman's (1984) Emotional Facial Action Coding System (EMFACS) is used to code facial expressions of clients and counselors potentially associated with affect. In using the EMFACS system, a target facial expression is matched to a dictionary of facial expressions and coded as (1) a primary emotion (happiness, anger, contempt, disgust, fear, sadness, surprise, or social smiles); (2) a blend (two primary emotions occurring simultaneously), (3) a mask (when happiness is used to cover a negative emotion), or (4) nonaffective.

In the Merten et al. (1996) study, 11 severely disturbed clients were treated for 15 sessions by one of 11 experienced therapists. All sessions were videotaped with two cameras, one recording the counselor's facial expressions and the other the client's. Upon completion of the 15 sessions, both clients and counselors completed ratings of success, goal attainment, helpfulness, and contentment with treatment. Based on these outcome ratings, one successful and one unsuccessful client–counselor dyad were selected for further study with the EMFACS.

Both the successful and unsuccessful counseling cases had a similar number of client facial events, 233 for the unsuccessful case and 239 for the successful case. For the unsuccessful case, 73% of the facial events were affective, and 62% of these affective events were primary emotions. By contrast, in the successful case, only 56% of the facial events were affective, and only 46% of these affective events were primary emotions. The counselor in the successful case displayed significantly more facial events ($N = 167$) than did the counselor in the unsuccessful case ($N = 125$). For the counselor in the unsuccessful case, 94% of the detected facial events were affective, with 36% of these affective events being primary emotions. By contrast, in the successful case, only 47% of the counselor's facial events were affective; however, 81% of these affective events were primary emotions.

The vast majority of the primary facial emotions expressed by the counselor in the unsuccessful dyad were happiness or social smiles. Likewise, the unsuccessful client's primary facial expressions were happiness and social smiles. As described by Merten et al. (1996), the facial behavior of the unsuccessful dyad was monotonous, consisting of a series of reciprocal expressions of happiness. The more successful client had a relatively equal balance of happiness, anger, and disgust facial expressions. The facial expressions of this client's counselor were predominantly surprise, disgust, and happiness. There was far less reciprocation of happiness in the successful dyad than in the unsuccessful dyad. It seems clear from this preliminary study that the nonverbal facial behaviors of clients and counselors in successfully and unsuccessfully treated dyads are dramatically different. This suggests that these types of micro-level ancillary behaviors are important topics to address in counseling process research.

ANCILLARY BEHAVIORS, GLOBAL LEVEL

Unlike the micro level, at which the kinesic and vocalic dimensions of ancillary behaviors have usually been measured separately, at the macro level these two dimensions have frequently been combined in a single measure. An example of this type of combined measure is the Arousal Measure developed by Burgoon, Kelly, Newton, and Keeley-Dyreson (1989). According to the authors, this scale was intended to measure both the positive and negative aspects of kinesic and vocalic arousal and affect. Trained raters use only the video portion of a videotape when rating the kinesic nonverbal dimensions, whereas vocalic ratings are made from only the audio portion of the tape. One rating, Arousal, is made using both auditory and visual channels.

The Arousal Measure consists of 21 dimensions, with most dimensions containing multiple items. Some items (for example, nodding) are rated on a frequency scale (1 = "none"; 7 = "frequent"), whereas other items are rated for intensity using bi-polar adjective pairs (for example, concern ratings are 1 = "indifferent"; 7 = "concerned"). The 21 nonverbal dimensions (with a representative item in parentheses) are: (1) Arousal (calm), (2) Orientation/Gaze (body orientation), (3) Random Movement (trunk/limb movement), (4) Facial/Head Animation (facial animation), (5) Facial Pleasantness (facial expression), (6) Gestural Animation (gestures), (7) Self-Adaptors (self-adaptors), (8) Object-Adaptors (object-adaptors), (9) Kinesic/Proxemic (involved), (10) Attentiveness (interested), (11) Bodily Coordination (movements), (12) Postural Relaxation (slumped), (13) Body Lean (body lean), (14) Vocal Expressiveness (loudness), (15) Pauses and Laughter (silences), (16) Fluency (nervous vocalizations), (17) Vocal Attentiveness (focused), (18) Vocal Relaxation (rhythm), (19) Vocal Warmth (warm), (20) Loudness (loud), and (21) Pitch (pitch).

Burgoon et al. (1993) compared nonverbal arousal for clients in cognitive group therapy (CT) to clients participating in focused expressive psychotherapy (FEP). As described by the authors, the focus of FEP was emotional arousal, awareness, and resolution of conflict; the focus of CT was identifying and changing dysfunctional cognitions associated with troubling life experiences. As would be expected from a description of the two therapeutic modalities, FEP clients had higher levels of arousal and gesture animation, and lower levels of vocal relaxation and fluency than CT clients. In addition, FEP clients had lower levels of kinesic pleasantness and vocalic pleasantness than CT clients.

Burgoon et al. (1993) also examined the relationship between clients' end of session ratings of resolution (the extent to which the problem worked on was resolved) and the nonverbal arousal measures for clients in the FEP groups. Random movement and vocal relaxation were both associated with client-judged resolution. Specifically, greater amounts of random movement and moderate amounts of vocal relaxation during middle sessions were associated with greater subjective resolution. The results of the Burgoon et al. (1993) study suggest that level of nonverbal arousal is differentially associated with various treatment modalities. In addition, the results suggest that some aspects of nonverbal arousal may be linked to client outcome. The results are encouraging for the continued assessment of macro-level ancillary behaviors in counseling process research.

Verbal Behaviors, Micro Level

Verbal behaviors refer to the communication between counselor and client—not the content of the communication, but rather the grammatical structure (Hill, 1982). Even though various studies have examined linguistic structure (see, for example, Meara & Patton, 1986; Meara, Shannon, & Pepinsky, 1979), most of them have relied on measures of response modes. Response mode refers to the grammatical structure of the response (for example, closed question, open question, or interpretation). Elliott et al. (1987) suggested that for the 20 to 30 systems developed for identifying counselor response modes, the breadth and quality of these systems vary greatly. Accordingly, researchers wanting to measure this level of counselor action are presented with a plethora of choices but little systematic help in choosing a particular response mode system for their studies. Elliott et al. addressed this problem by comparing six of the more widely used response-mode rating systems.

Elliott et al. (1987) found that a fundamental set of response-mode categories underlie the six systems they examined. These response modes include questions, advisements, information, responses, reflections, interpretations, and self-disclosures. In addition, three other response modes (reassurances, confrontations, and acknowledgments) were reliably represented in most of the six systems examined. Unfortunately, Elliott et al. concluded that there was no single best system for rating response modes. Rather, they suggested that researchers examining response modes should at least use systems that contain the six (and probably the three additional) primary response modes to promote comparability across studies. One frequently used example of a response mode rating system is the Hill Counselor Verbal Response Modes Category System (Hill, 1985).

One of the strengths of response-mode systems is conceptual clarity. In addition, most of the systems are atheoretical, which enables them to be used across a variety of treatment modalities. In addition, response-mode systems can reliably differentiate among various therapeutic approaches. Research linking therapist response modes to immediate or long-term outcome, however, has revealed only a weak relationship between response-mode use and outcome (Elliott et al., 1987; Hill et al., 1988a). These results suggest that other variables may be more important in accounting for counseling out-comes, and that perhaps the frequency of response-mode use in and of itself does not measure a critical ingredient of the change process. After all, the frequency of certain counselor responses tells us little about the myriad of possible client reactions. Given these findings, we recommend that future process researchers not examine response modes in isolation. More useful research could involve examining the interaction between response-mode use and the other aspects (content, style, intention, and quality) of counselor behavior.

An example of this type of research is the study by Hill et al. (1988a), which examined the effects of therapist response modes on immediate outcome (client helpfulness ratings, changes in level of client experiencing, and client reactions), on session outcome (client and therapist ratings of session depth and smoothness), and on treatment outcome (changes in anxiety, depression, and self-concept). Although certain response modes were significantly correlated with measures of session and treatment outcome, these response modes accounted for only 1% of the variance in immediate outcome. This small relationship between response modes and immediate outcome became more tenuous when other process variables were added to the analysis. In fact, counselor intentions (discussed later) were better predictors of immediate outcome than were response modes. Only when counselor response modes were combined with counselor intentions was an appreciable amount of variance in immediate outcome accounted for in this analysis. The results of this study underscore the need to examine the interaction between therapist response modes and other aspects of counselor behavior in counseling process research.

Unlike counselor verbal behavior, client verbal behavior has received little research attention. Thus, fewer systems have been developed to measure client response modes. Client verbal behavior, like that of the counselor, can be categorized in terms of its grammatical structure. This type of category system results in a measure of client response modes. One such system has been developed by Hill, Greenwald, Reed, Charles, O'Farrell, and Carter (1981). Using this system, client verbal behavior can be classified as simple responses, requests, descriptions, experiencing, insight, discussion of plans, discussion of client–counselor relationship, silence, and other. One problem with this system is that verbal behavior (that is, requests) is confused or confounded with content (that is, discussion of plans).

We suspect that client verbal behavior is a research area that deserves more attention. Not only are few ways available for comparing or contrasting different approaches to defining client responses, but few studies have examined the relationship between client response modes and other aspects of client or counselor behavior.

VERBAL BEHAVIORS, GLOBAL LEVEL

Verbal behaviors have also been examined at a more global level, particularly research examining the supervisory process. Almost all of the studies of counselor supervision (with the exception of those done by Holloway and colleagues;

see, for example, Holloway, Freund, Gardner, Nelson, & Walker, 1989) have relied on supervisor or supervisee ratings of supervision behavior. In this type of research, supervisors and/or supervisees are presented with a list of items describing supervisor behaviors and asked to indicate the general frequency with which the behaviors occurred in the supervision session or during the course of supervision. An example of an instrument in this area is the Supervision Questionnaire (Worthington & Roehlke, 1979).

An example of this type of research is provided by Krause and Allen (1988), who were interested in examining Stoltenberg's (1981) developmental model, which predicted that supervisors would use different behaviors with trainees at different developmental levels. These authors gave a list of 37 items describing supervisor behavior to 87 supervisors and 77 supervisees. The responses of the supervisees and supervisors were factor-analyzed separately. Eight factors accounted for the variance in supervisors' ratings: teacher, counselor, respectful sharing, satisfied colleague, dynamic counselor, perceived impact, laissez-faire, and preparation. A factor analysis of the same items from the supervisees' perspective yielded five factors: supervisor as mentor, supervisor as counselor, directive supervision, supervisor as dynamic counselor, and process supervision.

Krause and Allen (1988) used these factors to examine the hypothesis that supervisors would vary their behaviors with supervisees. Using the eight supervisor-derived factors to examine this hypothesis, supervisors rated three of these factors differently depending on the supervisees' training levels. Specifically, structuring and directing behaviors decreased, and collegial and consulting relationships increased as supervisees advanced in development. An identical analysis using the five supervisee-derived clusters yielded no differences in supervisees' ratings of supervisor behaviors for supervisees at different developmental levels. In sum, the supervisors saw themselves as varying their behaviors with supervisees of different developmental levels, but the supervisees did not.

Did the supervisors actually vary their behaviors with supervisees at different levels? Unfortunately, we cannot provide a complete answer to this question because of the measures used to examine supervisor verbal behavior. Without some outside perspective from which to examine the process at the micro level, it is impossible to determine the reliability of either the supervisors' or supervisees' accounts of the supervisors' behavior.

COVERT BEHAVIORS, MICRO LEVEL

Covert behavior refers to thoughts, feelings, and perceptions (Highlen & Hill, 1984). One aspect of covert behavior that has received increasing attention is the study of counselor or client self-talk. According to Hines, Stockton, and Morran (1995), counselor self-talk involves the self-reported thoughts that affect the counselor's intention-creation process. Counselor self-talk has been examined in both individual and group therapy. Most of the research on counselor self-talk has attempted to categorize the type of self-talk engaged in by counselors. For example, in individual counseling, Morran, Kurpius, and Brack (1989) found 14 distinct categories of counselor self-talk defined by four dimensions: (1) attending and assessing, (2) information seeking, (3) integrative understanding, and (4) intervention planning.

Counselor self-talk is typically assessed through a thought-listing procedure. Originally developed by social psychologists (for example, Brock, 1967; Greenwald, 1968), thought listing is a means of identifying a person's cognitive responses to a particular stimulus. The stimulus for thought listing can be an entire session, as in Heppner, Rosenberg, and Hedgespeth (1992), or every few minutes within a session, as in Hines et al. (1995). The thought-listing instrument usually consists of some instructions and several "thought-listing" pages containing blanks; research participants are instructed to list one thought in each blank. In addition, research participants are encouraged to not worry about spelling or grammar and to be as open and spontaneous as possible. For additional information about constructing a thought-listing form, see Meichenbaum, Henshaw, and Himel (1980) and Petty and Cacioppo (1977).

Hines et al. (1995) used thought listing to examine the self-talk of novice group leaders (participants who had never led a group), beginning group leaders (participants with one to three group-leadership experiences), and experienced group leaders (participants with six or more group-leadership experiences). The participants watched on videotape a 20-minute staged group counseling session depicting "normal group process occurring around the fourth group counseling session" (Hines et al., p. 243). Five times during the 20-minute session the tape went blank for 90 seconds, during which research participants were instructed to use the thought-listing forms to record the thoughts they had while viewing the videotape.

As in the Hines et al. (1995) study, thought-listing procedures typically result in a great deal of "qualitative" data that researchers must code or classify. Of the several strategies for dealing with the open-ended data generated by thought-listing procedures, the three most frequently used strategies are: (1) coding statements into a priori categories (positive, negative, and neutral; see, for example, Heppner, Rosenberg, and Hedgpeth, 1992); (2) developing a classification system based on a reading and analysis of the data collected (see, for example, Heppner, Rosenberg, and Hedgpeth, 1992); and (3) using a statistical technique such as cluster analysis or multidimensional scaling to empirically group the free sort ratings of several judges (see, for example, Morran et al., 1989).

Hines et al. (1995) used the second method to develop categories of self-talk for the group counselors they studied. The development of categories in this study involved a two-step process. First, two experienced group counselors independently free-sorted into mutually exclusive categories the 1,299 thoughts collected in the thought-listing process. These two judges then reached a consensus on the titles and definitions of 17 thought categories. Second, a panel of three judges trained in the definitions of the 17 categories independently coded the 1,299 thoughts generated by the research participants into the 17 predefined categories. An agreement level of 94% was achieved by the three judges.

Using this method, Hines et al. (1995) described 17 categories of group counselors' thoughts: (1) observations of group members, (2) observations of group process, (3) observations of co-leader, (4) observations of self, (5) interpretations of members, (6) interpretations of group process, (7) interpretations of co-leader, (8) internal questions regarding members, (9) internal questions regarding group process, (10) internal questions regarding intervention toward members, (11) internal questions regarding intervention toward group process, (12) therapeutic value judgments, (13) personal value judgments, (14) interventions directed toward members, (15) interventions directed toward group process, (16) intervention rehearsals toward members, and (17) intervention rehearsals toward group process. Once the proportion of use for the various thought categories were recorded, Hines et al. correlated these proportions with the number of groups that a participant had led. Four categories of group-leader thought were significantly correlated with group-leading experience. The self-talk of the more experienced group leaders had a relatively higher frequency of interpretations of group process, internal questions regarding members, and interpretations of members, and a relatively lower frequency of therapeutic value judgments, than did the self-talk of less experienced group counselors.

COVERT BEHAVIORS, GLOBAL LEVEL

On the global level, measures that operationalize counselor intention are not currently available. This is somewhat surprising given the emphasis these actions receive in counselor training and supervision. Among the most common questions addressed to supervisees are things that ask what he or she was trying to accomplish in a given session, or what his or her overall treatment plan involves. Development of this type of measure would be useful in future research and in conceptualizing the counseling process.

Clients also have intentions. In their analysis of the literature, Elliott and James (1989) found eight common themes across the studies that examined client intentions: understanding self and problems, avoiding, getting a personal response from the counselor, feeling relieved or better, changing behavior, getting counselor support, expressing feelings, and following therapeutic directives or procedures. Elliott and Shapiro's (1988) Brief Structured Recall method was designed as a global measure of client intentions. Clients complete a structured assessment that identifies their intentions during a significant event. The intentions include the eight categories described in Elliott and James. Elliot and his colleagues (see, for example, Elliott, James, Reimschuessel, Cislo, & Sack, 1985) have used free recall to study client intentions at a micro level, but these have not been systematized into a more replicable format. Investigating client intentions is a promising area for future research.

One of the most widely used measures of client reactions at the global level is the Session Evaluation Questionnaire (SEQ; Stiles & Snow, 1984). The SEQ consists of four scales. The Depth and Smoothness scales measure the client's reactions to characteristics of the session. (These scales are discussed in more detail later in this chapter when we address process measures of the relationship.) The Positivity and Arousal scales measure postsession mood. Positivity, as the name implies, is a measure of how positive or negative the client feels upon completing the session. The Arousal scale is a measure of how much emotional arousal the client feels after completing the session. These SEQ scales have been used to measure consequences (that is, the relationship between therapist response modes and client postsession mood) and antecedents (that is, the relationship between postsession mood and counseling outcome).

Counselor reactions have been measured at a global level with instruments parallel to those used to measure global client reactions. For instance, the SEQ has been used to record the counselor's session-by-session reactions.

A final instrument in this category is the Comprehensive Scale of Psychotherapy Session Constructs (CSPSC; Eugster & Wampold, 1996). Basically, the CSPSC measures nine aspects of the session (patient involvement, patient comfort, patient learning, patient real relationship, therapist involvement, therapist comfort, therapist expertness, therapist interpersonal style, and therapist real relationship) from the perspective of both patient and therapist, as well as a global evaluation of the session from both perspectives. Eugster and Wampold found that therapist session evaluation was best predicted by therapist expertness, and patient session evaluation was best predicted by the therapist real relationship. The therapist real relationship negatively predicted therapist session evaluation when all process variables were considered simultaneously. Patient learning and patient involvement significantly and positively predicted both therapist and patient evaluations of the session.

Content, Micro Level

Content refers to the topic or subject of counseling. The Hill Interaction Matrix (HIM; Hill, 1965), which is used in group process research, is an example of a micro-level rating system that focuses on the content of the interaction. The HIM is a statement-by-statement rating system that can be used to rate statements made by either group clients or therapists. The HIM consists of 20 cells formed by combining the dimensions of content style (four types) and work style (five types). The content-style categories in the HIM system are topic, group, personal, and relationship; the work-style categories are responsive, conventional, assertive, speculative, and confrontive. The HIM is used by an outside observer who reviews a transcript and places each client or counselor statement into one of the 20 HIM categories. As an example, a researcher could identify how often a group counselor used statements in each of the 20 cells and compare the counselor's rate of use to group members' use of the categories. Research has suggested that the rate of therapist sponsoring is related to the rate of member participation in the different HIM cells (see, for example, Hill, 1965). Hill therefore concluded that the content (and the style) of the counselor's speech is related to (influences) the content (and style) of the client's speech.

CONTENT, GLOBAL LEVEL

Research in counseling process would be enhanced by the development of another category system to classify the global content of the counselor's and client's responses. Several early process studies examined the content of discussion, or topical units of discussion. Dipboye (1954) defined a topical unit as the portion of an interview that is devoted to an obvious and clearly recognizable topic of discussion. He defined the following six topical units: (1) test discussion and interpretation, (2) interpersonal relations, (3) family relations, (4) educational and vocational problems and planning, (5) self-reference, and (6) study habits and skills. Dipboye found that the counselors he studied tended to vary their styles or actions as a function of the topical unit of discussion.

This finding was extended in a study by Cummings (1989), who classified problem type or the content of the counseling interaction as either interpersonal or intrapersonal. Like Dipboye (1954), she found that counselors varied their behavior as a function of problem type: Counselors used more information responses with intrapersonal problems and more reflection responses with interpersonal problems.

The research by Dipboye and by Cummings suggests that the content of the material affects the counseling process. Relatively few studies, however, focus on this content dimension, which is quite surprising given that most theories of counseling and therapy specifically advocate the focus on specific content areas, and that counselor training focuses a great deal on content.

One major problem is the lack of any well-developed system for categorizing content material. Diploye's system of classifying content seems biased toward a counselor's definition of "appropriate" content areas, and thus it may be limited. The intrapersonal-interpersonal categorization of Cummings seems useful but perhaps too simple; future research might explore the utility of developing several finer categories rather than the two global categories, and Cummings's distinction might be a starting point. A third major category—impersonal content (weather)—could be added, and each of the three main categories could be divided into subcategories. As an example, Horowitz et al. (1988) identified six types of interpersonal problems: hard to be assertive, hard to be sociable, hard to be submissive, hard to be intimate, too responsible, and too controlling. The categories of intrapersonal and nonpersonal content could be subdivided in a similar manner. Another reason for exploring such a differentiated system is that there is evidence in the coping, problem-solving literature that different problem types lead to different problem-solving activities (see Heppner & Krauskopf, 1987, for a review). In short, additional research is needed to further examine the utility of content and of various classification systems in the counseling relationship.

STRATEGIES, MICRO LEVEL

Strategies are defined as interventions or approaches for helping the client (Highen & Hill, 1984). Perhaps the two most frequently used measures in this area are counselor intentions and client reactions, which are the focus of our discussion in this category.

Counselor and client intentions are a relatively new and unexplored area of examination in process research. At present, all of the research has examined intentions at the speech act level, and most of the work has focused on counselor (as opposed to client) intentions. Hill and O'Grady (1985) define a counselor intention as the covert rationale for (or the "why" of) counselor behavior. These authors have developed a list of 19 pantheoretical, nominal, nonmutually exclusive intentions: set limits, get information, give information, support, focus, clarify, hope, cathart, cognitions, behaviors, self-control, feelings, insight, change, reinforce change, resistance, challenge, relationship, and therapist needs. Because intentions are covert, they are available only through counselor introspective reports. To obtain these introspective reports, researchers have counselors review a videotape or audiotape of a recently completed session. (Hill and O'Grady recommend that this review take place within 24 hours.) For each counselor turn, counselors list up to five intentions that described their goals for that intervention.

This intention measure has been used in numerous studies examining different aspects of counseling process (see, for example, Fuller & Hill, 1985; Kivlighan, 1989; Kivlighan & Angelone, 1991). For instance, Hill and O'Grady (1985) found that counselor theoretical orientation was related to differential intention use, and that intention use changed both within and across sessions. More important was Hill, Helms, Tichenor, Spiegel, O'Grady, and Perry's (1988) finding that counselor intentions were more adequate descriptors of counselor behavior than were response modes. Specifically, intentions either alone or in conjunction with response modes (counselor actions) accounted for significantly more of the variance in immediate outcome ratings than did response mode measures alone. This finding supports the continued use of intention measures for examining counselor behavior.

Some controversy surrounds the measurement of counseling intentions. Hill and colleagues have simply asked counselors to record their intentions while reviewing taped sessions, sometimes with little or no training in the use of the intentions measure. This method of ascertaining intentions makes it virtually impossible to obtain estimates of reliability. Martin, Martin, and Slemon (1989) have contended that counselors often use different intention categories to describe nominally identical reasons for behaving; consequently they have modified Hill and O'Grady's (1985) procedure for collecting intentions. Martin et al. had counselors review each videotape and for each turn describe their intentions or reasons for the intervention. These descriptions were then transcribed and submitted to judges, who placed the descriptions into the categories in the Hill and O'Grady intentions list. One advantage of this procedure is that the reliability of category placement can be assessed by examining agreement across judges.

Given the concerns of Martin et al. (1989) about counselors using the intentions list in an idiosyncratic manner, we recommend that researchers use one of two procedures for examining counselor intentions. First, researchers could use a procedure in which counselors orally (Martin et al.) or in writing (Kivlighan, 1990) describe their intentions, and then raters decide on category placement. Second, researchers could develop more extensive training procedures designed to ensure that counselors have a common understanding of the intentions list. A researcher could develop, for example, a list of counselor-stated reasons for intervening and have potential research participants practice placing these reasons into intention categories until an acceptable level of agreement is reached.

Reaction is the internal, subjective response of a client or a counselor to the other's speech act or person. Although counseling process research on the client's and counselor's subjective responses to the session has had a long history (see, for example, Orlinsky & Howard, 1978), examination of the client's or counselor's response to particular speech acts has occurred only recently.

Hill, Helms, Spiegel, and Tichenor (1988) developed a system for categorizing client reactions to counselor interventions. This system contains 21 categories of reactions, grouped into 14 positive reactions (felt understood, felt supported, felt hopeful, felt relief, became aware of negative thoughts or behaviors, gained better self-understanding, became more clear, became aware of feelings, took responsibility, got unstuck, gained new perspective, got educated, learned new ways to behave, and felt challenged) and 7 negative reactions (felt scared, worse, stuck, lack of direction, confused, misunderstood, and no reaction).

Clients review a videotape of their counseling session, stopping the tape after each therapist response. The clients then use the client reactions list (all 21 reactions) to record their recollected experience. The Client Reactions System has operationalized an important area of counseling process. Even though most counseling theories advocate attempting to alter both clients' external behavior and their internal processing, until the development of the Client Reactions System there was no way of documenting moment-to-moment changes in clients' internal processes. One strength of this system is its ability to differentiate among categories of reactions, which enables the researcher to examine specific effects of counselor interventions (for example, what type of counselor intervention precedes relief in clients, as compared to, say, better self-understanding).

The main concern with this rating system pertains to questions of reliability and validity. We noted that Martin et al. (1989) reported that counselors seemed to use the Counselor Intentions List in an idiosyncratic manner—that they would record different intentions for nominally similar statements of intent. It is likely that the same problem exists with the Client Reactions System. Researchers may want to consider collecting client reactions in a manner similar to that used by Martin et al. to collect intentions, which would involve having the client review a tape of a session and describe either orally or in writing his or her response to each counselor intervention. These descriptions could then be given to judges, who would categorize the reactions using the Hill, Helms, Spiegel, and Tichenor (1988) rating system. The researcher would then be able to examine the reliability of the categorizations. Moreover, in terms of validity, the extent to which client reactions are influenced by, for instance, self- or other-deception is presently unknown.

Although counselors certainly have reactions to what their clients do, few systematic investigations have explored this important area. Most researchers seem to view counseling as a one-way interaction, with the counselor influencing the client and the client passively accepting this influence. Heppner and Claiborn (1989) maintained that the client should be considered an active participant in the counseling process who also exerts influence on the counselor. From this perspective, counselors would be expected to have reactions to their clients. Unfortunately, the development of statement-by-statement or micro-level measures of counselor reactions has not kept pace with the theoretical formulations.

STRATEGIES, GLOBAL LEVEL

Hill and O'Grady's (1985) Counselor Intentions List was designed to capture the counselor's rationale for selecting a specific behavior, technique, or intervention on a moment-to-moment basis. The rationale of the counselor is clearly an aspect of strategy as defined by Highlen and Hill (1984). Recently, Stiles et al. (1996) argued that the same intentions list can be used to describe typical or principal intentions in a whole session. They used "the term session intention to denote the therapist's rationale for using a class of behaviors, response modes, techniques, or interventions with a client during one or more episodes within a session" (Stiles et al., p. 403). Stiles et al. called this revised measure the Therapist Session Intentions (TSI).

Like the Counselor Intentions List (Hill & O'Grady, 1985), the TSI consists of 19 items, each of which is rated on a five-point Likert-type scale: 1 = not at all, 2 = slightly, 3 = somewhat, 4 = pretty much, and 5 = very much. The instructions for the TSI are: "Please rate the extent to which you were carrying out or working toward the following activities or goals generally in this session. Rate each item on the basis of the descriptor which fits your intentions best (not every descriptor needs to fit)" (Stiles et al., 1996, p. 405).

Stiles et al. (1996) suggested that counselors use a combination of several different intentions to pursue a treatment goal, referring to this combined use of related session intentions as a focus. "For example, early in therapy, a therapist might seek to gather information from clients, give information about the treatment, and set limits and expectations . . . ; this cluster of session intentions might be called a treatment context focus" (Stiles et al., p. 403). One of the purposes of the Stiles et al. study was to identify the types of treatment foci that characterized cognitive-behavioral and psychodynamic-interpersonal approaches to counseling.

Stiles et al. (1996) found striking differences in session intention for cognitive-behavioral and psychodynamic-interpersonal sessions. Specifically, cognitive-behavioral sessions had higher levels of the following session-intention categories: reinforce change, cognitions, self-control, behaviors, and change session. Psychodynamic-interpersonal sessions had higher levels of the following session intention categories: feelings-awareness, insight, cathart, and relationship. Factor analysis was used to identify treatment foci in the two types of sessions. Both the cognitive-behavioral and the psychodynamic-interpersonal sessions had seven session foci: (1) treatment context (set limits, get information, give information), (2) session structure (focus, clarify), (3) affect (cathart, feelings-awareness), (4) obstacles (resistance, therapist needs, challenge, relationship), (5) encouraging change (hope, change, reinforce change), (6) behavior (self-control, behaviors), and (7) cognition-insight (insight, cognitions).

Stiles et al. (1996) also examined how the identified foci changed over time in the cognitive-behavioral and psychodynamic-interpersonal treatments. Overall, the cognitive-behavioral treatment sessions had greater focus on treatment context, encouraging change and behavior, whereas the psychodynamic-interpersonal treatment sessions had greater focus on affect and obstacles. In addition, all seven foci showed significant changes in pattern over time. For example, the treatment context and affect foci decreased over time, whereas the encouraging change and cognition-insight foci increased over time.

INTERPERSONAL MANNER, MICRO LEVEL

Interpersonal manner refers to subjective elements of the counseling relationship, such as attitudes, involvement, and communication patterns (Highen & Hill, 1984). Much of the early process literature involved measurement of the necessary and sufficient conditions described by Rogers (1955). The single most widely addressed research topic has been the assessment of counselor empathy (see the review by Parloff, Waskow, & Wolfe, 1978). This assessment has typically involved trained raters listening to or reading transcripts of segments of counseling sessions and rating the empathy of each counselor response. Although the focus of much early research, the examination of counselor empathy (at the micro level) has now slowed to a virtual standstill. (Research on empathy at the global level continues.) More recently, counselor and client interpersonal manner has also been assessed by using some variant of the Leary (1957) system to classify counselor speech along the dimensions of control and affiliation (see, for example, Penman, 1980). Another version of this system, an inventory called the Interpersonal Communication Rating Scale, was developed by Strong et al. (1988). They used the dimensions of control and affiliation to define eight types or styles of counselor or client communication: leading, self-enhancing, critical, distrustful, self-effacing, docile, cooperative, and nurturant.

Compared to the global level, far less research has examined counselor interpersonal manner at the micro level of speech acts. One study examined differences in counselor interpersonal manner with successfully versus unsuccessfully treated clients (Henry, Schacht, & Strupp, 1986). These authors classified counselor speech acts using Benjamin's (1974) system, which, like the Strong et al. (1988) system, is based on Leary's (1957) dimensions of control and affiliation. They found significant differences in counselor interpersonal manner between the successful and unsuccessful cases; specifically, counselors were less likely to reciprocate client hostility in successful cases.

We suspect that additional research addressing counselor interpersonal manner at the microscopic level may be fruitful. It may be especially helpful to conduct research that examines the relations between counselor interpersonal manner at the speech act level and more global ratings of interpersonal manner.

INTERPERSONAL MANNER, GLOBAL LEVEL

The Barrett-Lennard Relationship Inventory (Barrett-Lennard, 1962) was designed to measure client perceptions of counselor-offered conditions. Clients generally fill out this inventory after interacting with the counselor over a number of sessions. One of the interesting aspects of the research on counselor empathy is the divergence of findings on the connection between counselor empathy and counseling outcome (see Parloff et al., 1978). Research at the micro or speech act level has generally shown no relationship between counselor-offered empathy and client outcome (Gurman, 1977). At the global level, however, research reveals a moderate relationship between client ratings of counselor empathy and client outcome, suggesting that assessments of these global ratings of counselor interpersonal manner are important. In short, empathy at the global level is an important dimension of counselor behavior. Other aspects of counselor interpersonal manner that can be usefully assessed at this relationship level are unclear at this time.

Another widely used global measure of counselor interpersonal manner has been the Counselor Rating Form (Barak & LaCrosse, 1975). Strong (1968) had initially hypothesized that a counselor's power or ability to influence a client (for example, to change an opinion) was related to source characteristics of the counselor—namely, perceived counselor expertness, attractiveness, and trustworthiness. These constructs were operationalized in the Counselor Rating Form as counselor attractiveness, expertness, and trustworthiness. Like the Barrett-Lennard Relationship Inventory, this rating is usually (although not always) made on a session-to-session basis.

Scores from the Counselor Rating Form have been used as both dependent (or criterion) and independent (or predictor) variables in research using the social influence paradigm (see reviews by Corrigan et al., 1980; Heppner & Claiborn, 1989; Heppner & Dixon, 1981; Heppner & Frazier, 1992; Hoyt, 1996). In short, a large body of research has examined the influence of various independent variables (diplomas, communication style) on client ratings of counselor attractiveness, expertness, and trustworthiness. Another group of studies has examined the relationship of client-rated attractiveness, expertness, and trustworthiness to client outcome.

The client's interpersonal manner also has been measured at the global level; the work of Leary (1957) on interpersonal diagnosis has served as a foundation for most of the examination of client style of interacting. Elliott and James (1989) reviewed the literature on the client's experience in psychotherapy and proposed three dimensions to account for their findings: positive versus negative affiliation, control versus independence, and interpersonal versus task focus. Two instruments developed by Kiesler (1984,

1987) use the control and affiliation dimensions to describe client or counselor interpersonal manner. The Impact Message Inventory (IMI; Kiesler, 1987) assesses client interpersonal manner by recording the engagements or pulls that a client has on another interactant or observer (that is, what the person feels, thinks, or wants to do as he or she interacts or observes this client). The Check List of Psychotherapy Transactions (CLOPT) and the Check List of Interpersonal Transactions (CLOIT) define the client's style by describing overt interpersonal actions. The IMI, CLOPT, and CLOIT can characterize clients in terms of 16 interpersonal scores: dominant, competitive, mistrusting, cold, hostile, detached, inhibited, unassured, submissive, deferent, trusting, warm, friendly, sociable, exhibitionistic, and assured. These interpersonal scores can be combined to form octant, quadrant, or axes descriptions of client interpersonal style. We believe research in this area is promising. For example, Orlinsky and Howard (1986) noted a positive association between client openness and therapeutic outcome.

THERAPEUTIC RELATIONSHIP, MICRO LEVEL

The relationship in counseling is more than the sum of the interactants. Measuring only what the client and counselor or the group members do individually does not constitute a measure of this relationship. Process measures thus focus on the developing relationship between and among clients and counselors.

The quality of this relationship has received a great deal of theoretical and empirical attention. In individual counseling, the quality of the relationship is usually examined in terms of the therapeutic or working alliance (see, for example, Horvath & Greenberg, 1989). In group research, this dimension is usually examined in terms of cohesion (see the review by Bednar & Kaul, 1978). However, almost all of this work has been at the global level (see the next section); indeed, a major issue in assessing the quality of the relationship is the lack of micro-level speech act measures of the working alliance. Bordin's (1979) conceptualizations of the working alliance emphasized the "tear and repair" process, which is best conceptualized at the speech act level. It may be useful to develop speech act measures of the working alliance, so that an examination of the client and therapist behaviors that lead to tearing and repairing the alliance can be concluded.

We are aware of only one measure of cohesion at the speech act level. Friedlander, Thibodeau, Nichols, Tucker, and Snyder (1985) defined cohesion as the semantic relations within a spoken text that make it cohere or coalesce as a unit. They operationalized a cohesive tie as occurring when the interpretation of one speaker's message depends on information contained in the previous speaker's turn. According to these authors, there are five categories or types of cohesive ties: reference, conjunction, substitution, ellipsis, and lexical, known as the five Categories of Semantic Cohesion Analysis. Friedlander et al. argued that semantic cohesion is a measure of conversational involvement, an important component of all definitions of cohesion. The results of the Friedlander et al. study indicated that leader style was related to the number of cohesive ties produced in a group, and that groups with more cohesive ties had better client outcomes. These findings suggest that this speech act measure of cohesion may be a useful means of studying this elusive group phenomenon.

THERAPEUTIC RELATIONSHIP, GLOBAL LEVEL

Frank (1974), in summarizing 25 years of research, concluded that "the quality of the therapeutic interaction, to which the patient, therapist, and therapeutic method contribute, is probably the major determinant of short-term therapeutic response" (p. 328). The quality of therapeutic interaction at the global level is the focus of the various measures of the therapeutic or working alliance. Of the four commonly used measures of the working alliance, three were designed for use by trained observers: the California Psychotherapy Alliance Scales (CALPAS; Marmar et al., 1986), the Penn Helping Alliance Rating Scale (Alexander & Luborsky, 1986), and the Vanderbilt Therapeutic Alliance Scale (VTAS; Hartley & Strupp, 1983). The Working Alliance Inventory (WAI; Horvath & Greenberg, 1989), is designed to capture client and therapist perceptions of the working alliance.

A study by Tichenor and Hill (1989) compared these various measures of the working alliance. These authors also devised an observer form of the WAI (adopted by altering the pronouns to fit an observer's perspective). All of the working alliance measures had high internal consistency; coefficient alphas ranged from .90 for the CALPAS to .98 for the WAI-observer form. In addition, the four observer ratings forms had high inter-rater reliability; interclass correlations ranged from .71 for the Penn to .94 for the CALPAS. Three of the four observer measures (CALPAS, VTAS, and WAI-observer form) also had high intercorrelations, indicating that they were measuring a single working alliance construct. (The Penn was significantly correlated with the WAI-observer form only.) These findings suggest common elements across the four observer measures of the working alliance. In addition, the WAI-observer form was the most economical measure because it did not require any rater training. Replication of the Tichenor and Hill study would provide strong support for using the WAI-observer form to operationalize the working alliance.

Tichenor and Hill (1989) also found the lack of a relationship among observer, client, and counselor perspectives on working alliance ratings. Thus, it is unclear what the measurements of the working alliance from the different perspectives actually assess; further research is needed to address the lack of agreement across the working alliance perspectives.

Fuhriman and Burlingame (1990) described cohesion in groups as analogous to the relationship in individual counseling. Kaul and Bednar (1986) declared that the term *cohesion* has such an endemic use in group treatment that descriptions of what happens in "groups would be practically impossible without reference to cohesion." Despite its clinical utility, the concept of cohesion has been a "spectacular embarrassment" for group researchers (Kaul & Bednar, p. 707). Most researchers have attempted to measure cohesion at a global level. As implied in Kaul and Bednar's comment, there is no consensus on a definition of or way to operationalize cohesion. Most of the research that examines cohesion has developed idiosyncratic derivatives of the concept, resulting in inconclusive findings and little cumulative knowledge of the construct. It might be a useful step for the group counseling field to examine the relationship between the different measures of cohesion. A study similar in format to Tichenor and Hill (1989) that examines group cohesion measures might well provide both theoretical and operational clarity for this important but messy area.

In summary, the therapeutic relationship is a key ingredient of the counseling process. Additional research is needed to develop a speech act measure of the working alliance. Only with this type of measure can investigators begin to examine Bordin's (1979) notion of the "tear and repair" process in the actual formation of the working alliance. Moreover, additional research is needed to examine how the three perspectives (client, counselor, observer) on working alliance formation interact. Are they complementary, unrelated, or just different? Researchers interested in group cohesion research have a promising speech act measure. It appears that research at the global level could be enhanced by a comparative study of the different measures that purport to measure cohesion.

QUALITY, MICRO LEVEL

Quality refers to how well or how completely the counselor carries out a single or a series of interventions, or how well the client enacts his or her role or tasks. Clinically, counselor competence is extremely important, but until recently it has been virtually ignored in process research. For example, even though dynamically oriented counselors speak of the timing and correctness of an interpretation, most research on this topic has simply examined the presence or amount of interpretation (see the review by Claiborn, 1982).

At the speech act level, one of the most commonly used measures of the quality of the counselor's intervention is the Helpfulness Scale (Elliott, 1985). To use this measure, clients review a recently completed counseling session and rate each of their counselor's interventions on a nine-point scale measuring helpfulness. This method assumes that the client is in fact the best arbiter of the usefulness of counseling. At present it is unknown whether such a rating of the helpfulness of specific counselor interventions is related to client outcome. When a client rates therapist interventions as more helpful, for example, will he or she have a better outcome than a client who rates his or her therapist's interventions as less helpful?

A second method for examining quality of counselor interventions at the speech act level has been described by Silberschatz, Fretter, and Curtis (1986). These authors maintained that assessing the quality of counselor behaviors involves two processes: (1) identifying the client's problems and needs, and (2) deciding if a given intervention correctly addresses those problems and needs. Specifically, Silberschatz et al. assessed the quality of therapist interpretations using two steps. The first step involved formulating for each client a plan or conceptualization, a prominent part of which involved identifying insights that would be helpful to the client. Five clinicians independently prepared such a plan for each client using assessment instruments and transcripts from an assessment interview. The second step involved having a second group of judges rate the extent to which each counselor interpretation fit the plan that had been developed. These judges used a seven-point Likert scale ranging from –3 (strongly anti-plan) to +3 (strongly pro-plan) to measure the extent of agreement between the plan and the individual interpretation. Silberschatz et al. found that the compatibility of an interpretation with a plan was a better predictor of immediate outcome (change in client experience) than was type of interpretation (transference versus nontransference).

Silberschatz et al. (1986) suggested that their methods or procedures for assessing quality of counselor interventions were transferable to a variety of conceptual frameworks. We agree with this suggestion. To reiterate, this method of assessing quality requires two steps. First, an independent and reliable conceptualization of the client, including a specification of his or her particular learning needs, is needed. Second, an independent and reliable rating of the extent to which particular interventions fit the conceptualization is needed.

As was true for assessing the quality of therapist interventions, there is relatively little consensus concerning measures of client response quality. One obstacle to the development of standardized quality measures is that various theories define the client role differently, and hence the appropriateness or quality of various client responses is viewed in divergent ways. For example, a behavior therapist might construe a client response of questioning or disagreeing with the therapist as a sign of resistance to implementing a treatment protocol, and thus assign it a low quality rating. A dynamic therapist, on the other hand, might construe the same response as a sign of autonomy, and thus assign it a high quality rating. Despite these theoretical differences, there is surprising consistency in usage of two particular speech act ratings of client response quality, which we will now discuss.

One of the most widely used ratings of client response quality is the Client Experiencing Scale (Klein, Mathieu-Coughlin, & Kiesler, 1986), which is a seven-point scale used by trained raters to describe a client's level of involvement. Low levels are characterized by client disclosures that are impersonal or superficial. At high levels of experiencing, feelings and exploration are a basis for problem resolution and/or self-understanding. Klein et al. reported high inter-rater reliability and validity, as evidenced by the relationships between client experiencing and self-exploration, insight, working through, the absence of resistances, and high-quality free association.

The second measure that has been used to operationalize the quality of client responding at the speech act level is the Client Vocal Quality Scale (CVQ; Rice, Koke, Greenberg, & Wagstaff, 1979). Like the Client Experiencing Scale, the CVQ is designed to measure the quality of the client's involvement in the counseling process. Vocal quality is a measure of how the energy of a speech act is expressed. According to this system, voice quality can be characterized as limited, externalizing, emotional, or focused (from low to high voice quality). In limited vocal quality, there is a lack of energy; the voice has a thinness that seems to suggest a withdrawal of energy. Externalizing vocal quality involves an external or outward movement of energy designed to produce an effect in a listener. Emotional vocal quality contains an overflow of energy, whereas focused vocal quality involves energy that is concentrated and directed inward. Like the Client Experiencing Scale, the CVQ has good reliability and validity data (Rice et al., 1979).

It is worth noting that the two most widely used measures of client response quality (at the speech act level) were developed by researchers operating within a client-centered perspective, which more than any other theoretical formulation places a premium on the client's involvement in the counseling process. Thus, it is probably not surprising that client-centered researchers have concentrated on developing measures of client process. What is surprising is how widely these client response quality measures have been adopted by researchers from other theoretical perspectives. For example, Silberschatz et al. (1986) used the Client Experiencing Scale to examine the quality of analytic interpretations.

As noted earlier, it seems likely that other theoretical perspectives would define client response quality in terms other than the quality of client involvement. It may be important to develop process measures that offer complementary views of what constitutes client response quality. An example of an alternative perspective for defining client response quality was reported by Martin and Stelmaczonek (1988), who used categories of discourse analysis that were drawn from a theoretical framework of information processing to define the quality of a client's response. Specifically, they rated client speech acts on five information-processing dimensions: (1) deep-shallow, (2) elaborative-nonelaborative, (3) personal-impersonal, (4) clear-vague, and (5) conclusion oriented-description oriented. Martin and Stelmaczonek found that events clients recalled as being important (when compared to events not so recalled) were characterized by client speech acts that involved (1) interpretive, critical, and analytic thinking (deep); (2) thinking that involved unique language, images, or metaphors (elaborative); or (3) interpretations or hypotheses (conclusion-oriented). It would be especially interesting to see how these measures of client response quality, derived from information-processing theory, would relate to the more established measures (experiencing and voice quality) de-rived from client-centered theory.

QUALITY, GLOBAL LEVEL

There has been far less work measuring counselor quality at a global level. This lack of empirical investigation is probably because the measurement of counselor competence presents a number of thorny problems. Whereas naïve raters can be trained to rate adherence to a treatment model, rating of counselor competence presumes a level of general clinical sophistication and expertise in the particular treatment method being rated. For example, it its easier to train an observer to recognize whether or not a counselor makes an interpretation than it is to train an observer to rate the appropriateness (accuracy, timing) of an interpretation. Several researchers have attempted to measure therapist competence; for example, Barber and Crits-Christoph (1996) developed the Penn Adherence and Competence Scale for Supportive-Expressive Therapy (PACSE). As the name suggests, the PACSE is designed to rate both the frequency and quality of specific counselor responses associated with Luborky's manualized supportive-expressive treatment. Each item on the PACSE is rated twice: once for adherence (frequency) and once for competence (quality). The competence quality ratings are made on a seven-point scale ranging from 1 (poor quality) to 7 (excellent quality).

In the initial development of the PACSE (Barber & Crits-Christoph, 1996), two Ph.D.-level clinical psychologists rated audiotapes from 33 depressed patients receiving supportive-expressive therapy and seven patients receiving cognitive therapy. The PACSE contains 45 items covering general therapeutic skills (9 items), supportive techniques (9 items), and expressive techniques (27 items). Inter-rater reliabilities for the competence ratings were low when only supportive-expressive sessions were examined; when all sessions were examined, the inter-rater reliabilities were considerably higher. When Barber and Crits-Christoph examined the correlations between the PACSE adherence and competence ratings, they found that adherence and competence ratings are related but distinct constructs. Presumably, a counselor must have some level of adherence before she or he can demonstrate competence. In a more recent study, Crits-Christoph et al. (1998) used six of the original PACSE expressive items to rate competence in the delivery of a modified form of supportive-expressive counseling. The competence ratings in the Crits-Christoph et al. study were made by the clinical supervisors of the project counselors. The three very experienced supportive-expressive supervisors made competence ratings for both their own supervisees and the supervisees of the other supervisors. The Barber and Crits-Christoph and the Crits-Christoph et al. studies suggest that competence in supportive-expressive counseling can be rated relatively reliably (by experienced supervisors) and that adherence and competence are related but distinct constructs.

The PACSE has now been used in at least three studies (Barber & Crits-Christoph, 1996; Barber, Crits-Christoph, & Luborsky, 1996; Crits-Christoph et al., 1998). These studies show that supportive and expressive competence ratings are related to clients' level of psychopathology, depression, or psychological health and unrelated to current measures of the working alliance (Barber & Crits-Christoph). In a large-scale training study, expressive competence ratings were shown to change linearly (improve) across counseling sessions for the trainees' first training case (Crits-Christoph et al.). Finally, expressive competence ratings were related to improvement in depression for clients in supportive-expressive treatment for depression. The relationship between expressive competence and improvement remained after controlling for the therapists' use (adherence) of expressive techniques, previous improvement, the therapeutic alliance, and general therapeutic skills (Barber, Crits-Christoph, & Luborsky).

For our purposes, the most important aspects of the studies by Barber and colleagues are the procedures used to operationalize the global level of therapist competence. To do this, the researcher must first carefully and specifically define the parameters of the treatment. Once the treatment has been specified, then the therapist's behaviors within a session can be examined on the extent to which they match or represent competent expression of the specified behaviors. The critical question for counseling researchers concerns the qualifications of the competence raters/judges. For example, Barber (1998, personal communication) emphasizes that use of the PACSE scale requires training in both the use of the scale and supportive-expressive therapy. It is likely that only judges who are experts in a particular modality can make accurate competency judgments. The assessment of counselor quality is an exciting and virtually untapped area for process researchers. The methods and procedures developed by Silberschatz et al. (1986) and Barber and Crits-Christoph (1996) to assess counselor quality can serve as models for researchers seeking to measure the quality of counselor behavior from other theoretical perspectives.

The examination of client response quality at the global level has received even more limited attention. One of the most promising dimensions for characterizing client response quality at the global level is formulated in terms of openness versus defensiveness. Orlinsky and Howard (1986) reported that 88% of the studies examining client openness found a positive relationship between this variable and outcome measures. There is, however, little agreement on how this construct should be measured at the global level. In the 16 studies that examined client openness, the same process measure was seldom used to assess this construct. Nor is it known how the different measures that assess client openness relate to one another. Given the positive association between client openness and therapeutic outcome noted by Orlinsky and Howard, development of more standardized ways of assessing this construct at a global level seems important.

Two Postscripts

We have some final comments concerning two topics: client process measures and assessment strategies. With regard to the former, Hill (1982) observed that counselor process variables have attracted more theoretical and empirical attention than client process variables, perhaps because we as counselors/ researchers are most interested in examining what we do, as evidenced by the differential attention focused on counselor and client response modes.

We believe this relative lack of attention to client process variables is a critical omission that hampers our understanding of the counseling process. Moreover, we strongly recommend that the client be conceptualized not as a passive agent to whom interventions are administered, but rather as an active processor of information in the change process (see Heppner & Claiborn, 1989; Heppner & Krauskopf, 1987; Martin, 1984, 1987; McGuire, 1985; Petty & Cacioppo, 1986). The Martin and Stelmaczonek (1988) investigation is an excellent example of conceptualizing the client as an active processor of information. Because human reasoning is a key activity in how people cope with their problems, attention to the active process of human reasoning deserves a central place in counseling process research.

Such a perspective might best be examined in both the content and quality aspects of process research. With regard to content, it may be useful to examine how clients represent their presenting problems to themselves (for example, via schemas), and whether the client's views of the problem change over time in counseling. Are there changes in the client's knowledge of the problem over time, or in the way the client's knowledge is organized? (See Martin, 1985, for an excellent case illustration.) It also may be important to investigate how clients deal with their affective reactions and how they appraise the significance of their problems. In short, we believe it may be very fruitful to examine the internal processes that clients engage in (cognitive, affective, and physiological) as they struggle with their problems before, during, and after counseling. Whereas client satisfaction or perceptions of counselor expertness provide some information about the client, these variables tell us little about how clients process information about the pressing concerns that brought them into counseling (Heppner & Claiborn, 1989; Heppner & Frazier, 1992).

Finally, some comments on assessment strategies are warranted given the multifaceted nature of counseling process and outcome research. Whereas most instruments can be categorized within one of the cells in Table 19.1, some instruments contain items that provide assessments across more than one aspect of the counseling process. Given the need to obtain a broad assessment of the counseling process, and the time-consuming nature of multiple assessments, the advantages of such inventories are clear. For example, consider the Comprehensive Scale of Psychotherapy Session Constructs (CSPSC; Eugster & Wampold, 1996). The CSPSC measures session-level occurrences from either the client's or the therapist's perspective of nine counseling process components (patient involvement, client involvement, comfort, learning, therapist involvement, expertness, interpersonal style, real relationship) and session evaluation. In short, an 80-item, six-point Likert scale was developed by adapting items from the California Psychotherapy Alliance Scales (Barkham, Andrew, & Culverwell, 1993), the Empathy Scale (Burns, 1981), the Experiencing Scales (Klein, Mathieu, Kiesler, & Gendlin, 1969), the Patient and Therapist Behavior Ratings (Bennum, Hahlweg, Schindler, & Langlotz, 1986), the Patient and Therapist Therapy Session Reports (Orlinsky & Howard, 1978), the Penn Helping Alliance Scales (Luborsky et al., 1983), the Relationship Inventory (Barrett-Lennard, 1962), the Session Evaluation Questionnaire (Stiles & Snow, 1984), the Session Impacts Scale (Elliott & Wexler, 1994), the Therapist and Patient Action Scales (Hoyt, Marmar, Horowitz, & Alvarez, 1981), the Vanderbilt Psychotherapy Process Scale (Suh, O'Malley, Strupp, & Johnson, 1989), and the Working Alliance Inventory (Horvath & Greenberg, 1986). Eight items were devised for each of the nine constructs and for global session evaluation. Alpha coefficients revealed an average of .73 and .76 for subscales on the therapist and patient forms, respectively. Assessment strategies such as this, and instruments such as the CSPSC in particular, hold a great deal of promise for future research.

SUMMARY AND CONCLUSIONS

This chapter provided a general introduction to counseling process research, or investigations that examine events that occur within the therapeutic encounter. Researchers have examined a very wide range of activities, such as therapist self-disclosure, client reactions, the working alliance, perceived therapist empathy, client openness, and various interventions (for example, interpretations). We discussed Hill's (1991) scheme for classifying the various behaviors within process research, which consists of the following seven types of behaviors: (1) ancillary behaviors, (2) verbal behaviors, (3) covert behaviors, (4) content, (5) strategies, (6) interpersonal manner, and (7) the therapeutic relationship. The discovery of new knowledge pertaining to these categories of counseling process research can be exhilarating.

The research that examines counseling process and outcomes is vast; Orlinsky et al. (1994) counted more than 2,300 process and outcomes studies from 1950 to 1992. Clearly, process research has been a very important theme within the counseling literature. Perhaps one of the major stimulants for much of the process research in the early 1960s and 1970s was Rogers's (1957) formulation of the necessary and sufficient conditions for therapeutic gain.

Most of the counseling process research over the years has focused on individual counseling with European-American participants; relatively few empirical studies have been conducted on racial and cultural factors in the therapy process (Helms, 1994). Moreover, the process of career counseling remains largely unexplored (Swanson, 1995). Although much has been learned about the counseling process in the past 50 years, many basic research questions relative to various ethnic and nonethnic minority populations remain.

Many design considerations for conducting research (for example, selecting variables, experimenter bias) discussed earlier in this book apply to counseling process research. The second part of this chapter highlighted five methodological and measurement issues that are particularly relevant for counseling process researchers: (1) what to study, (2) what to measure, (3) whose perspective, (4) how much to measure, and (5) how to analyze process data. We maintained that it is very important for researchers to be very careful in selecting behaviors to examine in process research; examination of various classification schemes (see, for example, Elliott, 1991; Hill, 1991) might help guide researchers. In addition, it is important to consider at what level the researcher wants to examine the behaviors, from statement-by-statement speech acts to more global levels. Research clearly documents that the counseling process differs across various perspectives, such as from the client, counselor, or observer perspective. We encourage researchers to carefully think about the different perspectives in developing research questions, and if appropriate, to examine the counseling process from multiple perspectives.

We noted that important differences between the first and last session have also been observed in process research. Thus, in determining how much to measure it is critical to think through the research questions very carefully; it may be useful to include individual differences or time intervals in the research questions. With group designs, sampling a part of several sessions will likely yield acceptable results, whereas single-subject designs may need to examine the entire session without sampling. Finally, in terms of analyzing the data, we highlighted the critical issue of using nonparticipatory judges in rating data. The task of rating data from process studies merits careful consideration of a number of issues, including the number of judges, rater selection, rater bias, rater errors, rater training, maintaining morale among judges, and data aggregation. We also briefly discussed statistical strategies to analyze quantitative data, ranging from correlational designs to more powerful sequential analysis.

STIMULUS QUESTIONS

AN EXERCISE TO ANALYZE TWO COUNSELING PROCESS STUDIES

The following exercise is designed to help readers not only to become more aware of the intricacies of counseling process research, but also to become more aware of different types of counseling process methods.

First, identify two published articles that investigated the counseling process. One article should employ quantitative methods and the second qualitative methods. Study these two articles, and then respond to the following questions. In addition, if you want, ask a peer to join you in this exercise; independently respond to the questions for the same two articles, and then discuss and compare your responses.

1. What constructs or variables were investigated in each article?
2. How were the constructs or variables for each of these two articles measured or assessed?
3. How adequately do you think the constructs/variables were measured or assessed?
4. From whose perspective was the counseling process examined?
5. What were the pros and cons of examining the counseling process from these perspectives?
6. What were the pros and cons of the quantitative and the qualitative methodologies used across the two articles?
7. What conclusions were drawn from each article about the counseling process?
8. What limitations do you see about the conclusions from each study?
9. What would be some exciting "next best studies" to follow each of the two process articles?
10. What types of methodologies would you use to conduct those studies, and why?

20 CHAPTER | SCALE CONSTRUCTION

Dong-gwi Lee and Hyun-Woo Lim

Scale construction is a widely used research methodology in the field of counseling psychology research. According to Buboltz, Miller, and Williams (1999), 9% of the articles published in the *Journal of Counseling Psychology* from 1973 to 1998 concerned the development and validation of various scales and measures. The term *scale* in counseling research is typically defined as "a collection of items, the responses to which are scored and combined to yield a scale score" (Dawis, 1987, p. 481). A scale would be categorized into one of two types (Pett, Lackey, & Sullivan, 2003): (1) a criterion-referenced scale, which measures an individual's ability (e.g., achievement tests), or (2) a norm-referenced scale, which aims to differentiate individuals standing along dimensions of a given construct, typically "portrayed along a continuum of values" (e.g., personality or attitude tests) (pp. 14–15). The majority of scale construction in the field of counseling concerns the latter (i.e., "individual differences scales"; Dawis, p. 481). In this chapter, therefore, we limit our discussion to norm-referenced scales.

The purpose of this chapter is to demystify the process of scale construction. First, commonly observed misconceptions or myths pertaining to the scale construction process will be highlighted. Subsequently, a discussion of typical steps of scale construction along with examples from journal articles will be provided. Given that an in-depth discussion of statistical analyses (e.g., various scaling methods, factor analyses) is beyond the scope of this chapter, those more interested in statistical analyses are directed to additional resources (e.g., Dawis, 2000; Heppner & Heppner, 2004; Pett et al., 2003).

SEVEN COMMON MYTHS ON SCALE CONSTRUCTION

This section provides a discussion of seven common myths that researchers unwittingly assume in scale construction. The first four myths concern the scale construction process in general, and the latter three myths pertain to cross-cultural or multicultural considerations germane to scale construction.

MYTH 1: ITEM CONSTRUCTION CAN BE DONE IN A COUPLE OF WEEKS

Researchers are tempted to believe that they can develop items in a short period of time, or if they exert high levels of concentration due to an impending deadline. However, this common myth comes from a lack of understanding of the arduous and time-consuming processes of scale construction. For instance, the item generation process itself is not linear; researchers often add, delete, and revise the items multiple times to hone their meaning or focus. This recursive process is inevitable even after pilot testing, and such revisions take considerable time and effort; for example, it is not uncommon for item construction to take six months or longer. It is critical to remember that a scale is only as good as its items, and that hurried item construction often leads to disappointing results. As for the arduous processes in item construction, some examples are provided for illustrative purpose later in this chapter. It is very important that the reader understands the complex processes of scale construction, particularly item generation, pilot testing, and, if necessary, translation and back translation.

MYTH 2: ITEMS CAN BE EASILY CONSTRUCTED WITHOUT AN EXTENSIVE LITERATURE REVIEW

Sometimes researchers believe that items can be created through a couple of meetings where the research team members brainstorm the content and focus of items. This certainly is not true. A sound scale requires a clear definition and operationalization of the construct (Pett et al., 2003), and this can be achieved only from careful deliberation, a clear definition of the construct, and an extensive literature review. There is no substitute for this time- and energy-consuming process. In essence, the literature review is crucial because it can provide a solid theoretical/conceptual grounding of the construct and/or a wealth of information from previous research findings that investigated similar constructs. An example of adequate literature review in scale construction will be presented later in this chapter.

MYTH 3: IT IS BEST TO USE A CONVENIENCE SAMPLE WHENEVER POSSIBLE

Researchers typically face a situation in which scale construction is a component of a larger project (e.g., dissertations, grant proposals); thus, many want to collect data quickly. It is not surprising that a number of researchers utilize convenience samples (e.g., psychology undergraduates) for testing the psychometric properties of their scales. Although college student samples could be relevant for some cases (e.g., the development of a scale designed to measure college students' career decision-making style), this is not always the case. For example, if researchers want to develop a new scale to measure individuals' general trait of procrastination, not only should the researchers devise items relevant to trait procrastination (not procrastination specific to academia), but they also should administer the scale to a broader population rather than just college students. It is also important to note that psychology students may not be representative of all college students. In the same vein, even within psychology undergraduates, the external validity (i.e., generalizability) of the scale can be compromised by other factors such as race and ethnicity. Alexander and Suzuki (2001) cautioned against biases in assessment and measurement procedures that lack sensitivity to multicultural issues, and highlighted the importance of obtaining representative samples of various racial and ethnic populations.

Myth 4: Conducting a Factor Analysis Ensures the Validity of the Scale

Although statistical advancements in factor analytic techniques provide a useful tool for the researcher in testing the latent structure of the scale, which provides an estimate of construct validity, it should be noted that factor analysis alone cannot provide sufficient estimates of validity. Sometimes researchers skip the necessary steps to test validity, such as convergent and discriminant validity estimates. For example, sometimes researchers attempt to make the research packet as short as possible, and do not include extra measures for convergent and discriminant validity estimates. However, this approach may yield serious problems in terms of internal and construct validity. (See discussions on various validity issues in Chapter 5.) For example, if a scale was designed to measure individuals' attitudes toward seeking professional help but a measure for social desirability to test discriminant validity was not included, then it is difficult to determine whether the items developed actually measure the intended construct, or whether participants were simply responding in socially desirable ways. The discriminant validity of a scale can be established by providing a low correlation coefficient between the inventory and the social desirability measure. Likewise, when a scale designed to measure an individual's level of depression is developed, it is an imperative step to examine convergent validity (e.g., concurrent or predictive validity) estimates of the scale by including a more widely used measure of depression (e.g., the Beck Depression Inventory). It is desirable to have a high correlation between the two measures to support convergent validity that the new scale measures depression. Examples of testing convergent and discriminant validity estimates will be presented later in this chapter. In summary, it is crucial to include measures of convergent and discriminant estimates in addition to a plan to conduct a factor analysis in establishing the validity of a new inventory.

Myth 5: A Scale with Strong Psychometric Properties Developed in a Western Culture Is Universally Valid

Sometimes researchers may mistakenly assume that a scale that has been validated in a Western culture will also be suitable for people in other cultures, and thus a careful translation and back translation will ensure cross-cultural compatibility. Translating and back-translating the items of a scale only indicate that the *items* have been adequately translated into another language, but does not provide any estimates of the validity of the scale in the other culture. If an adequately translated version of a scale replicates its original factor structure or reveals a similar factor structure in another culture, such results provide one estimate of construct validity, and the scale may be potentially suitable for the new culture. However, satisfactory results in factor analyses on a scale do not always guarantee the equivalence of two versions of the scale (an original version developed in the Western culture and a translated version in a non-Western culture). A psychological construct measured by a scale is *culture-bound*. A scale developed in one culture about a particular target is based on the beliefs and assumptions of the particular cultural group, which may differ from the beliefs/assumptions about this construct in another culture. Thus, it is important to provide cross-cultural validation of a scale.

As an example, Lee, Park, Shin, and Graham (2005) conducted an exploratory factor analysis (EFA) with a sample of Korean college students by using the Frost Multidimensional Perfectionism Scales (Frost, Marten, Lahart, & Rosenblate, 1990), which was developed in the United States. Frost et al. reported six factors: (1) concerns over mistake, (2) doubts about action, (3) organization, (4) parental expectations, (5) parental criticism, and (6) personal standards. Although a five-factor solution was also found in some Western cultures (e.g., Harvey, Pallant, & Harvey, 2004; Purdon, Antony, & Swinson, 1999; Stöber, 1998; Stumpf & Parker, 2000), the EFA results by Lee et al. favored a five-factor solution with parental expectations and parental criticism combined into one new factor called parental pressure. In essence, the parental criticism factor almost disappeared. A similar finding was reported by Cheng, Chong, and Wong (1999) with a Chinese adolescent sample in Hong Kong. Thus, the majority of items in the parental criticism factor failed to be retained, indicating a culturally unique factor structure found in the two studies using Asian samples. Lee et al. described this culturally specific phenomenon as follows:

> It appears that parental pressure is a universal dimension of perfectionism across cultures at least in six different countries; however, we cannot conclude that the nature of the parental pressure factor is invariant between the Eastern and Western cultures. For example, in both Korean and Chinese cultures, items for the parental criticism factor almost disappeared; whereas, from the studies conducted in the Western culture (Harvey et al., 2004; Purdon et al., 1999; and Stumpf & Parker, 2000), all parental criticism items were still alive under parental influence/pressure. In other words, in the Western culture, parental expectations and parental criticism live together under one roof, keeping the unique characteristics of each dimension intact.

On the contrary, in Asian cultures, the majority of items for parental criticism disappeared. Specifically, Cheng et al. (1999) suggested that Chinese parents in Hong Kong do not frequently use criticism as a medium of parenting, which would inhibit the emergence of the parental criticism factor in Chinese adolescents' responses. They further suggested that Chinese adolescents would interpret the occasional existence of parental criticism "in a positive way such as parental care" (p. 1059). This hypothesis may be applicable to Korean culture as well, although it is unclear whether Korean parents do not perceive criticism as an effective ways of parenting. A plausible hypothesis is that Korean students *do* experience critical feedback from parents, but may not *perceive* it as criticism. This can be understood through the lens of unique parent-child relationships in Korea, which is best explained by the phrase, "*om bu ja mo*" that means disciplinary father and lenient mother (Kim & Choi, 1994, p. 244). It would be rare to regard Korean parents as *critical* or harsh. (p. 8)

In short, even though a scale has been carefully translated and back-translated, the items may mean different things in different cultures.

MYTH 6: A LITERAL TRANSLATION ENSURES LINGUISTIC AND CULTURAL EQUIVALENCE

A literal, word-for-word translation of each item or the instruction statements of a scale may not guarantee linguistic or cultural equivalence. It is crucial to conduct appropriate translations and back-translations and to seek consultations with cultural insiders regarding how the translated items would be interpreted by people from the target culture. A literal translation sometimes can bring about unintended consequences. For example, in some languages the literal translation puts a subordinate clause (e.g., if, when clauses) in the wrong place, resulting in a different meaning. Furthermore, such situations can be more complicated when a sentence contains two elements. Consider the following item, which was included in the initial item pool for the Collectivist Coping Styles Inventory (CCS; Heppner et al., 2006) but was modified due to its statement ambiguity as well as potential problems in translation:

> Item: To avoid family shame, only told a few people about the difficult event or my feelings about the event.

This item contains two elements (i.e., avoidance of family shame and only told a few people about the stressful event), and thus the respondents may be confused in determining which content they should respond to. If this item were literally translated into different languages where the order between the subordinate phrase and the main clause became different from that of the original item, then it would add more complexity. Specifically, after the factor analysis, if this item loaded on the avoiding family shame factor, it is unclear whether this item truly belongs to this factor or merely is an artifact of a different word order across the two cultures. Therefore, we strongly advise the researcher to avoid any item that contains two or more elements at any time, particularly when translating it into another language.

Myth 7: Structural Elements of a Scale, Such As a Likert Rating Scale, or Consent Forms, Are Universal Across Cultures

Likert scales (Likert, 1932) are one of the most widely used rating scales, and typically consist of "a number of positively or negatively worded declarative sentences followed by response options that indicate the extent to which the respondent agrees or disagrees with the statement" (Pett et al., 2003, p. 32). Given its popularity, researchers and students usually believe this response system may be universally accepted because it is an ordinal scale consisting of five- or six-degree points. Unfortunately, this is not the case at all. Literature suggests that some East Asians tend to frequently endorse the middle or center points of the scale (Chen, Lee, & Stevenson, 1995; Chia, Allred, & Jerzak, 1997; Gibbons, Hamby, & Dennis, 1997). This tendency may reflect Asians' avoidance of being extreme in their responses. Thus, it is difficult to interpret results from East Asian populations where the mean response is, let's say, a 3 on a 5-point scale.

Written consent forms are standard protocol in some countries like the United States. In fact, in the United States, consent forms are often so commonplace that it is easy to take them for granted as an essential part of a research packet. However, in some countries (e.g., South Korea), a request for a written consent or the respondent's signature is atypical, and may imply the researcher's mistrust in the respondent's willingness to provide honest responses, or the researcher's hidden intention to force the respondents into something bigger, such as a legal contract. Many people in those cultures often feel more secure and trusted when given verbal instructions and requests from the researcher in person. Insisting on a written consent for the purpose of the institutional review board from a Western culture could cause unintended negative consequences, and in essence could become an unwanted nuisance variable (e.g., reactivity), which may threaten the internal validity of the scale. Heppner et al. (2006) were quite aware of this issue, as evidenced by their description of procedures: "Based on consultations with Taiwanese professionals with sensitivity to cultural norms regarding research procedures, verbal consent instead of written consent was deemed to be more culturally appropriate and was approved by the Institutional Review Board of the first author" (p. 110). Researchers should consult with cultural experts about this issue when they administer scales in countries other than where the scale was originally constructed.

STEPS OF SCALE CONSTRUCTION

Thus far, common myths concerning scale construction have been highlighted. In the remainder of this chapter, we will provide a brief description of typical steps of scale construction, particularly in a cross-cultural or multicultural context. For more information, interested readers are encouraged to read Dawis (1987), Kline (2005), Patten (2001), and Pett et al. (2003).

A brief sketch of the process by which Heppner et al. (2006) developed the Collectivist Coping Styles Inventory (CCS) may be instructive. The process of developing the CCS not only reveals the complexity of the scale construction processes, but also highlights the importance of cross-cultural or multicultural considerations in scale construction.

First, the researchers formed a research team that consisted of two European-American doctoral-level counseling psychologists and three Asian-born doctoral students (one Taiwanese and two South Koreans) in a U.S. counseling psychology program, as well as one Taiwanese faculty member. It took a year for the team to develop, discuss, refine, pilot, and finalize the items for the CCS. The item generation processes involved debates and refinements of items. For example, the original 70 items developed across 13 theoretically driven categories (which will be described later in this chapter) were subject to numerous debates, brainstorming, and modifications. The 70 items were pilot tested with eight Asian graduate students in order to ensure the relevance of the items to Asian cultures. Numerous personal communications and consultations with Taiwanese colleagues regarding the cultural relevance of the scale were also necessary. The final version of the CCS was then subject to robust translations and back-translations in order to be used in Taiwan. The translation process was repeated until consensus was reached among all the parties involved in terms of linguistic equivalence and cultural relevance. In addition, the team spent a great deal of time incorporating culturally relevant categories for common stressful or traumatic life events. For example, issues such as social ostracism or academic failure were included among 17 stressful or traumatic events because these events may be perceived as traumatic, particularly in Asia where interpersonal harmony is extremely valued and keen competition in academic environments is prevalent. Details about testing the construct validity of the CCS (i.e., factor analyses and psychometric properties) can be found in Heppner et al. (2006).

In the following sections, we describe seven steps in scale construction: (1) conceptualizing and operationalizing the construct of interest; (2) conducting the literature review; (3) generating the items, indicators, and response formats; (4) conducting content analysis and pilot testing, revising, and administering the items; (5) sampling and data collection; (6) translating and back-translating the scale, if necessary; and (7) performing factor analyses, finalizing items, and testing the psychometric properties of the scale.

STEP 1: CONCEPTUALIZING AND OPERATIONALIZING THE CONSTRUCT OF INTEREST

The first step in scale construction involves identification of the construct of interest. Before deciding to develop a new scale, a researcher should consider (1) assessing the necessity for a new scale for the construct and the population of interest, (2) conceptualizing the content of the construct and writing its operational definition, and (3) consulting with other colleagues regarding the utility of the scale and the appropriateness of the definition. In order for the definition to be operationalized, the construct should be written in a statement that is measurable (Vogt, 1993). For example, Lee, Choe, Kim, and Ngo (2000) developed a scale that was designed to measure typical intergenerational family conflicts in Asian Americans. The construct of family conflicts was defined as "acculturation differences between parents and late adolescent and young adult children [in Asian American populations across various areas such as cultural values and behaviors]" (p. 212). Note that the researchers focused on two things: (1) the prevalent but underexplored phenomenon of family conflicts in Asian immigrants, and (2) particularly, the Asian-American adolescent population that is at risk of intergenerational gaps that lead to a broad array of mental health problems. Conceptualizing and operationalizing a construct necessitates a researcher's extensive knowledge of the target population.

STEP 2: CONDUCTING THE LITERATURE REVIEW

It is essential that researchers ground their scale construction in the previous literature and relevant theories related to the construct under investigation. Perhaps previous scholars have developed a scale on the same construct, or a closely related construct. Typically, the previous studies help researchers understand the construct of interest, as well as the strengths and limitations of the existing knowledge on the construct. Often a researcher uses a theory to guide the development of the items, which typically provides guidance in generating the domain of items. Thus, after conceptualizing the construct, the next step typically is to search for relevant literature to increase one's knowledge about the construct, and search for relevant theories to guide the item generation phase.

Heppner and Heppner (2004) highlighted the importance of understanding the nonlinear nature in the literature search processes, stating "Be careful! As you plan your time for the literature search, add more time for the nonlinear, looping-back process . . . These kinds of nonlinear processes generally mean that [you] are (a) critically analyzing a complex topic, [and] (b) refining [your] conceptualization of [your] study" (p. 56). In addition, Pett et al. (2003) provided practical guidelines in developing questions and evaluation criteria to guide the literature review:

> How is the construct defined conceptually and operationally in a published article?, What kind of and how many concerns about testing [this construct] does the author identify?, Were there specific empirical indicators [regarding the construct] listed in the article?, Does that author cite other authors who have studied the construct?"(p. 21)

For example, in Heppner et al.'s (2006) CCS project, identifying the relevant literature or theoretical background for the construct they purport to measure was a crucial task because it identified relevant theories related to the construct. For example, the CCS was guided by three theoretical/conceptual grounds or previous research findings: (1) Kim, Atkinson, and Yang's (1999) work on Asian values; (2) Weisz, Rothbaum, and Blackburn's (1984) concepts regarding primary and secondary control; and (3) Zeidner and Saklofske's (1996) adaptational model of coping. For example, Heppner et al. described how the construct, Collectivist Coping Styles, and items were derived from Weisz et al.'s work on both primary control (individuals achieve control by directly influencing their realities) and secondary control (individuals obtain control by reframing or accommodating their realities). This was an important component in generating items for the CCS project because the researchers' goal was to develop a broad range of coping items specifically for Asians, which would include items related to secondary control as well as primary control (which is prominent in Western coping instruments).

STEP 3: GENERATING THE ITEMS, INDICATORS, AND RESPONSE FORMATS

Item generation is a pivotal step in scale construction, because poor items jeopardize the construct validity of the scale, which in turn misleads future researchers who wish to use the scale. Generally speaking, careful item generation takes several months. The quality of items are often enhanced in several ways such as (1) basing the items on a solid literature review and conceptual models or theories, (2) using qualitative methods such as focus groups and interviews with relevant groups of people to identify prototypical dimensions or indicators of the construct, and (3) writing conceptually and linguistically clear items. Kline (2005) suggested the following nine rules to guide the development of writing items: (1) deal with only *one* central thought in each item, (2) be precise, (3) be brief, (4) avoid awkward wording or dangling constructs, (5) avoid irrelevant information, (6) present items in positive language, (7) avoid double negatives, (8) avoid terms like *all* and *none*, and (9) avoid indeterminate terms like *frequently* or *sometimes* (pp. 34–35).

Consider a study by Kim et al. (1999) to develop the Asian Values Scale. Specifically, the researchers were first guided by their literature review, which generated 10 Asian value dimensions and 60 statements. Subsequently, the researchers obtained feedback on the identified Asian value dimensions and statements from 103 psychologists, selected from the list of members in Division 45 (Society for the Psychological Study of Ethnic Minority Issues) of the American Psychological Association. Finally, Kim et al. performed focus discussion groups to generate Asian value dimensions and statements. These multiple processes resulted in 14 Asian values and 202 items for the Asian Value Scale. In essence, the researchers were able to identify sound items for their scale using multiple methods of item generation.

In addition, to achieve the clarity of items and response formats, researchers should avoid an item with negatives or double negatives. This is applicable to any scale construction project, but it would be more critical in a cross-cultural study necessitating translation. Consider the following example modified from Patten (2001, p. 11):

Item: "I *can't* stop ruminating about how the accident happened."

1. Very rarely   2. Rarely   3. Sometimes   4. Often   5. Very Often

The respondent may be confused because of the negative statement in the item (i.e., can't) and the anchor choices that also include negatives (i.e., rarely). Moreover, it would likely confuse respondents more from another culture in a different language. It is generally advisable to avoid using negatives or double negatives, particularly in cross-cultural contexts, unless the researchers have a strong rationale for using them.

STEP 4: CONDUCTING CONTENT ANALYSIS AND PILOT TESTING, REVISING, AND ADMINISTERING THE ITEMS

It is important for authors to go beyond just developing a list of items. Regardless of one's level of confidence in the validity of item content, the respondents may perceive/interpret the items quite differently from what researchers intended due to many systematic or nonsystematic errors. To enhance the construct validity of the scale (i.e., whether the scale measures what it purports to measure) researchers are advised to: (1) conduct content analyses and consult with domain experts, and (2) pilot items to identify potential problems with their wording. The following example from Neville, Lilly, Duran, Lee, and Browne (2000) illustrates the importance of conducting content analyses. Neville et al. developed a scale designed to measure color-blind racial attitudes. The researchers checked the content validity of the items by seeking consultation with five experts in the topic of interest. The following is an excerpt from the Neville et al. study. Note in this example that Neville et al. conducted multiple rounds of checking the clarity, appropriateness, and readability of the items from multiple sources. Researchers are advised to follow the model established by Neville and her colleagues in this study.

Items were generated on the basis of Schofield's (1986) and Frankenberg's (1993) working definitions of color-blind racial attitudes and their corollaries, the interdisciplinary literature on color-blindness, consultation with experts on racial attitudes, and informal individual and group discussions with racially diverse undergraduate and graduate students as well as community people. . . . To assess content validity, the original items were given to five experts in race-ethnic studies or psychological measurement. The experts rated each item on content appropriateness and clarity using a 5-point scale that ranged from 1 (*not at all appropriate or clear*) to 5 (*very appropriate or clear*). Items receiving ratings between 1 and 3 were reworded or dropped. On the basis of qualitative feedback from the experts, 2 items were deleted, 7 items reworded and 11 items added. Three of the original content experts evaluated the revised 26-item scale once more on appropriateness and clarity. To help reduce potential response biases, half of the items were worded in a negative direction. Using a computer software program, we identified the reading level of the scale as slightly above 6th grade comprehension. To assess further the readability and clarity of the items, one primary and one secondary school teacher, a high school student, and a newspaper editor evaluated the scale. On the basis of feedback from the content experts and community persons, four items were reworded for clarification. (p. 61)

In addition to content analysis, pilot testing of the items is another important activity in the development of items. Pilot testing involves asking participants not only to respond to the items as if they were a participant, but also to identify unclear or ambiguous elements about the items. Sometimes this is accomplished by having participants circle ambiguous terms, identify in writing what parts are confusing or ambiguous, or even write alternative wording to enhance the items. With such a strategy, participants are given not only very specific instructions to clearly identify the task, but also ample space below each item to make comments. In this way, pilot testing provides a powerful tool for the researcher to identify items that might be misunderstood or unclear to the respondents.

Sudman and Bradburn (1982) maintained that data collection should not be conducted if pilot testing of the scale was not performed. Following is an example from Juntunen and Wettersten (2006). Note that the authors sought pilot testing before they consulted with domain-specific experts. This strategy attempts to reduce ambiguity in the items before the content experts examine them.

> We eventually selected 28 items for the initial item pool. We structured each as a declarative sentence, and we selected a Likert scale response format. We then administered the 28-item WHS [Work Hope Scale] to a pilot sample of individuals from a northern Midwestern community. Although this varies slightly from the recommendations of DeVellis (2003), who suggested moving directly to expert review, we included the pilot study to identify items that performed poorly and to gain initial psychometric information to assist in decision making for inclusion, exclusion, and revision of items. (p. 97)

In essence, content analysis and pilot testing helped the authors to fine tune and revise their items. Readers should keep in mind that the revision processes are neither linear nor clear-cut; sometimes, the researchers repeatedly engage in numerous activities to revise and alter the items to achieve more clarity in content.

STEP 5: SAMPLING AND DATA COLLECTION

Sampling pertains to identifying the samples of the population of interest that the research intends to generalize to; data collection is the actual collection of data from the participants. The researcher must first consider (1) whether the sample is representative of the population of interest or a sample of convenience, and (2) whether the sample size is appropriate (e.g., typically at least 250–300 participants are needed for factor analyses; refer to Tabachnick and Fidell, 2001, for more details).

The sampling issue is a critical one. For example, when Heppner et al. (2006) were developing and validating the CCS inventory, they specifically sought an East Asian sample that would assess Asian-specific ways of coping with traumatic life events. A total of 24 universities in Taiwan were involved in the data collection procedures. The college student samples were also relevant for the study because several categories among the 17 common stressful or traumatic events assessed academic situations. It should be noted that the research team sought data from the four different geographic regions in Taiwan (north, south, central, and east) in order to obtain a geographically representative sample of Taiwanese college students. This was extremely important because the geographic region is one of the most distinct demographic characteristics in Taiwan. The data collection procedures required a great deal of work for a senior Taiwanese faculty member and one of the research team members, which was far from collecting the data from a "convenience" sample. As a result, college students from around the island participated in the study. For more information about sampling and screening, see Kline (2005).

Data collection is also a critical step in scale construction. A typical method of data collection involves distributing questionnaires to a group of participants; however, it is not uncommon to collect data through the mail, email, or the Internet. Internet-based surveys are increasingly being used because of their distinctive advantages, such as being less geographically constrained, quick and economical, and easy to convert into statistical software. However, the Internet's disadvantages should also be considered; these include limited accessibility to the Internet for some people, a tendency to obtain low response rates, and issues with privacy and confidentiality. For more information on survey methods, see Chapter 10 as well as Dillman (2000) and Heppner and Heppner (2004).

STEP 6: TRANSLATING AND BACK-TRANSLATING THE SCALE, IF NECESSARY

The issue concerning translation and its linguistic and cultural equivalence cannot be overemphasized; lack of care in this step not only introduces measurement error in the scale, but also misleads readers about the generalizability of the construct across cultures. Two resources that discuss enhancing the quality of translation and back-translation of the construct in cross-cultural studies are van de Vijver and Leung (1997) and Mallinckrodt and Wang (2004). Both references discuss challenges in cross-cultural studies such as equivalence issues. In particular, Mallinckrodt and Wang provided a thorough discussion of the procedure to enhance the equivalence (e.g., content, semantic, technical, criterion, and conceptual equivalence based on Flaherty et al.'s [1988] work) of a translated scale to the original instrument.

Following is an excerpt from Mallinckrodt and Wang (2004) pertaining to the back-translation procedure they employed to ensure linguistic and cultural equivalence in the translation and back-translation. Note that the researchers started by gaining permission from the original authors of a scale that they wanted to translate into Chinese (Mandarin). This is an important step concerning the ethics in cross-cultural validation of a scale.

> The study began by obtaining permission from the developers of the ECRS ([Experiences in Close Relationships Scale], Brennan, [Clark, & Shaver], 1998) to adapt the instrument (P. R. Shaver, personal communication, March 5, 2002). Next, two native speakers of Chinese (one man, one woman) who were doctoral students in counseling psychology and fluent in English independently translated the ECRS into Mandarin Chinese. (Mandarin is the official language of Taiwan and mainland China.) At this stage, there were three types of discrepancies between the two initial translations: (a) selection of an appropriate Chinese phrase for "romantic partner," (b) problems created by shifts across the English ECRS items from singular "partner" to plural "partners," and (c) finding a single Chinese referent for affect descriptors such as "feel bad" or "resent." Discrepancies between the two versions were thoroughly discussed and resolved until a new draft translation was agreed upon. This first draft of the Chinese version of the ECRS was then submitted for back-translation to a bilingual Taiwanese graduate student whose major was Translation and Interpretation. She was completely unfamiliar with the original English version of the ECRS. Next, a native English speaker, with a doctoral degree in counseling psychology and considerable familiarity with the ECRS, compared the back-translated English version with the original ECRS item-by-item, together with the instruction, to evaluate the semantic equivalence of the two versions. Two pairs of items were evaluated as not equivalent. The preceding steps were then repeated for these items in a second iteration. After this process, the back-translated version and the original ECRS were judged to be equivalent. The final Mandarin Chinese version was labeled the *ECRS-C*. Quantitative procedures for establishing equivalence of the ECRS and ECRS-C are described in the Results section. (p. 372)

STEP 7: PERFORMING FACTOR ANALYSES, FINALIZING ITEMS, AND TESTING THE PSYCHOMETRIC PROPERTIES OF THE SCALE

> Conducting factor analyses (both exploratory and confirmatory factor analyses) and examining the psychometric properties of a new scale (e.g., reliability and validity estimates) are critical steps in developing construct validity (see Chapter 10). Factor analysis is a set of statistical procedures for "theory and instrument development and assessing construct validity of an established instrument when administered to a specific population" (Pett et al., 2003, p. 3) and typically consists of two types (1) exploratory factor analysis (EFA) and (2) confirmatory factor analysis (CFA). EFA is conducted "when the researcher does not know how many factors [or underlying/latent dimensions] are necessary to explain the interrelationships among a set of characteristics, indicators, or items" (Pett et al., p. 3), whereas CFA is utilized when the researcher wants "to assess the extent to which the hypothesized organization [i.e., the researcher already knows the underlying structure or dimensions of the construct] of a set of identified factors fits the data" (Pett et al., p. 4).

Typically, a researcher performs EFA first with a sample in order to identify the underlying factor structure of a construct, and then attempts to cross-validate it with another sample via CFA. This process is actually quite complex; in order to fully understand the conceptual and statistical issues pertaining to factor analysis, readers should refer to some of the following resources to attain more complete information on those processes: (1) Pett et al. (2003) for the steps to conduct EFA using Statistical Package for Social Sciences (SPSS), (2) Thompson (2004) for conceptual understanding and application of both EFA and CFA along with SPSS syntax, and (3) the chapter by Lee and Park in Heppner and Heppner (2004) for practical guidelines and examples regarding how to report factor analysis results.

In general, when conducting EFA, particularly for new scale development, two points are noteworthy. First, researchers should use common factor analysis (CA) instead of principal components analysis (PCA) because CA provides a more realistic estimation of factor structure assuming that "the items are measured with errors" (Kline, 2005, p. 258). Second, the use of parallel analysis (Hayton, Allen, & Scarpello, 2004) is recommended in order to more accurately determine the number of factors to retain.

As a result of the EFA, typically a number of the original scale items are deleted, leaving only those items that correlate strongly with the factors identified in the EFA. The scale items are finalized and ready for the final stage of validation, testing of the psychometric properties of the scale. If another sample is available (which is usually encouraged), researchers will also conduct a CFA for cross-validation of the factor structure.

It is essential to establish the psychometric properties of any new scale. This can be achieved by examining estimates of reliability (e.g., coefficient alphas and test-retest reliability) and various types of validity (e.g., convergent and discriminant validity). With regard to reliability estimates, coefficient alphas (typically referred to as Cronbach's alpha) provide the researcher with information about the degree of the homogeneity or internal consistency among a set of items. Although there is not a commonly agreed upon cut-off for the acceptable magnitude of a coefficient alpha, often .70 or higher is desired in the social sciences. Another estimate of reliability is also recommended. A test-retest reliability coefficient informs researchers of the stability of the scale over time. The time interval between pre- and posttest needs to be at least two weeks, preferably a month. When reporting test-retest reliability (e.g., $r = .80$), it is essential to include the specific time interval (e.g., 2 weeks) because the longer the time interval (e.g., 2 weeks versus 2 years), typically the lower the correlation.

Estimates of validity, typically convergent and discriminant, are also very important in scale construction. The following is an example of an attempt to establish both convergent and discriminant validity of a scale developed by Neville et al. (2000). The researchers first examined the concurrent validity of the Color-Blind Racial Attitudes Scale (CoBRAS) by calculating its correlation coefficients with the Global Belief in a Just World Scale (GBJWS; Lipkus, 1991) and the Multidimensional Belief in a Just World Scale (MBJWS;

Furnham & Procter, 1988), two established measures of social justice attitudes. They expected moderate to high correlations with these two scales. In addition, they examined the discriminant validity of the CoBRAS by calculating its correlations with the Marlowe-Crowne Social Desirability Scale (MCSDS; W. M. Reynolds, 1982), expecting a small correlation. Following is an excerpt from Neville et al. Two points are noteworthy. First, in order to establish the discriminant validity of the CoBRAS, the researchers used a short version of the MCSDS (13 true-false items), which in the past was one of the most widely used measures of social desirability. More recently, another measure of social desirability, the 20-item Impression Management (i.e., deliberate self-presentation to an audience) of the Balanced Inventory of Desirable Responding (BIDR; Paulhus, 1984, 1991) is being used more frequently. (Those interested in the psychometric properties of the BIDR should refer to Paulhus, 1991.) Second, note that Neville et al. found one significant correlation between one of the CoBRAS factors and the MCSDS. This is not an ideal situation because it indicates some items of the CoBRAS may reflect that respondents' responses are associated with social desirability. However, this does not nullify the utility of the CoBRAS because the amount of variance accounted for in the correlation was very small ($.20 \times .20 = 4\%$). This is called a "coefficient of determination," which refers to "an indication of how much variance is shared by the X and the Y variable" (Cohen, Swerdlik, & Phillips, 1996, p. 133). We recommend that researchers report the amount of variance when the correlation between their new measure and social desirability is statistically significant.

Concurrent Validity

The correlations among the CoBRAS factors and the two Belief in a Just World scales were examined to investigate the concurrent validity of the CoBRAS. Results indicate significant correlation among the GBJW, MBJWS-sociopolitical subscales (SS), the three CoBRAS factors, and the CoBRAS total score. Correlations ranged from .39 (between Institutional Discrimination and GBJW) to .61 (among MBJWS and Racial Privilege as well as the CoBRAS total).

Discriminant Validity

The correlations among the CoBRAS factors and the MCSDS were examined to provide estimates of discriminant validity. Results suggest that generally there is no strong association among the MCSDS and the CoBRAS factors. There was one statistically significant relation: MCSDS was associated with Blatant Racial Issues ($r = .20$); however, the maximum amount of variance accounted for was 4%. (p. 65)

SUMMARY AND CONCLUSIONS

The following seven common myths that researchers often unwittingly assume have been discussed: (1) item construction can be done in a couple of weeks, (2) items can be easily constructed without an extensive literature review, (3) it is best to use a convenience sample whenever possible, (4) conducting a factor analysis ensures the validity of the scale, (5) a scale with strong psychometric properties developed in a Western culture is universally valid, (6) a literal translation ensures linguistic and cultural equivalence, and (7) structural elements of a scale, such as a Likert rating scale, or even ancillary forms like a consent form, are universal across cultures. In addition, our discussion of the seven steps in scale construction along with examples from several inventories developed in the field of counseling (e.g., CCS and CoBRAS) guides researchers and students who may develop their own scales, particularly in a cross-cultural or multicultural context.

Creating a new scale is very important in education and psychology in general because a psychometrically sound inventory can provide an effective tool to (1) assess individuals' differences across various domains such as personality, attitudes, cognitions, emotions, and behaviors; and (2) examine the interface of such domains and psychological adjustment. Furthermore, as Dawis (1987) stated, "scales are ubiquitous features of counseling psychology research" (p. 481), and in essence promote the development of psychometrically sound ways of assessing and promoting understanding of a new construct relevant to the counseling profession. Heppner (2006), in his presidential address to the Society of Counseling Psychology of the American Psychological Association, suggested many challenges to becoming a globally competent counseling psychologist. Some of the challenges, such as (1) ethnocentricity, (2) difficulty in accepting others' worldview, (3) accepting cultural differences across cultures as simply differences, and (4) universal assumptions, are also pertinent to the challenges that many face in developing a culturally sensitive scale. It is hoped that researchers and students in the field not only increase their awareness of the complex nature of scale construction, but also incorporate multicultural and cross-cultural issues into the construction of new inventories.

A 22-ITEM CHECKLIST OF SCALE CONSTRUCTION

The following list of items can be used as a checklist when conducting a scale construction project.

Did you . . .

1. Identify a construct or phenomenon that you want to measure?
2. Search for other instruments that measure similar constructs or phenomena?
3. Consider the advantages and disadvantages of developing a new scale?
4. Seek consultations from your colleagues about this project?
5. Decide on the target population?
6. Define the construct with statements that can be measured?
7. Conduct an extensive literature review?
8. Consider multiple ways of item generation (e.g., focus discussion groups, interviews)?
9. Generate a clear and sufficient number of items informed by the various methods in #8, as well as guided by theory?
10. Create response formats and directions with clarity?
11. Refine the items through content analysis from domain-specific experts as well as pilot testing?
12. Conduct translation and back-translation procedures along with permission from the original author(s), if necessary?
13. Finalize the questionnaire including items, response formats, directions, and necessary demographic information?
14. Identify a representative sample with a sufficient number of participants?
15. Identify inventories for providing estimates of convergent and discriminant validity?
16. Obtain approval from the institutional review board?
17. Consider a suitable method of data collection (including ways of obtaining informed consent, use of Scantron sheets, if necessary)?

18. Enter the data into a statistical analysis package (e.g., SPSS, SAS) and clean the data (see Heppner & Heppner, 2004; Meyers, Gamst, & Guarino, 2006)?

19. Calculate descriptive statistics (e.g., means, standard deviations)?

20. Identify the factor structure of the construct and finalize the items through a series of exploratory factor analyses including parallel analysis?

21. Determine reliability estimates (internal consistency, e.g., alpha coefficients) as well as various estimates of validity (e.g., convergent and discriminant), calculating correlation coefficients?

22. Collect additional data and examine the stability of the factor structure through confirmatory factor analysis and administer other inventories to promote additional estimates of validity?

Program Evaluation

Matrese Benkofske and Clyde C. Heppner

CHAPTER **21**

The focus of this book throughout has been on research design, its application in the counseling profession, and the conditions needed to conduct quality research. Turning to a slightly different topic, this chapter describes program evaluation—what it is, how it is similar to and differs from counseling research, and how it is used within counseling settings. The chapter describes in considerable detail the phases of program evaluation to introduce professionals to the field. The first step is to define program evaluation.

PROGRAM EVALUATION DESCRIBED

What is program evaluation, and how is it similar to and different from research? Willett et al. (1991) used a standardized scale (the Family Problem Checklist) to assess potential difficulties faced by several families in Project Good Start, and then used the Family Function Scale to measure the progress of each family as treatment progressed. From a research perspective, the use of a repeated measures design to provide a quantifiable measure of a family's functioning over time is far superior to the traditional "before and after" snapshot. We reexamine this study here to illustrate important differences between research endeavors and program evaluation.

Whereas researchers are typically most interested in enhancing the profession's knowledge base, such as comparing the efficacy of two particular treatments, program evaluators are most interested in the effectiveness of a particular program for a particular group of people. Thus, program evaluators would want to be involved while programs such as Project Good Start are being designed. For example, during planning meetings they might learn that the community and neighborhood citizenry wanted the counselors to come from the community so that they would be sensitive to the families' cultural differences and needs. However, this could have both positive and negative effects on the program's outcomes: If counselors are culturally sensitive, program recipients may be more likely to disclose to them so that real progress can occur, but the families may be so familiar with the counselors that they feel uncomfortable talking with a "friend" about their parenting style. By being present during the planning meetings and knowing the community's require-ment of selecting only local counselors, an evaluator could be sure to in-clude "level of familiarity between counselor and client" as a variable in the database.

By being involved during the planning stage, evaluators also learn more about how the particular counseling treatment was chosen. Perhaps it was the only counseling treatment considered; perhaps several counseling treatments were identified, and this particular treatment was judged by the community's counseling professionals as most likely to be most effective with dysfunctional families in violent environments; or perhaps part of the program is to create a new counseling treatment not guided by a theoretical perspective. In short, for program evaluators, knowing how a particular counseling treatment was chosen and what outcomes it can be expected to deliver has a direct impact on the choice of outcomes measures. It then becomes an evaluator's responsi-bility to determine if there is a match among the treatment, the anticipated outcomes, and the outcome measures.

After the program has begun, the evaluator typically carefully monitors the data collection procedures to ensure that the Family Problem Checklist is administered prior to the first counseling session. In addition, the evaluator periodically checks the family's file to record each time a family attends coun-seling and to ensure that the family completes the Family Function Scale each month. During these visits the evaluator also makes various observations. How are families treated when they enter the center for counseling? Is the receptionist friendly and welcoming, or disinterested and rude? This information may be needed if the evaluator finds a very high or a very low dropout rate at the program's end.

While at the center, the evaluator may also note who the clients are and whether they represent the targeted population. As an example, consider a drug rehabilitation program aimed at people arrested and charged with drug possession. When the program evaluator visited the treatment site, she was surprised to see that the court had required not only drug users, but also drug dealers to participate in the program. It was a common sight to see drug deals being made in front of the treatment center! So, returning to Project Good Start, if it were designed to address the needs of intact families, are all members of the family present for counseling? Perhaps the program evaluator should bring up in focus group discussions how important it is to have all family members involved in counseling and how the family and the ultimate success of counseling were affected when some family members did not participate in counseling. The evaluator might also raise the same issue with the counselors.

In addition to making periodic visits to the counseling site, the evaluator also includes home visits to observe the families before, during, and after the counseling sessions. Prior to these visits, the evaluator has worked with the counselors and program administrators to create a list of behaviors that would indicate that a family needs counseling in parenting skills and that the counseling has improved the family's interactions. After being pilot-tested and then refined, this list would serve with the Family Function Scale as a measure of change within each family.

By being actively involved in the program from conception to implementation, evaluators are in a position to (1) identify problems with the data collection procedures to minimize the risk of losing valuable data; (2) collect data to evaluate program effectiveness; (3) formulate and then test hypotheses that arise as the program matures; (4) document changes in the program's implementation over time; (5) give possible explanations for unanticipated results; and (6) document unanticipated positive outcomes. For the sake of this example, suppose that no significant difference in family functioning as measured by the Family Function Scale was detected. By being actively involved in the program, the program evaluator might, through a review of his or her field notes, be able to identify reasons for the lack of significant change in family functioning and modify the program before implementing it again at the same or another site.

Or suppose instead that the evaluator identified significant differences in family functioning over time, but through discussions with the program recipients and observations at the treatment center, the evaluator ascertained that because the program was housed within a community center, the families also availed themselves of social services other than counseling. In that case, to say that the improvement in family functioning was due solely to the counseling program would be erroneous. Without being engaged in many aspects of the program, the program evaluator might incorrectly ascribe the effects to the counseling treatments alone.

By looking at Project Good Start from a program evaluator's perspective, several distinctions between research and program evaluation become evident. Whereas the goals of research are primarily to enhance the profession's knowledge base, the program evaluator's goal is to evaluate the effectiveness of a particular program with a defined group of participants. The researcher develops specific hypotheses and emphasizes internal and/or external validity; the program evaluator typically collects a wide range of data to determine whether an intervention was effective and to formulate other hypotheses about the causes and effects that explain the outcomes. Whereas both researchers and evaluators carefully select assessment measures a priori, the program evaluator also collects a wide range of additional data as the program unfolds. Although program evaluators often use research methodologies standard in psychology, they may also use observational methods developed and refined by anthropologists or cost/benefit analyses used in the business sector.

Unlike counseling psychology, which can trace its roots back to Frank Parsons in the early 1900s, program evaluation is still rather young. Evaluators have a wide range of experiences, preferred data collection methodologies, formal training, and professional viewpoints. Thus, it can be difficult to define program evaluation. It is often described as a process for judging the worth of a program relative to other alternatives, based on defensible, previously defined criteria (Scriven, 1980). Put another way, program evaluation is undertaken when a program's decision makers, recipients, funders, and/or managers want to determine whether a program is effective, to what degree, under what conditions, at what financial or social costs, and with what intentional or unintentional outcomes.

The data collection methodologies used during an evaluation are evolving with the profession. In the previous chapters on outcome and process research, we saw that as the counseling field has matured, the focus of counseling research has shifted—from an almost exclusive emphasis on outcome or process measures, to more integration of both process and outcome measures and recognition of increased complexity in counseling. A similar evolution has occurred in program evaluation. Perhaps because of its roots in education and testing, early program evaluations focused almost exclusively on measures of program recipients' progress after exposure to a program—how many new life skills recipients had mastered after a program designed to build basic skills, or how much self-esteem had increased after attending a youth camp for "at risk" high school students. Yet, as we saw in the Project Good Start example, much more than just the program's outcomes must be measured during an evaluation of a program. The environment, the population, the political climate, the needs of the community where the program is being implemented, the beliefs of program administrators as to the targeted population's needs, and many other factors play an integral role in defining the program and must be measured in the evaluation of the program.

PHASES OF PROGRAM EVALUATION

The steps for conducting a program evaluation do not always follow a routine set of procedures. In essence, what an evaluation looks like—what aspects of a program it examines, what data are collected, and how its results are used—depends largely on what stage in the program the evaluation occurs. Typically we think of doing an evaluation at the end of a program, and often this is when it in fact occurs, but an evaluation can occur at one or a combination of four stages of a program: during conceptualization, design, or implementation, or upon completion (Rossi & Freeman, 1999). Consider the following example:

> A university counseling center wishes to offer a stress-reduction program intended to help students cope with the anxiety, frustration, and potential for self-abusive behaviors (such as excessive drinking and erratic sleeping patterns) common during the final weeks of each semester. As scientist-practitioners, the counseling center staff decide to "evaluate" the program.

An evaluation of this program could take on many different forms, depending on the stage of the program at which the evaluation occurs, the needs of "stakeholders" (that is, individuals and groups of individuals who have a stake in the program), and the time frame and resources available for the evaluation. The specific stakeholders who are asked for input can dramatically change the results of the evaluation. For example, in this case, the stakeholders could be the students who enroll in the stress-reduction program, the counseling staff providing the program, university administrators, and even nonparticipating students who feel the program would be beneficial. If an evaluator is called to conduct the evaluation during the program's initial planning meetings, what steps would the evaluator take during the course of the evaluation? Starting with the framework presented by Herman, Morris, and Fitz-Gibbon (1987), an evaluator undertakes four phases of program evaluation, applicable at any stage of a program: (1) setting the boundaries of the evaluation; (2) selecting appropriate evaluation methods; (3) collecting and analyzing information; and (4) reporting the findings. Within each of these four phases are specific steps, which we examine in the following sections.

SETTING THE EVALUATION'S BOUNDARIES

This first phase entails (1) determining the purposes of the evaluation, (2) collecting background information about the program, (3) writing a description of the program and then ascertaining whether your understanding matches that of others associated with the program, (4) making a preliminary agreement as to what the evaluation may include, and (5) coming to a final agreement concerning the program evaluator's role, and the specific services and final products the evaluator will provide. This same agreement also describes the resources available to the evaluator and a preliminary estimate of the costs associated with the evaluation.

During this initial phase, it is crucial that the evaluator understands the program, its mission, its scope, and its magnitude. The clearer the evaluator is as to what the program is designed to do, the less likely unforeseen issues will pop up after the evaluation's budget, time line, and methodology have been set. Much of the information about the program can be obtained by meeting with the program manager, but it is also wise to meet with others associated with the program—funders, program advocates, and perhaps even opponents—to get a broad view of the mission and scope of the program. The evaluator might request written summaries of the program to provide an initial understanding before these meetings. Through either the written documents, the initial meetings, or a combination of these sources, the evaluator should obtain at least preliminary answers to the following questions, using the university counseling center's stress-reduction program as an example:

1. What are the stress-reduction program's objectives, and how will this program be implemented to address these objectives? Knowledge of the program objectives are essential in order to link what the program was designed to accomplish and the measurable behaviors observed in the evaluation.

2. What will this stress-reduction program involve? How long will the program last? How many sessions will a participant typically attend? What type of stress-reduction techniques will be used? This information helps the evaluator to shape the evaluation, the time line, and the types of statistics (nonparametric or parametric) used in the analyses.

3. What types of effects do program planners anticipate? When should these effects be measurable? Does the program manager anticipate long-term benefits of the program? What type of evidence would the program manager need to claim that the program's mission has been met? Information about these questions enables the evaluator to tailor the evaluation methods to the informational needs of stakeholders and program planners alike.

4. Has anyone written a proposal for funding? Are any program requirements tied to program funding (for example, including a segment of a special population as program recipients, paying program providers, or using some specific treatment in the program)? If, for example, the women's center on campus provided a portion of the program's funding, they may require the program to address issues identified by women students such as finding child care for a few hours while attending class rather than paying for an entire day. These kinds of stipulations can have dramatic implications on the evaluation design, and it is better to know this before the evaluation has been set in motion.

5. What is the funding level for the program, and how much has been set aside for the evaluation process? A guideline used at times is that the funding for the evaluation should constitute approximately 10% of the cost of the program. This helps to prevent a very small project from having a far too expansive evaluation, and vice versa. Designers of programs often severely underestimate the cost of conducting a program evaluation.

6. What are the program manager's expectations for the evaluation? Does he or she have a preferred data collection strategy? What role will the evaluator play? Some agencies have staff members capable of helping with data collection, which reduces the billing cost of the evaluation. In some cases, the program manager expects the evaluator to be highly visible throughout the program's direction. Knowing what the program manager feels comfortable with in terms of evaluator exposure helps in planning the evaluation.

7. Why is an evaluation of the program being undertaken? Is it required by the funders? Have the outcome measures and the sampling procedures been predetermined? Knowing the reasoning behind the evaluation enables the evaluator to tailor the evaluation to the needs of the program manager and stakeholders. If the funders of the evaluation have clearly stated that objective, measurable, and scientifically rigorous data must be collected in order to be considered for continued funding, the evaluation will be quite different from one designed to help program implementers better serve and understand their clients.

8. What resources are available to the evaluator? Will counseling staff help with data collection? Are interns or clerical help available? What records are available to the evaluator? Given that the stress-reduction program is

aimed at improving the physical health of the recipients, will medical records be available to the evaluator? Academic records? Again, knowing what resources are readily available enables the evaluator to select data sources that provide reliable and easily accessible, understandable data.

Among the many purposes of these questions, first and foremost the evaluator seeks to understand what the program is designed to do, what people associated with the program expect it to accomplish, and what outcomes or results are anticipated. The evaluator uses the answers to these questions to begin formulating a strategy for carrying out the evaluation. Moreover, the evaluator is trying to understand what aspects of the evaluation have already been arranged or agreed upon, and what aspects are yet to be determined.

Experienced evaluators also try to ascertain whether a request for an evaluation is sincere, or an attempt to "rubber stamp" a program as being a quality program. Novice evaluators, especially eager ones, often find themselves caught up in these situations. Our advice: Do not get involved. It will come back to haunt you, perhaps by giving you the reputation for taking any work, regardless of its merit. All evaluators wish they had never undertaken certain projects because they did not conduct the type of evaluation they had envisioned. Normal experience gives evaluators enough of these experiences; do not take them on willingly! Evaluators can use the following questions to determine whether they want to agree to an evaluation: Are there sufficient time and resources to conduct the evaluation? Do I have the needed resources, background knowledge, and time to commit to the evaluation? Typically, an evaluator need not be a content expert—that is, an expert in stress reduction, in this case—to conduct the evaluation, but some program managers also rely on the evaluator to judge the worthiness of the treatment. If this is the case, and you are not a stress-reduction expert, is there sufficient funding to hire a content expert, or will the program evaluator take on that role, too?

Evaluators cannot expect all of these questions to be answered fully. Not all programs are precisely defined, and many of these questions may not be answerable, especially during the initial planning. Although this leaves a lot of gray area for constant negotiation between the evaluator and the program designers, we prefer that evaluators come to a program during its planning phase because that allows them to integrate the evaluation's data collection procedures into the day-to-day operations of the program, rather than coming in after the program has begun. In the latter case, the data collection procedures become "add-ons" that are often viewed by already overworked staff as optional, as time-fillers, or, worse yet, as mindless paperwork. But by asking these questions during the negotiations, the program evaluator is in a position to make an informed decision about whether or not to agree to conduct the evaluation.

During the initial meetings and throughout the evaluation process, the evaluator must develop the ability to listen to his or her intuition, "gut instincts," or "inner voice." Program evaluation is probably three-quarters science and one-quarter art. The art of program evaluation involves listening to and then coming to trust your intuition. Even though being a competent researcher, possessing above-average written and oral skills, and exhibiting excellent organizational skills will make for an above-average program evaluator, the ability to hear and then trust your intuition is required for entering the ranks of the expert. A good program evaluator often carries a notebook for keeping notes of meetings, interactions, and observations—and to jot down impressions and insights as well. Even though many of these notes and insights are never acted upon, some of them—especially those that keep reappearing—become working hypotheses for further investigation and study. Keeping a log of these impressions, insights, and hunches, and reviewing them from time to time, can take an evaluation from a regurgitation of facts to a more complete understanding of a program, including its benefits and its deficits.

At the end of this first phase, an evaluator should have a good understanding of the program's objectives, how it will be implemented, what outcomes it is intended to accomplish, and a preliminary understanding of what its designers anticipate the evaluation might entail. To help crystallize this understanding, the evaluator writes a description of the program, which has three purposes. First, by setting down on paper what he or she understands about the program, the evaluator can often identify loosely defined concepts or unanswered questions. Second, the evaluator should share this document with others in the program, as a reality check. Discussing points of disagreement often helps program designers identify and clarify fuzzy aspects of the program. Finally, this document can serve as the first section of the program report: the program description. The evaluator should include with the description a short memo stating that he or she has agreed to proceed with the evaluation, assuming that a final agreement can be reached concerning the cost and methodology of the evaluation. This memo can serve as an informal agreement until a more detailed one can be drafted.

SELECTING APPROPRIATE EVALUATION METHODS

During the second phase of the evaluation process, the focus moves from a description of the program and its objectives to the evaluation—how it will measure or provide information about the program's effects. One of the most difficult parts of conducting an evaluation is keeping the evaluation in focus—concentrating on those aspects of the evaluation that are important, and not being sidetracked by interesting but unimportant side issues. Taking specific steps to keep the evaluation in focus is a crucial but sometimes forgotten task. The results of such an omission include wasting valuable time and resources collecting data on unimportant aspects of the program; causing anxiety, frustration, and tension between the evaluator and stakeholders as they sort out what is supposed to be included in the evaluation; missing opportunities to collect important data; and perhaps even entirely missing the aim of the evaluation, such that results are deemed useless. Every evaluator likely has, at one time or another, failed to adequately plan for an evaluation and has suffered the frustration, professional embarrassment, and perhaps even panic associated with scrambling to fill in gaps in the evaluation as the final report comes due.

Enough forces and factors—political posturing, incompetent program staff, belligerent program recipients, and funding cuts—potentially lurk around some evaluations to derail the program and its evaluation; this confusion does not need to be intensified by a poorly focused evaluation.

The following seven steps are the key tasks in creating a focused evaluation:

1. Solicit input from stakeholders.
2. Design a plan for examining program implementation.
3. Design a plan for evaluating program progress.
4. Create a consolidated data collection plan.
5. Plan the data analyses.
6. Estimate the financial and time costs of the evaluation.
7. Come to a final agreement about services, costs, and responsibilities.

SOLICITING INPUT FROM STAKEHOLDERS   The process of creating the evaluation's focus begins with face-to-face meetings with the program managers, funders, and others who have some special interest in the program. Notice that this list does not include only those people responsible for carrying out the program.

This step is the first one in helping to foster investment and commitment by stakeholders. By believing in the evaluation process and then personally committing time to design the evaluation, periodically review the evaluation process, and perhaps even collect some data, stakeholders see their concerns about the program being addressed. When they become fully involved in the evaluation of the program, stakeholders are more likely to make certain that funds are set aside for the evaluation, that data are faithfully collected, and that the evaluation's results are disseminated and incorporated into the next cycle of the program.

Getting stakeholders actively involved in the evaluation process is one of the most counterintuitive steps of evaluation. Beginning evaluators often approach evaluation like research, setting down a protocol for collecting data, implementing it, and then analyzing the results. Allowing others to help shape the protocol, to suggest data-collection methods, and to help interpret the findings seems to fly in the face of scientific objectivity! Experience with involving stakeholders leads most evaluators to the following observations. First, stakeholders often take a very objective perspective, even when they are deeply committed to the program. They tend to quickly understand that using suspect evaluation methods jeopardizes the evaluation and the implementation of the evaluation's results. Rather than being too lax, stakeholders often favor the most objective methods available. Second, with even minimal guidance from the evaluator, stakeholders often create the type of evaluation the evaluator had originally envisioned. Third, evaluators should remember that they are soliciting input from the stakeholders, not turning the entire evaluation over to them. Ultimately it is the evaluator, not the stakeholders, who makes final decisions about the evaluation protocol. Fourth, choosing to involve stakeholders should not be mere "lip service," but rather a commitment to weigh the opinions of the stakeholders. Anything less can jeopardize the evaluation because it is the stakeholders who ultimately make the final decisions about the utility of the program.

Including stakeholders in the initial planning meetings allows the evaluator to include data collection strategies that meet these stakeholders' need for information when determining a program's worth. Inclusion helps to decrease the temptation of some stakeholders to claim that the evaluation was flawed, especially if the program does not fair well in the final report.

It is important, however, not to be disheartened if stakeholders show a lack of interest in becoming involved in the program evaluation planning process. Some people have a propensity to be silent or even uninvolved unless a program's continuance is threatened. In these cases it is helpful to actively solicit the opinions and suggestions of stakeholders. The key word here is "actively"; it may take more than one formal invitation of marginal stakeholders, plus a well-placed phone call from the evaluator, during which the importance of the stakeholder's participation is emphasized. Another strategy for garnering stakeholder input is for the same individuals to be involved in both the initial planning of the program and the planning of the evaluation, assuming that this group also includes people who will be using the program.

At the least, the evaluation plan, once prepared in first draft, should be presented publicly through existing meetings typically attended by program recipients and/or the general public. When evaluating the counseling program for stress reduction, for example, the evaluation plan should be presented to governing bodies involved in funding the counseling center. For other programs, this public body may be the PTA of a school program, the city council (for a city-sponsored program), or a steering committee for campus programs. It is very important that the input of such meetings be incorporated into the evaluation plan; this is not the time to force a plan without an adequate discussion or to solicit input only to dismiss it. If evaluators seek input from stakeholders, it is their responsibility to consider suggestions and input seriously.

During discussions in which the focus of the evaluation is being generated, a few questions should be kept in the forefront: What aspects of the program should be evaluated? Will the whole program be evaluated or only newly added components? At what point in the program will the evaluation begin, and when will it end? Will it focus on the conceptualization stage, the design stage, or the implementation stage of the program? Is the program sufficiently mature for the evaluator to expect any measurable efficacy? By reflecting on these questions while formulating the evaluation plan, the evaluator is more likely to keep the evaluation on track. Moreover, by keeping the program's time frame and maturity in mind while designing the evaluation, it is more likely that the evaluation will be appropriate for the program.

This is also the time that the evaluator heeds the specific questions to be answered during the evaluation. Conducting an evaluation with only the very general questions, "Is this program worthwhile?" or "Has this program been successful?" is not sufficient and violates the first standard of program evaluation—the need for utility (Joint Committee on Standards for Educational

Evaluation, 1994). Put another way, the evaluation must answer the questions of interest to the stakeholders.

These initial meetings are a good time for the evaluator to come to understand the needs and interests of the primary stakeholders, and their relationships with one another. During the meetings the evaluator should pay attention to how people are interacting with one another. Are there factions within various groups? How deep are these divisions, and on what are they based? How large an effect will these factions have on the evaluation process, and on the reception of the evaluation results? How are differing points of view dealt with? Are viewpoints in opposition to the key stakeholders' allowed to surface and be fully considered, or are they quickly dismissed? If the latter occurs, the evaluator should steer the conversation back to the overlooked viewpoint, perhaps by saying, "I'd like to come back to a point just made. Could you elaborate on . . . ?" It is the evaluator's responsibility to ensure that the concerns raised at meetings represent not just the opinions of the vocal, but also those of potentially disenfranchised, underrepresented, or overlooked stakeholders.

Throughout these initial meetings, the evaluator is typically considered by the program managers and other stakeholders to be an "expert" whose words are taken as fact. Thus, it is important that evaluators allow others to speak and facilitate the process. If the evaluator becomes too vocal, the evaluation can quickly become one devised by the evaluator, not the one envisioned by stakeholders.

DESIGNING A PLAN FOR EXAMINING PROGRAM IMPLEMENTATION   After the evaluator has heard what questions stakeholders would like the evaluation to answer, the evaluator creates two plans for data collection, each with a different focus. The first plan, which we cover in this section, addresses collecting evidence of what the program actually did or how it was actually implemented. The second plan (described in the next section) presents the data collection strategy for measuring the progress of the program. Both of these plans require the evaluator to work back and forth among the set of evaluation questions proposed by the stakeholders, the limited resources such as funds and time, and commonly accepted data collection methods. Perhaps the easiest way to begin is to create a matrix like that shown in Table 21.1. For each evaluation question, five categories are examined: (1) sources of information, (2) needed resources, (3) data collection methodology, (4) time line, and (5) data analyses.

Consider again the stress-reduction workshop provided through the campus counseling center. What information is needed to determine whether the program was a success? First, the evaluator would need to know that a stress-reduction workshop occurred, what it involved, who attended it, and how well it matched its attendees' needs. These are measures of program implementation. It may seem obvious to state that only after you knew that the workshop occurred would it make sense to judge its merits. However, it is important not to assume that what is supposed to happen in fact happens, or that the unexpected never occurs.

TABLE 21.1 | AN EXAMPLE OF AN EVALUATION PLANNING MATRIX FOR A WORKSHOP

Evaluation Questions	Sources of Information	Needed Resources	Data Collection Methodology	Time Line	Data Analyses
How is the information presented in the workshop?	Workshop; workshop's presenters	Planning documents	Structured observations; workshop planning documents	Throughout the duration of workshop	Descriptive statistics
Did the workshop meet the needs of attendees?	Workshop participants' journals; survey of attendees	Journals for a sample of attendees; possibly some payment for completion; printed surveys	Journals; survey	Journals to be returned at last workshop; survey to be administered at final workshop	Qualitative data

Every program evaluator has numerous examples of a disparity between what the program was intended to be and what it in fact turned out to be. And although there are numerous examples of a program failing because some of its components were omitted, other programs succeed in unintended ways. One example is a program designed to help physically challenged students attend a large, Midwestern university. The student services center's goal was to improve the study skills of these students, both through skill building workshops (for example, test-taking strategies, mnemonics) and by providing them cutting-edge technology to facilitate the access of information (for example, large-print computer monitors for students with poor vision, or a voice-activated word processor for quadriplegic and paraplegic students). These services were made available to students, and some students were quite successful because of the training. However, conversations with the students revealed that the two most important, beneficial aspects of the program were having a place to come between classes, where they could interact with other students with disabilities, and knowing that there were people who could assist them in more mundane activities such as buttoning a coat, fixing eyeglasses, or coming to get them if their wheelchairs became inoperable. It was these services that enabled them to be full-time students on a large college campus.

Some form of observational methodology is the most common way to determine whether the program took place and the form it took during implementation. One common form of observation requires the observer to be detached from the activity, and typically the observations sample the program's activities in a structured fashion. Structured observations for the stress-reduction program would require the evaluator to observe the workshops for a specified amount of time—for example, 25 times for five-minute intervals over the course of a six-hour workshop. In each of the five-minute intervals, the evaluator would mark on a standardized code sheet what is taking place in the workshop. If one of the goals of a counseling program is to use real examples from life as the vehicle for presenting information, rather than relying on a theoretical, lecture-style presentation, then a structured observation would, among other things, monitor how the counselor is providing information during one-minute segments. Potential categories of presenting information might be (1) statements of fact, (2) presentations of examples, (3) questions and answers, (4) other, and (5) no presentation of information. Having more than one observer reliably code human behavior in discrete categories can be tricky, so pilot-testing these forms before formally collecting the data is time well spent. Fitzpatrick, Sanders, and Worthen (2004) is a very good reference for learning how to construct and pilot-test observation forms and analyze structured observation data.

The other commonly used observation methodology is participant observation, which requires the observer to actually become involved in the process, typically as a program participant. Participant observation is much less structured and more qualitative, and it requires the observer to take notes throughout the course of the activity or as soon after the activity as possible. Readers wanting more information about participant observation methodologies are referred to Patton (2002). Whereas structured observations are designed to capture how much of various activities occurred, participant observations are especially useful when descriptions of the mood preceding, during, and following an activity are also desired.

Even though structured observations and participant observations provide two different data sets and typically answer different questions, it is not uncommon to use both observation methods during an evaluation (although not simultaneously!). Assessing program activities through periods of both structured and participant observations provides a rich data set. The program evaluator asked to evaluate the stress-reduction program may begin with participant observations. The evaluator might attend the first few workshops, describing the structure of these workshops, the extent to which the participants actually practice stress-reduction techniques, and how she or he felt during these workshops. During these observations, the evaluator might, in turn, create some potential hypotheses about the program, such as: "Discussions about stressors are often brought up by participants but not addressed by the counselor" or "These stress-reduction techniques sound easy here in class, but I don't think I would practice them outside of this workshop. My life is just too hectic to take the time." These hypotheses, as well as impressions, observations, and other hypotheses, can then be used to create questions for participant surveys or they can be followed up through a structured observation.

Although observational methods are especially useful in evaluating a program's implementation, other methods may be useful as well. Program records such as activity logs, sign-in sheets, and individual client records (with permission) can provide a useful paper trail as to what activities occurred during a program. For example, if one component of Project Good Start involved referring families to community support programs providing medical attention, food resources, or child-care classes, then reviewing a random sample of client records should document the extent to which these services were suggested by the program staff. These same records may even indicate whether the client sought these sources of assistance, and the extent to which these services were provided to the client. Other times, however, the client may have to be asked directly what services he or she was referred to and what services he or she actually experienced. There can, of course, be a difference between the number of clients referred to a community resource and the number of clients who ultimately receive services.

This example provides a good illustration of how, as an evaluation process unfolds, an evaluator can easily lose the focus of the evaluation. For example, even though it might be interesting to ask why clients referred to services never follow through with them—is it because they were referred to the wrong service agency, they did not qualify for the particular service, they never went to the initial appointment due to a lack of transportation or child care, or they do not trust social services agencies and refused to go?—the program evaluator must first stick to the evaluation questions, and then determine whether new questions are within the scope of the evaluation. If not, the new questions are set aside, at least for the time being.

DESIGNING A PLAN FOR EVALUATING PROGRAM PROGRESS   The evaluation must not only examine how the program was implemented, but also ascertain whether the anticipated effects of the program are evident and (if the program has not reached completion) whether the program is on track to achieve the stated program goals. As with monitoring program implementation, program documents and observations can be used to measure a program's progress related to the program's anticipated outcomes. In addition, satisfaction surveys, focus groups, self-report logs or journals, and content testing may be useful. We discuss each of these methods next.

Surveys are a fairly easy and inexpensive method to collect information about a program's effects on participants. Traditional surveys have several advantages that often make them the method of choice when soliciting input from program participants, but they also have some disadvantages (see Fowler, 2002, and Chapter 10 for more details). Surveys are relatively inexpensive to create and produce, and typically they require only simple descriptive statistics for reporting purposes. Surveys can be used to collect information about the participants before and after a program, so that changes in affect, cognition, and/or behaviors can be measured.

Surveys are also quickly and easily administered to a large number of people; most people are familiar with surveys, which makes them easy to administer. On the other hand, the program evaluator needs to assess the population asked to complete the survey. If, for example, illiteracy is an issue for this population, then the evaluator may wish to use an oral interview administered either individually or in a group setting. If a pre-post design is to be used, are the program participants easily located, or would tracking these individuals to collect the postprogram information be difficult? Is the information easily conveyed in a singular response, or is further clarification needed before a full understanding is possible? Written surveys should not be the data collection method of choice when detailed written responses are needed; people typically will not complete numerous open-ended questions, and generally the responses are never more than a sentence or two. Other methods, such as focus groups or interviews, are better means for collecting in-depth responses.

Situations that limit the usefulness of survey methodologies are often present in social programs. In one example, an agency hired to conduct evaluations of three independent programs had difficulties with all three surveys of program participants. The data for families in public housing were lost because of major difficulties in collecting the postprogram data; in the middle of the year-long program, the public housing units were renovated, thereby scattering the program's families across the city, and very few of the displaced families returned to the public housing units or provided a forwarding address. The evaluation of another program, again located in a public housing facility, required housing residents to respond to a written survey concerning aspects of their community they would like to change. Only after the data were analyzed did the evaluator, unable to see a consistent pattern of responses, realize that the respondents were illiterate and had randomly marked responses on the questionnaire! The third evaluation required the program staff to help program recipients complete a survey after completing a four-week course but before receiving services. The evaluator assumed that this was occurring but learned only after the program had ended that staff seldom had program recipients complete the survey before beginning the program; almost none of the respondents had both pre- and postprogram surveys.

Another methodology commonly used to collect data about the effects of a program is focus group methodology, which relies on the interaction of people as they discuss a common experience or viewpoint. Because the data are always qualitative and reflect people's experiences, thoughts, ideas, and impressions, this method is basically a self-report of how the program affected participants. Focus groups need not always involve program participants, however; program staff can also share their concerns and impressions about a program, its benefits, and its worth. Some specific skills are needed for conducting a successful focus group; see Krueger and Casey (2000) for an excellent discussion of focus group methodology as it applies to the social sciences.

Self-report logs or journals, which are often overlooked by program evaluators, represent an excellent method for capturing participant and staff reactions to a program or recording the frequency of specific behaviors. Self-report logs are typically in a checklist format on which the respondent periodically records the frequency of the behavior under study; journals are narrative descriptions of the behavior. With the stress-reduction program, program participants might carry a small notebook; every time they feel stressed they would jot down the stressor, their initial reaction to it, and a description of how this behavior either increased, decreased, or had no effect on the stress they were feeling. If quantitative data were needed, the program evaluator could generate a mutually exclusive list for each of the categories (stressor, behavior, and consequences) and ask participants to check off one item in each category. A more complex log might involve collecting information about the conditions surrounding the stressful event, the duration of the stressful feelings, and the time of day the stressor occurred. Logs and journals can provide specific data about behaviors *as they occur* rather than the broader statements about behaviors and feelings collected in more general surveys.

Content testing, yet another method for collecting data on a program's effect, evaluates program participants' knowledge about a topic, typically using some paper-and-pencil activity. Course exams are a form of content testing. This type of data is useful when distinct facts or information is being conveyed through the program. In the stress-reduction program, respondents might be asked to name the stress-reduction techniques introduced in the workshop, the physiological symptoms associated with stress, the psychological manifestations of stress, and the five most common stressors faced by people in their age group. An even better data set would result from administering the same test before and after the workshop to measure the amount of information respondents acquired from it. Of course, using content testing requires the test to be highly correlated with the material presented in the workshop, and the individual items must be specific and difficult enough that only workshop attendees can answer the questions correctly.

Another use of content testing is to determine respondents' familiarity with a specific topic. One evaluator used a content test to evaluate a city's biking and walking trails. Respondents were asked how familiar they were with the biking and walking trail system (using a 1 to 5 scale to assess the respondent's self-report of familiarity), as well as 20 questions about the trails. Only respondents who had used the trails were able to correctly answer a majority of the questions. These data then were used to subsequently classify the respondents into "high," "medium," and "low" trail users, a categorization that was subsequently used for other statistical analyses.

CREATING A CONSOLIDATED DATA COLLECTION PLAN   It is sometimes easy to become lost in the "forest" of data and end up with too much data in one area and no data in another. After considering all data collection options, it is good to make a matrix with the evaluation question in the first column and the various methods that will be used to answer the particular question in the other columns. In evaluation terms, an evaluator often will "triangulate" the data collection process (Denzin, 1978) using multiple methods, multiple data sources, and more than one data collector or observer for data collected over more than one time period. Such a strategy reduces the reliance on any particular source. Just as a medical diagnosis seems more reliable when it comes from several different physicians, so too is the judgment of a program's worth more reliable when based on several sorts of data. Thus, for observations of the stress-reduction workshop, an evaluator who uses triangulation would have more than one observer trained in the observation procedure (to minimize observer bias), and these observations would be distributed over the length of the workshop (to minimize situational bias). If the workshop is repeated within the time frame of the evaluation, the evaluator would collect observational data from the other workshops as well. Finally, if the observations were used to describe the workshop's content, then the evaluator would also examine the written descriptions of the workshop's curriculum or planned activities as yet another source of data.

PLANNING THE DATA ANALYSES The final column in the matrix of evaluation questions and data collection methods in Table 21.1 is "data analyses." If, for example, a survey is being used, will subscores be calculated, or will frequencies for each item be calculated? Will a respondent's survey data be correlated with workshop attendance, and if so, is there a way to match these two pieces of data, through either a name or a code? What statistical analysis will be performed on the data, and are the data in a form that allows the analysis to occur without extensive manipulation? If the data are qualitative, how will the data be analyzed? Will there be case studies or a summary of findings? Time spent planning for the data analyses, whether the data are qualitative, quantitative, or archival, can save considerable time in conducting the data analyses. Extensive planning can also prevent fatal data collection errors from occurring, such as collecting pre- and posttest data only to find that there is no way to link the data because no identifying names or codes were included on the survey instrument.

ESTIMATING THE FINANCIAL AND TIME COSTS OF THE EVALUATION "The cost of an evaluation is difficult to predict accurately" (Herman, Morris, & Fitz-Gibbon, 1987) is an assessment with which almost anyone who has conducted an evaluation will likely agree without hesitation. There are no hard-and-fast rules about how much time a survey, for example, will take to design, print, distribute, analyze, and interpret. Herman et al. suggest first determining the fixed costs—those over which you have no control, such as postage, consultant time, overhead costs (heat, electricity, phone, and so on), printing, test and instrument purchase, and supplies or equipment needed to complete the project. They also suggest that you then calculate the "per unit" cost for each of these items. Thus, printing costs should be "per page," and overhead costs might be calculated "per month." Similarly, "person-hours" should also be calculated on a monthly or daily basis. Per person costs should include all the expenses associated with individuals, such as benefits, income tax, and social security tax that routinely are charged for a person's employment.

After the per unit costs have been calculated, the evaluator can begin to create the actual budget. The exact level of detail and layout of the budget depend on funders' needs, any forms required by your own organization, and your experience. This process can be quite complex, especially for a large evaluation, but it can be made less daunting by creating a detailed list of specific tasks needed to complete each component of the program evaluation. Thus, for a survey, the evaluator would estimate the costs for each step needed to move the survey from creation to data interpretation. Experience makes this process easier; knowing some of the areas that can cause problems allows the evaluator to allocate sufficient resources within the budget. It is rare when an evaluator says, "I overestimated the amount of time this project would take" or "I have more resources than I know what to do with!" The more detailed this list of tasks is, the less likely it is that you will underestimate the time associated with each task. Clearly, the more information you can add to this list, the better estimate you will make. Some details result from specific decisions, such as how many surveys will be given out and how they will be distributed and returned; other details come from talking with others. For example, if you learn that the data entry specialist charges by the keystroke rather than by the hour, you might want to know what the survey will look like before moving forward on that line in the budget. Colleagues can be good resources in helping to create realistic time lines and budgets. Each component should be broken into its individual tasks, and then estimates of time to complete each task and the subsequent cost for that task should be made. Even though this procedure creates a budget with a built-in time line, the evaluator may wish to create a time line in calendar form, with target dates for each component's completion highlighted. Several commercially available computer programs can create a master calendar of projects, in addition to monthly calendars. This software can be very helpful for keeping track of target dates in projects, especially if the evaluator is working on several projects simultaneously.

COMING TO A FINAL AGREEMENT ABOUT SERVICES, COSTS, AND RESPONSIBILITIES
After outlining the data collection procedures and creating a time line and budget to encompass these activities, the program evaluator submits these materials for final approval to the agency commissioning the program evaluation. The documents submitted should contain the following items:

1. A document that provides an overview of what will and will not be covered in the evaluation process, how and to whom the data will be reported, the cost of the evaluation, and the terms for payment. This document, sometimes known as a letter of agreement, should be short and succinct. It serves as an overview of the entire evaluation process and should be signed by both the program evaluator and a representative of the agency commissioning the program evaluation.
2. A document that identifies the following for each component of the program evaluation: a brief rationale, what data will be collected, the procedures for collecting the data, the person responsible, the roles and responsibilities of assistants, the time line, and the costs.
3. A current vitae or resume of the program evaluator.

Modifications to these documents are common, both before the documents are signed and after the evaluation has begun. All modifications in the data collection procedures need to be documented in writing, and a copy of these written changes must be provided to the client. These documents can be invaluable should disputes arise concerning any component.

COLLECTING AND ANALYZING INFORMATION

All the steps we have described up to this point occur *before* one piece of data has been collected. With proper planning and documentation, collecting and analyzing the information and then reporting the findings are rather straightforward. With proper planning and good record keeping, the evaluator should know exactly what data need to be collected; when during the program the data will be collected, and by whom; and how the data will be analyzed and interpreted. More important, perhaps, the evaluator will have a framework for judging whether collecting additional data would be beneficial, whether funds allow for following up on a newly presented data collection opportunity, and how any follow-up data will fit into the overall evaluation. In essence, up to this point the program evaluator has been creating a road map that will be used to keep the evaluation on track once data collection is underway. Moreover, this road map will also guide decisions about the format, content, and style of the evaluation report.

The role the evaluator has negotiated determines how actively involved he or she is in the day-to-day data collection process. If the program is large and will be replicated at several sites, or if site employees will collect a majority of the data to keep the cost of the evaluation down, then the evaluator becomes a data manager. At other times the evaluator serves as the principal data collector. Regardless, *ultimately the evaluator is responsible for the data, their integrity, their validity, and their timely collection.* Thus, several steps must be undertaken to ensure that the data are clean, as error-free as possible, unbiased, and collected on time and within budget.

First, every data collection procedure should undergo pilot testing. This requires thoroughly training any data collectors or site personnel concerning how the data are to be collected. Do not rely simply on written instructions; actual face-to-face training with several opportunities for role playing and questions can eliminate many points of confusion. If a questionnaire is to be administered, data collectors should practice administering it; if observations are to be made, practice sessions should occur until all data collectors observe the same situation and collect exactly the same data 90% to 95% of the time. If such coding reliability does not happen within a reasonable amount of time, the evaluator should consider simplifying the observation form or replacing some observers.

When the evaluator is not the principal data collector, the second step is to establish a checks-and-balances system. All data should be examined. Are the surveys filled out correctly and completely? Are pretests being given to clients before the first counseling session? Are files complete enough so that clients can be tracked for a six-month follow-up interview? The evaluator should never assume that the data are being collected as instructed; periodic monitoring of the data collection process is essential. An inexperienced evaluator once failed to check on a data collector because this particular collector had been working with the evaluation group for a couple of years before working for the evaluator. You can imagine the evaluator's horror, dismay, and embarrassment when, while visiting the program site, she was asked when the data collector was going to observe the program; she had just looked over the data supposedly collected from that site the previous week! The combination of that and similar experiences has led the evaluator to hang above her desk the following sign, which summarizes her philosophy about data collection:

> If you haven't seen it, heard it, touched it, smelled it, rolled in it, felt it, and tasted it, you don't know it.

Periodic checks of the program site, both announced and unannounced, are essential for monitoring the program and helping to keep the data clean.

The task of checking the data does not end once they arrive on the evaluator's desk. Data entry must be checked for accuracy, especially if performed by someone new to the evaluator. Are missing data being coded properly? How many errors are there per 100 data entry keystrokes? A skilled data entry person probably has no more than one or two errors. Are the data being entered using standardized procedures to make data analyses easy and to minimize data transformation or manipulation? The evaluator should never assume that the person entering the data knows how to do so in a format that is usable by a given statistical computer package.

Once all of the data have been collected and readied for analyses (that is, quantitative data have been entered into a spreadsheet or statistical analysis package, field notes have been typed into case notes, tapes of focus groups have been transcribed, and either paper copies or computer files are available), then the evaluator is now ready to conduct the data analysis. We divide data analysis into two distinct steps: primary analyses and secondary analyses.

PRIMARY DATA ANALYSES   The first analyses, called primary analyses, are identical to those presented in the results sections of empirical articles. The data from each component of the evaluation are analyzed in isolation from other data. Thus, for example, the results of the survey that measured respondent happiness are analyzed and reported separate from the descriptions of the stress-reduction workshop activities prepared by the participant-observer; each component has its own methods, results, and summary sections, as if each were the only data collected for the evaluation.

There are several advantages to analyzing and interpreting each data component in isolation from the other components. First, these primary data reports are excellent vehicles for periodically presenting data to stakeholders. They give stakeholders some preliminary indication of some of the findings; moreover, they begin to prepare stakeholders for the final report. Second, they prevent the data from becoming backlogged. By analyzing and writing the report for each data set as soon as it is ready, program evaluators are not faced with piles and piles of data as the completion deadline approaches. Third, primary data reports help the evaluator see holes in the data or areas that need additional examination. Programs are fluid entities; despite the best planning, changes in the program, failed data collection procedures, or ambiguous results sometimes require the evaluator to augment planned data sources. By analyzing the data as they come in, the evaluator may have enough time to develop a plan for collecting additional data before the program has ended. Finally, conducting a primary data analysis also expedites the secondary data analyses, as we discuss next.

SECONDARY DATA ANALYSES   A secondary data analysis ties together the individual, primary analyses to describe a component of the program. Because multiple sources of data are used, the program evaluator must reexamine each of the primary analyses to determine where findings support one another and where there are discrepancies. When answering the question, "Did the stress-reduction program provide program participants with strategies they could implement?" the evaluator would look at all the data collected. The evaluator would look at the survey items (which had been summarized into frequencies and percentages in the primary analyses) that asked respondents how often they used a particular technique, as well as examine journals kept by the respondents and the field notes taken during the participant-observations. If program participants said they used meditation frequently to reduce stress, was this technique emphasized in the workshops? If "effective decision making" was a technique emphasized during training but did not appear in the participants' journals, was this because they did not understand the importance of decision making in stress reduction or because it was not presented clearly enough to be useful?

Although there are several differences between how a researcher and an evaluator conduct the study of a social program, one of the elemental differences comes in the collection and interpretation of several data sources. Multiple data sources that provide insight into the worth of a social program are a hallmark of program evaluation, and the multiplicity of data sources requires some method for weaving together these sources. This method involves secondary data analyses.

The evaluator begins with the program's goals and objectives and examines the primary data reports to see how the results of each data collection component support or refute the supposition that the program met its goals. What evidence is there that college students who have taken part in the stress-reduction program have learned several new stress-reduction techniques? Did items on the questionnaire given in the workshop address this question? What did respondents say in focus groups when asked if they learned new techniques? According to the field notes of the participant-observer, were workshop attendees introduced to "several" techniques? Perhaps another goal of the stress-reduction workshop was to have respondents feel better able to handle stressful situations. What evidence either supports or refutes this claim of the program? If workshop attendees kept journals, do they contain evidence that attendees improved their stress-coping skills over time?

The secondary analysis moves back and forth from stated program goals and objectives to data sources. The importance of reducing the data via primary data analyses should now be evident: Wading through raw data at this point would be inefficient and cumbersome, if not impossible; relying on the summary statements made in the primary report helps to expedite the writing of the secondary analyses.

The secondary analysis—this moving back and forth from the program's objectives to the evidence, the weaving together of the individual pieces of data into a holistic picture—*is* program evaluation. Combined with recommendations and comparisons to similar programs, the secondary analysis creates the evaluation of the program. A program evaluator should never leave the interpretation of the evaluation to the stakeholders. It is the program evaluator's role to pull the pieces together and to clearly state what he or she means in terms of the program's implementation, anticipated outcomes, and implications for the successful conduct of this or future programs.

REPORTING THE EVALUATION'S FINDINGS

The evaluation process is not finished with the analysis and interpretation of the data. The last step, writing the final report, includes a few aspects that may be new to researchers. A good evaluation report, according to Fitzpatrick, Sanders, and Worthen (2004), contains the following sections: (1) an executive summary; (2) an introduction to the report stating the evaluation's purpose, the audience for whom the report was intended, any needed disclaimers of limitations, and an overview of the report contents; (3) a section that describes the focus of the evaluation and the program under evaluation; (4) an overview of the evaluation procedures; (5) a presentation of the evaluation results (the primary and secondary analyses); (6) the conclusions and recommendations; (7) responses to the report (if any); and (8) appendices, including the detailed evaluation plan, copies of instruments, and detailed analyses (the primary analyses). Several very good references provide the reader detailed information about each of these sections (see Fitzpatrick, Sanders, & Worthen, 2004; Newman & Brown, 1996; Patton, 1997; Smith, 1982). We next present a few comments on two of these sections: the recommendations and the executive summary.

WRITING RECOMMENDATIONS FOR IMPROVEMENT   Although writing the recommendations for improvement is perhaps the most important part of the evaluation process, it is daunting, especially for people new to program evaluation. Even experienced evaluators can have doubts, thinking "Who do you think you are, making suggestions about the program? You are not a content expert in counseling, in education, or in whatever area the program functions." The solution is not to write the recommendations in isolation. Just as evaluators should work to establish a rapport and understanding between themselves and the stakeholders when designing the evaluation, and should update stakeholders during the data collection and analyses, the evaluator/stakeholder relationship should continue through the report- and recommendation-writing stage.

An experienced evaluator might write the recommendations and then present them to stakeholders for discussion, but a more inclusive method is to present the final report minus the recommendations. Then, after stakeholders have had an opportunity to digest the contents of the final report—and stakeholders will do this at different levels of intensity—the evaluator schedules a meeting at which the evaluator facilitates the group in the generation of recommendations based on the final report. As recommendations are written by the stakeholders, the evaluator notes the differences from his or her own prewritten recommendations. The evaluator also may need to draw the group's attention to points not yet brought into the discussion. By using this method of including stakeholders in writing the recommendations, two important goals are achieved. First, stakeholders are reminded that program evaluation is not something that happens to them and their program, but instead is a collaborative discussion in which several perspectives shape the final recommendations. Second, the evaluation report and the subsequent recommendations are not viewed as being the sole property of the evaluator but rather as reflecting the thoughts of several professionals closely related to the program.

Utilizing the experience of stakeholders to help formulate the recommendations can be very beneficial, but a successful meeting does not occur without proper planning. First, because it is likely that many stakeholders assembled have not read the report prior to the meeting, the evaluator should provide a 15- to 20-minute presentation that outlines the evaluation findings. Moreover, the evaluator should have a list of recommendations he or she feels are absolutely crucial for inclusion and should ensure their inclusion in the discussion. A block of uninterrupted time must be set aside for this meeting. No one has ever complained if a meeting does not fill the whole block of time, but trying to hurry through the discussion can leave stakeholders feeling that ideas have been thrust upon them. The evaluator should be the keeper of the agenda and move the meeting along at a reasonable pace, allowing for discussion but preventing it from straying from the stated purpose. Finally, it is extremely important to invite the full range of stakeholders to this meeting, *including those with dissenting views,* and everyone invited should be notified as to who else will be in attendance. The evaluator should act as a facilitator, encouraging people to express their opinions within the constraints of the program. This meeting is not the vehicle for settling longstanding disagreements.

Recommendations include both the positive and negative aspects of the program as it was implemented and the subsequent outcomes. The strengths of the program are always listed first, separate from the weaknesses (sometimes called the limitations) of the program. Careful wording of the recommendation section of the report is crucial; the goal is to write a recommendation that adequately describes the strengths and weaknesses of the program without being overly critical or mired in detail. One good perspective addresses the future—either in the next year of the program or the next time the program is replicated: What aspects of the program would be absolutely critical for success next time? What are the key, beneficial features of the program that need to be incorporated into future programs? What parts of the program were not implemented as anticipated, and what does this mean for future replications of the program? What is missing from the current program that, if included in future years, would make it stronger? What can be done to strengthen the program in future replications? Some evaluators simply list recommendations; others include a short rationale that describes the formulation of the conclusions drawn in the report.

WRITING THE EXECUTIVE SUMMARY   The other aspect of the evaluation report that may be unfamiliar to researchers is the executive summary. Attention to the style of this section and the recommendations is time well spent, because although few people read a report from cover to cover, the executive summary and the recommendations are read by most people who come in contact with the report. To illustrate this point, Fitzpatrick, Sanders, and Worthen (2004) described an experience in evaluating a statewide "controversial program" for which three separate reports were prepared for review by stakeholders: (1) the full report containing all of the technical detail of how the evaluation was conducted; (2) a medium-size summary of major interpretations drawn from the data; and (3) a brief executive summary:

> Availability of these three reports was broadly announced in the newspapers and on television. . . . Nearly 400 individuals [requested and] read the executive summary, 40 read the mid-size interpretive report, and only one person ever even requested the complete report (and he was an expert methodologist hired by opponents of the evaluation to see if he could find fault with it). As these results show, shorter reports will often be most widely disseminated. (Worthen et al., 1997, p. 416)

The executive summary should be no more than three pages, give the reader an overview of the goals of the program, and indicate the services provided, the outcomes anticipated, and the extent to which these objectives were met. An executive summary should stand on its own; it should contain enough detail so that a person can grasp the program, its purpose, and its impact by reading it alone.

DISSEMINATING THE REPORT   Who owns the data and to whom the written findings are disseminated are points negotiated prior to signing a letter of agreement. The evaluator and program administrators should come to an understanding about how many copies of the final report are needed, the number of presentations the evaluator is expected to make, and how the evaluation results should be disseminated. Some agencies are bound by the Public Information Act, which makes the report automatically available to anyone who requests a copy. But who is the spokesperson for the evaluation and its results? What are the limitations for using the evaluation data and the subsequent report? This answer lies in the *Program Evaluation Standards* (Joint Committee on Standards for Educational Evaluation, 1994). Suppose the local newspaper chooses to print only that portion of an evaluation that outlines a controversial program's weaknesses, or suppose the program administrator requests from the evaluator an updated summary but then forwards to a federal funding agency only those portions of the evaluator's report that favor the program. In both cases, the evaluator and the program administrator could have taken steps to prevent or minimize the effect of these actions.

In the *Program Evaluation Standards,* the "formal parties [in this case, the evaluator and program administrator] should ensure that the full set of evaluation findings along with pertinent limitations are made accessible to the persons affected by the evaluation, and any others with expressed legal rights to receive the results" (Propriety Standard 6). Both the evaluator and the program administrator are responsible for monitoring the release and use of the evaluation. In the second situation, it was the evaluator's responsibility to require the program administrator to provide a copy of the summary prior to releasing it to the funding agency. An evaluator should *never* give up editing responsibility to others; editing, summarizing, or releasing portions of an evaluation should remain exclusively in the evaluator's direct control.

CONCLUDING THE EVALUATION   The final two steps in conducting a program evaluation involve creating an evaluation trail and conducting a meta-evaluation. An evaluation trail is a file, either electronic or paper, that outlines the steps taken during the evaluation, beginning with a copy of the letter of agreement. All original data, including completed surveys, field notes, copies of transcribed tapes, and data files, should be organized, labeled, and included in this file. Paper copies of data files used in statistical analyses and the computer command files and output files should also be included and clearly labeled. Also needed are any internal review board documents, signed consent forms, and financial records outlining how money for the evaluation was spent. Finally, a clean copy of the final report, including any appendices, should be placed in this file. This evaluation trail should stand as an archival record of when and how the evaluation was completed, and should contain all original documents associated with the evaluation.

The last step in the evaluation process encourages growth and reflection by the evaluator. After each evaluation, the program evaluator should take some time to reflect on the evaluation process—what went well, and what aspects of the evaluation could have been completed more efficiently, professionally, or rigorously. Some evaluators keep a professional journal in which they keep a record of the pitfalls and triumphs of each evaluation. When completed honestly and reviewed periodically, these journals can help evaluators identify recurring themes that need to be addressed. They also can serve as personal histories of evaluators' growth and accumulating experience.

SUMMARY AND CONCLUSIONS

This chapter introduces program evaluation—how it differs from research and the steps used in conducting it. Although program evaluation uses many of the data collection methods used in empirical research, the scope of a program evaluation is often much broader than that of empirical research. Whereas empirical research often occurs in controlled settings, program evaluation typically occurs without a control group and in settings outside the control of the program evaluator. Rather than following experimental research protocols and methodologies, program evaluation at its best adheres to quasi-experimental designs.

Evaluations of social programs examine not only the effects of the program (outcomes), but also the program's implementation (process). An examination of how the program is implemented often reveals the reasons a program met or failed to meet specified outcomes. Documenting the factors that both limit and enhance the program as it was administered can help to strengthen the program or similar programs in the future. A defining feature of program evaluation is the use of and interpretation of *triangulated* data—data collected from more than one source, at more than one setting, using more than one data collection methodology. By using data triangulation, program evaluators increase the validity of the evaluation's findings.

This chapter describes four phases of program evaluation. An evaluator begins the process by setting the boundaries of the evaluation. A crucial step in this phase involves allowing all stakeholders to have a voice in the scope of the evaluation to ensure that the evaluation's findings are fair and unbiased. Utility is also enhanced by linking the program's goals and objectives to specific evaluation questions.

After setting the boundaries of the evaluation, the second phase involves selecting appropriate evaluation methods. The selection of the methodology depends on the information needs of the evaluation audience; the time, personnel, and financial resources available to the evaluator; and the constraints of the program. During this phase the program evaluator also plans how the data will be collected and prepared for analyses, and trains the program staff to ensure reliable collection.

The third phase entails the actual collection and analyses of the data. The evaluator pilot-tests all newly created or modified instruments and observation forms, monitors data collection by program staff or evaluation staff, and ensures that agreements of anonymity and/or confidentiality are upheld. Primary data analyses are conducted and reported in a manner similar to those conducted in empirical research. Secondary analyses examine the various primary data analyses to focus the findings on specific evaluation questions.

The final phase of evaluating a program requires the evaluator to report the findings of the evaluation. Methods of dissemination, report deadlines, and types of reports to be created should be agreed upon by the evaluator and client as part of the evaluation contract. All evaluation reports should contain sections that describe (1) the program, (2) the evalua-tion process, (3) the data collection procedures, and (4) the results and findings of the evaluation. In addition, all reports should contain an executive summary and a list of recommendations that include the positive aspects of the program as well as the areas that may need improvement. These two sections should not exceed five or six pages.

STIMULUS QUESTIONS

An Exercise in Program Evaluation

You have been asked to evaluate a week-long, overnight camping experience for girls ages 7 to 14. Use this example when answering the following questions:

1. What sources of information will you use to describe the program and understand its mission and goals?
2. Outline a couple of evaluation questions you might pose during the implementation phase of the program.
3. How would the evaluation questions change if the evaluation were conducted during the conceptualization phase of the program?
4. Who are the possible stakeholders for your program? Are there any silent stakeholders? Are there any disenfranchised stakeholders?
5. The second phase in the evaluation of a program involves outlining data collection steps and time lines. What is the relevance of this procedure?

6. What data collection strategies will you use?

7. What might be some of the advantages and disadvantages of using participant observation in your evaluation?

8. What does it mean to "triangulate the data sources"?

9. When does primary data analysis occur, and why is it important in the evaluation of a program?

10. What is secondary data analysis, and how does it differ from primary data analysis?

11. What are some of the advantages of involving the stakeholders when writing the evaluation recommendations?

12. What is an "evaluation trail," and what does it include?

13. How do research and program evaluation differ?

PROFESSIONAL ISSUES

PART 4

22 CHAPTER | PROFESSIONAL WRITING

This chapter discusses an important professional issue related to research—writing the research report. It is essential to realize that a study is not any better than the written report that discusses it. Although it could be argued that results of studies are disseminated in ways other than written reports (such as conference presentations), the research report is a very important mechanism for the dissemination of new knowledge. Journal articles, books, dissertations, and (to a lesser extent) written summaries of conference presentations are the permanent records of counseling research. Unless a study is discussed in one of these sources, it is unlikely that a researcher interested in the topic will be able to learn about the study. Nevertheless, a poorly written report, even if it is retrieved, will limit the usefulness of the research. It is a shame when the informative results of an elegantly conducted study are obscured by a contorted and confusing report. The preparation of a clear and informative research report is a critical step in the research process.

Few readers are likely to begin conducting research without having had at least some instruction in writing. A critical element in learning to write is to practice and to receive feedback. Of all the elements of the research process, writing is the most difficult to teach. Nevertheless, we would be remiss if we did not discuss important aspects of the research report writing process. Others have discussed psychological report writing (see, for example, American Psychological Association [APA], 1983; Dorn, 1985; Seeman, 1959; Sternberg, 1988). Several authors have also discussed writing various types of articles, including review articles (Bem, 1995), methodological articles (Maxwell & Cole, 1995), and meta-analytic reviews (Rosenthal, 1995).

Writing style is personal; the opinions of authors, critics, and educators in this matter differ. Furthermore, style varies according to the constraints of the publication in which the writing will appear. For example, the American Psychological Association (APA) carefully details the required elements of manuscripts submitted to APA journals in its *Publication Manual of the American Psychological Association* (APA, 2001). This reference book is indispensable for most authors who publish in counseling and related professional journals. Graduate schools typically have their own requirements for dissertations.

One chapter cannot cover the myriad of details involved in writing theses, dissertations, or manuscripts for publication. Our goal in this chapter is to introduce writers to the basic components of a research report. First, we present the major sections of a report and discuss their relation to the principles of research design previously discussed in this book. Although we could discuss various organizational formats, we focus on the title, abstract, introduction, method, results, and discussion. We also present some general principles for writing research reports. For a more detailed discussion of writing research reports, we suggest interested readers consult Heppner and Heppner (2004), which provides a more in depth guide to writing and publishing thesis and dissertation research, and offers many examples to illustrate writing each section of a research report.

It is also important to acknowledge at the beginning that everyone has difficulty in writing at one time or another. It may be due to writer's block, fatigue, a particularly complex writing task, or a myriad of fears and apprehensions about the product (for example, "I will make a mistake, which will be there for everyone to see"; "What I have to say is really not very important"; "If I can't write it perfectly, I won't write anything"). For inexperienced authors, many of these fears are particularly acute but developmentally normal. However, even the veteran author experiences fears and apprehensions. Writing is just one more skill the researcher needs to acquire, and like any other skill, it takes practice, feedback, analysis of successful models of writing such as published articles, and rewriting.

SECTIONS OF A RESEARCH REPORT

The exact organization of a research report varies, depending on the publication for which it is intended and the nature of the study. Nevertheless, a perusal of counseling journals reveals that articles are typically organized as follows:

- Title
- Abstract
- Introduction
- Method

- Participants
- Measures (or Variables or Instruments)
- Materials
- Design (or Design and Analysis)
- Procedure
- Results
- Discussion (or Conclusions)
- References
- Tables
- Figures

The nature of each of these components depends on the publication and its readership. Nevertheless, some aspects of each of these components are crucial to well-written research reports. In this discussion we will focus on those aspects of the components that relate to research design. (See APA, 2001; Dorn, 1985; Heppner & Heppner, 2004; and Sternberg, 1988, for other discussions related to these components.) We will not discuss reference lists, tables, and figures, because these are clearly described in the *APA Publication Manual*. As we discuss these components sequentially, keep in mind that they are held together by a common focus—the research questions and/or hypotheses—which help the reader comprehend the study as a whole. For this reason, presentation of the results, for example, should mirror presentation of the design used to examine the research questions and/or hypotheses, as discussed in the method section.

TITLE

The title of a research report does much more than just give it a name; it is used in a variety of ways to make the report accessible to readers. Many services depend on titles to index and abstract publications; users of these services often see only the title. Furthermore, readers perusing journals or other sources (such as *Current Contents* or *PsychLit*) often decide to read a report solely on the basis of its title. Therefore, choose the title carefully.

A title should accurately summarize the research, describing the topic, the variables, the design, and the outcome succinctly (in 12 to 15 words, according to most sources). Given the limitations on the length of titles, redundancies and irrelevancies must be avoided. Omit such phrases as "A Study of" or "The Relation Between." However, even within these constraints, interesting and stylistic titles can be developed.

Alloy and Abramson (1979) provide an example of a seminal article with a title that is both descriptive and attention-getting: "Judgment of Contingency in Depressed and Nondepressed Students: Sadder but Wiser?" The title describes the independent variable (depressed versus nondepressed), the dependent variable (judgment of contingency), the participants (students), and the results (sadder but wiser). The phrase "Sadder but Wiser?" not only adds interest, but also has become a mnemonic; it is often used to refer to this article.

ABSTRACT

The abstract is a summary of the research report. Like the title, the abstract is used for indexing and retrieving articles. After the title, the abstract is the most-often read portion of a research report, and thus it should be succinct, accurate, and comprehensive. It should summarize the content of each of the major sections of the report, including the hypotheses, method (participants, measures, materials, design, and procedure), results, and conclusions. Remember that nonsignificant results are informative; typically, it can be useful to report and discuss all results, not just those that were expected. The length of abstracts depends on the publication; APA journals require abstracts of empirical studies to be between 100 and 120 words. Writing accurate and informative abstracts is a difficult task.

The abstract should be self-contained; the reader should not need to depend on any other section of the report to make sense of the abstract. Therefore, avoid abbreviations and acronyms to the extent possible, or at the very least make sure that they are defined in the abstract. Explain unique and technical terms. Because readers of abstracts often do not have access to the entire research report, do not refer to other articles in an abstract. Exceptions to this rule include abstracts of reaction articles (for instance, an article written in response to a previous article or a reanalysis of data from a published article).

INTRODUCTION

The introduction to a research report sets the stage for the study. It should orient the reader to the problem, develop the rationale behind the study, and indicate as specifically as possible the hypotheses being tested. Several questions should be answered in the introduction: Why is this an important topic to study? What previous work (empirical and theoretical) bears on the topic? How does this previous work logically lead to the author's research question and hypotheses? How will this question be researched? What predictions can be made? To answer these questions, the introduction of a research report typically contains three elements: (1) an introduction to the problem, (2) a development of the framework for the study, and (3) a statement of the research questions and/or hypotheses.

The introduction to the problem should begin by orienting the reader to the topic, including why this is an important area to investigate. This discussion should be achieved with broad strokes. A study of child abuse might begin with some general statistics about the prevalence of child abuse and its implications for society; a study of supervision might begin by discussing difficulties involved in understanding the supervisory process (see, for example, Friedlander, Siegel, & Brenock, 1989); a study of social support vis-à-vis the effectiveness of group therapy might begin with a statement about the widespread finding that social support mediates stressful life changes (see Mallinckrodt, 1989). The introduction to the problem should begin to narrow the topic by identifying important developments relevant to the topic area. With regard to child abuse, the identification of stress as a precursor of abuse could be cited (if that is the direction the researcher will pursue). The introduction to the problem can be concluded with a statement of the problem in general terms.

The second element in an introduction is the development of a rationale for the study. The framework for the rationale is built through the logical interconnectedness of empirical results and theory that leads to a critical, unanswered research question. We quite deliberately avoid the use of the more traditional term *literature review,* because it implies (at least to some) a synopsis of one study after another, along with considerable integration and synthesis of the findings; in contrast, a *framework* consists of elements connected in some logical way. In some ways, the development of a framework is similar to that of a legal brief. When the case is solid, there is one inescapable conclusion; similarly, by the time the readers have completed reading this section, they should be saying, "I know exactly what research question should be asked" and then find that the author asked that research question.

The literature cited in the development of the framework should be pertinent to this particular research study. If reviews of the literature exist, cite the review articles rather than the original studies if this is sufficient to build the case. In any discussion of a previous study, discuss only the pertinent aspects of that study which build the rationale of your study—these are typically those aspects related to the findings of that study, but perhaps methodological issues (such as type of participants), design, and statistical tests as well. For example, reference to a study would not mention the number of participants used in that study unless those data were pertinent to the rationale of your study, which would be the case if the point being made was related to inadequate power to detect an effect. Discussion of previous findings and theories needs to be intertwined logically. When you discuss a particular study or theory, the purpose of the discussion vis-à-vis the framework should be clear to the reader. Do not hesitate to inform the reader directly: "Left and Write's (1980) application of the Direct Counseling Approach (DCA) is important because it extends previous studies using DCA to children." Furthermore, you should integrate the material reviewed. Often studies result in contradictory findings; you need to speculate about the reasons for the discrepancy and to indicate how these discrepancies (and the reasons behind them) relate to the present study.

A word about completeness is needed. Certainly, the scope of the framework and the literature discussed in it is determined by the publication for which it is intended; more completeness is needed for a dissertation than for a journal article. Nevertheless, the goal is the same: to develop a logical argument that will lead to a research question and/or hypothesis, not to review all the studies ever written on a topic. Generally, this element of the introduction should be complete enough that it touches on issues raised elsewhere in the research report; it should not be necessary to review literature when hypotheses are stated or when dependent variables are operationalized. One exception to this rule is that it is common to report psychometric information under the measures subsection of the method section.

If the framework has been developed properly, the purpose of the present research should be readily apparent. One purpose might be to reconcile discrepancies in previous research; in that case the study will explain why contradictory findings have been obtained. Another purpose might be to apply results from some noncounseling area to problems in counseling (see, for example, the social influence model, Strong, 1968). Still another purpose of the study might be to extend previous results to a different population.

The final element of the introduction is the statement of the research questions and/or hypotheses. The research questions and/or hypotheses should follow logically from the framework built previously. Research questions are typically used in descriptive studies, especially of a qualitative nature. In those studies the author may not have specific hypotheses because little is known about the topic, and the purpose of the study is more exploratory than predictive of relationships. Conversely, authors often use hypotheses as a critical test of some important theoretical or practical question (Shadish, Cook, & Campbell, 2002; Wampold, Davis, and Good, 1990). A good theory will allow several implications to be drawn from it; a hypothesis is critical to the extent that it tests an implication from a theory and that the implication is unique to that theory (see Wampold, Davis, and Good, 1990). In that way, knowledge progresses because unsubstantiated theories are winnowed out.

Research questions and/or hypotheses are written in terms of theoretical constructs; operationalization of the constructs comes later. For example, the research hypothesis might state that a cognitive-behavioral treatment will lower state anxiety but not trait anxiety. Unless there is some particular issue with operationalization that this study addresses directly, operationalization of state and trait anxiety is typically discussed under the measures subsection of the method section. Thus, discussion of particular measures used to operationalize a construct should not be included in the introduction, unless a particular operationalization is related to the research hypothesis (for example, the study differs from previous studies in the manner in which a construct is operationalized).

Research hypotheses should be stated unambiguously. Of course, the degree to which a hypothesis can be specific depends on the specificity of the theory. However, statements such as "the purpose of the present study is to explore the relation between" or "the purpose is to determine the relation between" are insufficient because some relation will always be discovered (even if the relation is null—that is, no relation). Such statements do not make clear how the discovered relation relates to theoretical predictions, and the researcher must create post-hoc explanations.

An example of an unambiguous research hypothesis is provided by Ponce and Atkinson (1989). The purpose of this study was to examine the effects of counselor ethnicity, participant acculturation, and counseling style on Mexican-American participants' perceptions of counselor credibility and influence. It was hypothesized that participant acculturation would interact with both counselor ethnicity and counseling style in such a way that unacculturated participants would prefer a Mexican-American counselor who used a directive style, whereas acculturated clients would have no preference for either counselor ethnicity or counseling style.

An example of a research question that guides the direction of a study is: What are the coping processes Mexican immigrants use in response to the stressors of acculturation in a rural Midwest community? For more on this topic, see Suarez-Renaud, 2002. Heppner and Heppner (2004) devote an entire chapter to discussing writing research questions and hypotheses, and provide examples of how the literature review can be used to establish research questions and hypotheses.

METHOD

The method section describes how the research questions and/or hypotheses were examined, including all aspects of how the study was conducted. Enough detail is needed so that a reader can (1) determine the validity of the study and (2) replicate the study. Of all the sections of a manuscript, the method section often has the highest correlation with editorial decisions concerning rejection or acceptance for publication (Munley, Sharkin, & Gelso, 1988); therefore, it is imperative that the method section be well written.

The method section is typically divided into subsections. Research in counseling usually contains subsections on participants, measures (or variables or instruments), materials, design, and procedures, each of which we briefly describe here. Organization of the method section depends, to a great extent, on the nature of the study. The order of the subsections may be altered (for instance, design often appears as either the first or last subsection), but they should fit together like a puzzle, providing at the end a very clear picture of what was done and how it was done. Furthermore, they should explain how the researcher analyzed the data so that the reader is primed for the presentation of the results.

PARTICIPANTS   The subsection on participants should indicate, at a minimum, (1) the total number of participants, (2) how the participants were selected, and (3) characteristics of the participants relevant to the outcome of the study (including, for example, age, educational level, gender, ethnicity, geographical area of residence, and pretest level of functioning, depending on the study; see Chapter 14 for a discussion of this issue). Other aspects that may be mentioned in this section include topics such as how many participants were recruited, what they were told about the study, assignment of participants to conditions of the independent variable (including number of participants in each condition), attrition, statistical power, and circumstances under which the participants participated (for instance, financial remuneration or course credit). If a power analysis was conducted to determine the number of participants needed, results of this analysis should be included either here or in the design subsection. In short, the participants section should allow the reader to ascertain: (1) the number of participants, (2) who the participants are and where you recruited them, and (3) the representativeness of the sample, and thus, relevant information to ascertain the external validity or generalizability of the study (see Heppner & Heppner, 2004, for more details).

MEASURES (OR VARIABLES OR INSTRUMENTS) The purpose of the measures subsection is to operationalize the constructs to which the research questions and/or hypotheses referred. Recall that Ponce and Atkinson (1989) mentioned counselor ethnicity, participant acculturation, counseling style, and perceptions of counselor credibility in their statement of the research hypothesis. Counselor ethnicity was a participant characteristic, and counseling style was a manipulated independent variable; participant acculturation and perceptions of counselor credibility were operationalized using the Acculturation Rating Scale for Mexican-Americans (ARSMA) and the Counselor Effectiveness Rating Scale (CERS), respectively. Therefore, Ponce and Atkinson discussed the ARSMA and the CERS under a subsection called "Instruments."

The measures subsection discusses the operationalization of constructs, including the rationale for choosing particular instruments. Why was a particular instrument chosen? Why were three measures of a construct used rather than one (or two, or four)? Why were commonly used measures omitted? Furthermore, the measures subsection should include a discussion of each instrument chosen, including its title, a citation (manual, article, or other primary source), a description (for example, number and type of items, direction of scoring), factors or subscales, and psychometric properties (such as reliability and validity). Statements about reliability and validity estimates should refer to the context in which these estimates were calculated (for example, the population).

In general, 11 elements are typically included in the description of each instrument, roughly in the following order: (1) instrument name, (2) acronym, (3) author(s), (4) key reference, (5) a brief description of the construct the instrument assesses, (6) number of items, (7) type of items (e.g., Likert format), (8) factors or subscales and their definitions, (9) indication of the direction of the scoring, i.e., what a high score means, (10) validity estimates, and (11) reliability estimates (Heppner & Heppner, 2004). In addition, for qualitative studies, the procedures section will often contain information such as assumptions and rationale for using an interpretive design, strategies of inquiry, data collection, the researchers and their biases, interview protocol, pilot of the protocol, training the research team, transcribing the interviews, and data analyses procedures (for more details see Heppner & Heppner).

Because of the need to justify choice of operationalizations, the measures subsection is one place in the method section where it is not unusual to cite various studies (for instance, studies of psychometric properties). However, if the operationalization of a crucial construct is controversial, then discussion of these issues probably fits best in the introduction (as a part of the development of the framework). This would be the case if the researcher claims that previous attempts to corroborate a theory were unsuccessful because of improper operationalization of the dependent variable and the present study used different instruments to measure the same construct.

In a treatment study, operationalization of the independent variable is vital, usually taking the form of describing the treatments for each condition. Sometimes the amount of detail needed to describe a particular treatment intervention adequately becomes prohibitive; in such cases it often is helpful to develop a detailed treatment manual to which interested readers can be directed via a footnote (see, for example, O'Neil & Roberts Carroll, 1988).

MATERIALS   The materials subsection describes any materials used in the study. Pilot testing of the materials would also be described in this section. Sufficient information should be given to enable an independent researcher to reproduce the materials and replicate the study. If space limitations make this impossible, it is customary to indicate in a footnote that additional information or the materials themselves are available from the author.

DESIGN (OR DESIGN AND ANALYSIS)   This subsection describes the design of the study. After this section, readers should have a clear understanding of, for example, the independent, status, and dependent variables and the manner in which participants were assigned to levels of the independent variables. For example, if a factorial design is used, the factors should be labeled, the number of conditions within a factor should be indicated, and the nature of the factors (such as between versus within, or random versus fixed) should be stated. If the analyses are mentioned (for example, a two-way analysis of variance applied to a factorial design), then the name of the subsection should include "Analysis." A power analysis, if conducted, can also be included in this subsection.

The connection between the design and the research questions and/or hypotheses should be clear. For example, after reading this subsection, the reader should understand how the hypotheses were tested (see Wampold, Davis, and Good, 1990). Often (especially in a dissertation), the research hypotheses are restated in operationalized form, such as "To test the research hypothesis that [statement of hypothesis], a two-way analysis of variance was conducted. [Explain factors and indicate dependent variable.] It was predicted that a statistically significant F test for the interaction would be obtained."

PROCEDURE   The procedure subsection describes how the research was conducted with the participants. Discuss everything that the researchers did with the participants, from beginning to end, including instructions to the participants, the formation of groups, experimental manipulations, interview questions, development of questionnaire items, and so on. The procedure subsection is typically organized chronologically. The goal of the procedure subsection is to provide enough detail so that the study can be replicated by another researcher. If a separate design subsection is not included, details related to randomization and other features of the design can be included in this subsection. The procedure section can vary greatly depending on whether the study is a survey study, a correlational study, a scale construction study, or a counseling process study (see examples in Heppner & Heppner, 2004).

RESULTS

The purpose of the results section is to summarize the data and the results of the analyses utilized in the study. It is important to note that the writing style is quite different for a results section depending on whether the methodology is quantitative or qualitative (see Heppner & Heppner, 2004). Generally, for a quantitative study, two types of results are reported: (1) data screening, summary statistics, and results of preliminary analyses; and (2) results related to the research hypotheses. The summary statistics typically include the means and standard deviations of the dependent variables for each level of the independent variable (or combination of levels, as in a factorial design) and the correlation matrix for all variables, when appropriate (for example, regression analyses, factor analyses, or structural equation modeling). Results of preliminary analyses may be related to manipulation checks, dropouts, verification of stimulus materials, and so forth (see Heppner & Heppner, 2004).

Results related to research hypotheses should be organized so that the reader can tie the results of specific statistical tests to research hypotheses stated earlier in the report. There should be a one-to-one correspondence between the hypotheses and the statistical tests (see Wampold, Davis, and Good, 1990). This organization is facilitated by appropriately titled subsections, such as "Preliminary Analyses," "Summary Statistics," or "Test of Hypothesis 1."

The results section should report the findings, but discussion of the results is saved for the discussion section. Nevertheless, introduce each result so that its purpose is clear. For example, indicate why a preliminary analysis was conducted and what various outcomes mean: "A preliminary analysis on the observers' ratings of the therapy sessions was conducted to determine whether or not the treatments were perceived as different. The [name of statistical test] was statistically significant [give information about test statistic], indicating that the observers did indeed rate the treatments differently."

Some confusion often exists about what information to include concerning statistical tests. The *APA Publication Manual* (2001) gives specifics about reporting statistical tests in the text and in tables. However, these specifications are inadequate because for the most part they indicate *how* to report rather than *what* to report. The trend has been to report less; for example, one rarely sees analysis of variance source tables anymore. More disturbing is the tendency not to report important information (such as size of test statistic and probability levels) when results are nonsignificant. This minimalist point of view puts the emphasis on statistical significance and ignores concepts such as effect size, estimation, and power. Failure to report information other than significance levels makes it difficult or impossible for readers to verify results, calculate other indexes (such as effect size or power), and conduct meta-analyses. A persuasive argument can be made for reporting size of test statistics, exact probability levels (rather than, say, $p < .05$) for significant and nonsignificant findings, some measure of effect size, power, and other indexes as appropriate (Rosnow & Rosenthal, 1988). An article by Ellis, Robbins, Shult, Ladany, and Banker (1990) provides a good example of reporting a variety of indexes other than level of significance. For more details about writing the results section for a wide range of research designs and corresponding statistical analyses, see Heppner and Heppner (2004).

For qualitative studies, the results section will typically differ based on the chosen strategy of inquiry (e.g., grounded theory, consensual qualitative research, or phenomenology/hermeneutics). Thus, the results section might contain subsections such as a dimensional analysis model, descriptions of categories or domains that emerge from the data, excerpts from the interviews to explain the meaning of the categories, cross-analysis of the results, and detailed descriptions of participants' lived experiences. For concrete examples of writing qualitative results sections, see Heppner and Heppner (2004).

For both quantitative and qualitative studies, results are often presented in tables or figures, which are useful because results can be understood while taking up a minimal amount of space. Locating important results in the text is much more difficult than finding them in a well-organized table. Figures are particularly useful for illustrating patterns of results, such as an interaction in an analysis of variance. When tables or figures are used, total recapitulation of the results in the text should be avoided, although sometimes it is useful to summarize key results presented in the tables. The writer must, however, tell the reader what to look for in the tables. For example, one might say, "The main effects of the 3 (treatment) by 2 (gender) analysis of variance were statistically significant, as shown in Table 1"; it is then unnecessary to note, for example, the degrees of freedom, the F statistics, and so forth, because that information is in the table.

DISCUSSION

The discussion typically includes: (1) an explanation of the results of the data analyses; (2) if appropriate, whether or not the data support the research hypotheses; (3) a statement of the conclusions; (4) an indication of the study's limitations; and (5) a discussion of the implications. This section allows the author to expand on the findings and to place them in the context of previous research and theory on this topic.

The discussion typically begins with a description of the strongest findings from the data analyses that were presented in the results section. For example, sometimes authors structure the discussion around the hypotheses, addressing each one sequentially (see Heppner & Heppner, 2004, for examples). In such cases, there are usually clear statements about whether the research hypotheses were supported. Has new knowledge been generated by support of the hypotheses? Do the results support or refute particular theories? If the data lead to reformulated hypotheses, state them, but indicate that they have been formulated post hoc (that is, they have not been tested directly). If future research is needed, indicate what types of hypotheses should be tested and how future studies should be designed (see Heppner & Heppner).

Every discussion of results should include a statement of the limitations, which typically are related to methodological issues such as low power, the analogue nature of the study, violated assumptions of statistical tests, confounds, and so forth. Remember that no study is perfect; it is best to be forthright about the limitations and discuss how the results are interpretable in spite of the limitations.

Finally, given the results of the data analyses, support (or nonsupport) for the hypotheses (if relevant), and the limitations, you are free to indicate the implications of the study for theory and for practice. However, because the results of one study are rarely important enough by themselves to revise theory or to change practice, avoid statements such as "Practitioners should refrain from Treatment X and only use Treatment Y."

GENERAL PRINCIPLES FOR WRITING RESEARCH REPORTS

Although it is difficult to identify general principles of writing, we can emphasize seven general rules of thumb: (1) Be informative, (2) be forthright, (3) do not overstate or exaggerate, (4) be logical and organized, (5) have some style, (6) write and rewrite, and (7) if all else fails, just write!

PRINCIPLE 1: BE INFORMATIVE

The goal of the research report is to inform the reader about the study. Provide enough detail for the reader to understand what you are explaining, but not so much that the reader becomes bogged down. Of course, the publication format determines the level of detail. Dissertations require the most detail. Some journals are more technical than others and thus require more detail. Are the readers of a particular journal primarily practitioners, other researchers, or statisticians? The best way to include the right amount of detail is to emulate the publication of interest. Most journals periodically present editorials or other information about the materials to be contained in their articles (see the inside covers of most journals for descriptions of appropriate articles).

In any report, discuss the central points and minimize digressions. Obviously, you should not report everything that you did, but only information that readers need to understand the study. For example, preparation of stimulus materials often involves many successive stages of development. It is not necessary to explain each iteration; rather, describe the final product and summarize the development process in a sentence or two. However, do not omit important details, either. Authors frequently refer to a decision that was made but do not discuss the decision rule; if, for example, "three outliers were omitted from the analysis," on what basis were the three data considered outliers? Was this decision rule formulated before the data were analyzed? (For more details on writing the discussion section, see Heppner and Heppner, 2004.)

PRINCIPLE 2: BE FORTHRIGHT

Every study has flaws (Gelso, 1979). It is rare that a researcher would not alter a study, given the chance to do so. Authors should be forthright and discuss the ramifications of a study's limitations, rather than trying to hide flaws in some way. Signs of hidden flaws include obtuse language, esoteric statistical tests (with improper justification), omitted information, and overstated justifications. Reviewers of manuscripts submitted for publication are especially annoyed when they uncover hidden flaws or when they have a vague (intuitive) sense that the author has not been forthright with regard to some limitation.

Such flaws necessitate a fundamental decision: If a flaw is fatal to the study (for example, a confound that cannot be minimized), then it is best to consider the study a time-consuming learning experience. If the flaw is problematic but the results of the study are informative nevertheless, then the author should indicate how the flaw affects the interpretation and why the study remains important. Keep in mind that judgments in this regard typically are made by others—by dissertation committees, editors, and reviewers. Although the author may think that a flaw is not fatal, a journal editor may decide otherwise, or vice versa.

PRINCIPLE 3: DO NOT OVERSTATE OR EXAGGERATE

There is a widely shared tendency to believe that every study will somehow change the course of the field. When expressed in written reports, it appears as unjustified claims about the importance of the results for the field of counseling. Put in the proper perspective, it is highly unusual that any one research study in counseling is sufficient to stand alone; it is only the accumulation of the results from many studies that adds to our knowledge. For example, progress toward the conclusion that a link exists between smoking and health was made inch by inch (P. W. Holland, 1986). The conclusion that smoking is detrimental to health was established by years of research; alternative explanations in one study were ruled out in other studies. Interestingly, it is not unusual for the results of seminal studies to be contradicted by subsequent research. For example, Rosenthal and Jacobson's (1968) conclusion that teacher expectations influence student achievement has not always been supported by subsequent research (Brophy & Good, 1974).

Unsupported statements usually appear in the discussion and conclusions sections of a report. Refrain from stating that, based on the results of your study, practitioners should change their practice or that researchers should abandon some theoretical position. If you feel strongly about a position, state that "the results of this study as well as previous studies [cite those studies] suggest that Theory X should be reconsidered." Let the scientific community decide whether Theory X should be abandoned.

An issue related to overstatement concerns the appraisal of other authors' work. Generally, it is not advisable to be overly critical of others, especially at the beginning of one's career. Again, let the scientific community make judgments about the worth of various schools of thought or of a researcher's contributions. It is acceptable to point out differences of opinion, but do so tactfully. Wampold and Kim (1989) reanalyzed a case study presented by Hill, Carter, and O'Farrell (1983) and came to different conclusions from those reached in the original study. Instead of arguing that their conclusions were justified, Wampold and Kim provided several possible explanations for the differences and made the following conclusion: "Whether Hill et al.'s observations or the patterns revealed by the sequential analysis [conducted by Wampold & Kim] are reflective of the essential nature of the counseling process in this study remains an unanswered epistemological question" (p. 362). Readers are left to draw their own conclusions.

PRINCIPLE 4: BE LOGICAL AND ORGANIZED

The written report is not a recitation of facts; it is the presentation of a position. Authors must persuade the reader that their claims are justified. As we indicated previously, the research question should be justified given the literature reviewed, and the logic and organization of the introduction should make the case for the research question. Don't force the reader to guess how the research question followed logically from the studies reviewed; explain it!

A few general considerations can aid in organization and logic. First, work from an outline that not only lists various parts of the report, but also neatly summarizes the logical organization. Second, provide advance organizers and summaries of complex materials; that is, tell the reader what is to follow and how it is organized, and, if necessary, summarize at the end of explanations. If the material is lengthy, use headings. Transition statements are particularly helpful when the logic shifts gears. (For more details and examples, see Heppner and Heppner, 2004.)

Writing can be an aid to logic. What may seem perfectly logical in one's own mind may indeed be illogical when expressed in writing. Writing the method section of a report before the study is conducted often reveals faulty logic. Of course, this is the utility of research proposals.

PRINCIPLE 5: HAVE SOME STYLE

Although technical writing is constrained by various parameters, style remains important. Make the research report interesting. Would a reader mildly interested in this topic want to read the entire report? Often, style is the determining factor. Of course, style must be congruent with the publication in which the article will appear. Still, even the most technical writing should be made readable to the fullest extent possible.

Several considerations aid in preparing readable reports. Interest the reader at the outset by choosing good titles, quotations from important sources (ancient Greek sources seem to be the most prestigious!), and so forth. Avoid abbreviations; many readers tend to focus on one or two sections of the report, and if they have to flip around to understand abbreviations, they tend to quit reading entirely. Particularly annoying are idiosyncratic abbreviations of variables used in statistical analysis programs that make sense only to the author (for example, NCOCLIN—number of counselor/client interactions). Finally, simpler words and sentence structures are preferable to more complex ones. The corollary of this suggestion is that precision of expression is desirable.

PRINCIPLE 6: WRITE AND REWRITE

One thing is clear: Except for the extraordinary few, authors need to do some rewriting to prepare a quality research report. Different writers use different methods: Some write as fast as possible and rely heavily on the revision process to create a polished product; others write the first draft carefully and minimize time with revisions. Some like to let the original "age" before revising, while others progress as quickly as possible to the final product.

Often authors become so absorbed with their project that they lose objectivity. Having discussed and thought about a procedure, they are convinced that their explanation of it is clear and concise. However, someone else may have a very different view. We strongly recommend that all authors have a colleague or advisor read and critique research reports as part of the revision process. Unjustified compliments are not helpful, so choose someone who will be properly critical. (Similarly, if asked to review someone else's report, provide direct and helpful comments.) Different types of comments will be provided by different types of readers. Consider readers who are unfamiliar with the area as well as those who are knowledgeable. Someone who disagrees with the author's point of view can often identify problems with the logic. Remember that these critiques are not binding and an author may choose to ignore them. As a courtesy, authors should ask those who provide critiques whether they wish to be credited in the author footnote (for example, "I express my appreciation to Ima Kritiq for her helpful comments").

PRINCIPLE 7: IF ALL ELSE FAILS, JUST WRITE!

We would be remiss if we did not mention problems related to procrastination. Many of us who enjoy conducting research avoid settling down to write the research report. We venture to say that at one time or another, all researchers have agonized about writing the research report. Rather than stating that "misery loves company," we give this suggestion: Write! Even if you think what you are writing is terrible, write anyway. Drafts can be changed or discarded. In fact, it is usually much easier to revise a draft than to create a first draft. Write a few pages and then decide later whether it is any good. Once started, writing becomes increasingly easy. (For more information on affective issues and writing blocks, see Heppner & Heppner, 2004.)

SUMMARY AND CONCLUSIONS

The research report is critical to the research endeavor because it is the vehicle by which the results of studies are typically disseminated. The entire research process is summarized in the research report, from the statement of the problem to the discussion of the results. A coherently organized and well-written report increases the likelihood that the research study will influence the scientific community.

Although organization of the research report varies, most reports contain a title, an abstract, an introduction, a description of the method (participants, measures, materials, design, and procedure), a presentation of the results, and a discussion or conclusion. The content of these sections is determined, to a great extent, by the design of the research.

The style of the written report varies, for each of us has our own style, which we in turn alter depending on the publication outlet for which our writing is intended. Nevertheless, as a rule authors should (1) be informative, (2) be forthright, (3) not overstate or exaggerate, (4) be logical and organized, (5) write in an interesting way, and (6) revise their reports to obtain a polished product.

Professional writing is a complex skill that takes years of practice and feedback. Moreover, it is a skill that involves one's personal style of communicating. Procrastination and other avoidance patterns are common reactions of inexperienced and experienced authors alike. One of the most effective strategies to improve one's professional writing is to work closely with a successful author, writing drafts, receiving feedback, rewriting, and polishing. It is not atypical for graduate students to spend two to three years co-writing with a faculty member to enhance both their professional writing skills and their research skills in general. We strongly urge students to actively solicit feedback on their writing and seek co-writing experiences with established authors.

In closing, it is our sincere hope that students are able to utilize scholarly inquiry to promote an inquisitive and pioneering attitude. As Enos Mills, an explorer of Rocky Mountain National Park, observed, pioneers lives suffer from no dull existence, but rather "are rich with hope and their future has all the promise of spring" (Mills, 1924, p. 9). We wish you happy trails!

STIMULUS EXERCISE

WRITING AN INTRODUCTION TO AN ARTICLE

Learning to write a compelling introduction is difficult. We have found that the following exercise is helpful in learning this complex skill. This exercise is best done as a class, or with a small group of four to six students. It is best if you can have a faculty advisor or advanced student with expertise in scientific writing leading the exercise or helping the group work through it together. We will describe the exercise using a class format, but it can be adapted for a small group of students as long as one of the students is more advanced in their writing skills and can give appropriate feedback to group members. In addition, the exercise can be done with all seven steps or just a few of the steps.

1. First, the class critiques an introduction to an article the instructor selected from a recent journal.
2. Then, as an individual assignment, each student critiques the introduction to an article in their area of interest and receives feedback on their critique from the instructor.
3. The next assignment involves a published article that contains an introduction citing seven other articles (but no books or book chapters). The students are given the published article without the introduction and the seven articles cited.
4. The next assignment is to read the seven cited articles and the published article (without the introduction). At the next class meeting, the class discusses various structures that could be used to construct the introduction to the published article (that is, the logic of the introduction, how the paragraphs would follow each other, how the case would be built for the hypotheses, and so on). In this discussion, it is emphasized that there is no one correct way to write this introduction, but the class agrees on a common structure.

5. The next assignment is for each student to write, in APA style (that is, in accordance with the *Publication Manual of the American Psychological Association,* 2001), an in.troduction that leads logically to the hypothesis, using only the seven articles as supporting evidence (this assignment is completed in one week). The instructor grades the papers, providing feedback at every level (that is, grammar, sentence construction, paragraph construction, logic, proper citation, and so forth) within one week.

6. The final assignment is to revise the introduction given the instructor's feedback. This revision is again evaluated by the instructor.

7. At the end, the original introduction is critiqued in a class discussion.

ACA Code of Ethics

PREAMBLE

The American Counseling Association is an educational, scientific, and professional organization whose members work in a variety of settings and serve in multiple capacities. ACA members are dedicated to the enhancement of human development throughout the life span. Association members recognize diversity and embrace a cross-cultural approach in support of the worth, dignity, potential, and uniqueness of people within their social and cultural contexts.

Professional values are an important way of living out an ethical commitment. Values inform principles. Inherently held values that guide our behaviors or exceed prescribed behaviors are deeply ingrained in the counselor and developed out of personal dedication, rather than the mandatory requirement of an external organization.

ACA CODE OF ETHICS PURPOSE

The *ACA Code of Ethics* serves five main purposes:

1. The *Code* enables the association to clarify to current and future members, and to those served by members, the nature of the ethical responsibilities held in common by its members.
2. The *Code* helps support the mission of the association.

3. The *Code* establishes principles that define ethical behavior and best practices of association members.
4. The *Code* serves as an ethical guide designed to assist members in constructing a professional course of action that best serves those utilizing counseling services and best promotes the values of the counseling profession.
5. The *Code* serves as the basis for processing of ethical complaints and inquiries initiated against members of the association.

The *ACA Code of Ethics* contains eight main sections that address the following areas:

Section A: The Counseling Relationship
Section B: Confidentiality, Privileged Communication, and Privacy
Section C: Professional Responsibility
Section D: Relationships With Other Professionals
Section E: Evaluation, Assessment, and Interpretation
Section F: Supervision, Training, and Teaching
Section G: Research and Publication
Section H: Resolving Ethical Issues

Each section of the *ACA Code of Ethics* begins with an Introduction. The introductions to each section discuss what counselors should aspire to with regard to ethical behavior and responsibility. The Introduction helps set the tone for that particular section and provides a starting point that invites reflection on the ethical mandates contained in each part of the *ACA Code of Ethics*.

When counselors are faced with ethical dilemmas that are difficult to resolve, they are expected to engage in a carefully considered ethical decision-making process. Reasonable differences of opinion can and do exist among counselors with respect to the ways in which values, ethical principles, and ethical standards would be applied when they conflict. While there is no specific ethical decision-making model that is most effective, counselors are expected to be familiar with a credible model of decision making that can bear public scrutiny and its application.

Through a chosen ethical decision-making process and evaluation of the context of the situation, counselors are empowered to make decisions that help expand the capacity of people to grow and develop.

A brief glossary is given to provide readers with a concise description of some of the terms used in the *ACA Code of Ethics*.

SECTION A: THE COUNSELING RELATIONSHIP

INTRODUCTION

Counselors encourage client growth and development in ways that foster the interest and welfare of clients and promote formation of healthy relationships. Counselors actively attempt to understand the diverse cultural backgrounds of the clients they serve. Counselors also explore their own cultural identities and how these affect their values and beliefs about the counseling process.

Counselors are encouraged to contribute to society by devoting a portion of their professional activity to services for which there is little or no financial return (pro bono publico).

A.1. WELFARE OF THOSE SERVED BY COUNSELORS

A.1.a. PRIMARY RESPONSIBILITY   The primary responsibility of counselors is to respect the dignity and to promote the welfare of clients.

A.1.b. RECORDS   Counselors maintain records necessary for rendering professional services to their clients and as required by laws, regulations, or agency or institution procedures. Counselors include sufficient and timely documentation in their client records to facilitate the delivery and continuity of needed services. Counselors take reasonable steps to ensure that documentation in records accurately reflects client progress and services provided. If errors are made in client records, counselors take steps to properly note the correction of such errors according to agency or institutional policies. *(See A.12.g.7., B.6., B.6.g., G.2.j.)*

A.1.c. COUNSELING PLANS   Counselors and their clients work jointly in devising integrated counseling plans that offer reasonable promise of success and are consistent with abilities and circumstances of clients. Counselors and clients regularly review counseling plans to assess their continued viability and effectiveness, respecting the freedom of choice of clients. *(See A.2.a., A.2.d., A.12.g.)*

A.1.d. SUPPORT NETWORK INVOLVEMENT   Counselors recognize that support networks hold various meanings in the lives of clients and consider enlisting the support, understanding, and involvement of others (e.g., religious/spiritual/community leaders, family members, friends) as positive resources, when appropriate, with client consent.

A.1.e. EMPLOYMENT NEEDS   Counselors work with their clients considering employment in jobs that are consistent with the overall abilities, vocational limitations, physical restrictions, general temperament, interest and aptitude patterns, social skills, education, general qualifications, and other relevant characteristics and needs of clients. When appropriate, counselors appropriately trained in career development will assist in the placement of clients in positions that are consistent with the interest, culture, and the welfare of clients, employers, and/or the public.

A.2. INFORMED CONSENT IN THE COUNSELING RELATIONSHIP

(See A.12.g., B.5., B.6.b., E.3., E.13.b., F.1.c., G.2.a.)

A.2.a. INFORMED CONSENT   Clients have the freedom to choose whether to enter into or remain in a counseling relationship and need adequate information about the counseling process and the counselor. Counselors have an obligation to review in writing and verbally with clients the rights and responsibilities of both the counselor and the client. Informed consent is an ongoing part of the counseling process, and counselors appropriately document discussions of informed consent throughout the counseling relationship.

A.2.B. TYPES OF INFORMATION NEEDED   Counselors explicitly explain to clients the nature of all services provided. They inform clients about issues such as, but not limited to, the following: the purposes, goals, techniques, procedures, limitations, potential risks, and benefits of services; the counselor's qualifications, credentials, and relevant experience; continuation of services upon the incapacitation or death of a counselor; and other pertinent information. Counselors take steps to ensure that clients understand the implications of diagnosis, the intended use of tests and reports, fees, and billing arrangements. Clients have the right to confidentiality and to be provided with an explanation of its limitations (including how supervisors and/or treatment team professionals are involved); to obtain clear information about their records; to participate in the ongoing counseling plans; and to refuse any services or modality change and to be advised of the consequences of such refusal.

A.2.C. DEVELOPMENTAL AND CULTURAL SENSITIVITY   Counselors communicate information in ways that are both developmentally and culturally appropriate. Counselors use clear and understandable language when discussing issues related to informed consent. When clients have difficulty understanding the language used by counselors, they provide necessary services (e.g., arranging for a qualified interpreter or translator) to ensure comprehension by clients. In collaboration with clients, counselors consider cultural implications of informed consent procedures and, where possible, counselors adjust their practices accordingly.

A.2.D. INABILITY TO GIVE CONSENT   When counseling minors or persons unable to give voluntary consent, counselors seek the assent of clients to services, and include them in decision making as appropriate. Counselors recognize the need to balance the ethical rights of clients to make choices, their capacity to give consent or assent to receive services, and parental or familial legal rights and responsibilities to protect these clients and make decisions on their behalf.

A.3. CLIENTS SERVED BY OTHERS

When counselors learn that their clients are in a professional relationship with another mental health professional, they request release from clients to inform the other professionals and strive to establish positive and collaborative professional relationships.

A.4. AVOIDING HARM AND IMPOSING VALUES

A.4.A. AVOIDING HARM   Counselors act to avoid harming their clients, trainees, and research participants and to minimize or to remedy unavoidable or unanticipated harm.

A.4.B. Personal Values   Counselors are aware of their own values, attitudes, beliefs, and behaviors and avoid imposing values that are inconsistent with counseling goals. Counselors respect the diversity of clients, trainees, and research participants.

A.5. Roles and Relationships with Clients

(See F.3., F.10., G.3.)

A.5.A. Current Clients   Sexual or romantic counselor–client interactions or relationships with current clients, their romantic partners, or their family members are prohibited.

A.5.B. Former Clients   Sexual or romantic counselor–client interactions or relationships with former clients, their romantic partners, or their family members are prohibited for a period of 5 years following the last professional contact. Counselors, before engaging in sexual or romantic interactions or relationships with clients, their romantic partners, or client family members after 5 years following the last professional contact, demonstrate forethought and document (in written form) whether the interactions or relationship can be viewed as exploitive in some way and/or whether there is still potential to harm the former client; in cases of potential exploitation and/or harm, the counselor avoids entering such an interaction or relationship.

A.5.C. Nonprofessional Interactions or Relationships (Other Than Sexual or Romantic Interactions or Relationships)   Counselor–client nonprofessional relationships with clients, former clients, their romantic partners, or their family members should be avoided, except when the interaction is potentially beneficial to the client. *(See A.5.d.)*

A.5.D. Potentially Beneficial Interactions   When a counselor–client nonprofessional interaction with a client or former client may be potentially beneficial to the client or former client, the counselor must document in case records, prior to the interaction (when feasible), the rationale for such an interaction, the potential benefit, and anticipated consequences for the client or former client and other individuals significantly involved with the client or former client. Such interactions should be initiated with appropriate client consent. Where unintentional harm occurs to the client or former client, or to an individual significantly involved with the client or former client, due to the nonprofessional interaction, the counselor must show evidence of an attempt to remedy such harm. Examples of potentially beneficial interactions include, but are not limited to, attending a formal ceremony (e.g., a wedding/commitment ceremony or graduation); purchasing a service or product provided by a client or former client (excepting unrestricted bartering); hospital visits to an ill family member; mutual membership in a professional association, organization, or community. *(See A.5.c.)*

A.5.e. Role Changes in the Professional Relationship   When a counselor changes a role from the original or most recent contracted relationship, he or she obtains informed consent from the client and explains the right of the client to refuse services related to the change. Examples of role changes include

1. changing from individual to relationship or family counseling, or vice versa;
2. changing from a nonforensic evaluative role to a therapeutic role, or vice versa;
3. changing from a counselor to a researcher role (i.e., enlisting clients as research participants), or vice versa; and
4. changing from a counselor to a mediator role, or vice versa.

Clients must be fully informed of any anticipated consequences (e.g., financial, legal, personal, or therapeutic) of counselor role changes.

A.6. Roles and Relationships at Individual, Group, Institutional, and Societal Levels

A.6.a. Advocacy   When appropriate, counselors advocate at individual, group, institutional, and societal levels to examine potential barriers and obstacles that inhibit access and/or the growth and development of clients.

A.6.b. Confidentiality and Advocacy   Counselors obtain client consent prior to engaging in advocacy efforts on behalf of an identifiable client to improve the provision of services and to work toward removal of systemic barriers or obstacles that inhibit client access, growth, and development.

A.7. Multiple Clients

When a counselor agrees to provide counseling services to two or more persons who have a relationship, the counselor clarifies at the outset which person or persons are clients and the nature of the relationships the counselor will have with each involved person. If it becomes apparent that the counselor may be called upon to perform potentially conflicting roles, the counselor will clarify, adjust, or withdraw from roles appropriately. *(See A.8.a., B.4.)*

A.8. Group Work

(See B.4.a.)

A.8.a. Screening   Counselors screen prospective group counseling/therapy participants. To the extent possible, counselors select members whose needs and goals are compatible with goals of the group, who will not impede the group process, and whose well-being will not be jeopardized by the group experience.

A.8.b. Protecting Clients   In a group setting, counselors take reasonable precautions to protect clients from physical, emotional, or psychological trauma.

A.9. END-OF-LIFE CARE FOR TERMINALLY ILL CLIENTS

A.9.A. QUALITY OF CARE   Counselors strive to take measures that enable clients

1. to obtain high-quality end-of-life care for their physical, emotional, social, and spiritual needs;
2. to exercise the highest degree of self-determination possible;
3. to be given every opportunity possible to engage in informed decision making regarding their end-of-life care; and
4. to receive complete and adequate assessment regarding their ability to make competent, rational decisions on their own behalf from a mental health professional who is experienced in end-of-life care practice.

A.9.B. COUNSELOR COMPETENCE, CHOICE, AND REFERRAL   Recognizing the personal, moral, and competence issues related to end-of-life decisions, counselors may choose to work or not work with terminally ill clients who wish to explore their end-of-life options. Counselors provide appropriate referral information to ensure that clients receive the necessary help.

A.9.C. CONFIDENTIALITY   Counselors who provide services to terminally ill individuals who are considering hastening their own deaths have the option of breaking or not breaking confidentiality, depending on applicable laws and the specific circumstances of the situation and after seeking consultation or supervision from appropriate professional and legal parties. *(See B.5.c., B.7.c.)*

A.10. FEES AND BARTERING

A.10.A. ACCEPTING FEES FROM AGENCY CLIENTS   Counselors refuse a private fee or other remuneration for rendering services to persons who are entitled to such services through the counselor's employing agency or institution. The policies of a particular agency may make explicit provisions for agency clients to receive counseling services from members of its staff in private practice. In such instances, the clients must be informed of other options open to them should they seek private counseling services.

A.10.B. ESTABLISHING FEES   In establishing fees for professional counseling services, counselors consider the financial status of clients and locality. In the event that the established fee structure is inappropriate for a client, counselors assist clients in attempting to find comparable services of acceptable cost.

A.10.C. NONPAYMENT OF FEES   If counselors intend to use collection agencies or take legal measures to collect fees from clients who do not pay for services as agreed upon, they first inform clients of intended actions and offer clients the opportunity to make payment.

A.10.D. BARTERING   Counselors may barter only if the relationship is not exploitive or harmful and does not place the counselor in an unfair advantage, if the client requests it, and if such arrangements are an accepted practice among professionals in the community. Counselors consider the cultural implications of bartering and discuss relevant concerns with clients and document such agreements in a clear written contract.

A.10.e. RECEIVING GIFTS   Counselors understand the challenges of accepting gifts from clients and recognize that in some cultures, small gifts are a token of respect and showing gratitude. When determining whether or not to accept a gift from clients, counselors take into account the therapeutic relationship, the monetary value of the gift, a client's motivation for giving the gift, and the counselor's motivation for wanting or declining the gift.

A.11. TERMINATION AND REFERRAL

A.11.a. ABANDONMENT PROHIBITED   Counselors do not abandon or neglect clients in counseling. Counselors assist in making appropriate arrangements for the continuation of treatment, when necessary, during interruptions such as vacations, illness, and following termination.

A.11.b. INABILITY TO ASSIST CLIENTS   If counselors determine an inability to be of professional assistance to clients, they avoid entering or continuing counseling relationships. Counselors are knowledgeable about culturally and clinically appropriate referral resources and suggest these alternatives. If clients decline the suggested referrals, counselors should discontinue the relationship.

A.11.c. APPROPRIATE TERMINATION   Counselors terminate a counseling relationship when it becomes reasonably apparent that the client no longer needs assistance, is not likely to benefit, or is being harmed by continued counseling. Counselors may terminate counseling when in jeopardy of harm by the client, or another person with whom the client has a relationship, or when clients do not pay fees as agreed upon. Counselors provide pretermination counseling and recommend other service providers when necessary.

A.11.d. APPROPRIATE TRANSFER OF SERVICES   When counselors transfer or refer clients to other practitioners, they ensure that appropriate clinical and administrative processes are completed and open communication is maintained with both clients and practitioners.

A.12. TECHNOLOGY APPLICATIONS

A.12.a. BENEFITS AND LIMITATIONS   Counselors inform clients of the benefits and limitations of using information technology applications in the counseling process and in business/billing procedures. Such technologies include but are not limited to computer hardware and software, telephones, the World

Wide Web, the Internet, online assessment instruments, and other communication devices.

A.12.b. Technology-Assisted Services   When providing technology-assisted distance counseling services, counselors determine that clients are intellectually, emotionally, and physically capable of using the application and that the application is appropriate for the needs of clients.

A.12.c. Inappropriate Services   When technology-assisted distance counseling services are deemed inappropriate by the counselor or client, counselors consider delivering services face to face.

A.12.d. Access   Counselors provide reasonable access to computer applications when providing technology-assisted distance counseling services.

A.12.e. Laws and Statutes   Counselors ensure that the use of technology does not violate the laws of any local, state, national, or international entity and observe all relevant statutes.

A.12.f. Assistance   Counselors seek business, legal, and technical assistance when using technology applications, particularly when the use of such applications crosses state or national boundaries.

A.12.g. Technology and Informed Consent   As part of the process of establishing informed consent, counselors do the following:

1. Address issues related to the difficulty of maintaining the confidentiality of electronically transmitted communications.
2. Inform clients of all colleagues, supervisors, and employees, such as Informational Technology (IT) administrators, who might have authorized or unauthorized access to electronic transmissions.
3. Urge clients to be aware of all authorized or unauthorized users including family members and fellow employees who have access to any technology clients may use in the counseling process.
4. Inform clients of pertinent legal rights and limitations governing the practice of a profession over state lines or international boundaries.
5. Use encrypted Web sites and e-mail communications to help ensure confidentiality when possible.
6. When the use of encryption is not possible, counselors notify clients of this fact and limit electronic transmissions to general communications that are not client specific.
7. Inform clients if and for how long archival storage of transaction records are maintained.
8. Discuss the possibility of technology failure and alternate methods of service delivery.
9. Inform clients of emergency procedures, such as calling 911 or a local crisis hotline, when the counselor is not available.

10. Discuss time zone differences, local customs, and cultural or language differences that might impact service delivery.
11. Inform clients when technology-assisted distance counseling services are not covered by insurance. *(See A.2.)*

A.12.H. SITES ON THE WORLD WIDE WEB   Counselors maintaining sites on the World Wide Web (the Internet) do the following:

1. Regularly check that electronic links are working and professionally appropriate.
2. Establish ways clients can contact the counselor in case of technology failure.
3. Provide electronic links to relevant state licensure and professional certification boards to protect consumer rights and facilitate addressing ethical concerns.
4. Establish a method for verifying client identity.
5. Obtain the written consent of the legal guardian or other authorized legal representative prior to rendering services in the event the client is a minor child, an adult who is legally incompetent, or an adult incapable of giving informed consent.
6. Strive to provide a site that is accessible to persons with disabilities.
7. Strive to provide translation capabilities for clients who have a different primary language while also addressing the imperfect nature of such translations.
8. Assist clients in determining the validity and reliability of information found on the World Wide Web and other technology applications.

SECTION B: CONFIDENTIALITY, PRIVILEGED COMMUNICATION, AND PRIVACY

INTRODUCTION

Counselors recognize that trust is a cornerstone of the counseling relationship. Counselors aspire to earn the trust of clients by creating an ongoing partnership, establishing and upholding appropriate boundaries, and maintaining confidentiality. Counselors communicate the parameters of confidentiality in a culturally competent manner.

B.1. RESPECTING CLIENT RIGHTS

B.1.A. MULTICULTURAL/DIVERSITY CONSIDERATIONS   Counselors maintain awareness and sensitivity regarding cultural meanings of confidentiality and privacy. Counselors respect differing views toward disclosure of information. Counselors hold ongoing discussions with clients as to how, when, and with whom information is to be shared.

B.1.B. RESPECT FOR PRIVACY   Counselors respect client rights to privacy. Counselors solicit private information from clients only when it is beneficial to the counseling process.

B.1.c. Respect for Confidentiality Counselors do not share confidential information without client consent or without sound legal or ethical justification.

B.1.d. Explanation of Limitations At initiation and throughout the counseling process, counselors inform clients of the limitations of confidentiality and seek to identify foreseeable situations in which confidentiality must be breached. *(See A.2.b.)*

B.2. Exceptions

B.2.a. Danger and Legal Requirements The general requirement that counselors keep information confidential does not apply when disclosure is required to protect clients or identified others from serious and foreseeable harm or when legal requirements demand that confidential information must be revealed. Counselors consult with other professionals when in doubt as to the validity of an exception. Additional considerations apply when addressing end-of-life issues. *(See A.9.c.)*

B.2.b. Contagious, Life-Threatening Diseases When clients disclose that they have a disease commonly known to be both communicable and life threatening, counselors may be justified in disclosing information to identifiable third parties, if they are known to be at demonstrable and high risk of contracting the disease. Prior to making a disclosure, counselors confirm that there is such a diagnosis and assess the intent of clients to inform the third parties about their disease or to engage in any behaviors that may be harmful to an identifiable third party.

B.2.c. Court-Ordered Disclosure When subpoenaed to release confidential or privileged information without a client's permission, counselors obtain written, informed consent from the client or take steps to prohibit the disclosure or have it limited as narrowly as possible due to potential harm to the client or counseling relationship.

B.2.d. Minimal Disclosure To the extent possible, clients are informed before confidential information is disclosed and are involved in the disclosure decision-making process. When circumstances require the disclosure of confidential information, only essential information is revealed.

B.3. Information Shared with Others

B.3.a. Subordinates Counselors make every effort to ensure that privacy and confidentiality of clients are maintained by subordinates, including employees, supervisees, students, clerical assistants, and volunteers. *(See F.1.c.)*

B.3.b. Treatment Teams When client treatment involves a continued review or participation by a treatment team, the client will be informed of the team's existence and composition, information being shared, and the purposes of sharing such information.

B.3.c. CONFIDENTIAL SETTINGS   Counselors discuss confidential information only in settings in which they can reasonably ensure client privacy.

B.3.d. THIRD-PARTY PAYERS   Counselors disclose information to third-party payers only when clients have authorized such disclosure.

B.3.e. TRANSMITTING CONFIDENTIAL INFORMATION   Counselors take precautions to ensure the confidentiality of information transmitted through the use of computers, electronic mail, facsimile machines, telephones, voicemail, answering machines, and other electronic or computer technology. *(See A.12.g.)*

B.3.f. DECEASED CLIENTS   Counselors protect the confidentiality of deceased clients, consistent with legal requirements and agency or setting policies.

B.4. GROUPS AND FAMILIES

B.4.a. GROUP WORK   In group work, counselors clearly explain the importance and parameters of confidentiality for the specific group being entered.

B.4.b. COUPLES AND FAMILY COUNSELING   In couples and family counseling, counselors clearly define who is considered "the client" and discuss expectations and limitations of confidentiality. Counselors seek agreement and document in writing such agreement among all involved parties having capacity to give consent concerning each individual's right to confidentiality and any obligation to preserve the confidentiality of information known.

B.5. CLIENTS LACKING CAPACITY TO GIVE INFORMED CONSENT

B.5.a. RESPONSIBILITY TO CLIENTS   When counseling minor clients or adult clients who lack the capacity to give voluntary, informed consent, counselors protect the confidentiality of information received in the counseling relationship as specified by federal and state laws, written policies, and applicable ethical standards.

B.5.b. RESPONSIBILITY TO PARENTS AND LEGAL GUARDIANS   Counselors inform parents and legal guardians about the role of counselors and the confidential nature of the counseling relationship. Counselors are sensitive to the cultural diversity of families and respect the inherent rights and responsibilities of parents/guardians over the welfare of their children/charges according to law. Counselors work to establish, as appropriate, collaborative relationships with parents/guardians to best serve clients.

B.5.c. RELEASE OF CONFIDENTIAL INFORMATION   When counseling minor clients or adult clients who lack the capacity to give voluntary consent to release confidential information, counselors seek permission from an appropriate third party to disclose information. In such instances, counselors inform clients consistent with their level of understanding and take culturally appropriate measures to safeguard client confidentiality.

B.6. RECORDS

B.6.A. CONFIDENTIALITY OF RECORDS   Counselors ensure that records are kept in a secure location and that only authorized persons have access to records.

B.6.B. PERMISSION TO RECORD   Counselors obtain permission from clients prior to recording sessions through electronic or other means.

B.6.C. PERMISSION TO OBSERVE   Counselors obtain permission from clients prior to observing counseling sessions, reviewing session transcripts, or viewing recordings of sessions with supervisors, faculty, peers, or others within the training environment.

B.6.D. CLIENT ACCESS   Counselors provide reasonable access to records and copies of records when requested by competent clients. Counselors limit the access of clients to their records, or portions of their records, only when there is compelling evidence that such access would cause harm to the client. Counselors document the request of clients and the rationale for withholding some or all of the record in the files of clients. In situations involving multiple clients, counselors provide individual clients with only those parts of records that related directly to them and do not include confidential information related to any other client.

B.6.E. ASSISTANCE WITH RECORDS   When clients request access to their records, counselors provide assistance and consultation in interpreting counseling records.

B.6.F. DISCLOSURE OR TRANSFER   Unless exceptions to confidentiality exist, counselors obtain written permission from clients to disclose or transfer records to legitimate third parties. Steps are taken to ensure that receivers of counseling records are sensitive to their confidential nature. *(See A.3., E.4.)*

B.6.G. STORAGE AND DISPOSAL AFTER TERMINATION   Counselors store records following termination of services to ensure reasonable future access, maintain records in accordance with state and federal statutes governing records, and dispose of client records and other sensitive materials in a manner that protects client confidentiality. When records are of an artistic nature, counselors obtain client (or guardian) consent with regard to handling of such records or documents. *(See A.1.b.)*

B.6.H. REASONABLE PRECAUTIONS   Counselors take reasonable precautions to protect client confidentiality in the event of the counselor's termination of practice, incapacity, or death. *(See C.2.h.)*

B.7. RESEARCH AND TRAINING

B.7.A. INSTITUTIONAL APPROVAL   When institutional approval is required, counselors provide accurate information about their research proposals and obtain approval prior to conducting their research. They conduct research in accordance with the approved research protocol.

B.7.B. ADHERENCE TO GUIDELINES   Counselors are responsible for understanding and adhering to state, federal, agency, or institutional policies or applicable guidelines regarding confidentiality in their research practices.

B.7.C. CONFIDENTIALITY OF INFORMATION OBTAINED IN RESEARCH   Violations of participant privacy and confidentiality are risks of participation in research involving human participants. Investigators maintain all research records in a secure manner. They explain to participants the risks of violations of privacy and confidentiality and disclose to participants any limits of confidentiality that reasonably can be expected. Regardless of the degree to which confidentiality will be maintained, investigators must disclose to participants any limits of confidentiality that reasonably can be expected. *(See G.2.e.)*

B.7.D. DISCLOSURE OF RESEARCH INFORMATION   Counselors do not disclose confidential information that reasonably could lead to the identification of a research participant unless they have obtained the prior consent of the person. Use of data derived from counseling relationships for purposes of training, research, or publication is confined to content that is disguised to ensure the anonymity of the individuals involved. *(See G.2.a., G.2.d.)*

B.7.E. AGREEMENT FOR IDENTIFICATION   Identification of clients, students, or supervisees in a presentation or publication is permissible only when they have reviewed the material and agreed to its presentation or publication. *(See G.4.d.)*

B.8. CONSULTATION

B.8.A. AGREEMENTS   When acting as consultants, counselors seek agreements among all parties involved concerning each individual's rights to confidentiality, the obligation of each individual to preserve confidential information, and the limits of confidentiality of information shared by others.

B.8.B. RESPECT FOR PRIVACY   Information obtained in a consulting relationship is discussed for professional purposes only with persons directly involved with the case. Written and oral reports present only data germane to the purposes of the consultation, and every effort is made to protect client identity and to avoid undue invasion of privacy.

B.8.C. DISCLOSURE OF CONFIDENTIAL INFORMATION   When consulting with colleagues, counselors do not disclose confidential information that reasonably could lead to the identification of a client or other person or organization with whom they have a confidential relationship unless they have obtained the prior consent of the person or organization or the disclosure cannot be avoided. They disclose information only to the extent necessary to achieve the purposes of the consultation. *(See D.2.d.)*

SECTION C: PROFESSIONAL RESPONSIBILITY

INTRODUCTION

Counselors aspire to open, honest, and accurate communication in dealing with the public and other professionals. They practice in a nondiscriminatory manner within the boundaries of professional and personal competence and have a responsibility to abide by the *ACA Code of Ethics*. Counselors actively participate in local, state, and national associations that foster the development and improvement of counseling. Counselors advocate to promote change at the individual, group, institutional, and societal levels that improves the quality of life for individuals and groups and remove potential barriers to the provision or access of appropriate services being offered. Counselors have a responsibility to the public to engage in counseling practices that are based on rigorous research methodologies. In addition, counselors engage in self-care activities to maintain and promote their emotional, physical, mental, and spiritual well-being to best meet their professional responsibilities.

C.1. KNOWLEDGE OF STANDARDS

Counselors have a responsibility to read, understand, and follow the *ACA Code of Ethics* and adhere to applicable laws and regulations.

C.2. PROFESSIONAL COMPETENCE

C.2.A. BOUNDARIES OF COMPETENCE Counselors practice only within the boundaries of their competence, based on their education, training, supervised experience, state and national professional credentials, and appropriate professional experience. Counselors gain knowledge, personal awareness, sensitivity, and skills pertinent to working with a diverse client population. *(See A.9.b., C.4.e., E.2., F.2., F.11.b.)*

C.2.B. NEW SPECIALTY AREAS OF PRACTICE Counselors practice in specialty areas new to them only after appropriate education, training, and supervised experience. While developing skills in new specialty areas, counselors take steps to ensure the competence of their work and to protect others from possible harm. *(See F.6.f.)*

C.2.C. QUALIFIED FOR EMPLOYMENT Counselors accept employment only for positions for which they are qualified by education, training, supervised experience, state and national professional credentials, and appropriate professional experience. Counselors hire for professional counseling positions only individuals who are qualified and competent for those positions.

C.2.D. Monitor Effectiveness   Counselors continually monitor their effectiveness as professionals and take steps to improve when necessary. Counselors in private practice take reasonable steps to seek peer supervision as needed to evaluate their efficacy as counselors.

C.2.E. Consultation on Ethical Obligations   Counselors take reasonable steps to consult with other counselors or related professionals when they have questions regarding their ethical obligations or professional practice.

C.2.F. Continuing Education   Counselors recognize the need for continuing education to acquire and maintain a reasonable level of awareness of current scientific and professional information in their fields of activity. They take steps to maintain competence in the skills they use, are open to new procedures, and keep current with the diverse populations and specific populations with whom they work.

C.2.G. Impairment   Counselors are alert to the signs of impairment from their own physical, mental, or emotional problems and refrain from offering or providing professional services when such impairment is likely to harm a client or others. They seek assistance for problems that reach the level of professional impairment, and, if necessary, they limit, suspend, or terminate their professional responsibilities until such time it is determined that they may safely resume their work. Counselors assist colleagues or supervisors in recognizing their own professional impairment and provide consultation and assistance when warranted with colleagues or supervisors showing signs of impairment and intervene as appropriate to prevent imminent harm to clients. *(See A.11.b., F.8.b.)*

C.2.H. Counselor Incapacitation or Termination of Practice   When counselors leave a practice, they follow a prepared plan for transfer of clients and files. Counselors prepare and disseminate to an identified colleague or "records custodian" a plan for the transfer of clients and files in the case of their incapacitation, death, or termination of practice.

C.3. Advertising and Soliciting Clients

C.3.A. Accurate Advertising   When advertising or otherwise representing their services to the public, counselors identify their credentials in an accurate manner that is not false, misleading, deceptive, or fraudulent.

C.3.B. Testimonials   Counselors who use testimonials do not solicit them from current clients nor former clients nor any other persons who may be vulnerable to undue influence.

C.3.C. STATEMENTS BY OTHERS   Counselors make reasonable efforts to ensure that statements made by others about them or the profession of counseling are accurate.

C.3.D. RECRUITING THROUGH EMPLOYMENT   Counselors do not use their places of employment or institutional affiliation to recruit or gain clients, supervisees, or consultees for their private practices.

C.3.E. PRODUCTS AND TRAINING ADVERTISEMENTS   Counselors who develop products related to their profession or conduct workshops or training events ensure that the advertisements concerning these products or events are accurate and disclose adequate information for consumers to make informed choices. *(See C.6.d.)*

C.3.F. PROMOTING TO THOSE SERVED   Counselors do not use counseling, teaching, training, or supervisory relationships to promote their products or training events in a manner that is deceptive or would exert undue influence on individuals who may be vulnerable. However, counselor educators may adopt textbooks they have authored for instructional purposes.

C.4. PROFESSIONAL QUALIFICATIONS

C.4.A. ACCURATE REPRESENTATION   Counselors claim or imply only professional qualifications actually completed and correct any known misrepresentations of their qualifications by others. Counselors truthfully represent the qualifications of their professional colleagues. Counselors clearly distinguish between paid and volunteer work experience and accurately describe their continuing education and specialized training. *(See C.2.a.)*

C.4.B. CREDENTIALS   Counselors claim only licenses or certifications that are current and in good standing.

C.4.C. EDUCATIONAL DEGREES   Counselors clearly differentiate between earned and honorary degrees.

C.4.D. IMPLYING DOCTORAL-LEVEL COMPETENCE   Counselors clearly state their highest earned degree in counseling or closely related field. Counselors do not imply doctoral-level competence when only possessing a master's degree in counseling or a related field by referring to themselves as "Dr." in a counseling context when their doctorate is not in counseling or a related field.

C.4.E. PROGRAM ACCREDITATION STATUS   Counselors clearly state the accreditation status of their degree programs at the time the degree was earned.

C.4.F. PROFESSIONAL MEMBERSHIP   Counselors clearly differentiate between current, active memberships and former memberships in associations. Members of the

American Counseling Association must clearly differentiate between professional membership, which implies the possession of at least a master's degree in counseling, and regular membership, which is open to individuals whose interests and activities are consistent with those of ACA but are not qualified for professional membership.

C.5. NONDISCRIMINATION

Counselors do not condone or engage in discrimination based on age, culture, disability, ethnicity, race, religion/spirituality, gender, gender identity, sexual orientation, marital status/ partnership, language preference, socioeconomic status, or any basis proscribed by law. Counselors do not discriminate against clients, students, employees, supervisees, or research participants in a manner that has a negative impact on these persons.

C.6. PUBLIC RESPONSIBILITY

C.6.A. SEXUAL HARASSMENT   Counselors do not engage in or condone sexual harassment. Sexual harassment is defined as sexual solicitation, physical advances, or verbal or nonverbal conduct that is sexual in nature, that occurs in connection with professional activities or roles, and that either

1. is unwelcome, is offensive, or creates a hostile workplace or learning environment, and counselors know or are told this; or
2. is sufficiently severe or intense to be perceived as harassment to a reasonable person in the context in which the behavior occurred.

Sexual harassment can consist of a single intense or severe act or multiple persistent or pervasive acts.

C.6.B. REPORTS TO THIRD PARTIES   Counselors are accurate, honest, and objective in reporting their professional activities and judgments to appropriate third parties, including courts, health insurance companies, those who are the recipients of evaluation reports, and others. *(See B.3., E.4.)*

C.6.C. MEDIA PRESENTATIONS   When counselors provide advice or comment by means of public lectures, demonstrations, radio or television programs, prerecorded tapes, technology-based applications, printed articles, mailed material, or other media, they take reasonable precautions to ensure that

1. the statements are based on appropriate professional counseling literature and practice,
2. the statements are otherwise consistent with the *ACA Code of Ethics,* and
3. the recipients of the information are not encouraged to infer that a professional counseling relationship has been established.

C.6.D. EXPLOITATION OF OTHERS   Counselors do not exploit others in their professional relationships. *(See C.3.e.)*

C.6.E. SCIENTIFIC BASES FOR TREATMENT MODALITIES Counselors use techniques/procedures/modalities that are grounded in theory and/or have an empirical or scientific foundation. Counselors who do not must define the techniques/procedures as "unproven" or "developing" and explain the potential risks and ethical considerations of using such techniques/procedures and take steps to protect clients from possible harm. *(See A.4.a., E.5.c., E.5.d.)*

C.7. RESPONSIBILITY TO OTHER PROFESSIONALS

C.7.A. PERSONAL PUBLIC STATEMENTS When making personal statements in a public context, counselors clarify that they are speaking from their personal perspectives and that they are not speaking on behalf of all counselors or the profession.

SECTION D: RELATIONSHIPS WITH OTHER PROFESSIONALS

INTRODUCTION

Professional counselors recognize that the quality of their interactions with colleagues can influence the quality of services provided to clients. They work to become knowledgeable about colleagues within and outside the field of counseling. Counselors develop positive working relationships and systems of communication with colleagues to enhance services to clients.

D.1. RELATIONSHIPS WITH COLLEAGUES, EMPLOYERS, AND EMPLOYEES

D.1.A. DIFFERENT APPROACHES Counselors are respectful of approaches to counseling services that differ from their own. Counselors are respectful of traditions and practices of other professional groups with which they work.

D.1.B. FORMING RELATIONSHIPS Counselors work to develop and strengthen interdisciplinary relations with colleagues from other disciplines to best serve clients.

D.1.C. INTERDISCIPLINARY TEAMWORK Counselors who are members of interdisciplinary teams delivering multifaceted services to clients keep the focus on how to best serve the clients. They participate in and contribute to decisions that affect the well-being of clients by drawing on the perspectives, values, and experiences of the counseling profession and those of colleagues from other disciplines. *(See A.1.a.)*

D.1.D. CONFIDENTIALITY When counselors are required by law, institutional policy, or extraordinary circumstances to serve in more than one role in judicial or administrative proceedings, they clarify role expectations and the parameters of confidentiality with their colleagues. *(See B.1.c., B.1.d., B.2.c., B.2.d., B.3.b.)*

D.1.e. ESTABLISHING PROFESSIONAL AND ETHICAL OBLIGATIONS   Counselors who are members of interdisciplinary teams clarify professional and ethical obligations of the team as a whole and of its individual members. When a team decision raises ethical concerns, counselors first attempt to resolve the concern within the team. If they cannot reach resolution among team members, counselors pursue other avenues to address their concerns consistent with client well-being.

D.1.f. PERSONNEL SELECTION AND ASSIGNMENT   Counselors select competent staff and assign responsibilities compatible with their skills and experiences.

D.1.g. EMPLOYER POLICIES   The acceptance of employment in an agency or institution implies that counselors are in agreement with its general policies and principles. Counselors strive to reach agreement with employers as to acceptable standards of conduct that allow for changes in institutional policy conducive to the growth and development of clients.

D.1.h. NEGATIVE CONDITIONS   Counselors alert their employers of inappropriate policies and practices. They attempt to effect changes in such policies or procedures through constructive action within the organization. When such policies are potentially disruptive or damaging to clients or may limit the effectiveness of services provided and change cannot be effected, counselors take appropriate further action. Such action may include referral to appropriate certification, accreditation, or state licensure organizations, or voluntary termination of employment.

D.1.i. PROTECTION FROM PUNITIVE ACTION   Counselors take care not to harass or dismiss an employee who has acted in a responsible and ethical manner to expose inappropriate employer policies or practices.

D.2. CONSULTATION

D.2.a. CONSULTANT COMPETENCY   Counselors take reasonable steps to ensure that they have the appropriate resources and competencies when providing consultation services. Counselors provide appropriate referral resources when requested or needed. *(See C.2.a.)*

D.2.b. UNDERSTANDING CONSULTEES   When providing consultation, counselors attempt to develop with their consultees a clear understanding of problem definition, goals for change, and predicted consequences of interventions selected.

D.2.c. CONSULTANT GOALS   The consulting relationship is one in which consultee adaptability and growth toward self-direction are consistently encouraged and cultivated.

D.2.d. Informed Consent in Consultation   When providing consultation, counselors have an obligation to review, in writing and verbally, the rights and responsibilities of both counselors and consultees. Counselors use clear and understandable language to inform all parties involved about the purpose of the services to be provided, relevant costs, potential risks and benefits, and the limits of confidentiality. Working in conjunction with the consultee, counselors attempt to develop a clear definition of the problem, goals for change, and predicted consequences of interventions that are culturally responsive and appropriate to the needs of consultees. *(See A.2.a., A.2.b.)*

SECTION E: EVALUATION, ASSESSMENT, AND INTERPRETATION

Introduction

Counselors use assessment instruments as one component of the counseling process, taking into account the client personal and cultural context. Counselors promote the well-being of individual clients or groups of clients by developing and using appropriate educational, psychological, and career assessment instruments.

E.1. General

E.1.a. Assessment   The primary purpose of educational, psychological, and career assessment is to provide measurements that are valid and reliable in either comparative or absolute terms. These include, but are not limited to, measurements of ability, personality, interest, intelligence, achievement, and performance. Counselors recognize the need to interpret the statements in this section as applying to both quantitative and qualitative assessments.

E.1.b. Client Welfare   Counselors do not misuse assessment results and interpretations, and they take reasonable steps to prevent others from misusing the information these techniques provide. They respect the client's right to know the results, the interpretations made, and the bases for counselors' conclusions and recommendations.

E.2. Competence to Use and Interpret Assessment Instruments

E.2.a. Limits of Competence   Counselors utilize only those testing and assessment services for which they have been trained and are competent. Counselors using technology-assisted test interpretations are trained in the construct being measured and the specific instrument being used prior to using its technology-based application. Counselors take reasonable measures to ensure the proper use of psychological and career assessment techniques by persons under their supervision. *(See A.12.)*

E.2.b. Appropriate Use   Counselors are responsible for the appropriate application, scoring, interpretation, and use of assessment instruments relevant to the needs of the client, whether they score and interpret such assessments themselves or use technology or other services.

E.2.c. Decisions Based on Results   Counselors responsible for decisions involving individuals or policies that are based on assessment results have a thorough understanding of educational, psychological, and career measurement, including validation criteria, assessment research, and guidelines for assessment development and use.

E.3. Informed Consent in Assessment

E.3.a. Explanation to Clients   Prior to assessment, counselors explain the nature and purposes of assessment and the specific use of results by potential recipients. The explanation will be given in the language of the client (or other legally authorized person on behalf of the client), unless an explicit exception has been agreed upon in advance. Counselors consider the client's personal or cultural context, the level of the client's understanding of the results, and the impact of the results on the client. *(See A.2., A.12.g., F.1.c.)*

E.3.b. Recipients of Results   Counselors consider the examinee's welfare, explicit understandings, and prior agreements in determining who receives the assessment results. Counselors include accurate and appropriate interpretations with any release of individual or group assessment results. *(See B.2.c., B.5.)*

E.4. Release of Data to Qualified Professionals

Counselors release assessment data in which the client is identified only with the consent of the client or the client's legal representative. Such data are released only to persons recognized by counselors as qualified to interpret the data. *(See B.1., B.3., B.6.b.)*

E.5. Diagnosis of Mental Disorders

E.5.a. Proper Diagnosis   Counselors take special care to provide proper diagnosis of mental disorders. Assessment techniques (including personal interview) used to determine client care (e.g., locus of treatment, type of treatment, or recommended follow-up) are carefully selected and appropriately used.

E.5.b. Cultural Sensitivity   Counselors recognize that culture affects the manner in which clients' problems are defined. Clients' socioeconomic and cultural experiences are considered when diagnosing mental disorders. *(See A.2.c.)*

E.5.c. Historical and Social Prejudices in the Diagnosis of Pathology
Counselors recognize historical and social prejudices in the misdiagnosis and pathologizing of certain individuals and groups and the role of mental health professionals in perpetuating these prejudices through diagnosis and treatment.

E.5.d. Refraining from Diagnosis   Counselors may refrain from making and/or reporting a diagnosis if they believe it would cause harm to the client or others.

E.6. Instrument Selection

E.6.a. Appropriateness of Instruments   Counselors carefully consider the validity, reliability, psychometric limitations, and appropriateness of instruments when selecting assessments.

E.6.b. Referral Information   If a client is referred to a third party for assessment, the counselor provides specific referral questions and sufficient objective data about the client to ensure that appropriate assessment instruments are utilized. *(See A.9.b., B.3.)*

E.6.c. Culturally Diverse Populations   Counselors are cautious when selecting assessments for culturally diverse populations to avoid the use of instruments that lack appropriate psychometric properties for the client population. *(See A.2.c., E.5.b.)*

E.7. Conditions of Assessment Administration

(See A.12.b., A.12.d.)

E.7.a. Administration Conditions   Counselors administer assessments under the same conditions that were established in their standardization. When assessments are not administered under standard conditions, as may be necessary to accommodate clients with disabilities, or when unusual behavior or irregularities occur during the administration, those conditions are noted in interpretation, and the results may be designated as invalid or of questionable validity.

E.7.b. Technological Administration   Counselors ensure that administration programs function properly and provide clients with accurate results when technological or other electronic methods are used for assessment administration.

E.7.c. Unsupervised Assessments   Unless the assessment instrument is designed, intended, and validated for self-administration and/or scoring, counselors do not permit inadequately supervised use.

E.7.d. Disclosure of Favorable Conditions   Prior to administration of assessments, conditions that produce most favorable assessment results are made known to the examinee.

E.8. MULTICULTURAL ISSUES/DIVERSITY IN ASSESSMENT

Counselors use with caution assessment techniques that were normed on populations other than that of the client. Counselors recognize the effects of age, color, culture, disability, ethnic group, gender, race, language preference, religion, spirituality, sexual orientation, and socioeconomic status on test administration and interpretation, and place test results in proper perspective with other relevant factors. *(See A.2.c., E.5.b.)*

E.9. SCORING AND INTERPRETATION OF ASSESSMENTS

E.9.A. REPORTING   In reporting assessment results, counselors indicate reservations that exist regarding validity or reliability due to circumstances of the assessment or the inappropriateness of the norms for the person tested.

E.9.B. RESEARCH INSTRUMENTS   Counselors exercise caution when interpreting the results of research instruments not having sufficient technical data to support respondent results. The specific purposes for the use of such instruments are stated explicitly to the examinee.

E.9.C. ASSESSMENT SERVICES   Counselors who provide assessment scoring and interpretation services to support the assessment process confirm the validity of such interpretations. They accurately describe the purpose, norms, validity, reliability, and applications of the procedures and any special qualifications applicable to their use. The public offering of an automated test interpretations service is considered a professional-to-professional consultation. The formal responsibility of the consultant is to the consultee, but the ultimate and overriding responsibility is to the client. *(See D.2.)*

E.10. ASSESSMENT SECURITY

Counselors maintain the integrity and security of tests and other assessment techniques consistent with legal and contractual obligations. Counselors do not appropriate, reproduce, or modify published assessments or parts thereof without acknowledgment and permission from the publisher.

E.11. OBSOLETE ASSESSMENTS AND OUTDATED RESULTS

Counselors do not use data or results from assessments that are obsolete or outdated for the current purpose. Counselors make every effort to prevent the misuse of obsolete measures and assessment data by others.

E.12. Assessment Construction

Counselors use established scientific procedures, relevant standards, and current professional knowledge for assessment design in the development, publication, and utilization of educational and psychological assessment techniques.

E.13. Forensic Evaluation: Evaluation for Legal Proceedings

E.13.a. Primary Obligations When providing forensic evaluations, the primary obligation of counselors is to produce objective findings that can be substantiated based on information and techniques appropriate to the evaluation, which may include examination of the individual and/or review of records. Counselors are entitled to form professional opinions based on their professional knowledge and expertise that can be supported by the data gathered in evaluations. Counselors will define the limits of their reports or testimony, especially when an examination of the individual has not been conducted.

E.13.b. Consent for Evaluation Individuals being evaluated are informed in writing that the relationship is for the purposes of an evaluation and is not counseling in nature, and entities or individuals who will receive the evaluation report are identified. Written consent to be evaluated is obtained from those being evaluated unless a court orders evaluations to be conducted without the written consent of individuals being evaluated. When children or vulnerable adults are being evaluated, informed written consent is obtained from a parent or guardian.

E.13.c. Client Evaluation Prohibited Counselors do not evaluate individuals for forensic purposes they currently counsel or individuals they have counseled in the past. Counselors do not accept as counseling clients individuals they are evaluating or individuals they have evaluated in the past for forensic purposes.

E.13.d. Avoid Potentially Harmful Relationships Counselors who provide forensic evaluations avoid potentially harmful professional or personal relationships with family members, romantic partners, and close friends of individuals they are evaluating or have evaluated in the past.

SECTION F: SUPERVISION, TRAINING, AND TEACHING

Introduction

Counselors aspire to foster meaningful and respectful professional relationships and to maintain appropriate boundaries with supervisees and students.

Counselors have theoretical and pedagogical foundations for their work and aim to be fair, accurate, and honest in their assessments of counselors-in-training.

F.1. Counselor Supervision and Client Welfare

F.1.a. Client Welfare   A primary obligation of counseling supervisors is to monitor the services provided by other counselors or counselors-in-training. Counseling supervisors monitor client welfare and supervisee clinical performance and professional development. To fulfill these obligations, supervisors meet regularly with supervisees to review case notes, samples of clinical work, or live observations. Supervisees have a responsibility to understand and follow the *ACA Code of Ethics*.

F.1.b. Counselor Credentials   Counseling supervisors work to ensure that clients are aware of the qualifications of the supervisees who render services to the clients. *(See A.2.b.)*

F.1.c. Informed Consent and Client Rights   Supervisors make supervisees aware of client rights including the protection of client privacy and confidentiality in the counseling relationship. Supervisees provide clients with professional disclosure information and inform them of how the supervision process influences the limits of confidentiality. Supervisees make clients aware of who will have access to records of the counseling relationship and how these records will be used. *(See A.2.b., B.1.d.)*

F.2. Counselor Supervision Competence

F.2.a. Supervisor Preparation   Prior to offering clinical supervision services, counselors are trained in supervision methods and techniques. Counselors who offer clinical supervision services regularly pursue continuing education activities including both counseling and supervision topics and skills. *(See C.2.a., C.2.f.)*

F.2.b. Multicultural Issues/Diversity in Supervision   Counseling supervisors are aware of and address the role of multiculturalism/diversity in the supervisory relationship.

F.3. Supervisory Relationships

F.3.a. Relationship Boundaries With Supervisees   Counseling supervisors clearly define and maintain ethical professional, personal, and social relationships with their supervisees. Counseling supervisors avoid nonprofessional relationships with current supervisees. If supervisors must assume other professional roles (e.g., clinical and administrative supervisor, instructor) with supervisees, they work to minimize potential conflicts and explain to supervisees the expectations and responsibilities associated with each role. They do not engage in any form of nonprofessional interaction that may compromise the supervisory relationship.

F.3.B. SEXUAL RELATIONSHIPS   Sexual or romantic interactions or relationships with current supervisees are prohibited.

F.3.C. SEXUAL HARASSMENT   Counseling supervisors do not condone or subject supervisees to sexual harassment. *(See C.6.a.)*

F.3.D. CLOSE RELATIVES AND FRIENDS   Counseling supervisors avoid accepting close relatives, romantic partners, or friends as supervisees.

F.3.E. POTENTIALLY BENEFICIAL RELATIONSHIPS   Counseling supervisors are aware of the power differential in their relationships with supervisees. If they believe nonprofessional relationships with a supervisee may be potentially beneficial to the supervisee, they take precautions similar to those taken by counselors when working with clients. Examples of potentially beneficial interactions or relationships include attending a formal ceremony; hospital visits; providing support during a stressful event; or mutual membership in a professional association, organization, or community. Counseling supervisors engage in open discussions with supervisees when they consider entering into relationships with them outside of their roles as clinical and/or administrative supervisors. Before engaging in nonprofessional relationships, supervisors discuss with supervisees and document the rationale for such interactions, potential benefits or drawbacks, and anticipated consequences for the supervisee. Supervisors clarify the specific nature and limitations of the additional role(s) they will have with the supervisee.

F.4. SUPERVISOR RESPONSIBILITIES

F.4.A. INFORMED CONSENT FOR SUPERVISION   Supervisors are responsible for incorporating into their supervision the principles of informed consent and participation. Supervisors inform supervisees of the policies and procedures to which they are to adhere and the mechanisms for due process appeal of individual supervisory actions.

F.4.B. EMERGENCIES AND ABSENCES   Supervisors establish and communicate to supervisees procedures for contacting them or, in their absence, alternative on-call supervisors to assist in handling crises.

F.4.C. STANDARDS FOR SUPERVISEES   Supervisors make their supervisees aware of professional and ethical standards and legal responsibilities. Supervisors of postdegree counselors encourage these counselors to adhere to professional standards of practice. *(See C.1.)*

F.4.D. TERMINATION OF THE SUPERVISORY RELATIONSHIP   Supervisors or supervisees have the right to terminate the supervisory relationship with adequate notice. Reasons for withdrawal are provided to the other party. When cultural, clinical, or professional issues are crucial to the viability of the supervisory relationship, both parties make efforts to resolve differences. When termination is warranted, supervisors make appropriate referrals to possible alternative supervisors.

F.5. COUNSELING SUPERVISION EVALUATION, REMEDIATION, AND ENDORSEMENT

F.5.a. EVALUATION   Supervisors document and provide supervisees with ongoing performance appraisal and evaluation feedback and schedule periodic formal evaluative sessions throughout the supervisory relationship.

F.5.b. LIMITATIONS   Through ongoing evaluation and appraisal, supervisors are aware of the limitations of supervisees that might impede performance. Supervisors assist supervisees in securing remedial assistance when needed. They recommend dismissal from training programs, applied counseling settings, or state or voluntary professional credentialing processes when those supervisees are unable to provide competent professional services. Supervisors seek consultation and document their decisions to dismiss or refer supervisees for assistance. They ensure that supervisees are aware of options available to them to address such decisions. *(See C.2.g.)*

F.5.c. COUNSELING FOR SUPERVISEES   If supervisees request counseling, supervisors provide them with acceptable referrals. Counselors do not provide counseling services to supervisees. Supervisors address interpersonal competencies in terms of the impact of these issues on clients, the supervisory relationship, and professional functioning. *(See F.3.a.)*

F.5.d. ENDORSEMENT   Supervisors endorse supervisees for certification, licensure, employment, or completion of an academic or training program only when they believe supervisees are qualified for the endorsement. Regardless of qualifications, supervisors do not endorse supervisees whom they believe to be impaired in any way that would interfere with the performance of the duties associated with the endorsement.

F.6. RESPONSIBILITIES OF COUNSELOR EDUCATORS

F.6.a. COUNSELOR EDUCATORS   Counselor educators who are responsible for developing, implementing, and supervising educational programs are skilled as teachers and practitioners. They are knowledgeable regarding the ethical, legal, and regulatory aspects of the profession, are skilled in applying that knowledge, and make students and supervisees aware of their responsibilities. Counselor educators conduct counselor education and training programs in an ethical manner and serve as role models for professional behavior. *(See C.1., C.2.a., C.2.c.)*

F.6.B. INFUSING MULTICULTURAL ISSUES/DIVERSITY   Counselor educators infuse material related to multiculturalism/diversity into all courses and workshops for the development of professional counselors.

F.6.C. INTEGRATION OF STUDY AND PRACTICE   Counselor educators establish education and training programs that integrate academic study and supervised practice.

F.6.D. TEACHING ETHICS   Counselor educators make students and supervisees aware of the ethical responsibilities and standards of the profession and the ethical responsibilities of students to the profession. Counselor educators infuse ethical considerations throughout the curriculum. *(See C.1.)*

F.6.E. PEER RELATIONSHIPS   Counselor educators make every effort to ensure that the rights of peers are not compromised when students or supervisees lead counseling groups or provide clinical supervision. Counselor educators take steps to ensure that students and supervisees understand they have the same ethical obligations as counselor educators, trainers, and supervisors.

F.6.F. INNOVATIVE THEORIES AND TECHNIQUES   When counselor educators teach counseling techniques/procedures that are innovative, without an empirical foundation, or without a well-grounded theoretical foundation, they define the counseling techniques/procedures as "unproven" or "developing" and explain to students the potential risks and ethical considerations of using such techniques/procedures.

F.6.G. FIELD PLACEMENTS   Counselor educators develop clear policies within their training programs regarding field placement and other clinical experiences. Counselor educators provide clearly stated roles and responsibilities for the student or supervisee, the site supervisor, and the program supervisor. They confirm that site supervisors are qualified to provide supervision and inform site supervisors of their professional and ethical responsibilities in this role.

F.6.H. PROFESSIONAL DISCLOSURE   Before initiating counseling services, counselors-in-training disclose their status as students and explain how this status affects the limits of confidentiality. Counselor educators ensure that the clients at field placements are aware of the services rendered and the qualifications of the students and supervisees rendering those services. Students and supervisees obtain client permission before they use any information concerning the counseling relationship in the training process. *(See A.2.b.)*

F.7. STUDENT WELFARE

F.7.A. ORIENTATION   Counselor educators recognize that orientation is a developmental process that continues throughout the educational and clinical training of students. Counseling faculty provide prospective students with information about the counselor education program's expectations:

1. the type and level of skill and knowledge acquisition required for successful completion of the training;
2. program training goals, objectives, and mission, and subject matter to be covered;
3. bases for evaluation;
4. training components that encourage self-growth or self-disclosure as part of the training process;
5. the type of supervision settings and requirements of the sites for required clinical field experiences;
6. student and supervisee evaluation and dismissal policies and procedures; and
7. up-to-date employment prospects for graduates.

F.7.B. SELF-GROWTH EXPERIENCES   Counselor education programs delineate requirements for self-disclosure or self-growth experiences in their admission and program materials. Counselor educators use professional judgment when designing training experiences they conduct that require student and supervisee self-growth or self-disclosure. Students and supervisees are made aware of the ramifications their self-disclosure may have when counselors whose primary role as teacher, trainer, or supervisor requires acting on ethical obligations to the profession. Evaluative components of experiential training experiences explicitly delineate predetermined academic standards that are separate and do not depend on the student's level of self-disclosure. Counselor educators may require trainees to seek professional help to address any personal concerns that may be affecting their competency.

F.8. STUDENT RESPONSIBILITIES

F.8.A. STANDARDS FOR STUDENTS   Counselors-in-training have a responsibility to understand and follow the *ACA Code of Ethics* and adhere to applicable laws, regulatory policies, and rules and policies governing professional staff behavior at the agency or placement setting. Students have the same obligation to clients as those required of professional counselors. *(See C.1., H.1.)*

F.8.B. IMPAIRMENT   Counselors-in-training refrain from offering or providing counseling services when their physical, mental, or emotional problems are likely to harm a client or others. They are alert to the signs of impairment, seek assistance for problems, and notify their program supervisors when they are aware that they are unable to effectively provide services. In addition, they seek appropriate professional services for themselves to remediate the problems that are interfering with their ability to provide services to others. *(See A.1., C.2.d., C.2.g.)*

F.9. EVALUATION AND REMEDIATION OF STUDENTS

F.9.A. EVALUATION   Counselors clearly state to students, prior to and throughout the training program, the levels of competency expected, appraisal methods, and timing of evaluations for both didactic and clinical competencies. Counselor educators provide students with ongoing performance appraisal and evaluation feedback throughout the training program.

F.9.b. LIMITATIONS   Counselor educators, throughout ongoing evaluation and appraisal, are aware of and address the inability of some students to achieve counseling competencies that might impede performance. Counselor educators

1. assist students in securing remedial assistance when needed,
2. seek professional consultation and document their decision to dismiss or refer students for assistance, and
3. ensure that students have recourse in a timely manner to address decisions to require them to seek assistance or to dismiss them and provide students with due process according to institutional policies and procedures. *(See C.2.g.)*

F.9.c. COUNSELING FOR STUDENTS   If students request counseling or if counseling services are required as part of a remediation process, counselor educators provide acceptable referrals.

F. 10. ROLES AND RELATIONSHIPS BETWEEN COUNSELOR EDUCATORS AND STUDENTS

F.10.a. SEXUAL OR ROMANTIC RELATIONSHIPS   Sexual or romantic interactions or relationships with current students are prohibited.

F.10.b. SEXUAL HARASSMENT   Counselor educators do not condone or subject students to sexual harassment. *(See C.6.a.)*

F.10.c. RELATIONSHIPS WITH FORMER STUDENTS   Counselor educators are aware of the power differential in the relationship between faculty and students. Faculty members foster open discussions with former students when considering engaging in a social, sexual, or other intimate relationship. Faculty members discuss with the former student how their former relationship may affect the change in relationship.

F.10.d. NONPROFESSIONAL RELATIONSHIPS   Counselor educators avoid nonprofessional or ongoing professional relationships with students in which there is a risk of potential harm to the student or that may compromise the training experience or grades assigned. In addition, counselor educators do not accept any form of professional services, fees, commissions, reimbursement, or remuneration from a site for student or supervisee placement.

F.10.e. COUNSELING SERVICES   Counselor educators do not serve as counselors to current students unless this is a brief role associated with a training experience.

F.10.f. POTENTIALLY BENEFICIAL RELATIONSHIPS   Counselor educators are aware of the power differential in the relationship between faculty and students.

If they believe a nonprofessional relationship with a student may be potentially beneficial to the student, they take precautions similar to those taken by counselors when working with clients. Examples of potentially beneficial interactions or relationships include, but are not limited to, attending a formal ceremony; hospital visits; providing support during a stressful event; or mutual membership in a professional association, organization, or community. Counselor educators engage in open discussions with students when they consider entering into relationships with students outside of their roles as teachers and supervisors. They discuss with students the rationale for such interactions, the potential benefits and drawbacks, and the anticipated consequences for the student. Educators clarify the specific nature and limitations of the additional role(s) they will have with the student prior to engaging in a nonprofessional relationship. Nonprofessional relationships with students should be time-limited and initiated with student consent.

F.11. MULTICULTURAL/DIVERSITY COMPETENCE IN COUNSELOR EDUCATION AND TRAINING PROGRAMS

F.11.a. FACULTY DIVERSITY   Counselor educators are committed to recruiting and retaining a diverse faculty.

F.11.b. STUDENT DIVERSITY   Counselor educators actively attempt to recruit and retain a diverse student body. Counselor educators demonstrate commitment to multicultural/diversity competence by recognizing and valuing diverse cultures and types of abilities students bring to the training experience. Counselor educators provide appropriate accommodations that enhance and support diverse student well-being and academic performance.

F.11.c. MULTICULTURAL/DIVERSITY COMPETENCE   Counselor educators actively infuse multicultural/diversity competency in their training and supervision practices. They actively train students to gain awareness, knowledge, and skills in the competencies of multicultural practice. Counselor educators include case examples, role-plays, discussion questions, and other classroom activities that promote and represent various cultural perspectives.

SECTION G: RESEARCH AND PUBLICATION

INTRODUCTION

Counselors who conduct research are encouraged to contribute to the knowledge base of the profession and promote a clearer understanding of the conditions that lead to a healthy and more just society. Counselors support efforts of researchers by participating fully and willingly whenever possible. Counselors minimize bias and respect diversity in designing and implementing research programs.

G.1. Research Responsibilities

G.1.a. Use of Human Research Participants   Counselors plan, design, conduct, and report research in a manner that is consistent with pertinent ethical principles, federal and state laws, host institutional regulations, and scientific standards governing research with human research participants.

G.1.b. Deviation from Standard Practice   Counselors seek consultation and observe stringent safeguards to protect the rights of research participants when a research problem suggests a deviation from standard or acceptable practices.

G.1.c. Independent Researchers   When independent researchers do not have access to an Institutional Review Board (IRB), they should consult with researchers who are familiar with IRB procedures to provide appropriate safeguards.

G.1.d. Precautions to Avoid Injury   Counselors who conduct research with human participants are responsible for the welfare of participants throughout the research process and should take reasonable precautions to avoid causing injurious psychological, emotional, physical, or social effects to participants.

G.1.e. Principal Researcher Responsibility   The ultimate responsibility for ethical research practice lies with the principal researcher. All others involved in the research activities share ethical obligations and responsibility for their own actions.

G.1.f. Minimal Interference   Counselors take reasonable precautions to avoid causing disruptions in the lives of research participants that could be caused by their involvement in research.

G.1.g. Multicultural/Diversity Considerations in Research   When appropriate to research goals, counselors are sensitive to incorporating research procedures that take into account cultural considerations. They seek consultation when appropriate.

G.2. Rights of Research Participants

(See A.2, A.7.)

G.2.a. Informed Consent in Research   Individuals have the right to consent to become research participants. In seeking consent, counselors use language that

1. accurately explains the purpose and procedures to be followed,
2. identifies any procedures that are experimental or relatively untried,
3. describes any attendant discomforts and risks,
4. describes any benefits or changes in individuals or organizations that might be reasonably expected,

5. discloses appropriate alternative procedures that would be advantageous for participants,
6. offers to answer any inquiries concerning the procedures,
7. describes any limitations on confidentiality,
8. describes the format and potential target audiences for the dissemination of research findings, and
9. instructs participants that they are free to withdraw their consent and to discontinue participation in the project at any time without penalty.

G.2.B. DECEPTION   Counselors do not conduct research involving deception unless alternative procedures are not feasible and the prospective value of the research justifies the deception. If such deception has the potential to cause physical or emotional harm to research participants, the research is not conducted, regardless of prospective value. When the methodological requirements of a study necessitate concealment or deception, the investigator explains the reasons for this action as soon as possible during the debriefing.

G.2.C. STUDENT/SUPERVISEE PARTICIPATION   Researchers who involve students or supervisees in research make clear to them that the decision regarding whether or not to participate in research activities does not affect one's academic standing or supervisory relationship. Students or supervisees who choose not to participate in educational research are provided with an appropriate alternative to fulfill their academic or clinical requirements.

G.2.D. CLIENT PARTICIPATION   Counselors conducting research involving clients make clear in the informed consent process that clients are free to choose whether or not to participate in research activities. Counselors take necessary precautions to protect clients from adverse consequences of declining or withdrawing from participation.

G.2.E. CONFIDENTIALITY OF INFORMATION   Information obtained about research participants during the course of an investigation is confidential. When the possibility exists that others may obtain access to such information, ethical research practice requires that the possibility, together with the plans for protecting confidentiality, be explained to participants as a part of the procedure for obtaining informed consent.

G.2.F. PERSONS NOT CAPABLE OF GIVING INFORMED CONSENT   When a person is not capable of giving informed consent, counselors provide an appropriate explanation to, obtain agreement for participation from, and obtain the appropriate consent of a legally authorized person.

G.2.G. COMMITMENTS TO PARTICIPANTS   Counselors take reasonable measures to honor all commitments to research participants. *(See A.2.c.)*

G.2.H. EXPLANATIONS AFTER DATA COLLECTION   After data are collected, counselors provide participants with full clarification of the nature of the study to remove any misconceptions participants might have regarding the research. Where scientific or human values justify delaying or withholding information, counselors take reasonable measures to avoid causing harm.

G.2.I. INFORMING SPONSORS   Counselors inform sponsors, institutions, and publication channels regarding research procedures and outcomes. Counselors ensure that appropriate bodies and authorities are given pertinent information and acknowledgment.

G.2.J. DISPOSAL OF RESEARCH DOCUMENTS AND RECORDS   Within a reasonable period of time following the completion of a research project or study, counselors take steps to destroy records or documents (audio, video, digital, and written) containing confidential data or information that identifies research participants. When records are of an artistic nature, researchers obtain participant consent with regard to handling of such records or documents. *(See B.4.a, B.4.g.)*

G.3. RELATIONSHIPS WITH RESEARCH PARTICIPANTS (WHEN RESEARCH INVOLVES INTENSIVE OR EXTENDED INTERACTIONS)

G.3.A. NONPROFESSIONAL RELATIONSHIPS   Nonprofessional relationships with research participants should be avoided.

G.3.B. RELATIONSHIPS WITH RESEARCH PARTICIPANTS   Sexual or romantic counselor–research participant interactions or relationships with current research participants are prohibited.

G.3.C. SEXUAL HARASSMENT AND RESEARCH PARTICIPANTS   Researchers do not condone or subject research participants to sexual harassment.

G.3.D. POTENTIALLY BENEFICIAL INTERACTIONS   When a nonprofessional interaction between the researcher and the research participant may be potentially beneficial, the researcher must document, prior to the interaction (when feasible), the rationale for such an interaction, the potential benefit, and anticipated consequences for the research participant. Such interactions should be initiated with appropriate consent of the research participant. Where unintentional harm occurs to the research participant due to the nonprofessional interaction, the researcher must show evidence of an attempt to remedy such harm.

G.4. REPORTING RESULTS

G.4.A. ACCURATE RESULTS   Counselors plan, conduct, and report research accurately. They provide thorough discussions of the limitations of their data and alternative hypotheses. Counselors do not engage in misleading or fraudulent research, distort data, misrepresent data, or deliberately bias their results. They explicitly mention all variables and conditions known to the investigator that may have affected the outcome of a study or the interpretation of data. They describe the extent to which results are applicable for diverse populations.

G.4.b. OBLIGATION TO REPORT UNFAVORABLE RESULTS   Counselors report the results of any research of professional value. Results that reflect unfavorably on institutions, programs, services, prevailing opinions, or vested interests are not withheld.

G.4.c. REPORTING ERRORS   If counselors discover significant errors in their published research, they take reasonable steps to correct such errors in a correction erratum, or through other appropriate publication means.

G.4.d. IDENTITY OF PARTICIPANTS   Counselors who supply data, aid in the research of another person, report research results, or make original data available take due care to disguise the identity of respective participants in the absence of specific authorization from the participants to do otherwise. In situations where participants self-identify their involvement in research studies, researchers take active steps to ensure that data are adapted/changed to protect the identity and welfare of all parties and that discussion of results does not cause harm to participants.

G.4.e. REPLICATION STUDIES   Counselors are obligated to make available sufficient original research data to qualified professionals who may wish to replicate the study.

G.5. PUBLICATION

G.5.a. RECOGNIZING CONTRIBUTIONS   When conducting and reporting research, counselors are familiar with and give recognition to previous work on the topic, observe copyright laws, and give full credit to those to whom credit is due.

G.5.b. PLAGIARISM   Counselors do not plagiarize; that is, they do not present another person's work as their own work.

G.5.c. REVIEW/REPUBLICATION OF DATA OR IDEAS   Counselors fully acknowledge and make editorial reviewers aware of prior publication of ideas or data where such ideas or data are submitted for review or publication.

G.5.d. CONTRIBUTORS   Counselors give credit through joint authorship, acknowledgment, footnote statements, or other appropriate means to those who have contributed significantly to research or concept development in accordance with such contributions. The principal contributor is listed first, and minor technical or professional contributions are acknowledged in notes or introductory statements.

G.5.E. AGREEMENT OF CONTRIBUTORS   Counselors who conduct joint research with colleagues or students/supervisees establish agreements in advance regarding allocation of tasks, publication credit, and types of acknowledgment that will be received.

G.5.F. STUDENT RESEARCH   For articles that are substantially based on students' course papers, projects, dissertations or theses, and on which students have been the primary contributors, they are listed as principal authors.

G.5.G. DUPLICATE SUBMISSION   Counselors submit manuscripts for consideration to only one journal at a time. Manuscripts that are published in whole or in substantial part in another journal or published work are not submitted for publication without acknowledgment and permission from the previous publication.

G.5.H. PROFESSIONAL REVIEW   Counselors who review material submitted for publication, research, or other scholarly purposes respect the confidentiality and proprietary rights of those who submitted it. Counselors use care to make publication decisions based on valid and defensible standards. Counselors review article submissions in a timely manner and based on their scope and competency in research methodologies. Counselors who serve as reviewers at the request of editors or publishers make every effort to only review materials that are within their scope of competency and use care to avoid personal biases.

SECTION H: RESOLVING ETHICAL ISSUES

INTRODUCTION

Counselors behave in a legal, ethical, and moral manner in the conduct of their professional work. They are aware that client protection and trust in the profession depend on a high level of professional conduct. They hold other counselors to the same standards and are willing to take appropriate action to ensure that these standards are upheld.

Counselors strive to resolve ethical dilemmas with direct and open communication among all parties involved and seek consultation with colleagues and supervisors when necessary. Counselors incorporate ethical practice into their daily professional work. They engage in ongoing professional development regarding current topics in ethical and legal issues in counseling.

H.1. STANDARDS AND THE LAW

(See F.9.a.)

H.1.A. KNOWLEDGE   Counselors understand the *ACA Code of Ethics* and other applicable ethics codes from other professional organizations or from certification and licensure bodies of which they are members. Lack of knowledge or misunderstanding of an ethical responsibility is not a defense against a charge of unethical conduct.

H.1.b. Conflicts Between Ethics and Laws   If ethical responsibilities conflict with law, regulations, or other governing legal authority, counselors make known their commitment to the *ACA Code of Ethics* and take steps to resolve the conflict. If the conflict cannot be resolved by such means, counselors may adhere to the requirements of law, regulations, or other governing legal authority.

H.2. Suspected Violations

H.2.a. Ethical Behavior Expected   Counselors expect colleagues to adhere to the *ACA Code of Ethics*. When counselors possess knowledge that raises doubts as to whether another counselor is acting in an ethical manner, they take appropriate action. *(See H.2.b., H.2.c.)*

H.2.b. Informal Resolution   When counselors have reason to believe that another counselor is violating or has violated an ethical standard, they attempt first to resolve the issue informally with the other counselor if feasible, provided such action does not violate confidentiality rights that may be involved.

H.2.c. Reporting Ethical Violations   If an apparent violation has substantially harmed, or is likely to substantially harm, a person or organization and is not appropriate for informal resolution or is not resolved properly, counselors take further action appropriate to the situation. Such action might include referral to state or national committees on professional ethics, voluntary national certification bodies, state licensing boards, or to the appropriate institutional authorities. This standard does not apply when an intervention would violate confidentiality rights or when counselors have been retained to review the work of another counselor whose professional conduct is in question.

H.2.d. Consultation   When uncertain as to whether a particular situation or course of action may be in violation of the *ACA Code of Ethics,* counselors consult with other counselors who are knowledgeable about ethics and the *ACA Code of Ethics,* with colleagues, or with appropriate authorities

H.2.e. Organizational Conflicts   If the demands of an organization with which counselors are affiliated pose a conflict with the *ACA Code of Ethics,* counselors specify the nature of such conflicts and express to their supervisors or other responsible officials their commitment to the *ACA Code of Ethics.* When possible, counselors work toward change within the organization to allow full adherence to the *ACA Code of Ethics.* In doing so, they address any confidentiality issues.

H.2.f. Unwarranted Complaints   Counselors do not initiate, participate in, or encourage the filing of ethics complaints that are made with reckless disregard or willful ignorance of facts that would disprove the allegation.

H.2.G. Unfair Discrimination Against Complainants and Respondents
Counselors do not deny persons employment, advancement, admission to academic or other programs, tenure, or promotion based solely upon their having made or their being the subject of an ethics complaint. This does not preclude taking action based upon the outcome of such proceedings or considering other appropriate information.

H.3. Cooperation with Ethics Committees

Counselors assist in the process of enforcing the *ACA Code of Ethics*. Counselors cooperate with investigations, proceedings, and requirements of the ACA Ethics Committee or ethics committees of other duly constituted associations or boards having jurisdiction over those charged with a violation. Counselors are familiar with the *ACA Policy and Procedures for Processing Complains of Ethical Violations* and use it as a reference for assisting in the enforcement of the *ACA Code of Ethics*.

B APPENDIX | ETHICAL PRINCIPLES OF PSYCHOLOGISTS AND CODE OF CONDUCT

INTRODUCTION

The American Psychological Association's (APA's) Ethical Principles of Psychologists and Code of Conduct (hereinafter referred to as the Ethics Code) consists of an Introduction, a Preamble, six General Principles (A–F), and specific Ethical Standards. The Introduction discusses the intent, organization, procedural considerations, and scope of application of the Ethics Code. The Preamble and General Principles are *aspirational* goals to guide psychologists toward the highest ideals of psychology. Although the Preamble and General Principles are not themselves enforceable rules, they should be considered by psychologists in arriving at an ethical course of action and may be considered by ethics bodies in interpreting the Ethical Standards. The Ethical Standards set forth *enforceable* rules for conduct as psychologists. Most of the Ethical Standards are written broadly, in order to apply to psychologists in varied roles, although the application of an Ethical Standard may vary depending on the context. The Ethical Standards are not exhaustive. The fact that a given conduct is not specifically addressed by the Ethics Code does not mean that it is necessarily either ethical or unethical.

This version of the American Psychological Association Ethics Code was adopted by the American Psychological Association's Council of Representatives during its meeting on August 13 and 16, 1992, and was published in *American Psychologist*, 1992, Vol. 47, 1597–1611. Copyright 1992. Reprinted by permission.

Membership in the APA commits members to adhere to the APA Ethics Code and to the rules and procedures used to implement it. Psychologists and students, whether or not they are APA members. should be aware that the Ethics Code may be applied to them by state psychology boards, courts, or other public bodies.

This Ethics Code applies only to psychologists' work-related activities, that is, activities that are part of the psychologists' scientific and professional functions or that are psychological in nature. It includes the clinical or counseling practice of psychology, research, teaching, supervision of trainees, development of assessment instruments, conducting assessments, educational counseling, organizational consulting, social intervention, administration, and other activities as well. These work-related activities can be distinguished from the purely private conduct of a psychologist, which ordinarily is not within the purview of the Ethics Code.

The Ethics Code is intended to provide standards of professional conduct that can be applied by the APA and by other bodies that choose to adopt them. Whether or not a psychologist has violated the Ethics Code does not by itself determine whether he or she is legally liable in a court action, whether a contract is enforceable, or whether other legal consequences occur. These results are based on legal rather than ethical rules. However, compliance with or violation of the Ethics Code may be admissible as evidence in some legal proceedings, depending on the circumstances.

In the process of making decisions regarding their professional behavior, psychologists must consider this Ethics Code, in addition to applicable laws and psychology board regulations. If the Ethics Code establishes a higher standard of conduct than is required by law, psychologists must meet the higher ethical standard. If the Ethics Code standard appears to conflict with the requirements of law, then psychologists make known their commitment to the Ethics Code and take steps to resolve the conflict in a responsible manner. If neither law nor the Ethics Code resolves an issue, psychologists should consider other professional materials* and the dictates of their own conscience, as well as seek consultation with others within the field when this is practical.

---

*Professional materials that are most helpful in this regard are guidelines and standards that have been adopted or endorsed by professional psychological organizations. Such guidelines and standards, whether adopted by the American Psychological Association (APA) or its Divisions, are not enforceable as such by this Ethics Code, but are of educative value to psychologists, courts, and professional bodies. Such materials include, but are not limited to, the APA's *General Guidelines for Providers of Psychological Services* (1987), *Specialty Guidelines for the Delivery of Services by Clinical Psychologists, Counseling Psychologists, Industrial/Organizational Psychologists, and School Psychologists* (1981), *Guidelines for Computer Based Tests and Interpretations* (1987), *Standards for Educational and Psychological Testing* (1985), *Ethical Principles in the Conduct of Research With Human Participants* (1982), *Guidelines for Ethical Conduct in the Care and Use of Animals* (1986), *Guidelines for Providers of Psychological Services to Ethnic, Linguistic, and Culturally Diverse Populations* (1990), and the *Publication Manual of the American Psychological Association* (3rd ed., 1983). Materials not adopted by APA as a whole include the APA Division 41 (Forensic Psychology)/American Psychology–Law Society's *Specialty Guidelines for Forensic Psychologists* (1991).

The procedures for filing, investigating, and resolving complaints of unethical conduct are described in the current Rules and Procedures of the APA Ethics Committee. The actions that APA may take for violations of the Ethics Code include actions such as reprimand, censure, termination of APA membership, and referral of the matter to other bodies. Complainants who seek remedies such as monetary damages in alleging ethical violations by a psychologist must resort to private negotiation, administrative bodies, or the courts. Actions that violate the Ethics Code may lead to the imposition of sanctions on a psychologist by bodies other than APA, including state psychological associations, other professional groups, psychology boards, other state or federal agencies, and payors for health services. In addition to actions for violation of the Ethics Code, the APA Bylaws provide that APA may take action against a member after his or her conviction of a felony, expulsion or suspension from an affiliated state psychological association, or suspension or loss of licensure.

PREAMBLE

Psychologists work to develop a valid and reliable body of scientific knowledge based on research. They may apply that knowledge to human behavior in a variety of contexts. In doing so, they perform many roles, such as researcher, educator, diagnostician, therapist, supervisor, consultant, administrator, social interventionist, and expert witness. Their goal is to broaden knowledge of behavior and, where appropriate, to apply it pragmatically to improve the condition of both the individual and society. Psychologists respect the central importance of freedom of inquiry and expression in research, teaching, and publication. They also strive to help the public in developing informed judgments and choices concerning human behavior. This Ethics Code provides a common set of values upon which psychologists build their professional and scientific work.

This Code is intended to provide both the general principles and the decision rules to cover most situations encountered by psychologists. It has as its primary goal the welfare and protection of the individuals and groups with whom psychologists work. It is the individual responsibility of each psychologist to aspire to the highest possible standards of conduct. Psychologists respect and protect human and civil rights, and do not knowingly participate in or condone unfair discriminatory practices.

The development of a dynamic set of ethical standards for a psychologist's work-related conduct requires a personal commitment to a lifelong effort to act ethically; to encourage ethical behavior by students, supervisees, employees, and colleagues, as appropriate; and to consult with others, as needed, concerning ethical problems. Each psychologist supplements, but does not violate, the Ethics Code's values and rules on the basis of guidance drawn from personal values, culture, and experience.

GENERAL PRINCIPLES

PRINCIPLE A: COMPETENCE

Psychologists strive to maintain high standards of competence in their work. They recognize the boundaries of their particular competencies and the limitations of their expertise. They provide only those services and use only those techniques for which they are qualified by education, training, or experience. Psychologists are cognizant of the fact that the competencies required in serving, teaching, and/or studying groups of people vary with the distinctive characteristics of those groups. In those areas in which recognized professional standards do not yet exist, psychologists exercise careful judgment and take appropriate precautions to protect the welfare of those with whom they work. They maintain knowledge of relevant scientific and professional information related to the services they render, and they recognize the need for ongoing education. Psychologists make appropriate use of scientific, professional, technical, and administrative resources.

PRINCIPLE B: INTEGRITY

Psychologists seek to promote integrity in the science, teaching, and practice of psychology. In these activities psychologists are honest, fair, and respectful of others. In describing or reporting their qualifications, services, products, fees, research, or teaching, they do not make statements that are false, misleading, or deceptive. Psychologists strive to be aware of their own belief systems, values, needs, and limitations and the effect of these on their work. To the extent feasible, they attempt to clarify for relevant parties the roles they are performing and to function appropriately in accordance with those roles. Psychologists avoid improper and potentially harmful dual relationships.

PRINCIPLE C: PROFESSIONAL AND SCIENTIFIC RESPONSIBILITY

Psychologists uphold professional standards of conduct, clarify their professional roles and obligations, accept appropriate responsibility for their behavior, and adapt their methods to the needs of different populations. Psychologists consult with, refer to, or cooperate with other professionals and institutions to the extent needed to serve the best interests of their patients, clients, or other recipients of their services. Psychologists' moral standards and conduct are personal matters to the same degree as is true for any other person, except as psychologists' conduct may compromise their professional responsibilities or reduce the public's trust in psychology and psychologists. Psychologists are concerned about the ethical compliance of their colleagues' scientific and professional conduct. When appropriate, they consult with colleagues in order to prevent or avoid unethical conduct.

PRINCIPLE D: RESPECT FOR PEOPLE'S RIGHTS AND DIGNITY

Psychologists accord appropriate respect to the fundamental rights, dignity, and worth of all people. They respect the rights of individuals to privacy, confidentiality, self-determination, and autonomy, mindful that legal and other obligations may lead to inconsistency and conflict with the exercise of these rights. Psychologists are aware of cultural, individual, and role differences, including those due to age, gender, race, ethnicity, national origin, religion, sexual orientation, disability, language, and socioeconomic status. Psychologists try to eliminate the effect on their work of biases based on those factors, and they do not knowingly participate in or condone unfair discriminatory practices.

PRINCIPLE E: CONCERN FOR OTHERS' WELFARE

Psychologists seek to contribute to the welfare of those with whom they interact professionally. In their professional actions, psychologists weigh the welfare and rights of their patients or clients, students, supervisees, human research participants, and other affected persons, and the welfare of animal subjects of research. When conflicts occur among psychologists' obligations or concerns, they attempt to resolve these conflicts and to perform their roles in a responsible fashion that avoids or minimizes harm. Psychologists are sensitive to real and ascribed differences in power between themselves and others, and they do not exploit or mislead other people during or after professional relationships.

PRINCIPLE F: SOCIAL RESPONSIBILITY

Psychologists are aware of their professional and scientific responsibilities to the community and the society in which they work and live. They apply and make public their knowledge of psychology in order to contribute to human welfare. Psychologists are concerned about and work to mitigate the causes of human suffering. When undertaking research, they strive to advance human welfare and the science of psychology. Psychologists try to avoid misuse of their work. Psychologists comply with the law and encourage the development of law and social policy that serve the interests of their patients and clients and the public. They are encouraged to contribute a portion of their professional time for little or no personal advantage.

ETHICAL STANDARDS

1. GENERAL STANDARDS

These General Standards are potentially applicable to the professional and scientific activities of all psychologists.

1.01 APPLICABILITY OF THE ETHICS CODE   The activity of a psychologist subject to the Ethics Code may be reviewed under these Ethical Standards only if the activity is part of his or her work-related functions or the activity is psychological in nature. Personal activities having no connection to or effect on psychological roles are not subject to the Ethics Code.

1.02 RELATIONSHIP OF ETHICS AND LAW   If psychologists' ethical responsibilities conflict with law, psychologists make known their commitment to the Ethics Code and take steps to resolve the conflict in a responsible manner.

1.03 PROFESSIONAL AND SCIENTIFIC RELATIONSHIP   Psychologists provide diagnostic, therapeutic, teaching, research, supervisory, consultative, or other psychological services only in the context of a defined professional or scientific relationship or role. (See also Standards 2.01, Evaluation, Diagnosis, and Interventions in Professional Context, and 7.02, Forensic Assessments.)

1.04 BOUNDARIES OF COMPETENCE

(a) Psychologists provide services, teach, and conduct research only within the boundaries of their competence, based on their education, training, supervised experience, or appropriate professional experience.

(b) Psychologists provide services, teach, or conduct research in new areas or involving new techniques only after first undertaking appropriate study, training, supervision, and/or consultation from persons who are competent in those areas or techniques.

(c) In those emerging areas in which generally recognized standards for preparatory training do not yet exist, psychologists nevertheless take reasonable steps to ensure the competence of their work and to protect patients, clients, students, research participants, and others from harm.

1.05 MAINTAINING EXPERTISE   Psychologists who engage in assessment, therapy, teaching, research, organizational consulting, or other professional activities maintain a reasonable level of awareness of current scientific and professional information in their fields of activity, and undertake ongoing efforts to maintain competence in the skills they use.

1.06 BASIS FOR SCIENTIFIC AND PROFESSIONAL JUDGMENTS   Psychologists rely on scientifically and professionally derived knowledge when making scientific or professional judgments or when engaging in scholarly or professional endeavors.

1.07 DESCRIBING THE NATURE AND RESULTS OF PSYCHOLOGICAL SERVICES

(a) When psychologists provide assessment, evaluation, treatment, counseling, supervision, teaching, consultation, research, or other psychological services to an individual, a group, or an organization, they provide, using language that is reasonably understandable to the recipient of those services, appropriate information beforehand about the nature of such services and appropriate information later about results and conclusions. (See also Standard 2.09, Explaining Assessment Results.)

(b) If psychologists will be precluded by law or by organizational roles from providing such information to particular individuals or groups, they so inform those individuals or groups at the outset of the service.

1.08 HUMAN DIFFERENCES　Where differences of age, gender, race, ethnicity, national origin, religion, sexual orientation, disability, language, or socioeconomic status significantly affect psychologists' work concerning particular individuals or groups, psychologists obtain the training, experience, consultation, or supervision necessary to ensure the competence of their services, or they make appropriate referrals.

1.09 RESPECTING OTHERS　In their work-related activities, psychologists respect the rights of others to hold values, attitudes, and opinions that differ from their own.

1.10 NONDISCRIMINATION　In their work-related activities, psychologists do not engage in unfair discrimination based on age, gender, race, ethnicity, national origin, religion, sexual orientation, disability, socioeconomic status, or any basis proscribed by law.

1.11 SEXUAL HARASSMENT
(a) Psychologists do not engage in sexual harassment. Sexual harassment is sexual solicitation, physical advances, or verbal or nonverbal conduct that is sexual in nature, that occurs in connection with the psychologist's activities or roles as a psychologist, and that either: (1) is unwelcome, is offensive, or creates a hostile workplace environment, and the psychologist knows or is told this, or (2) is sufficiently severe or intense to be abusive to a reasonable person in the context. Sexual harassment can consist of a single intense or severe act or of multiple persistent or pervasive acts.

(b) Psychologists accord sexual-harassment complainants and respondents dignity and respect. Psychologists do not participate in denying a person academic admittance or advancement, employment, tenure, or promotion, based solely upon their having made, or their being the subject of, sexual harassment charges. This does not preclude taking action based upon the outcome of such proceedings or consideration of other appropriate information.

1.12 OTHER HARASSMENT　Psychologists do not knowingly engage in behavior that is harassing or demeaning to persons with whom they interact in their work based on factors such as those persons' age, gender, race, ethnicity, national origin, religion, sexual orientation, disability, language, or socioeconomic status.

1.13 PERSONAL PROBLEMS AND CONFLICTS
(a) Psychologists recognize that their personal problems and conflicts may interfere with their effectiveness. Accordingly, they refrain from undertaking an activity when they know or should know that their personal problems are likely to lead to harm to a patient, client, colleague, student, research participant, or other person to whom they may owe a professional or scientific obligation.

(b) In addition, psychologists have an obligation to be alert to signs of, and to obtain assistance for, their personal problems at an early stage, in order to prevent significantly impaired performance.

(c) When psychologists become aware of personal problems that may interfere with their performing work-related duties adequately, they take appropriate measures, such as obtaining professional consultation or assistance, and determine whether they should limit, suspend, or terminate their work-related duties.

1.14 AVOIDING HARM Psychologists take reasonable steps to avoid harming their patients or clients, research participants, students, and others with whom they work, and to minimize harm where it is foreseeable and unavoidable.

1.15 MISUSE OF PSYCHOLOGISTS' INFLUENCE Because psychologists' scientific and professional judgments and actions may affect the lives of others, they are alert to and guard against personal, financial, social, organizational, or political factors that might lead to misuse of their influence.

1.16 MISUSE OF PSYCHOLOGISTS' WORK

(a) Psychologists do not participate in activities in which it appears likely that their skills or data will be misused by others, unless corrective mechanisms are available. (See also Standard 7.04, Truthfulness and Candor.)

(b) If psychologists learn of misuse or misrepresentation of their work, they take reasonable steps to correct or minimize the misuse or misrepresentation.

1.17 MULTIPLE RELATIONSHIPS

(a) In many communities and situations, it may not be feasible or reasonable for psychologists to avoid social or other nonprofessional contacts with persons such as patients, clients, students, supervisees, or research participants. Psychologists must always be sensitive to the potential harmful effects of other contacts on their work and on those persons with whom they deal. A psychologist refrains from entering into or promising another personal, scientific, professional, financial, or other relationship with such persons if it appears likely that such a relationship reasonably might impair the psychologist's objectivity or otherwise interfere with the psychologist's effectively performing his or her functions as a psychologist, or might harm or exploit the other party.

(b) Likewise, whenever feasible, a psychologist refrains from taking on professional or scientific obligations when preexisting relationships would create a risk of such harm.

(c) If a psychologist finds that, due to unforeseen factors, a potentially harmful multiple relationship has arisen, the psychologist attempts to resolve it with due regard for the best interests of the affected person and maximal compliance with the Ethics Code.

1.18 BARTER (WITH PATIENTS OR CLIENTS) Psychologists ordinarily refrain from accepting goods, services, or other nonmonetary remuneration from patients or clients in return for psychological services because such arrangements create inherent potential for conflicts, exploitation, and distortion of the professional relationship. A psychologist may participate in bartering *only* if (1) it is not clinically contraindicated, *and* (2) the relationship is not exploitative. (See also Standards 1.17, Multiple Relationships, and 1.25, Fees and Financial Arrangements.)

1.19 EXPLOITATIVE RELATIONSHIPS

(a) Psychologists do not exploit persons over whom they have supervisory, evaluative, or other authority such as students, supervisees, employees, research participants, and clients or patients. (See also Standards 4.05–4.07 regarding sexual involvement with clients or patients.)

(b) Psychologists do not engage in sexual relationships with students or supervisees in training over whom the psychologist has evaluative or direct authority, because such relationships are so likely to impair judgment or be exploitative.

1.20 CONSULTATIONS AND REFERRALS

(a) Psychologists arrange for appropriate consultations and referrals based principally on the best interests of their patients or clients, with appropriate consent, and subject to other relevant considerations, including applicable law and contractual obligations. (See also Standards 5.01, Discussing the Limits of Confidentiality, and 5.06, Consultations.)

(b) When indicated and professionally appropriate, psychologists cooperate with other professionals in order to serve their patients or clients effectively and appropriately.

(c) Psychologists' referral practices are consistent with law.

1.21 THIRD-PARTY REQUESTS FOR SERVICES

(a) When a psychologist agrees to provide services to a person or entity at the request of a third party, the psychologist clarifies to the extent feasible, at the outset of the service, the nature of the relationship with each party. This clarification includes the role of the psychologist (such as therapist, organizational consultant, diagnostician, or expert witness), the probable uses of the services provided or the information obtained, and the fact that there may be limits to confidentiality.

(b) If there is a foreseeable risk of the psychologist's being called upon to perform conflicting roles because of the involvement of a third party, the psychologist clarifies the nature and direction of his or her responsibilities, keeps all parties appropriately informed as matters develop, and resolves the situation in accordance with this Ethics Code.

1.22 DELEGATION TO AND SUPERVISION OF SUBORDINATES

(a) Psychologists delegate to their employees, supervisees, and research assistants only those responsibilities that such persons can reasonably be expected to perform competently, on the basis of their education, training, or experience, either independently or with the level of supervision being provided.

(b) Psychologists provide proper training and supervision to their employees or supervisees and take reasonable steps to see that such persons perform services responsibly, competently, and ethically.

(c) If institutional policies, procedures, or practices prevent fulfillment of this obligation, psychologists attempt to modify their role or to correct the situation to the extent feasible.

1.23 Documentation of Professional and Scientific Work

(a) Psychologists appropriately document their professional and scientific work in order to facilitate provision of services later by them or by other professionals, to ensure accountability, and to meet other requirements of institutions or the law.

(b) When psychologists have reason to believe that records of their professional services will be used in legal proceedings involving recipients of or participants in their work, they have a responsibility to create and maintain documentation in the kind of detail and quality that would be consistent with reasonable scrutiny in an adjudicative forum. (See also Standard 7.01, Professionalism, under Forensic Activities.)

1.24 Records and Data

Psychologists create, maintain, disseminate, store, retain, and dispose of records and data relating to their research, practice, and other work in accordance with law and in a manner that permits compliance with the requirements of this Ethics Code. (See also Standard 5.04, Maintenance of Records.)

1.25 Fees and Financial Arrangements

(a) As early as is feasible in a professional or scientific relationship, the psychologist and the patient, client, or other appropriate recipient of psychological services reach an agreement specifying the compensation and the billing arrangements.

(b) Psychologists do not exploit recipients of services or payors with respect to fees.

(c) Psychologists' fee practices are consistent with law.

(d) Psychologists do not misrepresent their fees.

(e) If limitations to services can be anticipated because of limitations in financing, this is discussed with the patient, client, or other appropriate recipient of services as early as is feasible. (See also Standard 4.08, Interruption of Services.)

(f) If the patient, client, or other recipient of services does not pay for services as agreed, and if the psychologist wishes to use collection agencies or legal measures to collect the fees, the psychologist first informs the person that such measures will be taken and provides that person an opportunity to make prompt payment. (See also Standard 5.11, Withholding Records for Nonpayment.)

1.26 Accuracy in Reports to Payors and Funding Sources

In their reports to payors for services or sources of research funding, psychologists accurately state the nature of the research or service provided, the fees or charges, and where applicable, the identity of the provider, the findings, and the diagnosis. (See also Standard 5.05, Disclosures.)

1.27 REFERRALS AND FEES   When a psychologist pays, receives payment from, or divides fees with another professional other than in an employer-employee relationship, the payment to each is based on the services (clinical, consultative, administrative, or other) provided and is not based on the referral itself.

2. EVALUATION, ASSESSMENT, OR INTERVENTION

2.01 EVALUATION, DIAGNOSIS, AND INTERVENTIONS IN PROFESSIONAL CONTEXT

(a) Psychologists perform evaluations, diagnostic services, or interventions only within the context of a defined professional relationship. (See also Standard 1.03, Professional and Scientific Relationship.)

(b) Psychologists' assessments, recommendations, reports, and psychological diagnostic or evaluative statements are based on information and techniques (including personal interviews of the individual when appropriate) sufficient to provide appropriate substantiation for their findings. (See also Standard 7.02, Forensic Assessments.)

2.02 COMPETENCE AND APPROPRIATE USE OF ASSESSMENTS AND INTERVENTIONS

(a) Psychologists who develop, administer, score, interpret, or use psychological assessment techniques, interviews, tests, or instruments do so in a manner and for purposes that are appropriate in light of the research on or evidence of the usefulness and proper application of the techniques.

(b) Psychologists refrain from misuse of assessment techniques, interventions, results, and interpretations and take reasonable steps to prevent others from misusing the information these techniques provide. This includes refraining from releasing raw test results or raw data to persons, other than to patients or clients as appropriate, who are not qualified to use such information. (See also Standards 1.02, Relationship of Ethics and Law, and 1.04, Boundaries of Competence.)

2.03 TEST CONSTRUCTION   Psychologists who develop and conduct research with tests and other assessment techniques use scientific procedures and current professional knowledge for test design, standardization, validation, reduction or elimination of bias, and recommendations for use.

2.04 USE OF ASSESSMENT IN GENERAL AND WITH SPECIAL POPULATIONS

(a) Psychologists who perform interventions or administer, score, interpret, or use assessment techniques are familiar with the reliability, validation, and related standardization or outcome studies of, and proper applications and uses of, the techniques they use.

(b) Psychologists recognize limits to the certainty with which diagnoses, judgments, or predictions can be made about individuals.

(c) Psychologists attempt to identify situations in which particular interventions or assessment techniques or norms may not be applicable or may require adjustment in administration or interpretation because of factors such as individuals' gender, age, race, ethnicity, national origin, religion, sexual orientation, disability, language, or socioeconomic status.

2.05 INTERPRETING ASSESSMENT RESULTS   When interpreting assessment results, including automated interpretations, psychologists take into account the various test factors and characteristics of the person being assessed that might affect psychologists' judgments or reduce the accuracy of their interpretations. They indicate any significant reservations they have about the accuracy or limitations of their interpretations.

2.06 UNQUALIFIED PERSONS   Psychologists do not promote the use of psychological assessment techniques by unqualified persons. (See also Standard 1.22, Delegation to and Supervision of Subordinates.)

2.07 OBSOLETE TESTS AND OUTDATED TEST RESULTS

(a) Psychologists do not base their assessment or intervention decisions or recommendations on data or test results that are outdated for the current purpose.

(b) Similarly, psychologists do not base such decisions or recommendations on tests and measures that are obsolete and not useful for the current purpose.

2.08 TEST SCORING AND INTERPRETATION SERVICES

(a) Psychologists who offer assessment or scoring procedures to other professionals accurately describe the purpose, norms, validity, reliability, and applications of the procedures and any special qualifications applicable to their use.

(b) Psychologists select scoring and interpretation services (including automated services) on the basis of evidence of the validity of the program and procedures as well as on other appropriate considerations.

(c) Psychologists retain appropriate responsibility for the appropriate application, interpretation, and use of assessment instruments, whether they score and interpret such tests themselves or use automated or other services.

2.09 EXPLAINING ASSESSMENT RESULTS   Unless the nature of the relationship is clearly explained to the person being assessed in advance and precludes provision of an explanation of results (such as in some organizational consulting, preemployment or security screenings, and forensic evaluations), psychologists ensure that an explanation of the results is provided using language that is reasonably understandable to the person assessed or to another legally authorized person on behalf of the client. Regardless of whether the scoring and interpretation are done by the psychologist, by assistants, or by automated or other outside services, psychologists take reasonable steps to ensure that appropriate explanations of results are given.

2.10 MAINTAINING TEST SECURITY   Psychologists make reasonable efforts to maintain the integrity and security of tests and other assessment techniques consistent with law, contractual obligations, and in a manner that permits compliance with the requirements of this Ethics Code. (See also Standard 1.02, Relationship of Ethics and Law.)

3. ADVERTISING AND OTHER PUBLIC STATEMENTS

3.01 DEFINITION OF PUBLIC STATEMENTS   Psychologists comply with this Ethics Code in public statements relating to their professional services, products, or publications or to the field of psychology. Public statements include but are not limited to paid or unpaid advertising, brochures, printed matter, directory listings, personal resumes or curricula vitae, interviews or comments for use in media, statements in legal proceedings, lectures and public oral presentations, and published materials.

3.02 STATEMENTS BY OTHERS
(a) Psychologists who engage others to create or place public statements that promote their professional practice, products, or activities retain professional responsibility for such statements.

(b) In addition, psychologists make reasonable efforts to prevent others whom they do not control (such as employers, publishers, sponsors, organizational clients, and representatives of the print or broadcast media) from making deceptive statements concerning psychologists' practice or professional or scientific activities.

(c) If psychologists learn of deceptive statements about their work made by others, psychologists make reasonable efforts to correct such statements.

(d) Psychologists do not compensate employees of press, radio, television, or other communication media in return for publicity in a news item.

(e) A paid advertisement relating to the psychologist's activities must be identified as such, unless it is already apparent from the context.

3.03 AVOIDANCE OF FALSE OR DECEPTIVE STATEMENTS
(a) Psychologists do not make public statements that are false, deceptive, misleading, or fraudulent, either because of what they state, convey, or suggest or because of what they omit, concerning their research, practice, or other work activities or those of persons or organizations with which they are affiliated. As examples (and not in limitation) of this standard, psychologists do not make false or deceptive statements concerning (1) their training, experience, or competence; (2) their academic degrees; (3) their credentials; (4) their institutional or association affiliations; (5) their services; (6) the scientific or clinical basis for, or results or degree of success of, their services; (7) their fees; or (8) their publications or research findings. (See also Standards 6.15, Deception in Research, and 6.18, Providing Participants with Information About the Study.)

(b) Psychologists claim as credentials for their psychological work, only degrees that (1) were carried from a regionally accredited educational institution or (2) were the basis for psychology licensure by the state in which they practice.

3.04 MEDIA PRESENTATIONS   When psychologists provide advice or comment by means of public lectures, demonstrations, radio or television programs, prerecorded tapes, printed articles, mailed material, or other media, they take reasonable precautions to ensure that (1) the statements are based on appropriate psychological literature and practice, (2) the statements are otherwise consistent with this Ethics Code, and (3) the recipients of the information are not encouraged to infer that a relationship has been established with them personally.

3.05 TESTIMONIALS   Psychologists do not solicit testimonials from current psychotherapy clients or patients or other persons who because of their particular circumstances are vulnerable to undue influence.

3.06 IN-PERSON SOLICITATION   Psychologists do not engage, directly or through agents, in uninvited in-person solicitation of business from actual or potential psychotherapy patients or clients or other persons who because of their particular circumstances are vulnerable to undue influence. However, this does not preclude attempting to implement appropriate collateral contacts with significant others for the purpose of benefiting an already engaged therapy patient.

4. THERAPY

4.01 STRUCTURING THE RELATIONSHIP

(a) Psychologists discuss with clients or patients as early as is feasible in the therapeutic relationship appropriate issues, such as the nature and anticipated course of therapy, fees, and confidentiality. (See also Standards 1.25, Fees and Financial Arrangements, and 5.01, Discussing the Limits of Confidentiality.)

(b) When the psychologist's work with clients or patients will be supervised, the above discussion includes that fact, and the name of the supervisor, when the supervisor has legal responsibility for the case.

(c) When the therapist is a student intern, the client or patient is informed of that fact.

(d) Psychologists make reasonable efforts to answer patients' questions and to avoid apparent misunderstandings about therapy. Whenever possible, psychologists provide oral and/or written information, using language that is reasonably understandable to the patient or client.

4.02 INFORMED CONSENT TO THERAPY

(a) Psychologists obtain appropriate informed consent to therapy or related procedures, using language that is reasonably understandable to participants. The content of informed consent will vary depending on many circumstances; however, informed consent generally implies that the person (1) has the capacity to consent, (2) has been informed of significant information concerning the procedure, (3) has freely and without undue influence expressed consent, and (4) consent has been appropriately documented.

(b) When persons are legally incapable of giving informed consent, psychologists obtain informed permission from a legally authorized person, if such substitute consent is permitted by law.

(c) In addition, psychologists (1) inform those persons who are legally incapable of giving informed consent about the proposed interventions in a manner commensurate with the persons' psychological capacities, (2) seek their assent to those interventions, and (3) consider such persons' preferences and best interests.

4.03 COUPLE AND FAMILY RELATIONSHIPS

(a) When a psychologist agrees to provide services to several persons who have a relationship (such as husband and wife or parents and children), the psychologist attempts to clarify at the outset (1) which of the individuals are patients or clients and (2) the relationship the psychologist will have with each person. This clarification includes the role of the psychologist and the probable uses of the services provided or the information obtained. (See also Standard 5.01, Discussing the Limits of Confidentiality.)

(b) As soon as it becomes apparent that the psychologist may be called on to perform potentially conflicting roles (such as marital counselor to husband and wife, and then witness for one party in a divorce proceeding), the psychologist attempts to clarify and adjust, or withdraw from, roles appropriately. (See also Standard 7.03, Clarification of Role, under Forensic Activities.)

4.04 PROVIDING MENTAL HEALTH SERVICES TO THOSE SERVED BY OTHERS   In deciding whether to offer or provide services to those already receiving mental health services elsewhere, psychologists carefully consider the treatment issues and the potential patient's or client's welfare. The psychologist discusses these issues with the patient or client, or another legally authorized person on behalf of the client, in order to minimize the risk of confusion and conflict, consults with the other service providers when appropriate, and proceeds with caution and sensitivity to the therapeutic issues.

4.05 SEXUAL INTIMACIES WITH CURRENT PATIENTS OR CLIENTS   Psychologists do not engage in sexual intimacies with current patients or clients.

4.06 THERAPY WITH FORMER SEXUAL PARTNERS   Psychologists do not accept as therapy patients or clients persons with whom they have engaged in sexual intimacies.

4.07 SEXUAL INTIMACIES WITH FORMER THERAPY PATIENTS

(a) Psychologists do not engage in sexual intimacies with a former therapy patient or client for at least two years after cessation or termination of professional services.

(b) Because sexual intimacies with a former therapy patient or client are so frequently harmful to the patient or client, and because such intimacies undermine public confidence in the psychology profession and thereby deter the public's use of needed services, psychologists do not engage in sexual intimacies with former therapy patients and clients even after a two-year interval except in the most unusual circumstances. The psychologist who engages in such activity after the two years following cessation or termination of treatment bears the burden of demonstrating that there has been no exploitation, in light of all relevant factors, including (1) the amount of time that has passed since therapy terminated, (2) the nature and duration of the therapy, (3) the circumstances of termination, (4) the patient's or client's personal history, (5) the patient's or client's current mental status, (6) the likelihood of adverse impact on the patient or client and others, and (7) any statements or actions made by the therapist during the course of therapy suggesting or inviting the possibility of a posttermination sexual or romantic relationship with the patient or client. (See also Standard 1.17, Multiple Relationships.)

4.08 INTERRUPTION OF SERVICES

(a) Psychologists make reasonable efforts to plan for facilitating care in the event that psychological services are interrupted by factors such as the psychologist's illness, death, unavailability, or relocation or by the client's relocation or financial limitations. (See also Standard 5.09, Preserving Records and Data.)

(b) When entering into employment or contractual relationships, psychologists provide for orderly and appropriate resolution of responsibility for patient or client care in the event that the employment or contractual relationship ends, with paramount consideration given to the welfare of the patient or client.

4.09 TERMINATING THE PROFESSIONAL RELATIONSHIP

(a) Psychologists do not abandon patients or clients. (See also Standard 1.25e, under Fees and Financial Arrangements.)

(b) Psychologists terminate a professional relationship when it becomes reasonably clear that the patient or client no longer needs the service, is not benefiting, or is being harmed by continued service.

(c) Prior to termination for whatever reason, except where precluded by the patient's or client's conduct, the psychologist discusses the patient's or client's views and needs, provides appropriate pretermination counseling, suggests alternative service providers as appropriate, and takes other reasonable steps to facilitate transfer of responsibility to another provider if the patient or client needs one immediately.

5. PRIVACY AND CONFIDENTIALITY

These Standards are potentially applicable to the professional and scientific activities of all psychologists.

5.01 DISCUSSING THE LIMITS OF CONFIDENTIALITY

(a) Psychologists discuss with persons and organizations with whom they establish a scientific or professional relationship (including, to the extent feasible, minors and their legal representatives) (1) the relevant limitations on confidentiality, including limitations where applicable in group, marital, and family therapy or in organizational consulting, and (2) the foreseeable uses of the information generated through their services.

(b) Unless it is not feasible or is contraindicated, the discussion of confidentiality occurs at the outset of the relationship and thereafter as new circumstances may warrant.

(c) Permission for electronic recording of interviews is secured from clients and patients.

5.02 MAINTAINING CONFIDENTIALITY   Psychologists have a primary obligation and take reasonable precautions to respect the confidentiality rights of those with whom they work or consult, recognizing that confidentiality may be established by law, institutional rules, or professional or scientific relationships. (See also Standard 6.26, Professional Reviewers.)

5.03 MINIMIZING INTRUSIONS ON PRIVACY

(a) In order to minimize intrusions on privacy, psychologists include in written and oral reports, consultations, and the like, only information germane to the purpose for which the communication is made.

(b) Psychologists discuss confidential information obtained in clinical or consulting relationships, or evaluative data concerning patients, individual or organizational clients, students, research participants, supervisees, and employees, only for appropriate scientific or professional purposes and only with persons clearly concerned with such matters.

5.04 MAINTENANCE OF RECORDS   Psychologists maintain appropriate confidentiality in creating, storing, accessing, transferring, and disposing of records under their control, whether these are written, automated, or in any other medium. Psychologists maintain and dispose of records in accordance with law and in a manner that permits compliance with the requirements of this Ethics Code.

5.05 DISCLOSURES

(a) Psychologists disclose confidential information without the consent of the individual only as mandated by law, or where permitted by law for a valid purpose, such as (1) to provide needed professional services to the patient or the individual or organizational client, (2) to obtain appropriate professional consultations, (3) to protect the patient or client or others from harm, or (4) to obtain payment for services, in which instance disclosure is limited to the minimum that is necessary to achieve the purpose.

(b) Psychologists also may disclose confidential information with the appropriate consent of the patient or the individual or organizational client (or of another legally authorized person on behalf of the patient or client), unless prohibited by law.

5.06 CONSULTATIONS   When consulting with colleagues, (1) psychologists do not share confidential information that reasonably could lead to the identification of a patient, client, research participant, or other person or organization with whom they have a confidential relationship unless they have obtained the prior consent of the person or organization or the disclosure cannot be avoided, and (2) they share information only to the extent necessary to achieve the purposes of the consultation. (See also Standard 5.02, Maintaining Confidentiality.)

5.07 Confidential Information in Databases

(a) If confidential information concerning recipients of psychological services is to be entered into databases or systems of records available to persons whose access has not been consented to by the recipient, then psychologists use coding or other techniques to avoid the inclusion of personal identifiers.

(b) If a research protocol approved by an institutional review board or similar body requires the inclusion of personal identifiers, such identifiers are deleted before the information is made accessible to persons other than those of whom the subject was advised.

(c) If such deletion is not feasible, then before psychologists transfer such data to others or review such data collected by others, they take reasonable steps to determine that appropriate consent of personally identifiable individuals has been obtained.

5.08 Use of Confidential Information for Didactic or Other Purposes

(a) Psychologists do not disclose in their writings, lectures, or other public media, confidential, personally identifiable information concerning their patients, individual or organizational clients, students, research participants, or other recipients of their services that they obtained during the course of their work, unless the person or organization has consented in writing or unless there is other ethical or legal authorization for doing so.

(b) Ordinarily, in such scientific and professional presentations, psychologists disguise confidential information concerning such persons or organizations so that they are not individually identifiable to others and so that discussions do not cause harm to subjects who might identify themselves.

5.09 Preserving Records and Data   A psychologist makes plans in advance so that confidentiality of records and data is protected in the event of the psychologist's death, incapacity, or withdrawal from the position or practice.

5.10 Ownership of Records and Data   Recognizing that ownership of records and data is governed by legal principles, psychologists take reasonable and lawful steps so that records and data remain available to the extent needed to serve the best interests of patients, individual or organizational clients, research participants, or appropriate others.

5.11 Withholding Records for Nonpayment   Psychologists may not withhold records under their control that are requested and imminently needed for a patient's or client's treatment solely because payment has not been received, except as otherwise provided by law.

6. Teaching, Training Supervision, Research, and Publishing

6.01 Design of Education and Training Programs   Psychologists who are responsible for education and training programs seek to ensure that the programs are competently designed, provide the proper experiences, and meet the requirements for licensure, certification, or other goals for which claims are made by the program.

6.02 Descriptions of Education and Training Programs

(a) Psychologists responsible for education and training programs seek to ensure that there is a current and accurate description of the program content, training goals and objectives, and requirements that must be met for satisfactory completion of the program. This information must be made readily available to all interested parties.

(b) Psychologists seek to ensure that statements concerning their course outlines are accurate and not misleading, particularly regarding the subject matter to be covered, bases for evaluating progress, and the nature of course experiences. (See also Standard 3.03, Avoidance of False or Deceptive Statements.)

(c) To the degree to which they exercise control, psychologists responsible for announcements, catalogs, brochures, or advertisements describing workshops, seminars, or other non–degree–granting educational programs ensure that they accurately describe the audience for which the program is intended, the educational objectives, the presenters, and the fees involved.

6.03 Accuracy and Objectivity in Teaching

(a) When engaged in teaching or training, psychologists present psychological information accurately and with a reasonable degree of objectivity.

(b) When engaged in teaching or training, psychologists recognize the power they hold over students or supervisees and therefore make reasonable efforts to avoid engaging in conduct that is personally demeaning to students or supervisees. (See also Standards 1.09, Respecting Others, and 1.12, Other Harassment.)

6.04 Limitation on Teaching   Psychologists do not teach the use of techniques or procedures that require specialized training, licensure, or expertise, including but not limited to hypnosis, biofeedback, and projective techniques, to individuals who lack the prerequisite training, legal scope of practice, or expertise.

6.05 Assessing Student and Supervisee Performance

(a) In academic and supervisory relationships, psychologists establish an appropriate process for providing feedback to students and supervisees.

(b) Psychologists evaluate students and supervisees on the basis of their actual performance on relevant and established program requirements.

6.06 Planning Research

(a) Psychologists design, conduct, and report research in accordance with recognized standards of scientific competence and ethical research.

(b) Psychologists plan their research so as to minimize the possibility that results will be misleading.

(c) In planning research, psychologists consider its ethical acceptability under the Ethics Code. If an ethical issue is unclear, psychologists seek to resolve the issue through consultation with institutional review boards, animal care and use committees, peer consultations, or other proper mechanisms.

(d) Psychologists take reasonable steps to implement appropriate protections for the rights and welfare of human participants, other persons affected by the research, and the welfare of animal subjects.

6.07 RESPONSIBILITY

(a) Psychologists conduct research competently and with due concern for the dignity and welfare of the participants.

(b) Psychologists are responsible for the ethical conduct of research conducted by them or by others under their supervision or control.

(c) Researchers and assistants are permitted to perform only those tasks for which they are appropriately trained and prepared.

(d) As part of the process of development and implementation of research projects, psychologists consult those with expertise concerning any special population under investigation or most likely to be affected.

6.08 COMPLIANCE WITH LAW AND STANDARDS   Psychologists plan and conduct research in a manner consistent with federal and state law and regulations, as well as professional standards governing the conduct of research, and particularly those standards governing research with human participants and animal subjects.

6.09 INSTITUTIONAL APPROVAL   Psychologists obtain from host institutions or organizations appropriate approval prior to conducting research, and they provide accurate information about their research proposals. They conduct the research in accordance with the approved research protocol.

6.10 RESEARCH RESPONSIBILITIES   Prior to conducting research (except research involving only anonymous surveys, naturalistic observations, or similar research), psychologists enter into an agreement with participants that clarifies the nature of the research and the responsibilities of each party.

6.11 INFORMED CONSENT TO RESEARCH

(a) Psychologists use language that is reasonably understandable to research participants in obtaining their appropriate informed consent (except as provided in Standard 6.12, Dispensing with Informed Consent). Such informed consent is appropriately documented.

(b) Using language that is reasonably understandable to participants, psychologists inform participants of the nature of the research; they inform participants that they are free to participate or to decline to participate or to withdraw from the research; they explain the foreseeable consequences of declining or withdrawing; they inform participants of significant factors that may be expected to influence their willingness to participate (such as risks, discomfort, adverse effects, or limitations on confidentiality, except as provided in Standard 6.15, Deception in Research); and they explain other aspects about which the prospective participants inquire.

(c) When psychologists conduct research with individuals such as students or subordinates, psychologists take special care to protect the prospective participants from adverse consequences of declining or withdrawing from participation.

(d) When research participation is a course requirement or opportunity for extra credit, the prospective participant is given the choice of equitable alternative activities.

(e) For persons who are legally incapable of giving informed consent, psychologists nevertheless (1) provide an appropriate explanation, (2) obtain the participant's assent, and (3) obtain appropriate permission from a legally authorized person, if such substitute consent is permitted by law.

6.12 DISPENSING WITH INFORMED CONSENT   Before determining that planned research (such as research involving only anonymous questionnaires, naturalistic observations, or certain kinds of archival research) does not require the informed consent of research participants, psychologists consider applicable regulations and institutional review board requirements, and they consult with colleagues as appropriate.

6.13 INFORMED CONSENT IN RESEARCH FILMING OR RECORDING   Psychologists obtain informed consent from research participants prior to filming or recording them in any form, unless the research involves simply naturalistic observations in public places and it is not anticipated that the recording will be used in a manner that could cause personal identification or harm.

6.14 OFFERING INDUCEMENTS FOR RESEARCH PARTICIPANTS

(a) In offering professional services as an inducement to obtain research participants, psychologists make clear the nature of the services, as well as the risks, obligations, and limitations. (See also Standard 1.18, Barter [with Patients or Clients]).

(b) Psychologists do not offer excessive or inappropriate financial or other inducements to obtain research participants, particularly when it might tend to coerce participation.

6.15 DECEPTION IN RESEARCH

(a) Psychologists do not conduct a study involving deception unless they have determined that the use of deceptive techniques is justified by the study's prospective scientific, educational, or applied value and that equally effective alternative procedures that do not use deception are not feasible.

(b) Psychologists never deceive research participants about significant aspects that would affect their willingness to participate, such as physical risks, discomfort, or unpleasant emotional experiences.

(c) Any other deception that is an integral feature of the design and conduct of an experiment must be explained to participants as early as is feasible, preferably at the conclusion of their participation, but no later than at the conclusion of the research. (See also Standard 6.18, Providing Participants with Information About the Study.)

6.16 SHARING AND UTILIZING DATA   Psychologists inform research participants of their anticipated sharing or further use of personally identifiable research data and of the possibility of unanticipated future uses.

6.17 MINIMIZING INVASIVENESS   In conducting research, psychologists interfere with the participants or milieu from which data are collected only in a manner that is warranted by an appropriate research design and that is consistent with psychologists' roles as scientific investigators.

6.18 PROVIDING PARTICIPANTS WITH INFORMATION ABOUT THE STUDY

(a) Psychologists provide a prompt opportunity for participants to obtain appropriate information about the nature, results, and conclusions of the research, and psychologists attempt to correct any misconceptions that participants may have.

(b) If scientific or humane values justify delaying or withholding this information, psychologists take reasonable measures to reduce the risk of harm.

6.19 HONORING COMMITMENTS   Psychologists take reasonable measures to honor all commitments they have made to research participants.

6.20 CARE AND USE OF ANIMALS IN RESEARCH

(a) Psychologists who conduct research involving animals treat them humanely.

(b) Psychologists acquire, care for, use, and dispose of animals in compliance with current federal, state, and local laws and regulations, and with professional standards.

(c) Psychologists trained in research methods and experienced in the care of laboratory animals supervise all procedures involving animals and are responsible for ensuring appropriate consideration of their comfort, health, and humane treatment.

(d) Psychologists ensure that all individuals using animals under their supervision have received instruction in research methods and in the care, maintenance, and handling of the species being used, to the extent appropriate to their role.

(e) Responsibilities and activities of individuals assisting in a research project are consistent with their respective competencies.

(f) Psychologists make reasonable efforts to minimize the discomfort, infection, illness, and pain of animal subjects.

(g) A procedure subjecting animals to pain, stress, or privation is used only when an alternative procedure is unavailable and the goal is justified by its prospective scientific, educational, or applied value.

(h) Surgical procedures are performed under appropriate anesthesia; techniques to avoid infection and minimize pain are followed during and after surgery.

(i) When it is appropriate that the animal's life be terminated, it is done rapidly, with an effort to minimize pain, and in accordance with accepted procedures.

6.21 REPORTING OF RESULTS

(a) Psychologists do not fabricate data or falsify results in their publications.

(b) If psychologists discover significant errors in their published data, they take reasonable steps to correct such errors in a correction, retraction, erratum, or other appropriate publication means.

6.22 PLAGIARISM

Psychologists do not present substantial portions or elements of another's work or data as their own, even if the other work or data source is cited occasionally.

6.23 PUBLICATION CREDIT

(a) Psychologists take responsibility and credit, including authorship credit, only for work they have actually performed or to which they have contributed.

(b) Principal authorship and other publication credits accurately reflect the relative scientific or professional contributions of the individuals involved, regardless of their relative status. Mere possession of an institutional position, such as Department Chair, does not justify authorship credit. Minor contributions to the research or to the writing for publications are appropriately acknowledged, such as in footnotes or in an introductory statement.

(c) A student is usually listed as principal author on any multiple-authored article that is substantially based on the student's dissertation or thesis.

6.24 DUPLICATE PUBLICATION OF DATA

Psychologists do not publish, as original data, data that have been previously published. This does not preclude republishing data when they are accompanied by proper acknowledgment.

6.25 SHARING DATA

After research results are published, psychologists do not withhold the data on which their conclusions are based from other competent professionals who seek to verify the substantive claims through reanalysis and who intend to use such data only for that purpose, provided that the confidentiality of the participants can be protected and unless legal rights concerning proprietary data preclude their release.

6.26 PROFESSIONAL REVIEWERS

Psychologists who review material submitted for publication, grant, or other research proposal review respect the confidentiality of and the proprietary rights in such information of those who submitted it.

7. FORENSIC ACTIVITIES

7.01 PROFESSIONALISM

Psychologists who perform forensic functions, such as assessments, interviews, consultations, reports, or expert testimony must comply with all other provisions of this Ethics Code to the extent that they apply to such activities. In addition, psychologists base their forensic work on appropriate knowledge of and competence in the areas underlying such work, including specialized knowledge concerning special populations. (See also Standards 1.06, Basis for Scientific and Professional Judgments; 1.08, Human Differences; 1.15, Misuse of Psychologists' Influence; and 1.23, Documentation of Professional and Scientific Work.)

7.02 FORENSIC ASSESSMENTS

(a) Psychologists' forensic assessments, recommendations, and reports are based on information and techniques (including personal interviews of the individual, when appropriate) sufficient to provide appropriate substantiation for their findings. (See also Standards 1.03, Professional and Scientific Relationship; 1.23, Documentation of Professional and Scientific Work; 2.01, Evaluation, Diagnosis, and Interventions in Professional Context; and 2.05, Interpreting Assessment Results.)

(b) Except as noted in (c), below, psychologists provide written or oral forensic reports or testimony of the psychological characteristics of an individual only after they have conducted an examination of the individual adequate to support their statements or conclusions.

(c) When, despite reasonable efforts, such an examination is not feasible, psychologists clarify the impact of their limited information on the reliability and validity of their reports and testimony, and they appropriately limit the nature and extent of their conclusions or recommendations.

7.03 CLARIFICATION OF ROLE   In most circumstances, psychologists avoid performing multiple and potentially conflicting roles in forensic matters. When psychologists may be called on to serve in more than one role in a legal proceeding—for example, as consultant or expert for one party or for the court and as a fact witness—they clarify role expectations and the extent of confidentiality in advance to the extent feasible, and thereafter as changes occur, in order to avoid compromising their professional judgment and objectivity and in order to avoid misleading others regarding their role.

7.04 TRUTHFULNESS AND CANDOR

(a) In forensic testimony and reports, psychologists testify truthfully, honestly, and candidly and, consistent with applicable legal procedures, describe fairly the bases for their testimony and conclusions.

(b) Whenever necessary to avoid misleading, psychologists acknowledge the limits of their data or conclusions.

7.05 PRIOR RELATIONSHIPS   A prior professional relationship with a party does not preclude psychologists from testifying as fact witnesses or from testifying to their services to the extent permitted by applicable law. Psychologists appropriately take into account ways in which the prior relationship might affect their professional objectivity or opinions and disclose the potential conflict to the relevant parties.

7.06 COMPLIANCE WITH LAW AND RULES   In performing forensic roles, psychologists are reasonably familiar with the rules governing their roles. Psychologists are aware of the occasionally competing demands placed upon them by these principles and the requirements of the court system, and attempt to resolve these conflicts by making known their commitment to this Ethics Code and taking steps to resolve the conflict in a responsible manner. (See also Standard 1.02, Relationship of Ethics and Law.)

8. Resolving Ethical Issues

8.01 Familiarity with Ethics Code Psychologists have an obligation to be familiar with this Ethics Code, other applicable ethics codes, and their application to psychologists' work. Lack of awareness or misunderstanding of an ethical standard is not itself a defense to a charge of unethical conduct.

8.02 Confronting Ethical Issues When a psychologist is uncertain whether a particular situation or course of action would violate this Ethics Code, the psychologist ordinarily consults with other psychologists knowledgeable about ethical issues, with state or national psychology ethics committees, or with other appropriate authorities in order to choose a proper response.

8.03 Conflicts Between Ethics and Organizational Demands If the demands of an organization with which psychologists are affiliated conflict with this Ethics Code, psychologists clarify the nature of the conflict, make known their commitment to the Ethics Code, and to the extent feasible, seek to resolve the conflict in a way that permits the fullest adherence to the Ethics Code.

8.04 Informal Resolution of Ethical Violations When psychologists believe that there may have been an ethical violation by another psychologist, they attempt to resolve the issue by bringing it to the attention of that individual if an informal resolution appears appropriate and the intervention does not violate any confidentiality rights that may be involved.

8.05 Reporting Ethical Violations If an apparent ethical violation is not appropriate for informal resolution under Standard 8.04 or is not resolved properly in that fashion, psychologists take further action appropriate to the situation, unless such action conflicts with confidentiality rights in ways that cannot be resolved. Such action might include referral to state or national committees on professional ethics or to state licensing boards.

8.06 Cooperating with Ethics Committees Psychologists cooperate in ethics investigations, proceedings, and resulting requirements of the APA or any affiliated state psychological association to which they belong. In doing so, they make reasonable efforts to resolve any issues as to confidentiality. Failure to cooperate is itself an ethics violation.

8.07 Improper Complaints Psychologists do not file or encourage the filing of ethics complaints that are frivolous and are intended to harm the respondent rather than to protect the public.

REFERENCES

Abramson, L. Y. (Ed.). (1988). *Social cognition and clinical psychology: A synthesis*. New York: Guilford Press.

Adler, P. A., & Adler, P. (1991). *Backboards and blackboards*. New York: Columbia University Press.

Adler, P. A., & Adler, P. (1994). Observational techniques. In N. K. Denzin & Y. S. Lincoln (Eds.), *Handbook of qualitative research* (pp. 377–392). Thousand Oaks, CA: Sage.

Albee, G. W. (1970). The uncertain future of clinical psychology. *American Psychologist, 25,* 1071–1080.

Aldenderfer, M. S., & Blashfield, R. K. (1984). *Cluster analysis*. Beverly Hills, CA: Sage.

Alexander, C. H., & Suzuki, L. A. (2001). Measurement of multicultural constructs: Integration and research directions. In J. G. Ponterotto, J. M. Casas, L. A. Suzuki, & C. M. Alexander (Eds.), *Handbook of multicultural counseling* (2nd ed., pp. 499–505). Thousand Oaks, CA: Sage.

Alexander, L. B., & Luborsky, L. (1986). The Penn Helping Alliance Scales. In L. S. Greenberg and W. M. Pinsof (Eds.), *The Psychotherapeutic Process: A Research Handbook* (pp. 325–366). New York: Guilford.

Alloy, L. B., & Abramson, L. Y. (1979). Judgment of contingency in depressed and nondepressed students: Sadder but wiser? *Journal of Experimental Psychology, 108,* 441–485.

Alvidrez, J., Azocar, F., & Miranda, J. (1996). Demystifying the concept of ethnicity for psychotherapy researchers. *Journal of Consulting and Clinical Psychology, 64,* 903–908.

American Cancer Society. (2003). *Cancer facts and figures*. Atlanta: Author.

American Counseling Association. (1995). *Code of ethics*. Washington, DC: Author.

American Counseling Association. (2005). *Code of ethics*. Alexandria, VA: Author.

American Psychological Association. (1983). *Publication manual of the American Psychological Association* (3rd ed.). Washington, DC: Author.

American Psychological Association. (1994). *Publication manual of the American Psychological Association* (4th ed.). Washington, DC: Author.

American Psychological Association. (2001). *Publication manual of the American Psychological Association* (5th ed.). Washington, DC: Author.

American Psychological Association. (2002). *Ethical principles of psychologists and code of conduct*. Washington, DC: Author.

American Psychological Association. (2003). Guidelines on multicultural education, training, research, practice, and organizational change for psychologists. *American Psychologist, 58,* 377–402.

American Psychological Association Ethics Committee. (1983, February 19). *Authorship guidelines for dissertation supervision*. Washington, DC: Author.

Andersen, B., & Anderson, W. (1985). Client perceptions of counselors using positive and negative self-involving statements. *Journal of Counseling Psychology, 32,* 462–465.

Anderson, J. R. (1983). *The architecture of cognition.* Cambridge, MA: Harvard University Press.

Anderson, W. P., & Heppner, P. P. (1986). Counselor applications of research findings to practice: Learning to stay current. *Journal of Counseling and Development, 65,* 152–155.

Anton, W. D., & Reed, J. R. (1991). *College adjustment scales.* Odessa, FL: Psychological Assessment Resources.

Areán, P. A., & Gallagher-Thompson, D. (1996). Issues and recommendations for the recruitment and retention of older ethnicity minority adults into clinical research. *Journal of Consulting and Clinical Psychology, 64,* 875–880.

Argyris, C. (1968). Some unintended consequences of rigorous research. *Psychological Bulletin, 70,* 185–197.

Arnold, C. L. (1992). An introduction to hierarchical linear models. *Measurement and Evaluation in Counseling and Development, 25,* 58–90.

Arredondo, P., Toporek, R., Brown, S. P., Sanchez, J., Locke, D. C., Sanchez, J., & Stadler, H. (1996). Operationalization of the multicultural counseling competencies. *Journal of Multicultural Counseling & Development, 24,* 42–78.

Asner-Self, K. K., & Marotta, S. A. (2005). Developmental indices among Central American immigrants exposed to war related trauma: Clinical implications for counselors. *Journal of Counseling and Development, 83,* 162–171.

Atkinson, D. (Ed.). (2004). *Counseling American minorities.* Boston, MA: McGraw-Hill.

Atkinson, D., & Hackett, G. (2004). *Counseling diverse populations.* Boston, MA: McGraw-Hill.

Atkinson, D. R. (1983). Ethnic similarity in counseling psychology: A review of the research. *The Counseling Psychologist, 11,* 79–92.

Atkinson, D. R., & Lowe, S. M. (1995). The role of ethnicity, cultural knowledge, and conventional techniques in counseling and psychotherapy. In J. G. Ponterotto, J. M. Casas, L. A. Suzuki, & C. M. Alexander (Eds.), *Handbook of multicultural counseling* (pp. 387–414). Thousand Oaks, CA: Sage.

Atkinson, D. R., Morten, G., & Sue, D. W. (Eds.). (1989). *Counseling American minorities: A cross-cultural perspective* (3rd ed.). Dubuque, IA: William C. Brown.

Atkinson, D. R., & Wampold, B. E. (1982). A comparison of the Counselor Rating Form and the Counselor Effectiveness Rating Scale. *Counselor Education and Supervision, 22,* 25–36.

Ayalon, L., & Young, M. (2003). A comparison of depressive symptoms in African Americans and Caucasian Americans. *Journal of Cross-Cultural Psychology, 34,* 111–124.

Azibo, D. A. (1988). Understanding the proper and improper usage of the comparative research framework. *Journal of Black Psychology, 15,* 81–91.

Babbie, E. (2001). *The practice of social research* (9th ed.). Belmont, CA: Wadsworth/Thomson Learning.

Babbie, E. R. (1979). *The practice of social research* (2nd ed.). Belmont, CA: Wadsworth.

Bakeman, R., & Gottman, J. M. (1986). *Observing interaction: An introduction to sequential analysis.* Cambridge: Cambridge University Press.

Baldwin, S. A., Murray, D. M., & Shadish, W. R. (2005). Empirically supported treatments or type I errors? Problems with the analysis of data from group-administered treatments. *Journal of Consulting and Clinical Psychology, 73,* 924–935.

Bamberger, M. (2000). *Integrating quantitative and qualitative research in development projects.* Washington, DC: World Bank.

Bangert, A. W. & Baumberger, J. P. (2005). Research designs and statistical techniques used in the *Journal of Counseling & Development,* 1990–2001. *Journal of Counseling & Development, 83,* 480–487.

Barak, A., & LaCrosse, M. B. (1975). Multidimensional perception of counselor behavior. *Journal of Counseling Psychology, 22,* 471–476.

Barber, J. P., & Crits-Christoph, P. (1996). Development of a therapist adherence competence rating scale for supportive-expressive dynamic psychotherapy: A prelimi-nary report. *Psychotherapy Research, 6,* 79–92.

Barber, J. P., Crits-Christoph, P., & Luborsky, L. (1996). Effects of therapist adherence and competence on patient outcome in brief dynamic therapy. *Journal of Consulting and Clinical Psychology, 64,* 619–622.

Barber, J. P., Gallop, R., Crits-Christoph, P., Frank, A., Thase, M. E., Weiss, R. D., et al., (2006). The role of therapist adherence, therapist competence, and alliance in predicting outcome of individual drug counseling: Results from the National Institute Drug Abuse Collaborative Cocaine Treatment Study. *Psychotherapy Research, 16,* 229–240.

Barber, T. X. (1976). *Pitfalls in human research: Ten pivotal points.* New York: Pergamon Press.

Barber, T. X., & Silver, M. J. (1968). Fact, fiction, and the experimenter bias effect. *Psychological Bulletin Monograph, 70,* 1–29.

Barkham, M., Andrew, R. M., & Culverwell, A. (1993). The California psychotherapy alliance scales: A pilot study of dimensions and elements. *British Journal of Medical Psychology, 66,* 157–165.

Barlow, D. H. (Ed.). (1981). *Behavioral assessment of adult disorders.* New York: Guilford Press.

Barlow, D. H., & Hersen, M. (1984). *Single case experimental designs: Strategies for studying behavior change* (2nd ed.). New York: Pergamon Press.

Baron, R. M., & Kenny, D. A. (1986). The moderator-mediator variable distinction in social psychological research: Conceptual, strategic, and statistical considerations. *Journal of Personality and Social Psychology, 51,* 1173–1182.

Barrett, K. A., & McWhirter, B. T. (2002). Counselor trainee's perceptions of clients based on client sexual orientation. *Counselor Education and Supervision, 41,* 219–232.

Barrett-Lennard, G. T. (1962). Dimensions of therapist response as causal factors in therapeutic change. *Psychological Monographs: General and Applied, 76,* Whole No. 562.

Baskin, T. W., Tierney, S. C., Minami, T., & Wampold, B. E. (2003). Establishing specificity in psychotherapy: A meta-analysis of structural equivalence of placebo controls. *Journal of Consulting and Clinical Psychology, 71,* 973–979.

Baumrind, D. (1976). *Nature and definition of informed consent in research involving deception.* Background paper prepared for the National Commission for the Protection of Human Subjects of Biomedical and Behavioral Research. Washington, DC: Department of Health, Education, and Welfare.

Beauchamp, T. L., & Childress, J. F. (2001). *Principles of biomedical ethics* (5th ed.). New York: Oxford University Press.

Beck, A. T., Rush, A. J., Shaw, B. F., & Emery, G. (1979). *Cognitive therapy of depression.* New York: Guilford Press.

Beck, A. T., Ward, C. H., Mendelson, M., Mock, J., & Erbaugh, J. (1961). An inventory for measuring depression. *Archives of General Psychiatry, 4,* 561–571.

Beck, K. A. (2005). Ethnographic decision tree modeling: A research method for counseling psychology. *Journal of Counseling Psychology, 52,* 243–249.

Bednar, R. L., & Kaul, T. J. (1978). Experiential group research: Current perspectives. In S. L. Garfield & A. E. Bergin (Eds.), *Handbook of psychotherapy and behavior change* (2nd ed., pp. 769–816). New York: Wiley.

Behrens, J. T. (1997). Does the white racial identity attitude scale measure racial identity? *Journal of Counseling Psychology, 44,* 3–12.

Behrens, J. T., Leach, M. M., Franz, S., & LaFleur, N. K. (1999, August). *Revising the Oklahoma racial attitudes scale: Work in progress.* Paper presented at the annual meeting of the American Psychological Association, Boston.

Belar, C. D., & Perry, N. W. (1992). National conference on scientist-practitioner education and training for the professional practice of psychology. *American Psychologist, 47,* 71–75.

Bem, D. J. (1995). Writing a review article for *Psychological Bulletin. Psychological Bulletin, 118,* 172–177.

Benjamin, L. S. (1974). Structural analysis of social behavior. *Psychological Review, 81,* 392–425.

Benn, S. I. (1967). Justice. In P. Edwards (Ed.), *The encyclopedia of philosophy* (Vol. 4, pp. 298–302). New York: Macmillan.

Bennum, I., Hahlweg, K., Schindler, L., & Langlotz, M. (1986). Therapist's and client's perceptions in behavior therapy: The development and cross-cultural analysis of an assessment instrument. *British Journal of Clinical Psychology, 25,* 275–283.

Berdie, R. F. (1972). The 1980 counselor: Applied behavioral scientist. *Personnel and Guidance Journal, 50,* 451–456.

Berg, I. A. (1954). Ideomotor response set: Symbolic sexual gesture in the counseling interview. *Journal of Counseling Psychology, 1,* 180–183.

Bergin, A. E., & Garfield, S. L. (Eds.). (1971). *Handbook of psychotherapy and behavior change.* New York: Wiley.

Bergin, A. E., & Garfield, S. L. (Eds.). (1994). *Handbook of psychotherapy and behavior change.* New York: Wiley.

Bergin, A. E., & Lambert, M. J. (1978). The evaluation of therapeutic outcomes. In S. L. Garfield & A. E. Bergin (Eds.), *Handbook of psychotherapy and behavior change* (2nd ed., pp. 139–190). New York: Wiley.

Bergin, A. E., & Strupp, H. H. (1970). New directions in psychotherapy research. *Journal of Abnormal Psychology, 76,* 13–26.

Berkowitz, A. D. (2003). Applications of Social Norms Theory to other health and social justice issues in H. W. Perkins (Ed.). *The Social Norms approach to preventing school and college substance abuse.* San Francisco: Jossey-Bass.

Bernard, J. M., & Goodyear, R. K. (1998). *Fundamentals of clinical supervision* (2nd ed.). Boston: Allyn & Bacon.

Bernstein, B. L., & Kerr, B. (1993). Counseling psychology and the scientist-practitioner model: Implementation and implications. *The Counseling Psychologist, 21,* 136–151.

Betancourt, H., & Lopez, S. R. (1993). The study of culture, ethnicity, and race in American psychology. *American Psychologist, 48,* 629–637.

Betz, N., & Fitzgerald, L. (1987). *The career psychology of women.* New York: Academic Press.

Betz, N. E. (1986). Research training in counseling psychology: Have we addressed the real issues? *The Counseling Psychologist, 14,* 107–113.

Betz, N. E., & Fitzgerald, L. F. (1993). Individuality and diversity: Theory and research in counseling psychology. *Annual Review of Psychology, 44,* 343–381.

Betz, N. E., & Hackett, G. (1981). The relationship of career-related self-efficacy expectations to perceived career options in college women and men. *Journal of Counseling Psychology, 28,* 399–410.

Betz, N. E., & Hackett, G. (1987). The concept of agency in educational and career development. *Journal of Counseling Psychology, 34,* 299–308.

Betz, N. E., & Taylor, K. M. (1982). Concurrent validity of the Strong-Campbell Interest Inventory for graduate students in counseling. *Journal of Counseling Psychology, 29,* 626–635.

Beutler, L. E., Brown, M. T., Crothers, L., Booker, K., & Seabrook, M. K. (1996). The dilemma of factitious demographic distinctions in psychological research. *Journal of Consulting and Clinical Psychology, 64,* 892–902.

Beutler, L. E., Moleiro, C. M., & Talebi, H. (2002). Resistance. In J. C. Norcross (Ed.), *Psychotherapy relationships that work: Therapist contributions and responsiveness to patients* (pp. 129–144). New York: Oxford University.

Bhaskar, R. (1975). *A realist theory of science.* Leeds, England: Leeds Books.

Bishop, J. B. (1992). The changing student culture: Implications for counselors and administrators. *Journal of College Student Psychotherapy, 6,* 37–57.

Blashfield, R. K. (1984). *The classification of psychopathology: Neo-Kraepelinian and quantitative approaches*. New York: Plenum.

Blos, P. (1946). Psychological counseling of college students. *American Journal of Orthopsychiatry, 16,* 571–580.

Bohus, M., Haaf, B., Simms, T., Limberger, M. F., Schmahl, C., Unckel, C., Lieb, K., & Linehan, M. M. (2004). Effectiveness of inpatient dialectical behavioral therapy for borderline personality disorder: A controlled trial. *Behaviour Research and Therapy, 42,* 487–499.

Bollen, K. A. (1989). *Structural equations with latent variables*. New York: John Wiley.

Bordin, E. S. (1965). Simplification as a research strategy in psychotherapy. *Journal of Consulting Psychology, 29,* 493–503.

Bordin, E. S. (1979). The generalizability of the psychoanalytic concept of working alliance. *Psychotherapy: Theory, Research and Practice, 16,* 252–260.

Borenstein, M., & Cohen, J. (1988). *Statistical power analysis: A computer program*. Hillsdale, NJ: Erlbaum.

Borgen, F. H. (1984a). Counseling psychology. *Annual Review of Psychology, 35,* 579–604.

Borgen, F. H. (1984b). Are there necessary linkages between research practices and the philosophy of science? *Journal of Counseling Psychology, 31,* 457–460.

Borgen, F. H. (1992). Expanding scientific paradigms in counseling psychology. In S. D. Brown & R. W. Lent (Eds.), *Handbook of counseling psychology* (2nd ed., pp. 111–139). New York: Wiley.

Borgen, F. H., & Barnett, D. C. (1987). Applying cluster analysis in counseling psychology research. *Journal of Counseling Psychology, 34,* 456–468.

Borgen, F. H., & Weiss, D. J. (1971). Cluster analysis and counseling research. *Journal of Counseling Psychology, 18,* 583–591.

Bracht, G. H., & Glass, V. V. (1968). The external validity of experiments. *American Educational Research Journal, 5,* 437–474.

Bradley, J. V. (1968). *Distribution-free statistical tests*. Englewood Cliffs, NJ: Prentice-Hall.

Brennan, K. A., Clark, C. L., & Shaver, P. R. (1998). Self-report measurement of adult attachment: An integrative overview. In J. A. Simpson & W. S. Rholes (Eds.), *Attachment theory and close relationships* (pp. 46–76). New York: Guilford Press.

Breuer, J., & Freud, S. (1955). Studies on hysteria. In J. Strachey (Ed. and Trans.), *The standard edition of the complete psychological works of Sigmund Freud* (Vol. 2). London: Hogarth Press. (Original work published 1893–1895.)

Bridgewater, C. A., Bornstein, P. H., & Walkenbach, J. (1981). Ethical issues and the assignment of publication credit. *American Psychologist, 36,* 524–525.

Brislin, R. W., Lonner, W. J., & Thorndike, R. M. (1973). *Cross-cultural research methods*. New York: Wiley.

Broad, W., & Wade, N. (1982). *Betrayers of the truth*. New York: Simon & Schuster.

Brock, T. C. (1967). Communication discrepancy and intent to persuade as determinants of counter-argument production. *Journal of Experimental Social Psychology, 3,* 269–309.

Brophy, J. E., & Good, T. L. (1974). *Teacher-student relationships: Causes and consequences*. New York: Holt, Rinehart & Winston.

Brotemarkle, R. A. (1927). College student personnel problems. *Journal of Applied Psychology, 11,* 415–436.

Brown, F. (1982). The ethics of psychodiagnostic assessment. In M. Rosenbaum (Ed.), *Ethics and values in psychotherapy*. New York: Free Press.

Brown, S. D., & Lent, R. W. (Eds.). (2000). *Handbook of counseling psychology* (3rd ed). New York: Wiley.

Brown, S. D., Lent, R. W., Ryan, N. E., & McPartland, E. B. (1996). Self-efficacy as an intervening mechanism between research training environments and scholarly productivity: A theoretical and methodological extension. *The Counseling Psychologist, 24,* 535–544.

Brown, S. D., & Krane, N. E. R. (2000). Four (or five) sessions and a cloud of dust: Old assumptions and new observations about career counseling. In S. D. Brown & R. W. Lent (Eds.), *Handbook of counseling psychology* (3rd ed., pp. 740–766). New York: Wiley.

Brown, W., & Holtzman, W. (1967). *Manual, survey of study habits and attitudes*. New York: The Psychological Corporation.

Bryk, A. S., & Raudenbush, S. W. (1992). *Hierarchical linear models: Applications and data analysis methods*. Newbury Park, CA: Sage.

Buboltz, W. C., Jr., Miller, M., & Williams, D. J. (1999). Content analysis of research in the *Journal of Counseling Psychology* (1973–1998). *Journal of Counseling Psychology, 46,* 496–503.

Buchler, J. (Ed.). (1955). *Philosophical writings of Peirce*. New York: Dover.

Burgoon, J. K., Beutler, L. E., Le Poire, B. A., Engle, D., Bergan, J., Salvio, M., & Mohr, D. C. (1993). Nonverbal indices of arousal in group therapy. *Psychotherapy, 30,* 635–645.

Burgoon, J. K., Kelly, D. L., Newton, D. A., & Keeley-Dyreson, M. P. (1989). The nature of arousal and nonverbal indices. *Human Communication Research, 16,* 217–255.

Burkard, A. W., & Knox, S. (2004). Effect of therapist color-blindness on empathy and attributions in cross-cultural counseling. *Journal of Counseling Psychology, 51,* 387–397.

Burns, B. D. (1981). *Feeling good: The new mood therapy*. New York: The New American Library.

Butler, S. F., Henry, W. P., & Strupp, H. H. (1992). *Measuring adherence and skill in time-limited dynamic psychotherapy*. Unpublished manuscript, Vanderbilt University.

Byrne, B. M., & Watkins, D. (2003). The issue of measurement invariance revisited. *Journal of Cross-Cultural Psychology, 34,* 155–175.

Campbell, A., Converse, P. E., Miller, W. E., & Stokes, D. E. (1990). *The American voter*. New York: Wiley.

Campbell, D. T., & Stanley, J. C. (1963). *Experimental and quasi-experimental designs for research.* Chicago: Rand McNally.

Campbell, L. M., III. (1973). A variation of thought stopping in a twelve-year-old boy: A case report. *Journal of Behavior Therapy and Experimental Psychiatry, 4,* 69–70.

Campbell, M. K., James, A., Hudson, M. A., Carr, C., Jackson, E., Oates, V., Demissie, S., Farrell, D., & Tessaro, I. (2004). Improving multiple behaviors for colorectal cancer prevention among African American church members. *Health Psychology, 23,* 492–502.

Caple, R. B. (1985). Counseling and the self-organization paradigm. *Journal of Counseling and Development, 64,* 173–178.

Carkhuff, R. R., & Burstein, J. W. (1970). Objective therapist and client ratings of therapist-offered facilitative conditions of moderate to low functioning therapist. *Journal of Clinical Psychology, 26,* 394–395.

Carney, C. G., & Barak, A. (1976). A survey of student needs and student personnel services. *Journal of College Student Personnel, 17,* 280–284.

Carter, R. (1995). *The influence of race and racial identity in psychotherapy: Toward a racially inclusive model.* New York: Wiley.

Casas, J. M. (2005). Race and racism: The efforts of counseling psychology to understand and address the issues associated with these terms. *The Counseling Psychologist, 33,* 501–512.

Casas, J. M., Ponterotto, J. G., & Gutierrez, J. M. (1986). An ethical indictment of counseling research and training: The cross-cultural perspective. *Journal of Counseling and Development, 64,* 347–349.

Chang, P. (1994). Effects of interviewer questions and response type on compliance: An analogue study. *Journal of Counseling Psychology, 41,* 74–82.

Chapman, L. J., & Chapman, J. P. (1969). Illusory correlations as an obstacle to the use of valid psychodiagnostic tests. *Journal of Abnormal Psychology, 74,* 271–280.

Charmaz, K. (2000). Grounded theory: Objectivist and constructivist

methods. In N. K. Denzin & Y. S. Lincoln (Eds.), *Handbook of qualitative research* (2nd ed., pp. 509–536). Thousand Oaks, CA: Sage.

Chartrand, J., Martin, W., Robbins, S., McAuliffe, G., Pickering, J., & Calliotte, J. (1994). Testing a level versus an interactional view of career indecision. *Journal of Career Assessment, 2,* 55–69.

Chen, C., Lee, S-Y., & Stevenson, H. W. (1995). Response style and cross-cultural comparisons of rating scales among East Asian and North American students. *Psychological Science, 6,* 170–175.

Cheng, S. K., Chong, G. H., & Wong, C. W. (1999). Chinese Frost Multidimensional Perfectionism Scale: A validation and prediction of self-esteem and psychological distress. *Journal of Clinical Psychology, 55,* 1051–1061.

Chia, R. C., Allred, L. J., & Jerzak, P. A. (1997). Attitudes toward women in Taiwan and China: Current status, problems, and suggestions for future research. *Psychology of Women Quarterly, 21,* 137–150.

Chickering, A. W. (1969). *Education and identity.* San Francisco: Jossey-Bass.

Christensen, L. B. (1980). *Experimental methodology* (2nd ed.). Boston: Allyn & Bacon.

Chwalisz, K. (2003). Evidence-based practice: A framework for the twenty-first century scientist practitioner training. *The Counseling Psychologist, 31,* 497–528.

Claiborn, C. D. (1982). Interpretation and change in counseling. *Journal of Counseling Psychology, 29,* 439–453.

Claiborn, C. D. (1985). Harold B. Pepinsky: A life of science and practice. *Journal of Counseling and Development, 64,* 5–13.

Claiborn, C. D. (1987). Science and practice: Reconsidering the Pepinskys. *Journal of Counseling and Development, 65,* 286–288.

Claiborn, C. D., & Lichtenberg, J. W. (1989). Interactional counseling. *The Counseling Psychologist, 17,* 355–453.

Cobb, A. K., & Hagemaster, J. N. (1987). Ten criteria for evaluating qualitative research proposals.

Journal of Nursing Education, 26(4), 138–143.

Cohen, J. (1968). Multiple regression as a general data-analytic strategy. *Psychological Bulletin, 70,* 426–443.

Cohen, J. (1988). *Statistical power analysis for the behavioral sciences* (2nd ed.). Hillsdale, NJ: Erlbaum.

Cohen, J., & Cohen, P. (1983). *Applied multiple regression/correlation analysis for the behavioral sciences* (2nd ed.). Hillsdale, NJ: Erlbaum.

Cohen, M. R., & Nagel, E. (1934). *An introduction to logic and scientific method.* New York: Harcourt, Brace & Company.

Cohen, R. J., Swerdlik, M. E., & Phillips, S. M. (1996). *Psychological testing and assessment: An introduction to tests and measurement.* Mountain View, CA: Mayfield.

Cokley, K. (2003a). What do we know about the motivation of African American students? Challenging the "anti-intellectual" myth. *Harvard Educational Review, 73,* 524–558.

Cokley, K. (2003b). *What do we really know about the academic motivation of African American college students? Challenging the "anti-intellectual" myth.* Presented at the 16th Annual National Conference on Race and Ethnicity, San Francisco, CA.

Cole, D. A. (1987). The utility of confirmatory factor analysis in test validation research. *Journal of Consulting and Clinical Psychology, 55,* 584–594.

Cole, D. A., Lazarick, D. L., & Howard, G. S. (1987). Construct validity and the relation between depression and social skill. *Journal of Counseling Psychology, 34,* 315–321.

Coleman, H. L. K., Wampold, B. E., & Casali, S. L. (1995). Ethnic minorities' ratings of ethnically similar and European American counselors: A meta-analysis. *Journal of Counseling Psychology, 42,* 55–64.

Condon, K. M., & Lambert, M. J. (1994, June). *Assessing clinical significance: Application to the State-Trait Anxiety Inventory.* Paper presented at the annual meeting of the Society for Psy-chotherapy Research, York, En-gland.

Constantine, M. G., Quintana, S. M., Leung, S. A., & Phelps, R. E. (1995). Survey of the professional needs of division 17's ethnic and racial minority psychologists. *The Counseling Psychologist, 23*, 546–561.

Cook, E. P. (1990). Gender and psychological distress. *Journal of Counseling and Development, 68*, 371–375.

Cook, T. D., & Campbell, D. T. (1979). *Quasi-experimentation: Design and analysis issues for field settings.* Boston: Houghton Mifflin.

Cooke, R. A. (1982). The ethics and regulation of research involving children. In B. B. Wolman (Ed.), *Handbook of developmental psychology.* Englewood Cliffs, NJ: Prentice-Hall.

Coopersmith, S. (1981). *SEI; self-esteem inventories.* Palo Alto, CA: Consulting Psychologists Press.

Corazzini, J. (1980). The theory and practice of loss therapy. In B. Mark Schoenberg (Ed.), *Bereavement counseling: A multi-disciplinary handbook* (pp. 71–85). Westport, CT: Greenwood Press.

Corning, A. F. (2002). Self-esteem as a moderator between perceived discrimination and psychological distress among women. *Journal of Counseling Psychology, 49*, 117–126.

Corrigan, J. D., Dell, D. M., Lewis, K. N., & Schmidt, L. D. (1980). Counseling as a social influence process: A review [monograph]. *Journal of Counseling Psychology, 27*, 395–441.

Corrigan, J. D., & Schmidt, L. D. (1983). Development and validation of revisions in the counselor rating form. *Journal of Counseling Psychology, 30*, 64–75.

Cournoyer, R. J., & Mahalik, J. R. (1995). Cross-sectional study of gender role conflict examining college-aged and middle-aged men. *Journal of Counseling Psychology, 42*, 11–19.

Creswell, J. W. (1994). *Research design: Qualitative and quantitative approaches.* Thousand Oaks, CA: Sage.

Creswell, J. W. (1998). *Qualitative inquiry and research design: Choosing among five traditions.* Thousand Oaks, CA: Sage.

Creswell, J. W. (2003). *Research design: Quantitative, qualitative, and mixed methods approaches* (2nd Ed.). Thousand Oaks, CA: Sage.

Crews, J., Smith, M. R., Smaby, M. H., Maddux, C. D., Torres-Rivera, E., Casey, J. A., & Urbani, S. (2005). Self-monitoring and counseling skills-based versus Interpersonal Process Recall Training. *Journal of Counseling and Development, 83*, 78–85.

Crites, J. O. (1978). *Career maturity inventory.* Monterey, CA: McGraw-Hill.

Crits-Christoph, P., Baranackie, K., Kurcias, J. S., Beck, A. T., Carroll, K., Perry, K., Luborsky, L., McLellan, A. T., Woody, G. E., Thompson, L., Gallagher, D., & Zitrin, C. (1991). Meta-analysis of therapist effects in psychotherapy outcome studies. *Psychotherapy Research, 1*, 81–91.

Crits-Christoph, P., Siqueland, L., Chittams, J., Barber, J. P., Beck, A. T., Frank, A., Liese, B., Luborsky, L., Mark, D. M. D., Onken, L. S., Najavits, L. M., Thase, M. E., & Woody, G. (1988). Training in cognitive, supportive-expressive, and drug counseling therapies for cocaine dependence. *Journal of Consulting and Clinical Psychology, 66*, 484–492.

Crosbie, J. (1993). Interrupted time series analysis with brief single subject data. *Journal of Consulting and Clinical Psychology, 61*, 966–974.

Cross, W. E. (1971). The Negro to black conversion experience: Toward a psychology of black liberation. *Black World, 20*(9), 13–27.

Cross, W. E. (1978). The Cross and Thomas models of psychological nigrescence. *Journal of Black Psychology, 5*(1), 13–19.

Cross, W. E., & Vandiver, B. J. (2001). Nigrescence theory and measurement: Introducing the cross racial identity scale (CRIS). In J. G. Ponterotto, J. M. Casas, L. A. Suzuki, & C. A. Alexander (Eds.), *Handbook of multicultural counseling* (2nd ed., pp. 425–456). Thousand Oaks, CA: Sage.

Cummings, A. L. (1989). Relationship of client problem type to novice counselor response modes. *Journal of Counseling Psychology, 36*, 331–335.

Cummings, A. L., Martin, J., Halberg, E., & Slemon, A. (1992). Memory for therapeutic events, session effectiveness, and working alliance in short-term counseling. *Journal of Counseling Psychology, 39*, 306–312.

Daniels, L. K. (1976). An extension of thought stopping in the treatment of obsessional thinking. *Behavior Therapy, 7*, 131.

Danskin, D. G., & Robinson, F. P. (1954). Differences in "degree of lead" among experienced counselors. *Journal of Counseling Psychology, 1*, 78–83.

Dar, R. (1987). Another look at Meehl, Lakatos, and the scientific practices of psychologists. *American Psychologist, 42*, 145–151.

Daus, J. A., III. (1995). *Changes in counseling efficacy across a semester of group supervision: A time series analysis.* Unpublished doctoral dissertation, University of Missouri, Columbia.

Dawis, R. V. (1987). Scale construction. *Journal of Counseling Psychology, 34*, 481–489.

Dawis, R. V. (2000). Scale construction and psychometric considerations. In H. E. A. Tinsley & S. D. Brown (Eds.), *Handbook of applied multivariate statistics and mathematical modeling* (pp. 65–94). San Diego, CA: Academic Press.

Day, S., & Schneider, P. L. (2002). Psychotherapy using distance technology: A comparison of face to face, video, and audio treatment. *Journal of Counseling Psychology, 49*, 499–503.

Deffenbacher, J. L., & Stark, R. S. (1992). Relaxation and cognitive-relaxation treatment of general anger. *Journal of Counseling Psychology, 39*, 158–167.

Deffenbacher, J. L., Thwaites, G. A., Wallace, T. L., & Oetting, E. R. (1994). Social skills and cognitive-relaxation approaches to general anger reduction. *Journal of Counseling Psychology, 41*, 386–396.

Delgado-Romero, E. A., Galván, N., & Maschino, P. (2005). Race and ethnicity in empirical counseling and counseling psychology research: A 10-year review. *The Counseling Psychologist, 33*, 419–448.

Dennin, M. K., & Ellis, M. V. (2003). Effects of a method of self-supervision for counselor trainees. *Journal of Counseling Psychology, 50,* 69–83.

Denzin, N. K. (1978). *The research act: A theoretical introduction to sociological methods.* New York: McGraw-Hill.

Denzin, N. K. (1997). Coffee with Anselm. *Qualitative family research, 11,* 16–18.

Denzin, N. K., & Lincoln, Y. S. (Eds.). (1998). *The landscape of qualitative research: Theories and issues.* Thousand Oaks, CA: Sage.

Denzin, N. K., & Lincoln, Y. S. (Eds.). (2000). *Handbook of qualitative research* (2nd ed.). Thousand Oaks, CA: Sage.

Department of Health and Human Services. (1989). Responsibilities of awardee and applicant institutions for dealing with and reporting possible misconduct in science. *Federal Register, 54*(151), 32446–32451.

DeProspero, A., & Cohen, S. (1979). Inconsistent visual analysis of intra-subject data. *Journal of Applied Behavior Analysis, 12,* 573–579.

Derogatis, L. R. (1983). *SCL-90-R administration, scoring and procedures manual.* Towson, MD: Clinical Psychiatric Research.

Derogatis, L. R. (1992). *The Brief Symptom Inventory (BSI): Administration, scoring, and procedures manual II.* Baltimore, MD: Clinical Psychometric Research.

DeRubeis, R. J., Hollon, S. E., Evans, M. D., & Bemis, K. M. (1982). Can psychotherapies for depression be discriminated? A systematic investigation of cognitive therapy and interpersonal therapy. *Journal of Consulting and Clinical Psychology, 50,* 744–756.

DeSena, P. A. (1966). Problems of consistent over-, under-, and normal-achieving college students as identified by the Mooney Problem Checklist. *Journal of Educational Research, 59,* 351–355.

DeVellis, R. F. (2003). *Applied social research methods* (Vol. 26). Thousand Oaks, CA: Sage.

Dhami, M. K., Hertwig, R., & Hoffrage, U. (2004). The role of representative design in an ecological approach to cognition. *Psychological Bulletin, 130,* 959–988.

Diener, E., & Crandall, R. (1978). *Ethics in social and behavioral research.* Chicago: University of Chicago Press.

Dillman, D. A. (2000). *Mail and Internet surveys: The tailored design method* (2nd ed.). New York: John Wiley & Sons.

Dillon, F. R., & Worthington, R. L. (2003). The Lesbian, Gay, and Bisexual Affirmative Counseling Self-Efficacy Inventory (LGB-CSI): Development, validation, and training implication. *Journal of Counseling Psychology, 50,* 235–251.

Dill-Standifond, T. J., Stiles, W. B., & Rorer, L. G. (1988). Counselor-client agreement on session impact. *Journal of Counseling Psychology, 35,* 47–55.

Dipboye, W. J. (1954). Analysis of counselor style by discussion units. *Journal of Counseling Psychology, 1,* 21–26.

Dixon, D. N., & Claiborn, C. D. (1981). Effects of need and commitment on career exploration behaviors. *Journal of Counseling Psychology, 28,* 411–415.

Dixon, D. N., & Glover, J. A. (1984). *Counseling: A problem-solving approach.* New York: Wiley.

Dixon, D. N., Heppner, P. P., Petersen, C. H., & Ronning, R. R. (1979). Problem-solving workshop training. *Journal of Counseling Psychology, 26,* 133–139.

Dixon, W. A. (1989). *Self-appraised problem solving ability, stress, and suicide ideation in a college population.* Unpublished masters thesis, University of Missouri, Columbia.

Dolliver, R. H. (1969). Strong vocational blank versus expressed vocational interests: A review. *Psychological Bulletin, 72,* 95–107.

Dorn, F. J. (1985). *Publishing for professional development.* Muncie, IN: Accelerated Development.

Dorn, F. J. (Ed.). (1986). *Social influence processes in counseling and psychotherapy.* Springfield, IL: Charles C Thomas.

Dorn, F. J. (1988). Utilizing social influence in career counseling: A case study. *Career Development Quarterly, 36,* 269–280.

Doss, B. D., Thum, Y. M., Sevier, M., Atkins, D. C., & Christensen, A. (2005). Improving relationships: Mechanisms of change in couple therapy. *Journal of Consulting and Clinical Psychology, 73,* 624–633.

Douglas, J. D. (1985). *Creative interviewing.* Thousand Oaks, CA: Sage.

Dovidio, J. F., Gaertner, S. L., Kawakami, K., & Hodson, G. (2002). Why can't we just get along? Interpersonal biases and interracial distrust. *Cultural Diversity and Ethnic Minority Psychology, 8,* 88–102.

Dowd, E. T., & Boroto, D. R. (1982). Differential effects of counselor self-disclosure, self-involving statements, and interpretation. *Journal of Counseling Psychology, 29,* 8–13.

Drane, J. F. (1982). Ethics and psychotherapy: A philosophical perspective. In M. Rosenbaum (Ed.), *Ethics and values in psychotherapy: A guidebook* (pp. 15–50). New York: Free Press.

Drew, C. F. (1980). *Introduction to designing and conducting research* (2nd ed.). St. Louis: C. V. Mosby.

Edgington, E. (1982). Nonparametric tests for single-subject multiple schedule experiments. *Behavioral Assessment, 4,* 83–91.

Edgington, E. S. (1980). *Randomization tests.* New York: Marcel Dekker.

Edgington, E. S. (1987). Randomized single-subject experiments and statistical tests. *Journal of Counseling Psychology, 34,* 437–442.

Elder, N. C., & Miller, W. L. (1995). Reading and evaluating qualitative research studies. *The Journal of Family Practice, 41*(3), 279–285.

Elkin, I., Falconnier, L. Martinovich, Z., & Mahoney, C. (2006). Therapist effects in the National Institute of Mental Health Treatment of Depression Collaborative Research Program. *Psychotherapy Research, 16,* 144–160.

Elkin, I., Shea, M. T., & Watkins, J. T. (1989). National Institute of Mental Health Treatment of Depression Collaborative Research Program: General effectiveness of treatments. *Archives of General Psychiatry, 46,* 971–982.

Elliot, R., & Wexler, M. M. (1994). Measuring the impact of sessions in process-experiential therapy of depression: The session impacts scale. *Journal of Counseling Psychology, 41,* 166–174.

Elliott, E. (1989). Comprehensive process analysis: Understanding the change process in significant therapy events. In M. J. Packer & R. B. Addison (Eds.), *Entering the circle: Hermeneutic investigation in psychology* (pp. 165–184). Albany, New York: State University of New York Press.

Elliott, E., Fischer, C. T., & Rennie, D. L. (1999). Evolving guidelines for publication of qualitative research studies in psychology and related fields. *British Journal of Clinical Psychology, 38,* 215–229.

Elliott, R. (1979). How clients perceive helper behaviors. *Journal of Counseling Psychology, 26,* 285–294.

Elliott, R. (1985). Helpful and nonhelpful events in brief counseling interviews: An empirical taxonomy. *Journal of Counseling Psychology, 32,* 307–322.

Elliott, R. (1988, June). Issues in the selection, training, and management of raters. In R. Moras & C. E. Hill (Co-chairs), *Selecting raters for psychotherapy process research.* Workshop conducted at the Society for Psychotherapy Research, Santa Fe, NM.

Elliott, R. (1991). Five dimensions of therapy process. *Psychotherapy Research, 1,* 92–103.

Elliott, R., Hill, C. E., Stiles, W. B., Friedlander, M. L., Mahrer, A. R., & Margison, F. R. (1987). Primary therapist response modes: Comparison of six rating systems. *Journal of Consulting and Clinical Psychology, 55,* 218–223.

Elliott, R., & James, E. (1989). Varieties of client experience in psychotherapy: An analysis of the literature. *Clinical Psychology Review, 9,* 443–467.

Elliott, R., James, E., Reimschuessel, C., Cislo, D., & Sack, N. (1985). Significant events and the analysis of immediate therapeutic impacts. *Psychotherapy, 22,* 620–630.

Elliott, R., & Shapiro, D. A. (1988). Brief structured recall: A more efficient method for studying significant therapy events. *British Journal of Medical Psychology, 61,* 141–153.

Elliott, R., Shapiro, D. A., Firth-Cozens, J., Stiles, W. B., Hardy, G. E., Llewelyn, S. P., & Margison, F. R. (1994). Comprehensive process analysis of insight events in cognitive-behavioral and psychodynamic-interpersonal psychotherapies. *Journal of Counseling Psychology, 41,* 449–463.

Ellis, A. (1962). *Reason and emotion in psychotherapy.* New York: Lyle Stuart.

Ellis, J. V., Robbins, E. S., Shult, D., Ladany, N., & Banker, J. (1990). Anchoring errors in clinical judgments: Type I error, adjustment, or mitigation. *Journal of Counseling Psychology, 37,* 343–351.

Ellis, M. V., Ladany, N., Krengel, M., & Schult, D. (1996). Clinical supervision research from 1981 to 1993: A methodological critique. *Journal of Counseling Psychology, 43,* 35–50.

Enns, C. Z., McNeilly, C. L., Corkery, J. M., & Gilbert, M. S. (1995). The debate about delayed memories of child sexual abuse: A feminist perspective. *The Counseling Psychologist, 23,* 181–279.

Erdur, O., Rude, S. S., & Baron, A. (2003). Symptom improvement and length of treatment in ethically similar and dissimilar client-therapist pairings. *Journal of Counseling Psychology, 50,* 52–58.

Erickson, C. D., & Al-Timimi, N. R. (2001). Providing mental health services to Arab Americans: Recommendations and considerations. *Cultural Diversity and Ethnic Minority Psychology, 7,* 308–327.

Ericsson, K. A., & Simon, H. A. (1984). *Protocol analysis: Verbal reports as data.* Cambridge, MA: MIT Press.

Eugster, S. L., & Wampold, B. E. (1996). Systematic effects of participant role on evaluation of the psychotherapy session. *Journal of Consulting and Clinical Psychology, 64,* 1020–1028.

Exner, J. E., Jr. (1974). *The Rorschach: A comprehensive system* (Vol. 1). New York: Wiley.

Eysenck, H. J. (1952). The effects of psychotherapy: An evaluation. *Journal of Consulting Psychology, 16,* 319–324.

Eysenck, H. J. (1960). *Behavior therapy and the neuroses.* Oxford: Pergamon Press.

Eysenck, H. J. (1961). The effects of psychotherapy. In H. J. Eysenck (Ed.), *Handbook of abnormal psychology* (pp. 697–725). New York: Basic Books.

Eysenck, H. J. (1965). The effects of psychotherapy. *International Journal of Psychology, 1,* 97–178.

Eysenck, H. J. (1969). *The effects of psychotherapy.* New York: Science House.

Fabrigar, L. R., Wegener, D. T., MacCallum. R. C., & Strahan, E. J. (1999). Evaluating the use of exploratory factor analysis in psychological research. *Psychological Methods, 4,* 272–299.

Fagley, N. S. (1985). Applied statistical power analysis and the interpretation of non-significant results by research consumers. *Journal of Counseling Psychology, 32,* 391–396.

Farmer, H. (1985). Model of career and achievement motivation for women and men. *Journal of Counseling Psychology, 32,* 363–390.

Farmer, H. S., Wardrop, J. L., Anderson, M. Z., & Risinger, R. (1995). Women's career choices: Focus on science, math, and technology careers. *Journal of Counseling Psychology, 42,* 155–170.

Farrell, A. D. (1999). Evaluation of the Computerized Assessment System for Psychotherapy Evaluation and Research (CASPER) as a measure of treatment effectiveness in an outpatient training clinic. *Psychological Assessment, 11,* 345–358.

Fassinger, R. (1990). Causal models of career choice in two samples of college women. *Journal of Vocational Behavior, 36,* 225–248.

Fassinger, R. E. (1987). Use of structural equation modeling in couseling psychology research. *Jour- nal of Counseling Psychology, 34,* 425–436.

Fassinger, R. E. (2005). Paradigms, praxis, problems, and promise: Grounded theory in counseling psychology research. *Journal of Counseling Psychology, 52(2),* 156–166.

Fassinger, R. E., & Richie, B. S. (1997). Sex matters: Gender and sexual orientation in training for multicultural counseling competency. In D. B. Pope-Davis & H. L. K. Coleman (Eds.), *Multicultural counseling competencies: Assessment, education and training, and supervision* (pp. 83–110). Thousand Oaks, CA: Sage.

Feldman, D. A., Strong, S. R., & Danser, D. B. (1982). A comparison of paradoxical and nonparadoxical interpretations and directives. *Journal of Counseling Psychology, 29,* 572–579.

Fine, M. (1992). *Disruptive voices: The possibilities of feminist research.* Ann Arbor, MI: University of Michigan Press.

Fisher, A. R., & Moradi, B. (2001). Racial and ethnic identity: Recent development and needed directions. In J. Ponterotto, J. Casas, L. Suzuki, & C. Alexander (Eds.), *Handbook of multicultural counseling* (pp. 341–370). Thousand Oaks, CA: Sage.

Fiske, S. T., & Taylor, S. E. (1984). *Social cognition.* Reading, MA: Addison-Wesley.

Fitzpatrick, J., Sanders, J., & Worthen, B. (2004). *Program evaluation: Alternative approaches and practical guidelines.* Boston: Pearson/Allyn & Bacon.

Flaherty, J. A., Gaviria, F. M., Pathak, D., Mitchell, T., Wintrob, R., & Richman, J. A. (1988). Developing instruments for cross-cultural psychiatric research. *Journal of Nervous and Mental Disorders, 176,* 257–263.

Flaskerud, J. H., & Nyamathi, A. M. (2000). Collaborative inquiry with low-income Latina women. *Journal of Health Care for the Poor and Underserved, 11,* 326–342.

Foa, E. B., Ehlers, A., Clark, D. M., Tolin, D. F., & Orsillo, S. M. (1999). The Posttraumatic Cognitions Inventory (PTCI): Development and validation. *Psychological Assessment, 11,* 303–314.

Foa, E. B., & Rauch, S. A. (2004). Cognitive changes during prolonged exposure versus prolonged exposure plus cognitive restructuring in female assault survivors with posttraumatic stress disorder. *Journal of Consulting and Clinical Psychology, 72,* 879–884.

Folger, R. (1989). Significance tests and the duplicity of binary decisions. *Psychological Bulletin, 106,* 155–160.

Folkman, S., & Lazarus, R. S. (1980). An analysis of coping in a middle-aged community sample. *Journal of Health and Social Behavior, 21,* 219–239.

Fong, M. L. (1992). When a survey isn't research. *Counselor Education and Supervision, 31,* 194–195.

Fong, M. L., & Malone, C. M. (1994). Defeating ourselves: Common errors in counseling research. *Counselor Education and Supervision, 33,* 356–362.

Fontana, A., & Frey, J. H. (1994). Interviewing: The art of science. In N. K. Denzin & Y. S. Lincoln (Eds.), *Handbook of qualitative research* (pp. 361–376). Thousand Oaks, CA: Sage.

Fontana, A., & Frey, J. H. (2000). The interviewing: From structured questions to negotiated text. In N. K. Denzin & Y. S. Lincoln (Eds.), *Handbook of qualitative research* (2nd ed., pp. 645–672). Thousand Oaks, CA: Sage.

Ford, D. H. (1984). Reexamining guiding assumptions: Theoretical and methodological implications. *Journal of Counseling Psychology, 31,* 461–466.

Forgy, E. W., & Black, J. D. (1954). A follow-up after three years of clients counseled by two methods. *Journal of Counseling Psychology, 1,* 1–8.

Forum Qualitative Sozialforschung (n.d.). Retrieved September 20, 2006, from http://www.qualitative-research.net/fqs/fqs-eng.htm

Fouad, N. A. (2002). Cross-cultural differences in vocational interests: Between-group differences on the Strong Interest Inventory. *Journal of Counseling Psychology, 49,* 283–289.

Fouad, N. A., Cudeck, R., & Hansen, J. (1984). Convergent validity of Spanish and English forms of the Strong-Campbell Interest Inventory for bilingual Hispanic high school students. *Journal of Counseling Psychology, 31,* 339–348.

Fouad, N. A., & Mohler, C. J. (2004). Cultural validity of Holland's theory and the Strong Interest Inventory for five racial/ethnic groups. *Journal of Career Assessment, 12,* 423–439.

Fowler, F. (2002). *Survey research methods* (3rd ed.). Thousand Oaks, CA: Sage.

Francis, D. J., Fletcher, J. M., Stuebing, K. K., Davidson, K. C., & Thompson, N. M. (1991). Analysis of change: Modeling individual growth. *Journal of Consulting and Clinical Psychology, 59,* 27–37.

Frank, G. (1984). The Boulder model: History, rationale, and critique. *Professional Psychology: Research and Practice, 15,* 417–435.

Frank, J. D. (1961). *Persuasion and healing: A comparative study of psychotherapy.* Baltimore: Johns Hopkins University Press.

Frank, J. D. (1974). Therapeutic components of psychotherapy. *Journal of Nervous and Mental Disease, 159,* 325–342.

Frankena, W. K. (1963). *Ethics.* Englewood Cliffs, NJ: Prentice-Hall.

Frankenberg, R. (1993). *White women, race matters: The social construction of whiteness.* Minneapolis: University of Minnesota Press.

Frazier, P. A., Tix, A. P., & Barron, K. E. (2004). Testing moderator and mediator effects in counseling psychology research. *Journal of Counseling Psychology, 51,* 115–134.

Fremont, S., & Anderson, W. P. (1986). What client behaviors make counselors angry? An exploratory study. *Journal of Counseling and Development, 65,* 67–70.

Fretz, B. R. (1982). Perspective and definitions. *The Counseling Psychologist, 10,* 15–19.

Friedlander, M. L., Ellis, M. V., Siegel, S. M., Raymond, L., Haase, R. F., & Highlen, P. S. (1988). Generalizing from segments to sessions: Should it be done? *Journal of Counseling Psychology, 35,* 243–250.

Friedlander, M. L., Heatherington, L., Johnson, B., & Showron, E. A. (1994). Sustaining engagement: A change event in family therapy. *Journal of Counseling Psychology, 41,* 438–448.

Friedlander, M. L., & Schwartz, G. S. (1985). Toward a theory of self-presentation in counseling and psychotherapy. *Journal of Counseling Psychology, 32,* 483–501.

Friedlander, M. L., Siegel, S. M., & Brenock, K. (1989). Parallel processes in counseling and supervision: A case study. *Journal of Counseling Psychology, 36,* 149–157.

Friedlander, M. L., Thibodeau, J. R., Nichols, M. P., Tucker, C., &

Snyder, J. (1985). Introducing semantic cohesion analysis: A study of group talk. *Small Group Behavior, 16*, 285–302.

Friedlander, M. L., Thibodeau, J. R., & Ward, L. G. (1985). Discriminating the "good" from the "bad" therapy hour: A study of dyadic interaction. *Psychotherapy, 22*, 631–642.

Friedman, N. (1967). *The social nature of psychological research.* New York: Basic Books.

Friesen, W. V., & Ekman, P. (1984). *EMFACS-7: Emotional facial action coding system.* Unpublished manual.

Frontman, K. C., & Kunkel, M. A. (1994). A grounded theory of counselors' construal of success in the initial session. *Journal of Counseling Psychology, 41*, 492–499.

Frost, R. O., Marten, P. A., Lahart, C., & Rosenblate, R. (1990). The dimensions of perfectionism. *Cognitive Therapy & Research, 14*, 449–468.

Fuhriman, A., & Burlingame, G. M. (1990). Consistency of matter: A comparative analysis of individual and group process variables. *The Counseling Psychologist, 18*, 6–63.

Fukuyama, M. (1990). Taking a universal approach to multicultural counseling. *Counselor Education & Supervision, 30*, 6–17.

Fuller, F., & Hill, C. E. (1985). Counselor and helpee perceptions of counselor intentions in relation to outcome in a single counseling session. *Journal of Counseling Psychology, 32*, 329–338.

Furlong, M. J., & Wampold, B. E. (1982). Intervention effects and relative variation as dimensions in experts' use of visual inference. *Journal of Applied Behavior Analysis, 15*, 415–421.

Furnham, A., & Procter, E. (1988). *The multi-dimensional Just World Belief Scale.* [Mimeograph] London: London University.

Furst, J. B., & Cooper, A. (1970). Combined use of imaginal and interoceptive stimuli in desensitizing fear of heart attacks. *Journal of Behavior Therapy and Experimental Psychiatry, 1*, 87–89.

Gade, E., Fuqua, D., & Hurlburt, G. (1988). The relationship of Holland's personality types to educational satisfaction with a native American high school population. *Journal of Counseling Psychology, 35*, 183–186.

Gambrill, E. (1990). *Critical thinking in clinical practice.* San Francisco: Jossey-Bass.

Gambrill, E. (2005). *Critical thinking in clinical practice; Improving the quality of judgments and decisions* (2nd Ed.). Hoboken, NJ: Wiley.

Garfield, S. L. (1993). Major issues in psychotherapy research. In D. K. Freedheim (Ed.), *History of psychotherapy* (pp. 335–360). Washington, DC: American Psychological Association.

Garfield, S. L., & Bergin, A. E. (Eds.). (1978). *Handbook of psychotherapy and behavior change* (2nd ed.). New York: Wiley.

Garfield, S. L., & Bergin, A. E. (Eds.). (1986). *Handbook of psychotherapy and behavior change* (3rd ed.). New York: Wiley.

Gelatt, H. B. (1989). Positive uncertainty: A new decision-making framework for counseling. *Journal of Counseling Psychology, 36*, 252–256.

Gelso, C. J. (1979). Research in counseling: Methodological and professional issues. *The Counseling Psychologist, 8*, 7–35.

Gelso, C. J. (1982). Editorial. *Journal of Counseling Psychology, 29*, 3–7.

Gelso, C. J. (1985). Rigor, relevance, and counseling research: On the need to maintain our course between Scylla and Charybdis. *Journal of Counseling and Development, 63*, 551–553.

Gelso, C. J. (1993). On the making of a scientist-practitioner: A theory of research training in professional psychology. *Professional Psychology: Research and Practice, 24*, 468–476.

Gelso, C. J. (1997). The making of a scientist in applied psychology: An attribute by treatment conception. *The Counseling Psychologist, 25*, 307–320.

Gelso, C. J., Betz, N. E., Friedlander, M. L., Helms, J. E., Hill, C. E., Patton, M. J., Super, D. E., & Wampold, B. E. (1988). Research in counseling psychology: Prospects and recommendations. *The Counseling Psychologist, 16*, 385–406.

Gelso, C. J., & Fassinger, R. E. (1990). Counseling psychology: Theory and research on interventions. *Annual Review of Psychology, 41*, 355–386.

Gelso, C. J., Mallinckrodt, B., & Judge, A. B. (1996). Research training environment, attitudes toward research, and research self-efficacy: The revised research training environment scale. *The Counseling Psychologist, 24*, 304–322.

Gelso, C. J., Raphael, R., Black, S. M., Rardin, D., & Skalkos, O. (1983). Research training in counseling psychology: Some preliminary data. *Journal of Counseling Psychology, 30*, 611–614.

Gibbons, J. L., Hamby, B. A., & Dennis, W. D. (1997). Researching gender-role ideologies internationally and cross-culturally. *Psychology of Women Quarterly, 21*, 151–170.

Giorgi, A. (1970). *Psychology as a human science: A phenomenological based approach.* New York: Harper & Row.

Giorgi, A. (1985). Sketch of a psychological phenomenological method. In A. Giorgi (Ed.), *Phenomenology and psychological research* (pp. 8–22). Pittsburgh, PA: Duquesne University Press.

Glaser, B., & Strauss, A. (1967). *The discovery of grounded theory: Strategies for qualitative research.* Chicago: Aldine.

Glaser, B. G. (1992). *Basics of grounded theory analysis: Emergence vs. forcing.* Mill Valley, CA: Sociology Press.

Glass, G. V., Willson, V. L., & Gottman, J. M. (1974). *Design and analysis of time-series experiments.* Boulder, CO: Colorado Associated University Press.

Gleitman, H. (1986). *Psychology* (2nd ed.). New York: Norton.

Glock, C. Y. (Ed.). (1967). *Survey research in the social sciences.* New York: Russell Sage Foundation.

Goetz, J. P., & LeCompte, M. D. (1984). *Ethnography and qualitative design in educational research.* New York: Academic Press.

Gold, R. L. (1958). Roles in sociological field observations. *Social Forces, 36*, 217–223.

Goldapple, K., Segal, Z., & Garson, C. (2004). Modulation of cortical-limbic pathways in major depression. *Archives of General Psychiatry, 61*, 34–41.

Goldman, L. (1976). A revolution in counseling research. *Journal of Counseling Psychology, 23*, 543–552.

Goldman, L. (Ed.). (1978). *Research methods for counselors: Practical approaches in field settings.* New York: Wiley.

Goldman, L. (1982). Defining non-traditional research. *The Counseling Psychologist, 10*, 87–89.

Goldstein, A. P., Heller, K., & Scchrest, L. B. (1966). *Psychotherapy and the psychology of behavior change.* New York: Wiley.

Good, G. E., Gilbert, L. A., & Scher, M. (1990). Gender aware therapy: A synthesis of feminist therapy and knowledge about gender. *Journal of Counseling and Development, 68*, 376–380.

Good, G. E., Robertson, J. M., O'Neil, J. M., Fitzgerald, L. F., Stevens, M., DeBord, K. A., Bartels, K. M., & Braverman, D. G. (1995). Male gender role conflict: Psychometric issues and relations to psychological distress. *Journal of Counseling Psychology, 42*, 3–10.

Good, G. E., Thoreson, R. W., & Shaughnessy, P. (1995). Substance use, confrontation of impaired colleagues, and psychological functioning among counseling psychologists: A national survey. *The Counseling Psychologist, 23*, 703–721.

Goodyear, R. K., & Benton, S. (1986). The roles of science and research in the counselor's work. In A. J. Palmo & W. J. Weikel (Eds.), *Foundations of mental health counseling* (pp. 287–308). Springfield, IL: Charles C Thomas.

Goodyear, R. K., Tracey, T. J. G., Claiborn, C. D., Lichtenberg, J. W., & Wampold, B. E. (2005). Ideographic concept mapping in counseling psychology research: Conceptual overview, methodology, and an illustration. *Journal of Counseling Psychology, 52*, 236–242.

Gottfredson, G. D., & Holland, J. L. (1990). A longitudinal test of the influence of congruence: Job satisfaction, competency utilization, and counterproductive behavior. *Journal of Counseling Psychology, 37*, 389–398.

Gottman, J. M. (1973). N-of-one and N-of-two research in psychotherapy. *Psychological Bulletin, 80*, 93–105.

Gottman, J. M. (1979). Detecting cyclicity in social interaction. *Psychological Bulletin, 86*, 338–348.

Gottman, J. M., & Markman, H. J. (1978). Experimental designs in psychotherapy research. In S. L. Garfield & A. E. Bergin (Eds.), *Handbook of psychotherapy and behavior change* (2nd ed., pp. 23–62). New York: Wiley.

Gottman, J. M., McFall, R. M., & Barnett, J. T. (1969). Design and analysis of research using time series. *Psychological Bulletin, 72*, 299–306.

Gottman, J. M., & Roy, A. K. (1990). *Sequential analysis.* Cambridge: Cambridge University Press.

Gould, S. J. (1994). The geometer of race. *Discover, 15*, 65–69.

Graham, J. R. (1990). *MMPI-2: Assessing personality and psychopathology.* New York: Oxford University Press.

Greenbaum, T. L. (1998). *The handbook for focus group research* (2nd ed.). Thousand Oaks, CA: Sage.

Greenberg, L. S. (1986a). Change process research. *Journal of Consulting and Clinical Psychology, 54*, 4–9.

Greenberg, L. S., & Foerster, F. S. (1996). Task analysis exemplified: The process of resolving unfinished business. *Journal of Consulting and Clinical Psychology, 64*, 439–446.

Greenberg, L. S., & Newman, F. L. (1996). An approach to psychotherapy change process research: Introduction to the special section. *Journal of Consulting and Clinical Psychology, 64*, 435–438.

Greenberg, L. S., & Pinsof, W. (Eds.). (1986). *The psychotherapeutic process: A research handbook.* New York: Guilford.

Greenberg, R. P., & Fisher, S. (1997). Mood-mending medicines: Probing drugs, psychotherapy, and placebo solutions. In S. Fisher & R. P. Greenberg (Eds.), *From placebo to panacea: Putting psychiatric drugs to the test* (pp. 115–172). New York: Wiley.

Greene, J. C., & Caracelli, V. J. (Eds.). (1997). *Advances in mixed-method evaluation: The challenges and benefits of integrating diverse paradigms* (New Directions for Evaluation, No. 74). San Francisco: Jossey-Bass.

Greene, J. C., Caracelli, V. J., & Graham, W. F. (1989). Toward a conceptual framework for mixed method evaluation designs. *Educational Evaluation and Policy Analysis, 11*, 255–274.

Greenwald, A. G. (1968). Cognitive learning, cognitive response to persuasion, and attitude change. In A. G. Greenwald, T. C. Brock, & T. M. Ostrom (Eds.), *Psychological foundations of attitudes* (pp. 147–190). New York: Academic Press.

Grieger, I., & Ponterotto, J. G. (1995). In J. G. Ponterotto, J. M. Casas, L. A. Suzuki, & C. M. Alexander (Eds.), *Handbook of multicultural counseling* (pp. 357–374). Thousand Oaks, CA: Sage.

Grummon, D. L., & Butler, J. M. (1953). Another failure to replicate Keet's study, two verbal techniques in a miniature counseling situation. *Journal of Abnormal and Social Psychology, 48*, 597.

Grundy, C. T., & Lambert, M. J. (1994a, June). *Assessing clinical significance: Application to the Child Behavior Checklist.* Paper presented at the annual meeting of the Society for Psychotherapy Research, York, England.

Grundy, C. T., & Lambert, M. J. (1994b, June). *Assessing clinical significance: Application to the Hamilton Rating Scale for Depression.* Paper presented at the annual meeting of the Society for Psychotherapy Research, York, England.

Grzegorek, J. L., Slaney, R. B., Franze, S., & Rice, K. (2004). Self-criticism, dependency, self-esteem and grade point average satisfaction among clusters of perfectionists and nonperfectionists. *Journal of Counseling Psychology, 51*, 192–200.

Guba, E. G., & Lincoln, Y. S. (1994). Competing paradigms in qualitative research. In N. K. Denzin & Y. S. Lincoln (Eds.), *Handbook of qualitative research* (pp. 105–117). Thousand Oaks, CA: Sage.

Guba, E. G., & Lincoln, Y. S. (1998). Competing paradigms in qualitative research. In N. K. Denzin & Y. S. Lincoln (Eds.), *The landscape of qualitative research: Theories and issues* (pp. 156–184). Thousand Oaks, CA: Sage.

Gurin, N. K., Veroff, G. J., & Feld, S. (1960). *Americans view their mental health*. New York: Basic Books.

Gurman, A. S. (1977). The patient's perception of the therapeutic relationship. In A. S. Gurman & A. M. Razin (Eds.), *Effective psychotherapy: A handbook of research* (pp. 503–543). New York: Pergamon Press.

Gurman, A. S., & Razin, A. M. (Eds.). (1977). *Effective psychotherapy: A handbook of research*. New York: Pergamon Press.

Gusheu, G. V., & Carter, R. T. (2000). Remembering race: White racial identity attitudes and two aspects of social memory. *Journal of Counseling Psychology, 47,* 199–210.

Gustav, A. (1962). Students' attitudes toward compulsory participation in experiments. *Journal of Psychology, 53,* 119–125.

Guthrie, R. V. (1998). *Even the rat was white: A historical view of psychology*. Boston, MA: Allyn & Bacon.

Haase, R. F., Waechter, D. M., & Solomon, G. S. (1982). How significant is a significant-difference? Average effect size of research in counseling psychology. *Journal of Counseling Psychology, 29,* 58–65.

Hackett, G. (1981). Survey research methods. *Personnel and Guidance Journal, 59,* 599–604.

Hair, J. F., Jr., Anderson, R. E., & Tatham, R. L. (1987). *Multivariate data analysis: With readings* (2nd ed.). New York: Macmillan.

Hair, J. K., & Black, W. C. (2000). Cluster analysis. In L. G. Grimm & P. R. Yarnold (Eds.), *Reading and understanding more multivariate statistics* (pp. 147–205). Washington, DC: American Psychological Association.

Hall, S., Weinman, J., & Marteau, T. M. (2004). The motivating impact of informing women smokers of the link between smoking and cervical cancer: The role of coherence. *Health Psychology, 23,* 419–424.

Hanfling, O. (1981). *Logical positivism*. Oxford: Blackwell.

Hanson, W. E., Creswell, J. W., Clark, V. L., Petska, K. S., & Creswell, J. D. (2005). Mixed methods research designs in counseling psychology. *Journal of Counseling Psychology, 52,* 224–235.

Hardin, S. I., Subich, L. M., & Holvey, J. M. (1988). Expectancies for counseling in relation to premature termination. *Journal of Counseling Psychology, 35,* 37–40.

Harding, S. (1991). *Whose science? Whose knowledge? Thinking from women's lives*. Ithaca, NY: Cornell University Press.

Harmon, L. (1977). Career counseling for women. In E. Rawlings & D. Carter (Eds.), *Psychotherapy for women* (pp. 197–206). Springfield, IL: Charles C Thomas.

Harmon, L. (1982). Scientific affairs: The next decade. *The Counseling Psychologist, 10,* 31–38.

Harmon, L. W. (1981). The life and career plans of young adult college women: A follow-up study. *Journal of Counseling Psychology, 28,* 416–427.

Harmon, L. W. (1989). Changes in women's career aspirations over time: Developmental or historical. *Journal of Vocational Behavior, 33,* 46–65.

Harre, R. (1970). *The principles of scientific thinking*. Chicago: University of Chicago Press.

Harre, R. (1972). *Philosophies of science: An introductory survey*. Oxford, England: Oxford University Press.

Harre, R. (1974). Blueprint for a new science. In A. Nigel (Ed.), *Reconstructing social psychology* (pp. 11–64). Baltimore: Penguin Books.

Harre, R. (1980). *Social being: A theory of social psychology*. Totowa, NJ: Rowman & Littlefield.

Hartley, D. E., & Strupp, H. H. (1983). The therapeutic alliance: Its relationship to outcome in brief psychotherapy. In J. Masling (Ed.), *Empirical studies of psychoanalytic theories* (Vol. 1, pp. 1–37). Hillsdale, NJ: The Analytic Press.

Harvey, B., Pallant, J., & Harvey, D. (2004). An evaluation of the factor structure of the Frost Multidimensional Perfectionism Scale. *Educational and Psychological Measurement, 64,* 1007–1018.

Hathaway, S. R., & McKinley, J. C. (1942). A multiphasic personality schedule (Minnesota): III. The measurement of symptomatic depression. *The Journal of Psychology, 14,* 73–84.

Haupt, S. G. (1990). *Client Christian belief issues in psychotherapy*. Unpublished doctoral dissertation, University of Missouri, Columbia.

Haverkamp, B. E., Morrow, S. L., & Ponterotto, J. G. (2005a). A time and place for qualitative and mixed methods in counseling psychology research. *Journal of Counseling Psychology, 52,* 123–125.

Haverkamp, B. E., Morrow, S. L., & Ponterotto, J. G. (2005b). Knowledge in context: Qualitative methods in counseling psychology research [special issue]. *Journal of Counseling Psychology, 52*.

Hayes, J. A., & Erkis, A. J. (2000). Therapist homophobia, client sexual orientation, and score of client HIV infection as predictor of therapist reaction to client with HIV. *Journal of Counseling Psychology, 47,* 71–78.

Hayes, J. A., McCracken, J. E., McClananhan, M. K., Hill, C. E., Harp, J. S., & Carozzoni, P. (1998). Therapist perspectives on countertransference: Qualitative data in search of a theory. *Journal of Counseling Psychology, 45,* 468–482.

Hays, W. L. (1988). *Statistics* (4th ed.). New York: Holt, Rinehart & Winston.

Hayton, J. C., Allen, D. G., & Scarpello, V. (2004). Factor retention decisions in exploratory factor analysis: A tutorial on parallel analysis. *Organizational Research Methods, 7,* 191–205.

Hazaleus, S. L., & Deffenbacher, J. L. (1986). Relaxation and cognitive treatments of anger. *Journal of Consulting and Clinical Psychology, 54,* 222–226.

Heesacker, M., Elliott, T. R., & Howe, L. A. (1988). Does the Holland code predict job satisfaction and productivity in clothing factory workers? *Journal of Counseling Psychology, 35,* 144–148.

Heller, K. (1971). Laboratory interview research as an analogue to treatment. In A. E. Bergin & S. L. Garfield (Eds.), *Handbook of psychotherapy and behavior change* (pp. 126–153). New York: Wiley.

Helms, J. E. (1976). Comparison of two types of counseling analogue. *Journal of Counseling Psychology, 23,* 422–427.

Helms, J. E. (1978). Counselor reactions to female clients: Generalizing from analogue research to a counseling setting. *Journal of Counseling Psychology, 25*, 193–199.

Helms, J. E. (1990). *Black and white racial identity: Theory, research, and practice.* Westport, CT: Greenwood Press.

Helms, J. E. (1994). How multiculturalism obscures racial factors in the therapy process: Comment on Ridley et al. (1994), Sodowsky et al. (1994), Ottavi et al. (1994), and Thompson et al. (1994). *Journal of Counseling Psychology, 41*, 162–165.

Helms, J. E., & Carter, R. T. (1990). Development of the white racial identity inventory. In J. E. Helms (Ed.), *Black and white racial identity: Theory, research and practice* (pp. 67–80). Westport, CT: Greenwood.

Helms, J. E., & Cook, D. A. (1999). *Using race and culture in counseling and psychotherapy: Theory and process.* Needham, MA: Allyn & Bacon.

Helms, J. E., & Parham, T. A. (1996). The racial identity attitudes. In R. L. Jones (Ed.), *Handbook of tests and measurements for black populations* (Vol. 1, pp. 53–72). Thousand Oaks, CA: Sage.

Helwig, A. A. (2004). A ten year longitudinal study of the career development of students: Summary findings. *Journal of Counseling and Development, 82*, 49–57.

Hembree, E. A., Street, G. P., & Riggs, D. S. (2004). Do assault-related variables predict response to cognitive behavioral treatment for PTSD? *Journal of Consulting and Clinical Psychology, 72*, 531–534.

Henry, W. P., Schacht, T. F., & Strupp, H. H. (1986). Structural analysis of social behavior: Application to a study of interpersonal processes in differential psychotherapeutic outcome. *Journal of Consulting and Clinical Psychology, 54*, 27–31.

Henry, W. P., Strupp, H. H., Butler, S. F., Schacht, T. E., & Binder, J. L. (1993). Effects of training in time-limited dynamic psychotherapy: Changes in therapist behavior. *Journal of Consulting and Clinical Psychology, 61*, 434–440.

Henwood, K., & Pidgeon, N. (2003). Grounded theory in psychology research. In P. M. Camic, J. E. Rhodes, & L. Yardley (Eds.), *Qualitative research in psychology: Expanding perspectives in methodology and design* (pp. 131–155). Washington, DC: American Psychological Association.

Heppner, M. J., & Hendricks, F. (1995). A process and outcome study examining career indecision and indecisiveness. *Journal of Counseling and Development, 73*, 426–437.

Heppner, M. J., & Heppner, P. P. (2003). Identifying process variables in career counseling: A research agenda. *Journal of Vocational Behavior, 62*, 429–452.

Heppner, M. J., Multon, K. D., Gysbers, N. C., Ellis, C., & Zook, C. E. (1998). Examining the relationship of counselor self-efficacy and selected client process and outcome measures in career counseling. *Journal of Counseling Psychology, 45*, 393–402.

Heppner, M. J., Multon, K. D., & Johnston, J. A. (1994). Assessing psychological resources during career change: Development of the career transitions inventory. *Journal of Vocational Behavior, 44*, 55–74.

Heppner, P. P. (1978a). A review of the problem-solving literature and its relationship to the counseling process. *Journal of Counseling Psychology, 25*, 366–375.

Heppner, P. P. (1978b). The clinical alteration of covert thoughts: A critical review. *Behavior Therapy, 9*, 717–734.

Heppner, P. P. (1979). The effects of client perceived need and counselor role on clients' behaviors (doctoral dissertation, University of Nebraska, 1979). *Dissertation Abstracts International, 39*, 5950A–5951A. (University Microfilms No. 79-07,542)

Heppner, P. P. (1989). Identifying the complexities within clients' thinking and decision-making. *Journal of Counseling Psychology, 36*, 257–259.

Heppner, P. P. (1995). On gender role conflict in men: Future directions and implications for counseling: Comment on Good et al. (1995) and Cournoyer and Mahalik (1995). *Journal of Counseling Psychology, 42*, 20–23.

Heppner, P. P. (2006). The benefits and challenges of becoming cross-culturally competent counseling psychologists. *The Counseling Psychologist, 34*, 147–172.

Heppner, P. P., & Anderson, W. P. (1985). The relationship between problem-solving self-appraisal and psychological adjustment. *Cognitive Therapy and Research, 9*, 415–427.

Heppner, P. P., Baumgardner, A. H., Larson, L. M., & Petty, R. E. (1988). The utility of problem-solving training that emphasizes self-management principles. *Counseling Psychology Quarterly, 1*, 129–143.

Heppner, P. P., Carter, J., Claiborn, C. D., Brooks, L., Gelso, C. J., Fassinger, R. E., Holloway, E. L., Stone, G. L., Wampold, B. E., & Galani, J. P. (1992). A proposal to integrate science and practice in counseling psychology. *The Counseling Psychologist, 20*, 107–122.

Heppner, P. P., Casas, J. M., Carter, J., & Stone, G. L. (2000). The maturation of counseling psychology: Multifaceted perspectives from 1978–1998. In S. D. Brown & R. W. Lent (Eds.), *Handbook of counseling psychology* (3rd ed., pp. 3–49). New York: Wiley.

Heppner, P. P., & Claiborn, C. D. (1989). Social influence research in counseling: A review and critique [monograph]. *Journal of Counseling Psychology, 36*, 365–387.

Heppner, P. P., Cooper, C. C., Mulholland, A. M., & Wei, M. F. (2001). A brief, multidimensional, problem-solving based psychotherapy outcome measure. *Journal of Counseling Psychology, 48*, 330–343.

Heppner, P. P., & Dixon, D. N. (1981). A review of the interpersonal influence process in counseling. *Personnel and Guidance Journal, 59*, 542–550.

Heppner, P. P, & Frazier, P. A. (1992). Social psychological processes in psychotherapy: Extrapolating basic research to counseling psychology. In S. D. Brown & R. W. Lent (Eds.), *Handbook of counseling psychology* (2nd ed., pp. 141–175) New York: Wiley.

Heppner, P. P., Gelso, C. J., & Dolliver, R. H. (1987). Three approaches to research training in counseling. *Journal of Counseling and Development, 66*, 45–49.

Heppner, P. P, & Heppner, M. J. (2004). *Writing and publishing your thesis, dissertation & research: A guide for students in the helping professions.* Belmont, CA: Brooks/Cole.

Heppner, P. P., Heppner, M. J., Lee, D-G., Wang, Y. W., Park, H-J., & Wang, L-F. (2006). Development and validation of a Collectivist Coping Styles Inventory. *Journal of Counseling Psychology, 53,* 107–125.

Heppner, P. P., Kivlighan, D. M., Jr., Good, G., Roehlke, H. J., Hills, H. I., & Ashby, J. S. (1994). Presenting problems of university counseling center clients: A snapshot and a multivariate classification scheme. *Journal of Counseling Psychology, 41,* 315–324.

Heppner, P. P., & Krauskopf, C. J. (1987). An information-processing approach to personal problem solving. *The Counseling Psychologist, 15,* 371–447.

Heppner, P. P., & Neal, G. W. (1983). Holding up the mirror: Research on the roles and functions of counseling centers in higher education. *The Counseling Psychologist, 11,* 81–89.

Heppner, P. P., & Petersen, C. H. (1982). The development and implications of a personal problem-solving inventory. *Journal of Counseling Psychology, 29,* 66–75.

Heppner, P. P., & Roehlke, H. J. (1984). Differences among supervisees at different levels of training: Implications for a developmental model of supervision. *Journal of Counseling Psychology, 31,* 76–90.

Heppner, P. P., Rogers, M. E., & Lee, L. A. (1984). Carl Rogers: Reflections on his life. *Journal of Counseling and Development, 63,* 14–20.

Heppner, P. P., Rosenberg, J. I., & Hedgespeth J. (1992). Three methods in measuring the therapeutic process: Clients' and counselors' constructions of the therapeutic process versus actual therapeutic events. *Journal of Counseling Psychology, 39,* 20–31.

Herman, J., Morris, L., & Fitz-Gibbon, C. (1987). *Evaluator's handbook.* Newbury Park, CA: Sage.

Hermansson, G. L., Webster, A. C., & McFarland, K. (1988). Counselor deliberate postural lean and communication of facilitative conditions. *Journal of Counseling Psychology, 35,* 149–153.

Heron, J. & Reason, P. (1997). A participatory inquiry paradigm. *Qualitative Inquiry, 3*(3), 274–294.

Hersen, M., & Barlow, D. H. (1976). *Single case experimental designs: Strategies for studying behavior change.* New York: Pergamon Press.

Herskovits, M. J. (1955). *Cultural anthropology.* New York: Knopf.

Highlen, P. S., & Hill, C. E. (1984). Factors affecting client change in counseling: Current status and theoretical speculations. In S. D. Brown & R. W. Lent (Eds.), *Handbook of counseling psychology* (pp. 334–396). New York: Wiley.

Hill, C. E. (1982). Counseling process researcher: Philosophical and methodological dilemmas. *The Counseling Psychologist 10,* 7–20.

Hill, C. E. (1984). A personal account of the process of becoming a counseling process researcher. *The Counseling Psychologist, 12,* 99–109.

Hill, C. E. (1985). *Manual for the Hill Counselor Verbal Response Modes Category System* (rev. ed.). Unpublished manuscript, University of Maryland.

Hill, C. E. (1990). A review of exploratory in-session process research. *Journal of Consulting and Clinical Psychology, 58,* 288–294.

Hill, C. E. (1991). Almost everything you ever wanted to know about how to do process research on counseling and psychotherapy but didn't know how to ask. In C. E. Watkins, Jr. & L. J. Scheider (Eds.), *Research in counseling* (pp. 85–118). Hillsdale, NJ: Lawrence Erlbaum.

Hill, C. E. (1992). Research on therapist techniques in brief individual therapy: Implications for practitioners. *The Counseling Psychologist, 20,* 689–711.

Hill, C. E. (1997). The effects of my research training environment: Where are my students now? *The Counseling Psychologist, 25,* 74–81.

Hill, C. E., Carter, J. A., & O'Farrell, M. K. (1983). A case study of the process and outcome of time-limited counseling. *Journal of Counseling Psychology, 30,* 3–18.

Hill, C. E., Greenwald, C., Reed, K. A., Charles, D., O'Farrell, M. K., & Carter, J. A. (1981). *Manual for the counselor and client verbal response category systems.* Columbus, OH: Marathon Consulting and Press.

Hill, C. E., Helms, J. E., Spiegel, S. B., & Tichenor, V. (1988a). Development of a system for categorizing client reactions to therapist interventions. *Journal of Counseling Psychology, 35,* 27–36.

Hill, C. E., Helms, J. E., Tichenor, V., Spiegel, S. B., O'Grady, K. E., & Perry, E. S. (1988b). Effects of therapist response modes in brief psychotherapy. *Journal of Counseling Psychology, 35,* 222–233.

Hill, C. E., Knox, S., Thompson, B. G., Williams, E. N., Hess, S. A., & Ladany, N. (2005). Consensual qualitative research: An update. *Journal of Counseling Psychology, 52*(2), 196–205.

Hill, C. E., & Lambert, M. J. (2004). Methodological issues in studying psychotherapy processes and outcomes. In M. J. Lambert (Ed.), *Bergin and Garfield's handbook of psychotherapy and behavior change* (5th ed., pp. 84–135) New York: Wiley.

Hill, C. E., & O'Grady, K. E. (1985). List of therapist intentions illustrated in a case study and with therapists of varying theoretical orientations. *Journal of Counseling Psychology, 32,* 3–22.

Hill, C. E., Rochlen, A. B., Zack, J. S., McCready, T., & Dematatis, A. (2003). Working with dreams using the Hill cognitive-experimental model: A comparison of computer-assisted, therapy empathy, and therapist empathy + input conditions. *Journal of Counseling Psychology, 50,* 211–220.

Hill, C. E., & Stephany, A. (1990). Relation of nonverbal behavior to client reactions. *Journal of Counseling Psychology, 37,* 22–26.

Hill, C. E., Thompson, B. J., & Williams, E. N. (1997). A guide to conducting consensual qualitative research. *The Counseling Psychologist, 25,* 517–572.

Hill, C. E., & Williams, E. N. (2000). The process of individual therapy.

In S. D. Brown & R. W. Lent (Eds.), *Handbook of counseling psychology* (3rd ed., pp. 670–710). New York: Wiley.

Hill, W. F. (1965). *HIM: Hill Interaction Matrix.* Los Angeles: University of Southern California, Youth Study Center.

Hillenbrand-Gunn, T., Heppner, M. J., Mauch, P. A., & Park, H. J. (2004, July). *Sexual violence in high school males: Investigating social norms theory.* Paper presented at the annual convention of the American Psychological Association, Honolulu, Hawaii.

Hines, P. L., Stockton, R., & Morran, D. K. (1995). Self-talk of group therapists. *Journal of Counseling Psychology, 42,* 242–248.

Hoch, P. H., & Zubin, J. (Eds.). (1964). *The evaluation of psychiatric treatment.* New York: Grune & Stratton.

Hodder, I. (1994). The interpretation of documents and material culture. In N. K. Denzin & Y. S. Lincoln (Eds.), *Handbook of qualitative research* (pp. 393–402). Thousand Oaks, CA: Sage.

Hoffman, J., & Weiss, B. (1987). Family dynamics and presenting problems in college students. *Journal of Counseling Psychology, 34,* 157–163.

Hoffman, M. A., & Carter, R. T. (2004). Counseling psychology and school counseling: A call to collaboration. *The Counseling Psychologist, 32,* 181–183.

Hogg, J. A., & Deffenbacher, J. L. (1988). A comparison of cognitive and interpersonal-process group therapies in the treatment of depression among college students. *Journal of Counseling Psychology, 35,* 304–310.

Hohmann, A. A., & Parron, D. L. (1996). How the new NIH guidelines on inclusion of women and minorities apply: Efficacy trials, effectiveness trials, and validity. *Journal of Consulting and Clinical Psychology, 64,* 851–855.

Holland, J. L. (1985a). *Making vocational choices: A theory of vocational personalities and work environments.* Englewood Cliffs, NJ: Prentice-Hall.

Holland, J. L. (1985b). *Professional manual for the Self-Directed Search* (3rd ed.). Palo Alto, CA: Consulting Psychologists Press.

Holland, J. L. (1987). *Manual supplement for the Self-Directed Search.* Odessa, FL: Psychological Assessment Resources.

Holland, J. L. (1992). *Making vocational choices: A theory of vocational personalities and work environment* (2nd ed.). Odessa, FL: Psychological Assessment Resources.

Holland, J. L., Daiger, D. C., & Power, P. G. (1980). Some diagnostic scales for research in decision-making and personality: Identity, information, and barriers. *Journal of Personality and Social Psychology, 39,* 1191–1200.

Holland, P. W. (1986). Statistics and causal inference. *Journal of the American Statistical Association, 81,* 945–960.

Hollon, S. D. (1996). The efficacy and effectiveness of psychotherapy relative to medications. *American Psychologist, 51,* 1025–1030.

Hollon, S. D., & Kendall, D. C. (1980). Cognitive self-statements in depression: Development of an Automatic Thoughts Questionnaire. *Cognitive Therapy and Research, 4,* 383–395.

Holloway, E. L. (1987). Developmental models of supervision: Is it development? *Professional Psychology; Research and Practice, 18,* 209–216.

Holloway, E. L. (1992). Supervision: A way of teaching and learning. In S. D. Brown & R. W. Lent (Eds.), *Handbook of counseling psychology* (2nd ed., pp. 177–214). New York: Wiley.

Holloway, E. L. (1995). *Clinical supervision: A systems approach.* Thousand Oaks, CA: Sage.

Holloway, E. L., Freund, R. D., Gardner, S. L., Nelson, M. L., & Walker, B. R. (1989). Relation of power and involvement to theoretical orientation in supervision: An analysis of discourse. *Journal of Counseling Psychology, 36,* 88–102.

Holloway, E. L., & Wampold, B. E. (1986). Relation between conceptual level and counseling-related tasks: A meta-analysis. *Journal of Counseling Psychology, 33,* 310–319.

Holloway, E. L., Wampold, B. E., & Nelson, M. L. (1990). Use of a paradoxical intervention with a couple: An interactional analysis. *Journal of Family Psychology, 3,* 385–402.

Honos-Webb, L., Stiles, W. B., & Greenberg, L. S. (2003). A method of rating assimilation in psychotherapy based on makers of change. *Journal of Counseling Psychology, 50,* 189–198.

Hoshmand, L.T. (1994). Supervision of predoctoral graduate research: A proactive oriented approach. *The Counseling Psychologist, 22,* 147–161.

Horan, J. J. (1979). *Counseling for effective decision making: A cognitive-behavioral perspective.* North Scituate, MA: Duxbury Press.

Horowitz, L. M., Rosenberg, S. E., Baer, B. A., Ureno, G., & Villasenor, V. S. (1988). Inventory of Interpersonal Problems: Psychometric properties and clinical applications. *Journal of Consulting and Clinical Psychology, 56,* 885–892.

Horvath, A. O., & Greenberg, L. S. (1986). The development of the Working Alliance Inventory. In L. S. Greenberg & W. M. Pinsof (Eds.), *The psychotherapeutic process: A research handbook* (pp. 529–556). New York: Guilford Press.

Horvath, A. O., & Greenberg, L. S. (1989). Development and validation of the Working Alliance Inventory. *Journal of Counseling Psychology, 36,* 223–233.

Hoshmand, L. L. S. T. (1989). Alternate research paradigms: A review and teaching proposal. *The Counseling Psychologist, 17,* 3–79.

Hoshmand, L. T. (1994). Supervision of predoctoral graduate research: A practice oriented approach. *The Counseling Psychologist, 22,* 147–161.

Hoshmand, L. T. (1997). The normative context of research practice. *The Counseling Psychologist, 25,* 599–605.

Hoshmand, L. T. (2005). Narratology, cultural psychology, and counseling research. *Journal of Counseling Psychology, 52,* 178–186.

Howard, G. S. (1982). Improving methodology via research on research methods. *Journal of Counseling Psychology, 29,* 318–326.

Howard, G. S. (1983). Toward methodological pluralism. *Journal of Counseling Psychology, 30,* 19–21.

Howard, G. S. (1984). A modest proposal for a revision of strategies in counseling research. *Journal of Counseling Psychology, 31,* 430–441.

Howard, G. S. (1985). Can research in the human sciences become more relevant to practice? *Journal of Counseling and Development, 63,* 539–544.

Howard, K. I., Moras, K., Brill, P. L., Martinovich, Z., & Lutz, W. (1996). Evaluation of psychotherapy. *American Psychologist, 51,* 1059–1064.

Hoyle, R. H. (1995). The structural equation modeling approach: Basic concepts and fundamental issues. In R. H. Hoyle (Ed.), *Structural equation modeling: Concepts, issues, and applications* (pp. 1–15). Thousand Oaks, CA: Sage.

Hoyt, M. R., Marmar, C. R., Horowitz, M. J., & Alvarez, W. F. (1981). The therapist actions scale and the patient actions scale: Instruments for the assessment of activities during dynamic psychotherapy. *Psychotherapy: Theory, Research and Practice, 18,* 109–116.

Hoyt, W. T. (1996). Antecedents and effects of perceived therapist credibility: A meta-analysis. *Journal of Counseling Psychology, 43,* 430–447.

Huberty, C. J., & Morris, J. D. (1989). Multivariate analysis versus multiple univariate analyses. *Psychological Bulletin, 105,* 302–308.

Huck, S. W., & McLean, R. A. (1975). Using a repeated measures ANOVA to analyze the data from a pretest-posttest design: A potentially confusing task. *Psychological Bulletin, 82,* 511–518.

Hughes, E. C. (1952). Psychology: Science and/or profession. *American Psychologist, 7,* 441–443.

Hunt, D. W., Butler, L. F., Noy, J. E., & Rosser, M. E. (1978). *Assessing conceptual level by the paragraph completion method.* Toronto, Canada: The Ontario Institute for Studies in Education.

Iberg, J. R. (1991). Applying statistical control theory to bring together clinical supervision and psychotherapy research. *Journal of Consulting and Clinical Psychology, 96,* 575–586.

Ibrahim, F. A., & Kahn, H. (1987). Assessment of worldviews. *Psychological Reports, 60,* 163–176.

Ibrahim, F. A., & Owen, S. V. (1994). Factor analytic structure of the Scale to Assess Worldview. *Current Psychology: Developmental, Learning, Personality, Social, 13,* 201–209.

Ibrahim, F. A., Roysircar-Sodowsky, G., & Ohnishi, H. (2001). Worldview: Recent developments and needed directions. In J. G. Ponterotto, J. M. Casas, L. A. Suzuki, & C. A. Alexander (Eds.), *Handbook of multicultural counseling.* (2nd ed., pp. 425–456). Thousand Oaks, CA: Sage.

Ingram, R. (Ed.). (1986). *Information processing approaches to clinical psychology.* Orlando, FL: Academic Press.

Ivey, A. E., Ivey, M. B., & Simek-Morgan, L. (1997). *Counseling and psychotherapy: A multicultural perspective* (4th ed.). Boston: Allyn & Bacon.

Jacobson, N. S. (1991). Behavioral versus insight-oriented marital therapy: Labels can be misleading. *Journal of Consulting and Clinical Psychology, 59,* 142–145.

Jacobson, N. S., & Christensen, A. (1996). Studying the effectiveness of psychotherapy. *American Psychologist, 51,* 1031–1039.

Jacobson, N. S., Dobson, K. S., & Truax, P. A. (1996). A component analysis of cognitive-behavioral treatment for depression. *Journal of Consulting and Clinical Psychology, 64,* 295–304.

Jacobson, N. S., Follette, W. C., & Revenstorf, D. (1984). Psychotherapy outcome research: Methods for reporting variability and evaluating clinical significance. *Behavior Therapy, 15,* 336–352.

Jacobson, N. S., & Revenstorf, D. (1988). Statistics for assessing the clinical significance of psychotherapy techniques: Issues, problems and new developments. *Behavior Assessment, 10,* 133–145.

Jacobson, N. S., & Truax, P. (1991). Clinical significance: A statistical approach to defining meaningful change in psychotherapy research. *Journal of Consulting and Clinical Psychology, 59,* 12–19.

Jayaratne, S., & Levy, R. L. (1979). *Empirical clinical practice.* New York: Columbia University Press.

Jensen, A. R. (1969). How much can we boost IQ and scholastic achievement? *Harvard Educational Review, 39,* 1–123.

Jensen, A. R. (1985). The nature of the black-white difference on various psychometric tests: Spearman's hypothesis. *The behavioral and Brain Sciences, 8,* 193–263.

Johnson, C. V., & Hayes, J. A. (2003). Troubled spirits: Prevalence and predictors of religious and spiritual concerns among university students and counseling center clients. *Journal of Counseling Psychology, 50,* 409–419.

Johnson, R. F. Q. (1976). The experimenter attributes effect: A methodological analysis. *Psychological Record, 26,* 67–78.

Johnston, J. A., Buescher, K. L., & Heppner, M. J. (1988). Computerized career information and guidance systems: Caveat emptor. *Journal of Counseling and Development, 67,* 39–41.

Joint Committee on Standards for Educational Evaluation. (1994). *The program evaluation standards* (2nd ed.). Thousand Oaks, CA: Sage Publications.

Jones, A. S., & Gelso, C. J. (1988). Differential effects of style of interpretation: Another look. *Journal of Counseling Psychology, 35,* 363–369.

Jones, E. E. (1993). Introduction to special section: Single case research in psychotherapy. *Journal of Consulting and Clinical Psychology, 61,* 371–372.

Jones, E. E., Ghannam, J., Nigg, J. T., & Dyer, J. F. P. (1993). A paradigm for single-case research: The time series study of a long-term psychotherapy for depression. *Journal of Consulting and Clinical Psychology, 61,* 381–394.

Jones, H. G. (1956). The application of conditioning and learning techniques to the treatment of a psychiatric patient. *Journal of Abnormal and Social Psychology, 52,* 414–419.

Josephson, G. S., & Fong-Beyette, M. L. (1987). Factors assisting female clients' disclosure of incest during counseling. *Journal of Counseling and Development, 65,* 475–478.

Juntunen, C. L., Barraclough, D. J., Broneck, C. L., Seibel, G. A., Winrow, S. A., & Morin, P. M. (2001). American Indian perspectives on the career journey. *Journal of Counseling Psychology, 48,* 274–285.

Juntunen, C. L., & Wettersten, K. B. (2006). Work hope: Development and initial validation of a measure. *Journal of Counseling Psychology, 53,* 94–106.

Kagan, N. (1975). Influencing human interaction: Eleven years with IPR. *Canadian Counselor, 9,* 44–51.

Kahn, J. H., & Gelso, C. J. (1997). Factor structure of the Research Training Environment Scale—Revised: Implications for research training in applied psychology. *The Counseling Psychologist, 25,* 22–37.

Kahn, J. H., & Scott, N. A. (1997). Predictors of research productivity and science-related career goals among counseling psychology doctoral students. *The Counseling Psychologist, 25,* 38–67.

Kandel, D. K. (1973). Adolescent marijuana use: Role of parents and peers. *Science, 181,* 1067–1070.

Kanfer, F. H., & Busemeyer, J. R. (1982). The use of problem solving and decision making in behavior therapy. *Clinical Psychological Review, 2,* 239–266.

Kaul, T., & Bednar, R. L. (1986). Experiential group research. In S. L. Garfield & A. E. Bergin (Eds.), *Handbook of psychotherapy and behavior change* (3rd ed., pp. 671–714). New York: Wiley.

Kazdin, A. D., & Kopel, S. A. (1975). On resolving ambiguities of the multiple-baseline design: Problems and recommendations. *Behavior Therapy, 6,* 601–608.

Kazdin, A. E. (1978). Methodology of applied behavior analysis. In A. C. Catania & T. A. Brigham (Eds.), *Handbook of applied behavior analysis: Social and instructional processes* (pp. 61–104). New York: Irvington Press/Halstead Press.

Kazdin, A. E. (1980). *Research design in clinical psychology.* New York: Harper & Row.

Kazdin, A. E. (1982). *Single-case research designs: Methods for clinical and applied settings.* New York: Oxford University Press.

Kazdin, A. E. (2003). *Research design in clinical psychology.* (4th ed.). Boston: Allyn & Bacon.

Keet, C. D. (1948). Two verbal techniques in a miniature counseling situation. *Psychological Monographs, 62*(7, Whole No. 294).

Keith-Spiegel, P., & Koocher, G. P. (1985). *Ethics in psychology: Professional standards and cases.* New York: Random House.

Kelerman, G., & Neu, C. (1976). *A manual for interpersonal treatment of depression.* Unpublished manuscript, Yale University, New Haven, CT.

Keller, M. B. (2004). Remission versus response: The new gold standard of antidepressant care. *Journal of Clinical Psychiatry, 65,* 53–59.

Kelly, A. E., & Achter, J. A. (1995). Self-concealment and attitudes toward counseling in university students. *Journal of Counseling Psychology, 42,* 40–46.

Kelly, A. E., Kahn, J. H., & Coulter, R. G. (1996). Client self-presentation at intake. *Journal of Counseling Psychology, 43,* 300–309.

Kelly, A. E., McKillop, K. J., & Neimeyer, G. S. (1991). Effects of counselor as audience on the internalization of depressed and nondepressed self-presentation. *Journal of Counseling Psychology, 38,* 126–132.

Kelly, K. R., & Pulver, C. A. (2003). Refining measurement of career indecision types: A validity study. *Journal of Counseling and Development, 81,* 445–454.

Kerlinger, F. N. (1986). *Foundations of behavioral research* (3rd ed.). New York: Holt, Rinehart & Winston.

Kerlinger, F. N., & Lee, H. B. (2000). *Foundations of behavioral research.* Fort Worth, TX: Harcourt College.

Kiesler, D. J. (1966). Some myths of psychotherapy research and the search for a paradigm. *Psychological Bulletin, 65,* 110–136.

Kiesler, D. J. (1971). Experimental designs in psychotherapy research. In A. E. Bergin & S. L. Garfield (Eds.), *Handbook of psychotherapy and behavior change* (pp. 36–74). New York: Wiley.

Kiesler, D. J. (1973). *The process of psychotherapy.* Chicago: Aldine.

Kiesler, D. J. (1984). *Check List of Psychotherapy Transactions (CLOPT) and Check List of Interpersonal Transactions (CLOIT).* Richmond: Virginia Commonwealth University.

Kiesler, D. J. (1987). *Research manual for the Impact Message Inventory.* Palo Alto, CA: Consulting Psychologists Press.

Kiesler, D. J. (1988). *Therapeutic metacommunication.* Palo Alto, CA: Consulting Psychologists Press.

Kiesler, D. J., Klein, M. H., & Mathieu, P. L. (1965). Sampling from the recorder therapy interview: The problem of segment location. *Journal of Consulting Psychology, 29,* 337–344.

Kim, B. S. K., & Atkinson, D. (2002). Asian American client adherence to Asian cultural values, counselor expression of cultural values, counselor ethnicity, and career counseling process. *Journal of Counseling Psyhology, 49,* 3–13.

Kim, B. S. K., Atkinson, D. R., & Yang, P. H. (1999). The Asian values scale: Development, factor analysis, validation, and reliability. *Journal of Counseling Psychology, 46,* 342–352.

Kim, B. S. K., Brenner, B. R., Liang, C. T. H., & Asay, P. A. (2003). A qualitative study of adaptation experiences of 1.5-generation Asian Americans. *Cultural Diversity & Ethnic Minority Psychology, 9,* 156–170.

Kim, B. S. K, Hill, C. E., Gelso, C. J., Goates, M. K., Asay, P. A., & Harbin, J. M. (2003). Counselor self-disclosure, East Asian American client adherence to Asian cultural values, and counseling process. *Journal of Counseling Psychology, 50,* 324–332.

Kim, D. M., Wampold, B. E., & Bolt, D. (2006). Therapist effects in psychotherapy: A random effects modeling of the NIMH TDCRP data. *Psychotherapy Research, 16,* 161–172.

Kim, U., & Choi, S-H. (1994). Individualism, collectivism, and child development: A Korean perspective. In P. M. Greenfield & R. R. Cocking (Eds.), *Cross-cultural roots of minority child development* (pp. 227–257). Hillsdale, NJ: Erlbaum.

Kim, Y. C., & Cho, J. (2005). Now and forever: Portraits of qualitative research in Korea. *International Journal of Qualitative Studies in Education, 18*(3), 355–377.

Kirshner, T., Hoffman, M. A., & Hill, C. E. (1994). A case study of the process and outcome of career counseling. *Journal of Counseling Psychology, 41,* 216–226.

Kiselica, M. S., Baker, S. B., Thomas, R. N., & Reedy, S. (1994). Effects of stress inoculation training on anxiety, stress, and academic performance among adolescents. *Journal of Counseling Psychology, 41,* 335–342.

Kitchener, K., & Anderson, S. K. (2000). Ethical issues in counseling psychology: Old themes—new problems. In S. D. Brown & R. W. Lent (Eds.), *Handbook of counseling psychology* (3rd ed., pp. 50–82). New York: John Wiley & Sons.

Kitchener, K. S. (1984). Intuition, critical evaluation and ethical principles: The foundation for ethical decision in counseling psychology. *The Counseling Psychologist, 12,* 43–55.

Kivlighan, D. M., Jr. (1989). Changes in counselor intentions and response modes and client reactions and session evaluation following training. *Journal of Counseling Psychology, 36,* 471–476.

Kivlighan, D. M., Jr. (1990). Relation between counselors' use of intentions and clients' perception of working alliance. *Journal of Counseling Psychology, 37,* 27–32.

Kivlighan, D. M., Jr., & Angelone, E. O. (1991). Helpee introversion, novice counselor intention use, and counseling session impact. *Journal of Counseling Psychology, 38,* 25–29.

Kivlighan, D. M., Jr., Coleman, M. N., & Anderson, D. C. (2000). Process, outcome, and methodology in group counseling research. In S. D. Brown & R. W. Lent (Eds.), *Handbook of counseling psychology* (3rd ed., pp. 767–796). New York: Wiley.

Kivlighan, D. M., Jr., Hageseth, J., Tipton, R., & McGovern, T. M. (1981). The effects of matching treatment approaches and personality types in group vocational counseling. *Journal of Counseling Psychology, 28,* 315–320.

Kivlighan, D. M., Jr., & Lilly, R. L. (1997). Developmental changes in group climate as they relate to therapeutic gain. *Group Dynamics: Theory, Research, and Practice, 1,* 208–221.

Kivlighan, D. M., Jr., Multon, K. M., & Patton, M. J. (1996). Development of the Missouri Addressing Resistance Scale. *Psychotherapy Research 6,* 291–308.

Kivlighan, D. M., Jr., & Shapiro, R. M. (1987). Holland type as a predictor of benefit from self-help career counseling. *Journal of Counseling Psychology, 34,* 326–329.

Kivlighan, D. M., Jr. & Shaughnessy, P. (1995). An analysis of the development of the working alliance using hierarchical linear modeling. *Journal of Counseling Psychology, 42,* 338–349.

Klare, G. R. (1974–1975). Assessing readability. *Reading Research Quarterly, 10,* 62–102.

Klein, M., Mathieu, P., Kiesler, O., & Gendlin, E. (1969). *The experiencing scale.* Madison: Wisconsin Psychiatric Institute.

Klein, M. H., Mathieu-Coughlan, P., & Kiesler, D. J. (1986). The experiencing scales. In L. Greenberg & W. Pinsof (Eds.), *The psychotherapeutic process* (pp. 21–77). New York: Guilford Press.

Kleinke, C. L. (1986). Gaze and eye contact: A research review. *Psychological Bulletin, 100,* 78–100.

Kline, T. J. B. (2005). *Psychological testing: A practical approach to design and evaluation.* Thousand Oaks, CA: Sage.

Klingelhofer, E. L. (1954). The relationship of academic advisement to the scholastic performance of failing college students. *Journal of Counseling Psychology, 1,* 125–131.

Klinger, E. (1971). *Structure and functions of fantasy.* New York: Wiley.

Knox, S., Burkard, A. W., Johnson, A. J., Suzuki, L. A., & Ponterotto, J. G. (2003). African American and European American therapists' experiences of addressing race in cross-racial psychotherapy dyads. *Journal of Counseling Psychology, 50,* 466–481.

Knox, S., Hess, S. A., Petersen, D. A., & Hill, C. E. (1997). A qualitative analysis of client perceptions of the effects of helpful therapist self-disclosure in long-term therapy. *Journal of Counseling Psychology, 44,* 274–283.

Knox, S., Hess, S. A., Williams, E. N., & Hill, C. E. (2003). "Here's a little something for you": How therapists respond to client gifts. *Journal of Counseling Psychology, 50,* 199–210.

Koile, E. A., & Bird, D. J. (1956). Preferences for counselor help on freshman problems. *Journal of Counseling Psychology, 3,* 97–106.

Kokotovic, A. M., & Tracey, T. J. (1987). Premature termination at a university counseling center. *Journal of Counseling Psychology, 34,* 80–82.

Koocher, G. P., & Keith-Spiegel, P. (1998). *Ethics in psychology: Professional standards and cases* (2nd ed.). New York: Oxford University Press.

Koplik, E. K., & DeVito, A. J. (1986). Problems of freshmen: Comparison of classes of 1976 and 1986. *Journal of College Student Personnel, 27,* 124–131.

Kraemer, H. C., & Thiemann, S. (1987). *How many subjects?: Statistical power analysis in research.* Newbury Park, CA: Sage.

Krause, A. A., & Allen, G. J. (1988). Perceptions of counselor supervision: An examination of Stoltenberg's model from the perspectives of supervisor and supervisee. *Journal of Counseling Psychology, 35,* 77–80.

Krebs, P. J., Smither, J. W., & Hurley, R. B. (1991). Relationship of vocational personality and research training environment to the research productivity of counseling psychologists. *Professional Psychology: Research and Practice, 22,* 362–367.

Krivatsky, S. E., & Magoon, T. M. (1976). Differential effects of three vocational counseling treatments. *Journal of Counseling Psychology, 23,* 112–117.

Krop, H., & Krause, S. (1976). The elimination of shark phobia by self-administered systematic desensitization: A case study. *Journal of Behavior Therapy and Experimental Psychiatry, 7,* 293–294.

Krueger, R., & Casey, M. A. (2000). *Focus groups* (3rd ed.). Thousands Oaks, CA: Sage.

Krumboltz, J. D. (1991). *Career beliefs inventory.* Palo Alto, CA: Consulting Psychologist Press.

Krumboltz, J. D., & Mitchell, L. K. (1979). Relevant rigorous research. *The Counseling Psychologist, 81,* 50–52.

Kruskal, W., & Mosteller, F. (1979). Representative sampling III: The current statistical literature. *International Statistical Review, 47,* 245–265.

Kuhn, T. S. (1970). *The structure of scientific revolutions* (2nd ed.). Chicago: University of Chicago Press.

Kushner, K. (1978). On the external validity of two psychotherapy analogues. *Journal of Consulting and Clinical Psychology, 46,* 1394–1402.

Kvale, S. (1996). *Interviews: An introduction to qualitative research interviewing.* Thousand Oaks, CA: Sage.

Ladany, N., O'Brien, K. M., Hill, C. E., Melincoff, D. S., Knox, S., & Petersen, D. A. (1997). Sexual attraction toward clients, use of supervision, and prior training: A qualitative study of predoctoral psychology interns. *Journal of Counseling Psychology, 44,* 413–424.

Lakatos, I. (1970). Falsification and the methodology of scientific research programmes. In I. Lakatos & A. Musgrave (Eds.), *Criticism and the growth of knowledge* (pp. 91–196). Cambridge, England: Cambridge University Press.

Lambert, M. J., & Bergin, A. E. (1993). Achievements and limitations of psychotherapy research. In D. K. Freedheim (Ed.), *History of psychotherapy* (pp. 360–390). Washington, DC: American Psychological Association.

Lambert, M. J., Bergin, A. E., & Collins, J. L. (1977). Therapist-induced deterioration in psychotherapy. In A. S. Gurman & A. M. Razin (Eds.), *Effective psychotherapy: A handbook of research* (pp. 452–481). New York: Pergamon Press.

Lambert, M. J., Christensen, E. R., & DeJulio, S. (1983). *The assessment of psychotherapy outcome.* New York: Wiley.

Lambert, M. J., DeJulio, S. S., & Stein, D. M. (1978). Therapist interpersonal skills: Process, outcome, methodological considerations, and recommendations for future research. *Psychological Bulletin, 85,* 467–489.

Lambert, M. J., & Hill, C. E. (1994). Assessing psychotherapy outcomes and processes. In A. E. Bergin & S. L. Garfield (Eds.), *Handbook of psychotherapy and behavior change* (4th ed., pp. 72–113). New York: Wiley.

Lambert, M. J., & Ogles, B. M. (2004). The efficacy and effectiveness of psychotherapy. In M. J. Lambert (Ed.), *Bergin and Garfield's handbook of psychotherapy and behavior change* (5th ed., pp. 139–193). New York: Wiley.

Lapan, R. T., Boggs, K. R., & Morrill, W. H. (1989). Self-efficacy as a mediation of investigative and realistic general occupational themes of the Strong-Campbell Interest Inventory. *Journal of Counseling Psychology, 36,* 176–182.

Larson, L. M. (1998). The social cognitive model of counselor training. *The Counseling Psychologist, 26,* 219–273.

Larson, L. M., & Besett-Alesch, T. M. (2000). Bolstering the scientist component in the training of scientist-practitioners: One program's curriculum modifications. *The Counseling Psychologist, 28,* 873–896.

Larson, L. M., & Daniels, J. A. (1998). Review of the counseling self-efficacy literature. *The Counseling Psychologist, 26,* 129–218.

Larson, L. M., Heppner, P. P., Ham, T., & Dugan, K. (1988). Investigating multiple subtypes of career indecision through cluster analysis. *Journal of Counseling Psychology, 35,* 439–446.

Larson, L. M., & Majors, M. S. (1998). Application of the coping with career indecision instrument with adolescents. *Journal of Career Assessments, 6,* 163–179.

Larson, L. M., Suzuki, L. A., Gillespie, K. N., Potenza, M. T., Bechtel, M. A., & Toulouse, A. L. (1992). Development and validation of the Counseling Self-Estimate Inventory. *Journal of Counseling Psychology, 39,* 105–210.

Lawless, E. J. (2001). *Women escaping violence: Empowerment through narrative.* Columbia, MO: University of Missouri Press.

Leary, T. (1957). *Interpersonal diagnosis of personality.* New York: Ronald Press.

Lee, D-G., Park, H-J., Shin, Y-J., & Graham, D. (2005, August). *Validation of the Frost Multidimensional Perfectionism Scale in South Korea.* Poster presented at the annual meeting of the Asian American Psychological Association, Washington, DC.

Lee, L. A., Heppner, P. P., Gagliardi, J., & Lee, J. S. (1987). Gender bias in subject samples in counseling psychology. *Journal of Counseling Psychology, 34,* 73–76.

Lee, R. (2003). Do ethnic identity and other-group orientation protect against discrimination for Asian Americans? *Journal of Counseling Psychology, 50,* 133–141.

Lee, R. M. (2005). Resilience against discrimination: Ethnic identity and other-group orientation as protective factors for Korean Americans. *Journal of Counseling Psychology, 52,* 36–44.

Lee, R. M., Choe, J., Kim, G., & Ngo, V. (2000). Construction of the Asian American Family Conflicts Scale. *Journal of Counseling Psychology, 47,* 211–222.

Lent, R. W., Brown, S. D., & Hackett, G. (1994). Toward a unifying social cognitive theory of career and academic interest, choice, and performance. *Journal of Vocational Behavior, 45,* 79–122.

Lent, R. W., Brown, S. D., & Lankin, K. C. (1987). Comparison of three theoretically derived variables in predicting career and academic behavior: Self-efficacy, interest-consequence, and consequence thinking. *Journal of Counseling Psychology, 34,* 293–298.

Lent, R. W., Russell, R. K., & Zamostny, K. P. (1981). Comparison of cue-controlled desensitization, rational restructuring, and a credible placebo in the treatment of speech anxiety. *Journal of Consulting and Clinical Psychology, 49,* 608–610.

Leong, F. T. L., & Ponterotto, J. G. (2003). A proposal for internationalizing counseling psychology in the United States: Rationale, recommendations, and challenges. *The Counseling Psychologist, 31,* 381–395.

Leong, F. T. L., Wagner, N. S., & Tata, S. P. (1995). Racial and ethnic variations in help seeking attitudes. In J. G. Ponterotto, J. M. Casas, L. A. Suzuki, & C. M. Alexander (Eds.), *Handbook of multicultural counseling* (pp. 415–438). Thousand Oaks, CA: Sage.

Levant, R. F. (2004). The empirically validated treatment movement: A practitioner/educator perspective. *Clinical Psychology: Science and Practice, 11,* 219–224.

Levin, J. R. & Wampold, B. E. (1999). Generalized single-case randomization tests: Flexible analyses for a variety of situations. *School Psychology Quarterly, 14,* 59–93.

Lewin, K. (1951). Formalization and progress in psychology. In D. Cartwright (Ed.), *Field theory in social science* (pp. 1–41). New York: Harper.

Lewinsohn, P. M., Mischel, W., Chapel, W., & Barton, R. (1980). Social competence and depression: The role of illusory self-perceptions. *Journal of Abnormal Psychology, 89,* 203–212.

Lewis, J. (2001). Career and personal counseling: Comparing process and outcome. *Journal of Employment Counseling, 38,* 82–90.

Liang, C. T. H., Li, L. C., & Kim, B. S. K. (2004). The Asian American racism-related stress inventory: Development, factor analysis, reliability, and validity. *Journal of Counseling Psychology, 51,* 103–114.

Lichtenberg, J. W. (1984). Believing when the facts don't fit. *Journal of Counseling and Development, 63,* 10–11.

Lichtenberg, J. W., & Heck, E. J. (1983). Use of sequential analysis in counseling process research: A reply to Hill, Carter, and O'Farrell and to Howard. *Journal of Counseling Psychology, 30,* 615–618.

Lichtenberg, J. W., & Heck, E. J. (1986). Analysis of sequence and pattern in process research. *Journal of Counseling Psychology, 33,* 170–181.

Lichtenberg, J. W., & Hummel, T. J. (1976). Counseling as a stochastic process: Fitting a Markov chain model to initial counseling interviews. *Journal of Counseling Psychology, 23,* 310–315.

Lichtenberg, J. W., & Tracey, T. J. L. (2003). Interaction rules and strategies in psychotherapy. *Journal of Counseling Psychology, 50,* 267–275.

Liddle, B. J. (1996). Therapist sexual orientation, gender, and counseling practices as they relate to ratings of helpfulness by gay and lesbian clients. *Journal of Counseling Psychology, 43,* 394–401.

Lieberman, M. A., Yalom, I., & Miles, M. (1973). *Encounter groups: First facts.* New York: Basic Books.

Likert, R. (1932). A technique for the measurement of attitudes. *Archives of Psychology, 140,* 44–53.

Lincoln, Y. S., & Guba, E. G. (1985). *Naturalistic inquiry.* Beverly Hills, CA: Sage.

Lincoln, Y. S., & Guba, E. G. (2000). Paradigmatic controversies, contradictions, and emerging confluences. In N. K. Denzin & Y. S. Lincoln (Eds.), *Handbook of qualitative research* (2nd ed., pp. 163–188). Thousand Oaks, CA: Sage.

Lindsey, R. T. (1984). Informed consent and deception in psychotherapy research: An ethical analysis. *The Counseling Psychologist, 12,* 79–86.

Lipkus, I. (1991). The construction and preliminary validation of a Global Belief in a Just World Scale and the exploratory analysis of the Multidimensional Belief in a Just World Scale. *Personality and Individual Differences, 12,* 1171–1178.

Locke, D. (1990). A not so provincial view of multicultural counseling. *Counseling Education & Supervision, 30,* 18–25.

Locke, D. C., Myers, J. E., & Herr, E. L. (2001). *The handbook of counseling.* Thousand Oaks, CA: Sage.

Loehlin, J. C. (1992). *Latent variable models: An introduction to factor, path, and structural analysis* (2nd ed.). Hillsdale, NJ: Lawrence Erlbaum Associates.

Lorr, M. (1983). *Cluster analysis for social scientists.* San Francisco: Jossey-Bass.

Luborsky, L. (1984). *Principles of psychoanalytic psychotherapy: A manual for supportive-expressive treatment.* New York: Basic Books.

Luborsky, L., & Barber, J. P. (1993). Benefits of adherence to treatment manuals, and where to get them. In N. Miller, L. Luborsky, J. P. Barber, & J. P. Docherty (Eds.), *Psychodynamic treatment research:* *A handbook for clinical practice* (pp. 211–226). New York: Basic Books.

Luborsky, L., Diguer, L., Seligman, D. A., Rosenthal, R., Krause, E. D., Johnson, S., et al., (1999). The researcher's own therapy allegiances: A "wild card" in comparisons of treatment efficacy. *Clinical Psychology: Science and Practice, 6*(1), 95–106.

Lucas, M. S., & Epperson, D. L. (1990). Types of vocational undecidedness: A replication and refinement. *Journal of Counseling Psychology, 37,* 382–388.

Lundervold, D. A. & Belwood, M. F. (2000). The best kept secret in counseling: Single-case (N = 1) experimental designs. *Journal of Counseling and Development, 78,* 92–102.

Mackay, H. C., Barkham, M., Rees, A., & Stiles, W. B. (2003). Appraisal of published reviews of research on psychotherapy and counseling with adults 1990–1998. *Journal of Consulting & Clinical Psychology, 71,* 652–656.

Madriz, E. (2000). Focus groups in feminist research. In N. K. Denzin & Y. S. Lincoln (Eds.), *Handbook of qualitative research* (2nd ed., pp. 835–850). Thousand Oaks, CA: Sage.

Magoon, T. M., & Holland, J. L. (1984). Research training and supervision. In S. D. Brown & R. W. Lent (Eds.), *Handbook of counseling psychology* (pp. 682–715). New York: Wiley.

Mahalik, J. R., & Kivlighan, D. M., Jr. (1988). Research training and supervision. In S. D. Brown & R. W. Lent (Eds.), *Handbook of counseling psychology* (pp. 682–715). New York: Wiley.

Mahrer, A. R., Paterson, W. E., Theriault, A. T., Roessler, C., & Quenneville, A. (1986). How and why to use a large number of clinically sophisticated judges in psychotherapy research. *Voices: The Art and Science of Psychotherapy, 22,* 57–66.

Maier, N. R. F. (1931). Reasoning in humans: II. The solution of a problem and its appearance in consciousness. *Journal of Comparative Psychology, 12,* 181–194.

Malkiewich, L. E., & Merluzzi, T. V. (1980). Rational restructuring versus desensitization with clients of diverse conceptual levels: A test of client-treatment matching model. *Journal of Counseling Psychology, 27,* 453–461.

Mallinckrodt, B. (1989). Social support and the effectiveness of group therapy. *Journal of Counseling Psychology, 36,* 170–175.

Mallinckrodt, B., Gelso, C. J., & Royalty, G. M. (1990). Impact of the research training environment and counseling psychology students' Holland personality type on interest in research. *Professional Psychology: Research and Practice, 21,* 26–32.

Mallinckrodt, B., & Helms, J. E. (1986). Effect of disabled counselor's self-disclosures on client perceptions of the counselor. *Journal of Counseling Psychology, 33,* 343–348.

Mallinckrodt, B., & Wang, C-C. (2004). Quantitative methods for verifying semantic equivalence of translated research instruments: A Chinese version of the Experiences in Close Relationship Scale. *Journal of Counseling Psychology, 51,* 368–379.

Manicas, P. T., & Secord, P. F. (1983). Implications for psychology of the new philosophy of science. *American Psychologist, 38,* 399–413.

Markowitz, J. C., Kocsis, J. H., Bleiberg, K. L., Christos, P. J., & Sacks, M. (2005). A comparative trial of psychotherapy and pharmacotherapy for "pure" dysthymic patients. *Journal of Affective Disorders, 89,* 167–175.

Markowitz, J. C., Kocsis, J. H., & Fishman, B. (1998). Treatment of depressive symptoms in human immunodeficiency virus-positive patients. *Archives of General Psychiatry, 55,* 452–457.

Marmar, C. R. (1990). Psychotherapy process research: Progress, dilemmas, and future directions. *Journal of Consulting and Clinical Psychology, 58,* 265–272.

Marmar, C. R., Marziali, E., Horowitz, M. J., & Weiss, D. S. (1986). The development of the therapeutic alliance rating system. In L. S. Greenberg & W. M. Pinsof (Eds.), *The psychotherapeutic process: A research handbook* (pp. 367–390). New York: Guilford Press.

Marotta S. A. & Garcia, J. G. (2003). Latinos in the United States 2000. *Hispanic Journal of Behavioral Sciences, 25,* 13–34.

Marsden, G. (1965). Content-analysis studies of therapeutic interviews: 1954–1964. *Psychological Bulletin, 63,* 298–321.

Marsden, G. (1971). Content analysis studies of psychotherapy: 1954 through 1968. In A. E. Bergin & S. L. Garfield (Eds.), *Handbook of psychotherapy and behavior change* (pp. 345–407). New York: Wiley.

Marteau, T. M., Rana, S., & Kubba, A. (2002). Smoking and cervical cancer: A qualitative study of the explanatory models of smokers with cervical abnormalities. *Psychology, Health and Medicine, 7,* 107–109.

Martin, J. (1984). The cognitive mediational paradigm for research on counseling. *Journal of Counseling Psychology, 31,* 558–571.

Martin, J. (1985). Measuring clients' cognitive competence in research on counseling. *Journal of Counseling and Development, 63,* 556–560.

Martin, J. (1987). *Cognitive-instructional counseling.* London, Ontario, Canada: Althouse Press.

Martin, J., Martin, W., & Slemon, A. G. (1989). Cognitive-mediational models of action-act sequences in counseling. *Journal of Counseling Psychology, 36,* 8–16.

Martin, J., & Stelmaczonek, K. (1988). Participants' identification and recall of important events in counseling. *Journal of Counseling Psychology, 35,* 385–390.

Martin, J. S., Goodyear, R. K., & Newton, F. B. (1987). Clinical supervision: An intensive case study. *Professional Psychology: Research and Practice, 18,* 225–235.

Maruyama, M. (1963). The second cybernetics: Deviation-amplifying mutual causal processes. *American Scientist, 51,* 169–179.

Marx, J. A., & Gelso, C. J. (1987). Termination of individual counseling in a university counseling center. *Journal of Counseling Psychology, 34,* 3–9.

Mash, E. J., & Terdal, L. G. (1988). *Behavioral assessment of childhood disorders* (2nd ed.). New York: Guilford Press.

Masling, J. (1966). Role-related behavior of the subject and psychologist and its effect upon psychological data. In D. Levine (Ed.), *Nebraska Symposium on Motivation, 14,* 67–103.

Matsumoto, D. (1994). *Cultural influences on research methods and statistics.* Pacific Grove, CA: Brooks/Cole.

Matsumoto, D. (2000). *Culture and psychology: People around the world.* Belmont, CA: Wadsworth/Thomson Learning.

Maxwell, S. E., & Cole, D. A. (1995). Tips for writing (and reading) methodological articles. *Psychological Bulletin, 118,* 193–198.

McCarn, S. R., & Fassinger, R. E. (1996). Revisioning sexual minority identity and its implications for counseling and research. *The Counseling Psychologist, 24,* 508–534.

McCarthy, P. R., Shaw, T., & Schmeck, R. R. (1986). Behavioral analysis of client learning style during counseling. *Journal of Counseling Psychology, 33,* 249–254.

McCullough, L., & Farrell, A. D. (1983). The Computerized Assessment for Psychotherapy Evaluation and Research [computer program]. New York: Beth Israel Medical Center, Department of Psychiatry.

McCullough, L., Farrell, A. D., & Longabaugh, R. (1986). The development of a microcomputer-based mental health information system: A potential tool for bridging the scientist-practitioner gap. *American Psychologist, 41,* 207–214.

McDaniel, M. A., Whetzel, D. L., Schmidt, F. L., & Maurer, S. (1994). The validity of employment interview: A comprehensive view and meta-analysis. *Journal of Applied Psychology, 79,* 599–616.

McGuire, W. J. (1985). Attitudes and attitude change. In G. Lindzey & E. Aronson (Eds.), *Handbook of social psychology* (3rd ed., Vol. 2, pp. 233–346). New York: Random House.

McKay, K. M., Imel, Z. E., & Wampold, B. E. (2006). Psychiatrist effects in the psychopharmacological treatment of depression. *Journal of Affective Disorders, 92,* 287–290.

McKinney, F. (1945). Four years of a college adjustment clinic: I. Organization of clinic and problems of counselors. *Journal of Consulting Psychology, 9,* 203–212.

McLeod, J. (2001). *Qualitative research in counseling and psychotherapy*. Thousand Oaks, CA: Sage.

McNamara, K., & Horan, J. J. (1986). Experimental construct validity in the evaluation of cognitive and behavioral treatments for depression. *Journal of Counseling Psychology, 33*, 23–30.

Meara, N. M., & Day, J. D. (2003). Possibilities and challenges for academic psychology. *American Behavioral Scientist, 47*(4), 459–478.

Meara, N. M., & Patton, M. J. (1986). Language use and social influence in counseling. In F. J. Dorn (Ed.), *The social influence process in counseling and psychotherapy* (pp. 85–93). Springfield, IL: Charles C Thomas.

Meara, N. M., Schmidt, L. D., Carrington, C. H., Davis, K. L., Dixon, D. N., Fretz, B. R., Myers, R. A., Ridley, C. R., & Suinn, R. M. (1988). Training and accreditation in counseling psychology. *The Counseling Psychologist, 16*, 366–384.

Meara, N. M., Schmidt, L. D., & Day, J. D. (1996). Principles and virtues: A foundation for ethical decisions, policies, and character. *The Counseling Psychologist, 24*, 4–77.

Meara, N. M., Shannon, J. W., & Pepinsky, H. B. (1979). Comparison of the stylistic complexity of the language of counselor and client across three theoretical orientations. *Journal of Counseling Psychology, 28*, 110–118.

Meehl, P. E. (1971). A scientific, scholarly nonresearch doctorate for clinical practitioners. In R. R. Holt (Ed.), *New horizon for psychotherapy: Autonomy as a profession* (pp. 37–81). New York: International Universities Press.

Meehl, P. E. (1978). Theoretical risks and tabular asterisks: Sir Karl, Sir Ronald, and the slow progress of soft psychology. *Journal of Consulting and Clinical Psychology, 46*, 806–834.

Meehl, P. E. (1987). Why summaries of research on a psychological theory are often uninterpretable. In R. Snow & D. E. Wiley (Eds.), *Strategic thinking: A volume in honor of Lee J. Cronbach*. San Francisco: Jossey-Bass.

Megargee, E. I., & Bohn, M. J. (1979). *Classifying criminal offenders: A new system based on the MMPI*. Beverly Hills, CA: Sage.

Meichenbaum, D., Henshaw, D., & Himel, N. (1980). Coping with stress as a problem-solving process. In W. Krohne & L. Laux (Eds.), *Achievement stress and anxiety* (pp. 127–142). Washington, DC: Hemisphere.

Melby, J. N., Hoyt, W. T., & Bryant, C. M. (2003). A generalizability approach to assessing the effects of ethnicity and training on observer ratings of family interactions. *Journal of Social and Personal Relationships, 20*, 171–191.

Mercer, R. C., & Loesch, L. C. (1979). Audio tape ratings: Comments and guidelines. *Psychotherapy: Theory, Research, and Practice, 16*, 79–85.

Merrill, R. M. (1952). On Keet's study, "Two verbal techniques in a miniature counseling situation." *Journal of Abnormal and Social Psychology, 47*, 722.

Merten, J., Anstadt, T., Ullrich, B., Krause, R., & Buchheim, P. (1996). Emotional experience and facial behavior during the psychotherapeutic process and its relation to treatment outcome: A pilot study. *Psychotherapy Research, 6*, 198–212.

Meyer, V. (1957). The treatment of two phobic patients on the basis of learning principles. *Journal of Abnormal and Social Psychology, 55*, 261–266.

Meyers, L. S., Gamst, G., & Guarino, A. J. (2006). *Applied multivariate research: Design and interpretation*. Thousand Oaks, CA: Sage.

Mill, J. S. (1953). A system of logic, Book VI; On the logic of the moral sciences. In P. P. Weiner (Ed.), *Readings in philosophy of science* (pp. 255–281). New York: Scribner's. (Original work published 1843)

Miller, A. (1981). Conceptual matching models and interactional research in education. *Review of Educational Research, 51*, 33–84.

Mills, E. A. (1924). *Rocky Mountain National Park*. Garden City, NY: Doubleday, Page, & Co.

Mintz, J., & Luborsky, L. (1971). Segments vs. whole sessions: Which is the better unit for psychotherapy research? *Journal of Abnormal Psychology, 78*, 180–191.

Mintz, L. B., O'Halloran, S. M., Mullholland, A. M., & Schneider, P. A. (1997). Questionnaire for eating disorder diagnosis: Reliability and validity of operationalizing DSM-IV criteria diagnosed into a self-report format. *Journal of Counseling Psychology, 44*, 63–79.

Mintz, L. B., & O'Neil, J. M. (1990). Gender roles, sex, and the process of psychotherapy: Many questions and few answers. *Journal of Counseling and Development, 68*, 381–387.

Miranda, J., Azocar, F., Organista, K. C., Muñoz, R. F., & Lieberman, A. (1996). Recruiting and retaining low-income Latinos in psychotherapy research. *Journal of Consulting and Clinical Psychology, 64*, 868–874.

Mitchell, K. M., Bozarth, J. D., & Kraft, C. C. (1977). A reappraisal of the therapeutic effectiveness of accurate empathy, nonpossessive warmth and genuineness. In A. S. Gurman & A. M. Razin (Eds.), *Effective psychotherapy: A handbook of research* (pp. 482–502). New York: Pergamon Press.

Mohr, D. C., Shoham-Salomon, V., Engle, D., & Beutler, L. E. (1991). The expression of anger in psychotherapy for depression: Its role and measurement. *Psychotherapy Research, 1*, 124–134.

Mohr, J. J., Israel, T., & Sedlacek, W. E. (2001). Counselor's attitudes regarding bisexuality as predictors of counselor's clinical responses: An analogue study of a female bisexual client. *Journal of Counseling Psychology, 48*, 212–222.

Monte, C. F. (1980). *Beneath the mask: An introduction to theories of personality* (2nd ed.). New York: Holt, Rinehart & Winston.

Mooney, R. L., & Gordon, L. V. (1950). *Manual: The Mooney problem checklists*. New York: Psychological Corporation.

Moradi, B., & Hasan, N. T. (2004). Arab American persons' reported experiences of discrimination and mental health: The mediating role of personal control. *Journal of Counseling Psychology, 51*, 418–428.

Moradi, B., & Subich, L. M. (2003). A concomitant examination of the relations of perceived racist and sexist events to psychological distress for African American women. *The Counseling Psychologist, 31*, 451–469.

Moras, K., & Hill, C. E. (1991). Rater selection in psychotherapy process research: Observation on the state-of-the-art. *Psychotherapy Research, 1,* 113–123.

Morgan, D. (1988). *Focus groups as qualitative research.* Newbury Park, CA: Sage.

Morgan, K. S., & Brown, L. S. (1991). Lesbian career development, work behavior, and vocational counseling. *The Counseling Psychologist, 19,* 273–291.

Morran, D. K., Kurpius, D. J., & Brack, G. (1989). Empirical investigation of counselor self-talk categories. *Journal of Counseling Psychology, 36,* 505–510.

Morrison, L. A., & Shapiro, D. A. (1987). Expectancy and outcome in prescription vs. exploratory psychotherapy. *British Journal of Clinical Psychology, 29,* 54–60.

Morrow, S. L. (2005). Quality and trustworthiness in qualitative research in counseling psychology. *Journal of Counseling Psychology, 52*(2), 250–260.

Morrow, S. L., Rakhasha, G., & Castañeda, C. L. (2001). Qualitative research methods for multicultural counseling. In J. G. Ponterotto, J. M. Casas, L. A. Suzuki, & C. M. Alexander (Eds.), *Handbook of multicultural counseling* (2nd ed., pp. 575–603). Thousand Oaks, CA: Sage.

Morrow, S. L., & Smith, M. L. (1995). Constructions of survivals and coping by women who have survived childhood sexual abuse. *Journal of Counseling Psychology, 42,* 24–33.

Morrow, S. L., & Smith, M. L. (2000). Qualitative research for counseling psychology. In S. D. Brown & R. W. Lent (Eds.), *Handbook of counseling psychology* (3rd ed., 199–230). New York: John Wiley & Sons.

Moustakas, C. (1994). *Phenomenological research methods.* Thousand Oaks, CA: Sage.

Mueller, R. O. (1996). *Basic principles of structural equation modeling: An introduction to LISREL and EQS.* New York: Springer.

Mueller, W. J. (1969). Patterns of behavior and their reciprocal impact in the family and in psychotherapy [monograph]. *Journal of Counseling Psychology, 16,* 1–25.

Multon, K. D., Ellis-Kalton, C. A., Heppner, M. J., & Gysbers, N. C. (2003). Counselor verbal response modes and working alliance in career counseling. *Career Development Quarterly, 51,* 259–273.

Multon, K. D., Heppner, M. J., & Lapan, R. T. (1995). An empirical derivation of career decision subtypes in a high school sample. *Journal of Vocational Behavior, 47,* 76–92.

Multon, K. D., Wood, R., Heppner, M. J., & Gysbers, N. C. (in press). A cluster-analytic investigation of subtypes of adult career counseling clients: Toward a taxonomy of career problems. *Journal of Career Assessment.*

Munley, P. H. (1974). A review of counseling analogue research methods. *Journal of Counseling Psychology, 21,* 320–330.

Munley, P. H., Sharkin, B., & Gelso, C. J. (1988). Reviewer ratings and agreement on manuscripts reviewed for the *Journal of Counseling Psychology. Journal of Counseling Psychology, 35,* 198–202.

Myers, J. E., & Sweeney, T. J. (2004). Advocacy for the counseling profession: Results of a national survey. *Journal of Counseling and Development, 82,* 466–471.

Nagel, D. P., Hoffman, M. A., & Hill, C. E. (1995). A comparison of verbal response modes used by master's level career counselors and other helpers. *Journal of Counseling and Development, 74,* 101–104.

Nagelberg, D. B., Pillsbury, E. C., & Balzor, D. M. (1983). The prevalence of depression as a function of gender and facility usage in college students. *Journal of College Student Personnel, 24,* 525–529.

National Institutes of Health. (1994). *NIH guidelines on the inclusion of women and minorities as subjects in clinical research* (59 FR 14508–14513). Washington, DC: U.S. Department of Health and Human Services.

Neimeyer, G., & Resnikoff, A. (1982). Major contribution: Qualitative strategies in counseling research. *The Counseling Psychologist, 101*(4), 75–85.

Neimeyer, G. J., Saferstein, J., & Rice, K. G. (2005). Does the model matter? The relationship between science-practice emphasis and outcomes in academic training programs in counseling psychology. *The Counseling Psychologist, 33,* 635–654.

Neisser, U. (1976). *Cognition and reality: Principles and implications of cognitive psychology.* San Francisco: Freeman.

Nelson, C., Treichler, P. A., & Grossberg, L. (1992). Cultural studies: An introduction. In L. Grossberg, C. Nelson, & P. A. Treichler (Eds.), *Cultural studies* (pp. 1–16). New York: Routledge.

Neville, H., & Carter, R. (2005). Race and racism in counseling psychology research, training, and practice: A critical review, current trends, and future directions. *The Counseling Psychologist, 33,* 413–418.

Neville, H. A., Heppner, P. P., Ji, P., & Thye, R. (2004). The relations among general and race-related stressors and psychoeducational adjustment in black students attending predominately white institutions. *Journal of Black Studies, 34,* 599–618.

Neville, H. A., Lilly, R. L., Duran, G., Lee, R. M., & Browne, L. (2000). Construction and initial validation of the Color-Blind Racial Attitudes Scale (CoBRAS). *Journal of Counseling Psychology, 47,* 59–70.

Newman, D., & Brown, R. (1996). *Applied ethics for program evaluation.* Beverly Hills, CA: Sage.

Newman, I., & Benz, C. R. (1998). *Qualitative-quantitative research methodology: Exploring the interactive continuum.* Carbondale: University of Illinois Press.

Nghe, L. T., & Mahalik, J. R. (2001). Examining racial identity statuses as predictors of psychological defenses in African American college students. *Journal of Counseling Psychology, 48,* 10–16.

Nickerson, R. S. (2000). Null hypothesis significance testing: A review of an old and continuing controversy. *Psychological Methods, 5,* 241–301.

Nisbett, R. E., & Ross, L. (1980). *Human inference: Strategies and shortcomings of social judgment.* Englewood Cliffs, NJ: Prentice-Hall.

Nisbett, R. E., & Wilson, T. D. (1977). Telling more than we can know: Verbal reports on mental processes. *Psychological Review, 84,* 231–259.

Nocita, A., & Stiles, W. B. (1986). Client introversion and counseling session impact. *Journal of Counseling Psychology, 33,* 235–241.

Noonan, B. M., Gallor, S. M., Hensler-McGinnis, N. F., Fassinger, R. E., Wang, S., & Goodman, J. (2004). Challenge and success: A qualitative study of the career development of highly achieving women with physical and sensory disabilities. *Journal of Counseling Psychology, 51,* 68–80.

Norcross, J. C. (2001). Purposes, processes, and products of the Task Force on Empirically Supported Therapy Relationships. *Psychotherapy: Theory/Research/Practice/Training, 38,* 345–356.

Norcross, J. C., Beutler, L. E., & Levant, R. F. (Eds.). (2006). *Evidence-based practices in mental health: Debate and dialogue on the fundamental questions.* Washington, DC: American Psychological Association.

Norton, I. M., & Manson, S. M. (1996). Research in American Indian and Alaska Native communities: Navigating the cultural universe of values and process. *Journal of Consulting and Clinical Psychology, 64,* 856–860.

Nunnally, J. C. (1978). *Psychometric theory.* New York: McGraw-Hill.

O'Farrell, M. K., Hill, C. E., & Patton, S. M. (1986). A comparison of two cases of counseling with the same counselor. *Journal of Counseling and Development, 65,* 141–145.

Ogles, B. M., Lambert, M. J., & Fields, S. A. (2002). *Essentials of outcome assessment.* New York: Wiley.

Okazaki, S., & Kallivayalil, D. (2002). Cultural norms and subjective disability as predictors of symptom reports among Asian Americans and White Americans. *Journal of Cross-Cultural Psychology, 33,* 482–491.

O'Neil, J. M., Helms, B., Gable, R., David, L., & Wrightsman, L. (1986). Gender Role Conflict Scale: College men's fear of femininity. *Sex Roles, 14,* 335–350.

O'Neil, J. M., & Roberts Carroll, M. (1987). *A six-day workshop on gender role conflict and strain: Helping adult men and women take the gender role journey.* Storrs, CT: University of Connecticut, Department of Educational Psychology, Counseling Psychology Program. (ERIC Document Reproduction Service No. ED275963).

O'Neil, J. M., & Roberts Carroll, M. (1988). A gender role workshop focused on sexism, gender role conflict, and the gender role journey. *Journal of Counseling and Development, 67,* 193–197.

O'Neill, J., Small, B. B., & Strachan, J. (1999). The use of focus groups within a participatory action research environment. In M. Kopala & L. A. Suzuki (Eds.), *Using qualitative methods in psychology* (pp. 199–209). Thousand Oaks, CA: Sage.

Orlinsky, D. E., Grawe, K., & Parks, B. K. (1994). Process and outcome in psychotherapy: Noch einmal. In A. E. Bergin & S. L. Garfield (Eds.), *Handbook of psychotherapy and behavior change* (4th ed., pp. 270–376). New York: Wiley.

Orlinsky, D. E., & Howard, K. I. (1975). *Varieties of psychotherapeutic experience: Multivariate analyses of patients' and therapists' reports.* New York: Teachers College Press.

Orlinsky, D. E., & Howard, K. I. (1978). The relation of process to outcome in psychotherapy. In S. L. Garfield & A. E. Bergin (Eds.), *Handbook of psychotherapy and behavior change* (2nd ed., pp. 283–330). New York: Wiley.

Orlinsky, D. E., & Howard, K. I. (1986). The relation of process to outcome in psychotherapy. In S. L. Garfield & A. E. Bergin (Eds.), *Handbook of psychotherapy and behavior change* (3rd ed., pp. 311–381). New York: Wiley.

Orlinsky, D. E., Ronnestad, M. H., & Willutzki, U. (2004). Fifty years of psychotherapy process-outcome research: Continuity and change. In M. J. Lambert (Ed.), *Bergin and Garfield's handbook of psychotherapy and behavior change* (5th ed., pp. 307–389). New York: Wiley.

Osipow, S. H. (1979). Counseling researchers: Why they perish. *The Counseling Psychologist, 8,* 39–41.

Osipow, S. H., Carney, C. G., Winer, J., Yanico, B., & Koschier, M. (1976). *Career Decision Scale* (3rd rev.). Odessa, FL: Psychological Assessment Resources.

Oyserman, D., Coon, H. M., & Kemmelmeier, M. (2002). Rethinking individualism and collectivism: Evaluation of theoretical assumptions and meta-analyses. *Psychological Bulletin, 128,* 3–72.

Paivio, S. C., & Greenberg, L. S. (1995). Resolving "unfinished business": Efficacy of experiential therapy using empty-chair dialogue. *Journal of Consulting and Clinical Psychology, 63,* 419–425.

Parham, T. A. (1989). Cycles of psychological nigrescence. *The Counseling Psychologist, 17,* 187–226.

Parham, T. A., & Helms, J. E. (1981). The influence of black students' racial identity attitudes on preference for counselor's race. *Journal of Counseling Psychology, 28,* 250–257.

Parham, T. A., & Helms, J. E. (1985a). Attitudes of racial identity and self-esteem of black students: An exploratory investigation. *Journal of College Student Personnel, 26,* 143–147.

Parham, T. A., & Helms, J. E. (1985b). The relationship of racial identity attitudes to self-actualization and affective states of black students. *Journal of Counseling Psychology, 32,* 431–440.

Parloff, M. B., Waskow, I. E., & Wolfe, B. E. (1978). Research on therapist variables in relation to process and outcome. In S. L. Garfield & A. E. Bergin (Eds.), *Handbook of psychotherapy and behavior change* (2nd ed., pp. 233–282). New York: Wiley.

Parr, J., & Neimeyer, G. J. (1994). Effects of gender, construct type, occupational information, and career relevance on vocational differentiation. *Journal of Counseling Psychology, 41,* 27–33.

Patten, M. L. (2001). *Questionnaire research: A practical guide* (2nd ed.). Los Angeles, CA: Pyrczak.

Patterson, G. R., & Forgatch, M. S. (1985). Therapist behavior as a determinant for client noncompliance: A paradox for the behavior modifier. *Journal of Consulting and Clinical Psychology, 53,* 846–851.

Patton, M. J. (1984). Managing social interaction in counseling: A contribution from the philosophy of science. *Journal of Counseling Psychology, 31,* 442–456.

Patton, M. J., Kivlighan, D. M., Jr., & Multon, K. D. (1997). The Missouri psychoanalytic counseling research project: Relation of changes in counseling process to client outcome. *Journal of Counseling Psychology, 44,* 189–208.

Patton, M. Q. (1987). *How to use qualitative methods in evaluation.* Newbury Park, CA: Sage.

Patton, M. Q. (1990). *Qualitative evaluation and research methods* (2nd ed.). Newbury Park, CA: Sage.

Patton, M. Q. (1997). *Utilization-focused evaluation: The new century text* (3rd ed.). Thousand Oaks, CA: Sage.

Patton, M. Q. (2002). *Qualitative evaluation and research methods* (3rd ed.). Thousand Oaks, CA: Sage.

Paul, G. L. (1967). Strategy of outcome research in psychotherapy. *Journal of Consulting Psychology, 31,* 109–118.

Paulhus, D. L. (1984). Two-component models of socially desirable responding. *Journal of Personality and Social Psychology, 46,* 598–609.

Paulhus, D. L. (1991). Balanced inventory of desirable responding. In J. P. Robinson, P. R. Shaver, & L. S. Wrightsman (Eds.), *Measures of personality and social psychological attitudes* (pp. 37–41). San Diego: Academic Press.

Pedersen, P. (1988). *A handbook for developing multicultural awareness.* Alexandria, VA: American Association for Counseling and Development.

Pedersen, P. B. (1994). *A handbook for developing multicultural awareness* (2nd ed.). Alexandria, VA: American Counseling Association.

Pedersen, P. B. (1995). Culture-centered ethical guidelines for counselors. In J. G Ponterotto, J. M. Casas, L. A. Suzuki, & C. M. Alexander (Eds.), *Handbook of multicultural counseling* (pp. 34–49). Thousand Oaks, CA: Sage.

Pedersen, P. B., Draguns, J. G., Lonner, W. J., & Trimble, J. E. (Eds.). (1996). *Counseling across cultures* (4th ed.). Thousand Oaks, CA: Sage.

Pedhazur, E. (1982). *Multiple regression in behavioral research: Explanation and prediction* (2nd ed.). New York: Holt, Rinehart & Winston.

Penman, R. (1980). *Communication processes and relationships.* London: Academic Press.

Pepinsky, H. B. (1984). Language and the production and interpretation of social interactions. In H. F. Fisher (Ed.), *Language and logic in personality and society* (pp. 93–129). New York: Columbia University Press.

Pepinsky, H. B., & Pepinsky, P. N. (1954). *Counseling theory and practice.* New York: Ronald Press.

Petersen, P. B., Draguns, J. G., Lonner, W. J. & Trimble, J. E. (in press) (Eds.) *Counseling across cultures* (sixth ed.) Thousand Oaks, CA: Sage.

Pett, M. A., Lackey, N. R., & Sullivan, J. J. (2003). *Making sense of factor analysis: The use of factor analysis for instrument development in health care research.* Thousand Oaks, CA: Sage.

Petty, R. E., & Cacioppo, J. T. (1977). Forewarning, cognitive responding, and resistance to persuasion. *Journal of Personality and a Social Psychology, 35,* 645–655.

Petty, R. E., & Cacioppo, J. T. (1981). *Attitudes and persuasion: Classic and contemporary approaches.* Dubuque, IA: William C. Brown.

Petty, R. E., & Cacioppo, J. T. (1986). *Communication and persuasion: Central and peripheral routes to attitude change.* New York: Springer-Verlag.

Pfungst, O. (1911). *A contribution to experimental, animal, and human psychology.* New York: Holt, Rinehart & Winston.

Phelps, A., Friedlander, M. L., & Enns, C. Z. (1997). Psychotherapy process variables associated with the retrieval of memories of childhood sexual abuse: A qualitative study. *Journal of Counseling Psychology, 44,* 321–332.

Phillips, J. C., & Russell, R. K. (1994). Research self-efficacy, the research training environment, and research productivity among graduate students in counseling psychology. *The Counseling Psychologist, 22,* 628–641.

Phillips, S. D., Friedlander, M. L., Pazienza, N. J., & Kost, P. P. (1985). A factor analytic investigation of career decision-making styles. *Journal of Vocational Behavior, 26,* 106–115.

Phinney, J. (1996). When we talk about American ethnic groups, what do we mean? *American Psychologist, 51,* 98–927.

Pidgeon, N. (1996). Grounded theory: Theoretical background. In J. T. E. Richardson (Ed.), *Handbook of qualitative research methods for psychology and the social sciences* (pp. 75–85). Leicester, UK: British Psychological Society Books.

Pidgeon, N., & Henwood, K. (1996). Grounded theory: Practical implementation. In J. T. E. Richardson (Ed.), *Handbook of qualitative research methods for psychology and the social sciences* (pp. 86–101). Leicester, UK: British Psychological Society Books.

Plummer, D. L., & Slane, S. (1996). Patterns of coping in racially stressful situations. *Journal of Black Psychology, 22,* 89–95.

Polkinghorne, D. (1983). *Methodology for the human sciences: Systems of inquiry.* Albany: State University of New York.

Polkinghorne, D. E. (1984). Further extensions of methodological diversity for counseling psychology. *Journal of Counseling Psychology, 31,* 416–429.

Polkinghorne, D. E. (2005). Language and meaning, data collection in qualitative research. *Journal of Counseling Psychology, 52,* 137–145.

Ponce, F. Q., & Atkinson, D. R. (1989). Mexican-American acculturation, counselor ethnicity, counseling style, and perceived credibility. *Journal of Counseling Psychology, 36,* 203–208.

Ponterotto, J. G. (1988a). Racial consciousness development among white counselor trainees: A stage model. *Journal of Multicultural Counseling and Development, 16,* 146–156.

Ponterotto, J. G. (1988b). Racial/ethnic minority research in the *Journal of Counseling Psychology:* A content analysis and methodological critique. *Journal of Counseling Psychology, 35,* 410–418.

Ponterotto, J. G. (1998). Charting a course for research in multicultural counseling training. *The Counseling Psychologist, 43,* 26–68.

Ponterotto, J. G. (2005a). Integrating qualitative research requirements into professional psychology training programs in North America: Rationale and curriculum model. *Qualitative Research in Psychology, 2,* 97–116.

Ponterotto, J. G. (2005b). Qualitative research in counseling psychology: A primer on research paradigms and philosophy of science. *Journal of Counseling Psychology, 52,* 126–136.

Ponterotto, J. G., & Casas, J. M. (1991). *Handbook of racial/ethnic minority counseling research.* Springfield, IL: Charles C Thomas.

Ponterotto, J. G., Casas, J. M., Suzuki, L. A., & Alexander, C. A. (Eds.). (1995). *Handbook of multicultural counseling.* Thousand Oaks, CA: Sage.

Ponterotto, J. G., Casas, J. M., Suzuki, L. A., & Alexander, C. A. (Eds.). (2001). *Handbook of multicultural counseling.* (2nd ed.). Thousand Oaks, CA: Sage.

Ponterotto, J. G., Fuertes, J. N., & Chen, E. C. (2000). Models of multicultural counseling. In S. D. Brown & R. W. Lent (Eds.), *Handbook of counseling psychology* (3rd ed., pp. 639–669). New York: Wiley.

Ponterotto, J. G., & Furlong, M. J. (1985). Evaluating counselor effectiveness: A critical review of rating scale instruments. *Journal of Counseling Psychology, 32,* 597–616.

Ponterotto, J. G., & Grieger, I. (1999). Merging qualitative and quantitative perspectives in research identity. In M. Kopala & L. Suzuki (Eds.), *Using qualitative methods in psychology* (pp. 49–62). Thousand Oaks, CA: Sage.

Ponterotto, J. G., & Grieger, I. (in press). Guidelines and competencies for cross-cultural counseling research. In P. B. Pedersen, J. G. Draguns, W. J. Lonner, & J. E. Trimble (Eds.), *Counseling across cultures* (6th ed.). Thousand Oaks, CA: Sage.

Ponterotto, J. G., & Pedersen, P. B. (1993). *Preventing prejudice: A guide for counselors and educators.* Newbury Park, CA: Sage.

Ponterotto, J. G., Rieger, B. P., Barrett, A., & Sparks, R. (1994). Assessing multicultural counseling competence: A review of instrumentation.

Journal of Counseling and Development, 72, 316–322.

Porter, A. C., & Raudenbush, S. W. (1987). Analysis of covariance: Its model and use in psychological research. *Journal of Counseling Psychology, 34,* 383–392.

Powell, C. J. (1984). Ethical principles and issues of competence in counseling adolescents. *The Counseling Psychologist, 121*(3), 57–68.

Pressley, M., Raphael, L., Gallagher, J. D., & DiBella, J. (2004). Providence-St. Mel school: How a school that works for African American students works. *Journal of Educational Psychology, 96,* 216–235.

Price, D. J. (1963). *Little science, big science.* New York: Columbia University Press.

Purdon, C., Antony, M. M., & Swinson, R. P. (1999). Psychometric properties of the Frost Multidimensional Perfectionism Scale in a clinical anxiety disorders sample. *Journal of Clinical Psychology, 55,* 1271–1286.

Putman, H. (1962). What theories are not. In E. P. Nagel, P. Suppes, & A. Tarski (Eds.), *Logic, methodology, and philosophy of science: Proceedings of the 1960 international congress* (pp. 240–251). Stanford, CA: Stanford University Press.

Quintana, S. M., Troyano, N., & Gaylor, G. (2001). Cultural validity and inherent challenges in quantitative methods for multicultural research. In J. G. Ponterotto, J. M. Casas, L. A. Suzuki, & C. A. Alexander (Eds.), *Handbook of multicultural counseling* (pp. 604–630). Thousand Oaks, CA: Sage.

Rabinowitz, F. E., Heppner, P. P., & Roehlke, H. J. (1986). Descriptive study of process and outcome variables of supervision over time. *Journal of Counseling Psychology, 33,* 292–300.

Rachman, S. L., & Wilson, G. T. (1980). *The effects of psychological therapy.* New York: Pergamon Press.

Raimy, V. (Ed.). (1950). *Training in clinical psychology.* New York: Prentice-Hall.

Ramsey, P. (1970). *The patient as person.* New Haven, CT: Yale University.

Rappaport, D. (1960). The structure of psychoanalytic theory. *Psychological Issues,* Monograph 6. New York: International Universities Press.

Raudenbush, S. W., & Bryk, A. S. (2002). *Hierarchical linear models* (2nd ed.). Thousand Oaks, CA: Sage.

Raudenbush, S. W., & Chan, W. S. (1993). Application of a hierarchical linear model to the study of adolescent deviance in an overlapping cohort design. *Journal of Consulting and Clinical Psychology, 61,* 941–951.

Ravets, P. C. (1993). Group supervision: A multiple case study. *Dissertation Abstracts International, 54,* 2768.

Reising, G. N., & Daniels, M. H. (1983). A study of Hogan's model of counselor development and supervision. *Journal of Counseling Psychology, 30,* 235–244.

Rennie, D. L. (1994a). Clients' accounts of resistance in counseling: A qualitative analysis. *Canadian Journal of Counselling, 28,* 43–57.

Rennie, D. L. (1994b). Client's deference in psychotherapy. *Journal of Counseling Psychology, 41,* 427–437.

Rennie, D. L. (1994c). Storytelling on psychotherapy: The client's subjective experience. *Psychotherapy, 31,* 234–243.

Rennie, D. L. (1996). Fifteen years of doing qualitative research on psychotherapy. *British Journal of Guidance & Counselling, 24*(3), 317–327.

Rennie, D. L. (2000). Grounded theory methodology as methodical hermeneutics. *Theory & Psychology, 10*(4), 481–502.

Rennie, D. L., Watson, K. D., & Monteiro, A. M. (2002). The rise of qualitative research in psychology. *Canadian Psychology, 43,* 179–189.

Resnikoff, A. (1978). Scientific affairs committee report, 1975–1977: A discussion of methodology. *The Counseling Psychologist, 71*(4), 67–71.

Revicki, D. A., May, H. J., & Whitley, T. W. (1990). Reliability and validity of the Work Related Strain Inventory among health professionals. *Behavioral Medicine, 17,* 111–120.

Reynolds, W. M. (1982). Development of reliable and valid short forms of the Marlowe-Crowne Social Desirability Scale. *Journal of Clinical Psychology, 38,* 119–125.

Rice, L., & Kerr, G. (1986). Measures of client and therapist vocal quality. In L. Greenberg & W. Pinsof (Eds.), *The psychotherapy process: A research handbook* (pp. 73–106). New York: Guilford Press.

Rice, L. N., Koke, L. J., Greenberg, L. S., & Wagstaff, A. K. (1979). *Manual for client vocal quality* (Vol. 1). Toronto: Counseling and Development Center, York University.

Richardson, M. S., & Johnson, M. (1984). Counseling women. In S. R. Brown & R. W. Lent (Eds.), *Handbook of counseling psychology* (pp. 832–877). New York: Wiley.

Richie, B. S., Fassinger, R. E., Linn, S. G., Johnson, J., Prosser, J., & Robinson, S. (1997). Persistence, connection, and passion: A qualitative study of the career development of highly achieving African American-Black and White women. *Journal of Counseling Psychology, 44,* 133–148.

Ridley, C. R. (1995). *Overcoming unintentional racism in counseling and therapy: A practitioner's guide to intentional intervention.* Thousand Oaks, CA: Sage.

Ridley, C. R., Mendoza, D. W., & Kanitz, B. E. (1994). Multicultural training: Reexamination, operationalization, and integration. *The Counseling Psychologist, 22,* 227–289.

Ridley, C. R., Mendoza, D. W., Kanitz, B. E., Angermeier, L., & Zenk, R. (1994). Cultural sensitivity in multicultural counseling: A perceptual schema model. *Journal of Counseling Psychology, 41,* 125–136.

Riggio, R. E. (1989). *Social Skills Inventory manual* (research ed.). Palo Alto, CA: Consulting Psychologists Press.

Robinson, F. P. (1950). *Principles and procedures in student counseling.* New York: Harper & Brothers.

Robinson, T. L., & Howard-Hamilton, M. F. (2000). *The convergence of race, ethnicity, and gender: Multiple identities in counseling.* Upper Saddle River, NJ: Prentice-Hall.

Rogers, C. R. (1955). Persons or science? A philosophical question. *American Psychologist, 10,* 267–278.

Rogers, C. R. (1957). The necessary and sufficient conditions of therapeutic personality change. *Journal of Consulting Psychology, 21,* 95–103.

Rogers, C. R. (1961). *On becoming a person.* Boston: Houghton Mifflin.

Rogers, L. B. (1954). A comparison of two kinds of test interpretation interview. *Journal of Counseling Psychology, 1,* 224–231.

Rojewski, J. W. (1994). Career indecision types for rural adolescents from disadvantaged and nondisadvantaged backgrounds. *Journal of Counseling Psychology, 41,* 356–363.

Rokeach, M. (1973). *The nature of human values.* New York: Free Press.

Romano, J. L., & Kachgal, M. M. (2004). Counseling psychology and school counseling: An underutilized partnership. *The Counseling Psychologist, 32,* 184–215.

Rosenbaum, M. (1982). Ethical problems of group psychotherapy. In M. Rosenbaum (Ed.), *Ethics and values in psychotherapy* (pp. 237–257). New York: Free Press.

Rosenberg, M. (1965). *Society and the adolescent self-image.* Princeton, NJ: Princeton University Press.

Rosenthal, D., & Frank, J. D. (1956). Psychotherapy and the placebo effect. *Psychological Bulletin, 53,* 294–302.

Rosenthal, R. (1966). *Experimenter effects in behavioral research.* New York: Meredith.

Rosenthal, R. (1995). Writing meta-analytic reviews. *Psychological Bulletin, 118,* 183–192.

Rosenthal, R., & Jacobson, L. (1968). *Pygmalion in the classroom: Teacher expectations of the disadvantaged.* New York: Holt, Rinehart & Winston.

Rosenthal, R., & Rosnow, R. L. (1969). The volunteer subject. In R. Rosenthal & R. L. Rosnow (Eds.), *Artifact in behavioral research* (pp. 61–118). New York: Academic Press.

Rosnow, R. L., & Rosenthal, R. (1988). Focused tests of significance and effect size estimation in counseling psychology. *Journal of Counseling Psychology, 35,* 203–208.

Rosnow, R. L., & Rosenthal, R. (1997). *People studying people: Artifacts and ethics in behavioral research.* New York: Freeman.

Ross, R. R., & Altmaier, E. M. (1990). Job analysis of psychology internships in counseling center settings. *Journal of Counseling Psychology, 37,* 459–464.

Ross, W. D. (1930). *The right and the good.* Oxford, England: Clarendon.

Rossi, P., & Freeman, H. (1999). *Evaluation: A systematic approach.* Thousand Oaks, CA: Sage.

Rowe, D. C., Vazsonyi, A. T., & Flannery, D. J. (1994). No more than skin deep: Ethnic and racial similarity in developmental process. *Psychological Review, 101,* 396–413.

Rowe, W., & Atkinson, D. R. (1995). Misrepresentation and interpretation: Critical evaluation of white racial identity development models. *The Counseling Psychologist, 23,* 364–367.

Rowe, W., Bennett, S. K., & Atkinson, D. R. (1994). White racial identity models: A critique and alternative proposal. *The Counseling Psychologist, 22,* 129–146.

Royalty, G. M., Gelso, C. J., Mallinckrodt, B., & Garrett, K. D. (1986). The environment and the student in counseling psychology: Does the research training environment influence graduate students' attitude toward research? *The Counseling Psychologist, 14,* 9–30.

Royalty, G. M., & Magoon, T. M. (1985). Correlates of scholarly productivity among counseling psychologists. *Journal of Counseling Psychology, 32,* 458–461.

Royalty, G. M., & Reising, G. N. (1986). The research training of counseling psychologists: What the professionals say. *The Counseling Psychologist, 14,* 49–60.

Rubinton, N. (1980). Instruction in career decision making and decision-making styles. *Journal of Counseling Psychology, 27,* 581–588.

Ruch, F. L., & Zimbardo, P. G. (1970). *Psychology and life* (8th ed.). Glenview, IL: Scott, Foresman.

Rumenik, D. K., Capasso, D. R., & Hendrick, C. (1977). Experimenter sex effects in behavioral research. *Psychological Bulletin, 84,* 852–877.

Rushton, J. P. (2000). *Race, evolution, and behavior: A life history perspective.* Port Huron, MI: Charles Darwin Research Institute.

Russel, D. E. (1986). *The secrete trauma: Incest in the lives of the girls and women.* New York: Basic Books.

Russell, R. K., & Lent, R. W. (1982). Cue-controlled relaxation and systematic desensitization versus nonspecific factors in treating test anxiety. *Journal of Counseling Psychology, 29,* 100–103.

Russell, R. K., & Sipich, J. F. (1973). Cue-controlled relaxation in the treatment of test anxiety. *Journal of Behavior Therapy and Experimental Psychiatry, 4,* 47–50.

Russell, R. L. (1987). *Language in psychotherapy: Strategies of discovery.* New York: Plenum.

Russell, R. L., & Stiles, W. B. (1979). Categories for classifying language in psychotherapy. *Psychological Bulletin, 86,* 404–419.

Rust, R. E., & Davie, J. S. (1961). The personal problems of college students. *Mental Hygiene, 45,* 247–257.

Sabnani, H. B., & Ponterotto, J. G. (1992). Racial/ethnic minority-specific instrumentation in counseling research: A review, critique, and recommendation. *Measurement & Evaluation in Counseling & Development, 24,* 161–187.

Salsman, N. L., & Linehan, M. M. (2006). Dialectic-behavioral therapy for borderline personality disorder. *Primary Psychiatry, 13,* 51–58.

Sax, G. (1989). *Principles of educational and psychological measurement and evaluation* (3rd ed.). Belmont, CA: Wadsworth.

Schechtman, Z., Gilat, I., Fos, L., & Flasher, A. (1996). Brief group therapy with low-achieving elementary school children. *Journal of Counseling Psychology, 43,* 376–382.

Scher, M., & Good, G. E. (1990). Gender and counseling in the twenty-first century: What does the future hold? *Journal of Counseling and Development, 68,* 388–391.

Schmidt, F. L., & Hunter, J. E. (1996). Measurement error in psychological research: Lessons from 26 research scenarios. *Psychological Methods, 1,* 199–223.

Schmidt, L. D., & Meara, N. M. (1984). Ethical, professional, and legal issues in counseling psychology. In S. D. Brown & R. W. Lent (Eds.), *Handbook of counseling psychology* (pp. 56–96). New York: Wiley.

Schmidt, L. D., & Strong, S. R. (1971). Attractiveness and influence in counseling. *Journal of Counseling Psychology, 18,* 348–351.

Schneidler, G. G., & Berdie, R. F. (1942). Representativeness of college students who receive counseling services. *Journal of Educational Psychology, 33,* 545–551.

Schofield, J. W. (1986). Causes and consequences of the colorblind perspective. In J. F. Dovidio & S. L. Gaertner (Eds.), *Prejudice, discrimination, and racism* (pp. 231–253). New York: Academic Press.

Schotte, D., & Clum, G. (1982). Suicide ideation in a college population: A test of a model. *Journal of Consulting and Clinical Psychology, 50,* 690–696.

Schuller, R., Crits-Christoph, P., & Connolly, M. B. (1991). The Resistance Scale: Background and psychometric properties. *Psychoanalytic Psychology, 8,* 195–211.

Schutz, A. (1964). *Collected papers II: Studies in social theory* (A. Broderson, Ed.). The Hague, The Netherlands: Martinus-Nijhoff.

Schwandt, T. A. (2000). Three epistemological stances for qualitative inquiry: interpretivism, hermeneutics, and social constructionism. In N. K. Denzin & Y. S. Lincoln (Eds.), *Handbook of qualitative research* (pp. 189–213). Thousand Oaks, CA: Sage.

Scriven, M. (1980). *The logic of evaluation.* Inverness, CA: Edgepress.

Seeman, J. (1959). Organizing a thesis proposal. *American Psychologist, 9,* 794–797.

Seeman, J. (1969). Deception in psychological research. *American Psychologist, 24,* 1025–1028.

Seggar, L., & Lambert, M. J. (1994, June). *Assessing clinical significance: Application to the Beck Depression Inventory.* Paper presented at the annual meeting of the Society for Psychotherapy Research, York, England.

Serlin, R. C. (1987). Hypothesis testing, theory building, and the philosophy of science. *Journal of Counseling Psychology, 34,* 365–371.

Serlin, R. C., & Lapsley, D. K. (1985). Rationality in psychological research: The good enough principle. *American Psychologist, 40,* 73–83.

Serlin, R. C., Wampold, B. E., & Levin, J. R. (2003). Should providers of treatment be regarded as a random factor? If it ain't broke, don't "fix" it: A comment on Siemer and Joorman (2003). *Psychological Methods, 8,* 524–534.

Shadish, W. R., Cook, T. D., & Campbell, D. T. (2002). *Experimental and quasi-experimental designs for generalized causal inference.* Boston: Houghton Mifflin.

Shaw, B. F., Elkin, I., Yamaguchi, J., Olmsted, M., Vallis, T. M., Dobson, K. S., et al., (1999). Therapist competence ratings in relation to clinical outcome in cognitive therapy of depression. *Journal of Consulting and Clinical Psychology, 67,* 837–846.

Shlien, J. M., Mosak, H. H., & Dreikurs, R. (1962). Effects of time limits: A comparison of two psychotherapies. *Journal of Counseling Psychology, 9,* 31–34.

Silberschatz, G., Fretter, P. B., & Curtis, J. T. (1986). How do interpretations influence the process of therapy? *Journal of Consulting and Clinical Psychology, 54,* 646–652.

Sipich, J. F., Russell, R. K., & Tobias, L. L. (1974). A comparison of covert sensitization and "nonspecific" treatment in the modification of smoking behavior. *Journal of Behavior, Therapy, and Experimental Psychiatry, 5,* 201–203.

Slaney, R. B., Mobley, M., Trippi, J., Ashby, J., & Johnson, D. G. (1996). *The Almost Perfect Scale—Revised.* Unpublished manuscript, Pennsylvania State University, University Park campus.

Slaney, R. B., Rice, K. G., Mobley, M. Trippi, J., & Ashby, J. S. (2001). The Revised Almost Perfect Scale, *Measurement and Evaluation in Counseling and Development, 34,* 130–145.

Slate, J. R., & Jones, C. H. (1989). Can teaching of the WISC-R be improved? Quasi-experimental exploration. *Professional Psychology Research and Practice, 20,* 408–410.

Slusher, M. P., & Anderson, C. A. (1989). Belief perseverance and self-defeating behavior. In R. Curtis (Ed.), *Self-defeating behaviors: Experimental research, clinical impressions, and practical implications* (pp. 11–40). New York: Plenum.

Smith, M. L., & Glass, G. V. (1977). Meta-analysis of psychotherapy outcome studies. *American Psychologist, 32,* 752–760.

Smith, M. L., Glass, G. V., & Miller, T. I. (1980). *The benefits of psychotherapy.* Baltimore: Johns Hopkins University Press.

Smith, N. (Ed.). (1982). *Communication strategies in evaluation.* Beverly Hills, CA: Sage.

Smith, N. G., & Ingram, K. M. (2004). Workplace heterosexism and adjustment among lesbian, gay, and bisexual individuals: The role of unsupportive social interaction. *Journal of Counseling Psychology, 51,* 57–67.

Smith, R. E., & Nye, S. L. (1989). Comparison of induced effect and covert rehearsal in the acquisition of stress management coping skills. *Journal of Counseling Psychology, 36,* 17–23.

Snijders, T., & Bosker, R. (1999). *Multilevel analysis: An introduction to basic and advanced multilevel modeling.* London: Sage.

Snyder, D., & Wills, R. M. (1989). Behavioral versus insight-oriented marital therapy: Effects on individual and interspousal functioning. *Journal of Consulting and Clinical Psychology, 57,* 39–46.

Snyder, D. K., Wills, R. M., & Grady-Fletcher, A. (1991). Long-term effectiveness of behavioral versus insight oriented therapy: A 4-year follow-up. *Journal of Consulting and Clinical Psychology, 59,* 138–141.

Spanierman, L. B., & Poteat, V. P. (2005). Moving beyond complacency to commitment: Multicultural research in counseling. *The Counseling Psychologist, 33,* 513–523.

Speight, S. L., & Vera, E. M. (2003). Social justice agenda: Ready, or not? *The Counseling Psychologist, 32,* 109–118.

Spengler, P. M., Strohmer, D. C., Dixon, D. N., & Shivy, V. A. (1995). A scientist-practitioner model of psychological assessment: Implications for training, practice, and research. *The Counseling Psychologist, 23,* 506–534.

Spiegel, D., & Keith-Spiegel, P. (1970). Assignment of publication credits: Ethics and practices of psychologists. *American Psychologist, 25,* 738–747.

Spitzer, R. L., Gibbon, M., Skodol, A. E., Williams, J. B. W., & First, M. B. (Eds.). (1994). *DSM-IV case book.* Washington, DC: American Psychiatric Press.

Stanton, J. M. (1998). An assessment of data collection using the internet. *Personnel Psychology, 51,* 709–725.

Sternberg, R. J. (1988). *The psychologist's companion: A guide to scientific writing for students and researchers* (2nd ed.). New York: Cambridge University Press.

Stewart, G. M., & Gregory, B. C. (1996). Themes of a long-term AIDS support group for gay men. *The Counseling Psychologist, 24,* 285–303.

Stiles, W. B. (1980). Measurement of the impact of psychotherapy sessions. *Journal of Consulting and Clinical Psychology, 48,* 176–185.

Stiles, W. B. (1988). Psychotherapy process-outcome correlations may be misleading. *Psychotherapy, 25,* 27–35.

Stiles, W. B., Shapiro, D. A., & Firth-Cozens, J. A. (1988). Do sessions of different treatments have different impacts? *Journal of Counseling Psychology, 35,* 391–396.

Stiles, W. B., & Snow, J. S. (1984). Counseling session impact as viewed by novice counselors and their clients. *Journal of Counseling Psychology, 31,* 13–21.

Stiles, W. B., Startup, M., Hardy, G. E., Barkham, M., Rees, A., Shapiro, D. A., & Reynolds, S. (1996). Therapist session intentions in cognitive-behavioral and psychodynamic-interpersonal psychotherapy. *Journal of Counseling Psychology, 43,* 402–414.

Stipek, D. (1998). Differences between Americans and Chinese in the circumstances evoking pride, shame, and guilt. *Journal of Cross-Cultural Psychology, 29,* 619–629.

Stöber, J. (1998). The Frost Multidimensional Perfectionism Scale revisited: More perfect with four (instead of six) dimensions. *Personality and Individual Differences, 24,* 481–491.

Stoltenberg, C. (1981). Approaching supervision from a developmental perspective: The counselor complexity model. *Journal of Counseling Psychology, 28,* 59–65.

Stone, G. L. (1984). Reaction: In defense of the "artificial." *Journal of Counseling Psychology, 31,* 108–110.

Strauss, A., & Corbin, J. (1990). *Basics of qualitative research: Grounded theory procedures and techniques.* Newbury Park, CA: Sage.

Strauss, A. L., & Corbin, J. (1998). *Basics of qualitative research: Techniques and procedures for developing grounded theory* (2nd ed.). Thousand Oaks, CA: Sage.

Stricker, G. (1982). Ethical issues in psychotherapy research. In M. Rosenbaum (Ed.), *Ethics and values in psychotherapy: A guidebook* (pp. 403–424). New York: Free Press.

Strickland, O. L., Maloney, M. F., Dietrich, A. S., Myerburg, S., Cotsonis, G. A., & Johnson, R. V. (2003). Measurement issues related to data collection on the World Wide Web. *Advances in Nurses Science, 26,* 246–256.

Strohmer, D. C., & Blustein, D. L. (1990). The adult problem solver as personal scientist. *Journal of Cognitive Psychotherapy: An International Quarterly, 4,* 281–292.

Strohmer, D. C., & Newman, L. J. (1983). Counselor hypothesis-testing strategies. *Journal of Counseling Psychology, 30,* 557–565.

Strong, S. R. (1968). Counseling: An interpersonal influence process. *Journal of Counseling Psychology, 15,* 215–224.

Strong, S. R. (1971). Experimental laboratory research in counseling. *Journal of Counseling Psychology, 18,* 106–110.

Strong, S. R. (1984). Reflections on human nature, science, and progress in counseling psychology. *Journal of Counseling Psychology, 31,* 470–473.

Strong, S. R., & Dixon, D. N. (1971). Expertness, attractiveness, and influence in counseling. *Journal of Counseling Psychology, 18,* 562–570.

Strong, S. R., Hills, H. I., Kilmartin, C. T., De Vries, H., Lanier, K., Nelson, B., Strickland, D., & Meyer, C. W. (1988). The dynamic relations among interpersonal behaviors: A test of complementarity and autocomplementarity. *Journal of Personality and Social Psychology, 54,* 798–810.

Strong, S. R., & Matross, R. P. (1973). Change processes in counseling and psychotherapy. *Journal of Counseling Psychology, 20,* 25–37.

Strong, S. R., & Schmidt, L. D. (1970). Expertness and influence in counseling. *Journal of Counseling Psychology, 17,* 81–87.

Strong, S. R., Welsh, J. A., Corcoran, J. L., & Hoyt, W. T. (1992). Social psychology and counseling psychology: The history, products, and promise of an interface. *Journal of Counseling Psychology, 39,* 139–157.

Strupp, H. H. (1980a). Success and failure in time-limited psychotherapy: A systematic comparison of two cases—Comparison 1. *Archives of General Psychiatry, 37,* 595–603.

Strupp, H. H. (1980b). Success and failure in time-limited psychotherapy: A systematic comparison of two cases—Comparison 2. *Archives of General Psychiatry, 37,* 708–716.

Strupp, H. H. (1980c). Success and failure in time-limited psychotherapy: Further evidence—Comparison 4. *Archives of General Psychiatry, 37,* 947–954.

Strupp, H. H. (1981). Clinical research, practice, and the crisis of confidence. *Journal of Consulting and Clinical Psychology, 49,* 216–219.

Strupp, H. H., & Binder, J. L. (1984). *Psychotherapy in a new key.* New York: Basic Books.

Strupp, H. H., & Howard, K. I. (1993). A brief history of psychotherapy research. In D. K. Freedheim (Ed.), *History of psychotherapy* (pp. 309–334). Washington, DC: American psychological Association.

Stumpf, H., & Parker, W. D. (2000). A hierarchical structural analysis of perfectionism and its relation to other personality characteristics. *Personality and Individual Differences, 28,* 837–852.

Suarez-Renaud, G. (2002). *Examining the relationships of acculturation, acculturative stress, problem solving appraisal and psychological symptoms among Mexican immigrants in the Midwest.* Unpublished doctoral dissertation, University of Missouri-Columbia.

Sudman, S., & Bradburn, N. M. (1982). *Asking questions: A practical guide to questionnaire design.* San Francisco: Jossey-Bass.

Sue, D. W. (2003). *Overcoming our racism: The journey to liberation.* San Francisco, CA: Wiley.

Sue, D. W., & Sue, D. (1990). *Counseling the culturally different: Theory and practice.* New York: Wiley.

Sue, D. W., & Sue, D. (2003). *Counseling the culturally diverse: Theory and practice.* New York: Wiley.

Sue, S., Zane, N., & Young, K. (1994). Research on psychotherapy with culturally diverse populations. In A. E. Bergin & S. L. Garfield (Eds.), *Handbook of psychotherapy and behavior change* (4th ed., pp. 783–817). New York: John Wiley and Sons.

Suen, H. K. (1988). Agreement, reliability, accuracy, and validity: Toward a clarification. *Behavioral Assessment, 10,* 343–366.

Suh, C. S., O'Malley, S. S., Strupp, H. H., & Johnson, M. E. (1989). The Vanderbilt Psychotherapy Process Scale (VPPS). *Journal of Cognitive Psychotherapy, 3,* 123–154.

Suppe, F. (1977). *The structure of scientific theories* (2nd ed.). Urbana: University of Illinois Press.

Swagler, M. A., & Ellis, M. V. (2003). Crossing the distance: Adjustment of Taiwanese graduate students in the United States. *Journal of Counseling Psychology, 50,* 420–437.

Swanson, J. (1995). The process and outcome of career counseling. In W. B. Walsh & S. H. Osipow (Eds.), *Handbook of vocational psychology: Theory practice and research* (2nd ed., pp. 217–260). Mahwah, NJ: Lawrence Erlbaum Associates.

Szarewski, A., & Cuzick, J. (1998). Smoking and cervical neoplasia: A review of the evidence. *Journal of Epidemiology and Biostatistics, 3,* 229–256.

Tabachnick, B. G., & Fidell, L. S. (1996). *Using multivariate statistics.* New York: Harper Collins College.

Tabachnick, B. G., & Fidell, L. S. (2001). *Using multivariate statistics* (4th ed.). Boston, MA: Allyn & Bacon.

Tashakkori, A., & Teddlie, C. (Eds.). (2003). *Handbook on mixed methods in the behavioral and social sciences.* Thousand Oaks, CA: Sage.

Tanaka-Matsumi, J., & Kameoka, V. A. (1986). Reliabilities and concurrent validities of popular self-report measures of depression, anxiety, and social desirability. *Journal of Consulting and Clinical Psychology, 54,* 328–333.

Task Force for the Promotion and Dissemination of Psychological Procedures. (1995). Training in and dissemination of empirically-validated psychological treatment: Report and recommendations. *The Clinical Psychologist, 48,* 2–23.

Taussig, I. M. (1987). Comparative responses of Mexican Americans and Anglo-Americans to early goal setting in a public mental health clinic. *Journal of Counseling Psychology, 34,* 214–217.

Teixeira, M. A. P., & Gomes, W. B. (2000). Autonomous career change among professionals: An empirical phenomenological study. *Journal of Phenomenological Psychology, 31*(1), 78–96.

Tesch, R. (1990). *Qualitative research: Analysis types and software tools.* New York: Falmer.

Thombs, D. L. (2000). A retrospective study of DARE: Substantive effects not detected in undergraduates. *Journal of Alcohol and Drug Education, 46,* 27–40.

Thompson, A. S., & Super, D. E. (Eds.). (1964). *The professional preparation of counseling psychologists. Report of the 1964 Greystone Conference.* New York: Bureau of Publications, Teachers College, Columbia University.

Thompson, B. (2004). *Exploratory and confirmatory factor analysis: Understanding concepts and applications.* Washington, DC: American Psychological Association.

Thompson, B. J., & Hill, C. E. (1993). Client perceptions of therapist competence. *Psychotherapy Research, 3,* 124–130.

Thompson, C. E. (1994). Helms white racial identity development (WRID) theory: Another look. *The Counseling Psychologist, 22,* 645–649.

Thompson, C. E., & Jenal, S. T. (1994). Interracial and intraracial quasi-counseling interactions when counselors avoid discussing race. *Journal of Counseling Psychology, 41,* 484–491.

Thompson, C. E., & Neville, H. A. (1999). Racism, mental health, and mental health practices. *The Counseling Psychologist, 27,* 155–223.

Thompson, C. E., Worthington, R., & Atkinson, D. R. (1994). Counselor content orientation, counselor race, and black women's cultural mistrust and self-disclosures. *Journal of Counseling Psychology, 41,* 155–161.

Thompson, E. E., Neighbors, H. W., Munday, C., & Jackson, J. S. (1996). Recruitment and retention of African American patients for clinical research: An exploration of response rates in an urban psychiatric hospital. *Journal of Consulting and Clinical Psychology, 64,* 861–867.

Thoreson, R. W., Budd, F. C., & Krauskopf, C. J. (1986). Alcoholism among psychologists: Factors in relapse and recovery. *Professional Psychology: Research and Practice, 17,* 497–503.

Thoreson, R. W., Kardash, K. A., Leuthold, D. A., & Morrow, K. A. (1990). Gender differences in the academic career. *Research in Higher Education, 3*(2), 193–209.

Thoreson, R. W., Miller, M., & Krauskopf, C. J. (1989). The distressed psychologist: Prevalence and treatment considerations. *Professional Psychology: Research and Practice, 20,* 153–158.

Tichenor, V., & Hill, C. E. (1989). A comparison of six measures of working alliance. *Psychotherapy, 26,* 195–199.

Tingey, R. C., Lambert, M. J., Burlingame, G. M., & Hansen, N. B. (1996). Assessing clinical significance: Proposed extensions to method. *Psychotherapy Research, 6,* 109–123.

Tinsley, D. J., Tinsley, H. E. A., Boone, S., & Shim-Li, C. (1993). Prediction of scientist-practitioner behavior using personality scores obtained during graduate school. *Journal of Counseling Psychology, 40,* 511–517.

Tinsley, H. E. A. (1992). Psychometric theory and counseling psychology research. In S. D. Brown & R. W. Lent (Eds.), *Handbook of counseling psychology* (2nd ed., pp. 37–70). New York: John Wiley & Sons.

Tinsley, H. E. A. (1997). Synergistic analysis of structured essays: A large sample discovery oriented qualitative research approach. *The Counseling Psychologist, 25,* 573–585.

Tinsley, H. E. A., Bowman, S. L., & Ray, S. B. (1988). Manipulation of expectancies about counseling and psychotherapy: Review and analysis of expectancy manipulation strategies and results. *Journal of Counseling Psychology, 35,* 99–108.

Tinsley, H. E. A., Roth, J. A., & Lease, S. H. (1989). Dimensions of leadership and leadership style among group intervention specialists. *Journal of Counseling Psychology, 36,* 48–53.

Tinsley, H. E. A., & Tinsley, D. J. (1987). Use of factor analysis in counseling psychology research. *Journal of Counseling Psychology, 34,* 414–424.

Tinsley, H. E. A., & Weiss, D. J. (1975). Interrater reliability and agreement of subjective judgments. *Journal of Counseling Psychology, 22,* 358–376.

Tinsley, H. E. A., Workman, K. R., & Kass, R. A. (1980). Factor analysis of the domain of client expectancies about counseling. *Journal of Counseling Psychology, 27,* 561–570.

Tobacco Advisory Group of the Royal College of Physicians. (2000). *Nicotine addiction in Britain.* London: Royal College of Physicians of London.

Toporek, R. L., Gerstein, L. H., Fouad, N. A., Roysircar, G., & Israel, T. (Eds.). (2005). *Handbook for social justice in counseling psychology.* Thousand Oaks, CA: Sage.

Toporek, R. L., & Williams, R. (2005). Ethics and professional issues related to the practice of social justice in counseling psychology. In R. L. Toporek, L. H. Gerstein, N. A. Fouad, G. Roysircar, & T. Israel (Eds.), *Handbook for social justice in counseling psychology* (pp. 17–36). Thousand Oaks, CA: Sage.

Toukmanian, S. G., & Rennie, D. (1992). *Psychotherapy process research: Paradigmatic and narrative approaches.* Newbury Park, CA: Sage.

Toulmin, S. (1972). *Human understanding: The collecting use and evolution of concepts.* Princeton, NJ: Princeton University Press.

Tracey, T. J. (1985). The N of 1 Markov chain design as a means of studying the stages of psychotherapy. *Psychiatry, 48,* 196–204.

Tracey, T. J., Glidden, C. E., & Kokotovic, A. M. (1988). Factor structure of the Counselor Rating Form—Short. *Journal of Counseling Psychology, 35,* 330–335.

Tracey, T. J., Hays, K. A., Malone, J., & Herman, B. (1988). Changes in counselor response as a function of experience. *Journal of Counseling Psychology, 35,* 119–126.

Tracey, T. J., Leong, F. T. L., & Glidden, C. (1986). Help seeking and problem perception among Asian Americans. *Journal of Counseling Psychology, 33,* 331–336.

Tracey, T. J., & Ray, P. B. (1984). Stages of successful time-limited counseling: An interactional examination. *Journal of Counseling Psychology, 31,* 13–27.

Triandis, H. C. (1972). *The analysis of subjective culture.* New York: Wiley.

Truax, C. B., & Carkhuff, R. R. (1967). *Toward effective counseling and psychotherapy: Training and practice.* Chicago: Aldine.

Truax, C. B., & Wargo, D. G. (1966). Psychotherapeutic encounters that change behavior: For better or for worse. *American Journal of Psychotherapy, 20,* 499–520.

Tryon, W. W. (2001). Evaluating statistical difference, equivalence, and indeterminacy using inferential confidence intervals: An integrated alternative method of conducting null hypothesis statistical tests. *Psychological Methods, 6,* 371–386.

Turk, D. C., & Salovey, P. (Ed.). (1988). *Reasoning, inference, and judgment in clinical psychology.* New York: Free Press.

Turnbull, H. R., III (Ed.). (1977). *Consent handbook.* Washington, DC: American Association on Mental Deficiency.

Turner, P. R., Valtierra, M., Talken, T. R., Miller, V. I., & DeAnda J. R. (1996). Effect of treatment on treatment outcome for college students in brief therapy. *Journal of Counseling Psychology, 43,* 228–232.

Tversky, A., & Kahneman, D. (1974). Judgment under uncertainty: Heuristics and biases. *Science, 185,* 1124–1131.

Tversky, A., & Kahneman, D. (1981). The framing of decisions and the psychology of choice. *Science, 211,* 453–458.

Underwood, B. J. (1966). *Experimental psychology*. New York: Appleton-Century-Crofts.

Valencia, R., & Suzuki, L.A. (Eds.). (2001) *Intelligence testing and minority students: Foundations, performance factors, and assessment issues*. Thousand Oaks, CA: Sage.

Van de Vijver, F. J. R., & Leung, K. (1997). *Methods and data analysis for cross-cultural research*. Thousand Oaks, CA: Sage.

Vandenbos, G. R. (1996). Outcome assessment of psychotherapy. *American Psychologist, 51*, 1005–1006.

Vaughn, S., Schumm, J. S., & Sinagub, J. M. (1996). *Focus group interviews in education and psychology*. Thousand Oaks, CA: Sage.

Vogt, W. P. (1993). *Dictionary of statistics and methodology: A nontechnical guide for the social sciences*. Newbury Park, CA: Sage.

Vontress, C. E. (1970). Counseling blacks. *Personnel and Guidance Journal, 48*, 713–719.

Vredenburg, K., O'Brien, E., & Krames, L. (1988). Depression in college students: Personality and experiential factors. *Journal of Counseling Psychology, 35*, 419–425.

Waehler, C. A., Kalodner, C. R., Wampold, B. E., & Lichtenberg, J. W. (2000). Empirically supported treatments (ESTs) in perspective: Implications for counseling psychology training. *The Counseling Psychologist, 28*, 657–671.

Waldo, C. R. (1999). Working in the majority context: A structural model of heterosexism as minority stress in the workplace. *Journal of Counseling Psychology, 46*, 218–232.

Wallenstein, R. S. (1989). The psychotherapy research project of the Menninger Foundation: An overview. *Journal of Consulting and Clinical Psychology, 57*, 195–205.

Walsh, W. B., & Heppner, M. J. (2006). *Handbook of career counseling for women*. Hillsdale, NJ: Lawrence Erlbaum.

Walsh, W. B., & Osipow, S. H. (Eds.). (1994). *Career counseling for women*. Hillsdale, NJ: Lawrence Erlbaum.

Waltz, J., Addis, M. E., Koerner, K., & Jacobson, N. S. (1993). Testing the integrity of a psychotherapy protocol: Assessment of adherence and competence. *Journal of Consulting and Clinical Psychology, 61*, 620–630.

Wampold, B. E. (1986a). State of the art in sequential analysis: Comment on Lichtenberg and Heck. *Journal of Counseling Psychology, 33*, 182–185.

Wampold, B. E. (1986b). Toward quality research in counseling psychology: Current recommendations for design and analysis. *The Counseling Psychologist, 14*, 37–48.

Wampold, B. E. (1995). Analysis of behavior sequences in psychotherapy. In J. Siegfried (Ed.), *Therapeutic and everyday discourse as behavior change: Towards a microanalysis in psychotherapy process research* (pp. 189–214). Norwood, NJ: Ablex.

Wampold, B. E. (1997). Methodological problems in identifying efficacious psychotherapies. *Psychotherapy Research, 7*, 21–43.

Wampold, B. E. (1998). Necessary (but not sufficient) innovation: Comment on Fox and Jones (1998), Koehly and Shivy (1998), and Russell et al. (1998). *Journal of Counseling Psychology, 45*, 46–49.

Wampold, B. E. (2001). The *great psychotherapy debate: Models, methods, and findings*. Hillsdale, NJ: Lawrence Erlbaum.

Wampold, B. E., Ankarlo, G., Mondin, G., Trinidad-Carrillo, M., Baumler, B., & Prater, K. (1995). Social skills of and social environments produced by different Holland types: A social perspective on person-environment fit model. *Journal of Counseling Psychology, 42*, 365–379.

Wampold, B. E., & Bhati, K. S. (2004). Attending to the omissions: A historical examination of evidence-based practice movements. *Professional Psychology: Research and Practice, 35*, 563–570.

Wampold, B. E., & Bolt, D. (2006). Therapist effects: Clever ways to make them (and everything else) disappear. *Psychotherapy Research, 16*, 184–187.

Wampold, B. E., & Brown, G. S. (2005). Estimating therapist variability: A naturalistic study of outcomes in managed care. *Journal of Consulting and Clinical Psychology, 16*, 184–187.

Wampold, B. E., Davis, B., & Good, R. H., III. (1990). Hypothesis validity of clinical research. *Journal of Consulting and Clinical Psychology, 58*, 360–367.

Wampold, B. E., & Drew, C. J. (1990). *Theory and application of statistics*. New York: McGraw-Hill.

Wampold, B. E., & Freund, R. D. (1987). Use of multiple regression in counseling psychology research: A flexible data-analytic strategy. *Journal of Counseling Psychology, 34*, 372–382.

Wampold, B. E., & Freund, R. D. (1991). Statistical issues in clinical research. In M. Hersen, A. E. Kazdin, & A. S. Bellack (Eds.), *The clinical psychology handbook* (2nd ed., pp. 313–326). Elmsford, NY: Pergamon Press.

Wampold, B. E., & Furlong, M. J. (1981a). The heuristics of visual inference. *Behavioral Assessment, 3*, 79–82.

Wampold, B. E., & Furlong, M. J. (1981b). Randomization tests in single-subject designs: Illustrative examples. *Journal of Behavioral Assessment, 3*, 329–341.

Wampold, B. E., & Kim, K. H. (1989). Sequential analysis applied to counseling process and outcomes: A case study revisited. *Journal of Counseling Psychology, 36*, 357–364.

Wampold, B. E., Minami, T., Tierney, S. C., Baskin, T. W., & Bhati, K. S. (2005). The placebo is powerful: Estimating placebo effects in medicine and psychotherapy from clinical trials. *Journal of Clinical Psychology, 61*, 835–854.

Wampold, B. E., Mondin, G. W., Moody, M., Stich, F., Benson, K., & Ahn, H. (1997). A meta-analysis of outcome studies comparing bonafide psychotherapies: Empirically, "all must have prizes." *Psychological Bulletin, 122*, 203–215.

Wampold, B. E., & Poulin, K. L. (1992). Counseling research methods: Art and artifact. In S. D. Brown & R. W. Lent (Eds.), *Handbook of counseling psychology* (2nd ed., pp. 71–109). New York: Wiley.

Wampold, B. E., & Serlin, R. C. (2000). The consequences of ignoring a nested factor on measures of effect size in analysis of variance. *Psychological Methods, 5*, 425–433.

Wampold, B. E., & White, T. B. (1985). Research themes in counseling psychology: A cluster analysis of citations in the process and outcomes section of the *Journal of Counseling Psychology*. *Journal of Counseling Psychology, 32,* 123–126.

Wampold, B. E., & Worsham, N. L. (1986). Randomization tests for multiple-baseline designs. *Behavioral Assessment, 8,* 135–143.

Wang, Y.-W., Heppner, P. P., & Heppner, M. J. (2004a). Qualitative methods: On the road to exploring the unknown. In P. P. Heppner & M. J. Heppner (Eds.), *Writing and publishing your thesis, dissertation & research: A guide for students in the helping profession* (pp. 136–178). Pacific Grove, CA: Brooks/Cole.

Wang, Y.-W., Heppner, P. P., & Heppner, M. J. (2004b). Qualitative results: The meaning making process. In P. P. Heppner & M. J. Heppner (Eds.), *Writing and publishing your thesis, dissertation & research: A guide for students in the helping profession* (pp. 305–326). Pacific Grove, CA: Brooks/Cole.

Warchal, P., & Southern, S. (1986). Perceived importance of counseling needs among adult students. *Journal of College Student Personnel, 27,* 43–48.

Watkins, C. E., Jr. (1994). On hope, promise, and possibility in counseling psychology, or some simple, but meaningful observations about our specialty. *The Counseling Psychologist, 22,* 315–334.

Watkins, C. E., Jr. (Ed.). (1997). *Handbook of psychotherapy supervision.* New York: Wiley.

Watkins, C. E., Lopez, F. G., Campbell, V. L., & Himmell, C. D. (1986). Contemporary counseling psychology: Results of a national survey. *Journal of Counseling Psychology, 33,* 301–309.

Watkins, C. E., & Terrell, F. (1988). Mistrust level and its effects on counseling expectations in Black-White counselor relationships: An analogue study. *Journal of Counseling Psychology, 35,* 194–197.

Watson, J. C., Gordon, L. B., & Stermac, L. (2003). Comparing the effectiveness of process-experiential with cognitive-behavioral psychotherapy in the treatment of depression. *Journal of Consulting and Clinical Psychology, 71,* 773–781.

Watson, J. C., & Rennie, D. L. (1994). Qualitative analysis of clients' subjective experience of significant moments during the exploration of problematic reactions. *Journal of Counseling Psychology, 41,* 500–509.

Webb, E. J., Campbell, D. T., Schwartz, R. C., & Sechrest, L. (1966). *Unobtrusive measures: Nonreactive research in the social sciences.* Chicago: Rand McNally.

Webb, E. J., Campbell, D. T., Schwartz, R. D., Sechrest, L., & Grove, J. B. (1981). *Nonreactive measures in the social sciences.* Boston: Houghton Mifflin.

Webster-Stratton, C. (1988). Mothers' and fathers' perceptions of child deviance: Roles of parent and child behaviors and parent adjustment. *Journal of Consulting and Clinical Psychology, 56,* 909–915.

Wei, M., & Heppner, P. P. (2005). Counselor and client predictors of the initial working alliance: A replication and extension to Taiwanese client-counselor dyads. *The Counseling Psychologist, 33,* 51–71.

Wei, M., Heppner, P. P., & Mallinckrodt, B. (2003). Perceived coping as a mediator between attachment and psychological distress: A structural equation modeling approach. *Journal of Counseling Psychology, 50,* 438–447.

Wei, M., Vogel, D. L., Ku, T-Y., & Zakalik, R. A. (2005). Adult attachment, affect regulation, negative mood, and interpersonal problems: The mediating roles of emotional reactivity and emotional cutoff. *Journal of Counseling Psychology, 52,* 14–24.

Weisz, J. R., Rothbaum, F. M., & Blackburn, T. C. (1984). Standing out and standing in: The psychology of control in America and Japan. *American Psychologist, 39,* 955–969.

Weiten, W. (1998). *Psychology: Themes and variations.* Pacific Grove, CA: Brooks/Cole.

Wertz, F. J. (2005). Phenomenological research methods for counseling psychology. *Journal of Counseling Psychology, 52*(2), 167–177.

Westen, D., Novotny, C. M., & Thompson-Brenner, H. (2004). The empirical status of empirically supported psychotherapies: Assumptions, findings, and reporting in controlled clinical trials. *Psychological Bulletin, 130,* 631–663.

White, M. D., & White, C. A. (1981). Involuntarily committed patients' constituted right to refuse treatment. *American Psychologist, 36,* 953–962.

White, O. R. (1974). *The "split middle": A "quickie" method for trend estimation.* Seattle: University of Washington, Experimental Education Unit, Child Development and Mental Retardation Center.

Whiteley, J. M. (1984). A historical perspective on the development of counseling psychology as a profession. In S. D. Brown & R. W. Lent (Eds.), *Handbook of counseling psychology* (pp. 3–55). New York: Wiley.

Wiley, M. O., & Ray, P. B. (1986). Counseling supervision by developmental level. *Journal of Counseling Psychology, 33,* 439–445.

Wilkinson, L., & Task Force on Statistical Inference. (1999). Statistical methods in psychology journals. *American Psychologist, 54,* 594–604.

Willett, J. B. (1997). Measuring change: What individual growth modeling buys you. In: E. Amsel & K. A. Renninge (Eds.), *Change and development: Issues of theory, method, and application* (pp. 213–243). Mahwah, NJ: Erlbaum.

Willett, J. B., Ayoub, C. C., & Robinson, D. (1991). Using growth modeling to examine systematic differences in growth: An example of change in the functioning of families at risk of maladaptive parenting, child abuse, or neglect. *Journal of Consulting and Clinical Psychology, 59,* 38–47.

Willett, J. B., & Sayer, A. G. (1994). Using covariance structure analysis to detect correlates and predictors of individual change over time. *Psychological Bulletin, 116,* 363–381.

Williams, E. N., Soeprapto, E., Like, K., Touradiji, P., Hess, S., & Hill, C. E. (1998). Perceptions of serendipity: Career paths of prominent academic women in counseling psychology. *Journal of Counseling Psychology, 45,* 379–389.

Williams, J. E. (1962). Changes in self and other perceptions following brief educational-vocational counseling. *Journal of Counseling Psychology, 9,* 18–30.

Williams, K. E., & Chambless, D. L. (1994). The results of exposure-based treatment in agoraphobia. In S. Friedman (Ed.), *Anxiety disorders in African Americans* (pp. 149–165). New York: Springer.

Wills, T. A. (1987). Help seeking as a coping mechanism. In C. R. Snyder & C. E. Ford (Eds.), *Coping with negative life events: Clinical and psychological perspectives* (pp. 19–50). New York: Plenum.

Wilson, L. S., & Ranft, V. A. (1993). The state of ethical training for counseling psychology doctoral students. *The Counseling Psychologist, 21,* 445–456.

Winston, Roger B., Jr. (1985). A suggested procedure for determining order of authorship in research publications. *Journal of Counseling and Development, 63,* 515–519.

Wolcott, H. F. (1992). Posturing in qualitative inquiry. In M. D. LeCompte, W. L. Millroy, & J. Preissle (Eds.), *The handbook of qualitative research in education* (pp. 3–52). San Diego: Academic Press.

Wolcott, H. F. (1994). *Transforming qualitative data: Description, analysis, and interpretation.* Thousand Oaks, CA: Sage.

Wolpe, J. (1969). *The practice of behavior therapy.* New York: Pergamon Press.

Woodhouse, S. S., Schlosser, L. Z., Crook, R. E., Ligiero, D. P., & Gelso, C. J. (2003). Client attachment to therapist: Relations to transference and client recollections of parental caregiving. *Journal of Counseling Psychology, 50,* 395–408.

World Values Survey. (n.d.). Retrieved November 21, 2005, from http://www.worldvaluessurvey.org

Worthington, E. L., Jr. (1984). Empirical investigation of supervision of counselors as they gain experience. *Journal of Counseling Psychology, 31,* 63–75.

Worthington, E. L., Jr., & Roehlke, H. J. (1979). Effective supervision as perceived by beginning counselors-in-training. *Journal of Counseling Psychology, 26,* 64–73.

Worthington, E. L., & Stern, A. (1985). Effects of supervision and supervisor degree level and gender on supervisory relationship. *Journal of Counseling Psychology, 32,* 252–262.

Worthington, R. L. (2004). Sexual identity, sexual orientation, religious identity, and change: Is it possible to depolarize the debate? *The Counseling Psychologist, 32,* 741–749.

Worthington, R. L., & Atkinson, D. R. (1996). Effects of perceived etiology attribution similarity on client ratings of counselor credibility. *Journal of Counseling Psychology, 43,* 423–429.

Worthington, R. L., Dillon, F. R., & Becker-Schutte, A. M. (2005). Development, reliability, and validity of the Lesbian, Gay, and Bisexual Knowledge and Attitudes Scale for Heterosexuals (LGB-KASH). *Journal of Counseling Psychology, 52,* 104–118.

Wrenn, R. L. (1985). The evolution of Anne Roe. *Journal of Counseling and Development, 63,* 267–275.

Wundt, W. (1904). *Principles of physiological psychology.* New York: Macmillan.

Wundt, W. (1916). *Elements of folk psychology.* London: Allen & Unwin. (Original work published 1900.)

Yalom, I. D. (1985). *The theory and practice of group psychotherapy* (3rd ed.). New York: Basic Books.

Yalom, I. D. (2005) *The theory and practice of group psychotherapy.* (5th ed.). New York: Basic Books.

Yates, A. J. (1958). The application of learning theory to the treatment of tics. *Journal of Abnormal and Social Psychology, 56,* 175–182.

Yee, A. H., Fairchild, H. H., Weizmann, F., & Wyatt, G. E. (1993). Addressing psychology's problem with race. *American Psychologist, 48,* 1132–1140.

Zane, N., Hall, G. C. N., Sue, S., Young, K., & Nunez, J. (2004). Overview, trends, and future issues. In M. J. Lambert (Ed.), *Bergin and Garfield's handbook of psychotherapy and behavior change* (5th ed., pp. 767–804) New York: Wiley.

Zane, N. W. S. (1989). Change mechanisms in placebo procedures: Effects of suggestion, social demand, and contingent success on improvement in treatment. *Journal of Counseling Psychology, 36,* 234–243.

Zeidner, M., & Saklofske, D. (1996). Adaptive and maladaptive coping. In M. Zeidner & N. S. Endler (Eds.), *Handbook of coping: Theory, research, and applications* (pp. 505–531). New York: John Wiley.

Zimbardo, P. G., & Ebbesen, E. B. (1970). *Influencing attitudes and changing behavior.* Reading, MA: Addison-Wesley.

Zuckerman, M. (1990). Some dubious premises in research and theory on racial differences: Scientific, social, and ethical issues. *American Psychologist, 45,* 1297–1303.

Author Index

Subject Index

TO THE OWNER OF THIS BOOK:

I hope that you have found *Research Design in Counseling,* Third Edition, useful. So that this book can be improved in a future edition, would you take the time to complete this sheet and return it? Thank you.

School and address:_____

Department:_____

Instructor's name:_____

1. What I like most about this book is:_____

_____

_____

2. What I like least about this book is:

_____

_____

3. My general reaction to this book is:

_____

_____

4. The name of the course in which I used this book is:

_____

5. Were all of the chapters of the book assigned for you to read?_____

   If not, which ones weren't?_____

6. In the space below, or on a separate sheet of paper, please write specific suggestions for improving this book and anything else you'd care to share about your experience in using this book.

_____

_____

_____

_____

FOLD HERE

- -

BUSINESS REPLY MAIL
FIRST-CLASS MAIL   PERMIT NO. 34   BELMONT CA

POSTAGE WILL BE PAID BY ADDRESSEE

Attn: Marquita Flemming, Counseling

BrooksCole/Thomson Learning
10 Davis Drive
Belmont CA 94002-9801

Ilil....l..ll.....ll.....ll.l.l...l.l.l.ll.....lll...ll

- -

FOLD HERE

OPTIONAL:

Your name:_____ Date: _____

May we quote you, either in promotion for *Research Design in Counseling,* Third
Edition, or in future publishing ventures?

Yes: _____ No: _____

Sincerely yours,

P. Paul Heppner

Bruce E. Wampold

Dennis M. Kivlighan, Jr.